Philosophy of Religion

PHILOSOPHY

Contemporary

NORBERT O. SCHEDLER
PURDUE UNIVERSITY—FORT WAYNE

OF RELIGION

Perspectives

MACMILLAN PUBLISHING CO., INC.
NEW YORK

Macmillan Publishing Co., Inc.
866 Third Avenue, New York, New York 10022

Collier-Macmillan Canada, Ltd.

Library of Congress Cataloging in Publication Data

Schedler, Norbert O.   comp.
  Philosophy of religion.

  Includes bibliographies.
  1. Religion—Philosophy—Collected works.
I. Title.
BL51.S419   200'.1   73–1959
ISBN 0–02–406720–2

Printing: 1 2 3 4 5 6 7 8   Year: 4 5 6 7 8 9 80

Acknowledgments

"Protean Man" by Robert Jay Lifton. Copyright © 1968, 1970 by Robert Lifton.
From *History and Human Survival,* by Robert Lifton. Reprinted by permission of
Random House, Inc.

"The Experience of Nothingness" by Michael Novak. From pp. 1–23 in *The Experience of Nothingness* by Michael Novak. Copyright © 1070 by Michael Novak. By permission of Harper & Row, Publishers, Inc.

"Religion in the Age of Aquarius" by Harvey Cox. Reprinted from *Psychology Today* Magazine, April 1970. Copyright © Communications/Research/Machines, Inc.

"Biblical Faith as Heilsgeschichte" by Will Herberg. Reprinted by permission of the author.

"Archaic Myth and Historical Man" by Mircea Eliade. From *McCormick Quarterly* (1965), pp. 23–36. Reprinted by permission of the author and the publisher.

"The Task of Demythologizing the New Testament Proclamation" by Rudolf Bultmann. From pp. 1–16 in *Kerygma and Myth* by Rudolf Bultmann (1961). Reprinted by permission of the publisher, Harper & Row, Publishers, Inc.

"Reflections on a Peach-Seed Monkey or Storytelling and the Death of God" by Sam Keen. From Chapter 3, pp. 82–105 in *To a Dancing God* by Sam Keen. Copyright © 1970 by Sam Keen. By permission of Harper & Row, Publishers, Inc.

"The Ghost in the Cosmos and the Ghost in the Machine" by Norbert O. Schedler. Reprinted by permission of the author.

"The Pseudonyms of God" by Robert McAfee Brown. Reprinted by permission of the publisher from *The Presence and Absence of God*, ed. Christopher F. Mooney, S.J. (New York: Fordham University Press, 1969). Copyright © 1969 by Christopher F. Mooney, S.J., pp. 109–128.

"Existentialism as a Humanism" by Jean-Paul Sartre. From pp. 13–51 in *Existentialism as a Humanism* by Jean-Paul Sartre. Reprinted by permission of Philosophical Library, Inc.

"Absurdity and the Meaning of Life" by Albert Camus. From *The Myth of Sisyphus and Other Essays*, by Albert Camus, translated by Justin O'Brien. Copyright © 1955 by Alfred A. Knopf, Inc. Reprinted by permission of the publisher.

"Dynamics of Faith" by Paul Tillich. From pp. 1–4, 30–40, 41–54 in *Dynamics of Faith* by Paul Tillich. Copyright © 1957 by Paul Tillich. By permission of Harper & Row, Publishers, Inc.

"The Meaning of Existence" by Paul Tillich. From *Systematic Theology*, Vol. 11, 1957 by Paul Tillich, pp. 20, 21, 44, 45, and 47. Reprinted by permission of The University of Chicago Press and Robert C. Kimball, Literary Executor of the Estate of Paul Tillich.

"The Courage to Be" by Paul Tillich. From Chapter 6, "Courage and Transcendence" in *The Courage to Be* by Paul Tillich. Reprinted by permission of Yale University Press.

"Professor Tillich's Confusions" by Paul Edwards. From *Mind*, Vol. 74, 1965. Reprinted by permission of Basil Blackwell, Publisher, and the author.

"Buber and Encounter Theology" by Ronald Hepburn. From *Christianity and Paradox* by Ronald Hepburn. Reprinted by permission of C.A. Watts & Co., Ltd., London.

"Talk About God-Talk: A Historical Introduction" by Norbert O. Schedler. Reprinted by permission of the author.

"In Defense of Atheism" by Kai Nielsen. Reprinted from *Perspectives in Education, Religion, and the Arts* by permission of the State University of New York Press and the author.

"Religious Faith as Experiencing-As" by John Hick. From *Royal Institute of Philosophy Lectures*, Vol. 2, pp. 20–35. Reprinted by permission of St. Martin's Press, Inc. and Macmillan & Co., Ltd.

"Lectures on Religious Belief" by Ludwig Wittgenstein. From pp. 53–72 in *L. Wittgenstein: Lectures and Conversations on Aesthetics, Psychology, and Religious Belief*, edited by Cyril Barrett. Originally published by the University of California Press. Reprinted by permission of The Regents of the University of California.

"Differences Between Scientific and Religious Assertions" by Donald Evans. From *Science and Religion* edited by Ian G. Barbour. Copyright © 1968 by Ian G. Barbour. By permission of Harper & Row, Publishers, Inc.

"The Radical Theologies" by Langdon Gilkey. From *Naming the Whirlwind: The Renewal of God Language*. Copyright © 1968 by Langdon Gilkey. Reprinted by permission of the publishers, The Bobbs-Merrill Company, Inc.

"The Many Faces of Evil" by Edward H. Madden. From *Philosophy and Phenomenological Research*, Vol. 24, pp. 481–492 (June 1964). Reprinted by permission of the publisher and the author.

"Grounds for Disbelief in God" by John Hick. From John H. Hick, *Philosophy of Religion*, 2nd ed., © 1973, pp. 31–47. Reprinted by permission of Prentice-Hall, Inc., Englewood Cliffs, New Jersey.

"Religion and Commitment" by Kai Nielsen. From *Religious Language and Knowledge*, edited by R. H. Ayers and W. T. Blackstone. Reprinted by permission of the University of Georgia Press.

"Religious Humanism" by Erich Fromm. From *Psychoanalysis and Religion* by Erich Fromm. Copyright © 1950 by Erich Fromm. Reprinted by permission of Yale University Press.

"The World and God: A Process Perspective" by Delwin Brown. Reprinted by permission of the author.

"Teilhard's Process Metaphysics" by Ian G. Barbour. From *Journal of Religion*, Vol. 49, 1969. Reprinted by permission of The University of Chicago Press and the author.

"The Panentheism of Charles Hartshorne" by L. Bryant Keeling. From the essay "The Philosophy of Charles Hartshorne" by L. Bryant Keeling. Reprinted by permission of the author.

"The Modern World and a Modern View of God" by Charles Hartshorne. Reprinted by permission of the author.

"Divine Persuasion and the Triumph of Good" by Lewis S. Ford. Reprinted by permission of the author.

"The Beauty of Earth" by Michael Novak. From *A Theology for Radical Politics* by Michael Novak. Copyright 1969 by Michael Novak. Published by Herder and Herder, Inc. Reprinted by permission.

"Manifesto for a Dionysian Theology" by Sam Keen. Reprinted by permission of the author.

"Religion and Peak-Experiences" by Abraham Maslow. From "Religions, Values, and Peak-Experiences" by Abraham Maslow. From The Kappa Delta Pi Lecture Series. Copyright © 1964 by Kappa Delta Pi. Reprinted by permission of Kappa Delta Pi, An Honor Society in Education, owners of the copyright.

"The Reach and the Grasp; Transcendence Today" by Huston Smith. From *Transcendence*, edited by Herbert W. Richardson and Donald R. Cutler. Copyright © 1969 by Beacon Press. Reprinted by permission of Beacon Press.

"Ernst Bloch and 'The Pull of the Future'" by Harvey Cox. Foreword by Harvey Cox to *Man on His Own* by Ernst Bloch. Copyright 1970 by Herder and Herder, Inc. Used by permission of the publisher, The Seabury Press, New York.

"The Cancellation of Hope by Myth" by Carl Braaten. From pp. 42–46 in *The Future of God* by Carl E. Braaten. Copyright © 1969 by Carl E. Braaten. By permission of Harper & Row, Publishers, Inc.

Dedicated to my students in philosophy of religion
whose "polymorphous diversity" never ceases to astonish me.

Preface

There is an elitist's view of philosophy of religion in which one deals only with the time-honored names and topics in the history of the discipline. Philosophers in the discipline talk to each other in academic contexts. Theologians in the discipline talk to each other in seminaries. Little conversation occurs between theologian and philosopher. The philosopher is less superstitious because he does not rely on faith and revelation; the theologian is more broad-minded because his concept of experience includes depths denied by the philosopher. But an interesting change has occurred in this situation. Philosophy and theology have been challenged today by their audiences, which are no longer the indoctrinated seminarian or the philosophy major. The audience is polymorphous —it plays with many ideas and life styles. Students in universities and seminaries are bored with the traditional topics and the time-honored names.

Philosophical and theological ideas must be *heard* to be entertained. This has forced philosophy of religion out of the academic ghetto. The result has been a rapid turnover in ideas following the general pattern in the marketplace, not like the "good old days" when one learned a system that was good for at least a decade. This is particularly true of theological standpoints where changes seem to occur yearly.[1] Professionals moan and complain about the lack of depth; old-time believers are bewildered—"What next?" Others celebrate this freedom and continuing novelty. Indeed, it is now philosophy that has become dogmatic and estab-

[1] See the excellent series published by Macmillan Publishing Co., Inc., *New Theology,* Martin Marty and Dean Peerman (eds.), 9 vols., 1964–1973.

lishmentarian while theology is continuously surprising. Philosophers get tenure and continue talking to themselves; theologians, aware that they must be heard to keep their vocations, are very sensitive to the changes in their audiences.[2]

The temptation in this situation is to become superficial—to worry more about the package than about its content. As long as it sells, it is viable. This criticism will be raised by certain essays in this book. But some theologians in the struggle for their very existence feel that the risk must be taken.

Anthologies in philosophy of religion have traditionally dealt with a set number of topics using materials drawn from a long history of debate on those topics: arguments for the existence of God, the nature of God, the problem of evil, the immortality of the soul, and so on. I grant the importance of such an approach because the fascination with the new often overlooks our debt to the past. The concern with relevance also tempts one to identify the new with the true. But there are already a great number of traditionally oriented anthologies, so I have sought in this volume an approach that is closer to the actual interest of the students and exponents of religion without giving in to relevance for relevance's sake.

I have chosen, therefore, to anthologize around a number of standpoints. My understanding of a "standpoint" is developed in Chapter 1. The advantage of this approach is that we are aware today that our position on most issues depends on our assumptions. The assumptions set what we consider to be true, significant, real, and so on. I have chosen a number of standpoints that are prevalent today and let exponents of these positions tell their own stories. Even within a standpoint different conclusions can be drawn. The student can see this, for example, in the case of existentialism where theism and atheism carry on a debate. Following an essay that expresses a particular standpoint, I have included a number of essays from other standpoints as a contrast. Students should not only debate the specific issues but also see that criticisms frequently arise because a different standpoint is assumed. They should learn to recognize both in the debates in the book and in the class what assumptions are held, what standpoint is being taken.

I have intentionally chosen material that is readable and lively without being simplistic. I grant that some of the material is a popularization of a standpoint, or even perhaps a fad item. I have chosen popularizations because I want the students to get into the standpoint without "a lot of sweat." If the position "turns them on," they can pursue the position in depth. The footnotes and bibliographies provide guidance for such an exploration. The instructor may also wish to supplement this volume with paperbacks that go into the different standpoints in greater depth. Some

---

[2] Recent introductory texts in philosophy show that philosophy is also becoming sensitive to the interests of students.

of the material is tough. There is, for example, no easy way into Whitehead.

And what about the charge of faddism? The material chosen for this book was all written in this century, and almost all of it was written in the last two decades. My defense is based on the following. First, we live in an age in which change is the essence of things. Everything is easily "disposable" as we face a rapid succession of options. One can see this either as a breakdown of permanent truth or as a sign of vitality. My position is that theology today is more imaginative, open to new experience, and less dogmatic than many disciplines in the academic community. If this is true, the charge of "faddism" is no longer pejorative but one willingly chosen. Second, if we are to engage in the contemporary debate we do not yet have the objectivity of history to see what in the current scene will have lasting value. We can, however, be part of that debate which will determine the choice. Third, although the material is new and some of it is genuinely new, the old questions and options still seem to be raised in the material.

I have sidestepped the question of defining philosophy of religion. A definition only shows the standpoint of the person who expresses that particular position. This volume represents a number of such standpoints but certainly is not exhaustive. But why these and not others? My answer is autobiographical. The standpoints in this book trace my theological and philosophical evolution.

I have made no attempt to represent equally positions usually identified as Roman Catholic, Protestant, or Jewish. These labels have become obsolete in philosophy of religion. One can find Roman Catholic thinkers in all the standpoints represented in this volume. The same is true of Protestant and Jewish thinkers. I have not included Thomism as a standpoint because it is easily added by using any number of texts. The same is true of Oriental thought. This standpoint is currently of great interest, but it deserves a separate volume.

Linguistic philosophy is still persuasive to many involved in philosophy of religion, but a book strictly limited to meta-theology is a bore and a chore for those who do not *know* theology. I have, therefore, represented the linguistic point of view, but have included more essays that develop options to the linguistic viewpoint. The analyst will be overjoyed to have these specimens available for dissection. I am also convinced that linguistic philosophers often do their analysis on theological specimens that are no longer viable even for theologians. Again, the linguistic philosopher can be glad for the opportunity to learn and interact with current "live options" in theology.

In this volume the student is confronted by the careful exact thinker who attempts to keep us from fanaticism, irrationalism, superstition, and the new paganism. I have also represented the wise who argue that we must learn again to "see" beyond the minutia; that we must again dream dreams, hear again rumors of angels, go into levels of consciousness beyond the simply rational. The tough-minded and the tender-minded, I suspect, we will always have with us. The reader will have to decide for himself which he is.

I wish to thank my colleagues at Purdue University, James S. Churchill, William Bruening, Clark Butler, and David Fairchild, for kindly playing with my enthusiasm for this book. Delwin Brown is especially to be thanked for his advice and his contribution of an essay. Kai Nielsen was good enough to make suggestions for several chapters. But it was my students in philosophy of religion who particularly challenged me by their involvement in the issues raised in this book. I wish especially to thank Mike Ellis, Jeff Gibson, Phil Luecke, and Bill Oliphant. I hasten to add that I am solely responsible for what happened here. I thank also Jan Hoagburg who typed many drafts from my scribbles. I especially thank my wife, Carol, with whom I have debated all of these issues and who has kept me Dionysian when I would become too Apollonian. And finally to my three little philosophers—Karen, the analyst; Ruth, the existentialist; and David, the Whiteheadian—who refused to keep quiet while I worked because they too had something to say, I leave the task of editing the sequel.

N. O. S.

Suggested Readings

(* = extensive bibliography)
(p = available in paperback)

There are a number of good anthologies that follow a traditional approach or an approach different from mine. The teacher may wish to supplement this anthology with one of the following: Ed. Miller (ed.), *Philosophical and Religious Issues* (Belmont, Calif.: Dickenson Publishing Co., 1971); John Hick (ed.), *Classical and Contemporary Readings in the Philosophy of Religion* (Englewood Cliffs, N.J.: Prentice-Hall, Inc., 1964); W. P. Alston (ed.), *Religious Belief and Philosophical Thought* (New York: Harcourt Brace Jovanovich, Inc., 1963); W. L. Rowe and W. J. Wainwright (eds.), *Philosophy of Religion: Selected Readings* (New York: Harcourt Brace Jovanovich, Inc., 1973p); Jerry Gill (ed.), *Philosophy and Religion: Some Contemporary Perspectives* (Minneapolis: Burgess Publishing Co., 1968p); Ed. Miller (ed.), *Classical Statements on Faith and Reason* (New York: Random House, Inc., 1970p); John Bowden and James Richmond (eds.), *A Reader in Contemporary Theology* (Philadelphia: Westminster Press, 1967p); George Abernethy and Thomas Langford (eds.), *Philosophy of Religion*, 2nd ed. (New York: Macmillan Publishing Co., Inc., 1968); N. Smart (ed.), *Historical Selections in the Philosophy of Religion* (New York: Harper & Row, 1962); and G. I. Mavrodes and S. C. Hackett (eds.), *Problems and Perspectives in the Philosophy of Religion* (New York: Harper & Row, 1970).

The two volumes that I have found to work out especially well with a volume such as this one are G. I. Mavrodes (ed.), *The Rationality of Belief in God*

(Englewood Cliffs, N.J.: Prentice-Hall, Inc., 1970p) and John Hick (ed.), *Existence of God* (New York: Macmillan Publishing Co., Inc., 1061p).

The following general introductions contain detailed discussions of the traditional issues in philosophy of religion: John Hick, *The Philosophy of Religion,* 2nd ed. (Englewood Cliffs, N.J.: Prentice-Hall, Inc., 1973p); H. D. Lewis, *Philosophy of Religion* (London: English University Press, 1965); George Mavrodes, *Belief in God* (New York: Random House, Inc., 1970p); R. B. Edwards, *An Introduction to the Philosophy of Religion* (New York: Harcourt Brace Jovanovich, Inc., 1972p); John Hick, *Arguments for the Existence of God* (New York: Herder and Herder, 1971); J. F. Ross, *Introduction to the Philosophy of Religion* (New York: Macmillan Publishing Co., Inc., 1970p); C. Thomas, *Religious Philosophies of the West* (New York: Scribners, 1965p); Ed. Miller, *God and Reason* (New York: Macmillan Publishing Co., Inc., 1972p); J. Collins, *God in Modern Philosophy* (Chicago: Henry Regnery, 1959p); and, still a classic with good historical account of key figures in western history, E. Burtt, *Types of Religious Philosophy,* rev. ed. (New York: Harper & Row, 1951).

Paul Edwards (editor-in-chief), *Encyclopedia of Philosophy* (New York: Macmillan Publishing Co., Inc., 1967) should be consulted. This eight volume encyclopedia contains a great number of articles on topics and key figures in philosophy of religion. Good bibliographies are also found at the end of each article.

All the volumes previously cited treat the arguments for the existence of God. Several anthologies that deal specifically with the arguments and might be used with this volume are Donald Burrill (ed.), *The Cosmological Arguments* (Garden City, N.Y.: Anchor Books, 1967p); Alvin Plantinga (ed.), *The Ontological Argument* (Garden City, N.Y.: Anchor Books, 1965p); and John Hick and A. C. McGill (eds.), *The Many-Faced Argument* (New York: Macmillan Publishing Co., Inc., 1967p).

For those interested in Oriental thought, a number of volumes are useful with this volume. A. T. Embree (ed.), *The Hindu Tradition* and W. T. deBary (ed.), *The Buddhist Tradition,* both Vintage Books (p), deserve special mention. S. Radhakrishnan and C. A. Moore (eds.), *A Source Book in Indian Philosophy* (Princeton: Princeton University Press, 1957p) is more complete. A great number of inexpensive printings of eastern scriptures are available. The works of A. Watts and D. T. Suzuki, which are widely read by students, are also available in paperback editions.

Contents

CHAPTER THREE

Existentialism: Good-Luck Charm of Theism or New Humanism?

CHAPTER FOUR

Analytic Philosophy: Linguistic Veto?

CHAPTER FIVE

Atheism: Failure of Nerve or Rational Belief?

CHAPTER SIX

Process Thought: Toward a New Theism?

Contents   xix

CHAPTER SEVEN

Rumor of Angels: New Forms of Transcendence

Philosophy of Religion

CHAPTER ONE

The Contemporary Situation:
Gift or Chaos?

In our common sense realism we assume that the world is made up of things with remarkably stable qualities and a perceiver who peers out into a world set over against him. The perceiver reads off the characteristics of the world of things in an objective fashion, at least most of the time. The more objective (free from subjective bias) they are, the more his perceptions *correspond* to the way reality actually is. For the world "out there" is objectively what it is. When I experience it, my experiencing it leaves it pretty much the way it is. A subject (experiencer) *interacts* with an object over against it. The word 'interact' assumes two items that have a *separate* existence colliding or connecting with each other.

In approaching a position other than our own we assume much the same happens. We interact with an object (another belief). My argument in this anthology is that this is not the case in our experience of the world of objects, nor is it the case in our experience of positions other than our own.

To *under stand* (notice the literal meaning of this word) a standpoint other than your own requires a change of perspective. This does not mean that you have to become a believer to understand a belief, but it does mean that you have to imaginatively assume the believer's standpoint. The reader is asked to bracket (put out of operation) his standpoint and get into the language-game, the forms of life, the perspective of positions other than his own. Try this experiment! Before you criticize a position other than your own try to translate it into your own words. A position

1

that at first seemed absolutely ridiculous, often becomes understandable, given that perspective.[1] Try another experiment! Before criticizing another position different from your own, try to criticize it from the *inside*. *As a believer* what problems arise internally to the system of ideas? *External* criticism is cheap! If I have a totally different standpoint, primitive religion *obviously* seems ridiculous. But after a reflective understanding from within that standpoint, one's own perspective may be enlarged.

In reading the essays in this book try to under-stand the assumptions, the *point*-of-view of the other position. When you read two essays that are in fundamental disagreement, before asking yourself which one is true, try to describe the nature of the fundamental difference. What does each standpoint consider *real, true,* or *significant?*

I have taken this approach (contrasting perspectives) because it highlights a view of experiencing that I consider crucial to understanding religion. Knowing that in this short introduction I cannot go into these issues completely or field all the questions that I am aware must be answered, I will simply state my position with audacity.[2]

We do not have "virgin" experience. Our sense of what is real comes as a *transaction* between a subject and an object (or other subject), neither of which is known outside of that relationship. In the process of experiencing, the subject and object are in a process of transacting with each other so that the experience sets what each becomes. The word *transact* implies that each element in the experience gives and takes. As a result of the transaction, subject and object change. The only "world" we know is the one with which we have transacted.

This is not to deny that there are givens, but we cannot know them except within our standpoint. We exist *within* a "horizon" or "standpoint." The *context* exists, therefore I am! *We* are, therefore I am! *Co-esse,* therefore I am! These are all expressions of the contemporary attack upon the Cartesian ego-centric predicament which holds that the only thing that I know without doubt is my own existence. Everything else is in doubt. But we must refuse this dualism of isolated self with an external world set over against it, or as M. Novak puts it, "a conscious ego trapped inside a bag of skin in a world of colliding objects." [3] We are defined by our relationships rather than the reverse.[4]

---

[1] A device taught me by Sherwin Kepes who uses it effectively in group dynamics.

[2] I am currently working on a volume in religious epistemology that will develop the ideas in this introduction.

[3] M. Novak, *The Experience of Nothingness* (New York: Harper and Row, 1970), p. 27. I am indebted to Novak for much of what is written in this introduction although my use of his ideas is my responsibility. Cf. M. Novak, *Story in Politics* (New York: The Council on Religion and International Affairs, 1970); *Ascent of the Mountain, Flight of the Dove* (New York: Harper and Row, 1971); and numerous articles.

[4] This theory that man is what he is related to is also developed by the existentialists and phenomenologists in what is called the "field theory of man." One also finds this theory defended by some psychologists, e.g., R. D. Laing. One could even make a case for Wittgenstein adopting this position with his notion of the "forms of life."

Existing within a horizon [5] sets one's sense of reality. This sense of reality is articulated in a story one tells and a "life-style" [6] one adopts. Who one is takes the form of a story one tells and a set of actions that follow from that story. It is through the story that one finds identity and community. In being true to one's self one is true to a narrative that connects the past with the future.[7] The story tells what and why things happen and how and why I intend to act in the future. Our myths do not point beyond themselves to reality; reality corresponds to our myths.

A standpoint is a complex that includes one's feelings, memories, key images, language games, attitudes, symbols, and relationships through which reality becomes what it is. My world is refracted, filtered, and interpreted from my standpoint. But as I have already pointed out, this is not subjectivism. A standpoint is checked as to the *range* of experiences it is capable of interpreting, by its ability to motivate one to desirable actions, by the assent given to it by others (intersubjective check), by its adequacy in interpreting present and future experience.[8]

To give *reasons* for one's standpoint already presupposes the sense of reality embodied in that outlook. To back up a standpoint with facts presupposes what the standpoint itself has already built into it, the concept of what constitutes a fact.[9] Most arguments are frustrated as to a resolution because what one counts as evidence another interprets differently. The argument is not about facts but about what interpretation of the facts is correct, or what is a fact, or what life-style should follow from the interpretation. The argument is really about fundamental ways of looking at the world. What one person considers evidence of God's indifference, for example, pimples, another considers a cross to bear in the strengthening of one's faith. Perhaps the only way to argue between, or among, standpoints is on a *pragmatic* standard.[10]

We do not change standpoints because they have been proven false. Standpoints die when they no longer inspire action or when there is a gap between the narratives we have learned to tell, for example, scientific standpoint and biblical standpoint. If no way is found to tie the stories together one dies from dis-use.[11]

[5] Also called a perspective, onlook, conceptual frame, standpoint, viewpoint, blik, story, myth, vantage point, seeing as, and so on. I use these terms interchangeably.

[6] Life-styles are the actions that follow from a particular standpoint.

[7] See essays by M. Novak in Chapter One and Sam Keen in Chapter Two.

[8] I cannot defend this position at great length here. My forthcoming book will develop this notion of standpoint.

[9] This position is defended by others, such as Whitehead. A recent study by Lyman Lundeen is particularly useful for the development of this insight. See *Risk and Rhetoric in Religion: Whitehead's Theory of Language and the Discourse of Faith* (Philadelphia: Fortress Press, 1972).

[10] W. V. O. Quine, *From a Logical Point of View* (Cambridge: Harvard University Press, 1953), p. 79. See also M. Novak, "What Is Theology's Standpoint?" *Theology Today*, Vol. 25, No. 1, April 1968, p. 44.

[11] Cf. Ludwig Wittgenstein, *Lectures and Conversations* (Berkeley: University of California Press, 1967).

If one is asked to state his position in a set of propositions, he finds that this cannot be done exhaustively. Stories and styles are more than their linguistic articulation. A standpoint can be *shown* but *not* fully *stated*. "You cannot state who are, what your standpoint is, but by all your words, gestures, intonations, actions, etc., you *show* it." [12] To understand someone is to get into his language-game *and* the form of life that surrounds it. This extra-linguistic context is part of the meaning of who one is. To understand another is to participate in his "fundamental picture," as Wittgenstein notes. [13]

Language is one way our experience is filtered through a web. Our childhood experience is rich and full, often *noticing* much that we now fail to see. As we learn a language we direct our experience into approved channels and become *in-formed*. We can give in-form-ation about our experiences. (Again, notice the word. Language has a way of forming experience.) A child has a hard time telling someone else of his experiences not only because he has a limited vocabulary, but because there is no language for his experience. When we learn the word for a thing it often becomes a way of short-circuiting the actual, full experience. But language also adds new dimensions to our experience. It enables us to notice, imagine, and communicate to others about what we experience. [14]

Standpoints are judged by their ability to put what happens into a perspective, by their conative use (to motivate one to specific actions as in the case of the story of Jesus), by their sense of adequacy to experience, [15] and by their ability to open to and integrate with new experiences.

A standpoint is not necessarily static because the human subject moves through varied experiences that require a change in criteria of relevance that cause a shift in one's horizon. A new insight may lead one to see everything in a new way. The subjective and objective poles in one horizon are both in process such that standpoints *may* be dynamic. [16]

In the following chapters a number of standpoints are developed. This particular chapter is not a standpoint but is about contemporary man. Robert Lifton describes what he calls "polymorphus diversity." We find so many standpoints viable that it is hard to identify with any of them. Michael Novak describes the myths that have died and the nothingness we experience as a result of that death. Harvey Cox celebrates the play of stories current in the counterculture.

These three essays raise questions about our current situation. Is our

[12] Novak, op. cit., p. 44.

[13] Op. cit.

[14] See M. Novak, *Ascent of the Mountain, Flight of the Dove,* op. cit., passim. Novak quotes Edward Sapir who writes, "Language is heuristic, not merely in the simple sense . . . but in the much more far-reaching sense that its form predetermines for us certain modes of observation and interpretation." p. 222.

[15] This is the necessary check against pure subjectivism.

[16] This is not to say that someone's standpoint may be static. A static standpoint is usually considered to be inferior to a dynamic one. For a more detailed account see M. Novak, *A Time to Build* (New York: Macmillan, 1967), p. 51 ff.

age in chaos or in the birth pangs of creativity? Is our age unique?
What stories are viable? What stories are dead? What place does religion have in our attempt to understand who we are?

PROTEAN MAN

Robert Jay Lifton

ROBERT JAY LIFTON is Foundations' Fund for Research in Psychiatry
Associate Professor at Yale University.

I should like to examine a set of psychological patterns characteristic of
contemporary life, which are creating a new kind of man—a "protean
man." As my stress is upon change and flux, I shall not speak much of
"character" and "personality," both of which suggest fixity and permanence. Erikson's concept of identity has been, among other things, an
effort to get away from this principle of fixity; I have been using the term
self-process to convey still more specifically the idea of flow. For it is
quite possible that even the image of personal identity, in so far as it
suggests inner stability and sameness, is derived from a vision of a traditional culture in which man's relationship to his institutions and symbols
are still relatively intact—hardly the case today. If we understand the
self to be the person's symbol of his own organism, then self-process refers
to the continuous psychic recreation of that symbol.

I came to this emphasis through work in cultures far removed from my
own, studies of young (and not so young) Chinese and Japanese. Observations I was able to make in America also led me to the conviction that a
very general process was taking place. I do not mean to suggest that
everybody is becoming the same, or that a totally new "world-self" is
taking shape But I am convinced that a new style of self-process is
emerging everywhere. It derives from the interplay of three factors responsible for human behavior: the psychobiological potential common
to all mankind at any moment in time; those traits given special emphasis
in a particular cultural tradition; and those related to modern (and particularly contemporary) historical forces. My thesis is that this third
factor plays an increasingly important part in shaping self-process.

My work with the Chinese was done in Hong Kong, in connection with
a study of the process of "thought reform" (or "brainwashing") as conducted on the mainland. I found that Chinese intellectuals of varying
ages, whatever their experience with thought reform itself, had gone
through an extraordinary set of what I at that time called identity fragments—combinations of belief and emotional involvement—each of which
they could readily abandon in favor of another. I remember particularly

the profound impression made upon me by the extraordinary history of one young man in particular: beginning as a "filial son" or "young master," that elite status of an only son in an upper-class Chinese family; then feeling himself an abandoned and betrayed victim, as traditional forms collapsed during civil war and general chaos, and his father, for whom he was to long all his life, was separated from him by political and military duties; then a "student activist" in rebellion against the traditional culture in which he had been so recently immersed (as well as against a Nationalist Regime whose abuses he had personally experienced); leading him to Marxism and to strong emotional involvement in the Communist movement; then, because of remaining "imperfections," becoming a participant in a thought reform program for a more complete ideological conversion; but which, in his case, had the opposite effect, alienating him, so he came into conflict with the reformers and fled the country; then, in Hong Kong, struggling to establish himself as an "anti-Communist writer"; after a variety of difficulties, finding solace and meaning in becoming a Protestant convert; and following that, still just thirty, apparently poised for some new internal (and perhaps external) move.

Even more dramatic were the shifts in self-process of a young Japanese whom I interviewed in Tokyo and Kyoto from 1960 to 1962. I shall mention one in particular as an extreme example of this protean pattern, though there were many others who in various ways resembled him. Before the age of twenty-five he had been all of the following: a proper middle-class Japanese boy, brought up in a professional family within a well-established framework of dependency and obligation; then, due to extensive contact with farmers' and fishermen's sons brought about by wartime evacuation, a "country boy" who was to retain what he described as a life-long attraction to the tastes of the common man; then, a fiery young patriot who "hated the Americans" and whose older brother, a kamikaze pilot, was saved from death only by the war's end; then a youngster confused in his beliefs after Japan's surrender, but curious about rather than hostile toward American soldiers; soon an eager young exponent of democracy, caught up in the "democracy boom" which swept Japan; at the same time a young devotee of traditional Japanese arts—old novels, Chinese poems, kabuki and flower arrangement; during junior high and high school, an all-round leader, outstanding in studies, student self-government and general social and athletic activities; almost simultaneously, an outspoken critic of society at large and of fellow students in particular for their narrow careerism, on the basis of Marxist ideas current in Japanese intellectual circles; yet also an English-speaking student, which meant, in effect, being in still another vanguard and having a strong interest in things American; then, midway through high school, experiencing what he called a "kind of neurosis" in which he lost interest in everything he was doing and, in quest of a "change in mood," took advantage of an opportunity to become an exchange student for one year at an American high school; became a convert to many aspects of American life, including actually being baptized as a Christian under the influence of a minister he admired who was also his American "father," and returned to Japan only reluctantly; as a "returnee," found himself in many ways at odds with his friends and was accused by one of "smelling like butter" (a traditional Japanese phrase for Westerners); therefore re-immersed himself in "Japanese" experience—sitting on *tatami*, indulging in quiet, melancholy moods, drinking tea and so on; then became a *ronin* —in feudal days, a samurai without a master, now a student without a university—because of failing his examinations for Tokyo University (a sort of Harvard, Yale, Columbia and Berkeley rolled into one), and as is the custom, spending the following year preparing for the next round rather than attend a lesser institution; once admitted, found little to interest him until becoming an enthusiastic *Zengakuren* activist, with full embrace of its ideal of "pure Communism" and a profound sense of fulfillment in taking part in the planning and carrying out of student demonstrations; but when offered a high position in the organization during his junior year, abruptly became an *ex-Zangakuren* activist by resigning, because he felt he was not suited for "the life of a revolutionary"; then an aimless dissipator, as he drifted into a pattern of heavy drinking, marathon mah-jongg games and affairs with bar-girls; but when the time came, had no difficulty gaining employment with one of Japan's mammoth industrial organizations (and one of the *bêtes noires* of his Marxist days) and embarking upon the life of a young executive or *sarariman* (salaried man)—in fact doing so with eagerness, careful preparation and relief, but at the same time having fantasies and dreams of kicking over the traces, sometimes violently, and embarking upon a world tour (largely Hollywood-inspired) of exotic and sophisticated pleasure-seeking.

There are, of course, important differences between the protean life styles of the two young men, and between them and their American counterparts—differences which have to do with cultural emphases and which contribute to what is generally called national character. But such is the intensity of the shared aspects of historical experience that contemporary Chinese, Japanese and American self-process turn out to have striking points of convergence.

I would stress two historical developments as having special importance for creating protean man. The first is the world-wide sense of what I have called *historical* (or *psychohistorical*) *dislocation*, the break in the sense of connection which men have long felt with the vital and nourishing symbols of their cultural tradition—symbols revolving around family, idea systems, religions, and the life cycle in general. In our contemporary world one perceives these traditional symbols (as I have suggested elsewhere, using the Japanese as a paradigm) as irrelevant, burdensome or inactivating, and yet one cannot avoid carrying them within or having one's self-process profoundly affected by them. The second large historical tendency is the *flooding of imagery* produced by the extraordinary flow of post-modern cultural influences over mass communication networks. These cross readily over local and national boundaries, and permit each individual to be touched by everything, but at the same time cause him to be overwhelmed by superficial messages and undigested cultural elements, by headlines and by endless partial alternatives in every sphere of life. These alternatives, moreover, are universally and simultaneously shared—if not as courses of action, at least in the form of significant inner imagery.

We know from Greek mythology that Proteus was able to change his shape with relative ease—from wild boar to lion to dragon to fire to flood. But what he did find difficult, and would not do unless seized and chained, was to commit himself to a single form, the form most his own, and carry out his function of prophecy. We can say the same of protean man, but we must keep in mind his possibilities as well as his difficulties.

The protean style of self-process, then, is characterized by an interminable series of experiments and explorations—some shallow, some profound —each of which may be readily abandoned in favor of still new psychological quests. The pattern in many ways resembles what Erik Erikson has called "identity diffusion" or "identity confusion," and the impaired psychological functioning which those terms suggest can be very much present. But I would stress that the protean style is by no means pathological as such, and, in fact, may well be one of the functional patterns of our day. It extends to all areas of human experience—to political as well as sexual behavior, to the holding and promulgating of ideas and to the general organization of lives.

I would like to suggest a few illustrations of the protean style, as expressed in America and Europe, drawn both from psychotherapeutic work with patients and from observations on various forms of literature and art.

One patient of mine, a gifted young teacher, spoke of himself in this way:

I have an extraordinary number of masks I can put on or take off. The question is: is there, or should there be, one face which should be authentic? I'm not sure that there is one for me. I can think of other parallels to this, especially in literature. There are representations of every kind of crime, every kind of sin. For me, there is not a single act I cannot imagine myself committing.

He went on to compare himself to an actor on the stage who "performs with a certain kind of polymorphous versatility"—and here he was referring, slightly mockingly, to Freud's term, "polymorphous perversity," for diffusely inclusive (also protean) infantile sexuality. And he asked:

Which is the real person, so far as an actor is concerned? Is he more real when performing on the stage—or when he is at home? I tend to think that for people who have these many many masks, there is no home. Is it a futile gesture for the actor to try to find his real face?

My patient was by no means a happy man, but neither was he incapacitated. And although we can see the strain with which he carries his "polymorphous versatility," it could also be said that, as a teacher and a thinker, and in some ways as a man, it served him well.

In contemporary American literature, Saul Bellow is notable for the protean men he has created. In *The Adventures of Augie March,* one of his earlier novels, we meet a picaresque hero with a notable talent for adapting himself to divergent social worlds. Augie himself says: "I touched all sides, and nobody knew where I belonged. I had no good idea of that myself." And a perceptive young English critic, Tony Tanner, tells us: "Augie indeed celebrates the self, but he can find nothing to do with it." Tanner goes on to describe Bellow's more recent protean hero, Herzog, as "a representative modern intelligence, swamped with ideas, metaphysics, and values, and surrounded by messy facts. It labours to cope with them all."

A distinguished French literary spokesman for the protean style—in his life and in his work—is, of course, Jean-Paul Sartre. Indeed, I believe that it is precisely because of these protean traits that Sartre strikes us as such an embodiment of twentieth century man. An American critic, Theodore Solotaroff, speaks of Sartre's fundamental assumption that "there is no such thing as even a relatively fixed sense of self, ego, or identity—rather there is only the subjective mind in motion in relationship to that which it confronts." And Sartre himself refers to human consciousness as "a sheer activity transcending toward objects," and "a great emptiness, a wind blowing toward objects." These might be overstatements, but I doubt that they could have been written thirty years ago. Solotaroff further characterizes Sartre as

constantly on the go, hurrying from point to point, subject to subject; fiercely intentional, his thought occupies, fills, and distends its material as he endeavors to lose and find himself in his encounters with other lives, disciplines, books, and situations.

This image of repeated, autonomously willed death and rebirth of the self, so central to the protean style, becomes associated with the themes of fatherlessness—as Sartre goes on to tell us in his autobiography with his characteristic tone of serious self-mockery:

There is no good father, that's the rule. Don't lay the blame on men but on the bond of paternity, which is rotten. To beget children, nothing better; *to have* them, what iniquity! Had my father lived, he would have lain on me at full length and would have crushed me. . . . Amidst Aeneas and his fellows who carry their Anchises on their backs, I move from shore to shore, alone and hating those invisible begetters who bestraddle their sons all their life long. I left behind me a young man who did not have time to be my father and who could now be my son. Was it a good thing or bad? I don't know. But I readily subscribed to the verdict of an eminent psychoanalyst: I have no Superego.

We note Sartre's image of interchangeability of father and son, of "a young man who did not have time to be my father and who could now be my son"—which, in a literal sense refers to the age at which his father died, but symbolically suggests an extension of the protean style to intimate family relationships. And such reversals indeed become necessary in a rapidly changing world in which the sons must constantly "carry their fathers on their backs," teach them new things which they, as older people, cannot possibly know. The judgment of the absent superego, however, may be misleading, especially if we equate superego with susceptibility to guilt. What has actually disappeared—in Sartre and in protean man in general—is the *classic* superego, the internalization of clearly defined criteria of right and wrong transmitted within a particular culture by parents to their children. Protean man requires freedom from precisely that kind of superego—he requires a symbolic fatherlessness—in order to carry out his explorations. But rather than being free of guilt, we shall see that his guilt takes on a different form from that of his predecessors.

There are many other representations of protean man among contemporary novelists: in the constant internal and external motion of "beat generation" writings, such as Jack Kerouac's *On the Road;* in the novels of a gifted successor to that generation, J. P. Donleavy, particularly *The Ginger Man;* and of course in the work of European novelists such as Günter Grass, whose *The Tin Drum* is a breathtaking evocation of prewar Polish-German, wartime German and postwar German environments, in which the protagonist combines protean adaptability with a kind of perpetual physical-mental "strike" against any change at all.

In the visual arts, one of the most important postwar movements has been aptly named "action painting" to convey its stress upon process rather than fixed completion. And a more recent and related movement in sculpture, called Kinetic Art, goes further. According to Jean Tinguely, one of its leading practitioners, "artists are putting themselves in rhythm with their time, in contact with their epic, especially with permanent and perpetual movement." As revolutionary as any style or approach is the stress upon innovation per se which now dominates painting. I have frequently heard artists, themselves considered radical innovators, complain bitterly of the current standards dictating that "innovation is all," and of a turnover in art movements so rapid as to discourage the idea of holding still long enough to develop a particular style.

We also learn much from film stars. Marcello Mastroianni, when asked whether he agreed with *Time* magazine's characterization of him as "the neo-capitalist hero," gave the following answer:

In many ways, yes. But I don't think I'm any kind of hero, neo-capitalist or otherwise. If anything I am an *anti*-hero or at most a non hero. *Time* said I had the frightened, characteristically 20th-century look, with a spine made of plastic napkin rings. I accepted this—because modern man is that way; and being a product of my time and an artist, I can represent him. If humanity were all one piece, I would be considered a weakling.

Mastroianni accepts his destiny as protean man; he seems to realize that there are certain advantages to having a spine made of plastic napkin rings, or at least that it is an appropriate kind of spine to have these days.

John Cage, the composer, is an extreme exponent of the protean style, both in his music and in his sense of all of us as listeners. He concluded a recent letter to the *Village Voice* with the sentence: "Nowadays, everything happens at once and our souls are conveniently electronic, omniattentive." The comment is McLuhan-like, but what I wish to stress particularly is the idea of omniattention—the sense of contemporary man as having the possibility of "receiving" and "taking in" everything. In attending, as in being, nothing is "off limits."

To be sure, one can observe in contemporary man a tendency which seems to be precisely the opposite of the protean style. I refer to the closing off of identity or constriction of self-process, to a straight-and-narrow specialization in psychological as well as in intellectual life, and to reluctance to let in any "extraneous" influences. But I would emphasize that where this kind of constricted or "one-dimensional" self-process exists, it has an essentially reactive and compensatory quality. In this it differs from earlier characterological styles it may seem to resemble (such as the "inner-directed" man described by Riesman, and still earlier patterns in traditional society). For these were direct outgrowths of societies which then existed, and in harmony with those societies, while at the present time a constricted self-process requires continuous "psychological work" to fend off protean influences which are always abroad.

Protean man has a particular relationship to the holding of ideas which has, I believe, great significance for the politics, religion, and general intellectual life of the future. For just as elements of the self can be experimented with and readily altered, so can idea systems and ideologies be embraced, modified, let go of and reembraced, all with a new ease that stands in sharp contrast to the inner struggle we have in the past associated with these shifts. Until relatively recently, no more than one major ideological shift was likely to occur in a lifetime, and that one would be long remembered as a significant individual turning point accompanied by profound soul-searching and conflict. But today it is not unusual to encounter several such shifts, accomplished relatively painlessly, within a year or even a month; among many groups, the rarity is a man who has gone through life holding firmly to a single ideological vision.

In one sense, this tendency is related to "the end of ideology" spoken of by Daniel Bell, since protean man is incapable of enduring an unquestioning allegiance to the large ideologies and utopian thought of the nineteenth and early twentieth centuries. One must be cautious about speaking of the end of anything, however, especially ideology, and one also encounters in protean man what I would call strong ideological hunger. He is starved for ideas and feelings that can give coherence to his world, but here too his taste is toward new combinations. While he is by no means without yearning for the absolute, what he finds most acceptable are images of a more fragmentary nature than those of the ideologies of the past; and these images, although limited and often fleeting, can have great influence upon his psychological life. Thus political and religious movements, as they confront protean man, are likely to experience less difficulty convincing him to alter previous convictions than they do providing him a set of beliefs which can command his allegiance for more than a brief experimental interlude.

Intimately bound up with his flux in emotions and beliefs is a profound inner sense of absurdity, which finds expression in a tone of mockery. The sense and the tone are related to a perception of surrounding activities and belief as profoundly strange and inappropriate. They stem from a breakdown in the relationship between inner and outer worlds—that is, in the sense of symbolic integrity—and are part of the pattern of psychohistorical dislocation I mentioned earlier. For if we view man as primarily a symbol-forming organism, we must recognize that he has constant need of a meaningful inner formulation of self and world in which his own actions, and even his impulses, have some kind of "fit" with the "outside" as he perceives it.

The sense of absurdity, of course, has a considerable modern tradition, and has been discussed by such writers as Camus as a function of man's spiritual homelessness and inability to find any meaning in traditional belief systems. But absurdity and mockery have taken much more extreme forms in the post-World War II world, and have in fact become a prominent part of a universal life style.

In American life, absurdity and mockery are everywhere. Perhaps their most vivid expression can be found in such areas as Pop Art and the more general burgeoning of "pop culture." Important here is the complex stance of the pop artist toward the objects he depicts. On the one hand he embraces the materials of the everyday world, celebrates and even exalts them—boldly asserting his creative return to representational art (in active rebellion against the previously reigning nonobjective school), and his psychological return to the "real world" of *things*. On the other hand, everything he touches he mocks. "Thingness" is pressed to the point of caricature. He is indeed artistically reborn as he moves freely among the physical and symbolic materials of his environment, but mockery is his birth certificate and his passport. This kind of duality of approach is formalized in the stated "duplicity" of Camp, a poorly defined aesthetic in which (among other things) all varieties of mockery converge under the guiding influence of the homosexual's subversion of a heterosexual world.

Also relevant are a group of expressions in current slang, some of them derived originally from jazz. The "dry mock" has replaced the dry wit; one refers to a segment of life experience as a "bit," "bag," "caper," "game," (or "con game"), "scene," "show" or "scenario"; and one seeks to "make the scene" (or "make it"), "beat the system" or "pull it off"—or else one "cools it" ("plays it cool") or "cops out." The thing to be experienced, in other words, is too absurd to be taken at its face value; one must either keep most of the self aloof from it, or if not, one must lubricate the encounter with mockery.

A similar spirit seems to pervade literature and social action alike. What is best termed a "literature of mockery" has come to dominate fiction and other forms of writing on an international scale. Again Günter Grass's *The Tin Drum* comes to mind, and is probably the greatest single example of this literature—a work, I believe, which will eventually be appreciated as much as a general evocation of contemporary man as of the particular German experience with Nazism. In this country the divergent group of novelists known as "black humorists" also fit into the general category— related as they are to a trend in the American literary consciousness which R. W. B. Lewis has called a "savagely comical apocalypse" or a "new kind of ironic literary form and disturbing vision, the joining of the dark thread of apocalypse with the nervous detonations of satiric laughter." For it is precisely death itself, and particularly threats of the contemporary apocalypse, that protean man ultimately mocks.

The relationship of mockery to political and social action has been less apparent, but is, I would claim, equally significant. There is more than coincidence in the fact that the largest American student uprising of recent decades, the Berkeley Free Speech Movement of 1965, was followed immediately by a "Dirty Speech Movement." While the object of the Dirty Speech Movement—achieving free expression of forbidden language, particularly of four-letter words—can be viewed as a serious one, the predominant effect, even in the matter of names, was that of a mocking caricature of the movement which preceded it. But if mockery can undermine protest, it can also enliven it. There have been signs of craving for it in major American expressions of protest such as the Negro movement and the opposition to the war in Vietnam. In the former a certain chord can be struck by the comedian Dick Gregory, and in the latter by the use of satirical skits and parodies, a chord that revives the flagging attention of protestors becoming gradually bored with the repetition of their "straight" slogans and goals. And on an international scale, I would say that during the past decade, Russian intellectual life has been enriched by a leavening spirit of mockery—against which the Chinese leaders are now, in the extremes of their "Cultural Revolution," fighting a vigorous but ultimately losing battle.

Closely related to the sense of absurdity and the spirit of mockery is another characteristic of protean man which can be called "suspicion of counterfeit nurturance." Involved here is a severe conflict of dependency, a core problem of protean man. I first began to think of the concept several years ago while working with survivors of the atomic bomb in Hiroshima. I found that these survivors both felt themselves in need of special help, and resented whatever help was offered them because they equated it with weakness and inferiority. In considering the matter more generally, I found this equation of nurturance with a threat to autonomy a major theme of contemporary life. The increased dependency needs resulting from the breakdown of traditional institutions lead protean man to seek out replacements wherever he can find them. The large organizations (such as government, business and academic) to which he turns, and which contemporary society more and more holds out as a substitute for traditional institutions, present an ambivalent threat to his autonomy in one way, and the intense individual relationships in which he seeks to anchor himself in another. Both are therefore likely to be perceived as counterfeit. But the obverse side of this tendency is an expanding sensitivity to the unauthentic, which may be just beginning to exert its general creative force on man's behalf.

Technology (and technique in general), together with science, have special significance for protean man. Technical achievement of any kind can be strongly embraced to combat inner tendencies toward diffusion, and to transcend feelings of absurdity and conflicts over counterfeit nurturance. The image of science itself, however, as the ultimate power behind technology and, to a considerable extent, behind contemporary thought in general, becomes much more difficult to cope with. Only in certain underdeveloped countries can one find, in relatively pure form, those expectations of scientific-utopian deliverance from all human want and conflict which were characteristic of eighteenth and nineteenth century western thought. Protean man retains much of this utopian imagery, but he finds it increasingly undermined by massive disillusionment. More and more he calls forth the other side of the God-devil polarity generally applied to science, and sees it as a purveyor of total destructiveness. This kind of profound ambivalence creates for him the most extreme psychic paradox: the very force he still feels to be his liberator from the heavy burdens of past irrationality also threatens him with absolute annihilation, even extinction. But this paradox may well be—in fact, I believe, already has been—the source of imaginative efforts to achieve new relationships between science and man, and indeed, new visions of science itself.

I suggested before that protean man was not free of guilt. He indeed suffers from it considerably, but often without an awareness of what is causing his suffering. For his is a form of hidden guilt: a vague but persistent kind of self-condemnation related to the symbolic disharmonies I have described, a sense of having no outlet for his loyalties and no symbolic structure for his achievements. This is the guilt of social breakdown, and it includes various forms of historical and racial guilt experienced by whole nations and peoples, both by the privileged and the abused. Rather than a clear feeling of evil or sinfulness, it takes the form of a nagging sense of unworthiness all the more troublesome for its lack of clear origin.

Protean man experiences similarly vague constellations of anxiety and resentment. These too have origin in symbolic impairments and are particularly tied in with suspicion of counterfeit nurturance. Often feeling himself uncared for, even abandoned, protean man responds with diffuse fear and anger. But he can neither find a good cause for the former, nor a consistent target for the latter. He nonetheless cultivates his anger because he finds it more serviceable than anxiety, because there are plenty of targets of one kind or another beckoning, and because even moving targets are better than none. His difficulty is that focused indignation is as hard for him to sustain as is any single identification or conviction.

Involved in all of these patterns is a profound psychic struggle with the idea of change itself. For here too protean man finds himself ambivalent in the extreme. He is profoundly attracted to the idea of making all things, including himself, totally new—to the "mode of transformation." But he is equally drawn to an image of a mythical past of perfect harmony and prescientific wholeness, to the "mode of restoration." Moreover, beneath his transformationism is nostalgia, and beneath his restorationism is his fascinated attraction to contemporary forms and symbols. Constantly balancing these elements midst the extraordinarily rapid change surrounding his own life, the nostalgia is pervasive, and can be one of his most explosive and dangerous emotions. This longing for a "Golden Age" of absolute oneness, prior to individual and cultural separation or delineation, not only sets the tone for the restorationism of the politically Rightist antagonists of history: the still-extant Emperor-worshiping assassins in Japan, the Colons in France and the John Birchites and Ku Klux Klanners in this country. It also, in more disguised form, energizes that transformationist totalism of the Left which courts violence, and is even willing to risk nuclear violence, in a similarly elusive quest.

Following upon all that I have said are radical impairments to the symbolism of transition within the life cycle—the *rites de passage* surrounding birth, entry into adulthood, marriage and death. Whatever rites remain seem shallow, inappropriate, fragmentary. Protean man cannot take them seriously, and often seeks to improvise new ones with whatever contemporary materials he has available, including cars and drugs. Perhaps the central impairment here is that of symbolic immortality—of the universal need for imagery of connection predating and extending beyond the individual life span, whether the idiom of this immortality is biological (living on through children and grandchildren), theological (through a life after death), natural (*in* nature itself which outlasts all) or creative (through what man makes and does). I have suggested elsewhere that this sense of immortality is a fundamental component of ordinary psychic life, and that it is now being profoundly threatened: by simple historical velocity, which subverts the idioms (notably the theological) in which it has traditionally been maintained, and, of particular importance to protean man, by the existence of nuclear weapons, which, even without being used, call into question all modes of immortality. (Who can be certain of living on through children and grandchildren, through teachings or kindnesses?)

Protean man is left with two paths to symbolic immortality which he tries to cultivate, sometimes pleasurably and sometimes desperately. One is the natural mode we have mentioned. His attraction to nature and concern at its desecration has to do with an unconscious sense that, in whatever holocaust, at least nature will endure—though such are the dimensions of our present weapons that he cannot be absolutely certain even of this. His second path may be termed that of "experiential transcendence"—of seeking a sense of immortality in the way that mystics always have, through psychic experience of such great intensity that time and death are, in effect, eliminated. This, I believe, is the larger meaning of the "drug revolution," of protean man's hunger for chemical aids to "expanded consciousness." And indeed all revolutions may be thought of, at bottom, as innovations in the struggle for immortality, as new combinations of old modes.

We have seen that young adults individually, and youth movements collectively, express most vividly the psychological themes of protean man. And although it is true that these themes make contact with what we sometimes call the "psychology of adolescence," we err badly if we overlook their expression in all age groups and dismiss them as "mere adolescent phenomena." Rather, protean man's affinity for the young—his being metaphorically and psychologically so young in spirit—has to do with his never-ceasing quest for imagery of rebirth. He seeks such imagery from all sources: from ideas, techniques, religious and political systems, mass movements and drugs; or from special individuals of his own kind whom he sees as possessing that problematic gift of his namesake, the gift of prophecy. The dangers inherent in the quest seem hardly to require emphasis. What perhaps needs most to be kept in mind is the general principle that renewal on a large scale is impossible to achieve without forays into danger, destruction and negativity. The principle of "death and rebirth" is as valid psychohistorically as it is mythologically. However misguided many of his forays may be, protean man also carries with him an extraordinary range of possibility for man's betterment, or more important, for his survival.

THE EXPERIENCE OF NOTHINGNESS

Michael Novak

MICHAEL NOVAK is Associate Professor of Philosophy and Religious
Studies at the experimental Old Westbury campus of The State
University of New York..He is the author of many novels, books,
and articles. His latest books include *Ascent of the Mountain, Flight
of the Dove* (1971), *The Experience of Nothingness* (1970), and
Theology for a Radical Politics (1969).

The experience of nothingness is an incomparably fruitful starting place
for ethical inquiry. It is a vaccine against the lies upon which every
civilization, American civilization in particular, is built. It exposes man as
animal, question-asker, symbol-maker.

I wish to show from the experience of nothingness that no man *has* a
self or an identity; in a society like ours he must constantly be *inventing*
selves. I also wish to show that even the most solid and powerful social
institutions, though they may imprison us, impoverish us, or kill us, are
fundamentally mythical structures designed to hold chaos and formlessness
at bay: they are more like dreams than like reality. The experience of
nothingness, with or without psychoanalytic, social, and theological criticism, dissolves the pragmatic solidity of the American way of life.

The hopes of those young people who desire to bring about a revolution
in America seem doomed to bitter and painful frustration; the experience
of nothingness, carefully reflected upon, might arm them against that
event. I hope to write of that experience in a way that leads not to passivity
or to a sense of defeat, but to calm ardor and revolutionary expectation.[1]

THE PURSUIT OF HAPPINESS

In American society the pursuit of happiness has almost attained the
status of a constitutional right. Yet is it wise, or human, or good to pursue
happiness? At any cost? At anyone's expense? By any deeds whatever? A
small number of men and women have no special right, have they, to
accept a major part of the wealth of the entire planet? May they pursue
their own happiness with little regard for the lot of the vast majority of
men?

[1] My purpose is not altogether different from that of Josiah Royce, in one of the
first volumes of the Bross Library, *The Sources of Religious Insight* (New York:
Scribners, 1912).

Americans think of happiness as a psychological state of contentment or fulfillment, in which pleasure outbalances pain.[2] Yet the psychological states of essentially white, middle class Americans may not be so sacred that all other values, purposes, and meanings in the universe must be subservient to them. Many Americans imagine that the conditions of happiness can be satisfied by a balanced diet, suburban living, social status, and success in one's marriage and work. If a college coed writes home to her mother that she is restless and ill at ease, her mother is not likely to write back: "Don't worry, darling, it's only the ontological anxiety that all of us must share." She will more likely write: "Are you sure you're eating well? Are you getting enough sleep?" One would think, to watch the frequency with which Americans smile and assure each other that they are happy, that it is unpatriotic for an American to be discontent. "AMERICA: LOVE IT OR LEAVE IT!" the bumper stickers say.

From 1870 to 1940, the experience of nothingness swept through the educated class of Europe. The "disease" hardly seemed to touch well-fed, active, busy Americans. Even philosophers like Sidney Hook[3] and Charles Frankel[4] found existentialist literature on the subject vague, foreign, and self-serving. In America things were always looking up.

It seems indispensable to a technological society like ours to be future-oriented, forward-looking, fascinated by hope. The illusion of progress is the prop that takes the place of God; many cling to it. Could Americans endure life without ever new frontiers? Our national psyche is ill at ease wherever progress, our most important product, is not evident. Our image of world history places Washington (why not Peking—older, more various, more populous, more deeply cultured?) at the cutting edge of the line of progress that passes from ancient Israel to Athens to Rome to Paris and to London. Other nations are called developed or underdeveloped by comparison with us. In American eyes the march of time is linear; its direction, despite temporary setbacks, is up.

Suppose the American myth of progress, pragmatism, and fulfillment is wrong. Suppose history is going—precisely nowhere. Suppose the human costs of progress, for which we now have no measure, are steeper than

2 "Where family and nation once stood, or Church and Party, there will be hospital and theater too, the normative institutions of the next culture. . . . Religious man was born to be saved; psychological man is born to be pleased. The difference was established long ago, when 'I believe,' theory of the ascetic, lost precedence to 'one feels,' the caveat of the therapeutic. And if the therapeutic is to win out, then surely the psychotherapist will be his secular spiritual guide." Philip Rieff, *The Triumph of the Therapeutic: Uses of Faith After Freud* (New York: Harper & Row, Harper Torchbooks, 1966), pp. 24–25.

3 Sidney Hook says the question asked by Schelling and Heidegger, "Why is there something: why is there not nothing?" is "devoid of sense except as a sign of emotional anxiety." *The Quest for Being* (New York: St. Martin's Press, 1961), p. 147.

4 Charles Frankel, *The Love of Anxiety and Other Essays* (New York: Dell, Delta, 1967), pp. 1–11.

the technical gains we are so fond of measuring.[5] By assuming a new way of looking at the world, a great many young Americans have begun to disabuse themselves of the myths of the American way of life. Their precious years have sunk deep into the mud of Vietnam until they choke for breath. Ours is, they say with horror, a militarist, counterrevolutionary, racist nation.[6] For several years now, some young people have pinned their hopes upon the possibility of a revolution in American values. Many grow discouraged, disillusioned, sad. They can't go home to the suburban way of life they fled with abhorrence; the ledge ahead seems impassable. They are suspended, unable to talk with those five years older than they, some perhaps unable to talk with those five years younger.

I want to set a question before them: Have not you, too, sometimes tried with your theater of the streets, your frantic politics, to escape the feeling of nothingness? Have not you, too, like your parents, frequently turned to action as if it were a potion of forgetfulness? Are you not true children of your parents, clinging to the belief in essential human goodness, in love with quick solutions, dreaming of a gentle paradise? . . . Can action based upon evasion fail to end in bitterness?

THE EXPERIENCE OF AMERICA

"The experience of nothingness" is an experience, not a concept. It can be pointed to, described, built up indirectly, but not defined. Meursault's experience in *The Stranger*, Tolstoy's *The Death of Ivan Illich*, Kafka's "Metamorphosis," Sartre's *The Age of Reason*, and Saul Bellow's *The Dangling Man* are among its literary expressions. The experience of nothingness, however, arises in original forms today. The literature of preceding generations comforts us that we are not alone, but it does not precisely define our state of soul.

Today, for the young, consciousness is shaped by the fluidity of percepts.[7] Undifferentiated time is the medium of consciousness, like a sea on which and in which images float. The shaper of an alert, intelligent

[5] "Developed societies may well experience, in the not-too-distant future, occupational and geographical migrations or internal conflicts whose disruptive effects will dwarf those now occurring in non-developed lands. What ecological tragedies may not await the United States, generated by the very 'success' it has had in industrializing and producing goods efficiently? Will these be less destructive than those suffered by the victims of nature's ecological caprices (droughts, floods, plagues)? While it is easy for us to measure the high price paid for remaining underdeveloped, we lack instruments to gauge the price paid for the vaunted 'efficiency' attendant upon development." Denis Goulet, "Development for What?," *Comparative Political Studies*, July 1968, p. 303.
[6] See my *Theology for a Radical Politics* (New York: Herder & Herder, 1969).
[7] Siegfried Kraucauer, *Theory of Film* (New York: Oxford University Press, 1965).

consciousness is no longer a corpus of writings ("literature") nor the pursuit of a rigorous, analytical line of argument ("the sciences"). Many good students, of good will, who really want to read and to learn about the past, find it very difficult to concentrate. The new shaper of alert, discerning consciousness is the camera. The images on a screen are not sequential; time is dissolved, turned upon itself, defeated. The present gains at the expense of past and future. The attention of the camera zooms in, pulls back, superimposes, cuts away suddenly, races, slows, flashes back, flicks ahead, juxtaposes, repeats, spins. A turn of the wrist at the channel indicator alters reality. For those introduced to consciousness by such a teacher, the world is fluid. The percepts are too many and too rich to order, except by certain rhythms of emotion.

Roland Barthes describes in *Writing Degree Zero* the gradual collapse after 1850 of the canonical "literature" of the European aristocracy and bourgeoisie.[8] The language of the poor, the prostitutes, and the beggars entered the consciousness of writers; the pretensions of the classical and bourgeois traditions to universality were shattered. The use by middle class historians and novelists of the narrative past tense ("The marchioness went out at five o'clock") and of the third person ("he") had masked an ordered worldview, a definiteness, a position in the cosmos, safely observed. Such a universe could easily be shaped by stories: beginning, middle, end. Madness, chaos, and profound diversity were neatly kept outside. After the revolution of 1848, the writer began to feel uneasy in the literary tradition; that tidy image had been shattered. He listened for a voice of his own, listened, finally, for the neutral, clear, amoral voice achieved most flawlessly by Camus in *The Stranger*. Writing moved outside "Literature," "Tradition," "Society." The human race lacks unity; the writer recognized the absence of a language of unity. He continues today to trace his personal mythic history, defeated even by his own successes: he renders his isolation only to find it debased as common currency.

But the dispersal of consciousness experienced by the younger generation in the United States goes further still. In the classic French myth, the center of consciousness is a clear eye, focusing on "clear, distinct ideas." "I *think*, therefore I am." Hence the painful clarity of French sensibility and consciousness. In the United States, in an ever growing sub-culture at least, the equivalent affirmation is simply: "I feel." No "therefore" is available, or needed. The eye of consciousness yields to affect, percept, kaleidoscope. The self is a recipient of stimuli in a darkened room. I know I am alive when a warm body is next to mine. Connections come through skin.

In the new civilization then, the primary sense of reality is shaped partly by parents and neighbors (local customs, raised eyebrows), partly

---

[8] Roland Barthes, *Writing Degree Zero* (London: Jonathan Cape, 1967).

by books ("the liberal tradition"), but mostly by cinema, television, and records. It is a civilization of massive dissolution.

Those whose sense of the meaningful, the relevant, and the real is not entirely shaped by the new media may feel themselves caught between two barbarisms. If they imagine the self to be a seeing eye, a fierce and mastering awareness—Reason—then they stand accused of the barbaric rationalization of human life that has yielded Dallas, airline terminals, body count, and painful inner emptiness. If they imagine the self to be a center of feeling, they will certainly be drawn to darkness, blood and destruction. (The "gentle revolution" is innocent when no threat faces it. The young have learned to cope when they are shown approval. Denied their will, their aspect is terrifying. Events, inevitably harsh, will surely make them bitter; filled with resentment, distrustful, they will feel trapped, a thousand times betrayed.) Apollo sheered from Dionysus yields two tribes of beasts.

The experience of nothingness in America, however, cuts across all networks: neighbor culture, book culture, electronic culture. In every part of America the sense of security has been undermined; nearly everything must be defended. All the more because the Republic was established to ensure our happiness, we find reality too much to bear. The experience of nothingness seeps into our awareness through a sieve.

Boredom is the first taste of nothingness. Today, boredom is the chief starting place of metaphysics. For boredom leads instantly to "killing time." And why is time a threat? Time, on the stage of consciousness, stands still. For the bored, no action is more attractive than any other. The self cannot be drawn into action; it lives by and for distractions; it waits. The world acts; the self is acted on. The fighter pilot whose skeleton is supported by the web straps of a plane crashed long ago in the jungles of Iwo Jima might today be supported by the web strap of a commuter train. Death seems continuous with death-in-life. Many have an overpowering urge to sleep. When Superman meets the social worker (Jules Feiffer), he learns that he is not an agent; he is acted on, his behavior has been determined. He loses strength. He droops.

Boredom: the discovery that everything is a game. A friend of mine decided that, short of suicide, one bulwark against time is a game sufficiently complicated to hold his attention until death. He made enough money as an electronics engineer (a specialist in game theory) to have free at least one year in every three. He determined to visit every town on the planet with a population over twenty-five thousand. During his working years he pored over maps; during his traveling years he concentrated on one continent after another. He often stayed in a town only long enough to lunch and to make a mark on his list. The beauty of it is, he told me, that a booming population, wars, and refugees guarantee an ever changing list.

Besides boredom, there is the collapse of a strongly inculcated set of values. I have heard students say with bitterness that high school is "enough betrayal for a lifetime." A seeing-eye God who turns out to be on the side of parents, society, philistinism, law and order, mind and dessication. But after that, what? Many search for a new social order, a new community of love. Without a vision they would perish; a utopia becomes their crutch, filling the psychological need once filled by God. Social scientists leap in to tell the adolescent that everything is relative, that everything is determined, and to suggest that the social system is the source of his inner emptiness. (The "system" plays, today, the role of devil.) Plato: the system is the self writ large; the alienation of the self comes from the system. The young are left with the inner helplessness they learned in grammar school. Their rage is legitimated; it is projected outward. They flail against "the dehumanization of the American way of life." Although the new imperative is "Humanize the system," it is impossible to discern the criteria for "humanization." No society in history ever met all the needs the young feel. Slowly the young learn that even warm, close lovers betray one another, and each discovers in himself countless self-betrayals. Gone are the old firm values; gone also the innocent world that replaced them. Alienation projected onto the system is evasion. It evades a more terrifying emptiness.

Thirdly, there is helplessness. It is not only the large, impersonal bureaucracy that engenders feelings of helplessness. It is not only the feeling that "I have no control over my life." It is also the recognition that those who wield power are also empty, and that I, too, if I had power over my life, am most confused about what I would do with it. The sense of helplessness today is not, in the end, political; power, even pressed down and running over, does not fill the void; it merely masks it. In the eyes of the successful leaders of the Students for a Democratic Society, as in those of the occupants of the White House, one may still see nothingness.

Fourthly, there is the betrayal by permissiveness, pragmatism, and value-neutral discourse. "To every child a childhood." The young have a right to learn a way of discriminating right from wrong, the posed from the authentic, the excellent from the mediocre, the brilliant from the philistine, the shoddy from the workmanlike. When no one with experience bothers to insist—to insist—on such discrimination, they rightly get the idea that discernment is not important, that no one cares, that no one cares either about such things—or about them. For it is demanding to teach children ethics, beauty, excellence; demanding in itself, and even more demanding to do so with authenticity. The laissez-faire attitude of American society in matters of the human spirit represents one of the greatest mass betrayals of responsibility by any civilization in human history. (Ironically, the young in their rebellion often manifest in the form of "Do your own thing" precisely this profound sickness of their elders.)

Fifthly, there are drug experiences, and uncounted experiences with intimacy unwanted but given anyway. The young are forced to live through the problems of technological consciousness, problems created by generations who built a rational, efficient society without calculating in advance its effect upon human beings. The apocalypse may come, not by fire or flood, but by mass insanity. The civilization in and around New York City surely manifests insanity's advancing stages: everywhere there is hostility, bitterness, resentment—that grinding, bitter resentment of which Nietzsche and Scheler warned. People lash out at one another. Parents ridicule children. Wives scream at husbands.

Everywhere there is the experience of mechanical relationships. Has anyone ever counted how many persons in the United States are paid for telling lies? Has anyone ever counted the proportion of human transactions in which Americans are forced to treat one another impersonally, superficially, without interest? It is quite plain that Americans, the most nomadic people since the medieval Arabs, seldom grow organically into marriage. When they marry, they know only a small segment—hardly the least decisive—of their partners' lives. After they marry, the lives of husbands and wives are commonly attracted into separate orbits, sheering apart from one another. Nothing organic, nothing mutually rooted.

The enormous weight, meanwhile, put upon mutual sexual fulfillment is insupportable; intercourse is an organic expression of entire psyches, not a mechanical plugging in. Among young people, the weakening of cultural forms supporting sexual rituals and restraints deprives sexual intercourse of sustenance for the imagination and the spirit. It comes too cheaply: its intimacy is mainly fake; its symbolic power is reduced to the huddling warmth of kittens in the darkness—not to be despised, but open as a raw wound to the experience of nothingness. Close your eyes and plummet through the empty space where a lover ought to be.

A complete phenomenology of the experience of nothingness in our generation is neither possible nor desirable. There are as many ways for that unmistakable experience to break into one's consciousness as there are personal histories. Some feel its touch by way of sickness or disaster, some by way of external event and others by inner breakdown, some in the flush of power and others in irretrievable despair. The experience of nothingness comes uninvited; it may also be pursued. It is not found at the boundaries of life merely, at the broken places; [9] it comes also from

---

[9] Contrast Dietrich Bonhoeffer: "Religious people speak of God when human knowledge (perhaps simply because they are too lazy to think) has come to an end, or when human resources fail—in fact it is always the *deus ex machina* that they bring on to the scene, either for the apparent solution of insoluble problems, or as strength in human failure—always, that is to say, exploiting human weakness or human boundaries. . . . It always seems to me that we are trying anxiously in this way to reserve some space for God; I should like to speak of God not on the boundaries but at the centre, not in weakness but in strength; and therefore not in death and guilt but in man's life and goodness." *Letters and Papers From Prison,* rev. ed. (New York: Macmillan paperback, 1967), p. 142.

the very center, from the core of joy and pride and dignity. The strong
nod at its voice with familiarity no less than the weak. The men and
women from the lower middle class lack fancy words for it, but behind
the skin of their faces it sits with the same mask it wears under the faces
of television commentators.

Nor is the experience of nothingness accurately named *Angst* (Kierkegaard, Heidegger). Somehow the European hungers to possess his own
being, to be the cause of his own existence, to be God.[10] When he discovers
that his own being is partial and invaded by nonbeing, he feels an icy
threat. But the experience of nothingness in America is more often a
peculiar and quiet vulnerability, a dead stillness at the center of activity,
a lack of drive, an ignorance of Being and Life and Faith, a bafflement
that a future that should have been so lovely turns out so bleak. The
American experience of nothingness is a certain sadness. We do not have,
despite our reputation, the European willfulness; behind our frenetic
activity and self-assurance lurks a soft, purring, wounded kitten. We are
not metaphysical but sentimental.

In Europe: Nihilism

One cannot, however, give the American experience voice without turning to its European background. European thinkers, of course, immediately turned the experience of nothingness, which began to "infect"
Europeans with increasing frequency in the nineteenth century, into an
"ism"; they spoke of it ideologically, as nihilism. They wrote from a history
of unsurpassed intellectual energy. They had seen mythology, religion,
and science express themselves in a brilliant sunrise of cultural history,
each stage "higher" than the preceding; and then in the nineteenth century
as they were stepping toward the peak of their achievement, on the
threshold of a golden age, during nearly a century of relative world
peace, they peered down into a fathomless abyss. Friedrich Nietzsche,
like a tongue darting into a cavity, could not divert his attention. He
asked himself again and again: "What does nihilism mean?" In a single
felicitous sentence he answered: "The aim is lacking; 'why?' finds no
answer." [11]

The experience of nothingness is a mode of human consciousness; it
occurs in human beings, not in cats or trees.[12] It is, often, a kind of
exhaustion of spirit that comes from seeking "meaning" too long and too

[10] See Jean-Paul Sartre, "The Desire to Be God," in *Existentialism and Human
Emotions* (New York: Philosophical Library, 1957), pp. 60–67.

[11] Friedrich Nietzsche, *The Will to Power*, ed. Walter Kaufmann (New York:
Random House, 1967), p. 9.

[12] Albert Camus, *The Myth of Sisyphus and Other Essays* (New York: Random
House, Vintage Books, 1960), p. 38.

ardently. It is accompanied by terror. It seems like a kind of death, an inertness, a paralysis. Meanwhile, the dark impulses of destruction find only thin resistance, they beat upon the doors for instantaneous release. The threshold of rage, suicide, and murder is frighteningly low. (Does death make any difference?) Yet even more vivid than the dark emotions are a desert-like emptiness, a malaise, an illness of the spirit and the stomach. One sees all too starkly the fraudulence of human arrangements. Every engagement seems so involved in half-truth, lie, and unimportance that the will to believe and the will to act collapse like ash.

Nietzsche distinguished three phases in the experience of nothingness, and it may be helpful to follow his notes on the subject, which are too long to quote in full.[13] "Nihilism," he wrote, "will have to be reached, *first,* when we have sought in all events a 'meaning' that is not there." Nihilism, then, is a "recognition of the long *waste* of strength"; one is "ashamed in front of oneself, as if one had *deceived* oneself all too long." One had hoped to *achieve* something through one's actions, "and now one realizes that becoming aims at *nothing* and achieves *nothing.*"

Nihilism "as a psychological state is reached, *secondly,*" he writes, "when one has posited a totality," an organization, a unity "in all events, and underneath all events," so that a man will have "a deep feeling of standing in the context of, and being dependent on, some whole that is infinitely superior to him." This whole need not be God, but it is, at least, some scheme like that of progress, or the advance of science, or the fate of civilization, all of which function as some form of deity.[14] "But, behold, there is no such universal! At bottom, man has lost the faith in his own value when no infinitely valuable whole works through him; i.e., he conceived such a whole *in order to be able to believe in his own value.*"

The experience of nothingness has yet a third and last form:

Given these two insights, that becoming has no goal and that underneath all becoming there is no grand unity in which the individual could immerse himself completely as in an element of supreme value, an escape remains: to pass sentence on this whole world of becoming as a deception and to invent a world beyond it, a *true* world. Having reached this standpoint, one grants the reality of becoming as the *only* reality, forbids oneself every kind of clandestine access to afterworlds and false divinities—*but cannot endure this world though one does not want to deny it.*

What has happened, at bottom? The feeling of valuelessness was reached with the realization that the overall character of existence may not be interpreted by means of the concept of an "aim," the concept of "unity," or the concept of "truth." Existence has no goal or end; any comprehensive unity in the plurality of events is lacking: the character of existence is not "true," is *false.* One simply lacks any reason for convincing oneself that there is a *true* world. Briefly: the

13 Nietzsche, op. cit., pp. 12–13.

14 Here I depart from Nietzsche's words. His sentence reads: ". . . and a soul that longs to admire and revere has wallowed in the idea of some supreme form of domination and administration (—if the soul be that of logician, complete consistency and real dialectic are quite sufficient to reconcile it to everything)." Ibid.

categories "aim," "unity," "being," which we used to project some values into the world—we *pull out* again; so the world looks valueless.

I recognize that I put structure into my own world. Such recognition is a necessary condition of the experience of nothingness. There is no "real" world out there, given, intact, full of significance. Consciousness is constituted by random, virtually infinite barrages of experience; these experiences are indistinguishably "inner" and "outer." The mad are aware of that buzzing confusion. The sane have put structure into it.[15] Structure *is put into experience by culture and the self*, and may also be pulled out again. Sociological consciousness recognizes such an insight under the rubric of "relativism." But the experience of nothingness casts doubt, also, on the reasons and methods of sociology (and every other science or philosophy). In its light they, too, seem like useless passions. The experience of nothingness is an experience beyond the limits of reason. It arises near the borderline of insanity. It is terrifying. It makes all attempts at speaking of purpose, goals, aims, meaning, importance, conformity, harmony, unity—it makes all such attempts seem doubtful and spurious. The person gripped by the experience of nothingness sees nearly everything *in reverse image*. What other persons call certain, he sees as pretend; what other persons call pragmatic or effective, he sees as a most ironical delusion. There is no real world out there, he says. Within human beings and outside them, there is only a great darkness, in which momentary beams of attention flash like fireflies. The experience of nothingness is an awareness of the multiplicity and polymorphousness of experience, and of the tide urging the conscious self to shape its own confusion by projecting myths.

Most people, of course, are instructed by their parents, schools, churches, economic and social roles, and other instruments of culture to shape their inner and outer confusion in clear, direct ways. A person who is "well brought up" is balanced, well adjusted, well rounded, purposive, dutiful, clear in his aims, views, and values. The well-brought-up person has been sheltered from the experience of nothingness. His feet are planted on solid ground. His perceptions of himself, others, and the world have been duly arranged.[16] For him the question of reality has been settled. That is real

---

[15] Experience, R. D. Laing writes, is neither "subjective" nor "objective," neither "inner" nor "outer." In ordinary and scholarly discourse, "inner" and "outer" distinguish between experience and behavior. "More accurately this a distinction between different modalities of experience, namely, perception (as outer) in contrast to imagination, etc. (as inner). But perception, imagination, fantasy, reverie, dreams, memory, are simply different *modalities of experience*, none more 'inner' or 'outer' than any other" (p. 20). In our society, socialization creates a "split between experience and behavior" in which the inner is split from the outer (p. 54). *The Politics of Experience* (New York: Ballantine Books, 1967).

[16] "The family's function is to repress Eros; to induce a false consciousness of security; to deny death by avoiding life; to cut off transcendence; to believe in God, not to experience the Void; to create, in short, *one dimensional man;* to promote respect, conformity, obedience; to con children out of play; to induce a fear of failure, to promote a respect for work; to promote a respect for 'respectability.' " Ibid., p. 65.

which his culture says is real; that is of value which his culture values. His convictions about the aim of life have been formed in him by his culture. What he is to perceive and experience in life is determined in advance, and he *will* not allow himself to perceive or to experience otherwise.

To choose against the culture is not merely to disobey; it is to "die." Against what the culture knows is real, true, and good, one has chosen the evil, the false, and the unreal. To be or not to be, that is the question. To choose against the culture is to experience nothingness.

Nihilism is an ideological interpretation imposed on the experience of nothingness. Most writers on nihilism have placed the experience of nothingness in opposition to the values of the culture, as though that experience were a threat to it.[17] I want to argue that the power of the experience of nothingness has been misperceived. Its root and source have not been detected, or else have been wrongly identified. The experience of nothingness was so new, so powerful, and so unexpected that it arrived *inconnu*. All who have since reflected upon it stand in the debt of Nietzsche and Heidegger, Freud and Sartre, but in probing for its source and power no one has yet driven an arrow into the center of the circle. The unassimilable horror of the regime of Adolf Hitler showed that the experience of nothingness may be put to the most horrible uses; the experience of nothingness may be murderous.[18] Nevertheless, the experience of nothingness is now the point from which nearly every reflective man begins his adult life. We have seen too much blood to be astonished that Hitlers are possible. History, Hegel said, is a butcher's bench.

Still, the sorrows of this century have distorted our reflections on the experience of nothingness. That experience leads not only to murder; it is also the source of creativity and plenitude. We need not avert our eyes from the nihilism of the Fascists, or evade the ambiguities of nothingness. We can also reflect upon the preconditions and fertile possibilities of that experience, which in any case already occupies our hearts.

The source of the experience of nothingness lies in the deepest recesses of human consciousness, in its irrepressible tendency to ask

[17] For Freud, ". . . besides the instinct to preserve living substance and to pin it into ever larger units, there must exist another, contrary instinct seeking to dissolve those units and to bring them back to their primeval, inorganic state. That is to say, as well as Eros there was an instinct of death." *Civilization and Its Discontents* (New York: W. W. Norton, 1961), pp. 65–66, 92.

[18] The Nazis taught Camus that the word "nihilism" cannot be used lightly; it has consequences. "What is truth, you used to ask? To be sure, but at least we know what falsehood is; that is just what you have taught us. What is spirit? We know its contrary, which is murder. What is man? There I stop you, for we know. Man is that force which ultimately cancels all tyrants and gods. He is the force of evidence. Human evidence is what we must preserve, and our certainty at present comes from the fact that its fate and our country's fate are linked together. If nothing had any meaning, you would be right. But there is something that still has a meaning." Camus, "Letters to a German Friend: Second Letter," *Resistance, Rebellion and Death* (New York: Alfred A. Knopf, 1961), p. 14.

questions. The necessary condition for the experience of nothingness is that everything can be questioned. Whatever the presuppositions of a culture or a way of life, questions can be addressed against them and other alternatives can be imagined. Whatever the massive solidity of institutions, cultural forms, or basic symbols, accurately placed questions can shatter their claims upon us. The drive to ask questions is the most persistent and basic drive of human consciousness. It is the principle of the experience of nothingness. By exercising that drive, we come to doubt the definitions of the real, the true, and the good that our culture presents to us. Without this drive, cultural change would not be possible. What was sacred once would for all time be locked in unchanging sacredness.

Because it is the principle of cultural change, the experience of nothingness is ambiguous, for cultural change is in itself of dubious value. Because it lies so near to madness, the experience of nothingness is a dangerous, possibly destructive experience. But when it leads to changes in cultural or personal consciousness that are liberating and joyful, it is called, deservedly, a "divine madness." Those whom the city must put to death for corrupting its youth sometimes fire the consciousness of many others with a madness that comes to define a new sanity, a corruption that becomes a new morality, a nothingness that yields a new being. And then the process may begin again.

When, meanwhile, the drive to raise questions makes us aware of its total range and depth, a feeling of formlessness, or nausea, or lassitude arises. When I perceive the drive to question in its purity, apart from the products to which it leads me, I perceive the ambiguity of my own conscious life. I recognize the formlessness, the aimlessness, and the disunity implicit in my own insignificance, my mortality, my ultimate dissolution. I peer into madness, chaos, and death. These insights are true insights. Not to experience them is to evade the character of one's own consciousness. It is to live a lie. The experience of nothingness bears the taste of honesty.

The truth of the human situation, however, remains to be decided. Is the character of human consciousness so inherently chaotic that the only genuine way to mirror our situation is insanity? Quite possibly. I wish to argue tentatively that the character of human consciousness is merely tragic; that is, that the experience of nothingness may be absorbed in full sanity; that a clear and troubling recognition of our fragility, our mortality, and our ignorance need not subvert our relation to the world in which we find ourselves. The experience of nothingness may lead either to madness or to wisdom. The man who shares it, however wise, appears to those who do not share it (and sometimes to himself) as mad. Wisdom lies on the edge of insanity, just as those who wish to see themselves as sane and well adjusted in this bloody and absurd world may be foolish and insane. Our lives seem to be tragic rather than absurd, but I am far from certain on that point. The issue falls one way rather than the other only by a hair.

THE FOUR MYTHS OF THE UNIVERSITY

"Even within nihilism," Albert Camus wrote in 1940, "it is possible to find the means to proceed beyond nihilism." [19] Today in Rio de Janeiro children are starving. While in San Francisco children lie on laundered sheets, in Vietnam others lie in pools of blood. The earth is rich enough so that no one has to starve, and men are not obliged to murder one another. Exactly in proportion as we are free men, we are responsible for the social, economic, and political practices of our nation that terminate in uncounted deaths.[20] Occasionally we lift our eyes from our daily routine and glimpse briefly the worldwide consequences of the American way of life. The structure of rationalization collapses.[21] We went to bed imagining ourselves decent and good; we awake to find blood on our hands. Camus wrote: "Every action today leads to murder, direct or indirect." [22]

The experience of nothingness always arises in contrast to the values of a culture. To understand the character of the experience of nothingness in America, therefore, we must penetrate the foundations of the American way of life. One culture differs from another according to the constellation of myths that shapes its attention, its attitudes, and its practices. No culture perceives human experience in a universal, direct way; each culture selects from the overwhelming experience of being human certain salient particulars. One culture differs from another in the meaning it attaches to various kinds of experience, in its image of the accomplished man, in the stories by which it structures its perceptions.[23]

Of course, men are not fully aware that their own values are shaped

[19] Camus, *The Myth of Sisyphus*, op. cit., p. v.

[20] Paul Hanly Furfey, *The Respectable Murderers: Social Evil and Christian Conscience* (New York: Herder & Herder, 1966), p. 160.

[21] Richard Barnet, *Intervention and Revolution* (New York: New American Library, 1968).

[22] Camus, *The Rebel* (New York: Random House, Vintage Books, 1956), p. 4.

[23] In a critical survey of several hundred definitions of culture, A. L. Kroeber and Clyde Kluckhohn concluded that most social scientists would accept the following: "Culture consists of patterns, explicit and implicit, of and for behavior acquired and transmitted by symbols, constituting the distinctive achievement of human groups, including their embodiment in artifacts; the essential core of culture consists of traditional (i.e., historically derived and selected) ideas and especially their attached values; culture systems may, on the one hand, be considered as products of action, on the other as conditioning elements of further action." *Culture* (New York: Random House, Vintage Books, 1952), p. 357.

by myths. Myths are what men in other cultures believe in; in our own
culture we deal with reality. In brief, the word "myth" has a different
meaning depending upon whether one speaks of other cultures or of
one's own. When we speak of others, a myth is the set of stories, images,
and symbols by which human perceptions, attitudes, values, and actions
are given shape and significance. When we speak of our own culture, the
ordinary sense of reality performs the same function. In order to identify
the myths of one's own culture, therefore, it suffices to ask: "What constitutes my culture's sense of reality?"

In the United States, as elsewhere, the issue is complicated because
several versions of reality are in competition. Academic persons and
artists criticize the myths of the ordinary people of America: their religiousness, their chauvinism in foreign policy, their prejudices in do-
mestic affairs, their commercialism, their need to be boosters, and the like.
Moreover, ordinary people are quick to discern that intellectuals do not
share the assumptions, viewpoints, and values of the people. The intellectuals do not believe that the people see things as they are; the people
do not believe that the intellectuals have their feet on the ground. What
one group calls moral, the other believes the depth of immorality; what
one calls patriotic, the other calls treasonous. Social, political, religious,
and educational differences intensify the gap between the intellectuals
and the people.[24] Instead of entering the dispute between these two
shifting senses of reality, however, I would like to construct a third. It
will be more helpful in defining this third myth to contrast it to the myths
that dominate the American university rather than to the myths of the
people. Criticism of the people is too easy; criticism of the university, until
recently, has been seldom attempted.

Four basic stories shape the sense of reality in leading American universities. The first is the story of enlightenment through hardheaded,
empirical intelligence (and in psychology through behavioral methods).
The second is the story of the solitary, autonomous individual. The
third is the story of achievement through arduous competitive work.
And the fourth is the story of working within the system and concentrating upon one's own functional tasks until recognition comes. The most
realistic man, in the eyes of the university circles I am describing, would
be a hardnosed scholar, whose "lonely and heretical toil" (warmly supported by his colleagues) challenged the values of the community, but
who persevered until the system itself turned and rewarded him with a
Nobel Prize. Let us take up each strand of the myth separately.

[24] See my "The Gap Between Intellectuals and People," *A New Generation* (New
York: Herder & Herder, 1964), and the profounder interpretation of the phenomena
opened up by Robert N. Bellah's essay, "Civil Religion in America," with commentaries and a response in, *The Religious Situation: 1968,* ed. Donald R. Cutler (Boston:
Beacon Press, 1968).

The first means of giving structure to life is to place one's trust in
empirical reason and behavorial methods. The decision to attempt to
speak "objectively" and in "value-free discourse" is a decision to abstract
from the thick, complex stream of life. So is the decision to study behavior
rather than experience; that is, to observe actions from "outside," and to
distrust the introspective view of the one who experiences the actions
from "within." So is the decision to treat all issues, even human issues,
analytically and quantitatively.[25] Moreover, the stream of life does not
come to us ready-made for such abstraction.

It takes a great many years of rigorous socialization to make a scientist
out of a young man or woman, and neophytes must be initiated into the
difficult language, procedures, and viewpoints required for successful
performance. Most laymen cannot understand the speech or the disciplined, technical behavior of experts. But the employment of the techniques of objective reason for the last several generations has generated
power: napalm, atomic bombs, gases and chemicals that can incapacitate
or destroy the human nervous system, personality, or body, and genetic
mutants and machines that may develop into creatures more able and
more flexible than human beings. The speech and actions of the astronauts under pressure have given us a televised demonstration of the
"new type of man"; it is not a type that is wholly admirable.

The decision to choose scientific methods and, in particular, behavioral
methods as a way of life is first of all *to select* certain features of human
life (clarity, quantifiability, function, instrumentality) from among others.
It is, secondly, *to evade* other sorts of questions and values, and thus to
rig the meaning of "fact." And it is, thirdly, *to make a political choice.*
Behavioral science is far from value-free; it is certainly not power-free,
and someone somewhere will use the power it generates to secure his own
interests. In the United States, the federal government willingly pays the
incomes of sixty-five per cent of all scientists and engineers by direct or
indirect subsidy. The uses to which scientific and technological work

[25] ". . . Behavioral scientists who believe themselves to be in possession of certain
techniques of control and manipulation will tend to search for problems to which
their knowledge and skills might be relevant, defining these as 'important problems.'" Noam Chomsky, "The Menace of Liberal Scholarship," *New York Review
of Books,* II, no. 12 (January 2, 1969): 29, 35. "Gide has said somewhere that
he distrusts the carrying out of one possibility because it necessarily restricts
other possibilities. Call the possibilities 'imaginative.' And call the carrying-out
of *one* possibility the bureaucratization of the imaginative. An imaginative possibility
. . . is bureaucratized when it is embodied in the realities of a social texture,
in all the complexity of language and habits, in the property relationship, the method
of government, production and distribution, and in the development of rituals that
reinforce the same emphasis. . . . In the modern laboratory, the procedure of
invention itself (the very essence of the imaginative) has been bureaucratized. . . .
Science, knowledge, is the bureaucratization of wisdom." Kenneth Burke, *Attitudes
Toward History* (Boston: Beacon Press, 1961), pp. 225–28.

are put, and the direction of inquiry and research, are governed by political considerations.[26]

The second myth is that of the solitary autonomous individual. One of the most effective ways to manipulate men is to isolate them: "Divide and conquer." More effective still is to isolate them, while convincing them that their isolation is really their strength, and that rugged individualism is their chief protection against tyranny. In this respect, the Anglo-American tradition has perpetrated one of the coolest frauds in political history. Millions of Englishmen and Americans, divided against their fellows, believe themselves to be autonomous and free, while all the while giving evidence in their schools, their dress, their economic practices, and their habits of life of the most striking forms of docility, social conformity, and amenability to political control.[27] As the decline of English and American society continues, our former notions of superiority in these respects over Latin, French, Germanic, African, and Asian cultures are suitably humbled. Young people who serve in the Peace Corps or elsewhere experience "culture shock" on discovering that "underdeveloped" people are in many ways more fully developed than any Americans they know: in the subtlety and range of their emotions, in their sensitivities in human interaction, in their capacity to endure pain, in their skepticism regarding authority, and so on.

The myth of empirical reason has alienated many Americans from their own experience, leading them to think of themselves as objective minds. The myth of the autonomous individual has alienated many from their fellows and led them to think of themselves as atomic bits of private consciousness, turreted and protected against the encroachments of others. Thus unnaturally isolated, many experience as a leading characteristic of American life a poignant loneliness. Many imagine that their

[26] ". . . there is an ethically sinister possibility in knowing the machinery of rules. . . . In this sense, every sociologist is a potential saboteur or swindler, as well as a putative helpmate of oppression. . . . The social scientist shares this ethical predicament with his colleagues in the natural sciences, as the political use of nuclear physics has more than amply demonstrated in recent years. . . . As the physicists are busy engineering the world's annihilation, the social scientists can be entrusted with the smaller mission of engineering the world's consent." Peter Berger, *Invitation to Sociology: A Humanistic Perspective* (Garden City, N.Y.: Doubleday & Co., Anchor Books, 1963), p. 152. See also Chomsky, "Philosophers and Public Philosophy," *Ethics: An International Journal of Social, Political and Legal Philosophy* 79, no. 1 (October 1968): 1–9.

[27] "The function of education has never been to free the mind and the spirit of man, but to bind them; and to the end that the mind and spirit of his children should never escape Homo sapiens has employed praise, ridicule, admonition, accusation, mutilation, and even torture to chain them to the cultural pattern. . . . American classrooms, like educational institutions anywhere, express the values . . . and fears found in the culture as a whole. School has no choice; . . [it] can give training in skills; it cannot teach creativity." Jules Henry, *Culture Against Man* (New York: Random House, Vintage Books, 1963), pp. 286–87; on American conformity in work, pp. 34–35. On political quiescence, see Murray Edelman, *The Symbolic Uses of Politics* (Chicago: University of Chicago Press, 1967), pp. 27–28, 32–33.

most urgent personal need is for security and status. In England and
America we boast of democracy and free enterprise. But we are neither
as free nor as united as we imagine ourselves; on the contrary, we are
isolated, conformist, and manipulated.

The third major myth in leading universities is the need for hard,
competitive work. Perhaps no other myth in our society is so painstakingly
reinforced from birth—by story and example, exhortation and practice,
the contriving of roles and direct schooling—as the value of hard, competitive work.[28] Without that myth, our society is inconceivable; its
contradiction threatens society's very foundations. So powerful is that
myth in shaping American experience and perception, that it is virtually
impossible for Americans to understand how achievement is possible
under any other system. Jules Henry gives the following example of
how the myth is taught:

Boris had trouble reducing 12/16 to the lowest terms, and could only get as
far as 6/8. The teacher asked him quietly if that was as far as he could reduce it.
She suggested he "think." Much heaving up and down and waving of hands by
the other children, all frantic to correct him. Boris pretty unhappy, probably
mentally paralyzed. The teacher quiet, patient, ignores the others and concentrates with look and voice on Boris. After a minute or two she turns to the
class and says, "Well, who can tell Boris what the number is?" A forest of hands
appears, and the teacher calls Peggy. Peggy says that four may be divided
into the numerator and the denominator.

Henry remarks:

Boris's failure made it possible for Peggy to succeed; his misery is the occasion
for her rejoicing. This is a standard condition of the contemporary American
elementary school. To a Zuni, Hopi or Dakota Indian, Peggy's performance
would seem cruel beyond belief, for competition, the wringing of success
from somebody's failure, is a form of torture foreign to those noncompetitive
cultures. Looked at from Boris's point of view, the nightmare at the blackboard
was, perhaps, a lesson in controlling himself so that he would not fly shrieking
from the room under enormous public pressure. Such experiences force every
man reared in our culture, over and over again, night in, night out, even at
the pinnacle of success, to dream not of success, but of failure. In school the
external nightmare is internalized for life. Boris was not learning arithmetic

---

28 "Any well knit way of life molds human behavior into its own design. The
individualism of bourgeois society like the communism of a socialized state must be
inculcated from the nursery to the grave. In the United States, as one among the
bourgeois nations, the life of personal achievement and personal responsibility is
extolled in song and story from the very beginning of consciousness. Penny banks
instill the habit of thrift; trading in the schoolyard propagates the bourgeois scale
of values. Individual marks at school set the person at rivalrous odds with his fellows.
'Success and failure depend on you.' 'Strive and succeed' means 'If you strive,
success comes; if success does not come, you have not striven hard enough.' When
such an ideology impregnates life from start to finish, the thesis of collective responsibility runs against a wall of noncomprehension." Harold D. Lasswell, *Politics: Who
Gets What, When, How?* (New York: Meridan Books, 1958), pp. 32–34.

only; he was learning the *essential nightmare also. To be successful in our culture one must learn to dream of failure.*[29]

Apart from motives of competition, there are many motives for action, for self-realization, for supreme achievement, and for overcoming scarcity. And even competition may be conceived in two ways. A friend of mine witnessed a brilliant soccer match in southern France. Afterward, he congratulated the captain of the winning team for having won: The French peasant was embarrassed. One does not congratulate a man for "winning"; the point of the competition was not to vanquish the other side but, by facing worthy opponents, to force oneself to new levels of exertion.

In America, the emphasis on "success" dramatized by Miss America contests, bowl games, television quizzes, and spelling bees dehumanizes human performance; atomic individual is set over against atomic individual, and it is not the worth of their performance that is honored but the mere, almost independent fact of the success of one of them. Success is perceived as luck, a grace, a gift; failure as the lot of the damned. The myth of success renders useless the concept of internal worth, and countless Americans seem to feel insecure, helpless, and worthless when the lottery of success has not selected them. Even the notion that one must work hard in order to be worthy of success is commonly absorbed into the syntax of success: one works hard, not with the sense of dignity that comes from inner growth, risk and expansion, but with the hope of a vindication from beyond. The myth of competitive work is seldom oriented toward an internal sense of dignity; it is other-regarding, outwardly expectant, full of foreboding. An astonishing number of intelligent students, who should know better, want to satisfy two myths at once: *both* to study what is of intrinsic value to themselves *and* to get an "A."

The fourth way of life in the university emphasizes working within the system. The trap that a pragmatic, empirical way of life sets for itself grows from its refusal to question its own presuppositions, goals, values, or methods. The empiricist or pragmatist deals with answerable questions and measurable results. He defines "reality" according to what is "realizable" by his methods and in terms of the given situation; he concentrates upon clear next steps.[30] He cannot be bothered with "theologi-

[29] Henry, op. cit., pp. 27, 295–96.
[30] "We could state the principle of the laboratory in this proposition: 'Every machine contains a cow-path.' That is: there are embodied somewhere in its parts . . . a process that remains simply because the originators of the machine embodied this process in their invention. It has been retained . . . because no one ever thought of questioning it. . . . As it stands, the process is a 'cow-path' in pious obedience to its secret grounding in the authority of custom." Burke, op. cit., p. 228. "The state of having turbulent notions about things that seem to belong together, although in some unknown way, is a prescientific state, a sort of intellectual gestation period. This state the 'behavioral sciences' have sought to skip, hoping to learn its lessons by the way. . . . The result is that they have modeled themselves on physics, which is not a suit-

cal" or "metaphysical" speculation about experience, values, or long-range goals. In an important paper on the quest for peace in Vietnam, for example, Henry A. Kissinger describes in detail how realistic American bureaucrats fail to comprehend, and dislike dealing with, fundamental realities, basic issues, and long-range goals. They prefer dealing with daily, pragmatic, functional issues.[31] (Kissinger does not, himself, escape the limitations of realism.[32])

Realism effectively makes one a participant in the ongoing system. It stifles the revolutionary, utopian, visionary impulse. It teaches one compromise, patience, and acquiescence. It rewards dissent that strengthens the system, not dissent directed at the heart of the system or insisting on the constuction of a significantly new system. There is compelling evidence that realistic social and political reforms do not, in fact, alter power arrangements or weaken key interest groups in our society; political symbols change, but the same elites remain in unchallenged power.[33]

A precise analysis of American society shows that the analysis of myths, rituals, and symbols touches the heart of American reality much more accurately than the analysis of the pragmatist.[34] The pragmatist likes to believe that hardheaded, factual, toughminded analysis, in quantifiable terms, will change American society (and the world?) more effectively than any alternative. But the more the pragmatist has his way, the more hardened and obtuse the American system becomes. (Some Americans would call it progress to turn the whole world into an extended New Jersey.) The choice of the pragmatist myth of "working within the system" is not value-free; to assure oneself of this, it suffices to call that choice the radical disease from which we suffer. Many will leap to its defense as normal, ordinary, and inevitable. They will do so with passion.

Perhaps I have said enough about the central stories that shape American life. Americans, like all other peoples in history, live by myths because

able model. . . . The commitment to 'scientific method' could be seriously inimical to any advance of knowledge in such important but essentially humanistic pursuits [as the growing interrelationship of disciplines like psychology and biology]." Susanne Langer, *Mind: An Essay on Human Feeling* (Baltimore: Johns Hopkins Press, 1966), I:52–53.

[31]"We prefer to deal with cases as they arise, 'on their merits'. . . . Pragmatism and bureaucracy thus combine to produce a diplomatic style marked by rigidity in advance of formal negotiations and excessive reliance on tactical considerations once negotiations start. . . . The overriding concern with tactics suppresses a feeling for nuance and for intangibles." Henry A. Kissinger, "The Vietnam Negotiations," *Foreign Affairs* 47, no. 2 (January 1969): 221–22.

[32] Note how Kissinger's analysis accepts the basic presuppositions of American policy. For example, though he insists that decisions about "ultimate goals" cannot be avoided, he concludes: "However we got into Vietnam, whatever the judgment of our actions, ending the war honorably is essential for the peace of the world. Any other solution may unloose forces that would complicate prospects of international order." Ibid., p. 234. It does not occur to him to question in whose interest that "order" might be, or how questionable the existent definition of that interest might be.

[33] Edelman, op. cit., pp. 74–75; Lasswell, op. cit., pp. 168–71.

[34] Lasswell, op. cit., pp. 13–21, 172–73; Henry, op. cit., pp. 3–44.

human beings have no other choice. Experience rushes in upon us in such floods that we must break it down, select from it, abstract, shape, and relate. A culture is constituted by the meaning it imposes on human experience.[35] It imposes that meaning by every means at its disposal, and by so doing it shapes human life into a manageable sequence. A culture comes into being and endures through its ability to create a myth. The experience of nothingness is the origin of all mythmaking. Is it any wonder that every myth leads back to that primal experience? Culture begins and ends in the void. An honest culture does not evade its origin or its end.

RELIGION IN THE AGE OF AQUARIUS

Harvey Cox

HARVEY COX is a Professor of Church and Society at the Harvard
Divinity School. His books include *The Secular City* (1965) and
Feast of Fools (1969).

T George Harris: Do you worry, as a theologian, about the general re-surgence of superstition and magic? What do you do when students ask about your zodiac sign?

Harvey Cox: You know, I hate to admit it, but they did bug me at first. When somebody would come up and say, "What's your sign?" I used to say, "I don't know. I'm not interested in that stuff." Then I got to the point where I would say in my skeptical Harvard-professor voice, "If you believe there is really some correlation between signs and character, you ought to tell me what sign I am. What sign am I?" Mine was the typical rationalistic approach: "Look at me. Ask me questions. Guess. Let's test it."

Sometimes they would play my game, but it was wrong. I now know why. Do you know what people are saying when they ask your sign? They are saying *I want to relate to you, to be intimate with you in this kooky, interesting, groovy way—a way that is going to blow the minds of those god-damned rationalists. The logical people who have organized our society have defined us into categories that we can't live in.*

Well, that's true. There's no room to move around in, to grow in, in these little boxes reserved for white people, Protestants, Jews, men, women, students, Americans, Russians, Democrats, suburbanites, New

---

[35] "Culture is the creation by man of a world of adjustment and meaning, in the context of which human life can be significantly lived." Thomas F. O'Dea, *The Sociology of Religion* (Englewood Cliffs, N.J.: Prentice-Hall, 1966), p. 3.

Left, rich people, poor. The whole thing is sick, and we can't do without some kind of empathy.

So along comes this absolutely weird group of categories unrelated to social status or anything else. Nobody's defining you, and you're not putting a tag on him. If you're a Taurus and I'm a Taurus, my god, immediately we've got a secret intimacy. We enter into this little conspiracy . . .

Harris: . . . like prisoners talking a secret slang . . .

Cox: . . . yeah, you and I have this little conspiracy going against the prisonkeepers, the people who put down everything that is not scientifically demonstrable or socially presentable. So we find our own way to define ourselves.

Harris: I'm always afraid my sign, Libra, will be a turnoff.

Cox: Don't worry, the possibilities are unlimited. See, there are earth signs, air signs, water signs and fire signs. The air sign goes with the earth sign, and the water sign goes with the fire sign, or something like that. And there are other relationships connecting them up. If this doesn't pan out, there's the really esoteric thing about moon signs. You could be a Capricorn born under an Aries moon. It's such an intricate and general-purpose set of symbols that you can use it to build whatever relationship you want.

The astrology trip is a form of play, of relating to each other in ways we don't have to take too seriously until we know we want to. In a broader sense, astrology and drugs and Zen are forms of play, of testing new perceptions of reality without being committed to their validity in advance—or ever.

Harris: That word *play* keeps cropping up. In the new book, *The Feast of Fools,* you developed a general theory of play to make a radical indictment of the work-compulsive society.

Cox: I'm not alone, of course, in feeling that in our frantic rush to affluence we have paid a high price in psychic damage. The convincing evidence is beginning to come out of psychology and anthropology. It suggests that we have almost lost, or mutilated, our gift for true festivity and celebration, for pure imagination and playful fantasy.

Two French psychologists, Roger Frétigny and André Virel, began some time ago to use what they call "directed fantasy" in therapy. What I like about their work is that they related their findings to previous studies of mental imagery in anthropology and comparative religion. I think it has immeasurable importance to theology—and not just to theology. It isn't just the church but all of Western culture that has in the name of efficiency become the tribe that lost its head.

Frétigny and Virel talk about four states of consciousness—imaginative, active, reflexive and contemplative. Each has a significant function. The imaginative, of which fantasy is the best example, not only systematizes the materials of experience; it also takes apart both materials and systems in order to construct new configurations. They show how merely rational thought leaves the mind "incurably crippled in a closed and ossified system." It can only extrapolate from the past.

Persons and groups establish rhythms of movement back and forth between the world of facts and the world of fantasies. In tribal societies the period of group fantasy corresponds to the seasonal celebrations of the myths and legends of the tribe. In more complex societies the period is not as well marked and may come less frequently. Virel and Frétigny speculate that a culture such as ours may devote obsessive attention to the fact world for centuries, then move into an era of imaginative creativity and heightened fantasy.

Harris: Are we headed that way now?

Cox: Maybe, though today's partial rebirth of fantasy may be a deceptive flush on the cheek of a dying age. We're overdue. We have spent the last few hundred years with our cultural attention focused dourly on the "outside" factual world—exploring, investigating and mastering it.

Those who had a penchant for fantasy never really felt at home. They were even driven out of religious institutions, the shelter where the fantasies of the mystic would normally be cherished and cultivated. Christianity, especially its Protestant versions, conned itself, and got conned, into providing the spiritual cement and stick-and-carrot values for Western industrialization. Only in the black church and in folk Catholicism such as Mexico has do you find much of Christ's festive spirit still alive.

Harris: And the Methodists have cut the gut-busting tunes out of the *Cokesbury Hymnal*. You have to go to a bar to sing an ecstatic hymn.

Cox: Sure. A bar certainly is one of the few places remaining where you can really let go without somebody taking you seriously. You can play.

It's my conviction that conventional religion has declined not because of the advance of science or the spread of education or any of the reasons normally advanced for secularization. The reason is simple but hard to see because it is embedded in our total environment: the tight, bureaucratic and instrumental society—the only model we've known since the industrial revolution—renders us incapable of experiencing the nonrational dimensions of existence. The absurd, the inspiring, the uncanny, the awesome, the terrifying, the ecstatic—none of these fits into a production- and efficiency-oriented society. They waste time, aren't dependable. When they appear we try to ban them by force or some brand-name therapy. Having systematically stunted the Dionysian side of the whole human, we assume that man is naturally just a reliable, plane-catching Apollonian. [Editor's note: see essay by Sam Keen for an extended description of "Dionysian" and "Apollonian."]

The blame for this distortion usually gets hung on something called "puritanism" or the "Protestant ethic." But that analysis, I believe, is not entirely adequate. No religion yet tested seems to stand unbent by the pressure of the managerial faith known as "Economic Development." Communism, nationalism and other ideologies have gone the same route elsewhere on the globe.

Harris: So how does anybody see out, let alone break out?

Cox: We are never completely the captives of our culture or its language. People all over the world are turning, often desperately, to the overlooked corners and freaks that were never completely systematized. Hence our fascination for pop art—and gloriously, for Fellini's films— with the junk and rejects of the industrial process. Also with the slippery stuff that never found a place in it: astrology, madness, witches, drugs, non-Western religions, palmistry and mysticism, shoddy or serious.

Even the current preoccupation with sex and violence can, to some extent, be understood in terms of this reaction. Both blood and sperm are explosive, irregular, feeling-pitched, messy and inexplicably fascinating. You can't store either one safely in the humming memory of an IBM 360, to be smoothly printed out only when needed in the program. To use a theological term, they *transcend* routine experience.

Harris: In *The Secular City,* which stirred up many sociologists and city planners, you argued that urban-age man has become the creator of his own world, heaven or hell, including his value system. We can't blame it on fate or God anymore. With that weight on our heads, you now urge us, in *Feast,* to go dancing in the streets.

Cox: Maybe I've learned something. Must there be a gap between those who are working and hoping for a better world and those for whom life is affirmative, a celebration? Must the radicals and revolutionaries—the *new militants*—be at cross purposes with the *neo-mystics*—the hippies and Yippies and all those who are experimenting with new styles of being? I think not, and I hope not. They are, I think, tied together.

So *Feast* is not a recantation of *Secular City;* it's an extension, a recognition that the changes we need are much more fundamental than I thought five years ago, and that the method for achieving them must be much more drastic. Man actually took charge of his own history back in the 19th Century. In *City* I was trying to help us face that fact— defatalization—on the conscious level and work out the consequences. In *Feast* the point is that we can't handle the burden of making history if we are ourselves buried in it, unaware of the timeless dimension that we touch only in fantasy and festivity.

Have you noticed, George, how the past has become an intolerable weight? Except for conservatives who want to use the good-old-days as a club to beat everybody else with, people have a desperate impulse to destroy the past, to curse it, blow it up, burn it. That impulse explains the popularity of books like Norman O. Brown's *Life Against Death* and *Love's Body.* Brown calls on us to "be ready to live instead of making history, to enjoy instead of paying back old scores and debts, and to enter that state of Being which has the goal of Becoming." He begins with Freud's view that repression is the price we pay for civilization, and he thinks the price is exorbitant. History to Brown is not just one damned thing after another; it's one big mistake. He wants to get away from it all.

More calmly, Claude Lévi-Strauss and other French structuralists suggest that we are all over-committed to decision-making, temporal aims and historical objectives. Lévi-Strauss argues that Jean-Paul Sartre, the philosopher of free decision and human world-making, must be left behind.

Much of music and theater seeks to immolate the past quite literally. Take John Cage, for instance. He's certainly the most self-conscious avant-gardist in American music. He undermines the whole axiom of continuity by eliminating the idea of melody. He wants us to listen to one sound at a time, not to hear it in terms of the note that came before it.

In his theater of cruelty, Antonin Artaud invited playwrights to deal in the raw, instant aspects of existence. Lights should be selected not to enhance the play but to blister the eyes of the audience. He wanted to destroy our veneration of what had been done so that we would have to create life in our own idiom. Since Artaud, theater has been used to shock, outrage and seduce the audience out of cool spectator seats to participate in violence, magic and, at times, in joy.

Harris: Are you putting down such things as guerrilla theater?

Cox: Hell, no. Artaud's mix of spoken and written work lights up the visionary quality of some of the student radicals, the ones who are insistently anti-ideological. Cage, on the other hand, symbolizes the mystical, Dionysiac, experience-believing portion of the present generation: the *now* mentality that is dedicated to pursuit of direct experience—erotic, visual or auditory.

There's a close connection between sensory overload and sensory deprivation. John Lilly discovered in his experiments that for a man suspended in dark silence, a tiny stimulus becomes agonizingly intense. Now go the other way. With an acid-rock band imploding you with sound and a light show chopping your eyeballs, you are totally isolated and must turn intensely inward. It's not exactly like silent contemplation, but it's one way to cut yourself off from this harried culture.

Why bother? Is there any reason for people's desperate impulse to cut out of the orderly, tense roles assigned to us? Despite the battles between Christianity and Marxism, both have tended to harness us into a sense of doing whatever history bids us do. "History" is the name we give the horizon of consciousness within which we live. It's all we see. We've lost sight of the larger environment—the cosmic phenomena open to us through intuition, awe and ecstasy—because of our enormous self-consciousness about the events of the past, present and future. Michael Polanyi calls this larger reality the "tacit dimension." Teilhard de Chardin called it the "divine milieu." History is defined by time; the cosmic circle suggests eternity. To be fully human we need to be in touch with both— to apprehend, as T. S. Eliot said, the point of intersection of the timeless with time.

Gestalt psychologists and Marshall McLuhan have both pointed out the necessity for an "anti-environment," the background needed to frame anything before we can see it. If something fills our whole environment, we can't see it.

Harris: The fish, Marshall says, did not discover water.

Cox: Or the Age of Aquarius. Anyway, without a timeless perspective, a frame, we cannot regain the humility, the humor to see ourselves and our time honestly or the courage to act sensibly upon our insights. Otherwise we are driven to desperate attempts to "solve" everything. Richard L. Rubenstein wrote in *After Auschwitz* that the West's logical impulse toward solutions could but lead to the Nazi ovens, the "final solution."

Harris: Does theology have a way out?

Cox: It will, but not without a little help from its friends—the artists, the students and the social scientists. Most of the sophisticated, critical theology being written today—and this has been true for several decades —comes out of the 19th Century discovery of the historically conditioned character of our tradition, of our Bible, of our encyclicals and rituals. Everything in conventional religion has become second-hand. We are allowed to feel it *only* through careful study of the people who first experienced it long, long ago.

Look, my thesis here is that the sociology of religion is posing problems that theology has to give attention to now—the problems of present experience. Theology has to go much deeper into the social sciences, which suffer from an overweening presentism but can offset the obsessional past in theology. Ever since Emile Durkheim, sociologists have been laying the base for systematic study of the nonhistoric dimension of experience, often without meaning to. I tried to open up this prospect in *Feast*, but to go further I need to do a technical book on theology and the social sciences.

Harris: Marcello Truzzi at the University of Michigan has done a paper on contemporary witchcraft and Satanism, Harvey. He's positive that the upsurge is trivial because the people involved are not serious about it.

Cox: That's exactly the reason it's important—people are playing with new perceptions. It's not just the girls who join witches' covens or put on benign hexes. Arthur Waskow reports in *Liberation* on the whole range of rituals among radical groups, who at times are too serious to play in the way that I mean it. They have underground churches, exorcism, Buddhist communities, immolations, confessionals, tie-dye vestments, burn-the-money offerings, encounter groups, monastic contemplations, Indian runes, freedom Seders, commune liturgies, the whole bit. Did you ever notice how often Herbert Marcuse, whose writings gave the New Left its early base, uses the word "transcendent"? A friend of mine went through Marcuse's *One Dimensional Man* underscoring each use of the word. He had marks on just about every page.

Harris: Irving Kristol makes a good case in *Fortune* for Marcuse's being more of a religious figure than an intellectual leader.

Cox: In many ways that's true, though I'm sure Kristol means it to be a put-down.

The search for new perceptions, however, isn't limited to radicals or neo-mystics. I noticed a while back that my students were reading—really hooked on—six books that ordinarily would not seem to have anything in common. Here they are:

Stranger in a Strange Land, Robert Heinlein's science fiction on the human-from-Mars. Valentine Michael Smith, the hero, could "grok," that beautiful verb for total comprehension, in a way that we earthlings have trained ourselves not to do.

I Ching, the "book of changes" or the sacred books of ancient China.

The Double Helix, the account of how the genetic code was broken— by imagining pretty molecular structures and finding out which one could, by inference, be assumed to exist. Also, there were so many completely non-scientific factors—trying to beat Linus Pauling, and coping with ill-tempered Rosie, the chick in the next lab.

The Teachings of Don Juan, Carlos Castaneda's account of the romantic who refused to see things as practical men did, and do.

The Politics of Experience, psychiatrist R. D. Laing's wild, wonderful application of the theory that schizophrenia is double vision, a survival reaction.

The Mind of the Dolphin, John C. Lilly's research on what the comics of the sea say to each other.

These books all deal with unorthodox, often spooky ways of knowing and feeling, even with seeing things as the dolphin does.

But getting into a nonliteral mode of thought, let alone trying to write about it, is nearly impossible for many people. Remember the weekend we had a few years ago, George, at the American Academy of Arts and Sciences? Henry Murray and Talcott Parsons and Martin Marty and David Riesman—a combination of social scientists and theologians— were all sitting around the table. Remember how miffed Daniel Callahan got over the point you made about the emotional content in religion? He called you a Baptist. Well, my Baptist upbringing helps me to respect the experiential, the validity of the Dionysian. You know, Timothy Leary's wife—second wife—was once a Southern Baptist. I remember spending an evening with them on a hillside, lying under the stars up in New York State. She laughed and said to me, "We Baptists are just natural heads." Beautiful. What she meant was, you know, how could a Unitarian ever see a white flash? What liberal Congregationalist ever had a bad trip in church?

Harris: Getting back to behavioral studies, what did you mean about Durkheim's opening up the study of religion?

Cox: Oh, he took on very early the sociologists who wanted to get rid of religion. Religion is not a carry-over from the age of superstition, he pointed out, because religious symbols are essential. They unify the social group. Maybe the best behavioral definition of religion is simply that it's the highest order of symbol system—the one by which other symbol systems and metaphors and myths and values of a culture are ultimately legitimatized. The clammy inanities of present church liturgy have no power to bring us together.

Harris: And since the religious symbols come out of man's encounter with the suprarational, we've cut ourselves off from the source of unifying values.

Cox: Yes, but to comprehend religion's place in industrial, urban society, you have to look at more than the church. In *The Invisible Religion*, Thomas Luckmann showed that the church has lost its monopoly on religious symbols. Luckmann, who is a German, is very important to me because he showed that we have been looking at far too narrow a phenomenon—the church.

Another guy who has influenced me is Robert Bellah, who teaches sociology at the University of California. Remember Bellah? He did that brilliant paper for *Daedalus* on "civil religions." Focusing on Presidential inaugurals, he caught the religious overtones and rituals in national life.

Wouldn't it be interesting to analyze The Movement as a kind of counter-civil religion emerging in America with, already, its own sacred texts: "I Have a Dream," for instance, and "Damn Americans who Build Coffins," and a section of "Marcuse" and one on "draft-card immolations." Every radical has to find symbols that are extrinsic, esoteric and have the power to keep him from being encapsulated in the existing culture.

Lloyd Warner would have done it right. He's emeritus and not completely acceptable among sociologists today. But Warner used a good methodology for the study of festivity and symbolism. First he went to Central Australia among the Murngin aborigines. One of his focal points is their annual festival, the Kunapipi. You know how Warner worked, everything in excruciating detail, including the different positions of intercourse—the ritual intercourse as opposed to the ordinary kind. Then Warner came back for his Yankee City series. In the fifth of the series, *The Symbolic Life of Americans*, he reported how Yankee City celebrated its 250th Anniversary, just as he had reported the Kunapipi. He concentrated not on where symbols came from—their history—but on how they were appropriated into meaningful ritual, which is the theological problem today.

Harris: Sister Mary Corita—I guess she'd rather be known as artist Corita Kent——is appropriating secular symbols like bread wrappers for sacramental meaning.

Cox: Corita's enormously important. People saw her as just a cute nun, but she's the chick who saw slogans like "the Pepsi generation" and "come alive" and "care enough to send the best" and all that stuff in a way that would let us appropriate it. With her paintings she lets us say that man's creations, even the venial ones, are sacred.

Harris: Maybe the whole pop-art movement is a sacramentalizing of the environment. The artist lets us see it in a fresh way so we can laugh at it and celebrate it.

Cox: Yeah, yeah, Corita's humanizing the environment and also reminding us that the world is, as she says, unfinished. There's a new universe to create. She brings off these two master strokes at once, and she's got the love to put an ironic twist on slogans that have been used for manipulation. Wouldn't it be great if Corita would paint the cover for this issue of *Psychology Today!*

You know about the thing Corita and some of us did at that discotheque, The Boston Tea Party? We called it "An Evening with God." Everybody came, hundreds, and I started out by saying, a little lamely, "This isn't a church . . ." Somebody in the back yelled, "It *is* a church . . ." The ushers in beads and 20 wonderful girls in miniskirts passed out the wine and the home-baked bread. Dan Berrigan read his poems and Judy Collins sang. Corita had a rock band and strobe lights going, and pretty soon everybody was dancing in the aisles.

It worked well, maybe too well, because people keep coming back to ask when we're going to do it again. What we want is for them to do their own celebrations, not lean on us.

Post-industrial man is rediscovering festivity. In churches all over the country there's been this eruption of multimedia masses, jazz rituals, folk and rock worship services, new art and dance liturgies. You know, there's always a John Wesley around to wonder why the Devil should have all the good things. Judson Memorial in New York and a few other churches have had "revelations," the nude dancers in psychedelic lights at the altar. Some people oppose the guitar and the leotard in church for the same reasons their forebears opposed the use of the pipe organ—it never had been done before, or so they think. Others reject the festive new liturgies as merely the latest example of the Establishment's exploitation of flashy gimmicks to lure the recalcitrant back into the fold. They've got a point. Ecclesiastical imperialism is always a threat.

What matters is that the renaissance of festivity is comprehensive, and at the moment there's far more of it outside the church than inside. That's why Corita and I used a discotheque, not a church.

We're now working on an Easter service—for April 26, the Byzantine Easter, three weeks after the regular one. We'll sing things like *Amazing Grace;* Arlo Guthrie made it an ecumenical hymn. The liturgical dancers in Boston specialize in getting everybody to participate. In the midst of the multimedia rejoicing we'll have small group interactions and meditation. And the Woodstock Eucharist, home-baked bread and jugs. It'll start at 4 a.m. in The Boston Tea Party. At 6 a.m. the trumpets will blow for the resurrection of Christ—whatever that means to you. It's bring-your-own theology. We didn't think too many would come, but so many alienated Protestant and Jewish kids want to participate that we can't find enough things for them to do.

Harris: Your emphasis on sensuality blows a lot of clerical minds.

Cox: So what do we do, pretend that God created us as disembodied spirits? This is not a new question. Suspicion of the flesh has plagued Christianity off and on for most of its history. I suspect that we've inherited a perverted form of Christianity, deodorized and afraid of smell. That's one reason I used the title *Feast of Fools,* which comes from a Medieval celebration. It was not exactly prim and proper. Ordinarily pious priests and townsfolks put on bawdy masks, sang outrageous ditties and generally kept the world awake with revelry and satire. They made sport of the most sacred royal and religious practices. Of course, the feast was never popular with the higher-ups, who recognized that pure revelry is always radical. As the church became more and more worried about its authority, with running things on time, the bureaucrats managed to stamp out the feast, leaving only a memory of it in Halloween and New Year's.

Our feasting is now sporadic and obsessive, our fantasies predictable and our satire politically impotent. Our celebrations do not relate us, as they once did, to the parade of cosmic history or to the great stories of man's spiritual quest. If discovering that people have bodies is one of the risks we have to take, that seems to be a small—indeed pleasant— price to pay.

Harris: How about the risks you've taken in antidraft demonstrations?

Cox: I had to be pushed into that. The first time I heard about a guy burning a draft card I was horrified, shocked. Then about three years ago some students who had burned their cards had to go over to South Boston Courthouse for their trial. They were beaten and pummeled by a mob and the police wouldn't even intervene. Next day I joined the march—you know, just demanding the right of police protection. That now seems like a long time ago. We were only about 60 people—resistance kids with beards and peace symbols and a couple of black marchers and clergy—but a mob of 300 or 400 came throwing rocks and fruit at us. One guy waved a sword at us with a freshly killed chicken on the point and the blood running down. He had a sense of symbolism.

When we got to the church—it was Good Friday—one of the resistance kids spoke first. He had a swollen eye from the day before. He said the only thing he was sorry about was that the police had separated us from the mob, kept us from really having an encounter with those people. My first thought was, "this is where I leave you people—you're crazy." And my second thought was, "something's happening here that I don't

understand." He really felt warmth and regard for the people who wanted
to beat him up. I started out with my speech, but I couldn't say much.
It was a turning point for me.

Then came a student who was going to refuse to take the symbolic
step forward in the induction center. But he didn't want it to be a dour
affair. Since he was doing it to affirm life, refusing to kill, he got his
girl friend to make bread and strawberry jam, and all his friends came
with him, girls handing out flowers to the military and being festive.
Even the people at their desks got caught in the spirit of it.

This kind of thing upsets many adults, not only because they disagree
on ideas but because they think the kids are putting them on. They're
afraid they're being had. What they don't understand is the whole idea
of festivity and celebration.

Harris: You felt that way, as I recall, the first time you went to Esalen
Institute.

Cox: Well, Allen Ginsberg was there talking about his masturbatory
experiences and Gary Snyder was doing guru grunts. Old Jim Pike was
there, troubled and outrageous as usual. He was discussing his communication with the other side. Candles and incense. I never felt more
like a rigid defender of orthodoxy in my life. But they really changed my
teaching style. I was pretty proud of my lecture technique, but they said
"sit down and let's rap."

Harris: You're betting on the social sciences to deal with angel feathers,
Harvey—things like festivity are too gossamer to inspire serious work.

Cox: No, I don't think so. Didn't you publish Jerome L. Singer's research
into daydreaming? [See PT, "The Importance of Daydreaming," April
1968.] He and John Antrobus discovered that fantasies are richer among
what sociologists call the "marginality" people—richer among immigrant
Italians and Jews, richer still among black Americans. Apparently fantasy
thrives among the disenfranchised. The symbolism in the black church,
which, being marginal, never lost its festivity, should produce very rich
possibilities. We may yet see comparative religion turn from its Protestant fixation on the texts of other faiths—surely a distorted and limiting
view—to a more promising study of the whole religious ritual of a culture.

Harris: Where does that leave the institutional church?

Cox: Some form of institutionalized religious expression is going to
survive. Man is not only a religious being but a social one as well. He's
not going to accept a completely do-it-yourself approach on anything
this central to survival. Oh, the denominational type of Christianity
headquartered in skyscrapers with branch offices in the suburbs is fated
for rapid extinction, and it can't disappear too quickly for me. Yet,
some form will rise out of the present resurgence of spiritual concern.

The figure of Christ is ubiquitous. He is now beginning to appear as
Christ the Harlequin: the personification of celebration and fantasy in
an age that has lost both. It is a truer sense of Christ than the saccharine,

bloodless face we see painted so often. He was part Yippie and part revolutionary, and part something else. On His day of earthly triumph, Palm Sunday, He rode to town on a jackass. One of the earliest representations of Jesus in religious art depicts a crucified figure with the head of an ass. A weak, even ridiculous church somehow peculiarly at odds with the ruling assumption of its day can once again appreciate the harlequinesque Christ.

SUGGESTED READINGS

The student who wishes to acquaint himself with current theological thought may consult the following: John Cobb, Jr., *Living Options in Protestant Theology* (Philadelphia: Westminster, 1962); W. E. Hordern, *A Layman's Guide to Protestant Theology* (New York: Macmillan, 1968); James C. Livingston, * *Modern Christian Thought* (New York: Macmillan, 1971); John Macquarrie, * *Twentieth-Century Religious Thought* (New York: Harper & Row, 1963); and D. D. Williams, *What Present Day Theologians Are Thinking* (New York: Harper & Row, 3rd ed., revised, 1967p).

The following volumes give witness to the turmoil in contemporary religious thought: John A. T. Robinson, *Honest to God* (Philadelphia: Westminster, 1963p); Alan Richardson, *Religion in Contemporary Debate* (Philadelphia: Westminster, 1966). Martin E. Marty's *Varieties of Unbelief* (New York: Holt, Rinehart and Winston, 1964p) gives a lucid account of our age attempting to build its culture on a dead God. Michael Novak, *The Experience of Nothingness* (New York: Harper & Row, 1970p) and Sam Keen, *To a Dancing God* (New York: Harper & Row, 1970p) introduce the reader to a new awareness of religious themes. The continuing series edited by Martin E. Marty and Dean G. Peerman, *New Theology No. 1–9* (New York: Macmillan, 1964–1973p) witnesses the rapid change in theology over the last decade. The popularity of Charles Reich, *Greening of America* (New York: Bantam Book, 1971p); Theodore Roszak, *The Making of a Counter Culture* (Garden City, N.Y.: Anchor Books, 1969p), and his edited volume *Sources* (New York: Harper & Row, 1972p); Alvin Toffler, *Future Shock* (New York: Bantam Book, 1970p); Philip Slater, *The Pursuit of Loneliness* (Boston: Beacon Press, 1970p); and William Braden, *The Age of Aquarius* (New York: Quadrangle Books, 1970p) all show the current change in our contemporary consciousness. Jacob Needleman's *The New Religions* (New York: Doubleday, 1970) is a brilliant analysis of current issues in religion particularly on the campuses. See also his *Religion for a New Generation* (New York: Macmillan, 1973p) which covers current issues in religion that are in debate. In the last chapter we will come back to these issues.

CHAPTER TWO

Theology as the Recital of God's Mighty Acts: Outmoded Myths or Eternal Truths?

If a twentieth-century *seeker* is to understand biblical religion he must first get inside the world-view of biblical man. If a twentieth-century *believer* is to proclaim the biblical story to our time he must understand the world-view of contemporary man. This chapter begins with essays depicting the biblical point of view and follows with essays that are in dialogue with it from the contemporary standpoint.

THE BIBLICAL VIEW OF RELIGION [1]

In biblical religion, to know God is not to *see* him. Whereas the Greek mind makes seeing (*mental*—"Now I *see* what you mean!"; *physical*—"Open your eyes and *see* if I'm not right!") the model for knowing, the Hebrew makes the ear or hearing central—"Did you *hear* what God commanded us to do?" "Did you *hear* what God did for us in days of old?"

In the Greek view (notice the last word), when you know something or someone you are able to describe it by the use of predicates running from the class predicate down to physical and temporal predicates. "X is a horse of brown color being two years old, etc." To know God is to be able to describe the class of things to which he belongs and the

[1] I have purposely stressed this contrast to help the reader into the biblical standpoint. The reader should be cautioned that there are elements of the other model in each tradition.

characteristics (predicates) that apply to him. "God is a perfect being who is self caused, omniscient, eternal, and so on." The Hebrew tradition is quite different. To know something or someone involves more than a description; it means knowing a name. A Hebrew asks not what is God but *who* is God. Who is God? Yahweh! [2] Not, *what* is God? A perfect being beyond space and time.

And what is in a name? Names are personal and relational. Names relate entities into a history. Names *create*. If one does not have a name, he is a no-person, a no-body. If a place does not have a name, it is a no-place, a no-where. If a time does not have a name that ties it into a history, it is a no-time. To name is to create an identity. To be nameless is not to be. I am David ("beloved of Yahweh") from Bethlehem in the reign of King Saul. Notice the relational predicates that place an entity into the history of Yahweh and Israel. So "Yahweh" is a *proper name* like "David" or "Ruth" or "Karen."

The issue for the Hebrew tradition is not seeing God but hearing and knowing his name. The surprise that initiates the Judeo-Christian tradition is that Yahweh gives Israel his name and speaks to her about what he wills for a world that he made. A person who knows Yahweh knows his name, which he does not take in vain, for an entity's name *is* in some way identified with the being of that entity. If I have your name I have control over you in some sense. And Yahweh gives Israel from all the nations of the earth the responsibility of having his name. A person who knows Yahweh hears and obeys his word. Prophets and apostles are persons who hear Yahweh in the events of their lives and serve as Yahweh's voice to his people. The people of Yahweh are those who have been *called* by Yahweh to do his will because they have *heard* his voice. Yahweh's *call* elects (gives a name that creates-redeems), promises, judges. The Judeo-Christian tradition is a religion of the word, of the message. "Have you a word from the Lord?" Judaism and Christianity believe they do because they have heard.

There is another significant contrast between seeing and hearing. I can look at you and be passive, making no decisions about how I should relate to you. But to hear a person requires a self-involving act that is not necessarily the case in seeing someone. When someone speaks to you, you are almost forced to respond. "Hi! My name is John!"

Also, is it not the case that I can see *what* you are but not know you? I learn to know *who* you are by hearing your name and hearing you through your interpretation of your actions. "I did that because I love you."

Biblical religion comes out of this understanding of knowing. Every event, person, time, place, thing, becomes as it is caught up in the drama of Yahweh's purpose or history. For Yahweh is the Lord of history.

---

[2] The name that was given out of the burning bush when Moses asked, "*Who* shall I say sent me?" Its exact meaning is much in debate.

It is within this history that I become someone, Johnathan ("gift of God"), and hear who I am to be. *Everything* calls out to me of its mission (sent for a purpose) under Yahweh's word. Even nature becomes only as it is seen in this light. For by itself nature is chaos until it is seen in Yahweh's plan. As such is becomes a creation [3]—elected, given a name, having a purpose.

Questions about whom to trust, Yahweh or Baal, were central in this tradition, not the so-called cognitive issue.[4] The issue was not is there a God, but whom do you obey (hear)?[5]

THE BIBLICAL VIEW OF HISTORY

It is interesting that the Hebrew makes no distinction between the word and the thing or event signified by the word. "Dabar" or "word" [6] meant an event in nature or history as well as a spoken or written word. Words were not only *spoken;* they were also *done*. The actions of a person are the words he speaks. Those words are the person. The word is a complete revelation of a person or thing. The Hebrew also does not make a distinction between the word and the person who utters it. Speaking is a mode of being of the person himself. So when one speaks of a word it can include an event and a person as part of its meaning. Also, an *event* can include a word and a person. God's word creates and his creation is a word from God. The events of creation and history are part of a dialogue between Yahweh and man. Revelation is a dialogue between God and man. The dialogue occurs through historical events that speak and prophets hear and speak back, thereby interpreting the word heard in the event. The word of God is an event and a hearing. Just as I cannot but respond to your words, so a prophet cannot but speak of what he has *seen* and *heard*. For truly seeing an event is hearing its meaning.

In the Exodus, Yahweh calls Israel out of no-place and gives her a name, a land, a time, and a law. Only under this rubric is everything to be understood. Therefore, there are two ways of knowing an event. One, on the natural plane where every event is followed by another with no word about its meaning. But by faith I can know this event as

---

[3] Note that Adam creates by naming the animals as does every father when he names his child. Before a child is named he really is not.

[4] What can I know about God? Does he exist? What are his attributes?

[5] It is the weakness of some who after making this factual point consider the cognitive questions irrelevant to us today. Just because the Hebrews did not make the cognitive issues central is no reason why we must not ask them today. Maybe these cognitive questions are the very questions we *must* ask today! Being Hebrew is no more being right than making contemporary the standard for being right.

[6] It is interesting that the Greek word for "word" is "LOGOS" which also means *reason*. Again, one sees the stress in the Greek point of view for knowing through mental activity, whereas in the Hebrew tradition one knows through hearing and concrete events.

part of Yahweh's word. This is truly to know or hear. The event is understood when it speaks Yahweh's word, is incorporated into a past and a future that are in Yahweh's hand.

Just as a human being reveals himself more fully in certain events, so Yahweh reveals himself more fully in certain events, for example, Exodus, the person of Jesus Christ. The Bible is the record of these revelatory events to which men of faith responded in a personal way. Men of faith used various images to articulate their appreciation of the event as a mighty act of Yahweh. The complete act of revelation is the event through which God speaks and the faithful hear through men who interpret the word for their time. Theology is then remembering God's mighty acts and constantly listening for new hierophanies (revelations of God) of Yahweh in the present and the future.

BIBLICAL RELIGION AND COVENANT

A central theme in biblical religion is the covenant Yahweh makes with a people *he* elects. Yahweh takes the initiative and through his mighty acts elects a people who become a comm-unity. An individual is made whole as he becomes part of the covenant people. This is why rites of initiation are important, for they represent passage into the promises and responsibilities of the covenant people.

As a member of the comm-unity I am given a name-identity, a mission (call out for special service), a set of laws and promises. As such I become "holy," which does not mean without sin but set apart for a special task in God's plan. The Bible is the record of God's covenanting with the old and the new Israel. It portrays the continuing dialogue between God and man in which God remains faithful, while man continually breaks his covenant with God. A good summary of biblical religion is found in Yahweh's command to Moses.

Thus you shall say to the house of Jacob, and tell the people of Israel: You have seen what I did to the Egyptians, and how I bore you on eagles' wings and brought you to myself. Now therefore, if you will obey my voice and keep my covenant, you shall be my own position among all peoples; for all the earth is mine, and you shall be to me a kingdom of priests and a holy nation. These are the words which you shall speak to the children of Israel.[7]

The position introduced above we will call "heilsgeschichte" theology. Will Herberg and Mircea Eliade develop this position by contrasting heilsgeschichte theology with other ancient and contemporary theologies. In what ways is biblical religion different from other religions? What is the role of myth in biblical religion? What does it mean that the

[7] Exodus 19:3–6.

Judeo-Christian tradition is a theology of history? Can we do without myth?

The remaining essays in this section are in dialogue with heilsgeschichte theology. Rudolf Bultmann argues that biblical religion is couched in a cosmology or mythology that is no longer acceptable to contemporary man. The contemporary theologian must demythologize the Bible by interpreting it existentially. The Bible is to be understood as man's understanding of his existential [8] situation. The essay by Sam Keen grants the necessity of man telling his story but argues that we need *new* stories which articulate our individual self-understanding. We must find new ways to articulate the sacred dimension of our experience including what heilsgeschichte slights—nature. My essay raises the questions of the analytic tradition. I have attempted to do this in a nontechnical way, leaving future essays to deal with the intelligibility of God-talk in a more detailed way.[9] The section ends with an essay by Robert McAfee Brown who attempts to show that God is active in our history *now*, though not where one might expect him. But God is a person who often does the unexpected.

BIBLICAL FAITH AS HEILSGESCHICHTE

Will Herberg

WILL HERBERG is Professor of Judaic Studies and Social Philosophy at Drew University. He is the author of *Judaism and Modern Man* (1970) and *Protestant-Catholic-Jew* (1955), among others.

The uniqueness—the "scandal"—of biblical faith is revealed in its radically historical character. Biblical faith is historical not merely because it has a history, or deals with historical events; there is nothing particularly novel in that. Biblical faith is historical in the much more profound sense that it is itself essentially a history. The message biblical faith proclaims, the judgments it pronounces, the salvation it promises, the teachings it communicates, are all defined historically and understood as historical realities, rather than as timeless structures of ideas or values. The historicity of biblical faith has long been a source of embarrassment to philosopher and mystic, yet it cannot be eliminated without virtually eliminating the faith itself. Dehistoricizing biblical faith is like paraphrasing poetry; something called an "idea content" remains, but everything that gave power and significance to the original is gone. Biblical faith is *faith enacted as history*, or it is nothing at all.

[8] For a fuller treatment of this position see Chapter Three.
[9] For a fuller treatment of this position see Chapter Four.

I

How shall we understand this radically historical character of biblical faith? Is it merely a cultural trait of the "Hebraic mind," or does it reflect something deeper, something in the very grain of reality, particularly human reality?

There are, fundamentally, three ways in which man has attempted to understand himself, to establish his being, and to relate himself to what is ultimate. One of these, culturally perhaps the oldest, is the way of heathenism. Heathen man sees reality as *nature;* nature—divine since it is the locus of all ultimate sanctities, that beyond which there is nothing—is the context in which heathen man strives to understand himself and establish the meaning of his existence. The reality of his being is the "nature" in him, and rightness is to be achieved by engulfing himself in nature and its cyclical rhythms as an organic part of it. This is heathen man's way of realizing his humanness; heathen man feels wrong, and (if I may so put it) not truly himself, to the degree that he stands out of nature as an incommensurable element. Heathenism is thus at bottom total immanence, a primal unity of the divine, nature, and man.

Heathenism in this sense is obviously not something confined to primitive peoples remote in time and place. On the contrary, the heathen way of understanding man in his relation to ultimate reality seems to enter into the spirituality of men at all times and places, including our own. It emerges in the nature-pantheism of so many spiritually minded people of our time, as well as in the "hard-boiled" scientistic naturalism that holds nature to be ultimate and sees man as nothing more than a biological organism adjusting to its environment.

Standing in a kind of polar opposition to the heathen outlook is the outlook characteristic of the tradition of Greek philosophy and Oriental mysticism. Here it is not nature which is held to be ultimate and really real—though it is often spoken of as in some sense divine—but the *timelessly eternal* behind nature. A sharp dualism of appearance and reality is basic to this view: appearance is material and empirical, multiple, mutable, temporal, engrossed in flux; reality is one, immutable, timeless, eternal, spiritual. This ontological dualism of appearance and reality, the temporal and the eternal, is mirrored in a body-soul dualism in terms of which the human being is analyzed. The real self is the soul, and human self-realization becomes essentially the extrication of the self from nature and time (the body) and its elevation to the timeless realm of spirit. It is surely unnecessary to document the pervasiveness of this type of outlook, with its spiritualistic emphasis and its disparagement of time and history, among the religious people of our time. It is perhaps necessary to remind ourselves that however highminded and spiritual it may appear, this outlook, like the heathenism it replaces, is utterly alien to biblical faith, which understands human existence and ultimate reality in very different categories.

II

Biblical faith defines a view of reality and human existence that marks a sharp break with the presuppositions of both heathenism and Greek-Oriental spirituality. In biblical faith, nature is real and time no illusion since they are the creation of God: this is the biblical witness against the spiritualistic devaluation of the natural and the temporal. Yet though real, they are not self-subsistent or ultimate, since they look to God as their creator: here biblical faith takes its stand against heathen immanentism. In exactly the same way, biblical faith refuses to dissolve man into nature, as does heathenism, or into timeless spirit, as is the effort of so much of philosophy and mysticism. In biblical faith, man is understood as (to use a modern and perhaps inexact term) a psychophysical unit, really and truly part of nature, yet transcending it by virtue of his "spirit," his freedom, his self-awareness, his capacity to get beyond and outside of himself, by virtue of the "image of God" in which he is made.

This complex, multidimensional conception makes it possible, for the first time, to understand man as a genuinely personal and historical being. Heathen naturalism assimilates man's time (history) to nature's time, and feels the uniqueness of the self—insofar as that emerges—as a threat to the oneness with nature which is blessedness. Greek-Oriental eternalism necessarily devaluates history as pure temporality and finds no place for the self, with its uniqueness and multiplicity, in the realm of the really real. It is in biblical faith that the self and history come into their own, for in biblical faith it is man's "essential dignity" that he is a self and ". . . can have a history." [1] Indeed, the two are really one; in biblical faith, human history is intrinsically personal, and the self is an historical structure.

Here we come close to the heart of the matter. Biblical faith understands human existence and human destiny in irreducibly historical terms. If the question is asked what is the real reality of man, what is the actualization of which constitutes the fullness of his being, the heathen (turned philosopher) would say nature; the Greek metaphysician and the Oriental mystic would say that which is timeless and eternal in him; but the biblical thinker would say his *history*. History is the very stuff out of which human being is made: human existence is potential or implicit history; history is explicit or actualized existence. And it is not

---

[1] Søren Kierkegaard, *Either/Or* (Princeton, 1946), Vol. II, p. 209.

very different on the corporate level. In attempting to explain to someone who really does not know what it means to be an American, it would be futile to try to contrive some conceptual definition of "Americanness." Would it not prove more appropriate to tell the story of America and rely upon that story to communicate the fullness of what it means to be an American? "The human person and man's society," Reinhold Niebuhr has profoundly observed, "are *by nature historical* . . . [and] the ultimate truth about life must be mediated historically" [2] (emphasis added).

This is the biblical understanding of man as an historical being. On the basis of this understanding, biblical faith insists that man can realize himself only in and through his life in history. It is in and through history, that God calls to man; it is in and through history, human action in history, that man responds; and it is in and through history that God judges. Heathen man pursues his life in nature below the level of history; Greek-Oriental man aspires to escape from history into the realm of timeless eternity. Biblical man, on the contrary, seeing human existence as essentially historical, strives to redeem history, though realizing that it is not in his time or by his hand that the work can be completed.

It is in this context that the biblical notion of *Heilsgeschichte* (redemptive history, "sacred history") emerges and becomes intelligible. Lessing, in his inaugural address at Jena, protested that ". . . particular facts of history cannot establish eternal truths," least of all the truths of religion; and Fichte reiterated that ". . . the metaphysical only and not the historical can give blessedness." They were both repeating Celsus' outraged remonstrance against the "scandal of particularity," which is the "scandal" of history. But he who understands the reality of human being in biblical terms will find no difficulty in understanding that the ultimate truth about human life and destiny, about man's plight and man's hope alike, is truly and inexpugnably historical, and can be expressed in no other way. (Hence the Bible is composed so largely of stories, recitals, histories.) The structure of faith is an historical structure, because being, living, and acting are, in the biblical conviction, radically historical in character.

III

Once we come to understand our existence in terms of history, and to analyze the human situation in historical terms, we begin to grasp what it means to think of faith as *Heilsgeschichte*. Examining the structure of our existence, we see that each of us has—or rather *is*—many partial

[2] Reinhold Niebuhr, "Religion and Education," *Religious Education*, November–December, 1953.

histories, reflecting the many concerns and interests of life. We are Americans, members of a particular family and ethnic group, intimately associated with particular social institutions and movements. Each of these concerns, allegiances, and associations has its own special history through which it is expressed and made explicit. But most of these histories, we ourselves realize, are merely partial histories; they define only fragments of our being and do not tell us who we "really" are. Underlying and including the partial histories of life, there must be some "total" history, in some way fundamental and comprehensive, some really ultimate history. Such a history, the history which one affirms in a total and ultimate manner, is one's *redemptive history* (*Heilsgeschichte*), for it is the history in terms of which the final meaning of life is established and the self redeemed from the powers of meaninglessness and non-being. This is the history that defines, and is defined by, one's faith; it is, indeed, the history that *is* one's faith. "To be a self," H. Richard Niebuhr has said, "is to have a god; to have a god is to have a history." [3] If we reverse this—"To have a history is to have a god; to have a god is to be a self"— we get a glimpse of the full significance of the relation of faith and history.

Whatever history I take to tell me who I "really" am may thus be taken to define my actual faith. If I take my American history to define not merely the American aspect of my life, but also the fullness and ultimacy of my being as a person, I make "Americanism" (the American Way of Life) my faith and the nation my god. A moment's thought will show us how real this faith is in the lives of most of us today, and how clearly it is expressed as *Heilsgeschichte*. It has its symbols, liturgy, and ceremony, its holy days and cultic observances; it has its "sacred history" and its sense of messianic vocation. [4] Marxism, the great rival of Amer-

---

[3] Richard Niebuhr, *The Meaning of Revelation* (Macmillan, 1941), p. 80.

[4] In this country, more than anywhere else in the world perhaps, the old Christian church year has been all but replaced in law and in fact by a round of holidays (Columbus Day, Washington's Birthday, Independence Day, Memorial Day, Armistice [or Veterans] Day, etc., etc.) that mark great events in our national history: these are the days that Americans, insofar as they celebrate anything, celebrate as the "holy days" that really count. (Christmas and Easter are virtually all that remain of the old church calendar for the mass of Americans, and even these holidays have been largely voided of their religious content.) Perhaps even more revealing is the response of a group of outstanding Americans to the request that they rate the hundred most significant events in universal history. First place was given to Columbus' discovery of America, while Christ, either his birth or crucifixion, came fourteenth, tied with the Wright brothers' first plane flight (see the report in *Time*, May 24, 1954). This order of priority, so shocking in terms of Christian faith, becomes quite intelligible, even inevitable, once it is realized that the framework of faith in which it is made is the faith of "Americanism." This faith is defined by American history taken as ultimate and redemptive; it is only natural that those who hold this faith and this redemptive history should see Columbus' discovery of America (or alternatively, the American War of Independence) as the most important event in the anals of mankind. See also Will Herberg, *Protestant-Catholic-Jew: An Essay in American Religious Sociology* (Doubleday, 1955), chap. V.

icanism in the conflict of secular religions, is as thoroughly historical in
structure, and even more obviously the reflection of the absolutization of
a partial history. Marxism takes the partial history defined by the modern
worker's being a proletarian as the ultimate and "total" history, and this
history it proclaims as redemptive. From this standpoint, Marxism is,
fundamentally, a secularized version—and therefore perversion—of biblical "sacred history," in which God is replaced by the Dialectic, the
"chosen people" by the proletariat, the "faithful remnant" and even
the Messiah by the Party, while the "beginning" and "end" of history, the
"original rightness" lost and the "restored rightness" to come, are robbed
of their transcendence and made points *within* the historical process. That
Marxism is essentially a faith—an idolatrous faith—enacted as history,
and therefore a *Heilsgeschichte,* is now almost a commonplace.

And so generally. Idolatrous faiths (particularly those emerging in the
history-conscious West) are faiths defined by, and defining, partial histories made ultimate. They bear witness to gods that are idolatrous, in the
sense that they are gods who are something of this world—some idea,
institution, movement, power, or community—divinized and turned into
absolutes. The idolatrous god thus has his idolatrous "sacred history";
very frequently, it is the idolatrous "sacred history" that is more vivid in
men's minds than the god to whom it points.

Biblical faith, because it is faith in the living God, the God who is
"beyond the gods" of the world, expresses itself in a redemptive history
in which this God is central and the "holy people of God" the crucial
historical community. And just as faith in the living God is the only
alternative to idolatrous faiths, so, in the last analysis, the definition of
life in terms of the "sacred history" of God's dealings with men given in
biblical tradition is the only alternative to the idolatrous "totalization" of
one or another of the partial histories which make up our lives. The
ultimate existential decision is a choice between "sacred histories" as it is
a choice between gods.

IV

Biblical faith, understood as history, presents us with a grand and stirring drama of human existence and destiny. It is not my purpose to describe this cosmic drama, since that has been done and magnificently done
in a number of recent works on biblical religion. In its essentials, it defines
a three-phase pattern in which the present "wrong" and contradictory
existence of man and society is seen as a falling away from the original
"rightness" of God's creation, and as destined for restoration and rectifi-
cation in the final fulfillment of the kingdom of God. Within this vast
orbit, it traces the history of the "people of God," God's instrument for

the redemption of mankind. All human history falls under its range and sweep, since its purpose is universal, though its center—the crucial revelatory, community-creating event (Exodus-Sinai in Judaism, Calvary-Easter in Christianity)—is particular. But no attempt is made to impose a final "philosophy of history" upon the historical material, which is drawn from legend, saga, oral tradition, and written documents. Every understanding of history is felt to be partial and fragmentary; in the end, everything is swallowed up in the mystery of divine providence. Yet, however limited and uncertain our grasp of it may be, it is the "sacred history" that tells us who we are, where we stand, and what we hope for—that, in short, gives meaning to existence.

It has been repeatedly pointed out in recent years, and not by theologians alone, that this understanding of history tends to make for a creative realism that escapes utopianism on the one side and despair on the other. It is, in fact, the only real alternative to the many historical idolatries of our time, which are now seen to be distortions, often demonic distortions, of the historical faith and hope of the Bible.

Yet even with this understanding we have not penetrated to the heart of biblical faith as *Heilsgeschichte*. For we are still, as it were, on the outside looking in. Biblical "sacred history" possesses a double inwardness. It is, first of all, an interpretation through the eyes of faith of acts and events that, from another standpoint, might well be interpreted in an altogether different way: to Thucydides, the victorious Assyrian would hardly have appeared as the rod of God's anger against a wayward Israel. But it is inward also in another and perhaps deeper sense, in the sense that, as the history of God's redemptive work, it can become actually redemptive *for me*, redemptive existentially, only if I appropriate it in faith as *my personal history*, the history of my own life. "Faith in the New Testament sense," writes Oscar Cullmann, "is the way by which the past phase of redemptive history becomes effective for me. . . . Faith in the New Testament sense means to be convinced that this entire happening takes place for me." [5] Remembrance and expectation are the two foci of existence in faith. "He who does not himself remember that God led him out of Egypt, he who does not himself await the Messiah," says Martin Buber, "is no longer a true Jew." [6] Religion is thus not the apprehension of eternal truths or loyalty to eternal values; it is rather the personal acceptance, through commitment and action, of what God has done, is doing, and will do for the redemption of mankind, in the first place of oneself. [7] From this angle, the act of faith is double: the existential affirmation of a history as one's redemptive history and the existential appropriation of this redemptive history as one's personal background

[5] Oscar Cullmann, *Christ and Time* (Westminster, 1949), p. 219.
[6] Martin Buber, "Der Preis," *Der Jude*, October, 1917.
[7] In other words, redemption in the biblical sense is history, though history is not, as the Marxists or liberal utopians think, redemptive.

history, and therefore in a real sense the foundation of one's personal existence "In the history of Israel," to quote Buber once more, "we see the prehistory of our own life, each of us the prehistory of his own life." [8]

But this means that redemptive history is not merely a recital that we hear and understand. It is also a demand upon us, for out of it comes the voice of God. Faith is responding to the call of God that comes to us from out of the midst of redemptive history. It is (to borrow from Kierkegaard) as though we sat witnessing some tremendous epic drama being performed on a vast stage, when suddenly the chief character of the drama, who is also its director, steps forward to the front of the stage, fixes his eye upon us, points his finger at us, and calls out: "You, you're wanted. Come up here. Take your part!" This is the call of faith coming from out of "sacred history," the call to cease to be a spectator and come forward to be an actor in the great drama of redemption. We are none of us comfortable with this call; we much prefer the anonymity and irresponsibility of being spectators, and we resent the demand that we come forward, assume responsibility, and become actors. But precisely this is the demand of biblical faith as redemptive history. Unless we receive this call and respond to it, the redemptive history that we apprehend is not redemptive. It does not really tell us who we are, where we stand, and what we may hope for; it does not really give meaning to existence. The history which redeems is a history in which one is both object and subject, both spectator and actor; but paradoxically, it is a history in which one is not object unless he is subject, one is not spectator unless he is actor, for unless one is really actor and subject, the "sacred history" ceases to be personal history and loses all religious significance. Redemptive history, to be truly redemptive, must be existential, appropriated in inwardness in personal existence as a demand and a responsibility. This is the meaning of biblical faith as *Heilsgeschichte*.

[8] Martin Buber, "Hasidism in Religion," *Hasidism* (Philosophical Library, 1948), p. 199. This is true for both Jew and Christian, though the Christian, of course, extends the "old Israel" into the "new Israel" of the Church.

ARCHAIC MYTH AND HISTORICAL MAN

Mircea Eliade

MIRCEA ELIADE is Sewell Avery Distinguished Service Professor at the
University of Chicago. His works in the phenomenology of religion are
widely read. See especially *The Sacred and the Profane* (1959),
Cosmos and History (1959), and *Yoga, Immortality and Freedom*
(1958).

It would be hard to find a definition of myth that would be acceptable
to all scholars and at the same time intelligible to nonspecialists. Myth
is an extremely complex cultural reality, which can be approached and
interpreted from various and complementary viewpoints. The definition
that seems least inadequate because most embracing is this. Myth narrates a sacred history: it relates an event that took place in primordial
time, the fabled time of the "beginnings." In other words, myth tells how,
through the deeds of Supernatural Beings, a reality came into existence,
be it the whole of reality, the Cosmos, or only a fragment of reality—
an island, a species of plant, a particular kind of human behavior, an
institution. Myth, then, is always an account of a "creation"; it relates
how something was produced, began to be.

Myth tells only of that which *really happened*, which manifested itself
completely. The actors in myths are Supernatural Beings. They are known
primarily by what they did in the times of the "beginnings." Hence myths
disclose their creative activity and reveal the sacredness (or simply the
"supernaturalness") of their works. In short, myths describe the various
and sometimes dramatic breakthroughs of the sacred that really establishes the world and makes it what it is today. Furthermore, it is as a result
of the intervention of Supernatural Beings that man himself is what he is
today, a mortal, sexed, and cultural being. The myth is regarded as a
sacred story, and hence a "true history," because it always deals with
realities. The cosmogonic myth is "true" because the existence of the
World is there to prove it; the myth of the origin of death is equally true
because man's mortality proves it, and so on.

Because myth relates the *gesta* of Supernatural Beings and the manifestation of their sacred powers, it becomes the *exemplary model* for
all significant human activities. When the missionary and ethnologist, G.
Strehlow asked the Australian Arunta why they performed certain ceremonies, the answer was always: "Because the ancestors so commanded
it." The Kai of New Guinea refused to change their way of living and
working, and they explained: "It was thus that the Nemu (the Mythical
Ancestors) did, and we do likewise." Asked the reason for a particular

detail in a ceremony, a Navaho chanter answered: "Because the Holy People did it that way in the first place. The same justification is alleged by the Hindu theologians and ritualists. "We must do what the gods did in the beginning" (*Satapatha* Brāhmana, VII, 2, 1, 4). "Thus the gods did: thus men do" (*Taittiriya* Brāhmana, I, 5, 9, 4). In summary, the foremost function of myth is to reveal the exemplary models for all human rites and all significant human activities—alimentation or marriage, work or education, art or wisdom, and so on.

We might add that in societies where myth is still alive the natives carefully distinguish myths—"true stories"—from fables or tales, which they call "false stories." . . .

The distinction made by natives between "true stories" and "false stories" is significant. Both categories of narratives present "histories," that is, relate a series of events that took place in a distant and fabulous past. Although the actors in myths are usually Gods and Supernatural Beings, while those in tales are heroes or miraculous animals, all the actors share the common trait that they do not belong to the everyday world. Nevertheless, the natives have felt that the two kinds of "stories" are basically different. For everything that the myths relate concerns them directly, while the tales and fables refer to events that, even when they have caused changes in the world (such as the anatomical or physiological peculiarities of certain animals), have not altered the human condition as such.

Myths narrate not only the origin of the World, of animals, plants, and of man, but also all the primordial events in consequence of which man became what he is today—mortal, sexed, organized in a society, obliged to work in order to live, and working in accordance with certain rules. If the World exists, if man exists, it is because Supernatural Beings exercised creative powers in the "beginning." But after the cosmogony and the creation of man other events occurred, and man as he is today is the direct result of those mythical events; he is constituted by those events. He is mortal because something happened in the mythical time. If that thing had not happened, man would not be mortal—he would have gone on existing indefinitely, like rocks; or he might have changed his skin periodically like snakes, and hence would have been able to renew his life, that is, begin it over again indefinitely. But the myth of the origin of death narrates what happened *in illo tempore*, and, in telling the incident, explains why man is mortal.

Similarly, a certain tribe lives by fishing—because in mythical times a Supernatural Being taught their ancestors to catch and cook fish. The myth tells the story of the first fishery, and, in so doing, at once reveals a superhuman act, teaches men how to perform it, and finally, explains why this particular tribe must procure their food in this way.

It would be easy to multiply examples. But those already given show why, for archaic man, myth is a matter of primary importance,

while tales and fables are not. Myth teaches him the primordial "stories"
that have constituted him existentially; and everything connected with his
existence and his legitimate mode of existence in the Cosmos concerns
him directly. However, what happened *ab origine* can be repeated by the
power of rites. For the man of archaic societies, it is essential to know the
myths. By recollecting the myths, by re-enacting them, he is able to
repeat what the Gods, the Heroes, or the Ancestors did *ab origine.* To
know the myths is to learn the secret of the origin of things. In other
words, one learns not only how things came into existence but also where
to find them and how to make them reappear. . . . .

In most cases it is not enough to know the origin myth; it must
also be recited. This, in a sense, is a proclamation of one's knowledge, a
display of it. But this is not all. He who recites or performs the origin
myth is thereby steeped in the sacred atmosphere in which these miraculous events took place. The mythical time of origins is a "strong" time
because it was transfigured by the active, creative presence of the Supernatural Beings. By reciting the myths one reconstitutes that fabulous time
and hence in some way becomes "contemporary" with the events described; one is in the presence of the Gods or Heroes. As a summary
formula, we might say that by "living" the myths one emerges from
profane, chronological time and enters a time that is of a different
quality, a "sacred" Time at once primordial and indefinitely recoverable.

In general it can be said that myth, as experienced by archaic
societies, 1) constitutes the history of the acts of the Supernaturals; 2)
that this history is considered to be absolutely *true* (because it is concerned with realities) and *sacred* (because it is the work of the Supernaturals); 3) that myth is always related to a "creation"; it tells *how
something came into existence,* or how a pattern of behavior, an institution, a manner of working were established (this is why myths *constitute
the paradigms for all significant human acts*); 4) that by knowing the
myth one knows the "origin" of things and hence we can control and manipulate them at will (this is not an "external," "abstract" knowledge but a
knowledge that one "experiences" ritually, either by ceremonially recount-
ing the myth or by performing the ritual for which it is the justification);
5) that in one way or another one "lives" the myth, in the sense that one
is seized by the sacred, exalting power of the events re-collected or re-
enacted.

"Living" a myth, then, implies a genuinely religious experience,
since it differs from the ordinary experience of everyday life. The "religiousness" of this experience is due to the fact that one re-enacts
fabulous, exalting, significant events, one again witnesses the creative
works of the Supernaturals; one ceases to exist in the everyday world and
enters a transfigured, auroral world impregnated with the Supernaturals'
presence. What is involved *is not a commemoration of mythical events
but a reiteration of them.* The protagonists of the myth are made present;

one becomes their contemporary. This also implies that one is no longer living in chronological time, but in the primordial Time, the Time when the event took place. This is why we can use the term the "strong time" of myth; it is the prodigious, "sacred" time when something new, strong, and significant was manifested. To re-experience that time, to re-enact it as often as possible, to witness again the spectacle of the divine works, to meet with the Supernaturals and relearn their creative lesson is the desire that runs like a pattern through all the ritual reiterations of myths. In short, myths reveal that the World, man and life have a supernatural origin and history, and that this history is significant, precious, and exemplary.

Every mythical account of the origin of anything presupposes and continues the cosmogony. From the structural point of view, origin myths can be homologized with the cosmogonic myth. The creation of the World being the pre-eminent instance of creation, the cosmogony becomes the exemplary model for "creation" of every kind. This does not mean that the origin myth imitates or copies the cosmogonic model, for no concerted or systematic reflection is involved. But every new appearance—an animal, a plant, an institution—implies the existence of a World. Every origin myth narrates and justifies a "new situation"—new in the sense that it did not exist from the beginning of the World. Origin myths continue and complete the cosmogonic myth; they tell how the world was changed, made richer or poorer.

This is why some origin myths begin by outlining a cosmogony. The history of the great families and dynasties of Tibet opens by rehearsing the birth of the Cosmos from an Egg. The Polynesian genealogical chants begin in the same way. Such ritual genealogical chants are composed by the bards when the princess is pregnant, and they are communicated to the *hula* dancers to be learned by heart. The dancers, men and women, dance and recite the chant continuously until the child is born. It is as if the embryological development of the future chief were accompanied by a recapitulation of the cosmogony, the history of the World, and the history of the tribe. The gestation of a chief is the occasion for a symbolic "recreation" of the World. The recapitulation is at once a reminder and a ritual reactualization, through song and dance, of the essential mythical events that have taken place since the Creation.

The close connection between the cosmogonic myth, the myth of the origin of sickness and its remedy, and the ritual of magical healing is clearly exemplified in, for example, the Ancient Near East or among the Tibetans. Sometimes a solemn recitation of the cosmogonic myth is enough to cure certain sicknesses or imperfections. As the exemplary model for all "creation," the cosmogonic myth can help the patient to make a "new beginning" of his life. The return to origins gives the hopes of a rebirth. . . .

A contemporary Polynesian, Hare Hongi, puts it this way:

The words by which Io fashioned the Universe—that is to say, by which it was implanted and caused to produce a world of light—the same words are used in the ritual for implanting a child in a barren womb. The words by which Io caused light to shine in the darkness are used in rituals for cheering a gloomy and despondent heart, the feeble aged, the decrepit; for shedding light into secret places and matters, for inspiration in song—composing and in many other affairs, affecting men to despair in times of adverse war. For all such the ritual includes the words (used by Io) to overcome and dispel darkness. (E. S. C. Handy, *Polynesian Religion* [Honolulu, 1927], pp. 10–11.)

This remarkable text presents direct and incontrovertible testimony concerning the function of the cosmogonic myth in a traditional society. As we have just seen, this myth serves as the model for every kind of "creation"—the procreation of a child as well as the reestablishment of a military situation in jeopardy or of a psychic equilibrium threatened by melancholy and despair. . . .

All this is clearly apparent from the many ritual applications of the Polynesian cosmogonic myth. According to this myth, in the beginning there were only the Waters and Darkness. Io, the Supreme God, separated the Waters by the power of thought and of his words, and created the Sky and the Earth. He said: "Let the Waters be separated, let the Heavens be formed, let the Earth be!" These cosmogonic words of Io's, by virtue of which the world came into existence, are creative words, charged with sacred power. Hence men utter them when there is something to do, to create. They are repeated during the rite for making a suckling drink water or eat solid food. The child is ritually projected into the time of "origin" when milk, water, and grains first appeared on earth. The idea implicit in this belief is that it is *the first manifestation of a thing which is significant and valid,* and not its successive epiphanies.

Through the reactualization of his myths, the man of primitive societies attempts to approach the gods and to participate in *being;* the imitation of paradigmatic divine models expresses at once his desire for sanctity and his ontological nostalgia.

In the primitive and archaic religions the eternal repetition of divine exploits is justified as an *imitatio dei.* The sacred calendar annually repeats the same festivals, repeats, that is, the reactualizations of the same mythical events. Strictly speaking, the sacred calendar proves to be the "eternal return" of a limited number of divine *gesta* and this is true not only for primitive religions but for all others. The festal calendar everywhere constitutes a periodical return of the same primordial situations and hence a reactualization of the same sacred time. For religious man, reactualization of the same mythical events constitutes his greatest hopes, for which each reactualization he again has the opportunity to transfigure his existence, to make it like its divine model. In short, for religious man of the primitive and archaic societies, the eternal repetition of paradigmatic gestures and the eternal recovery of the same mythical time of origin, sanctified by the gods, in no sense implies a pessimistic vision of life. On the contrary, for him it is by virtue of this eternal return to the sources of the sacred and the real that human existence appears to be saved from nothingness and death.

The perspective changes completely when the sense of the *sacrality of the Cosmos becomes lost*. This is what occurs when, in certain more highly evolved societies, the intellectual élites progressively detach themselves from the patterns of the traditional religion. The religious meaning of the repetition of paradigmatic gestures is forgotten. But *repetition emptied of its religious content necessarily leads to a pessimistic vision of existence*. When it is no longer a vehicle for reintegrating a primordial situation, and hence for recovering the mysterious presence of the gods, that is, *when it is desacralized,* the mythical time becomes terrifying; it is seen as a circle forever turning on itself, repeating itself to infinity.

This is what happened in India, where the doctrine of cosmic cycles (*yugas*) was elaborately developed. To Indian thought, time was homologized to the cosmic illusion (*mâyâ*) and the eternal return to existence signified indefinite prolongation of suffering and slavery. In the view of these religious and philosophical élites, the only hope was non-return-to-existence, the abolition of *karma;* in other words, final deliverance (*mokska*) implying a transcendence of the cosmos. Greece, too, knew the myth of the eternal return, and the Greek philosophers of the late period carried the conception of circular time to its furthest limits.

Compared with the archaic and palaeo-oriental religions, as well as with the mythic-philosophical conception of the eternal return, as they were elaborated in India and Greece, Judaism presents an innovation of the first importance. For Judaism, time has a beginning and will have an end. The idea of cyclic time is left behind. Yahweh no longer manifests himself in *mythical time* (like the gods of other religions) but in a *historical time,* which is irreversible. Each new manifestation of Yahweh in history is no longer reducible to an earlier manifestation. The fall of Jerusalem expresses Yahweh's wrath against his people, but it is no longer the same wrath that Yahweh expressed by the fall of Samaria. His gestures are *personal* interventions in history and reveal their deep meaning *only for his people,* the people that Yahweh had *chosen.* Hence, the historical event acquires a new dimension; it becomes a theophany.

Christianity tried to go even further in valorizing *historical time*. The Christian Fathers insisted on the historicity of the life of Jesus and attempted to substantiate all the historical testimonies. Justin, for example, held that the Nativity could be proved by the "tax declarations submitted under the procurator Quirinus and available at Rome a century later." Origen thinks that the earthquake and the darkness can be confirmed by the historical narrative of Phlegon of Tralles. The Last Supper is a historical event that can be dated with absolute precision. Origen admits that the Gospels contain episodes that are not "authentic" historically though they are "true" on the spiritual plane. But in answering Celsus' criticisms, he also admits the difficulty of proving the historicity of a historical event. He writes: "An attempt to substantiate the truth of almost any story as historical fact, even if the story is true, and to produce complete certainty about it, is one of the most difficult tasks and in some cases impossible" (*Contra Celsum* I, 42).

Though he does not doubt the historicity of the life, passion, and resurrection of Jesus Christ, Origen is more concerned with the spiritual, nonhistorical meaning of the Gospel text. The true meaning is "beyond history." The exegetist must be able to "free himself from the historical materials," for these are only a "steppingstone." To overstress the historicity of Jesus and neglect the deeper meaning of his life and message is, in fact, to mutilate Christianity. "People marvel at Jesus," he writes in his *Commentary on the Gospel of John,* "when they look into the history about him, but they no longer believe when the deeper meaning is disclosed to them; instead they suppose it to be false."

In proclaiming the Incarnation, Resurrection, and Ascension of the Word, the Christian Fathers were sure that they were not putting forth a new myth. Actually, they were employing the categories of mythical thought. Obviously they could not recognize this mythical thought in the desacralized mythologies of the pagan scholars who were their contemporaries. But it is clear that for Christians of all creeds the center of religious life is constituted by the drama of Jesus Christ. Although played out in History, this drama first established the possibility of salvation; hence there is only one way to gain salvation—to reiterate this exemplary drama ritually and to imitate the supreme model revealed by the life and teaching of Jesus. Now, this type of religious behavior is bound up with genuine mythical thought.

It must at once be added that, by the *very fact that it is a religion,* Christianity had to keep at least one mythical aspect—liturgical Time, that is, the periodical recovery of the *illud tempus* of the "beginnings." The religious experience of the Christian is based upon an *imitation* of the Christ as *exemplary pattern,* upon the liturgical repetition of the life, death, and resurrection of the Lord, and upon the *contemporaneity* of the Christian with *illud tempus* which begins with the Nativity at Bethlehem and ends with the Ascension. Now, as we have seen, the imitation of a transhuman model, the repetition of an exemplary scenario and the breakaway from profane time through a moment which opens out into the Great Time, are the essential marks of "mythical behavior"— that is, the behavior of the man of the archaic societies, who finds the very source of his existence in the myth.

Ultimately, Christianity arrives, not at a *philosophy,* but at a *theology* of history. For God's intervention in history, and above all his incarnation in the historical person of Jesus the Christ, have a transhistorical purpose —the *salvation* of man.

Hegel takes over the Judaeo-Christian ideology and applies it to universal history in its totality: the universal spirit *continually* manifests itself in historical events and manifests itself *only* in historical events. Thus *the whole* of history becomes a theophany; everything that has happened in history *had to happen as it did,* because the universal Spirit so willed it. The road is thus opened to the various forms of twentieth-century historicistic philosophies. Yet we must add that historicism arises as a decomposition product of Christianity; it accords decisive importance to the historical event (which is an idea whose origin is Christian), but to the *historical event as such,* that is, by denying it any possibility of revealing a tranhistorical, soteriological intent.

The modern, nonreligious, "historical" man can be considered the result of a radical secularization of the Hegelian understanding of History. The nonreligious man refuses transcendence, accepts the relativity of "reality," and may even come to doubt the meaning of existence. The great cultures of the past too have not been entirely without nonreligious men. But it is only in the modern western societies that nonreligious man has developed fully. Modern nonreligious man assumes a new existential situation; he regards himself solely as the subject and agent of history, and he refuses all appeal to transcendence. In other words, he accepts no model for humanity outside the human condition as it can be seen in the various historical situations. Man *makes himself,* and he only makes himself completely in proportion as he desacralized himself and the world. The sacred is the prime obstacle to his freedom. He will become himself only when he is totally demystified. He will not be truly free until he has killed the last god.

The modern nonreligious man assumes a tragic existence and his existential choice is not without its greatness. But this nonreligious man descends from *homo religiosus* and, whether he likes it or not, he is also the work of religious man. In short, he is the result of a desacralization of human existence. But this means that nonreligious man has been formed by opposing his predecessor, by attempting to "empty" himself of all religion and all transhuman meanings. He recognizes himself in proportion as he "frees" and "purifies" himself from the "superstitions" of his ancestors. In other words, profane man cannot help preserving some vestiges of the behavior of religious man, though they are emptied of religious meaning. Do what he will, he is an inheritor. He cannot utterly abolish his past, since he is himself the product of his past. He forms himself by a series of denials and refusals, but he continues to be haunted by the realities that he has refused and denied. To acquire a world of his own, he has desacralized the world in which his ancestors lived; but to do so he has been obliged to adopt the opposite of an earlier type of behavior, and that behavior is still emotionally present to him, in one form or another, ready to be reactualized in his deepest being.

The nonreligious man *in the pure state* is a comparatively rare phenomenon, even in the most desacralized of modern societies. The majority of the "irreligious" still behave religiously, even though they are not aware of the fact. We refer not only to the modern man's many "superstitions" and "taboos," all of them magico-religious in structure. But the modern man who feels and claims that he is nonreligious still retains a large stock of camouflaged myths and degenerated rituals. The festivities that go with the New Year or with taking up residence in a new house, still exhibit the structures of a ritual of renewal.

A whole volume could well be written on the myths of modern man, on the mythologies camouflaged in the plays that he enjoys, in the books that he reads. The cinema, that "dream factory," takes over and employs countless mythical motifs—the fight between hero and monster, initiatory combats and ordeals, paradigmatic figures and images (the Maiden, the Hero, the Paradisal Landscape, Hell, and so on). Even reading includes a mythological function, not only because it replaces the recitation of myths in archaic societies and the oral literature that still lives in the rural communities of Europe, but particularly because through reading the modern man succeeds in obtaining an "escape from time" comparable to the "emergence from Time" effected by myths.

Strictly speaking, the great majority of the irreligious are not liberated from religious behavior, from theologies and mythologies. They sometimes stagger under a whole magico-religious paraphernalia, which, however, has degenerated to the point of caricature and hence is hard to recognize for what it is. We do not refer to the countless "little religions" that proliferate in all modern cities, to the pseudo-occult, neo-spiritualistic, or so-called hermetic churches, sects or movements; for all these phenomena still belong to the sphere of religion, even if they almost always present the aberrant aspects of pseudo-morphs. Nor do we allude to the various political movements and social utopianisms whose mythological structure and religious fanaticism are visible at a glance. For but one example we need only refer to the mythological structure of communism and its eschatological content. Marx takes over and continues one of the great eschatological myths of the Asian Mediterranean world—the redeeming role of the Just (the "chosen," the "anointed," the "innocent"; in our day, the proletariat), whose sufferings are destined to change the ontological status of the world. In fact, Marx's classless society and the consequent disappearance of historical tensions find their closest precedent in the myth of the Golden Age that many traditions put at the beginning and the end of history. Marx enriched this venerable myth by a whole Judaeo-Christian messianic ideology: on the one hand, the prophetic role and soteriological function that he attributes to the proletariat; on the other, the final battle between Good and Evil, which is easily comparable to the apocalyptic battle between Christ and Antichrist, followed by the total victory of the former.

But it is not only in the "little religions" or in the political mystiques that we find degenerated or camouflaged religious and mythical behavior. It is no less to be seen in movements that openly avow themselves to be secular or even antireligious. Examples are of nudism or the movements for complete sexual freedom, ideologies in which we can discern traces of the "nostalgia for Eden," the desire to reestablish the paradisal state before the Fall, when sin did not exist.

Then, too, it is interesting to observe to what an extent the scenarios of initiation still persist in the modern world—for instance, in psychoanalysis. The patient is asked to descend deeply into himself, to make his past live, to confront his traumatic experience again; structurally, this dangerous operation resembles initiatory descents into hell, the realm of ghosts, and combats with monsters. Just as the initiate was expected to emerge from his ordeals victorious—so the patient undergoing analysis today must confront his own unconscious, haunted by ghosts and monsters, in order to find psychic health and integrity and hence the world of cultural values.

In short, the majority of men "without religion" and "without myths" still hold to pseudo-religions and degenerated mythologies. There is nothing surprising in this, for as we saw, profane man is the descendant *homo religiosus* and he cannot wipe out his own history—that is, the behavior of his religious ancestors which has made him what he is today. This is all the more true because a great part of his existence is fed by impulses that come to him from the depths of his being, from the unconscious. Now, the contents and structures of the unconscious exhibit astonishing similarities to mythological images and figures. We do not mean to say that mythologies are the "product" of the unconscious, for the mode of being of the myth is precisely that it *reveals itself as myth*. That is, it announces that something *has been manifested in a paradigmatic manner*. A myth is "produced" by the unconscious in the same sense in which we could say that *Madame Bovary* is the "product" of an adultery.

Yet the contents and structures of the unconscious are the results of immemorial existential situations, especially of critical situations, and this is why the unconscious has a religious aura. Thus, the nonreligious man of modern societies is still nourished and aided by the activity of his unconscious, but without thereby attaining to a properly religious experience and vision of the world. From one point of view, it could almost be said that in the case of those moderns who proclaim that they are nonreligious, religion and mythology are "eclipsed" in the darkness of their unconscious. Or, from the Christian point of view, it could also be said that nonreligion is equivalent to a new "fall" of man—in other words, that nonreligious man has lost the capacity to live religion consciously, and hence to understand and assume it; but that, in his deepest being, he still retains a memory of it, as, after the first "fall," his ancestor, the primordial man, retained intelligence enough to enable him to rediscover the traces of God that are visible in the world. After the first "fall," the religious sense descended to the level of the "divided consciousness"; now, after the second, it has fallen even further, into the depths of the unconscious; it has been "forgotten."

THE TASK OF DEMYTHOLOGIZING THE
NEW TESTAMENT PROCLAMATION

Rudolf Bultmann

RUDOLF BULTMANN was Professor of New Testament at the University of Marburg. Among his many works are *Theology of the New Testament, Jesus Christ and Mythology, and History and Eschatology.*

A. THE PROBLEM

1. The Mythical View of the World and the Mythical Event of Redemption

The cosmology of the New Testament is essentially mythical in character. The world is viewed as a three-storied structure, with the earth in the centre, the heaven above, and the underworld beneath. Heaven is the abode of God and of celestial beings—the angels. The underworld is hell, the place of torment. Even the earth is more than the scene of natural, everyday events, of the trivial round and common task. It is the scene of the supernatural activity of God and his angels on the one hand, and of Satan and his daemons on the other. These supernatural forces intervene in the course of nature and in all that men think and will and do. Miracles are by no means rare. Man is not in control of his own life. Evil spirits may take possession of him. Satan may inspire him with evil thoughts. Alternatively, God may inspire his thought and guide his purposes. He may grant him heavenly visions. He may allow him to hear his word of succour or demand. He may give him the supernatural power of his Spirit. History does not follow a smooth unbroken course; it is set in motion and controlled by these supernatural powers. This aeon is held in bondage by Satan, sin, and death (for "powers" is precisely what they are), and hastens towards its end. That end will come very soon, and will take the form of a cosmic catastrophe. It will be inaugurated by the "woes" of the last time. Then the Judge will come from heaven, the dead will rise, the last judgment will take place, and men will enter into eternal salvation or damnation.

This then is the mythical view of the world which the New Testament presupposes when it presents the event of redemption which is the sub-

ject of its preachings. It proclaims in the language of mythology that the last time has now come, "In the fulness of time" God sent forth his Son, a pre-existent divine Being, who appears on earth as a man. He dies the death of a sinner on the cross and makes atonement for the sins of men. His resurrection marks the beginning of the cosmic catastrophe. Death, the consequence of Adam's sin, is abolished, and the daemonic forces are deprived of their power. The risen Christ is exalted to the right hand of God in heaven and made "Lord" and "King." He will come again on the clouds of heaven to complete the work of redemption, and the resurrection and judgment of men will follow. Sin, suffering and death will then be finally abolished. All this is to happen very soon; indeed, St. Paul thinks that he himself will live to see it.

All who belong to Christ's Church and are joined to the Lord by Baptism and the Eucharist are certain of resurrection to salvation, unless they forfeit it by unworthy behavior. Christian believers already enjoy the first instalment of salvation, for the Spirit is at work within them, bearing witness to their adoption as sons of God, and guaranteeing their final resurrection.

2. The Mythological View of the World Obsolete

All this is the language of mythology, and the origin of the various themes can be easily traced in the contemporary mythology of Jewish Apocalyptic and in the redemption myths of Gnosticism. To this extent *the kerygma is incredible to modern man, for he is convinced that the mythical view of the world is obsolete.* We are therefore bound to ask whether, when we preach the Gospel to-day, we expect our converts to accept not only the Gospel message, but also the mythical view of the world in which it is set. If not, does the New Testament embody a truth which is quite independent of its mythical setting? If it does, theology must undertake the task of stripping the kerygma from its mythical framework, of "demythologizing" it

Can Christian preaching expect modern man *to accept the mythical view of the world as true?* To do so would be both senseless and impossible. It would be senseless, because there is nothing specifically Christian in the mythical view of the world as such. It is simply the cosmology of a pre-scientific age. Again, it would be impossible, because no man can adopt a view of the world by his own volition—it is already determined for him by his place in history. Of course such a view is not absolutely unalterable, and the individual may even contribute to its change. But he can do so only when he is faced by a new set of facts so compelling as to make his previous view of the world untenable. He has then no alternatives but to modify his view of the world or produce a new one. The discoveries of Copernicus and the atomic theory are instances of this, and so was romanticism, with its discovery that the human sub-

ject is richer and more complex than elightenment or idealism had
allowed, and nationalism, with its new realization of the importance of
history and the tradition of peoples.

It may equally well happen that truths which a shallow enlightenment
had failed to perceive are later rediscovered in ancient myths. Theologians
are perfectly justified in asking whether this is not exactly what has
happened with the New Testament. At the same time it is impossible to
revive an obsolete view of the world by a mere fiat, and certainly not a
mythical view. For all our thinking to-day is shaped irrevocably by modern science. A blind acceptance of the New Testament mythology would
be arbitrary, and to press for its acceptance as an article of faith would
be to reduce faith to works. Wilhelm Hermann pointed this out, and one
would have thought that his demonstration was conclusive. It would involve a sacrifice of the intellect which could have only one result—a curious form of schizophrenia and insincerity. It would mean accepting a
view of the world in our faith and religion which we should deny in our
everyday life. Modern thought as we have inherited it brings with it
criticism of *the New Testament view of the world.*

Man's knowledge and mastery of the world have advanced to such an
extent through science and technology that it is no longer possible for
anyone seriously to hold the New Testament view of the world—in fact,
there is no one who does. What meaning, for instance, can we attach to
such phrases in the creed as "descended into hell" or "ascended into
heaven?" We no longer believe in the three-storied universe which the
creeds take for granted. The only honest way of reciting the creeds is to
strip the mythological framework from the truth they enshrine—that is,
assuming that they contain any truth at all, which is just the question that
theology has to ask. No one who is old enough to think for himself supposes that God lives in a local heaven. There is no longer any heaven in
the traditional sense of the word. The same applies to hell in the sense
of a mythical underworld beneath our feet. And if this is so, the story of
Christ's descent into hell and of his Ascension into heaven is done with.
We can no longer look for the return of the Son of Man on the clouds
of heaven or hope that the faithful will meet him in the air (I Thess.
4. 15ff.).

Now that the forces and the laws of nature have been discovered, we
can no longer believe in *spirits, whether good or evil.* We know that the
stars are physical bodies whose motions are controlled by the laws of
the universe, and not daemonic beings which enslave mankind to their
service. Any influence they may have over human life must be explicable
in terms of the ordinary laws of nature; it cannot in any way be attributed
to their malevolence. Sickness and the cure of disease are likewise at-
tributable to natural causation; they are not the result of daemonic activity or of evil spells. The *miracles of the New Testament* have ceased to be
miraculous, and to defend their historicity by recourse to nervous dis-

orders or hypnotic effects only serves to underline the fact. And if we are
still left with certain physiological and psychological phenomena which
we can only assign to mysterious and enigmatic causes, we are still
assigning them to causes, and thus far are trying to make them scientifically intelligible. Even occultism pretends to be a science.

It is impossible to use electric light and the wireless and to avail ourselves of modern medical and surgical discoveries, and at the same time
to believe in the New Testament world of spirits and miracles. We may
think we can manage it in our own lives, but to expect others to do so is
to make the Christian faith unintelligible and unacceptable to the modern
world.

The mythical eschatology is untenable for the simple reason that the
parousia of Christ never took place as the New Testament expected. History did not come to an end, and, as every schoolboy knows, it will continue to run its course. Even if we believe that the world as we know it
will come to an end in time, we expect the end to take the form of a
natural catastrophe, not of a mythical event such as the New Testament
expects. And if we explain the parousia in terms of modern scientific
theory, we are applying criticism to the New Testament, albeit unconsciously.

But natural science is not the only challenge which the mythology of
the New Testament has to face. There is the still more serious challenge
presented by *modern man's understanding of himself.*

Modern man is confronted by a curious dilemma. He may regard himself as pure nature, or as pure spirit. In the latter case he distinguishes
the essential part of his being from nature. In either case, however, *man
is essentially a unity.* He bears the sole responsibility for his own feeling,
thinking, and willing. He is not, as the New Testament regards him, the
victim of a strange dichotomy which exposes him to the interference of
powers outside himself. If his exterior behaviour and his interior condition are in perfect harmony, it is something he has achieved himself, and
if other people think their interior unity is torn asunder by daemonic
or divine interference, he calls it schizophrenia.

Although biology and psychology recognize that man is a highly dependent being, that does not mean that he has been handed over to
powers outside of and distinct from himself. This dependence is inseparable from human nature, and he needs only to understand it in order
to recover his self-mastery and organize his life on a rational basis. If he
regards himself as spirit, he knows that he is permanently conditioned
by the physical, bodily part of his being, but he distinguishes his true
self from it, and knows that he is independent and responsible for his
mastery over nature.

In either case he finds *what the New Testament has to say about the
"Spirit" (πνευμα) and the sacraments utterly strange and incomprehensible.* Biological man cannot see how a supernatural entity like the πνευμα

can penetrate within the close texture of his natural powers and set to work within him. Nor can the idealist understand how πνευμα working like a natural power can touch and influence his mind and spirit. Conscious as he is of his own moral responsibility, he cannot conceive how baptism in water can convey a mysterious something which is henceforth the agent of all his decisions and actions. He cannot see how physical food can convey spiritual strength, and how the unworthy receiving of the Eucharist can result in physical sickness and death (I Cor. 11. 30). The only possible explanation is that it is due to suggestion. He cannot understand how anyone can be baptized for the dead (I Cor. 15. 29).

We need not examine in detail the various forms of modern *Weltanschauung,* whether idealist or naturalist. For the only criticism of the New Testament which is theologically relevant is that which arises *necessarily* out of the situation of modern man. The biological *Weltanschauung* does not, for instance, arise necessarily out of the contemporary situation. We are still free to adopt it or not as we choose. The only relevant question for the theologian is the basic assumption on which the adoption of a biological as of every other *Weltanschauung* rests, and that assumption is the view of the world which has been moulded by modern science and the modern conception of human nature as a self-subsistent unity immune from the interference of supernatural powers.

Again, the biblical doctrine that *death is the punishment of sin* is equally abhorrent to naturalism and idealism, since they both regard death as a simple and necessary process of nature. To the naturalist death is no problem at all, and to the idealist it is a problem for that very reason, for so far from arising out of man's essential spiritual being it actually destroys it. The idealist is faced with a paradox. On the one hand man is a spiritual being, and therefore essentially different from plants and animals, and on the other hand he is the prisoner of nature, whose birth, life, and death are just the same as those of the animals. Death may present him with a problem, but he cannot see how it can be a punishment for sin. Human beings are subject to death even before they have committed any sin. And to attribute human mortality to the fall of Adam is sheer nonsense, for guilt implies personal responsibility, and the idea of original sin as an inherited infection is sub-ethical, irrational, and absurd.

The same objections apply to *the doctrine of the atonement.* How can the guilt of one man be expiated by the death of another who is sinless— if indeed one may speak of a sinless man at all? What primitive notions of guilt and righteousness does this imply? And what primitive idea of God? The rationale of sacrifice in general may of course throw some light on the theory of the atonement, but even so, what a primitive mythology it is, that a divine Being should become incarnate, and atone for the sins of men through his own blood! Or again, one might adopt an analogy from the law courts, and explain the death of Christ as a transaction between God and man through which God's claims on man were satisfied. But that would make sin a juridical matter· it would be no more than an external transgression of a commandment, and it would make nonsense of all our ethical standards. Moreover, if the Christ who died such a death was the pre-existent Son of God, what could death mean for him? Obviously very little, if he knew that he would rise again in three days!

The *resurrection of Jesus* is just as difficult for modern man, if it means an event whereby a living supernatural power is released which can henceforth be appropriated through the sacraments. To the biologist such language is meaningless, for he does not regard death as a problem at all. The idealist would not object to the idea of a life immune from death, but he could not believe that such a life is made available by the resuscitation of a dead person. If that is the way God makes life available for man, his action is inextricably involved in a nature miracle. Such a notion he finds incomprehensible, for he can see God at work only in the reality of his personal life and in his transformation. But, quite apart from the incredibility of such a miracle, he cannot see how an event like this could be the act of God, or how it could affect his own life.

Gnostic influence suggests that this Christ, who died and rose again, was not a mere human being but a God-man. His death and resurrection were not isolated facts which concerned him alone, but a cosmic event in which we are all involved. It is only with effort that modern man can think himself back into such an intellectual atmosphere, and even then he could never accept it himself, because it regards man's essential being as nature and redemption as a process of nature. And as for the pre-existence of Christ, with its corollary of man's translation into a celestial realm of light, and the clothing of the human personality in heavenly robes and a spiritual body—all this is not only irrational but utterly meaningless. Why should salvation take this particular form? Why should this be the fulfilment of human life and the realization of man's true being?

B. THE TASK BEFORE US

1. Not Selection or Subtraction

Does this drastic criticism of the New Testament mythology mean the complete elimination of the kerygma?

Whatever else may be true, we cannot save the kerygma by selecting some of its features and subtracting others, and thus reduce the amount of mythology in it. For instance, it is impossible to dismiss St. Paul's teaching about the unworthy reception of Holy Communion or about baptism for the dead, and yet cling to the belief that physical eating and drinking can have a spiritual effect. If we accept *one* idea, we must accept everything which the New Testament has to say about Baptism and Holy Communion, and it is just this one idea which we cannot accept.

It may of course be argued that some features of the New Testament mythology are given greater prominence than others: not all of them appear with the same regularity in the various books. There is for example only one occurrence of the legends of the Virgin birth and the Ascension; St. Paul and St. John appear to be totally unaware of them. But, even if we take them to be later accretions, it does not affect the mythical character of the event of redemption as a whole. And if we once start subtracting from the kerygma, where are we to draw the line? The mythical view of the world must be accepted or rejected in its entirety.

At this point absolute clarity and ruthless honesty are essential both for the academic theologian and for the parish priest. It is a duty they owe to themselves, to the Church they serve, and to those whom they seek to win for the Church. They must make it quite clear what their hearers are expected to accept and what they are not. At all costs the preacher must not leave his people in the dark about what he secretly eliminates, nor must he be in the dark about it himself. In Karl Barth's book *The Resurrection of the Dead* the cosmic eschatology in the sense of "chronologically final history" is eliminated in favour of what he intends to be a non-mythological "ultimate history." He is able to delude himself into thinking that this is exegesis of St. Paul and of the New Testament generally only because he gets rid of everything mythological in I Corinthians by subjecting it to an interpretation which does violence to its meaning. But that is an impossible procedure.

If the truth of the New Testament proclamation is to be preserved, the only way is to demythologize it. But our motive in so doing must not be to make the New Testament relevant to the modern world at all costs. The question is simply whether the New Testament message consists exclusively of mythology, or whether it actually demands the elimination of myth if it is to be understood as it is meant to be. This question is forced upon us from two sides. First there is the nature of myth in general, and then there is the New Testament itself.

2. The Nature of Myth

The real purpose of myth is not to present an objective picture of the world as it is, but to express man's understanding of himself in the world in which he lives. Myth should be interpreted not cosmologically, but anthropologically, or better still, existentially. Myth speaks of the power or the powers which man supposes he experiences as the ground and limit of his world and of his own activity and suffering. He describes these powers in terms derived from the visible world, with its tangible objects and forces, and from human life, with its feelings, motives, and potentialities. He may, for instance, explain the origin of the world by speaking

of a world egg or a world tree. Similarly he may account for the present
state and order of the world by speaking of a primeval war between the
gods. He speaks of the other world in terms of this world, and of the gods
in terms derived from human life.

Myth is an expression of man's conviction that the origin and purpose
of the world in which he lives are to be sought not within it but beyond
it—that is, beyond the realm of known and tangible reality—and that this
realm is perpetually dominated and menaced by those mysterious powers
which are its source and limit. Myth is also an expression of man's
awareness that he is not lord of his own being. It expresses his sense of
dependence not only within the visible world, but more especially on those
forces which hold sway beyond the confines of the known. Finally, myth
expresses man's belief that in this state of dependence he can be delivered
from the forces within the visible world.

Thus myth contains elements which demand its own criticism—namely,
its imagery with its apparent claim to objective validity. The real purpose
of myth is to speak of a transcendent power which controls the world and
man, but that purpose is impeded and obscured by the terms in which
it is expressed.

Hence the importance of the New Testament mythology lies not in its
imagery but in the understanding of existence which it enshrines. The
real question is whether this understanding of existence is true. Faith
claims that it is, and faith ought not to be tied down to the imagery of
New Testament mythology.

3. The New Testament Itself

The New Testament itself invites this kind of criticism. Not only are
there rough edges in its mythology, but some of its features are actually
contradictory. For example, the death of Christ is sometimes a sacrifice
and sometimes a cosmic event. Sometimes his person is interpreted as the
Messiah and sometimes as the Second Adam. The kenosis of the pre-
existent Son (Phil. 2. 6ff.) is incompatible with the miracle narratives
as proofs of his messianic claims. The Virgin birth is inconsistent with
the assertion of his pre-existence. The doctrine of the Creation is incompatible with the conception of the "rulers of this world" (I Cor. 2. 6ff.),
the "god of this world" (2 Cor. 4. 4) and the "elements of this world"
στοιχεῖα τοῦ κοβμου (Gal. 4. 3). It is impossible to square the belief
that the law was given by God with the theory that it comes from the
angels (Gal. 3. 19f.).

But the principal demand for the criticism of mythology comes from a
curious contradiction which runs right through the New Testament.
Sometimes we are told that human life is determined by cosmic forces,
at others we are challenged to a decision. Side by side with the Pauline
indicative stands the Pauline imperative. In short, man is sometimes re-

garded as a cosmic being, sometimes as an independent "I" for whom decision is a matter of life or death. Incidentally, this explains why so many sayings in the New Testament speak directly to modern man's condition while others remain enigmatic and obscure. Finally, attempts at demythologization are sometimes made even within the New Testament itself. But more will be said on this point later.

4. Previous Attempts at Demythologizing

How then is the mythology of the New Testament to be reinterpreted? This is not the first time that theologians have approached this task. Indeed, all we have said so far might have been said in much the same way thirty or forty years ago, and it is a sign of the bankruptcy of contemporary theology that it has been necessary to go all over the same ground again. The reason for this is not far to seek. The liberal theologians of the last century were working on the wrong lines. They threw away not only the mythology but also the kerygma itself. Were they right? Is that the treatment the New Testament itself required? That is the question we must face to-day. The last twenty years have witnessed a movement away from criticism and a return to a naïve acceptance of the kerygma. The danger both for theological scholarship and for the Church is that this uncritical resuscitation of the New Testament mythology may make the Gospel message unintelligible to the modern world. We cannot dismiss the critical labours of earlier generations without further ado. We must take them up and put them to constructive use. Failure to do so will mean that the old battles between orthodoxy and liberalism will have to be fought out all over again, that is assuming that there will be any Church or any theologians to fight them at all! Perhaps we may put it schematically like this: whereas the older liberals used criticism to *eliminate* the mythology of the New Testament, our task to-day is to use criticism to *interpret it.* Of course it may still be necessary to eliminate mythology here and there. But the criterion adopted must be taken not from modern thought, but from the understanding of human existence which the New Testament itself enshrines.

To begin with, let us review some of these earlier attempts at demythologizing. We need only mention briefly the allegorical interpretation of the New Testament which has dogged the Church throughout its history. This method spiritualizes the mythical events so that they become symbols of processes going on in the soul. This is certainly the most comfortable way of avoiding the critical question. The literal meaning is allowed to stand and is dispensed with only for the individual believer, who can escape into the realm of the soul.

It was characteristic of the older liberal theologians that they regarded mythology as relative and temporary. Hence they thought they could safely eliminate it altogether, and retain only the broad, basic principles of religion and ethics. They distinguished between what they took to be the essence of religion and the temporary garb which it assumed. Listen to what Harnack has to say about the essence of Jesus' preaching of the Kingdom of God and its coming: "The kingdom has a triple meaning. Firstly, it is something supernatural, a gift from above, not a product of ordinary life. Secondly, it is a purely religious blessing, the inner link with the living God; thirdly, it is the most important experience that a man can have, that on which everything else depends; it permeates and dominates his whole existence, because sin is forgiven and misery banished." Note how completely the mythology is eliminated: "The kingdom of God comes by coming to the individual, by entering into his *soul* and laying hold of it."

It will be noticed how Harnack reduces the kerygma to a few basic principles of religion and ethics. Unfortunately this means that *the kerygma has ceased to be kerygma:* it is no longer the proclamation of the decisive act of God in Christ. For the liberals the great truths of religion and ethics are timeless and eternal, though it is only within human history that they are realized, and only in concrete historical processes that they are given clear expression. But the apprehension and acceptance of these principles does not depend on the knowledge and acceptance of the age in which they first took shape, or of the historical persons who first discovered them. We are all capable of verifying them in our own experience at whatever period we happen to live. History may be of academic interest, but never of paramount importance for religion.

But the New Testament speaks of an *event* through which God has wrought man's redemption. For it, Jesus is not primarily the teacher, who certainly had extremely important things to say and will always be honoured for saying them, but whose person in the last analysis is immaterial for those who have assimilated his teaching. On the contrary, his person is just what the New Testament proclaims as the decisive event of redemption. It speaks of this person in mythological terms, but does this mean that we can reject the kerygma altogether on the ground that it is nothing more than mythology? That is the question.

Next came the History of Religions school. Its representatives were the first to discover the extent to which the New Testament is permeated by mythology. The importance of the New Testament, they saw, lay not in its teaching about religion and ethics but in its actual religion and piety; in comparison with that all the dogma it contains, and therefore all the mythological imagery with its apparent objectivity, was of secondary importance or completely negligible. The essence of the New Testament lay in the religious life it portrayed; its high-watermark was the experience of mystical union with Christ, in whom God took symbolic form.

These critics grasped one important truth. Christian faith is not the same as religious idealism; the Christian life does not consist in developing the individual personality, in the improvement of society, or in making the world a better place. The Christian life means a turning away from the world, a detachment from it. But the critics of the History of Religions school failed to see that in the New Testament this detachment is essentially eschatological and not mystical. Religion for them was an expression of the human yearning to rise above the world and transcend it: it was the discovery of a supramundane sphere where the soul could detach itself from all early care and find its rest. Hence the supreme manifestation of religion was to be found not in personal ethics or in social idealism but in the cultus regarded as an end in itself. This was just the kind of religious life portrayed in the New Testament, not only as a model and pattern, but as a challenge and inspiration. The New Testament was thus the abiding source of power which enabled man to realize the true life of religion, and Christ was the eternal symbol for the cultus of the Christian Church. It will be noticed how the Church is here defined exclusively as a worshipping community, and this represents a great advance on the older liberalism. This school rediscovered the Church as a *religious* institution. For the idealist there was really no place for the Church at all. But did they succeed in recovering the meaning of the Ecclesia in the full, New Testament sense of the word? For in the New Testament the Ecclesia is invariably a phenomenon of salvation history and eschatology.

Moreover, if the History of Religion school is right, the kerygma has once more ceased to be kerygma. Like the liberals, they are silent about a decisive act of God in Christ proclaimed as the event of redemption. So we are still left with the question whether this event and the person of Jesus, both of which are described in the New Testament in mythological terms, are nothing more than mythology. Can the kerygma be interpreted apart from mythology? Can we recover the truth of the kerygma for men who do not think in mythological terms without forfeiting its character as kerygma?

5. An Existentialist Interpretation the Only Solution

The theological work which such an interpretation involves can be sketched only in the broadest outline and with only a few examples. We must avoid the impression that this is a light and easy task, as if all we have to do is to discover the right formula and finish the job on the spot. It is much more formidable than that. It cannot be done single-handed. It will tax the time and strength of a whole theological generation.

The mythology of the New Testament is in essence that of Jewish apocalyptic and the Gnostic redemption myths. A common feature of them both is their basic dualism, according to which the present world and its human inhabitants are under the control of daemonic, satanic powers, and stand in need of redemption. Man cannot achieve this redemption by his own efforts; it must come as a gift through divine intervention. Both types of mythology speak of such an intervention: Jewish apocalyptic of an imminent world crisis in which this present aeon will be brought to an end and the new aeon ushered in by the coming of the Messiah, and Gnosticism of a Son of God sent down from the realm of light, entering into this world in the guise of a man, and by his fate and teaching delivering the elect and opening up the way for their return to their heavenly home.

The meaning of these two types of mythology lies once more not in their imagery with its apparent objectivity but in the understanding of human existence which both are trying to express. In other words, they need to be interpreted existentially. A good example of such treatment is to be found in Hans Jonas's book on Gnosticism.

Our task is to produce an existentialist interpretation of the dualistic mythology of the New Testament along similar lines. When, for instance, we read of daemonic powers ruling the world and holding mankind in bondage, does the understanding of human existence which underlies such language offer a solution to the riddle of human life which will be acceptable even to the non-mythological mind of to-day? Of course we must not take this to imply that the New Testament presents us with an anthropology like that which modern science can give us. It cannot be proved by logic or demonstrated by an appeal to factual evidence. Scientific anthropologies always take for granted a definite understanding of existence, which is invariably the consequence of a deliberate decision of the scientist, whether he makes it consciously or not. And that is why we have to discover whether the New Testament offers man an understanding of himself which will challenge him to a genuine existential decision.

REFLECTIONS ON A PEACH-SEED MONKEY OR STORYTELLING AND THE DEATH OF GOD

Sam Keen

SAM KEEN is currently a free-lance writer and lecturer. His books included *Apology for Wonder* (1969) and *To a Dancing God* (1970).

When the great Rabbi Israel Baal Shem-Tov saw misfortune threatening the Jews it was his custom to go into a certain part of the forest to meditate. There he would light a fire, say a special prayer, and the miracle would be accomplished and the misfortune averted. Later, when his disciple, the celebrated Magid of Mezritch, had occasion, for the same reason, to intercede with heaven, he would go to the same place in the forest and say: "Master of the Universe, listen! I do not know how to light the fire, but I am still able to say the prayer," and again the miracle would be accomplished. Still later, Rabbi Moshe-Leib of Sasov, in order to save his people once more, would go into the forest and say: "I do not know how to light the fire, I do not know the prayer, but I know the place and this must be sufficient." It was sufficient and the miracle was accomplished. Then it fell to Rabbi Israel of Rizhyn to overcome misfortune. Sitting in his armchair, his head in his hands, he spoke to God: "I am unable to light the fire and I do not know the prayer; I cannot even find the place in the forest. All I can do is to tell the story, and this must be sufficient." And it was sufficient.

God made man because he loves stories.

Elie Wiesel, *The Gates of the Forest* [1]

All sorrows can be borne if you put them into a story or tell a story about them . . . .   Isak Dinesen [2]

The first shock wave created by the recent use of the metaphor "the death of God" is beginning to subside. The religiously secure were briefly irritated because it was Christian theologians rather than atheists who were daring to use such irreverent language. But the reassurances that all was well in the world of religion began to appear. Bulletin boards in every hamlet announced sermons proclaiming, "God is *not* dead" or asking, "Is *your* God dead?" And the inevitable jokes began to be manufactured. Billy Graham is supposed to have said, "God isn't dead; I talked to him this morning." A less pious rumor circulated that God wasn't dead, only hiding in Argentina, etc. The more thoughtful members of the religious establishment took the occasion to confess the sins of the church and suggested that if only we could get on with the task of liturgical renewal, ecumenical theology, or the ministering to the social ills of the secular city, the crisis would pass. Religious language and institutions might be in need of renewal, but God remained alive and in good health.

Nor did the death-of-God theology seem to have any more profound and lasting effect upon the nonreligious community. The silent atheism of our culture, which is hidden under the pragmatic axiom which excludes all ultimate concerns from the arena of decision-making, took no notice of the supposed withdrawal of the Absolute. After all, how could such considerations bear upon the practical problems of the manufacture of napalm or the escalating inequality between the haves and the have-nots? And those few unorthodox but questing persons who were conscious of the vacuum at the heart of secularism and who were aware of living in what Koestler described as "the age of longing" seemed as puzzled by the solutions offered by the death-of-God theologians as the religiously pious. How confusing it was to them to find the radical rhetoric of the death-of-God theologians compromised by the conserva-

[1] New York: Holt, Rinehart & Winston, 1966.
[2] Quoted in Hannah Arendt, *The Human Condition* (Garden City: Doubleday Anchor Books, 1958), p. 175.

tive suggestion that, even if there were no longer any God, we might, nevertheless, believe in "the fully incarnate Word" (Altizer) or in the man, Jesus, who infected us with the quality of "contagious freedom" (Van Buren).

Everything seems to have settled down once again, and, as William Hamilton remarked, theologians have gone back to the libraries, and the religious press is looking for a new story. If no one is quite sure where we go from here, it is little wonder. The dramatic announcement of the death of God is a rough act to follow! With all of the drama, publicity, and subsequent fatigue, we stand in danger of missing the real significance of this event. Any metaphor which becomes the darling of the mass media is likely to be overexposed and underexplored. This is the fate of "the death of God," for, while the metaphor is fast becoming a cliché, we have yet to deal seriously with the momentous change in the self-consciousness of Western man which gave birth to the metaphor. The crisis in the metaphysical identity of man reflected in the metaphor "the death of God" remains *the* unsolved philosophical and spiritual dilemma of modern times. How we are to come to terms with the tragic character of human existence in an age in which there is widespread loss of confidence in all absolute or transcendent points of reference will remain the agonizing philosophical problem for generations after the popular press has tired of "death-of-God" theologians.

Belief or disbelief in God involves a whole hierarchy of ideas, attitudes, and feelings about nature, history, and the manner in which one aspires and acts within human community. Both theism and atheism are long-range, radical commitments. As Sartre has pointed out, it is not possible, without bad faith, merely to cross out the word "God" and go on existing within a theistic world of feeling and action. Thus, "the death of God" refers to a total change in the way many modern men perceive the context of their existence. The metaphysical matrix, or the spiritual ecology, of modern life is changing. The basic analogies, images, and metaphors which served to establish the metaphysical identity of traditional Western man are losing their credibility and their power to inform life.

The purpose of this essay is to explore one of the most fundamental Western metaphysical or, better, *metamundane* metaphors—the metaphor of the story. We may say that, symbolically, the identity of traditional man was based upon his ability to find his way in the forest, to light the fire, to say the prayer, and to tell a story that placed his life within an ultimate context. By the fire of sacrifice, by the practice of prayer, or by the use of some other technique of transcendence, the will of God or the gods could be determined and man could live in harmony with the powers of the overworld that exerted a mysterious influence on his existence. Each people had its own cycle of stories which located the individual within the tribe, the tribe within the cosmos, and the cosmos within the overworld. Modern man has lost his way in the forest, he cannot light the fire or say the prayer, and he is dangerously close to losing his ability to see his life as part of any story. In the bungaloid world that we are able to know with intelligence untouched by tenderness and can verify with senses which have been disciplined to exclude ecstasy, there is no transcendence. Even where the modest self-transcendence of love has remained a source of identity, there is deep suspicion that those who claim, by fire or prayer or sacred authority, to transcend the time-bound capsule in which we are all exiled are fools trafficking in dreams, fantasies, and illusions. It now appears that the ahistorical attitude created by the triumph of technological mentality and American ideology may be destroying the function of the story as a source of metamundane identity. The hero of the American story is Adam —the man without a history, living in the wonderland of the innocent present. Henry Ford stated the American dream in a manner that can hardly be surpassed: "History is bunk." In the non-story we tell in the new world, a man's identity is fashioned by doing rather than remembering; his credentials for acceptance are the skills of a trade rather than the telling of stories.

In exploring the significance of the metaphor of the story, I will suggest that telling stories is functionally equivalent to belief in God, and, therefore, "the death of God" is best understood as modern man's inability to believe that human life is rendered ultimately meaningful by being incorporated into a story. After exploring the history of storytelling and of the metaphor of the happening which is the contemporary candidate to replace the story as the clue to the ultimate context of human existence, I shall try to rehabilitate the story as a basic tool for the formation of identity. This is where the peach-seed monkey comes in. I will try to find out from him whether theology may find a new method for telling stories and for locating the presence of the holy in a time when the orthodox stories about the "mighty acts of God" no longer inform Western identity.

I. A SHORT HISTORY OF STORYTELLING

The significance of the story in archaic or preliterate cultures is well illustrated in a remark Laurens Van Der Post made about the Kalahari Bushmen:

The supreme expression of his spirit was in his stories. He was a wonderful storyteller. The story was his most sacred possession. These people knew what we do not: that without a story you have not got a nation, or a culture, or a civilization. Without a story of your own to live you haven't got a life of your own.[3]

[3] *Patterns of Renewal* (Wallingford, Penn.: Pendle Hall Pamphlets, 1962), p. 9.

Preliterate man lived in a world which received its intellectual, religious, and social structure through the story. Each tribe had its own set of tales, myths, and legends which defined the metaphysical context within which it lived, gave a history of the sacred foundation of its social rituals, and provided concrete models of authentic life. Membership in the tribe involved retelling and acting out the shared stories which had been passed on from generation to generation since the beginning of time. As the studies of Eliade show, archaic man sought to avoid the profane and to live in the realm of the sacred. Sacred acts were those which could be traced back to some archetype which had been originated by a god or hero. Thus, the telling of stories was a way of justifying and sanctioning those values which were essential to the preservation of the community. Wealth and status were often measured in archaic societies more by the stories a man knew, the rituals he was authorized to conduct, and the dances he could perform than by the cattle and possessions he had accumulated. The story served the diverse functions of philosophy, theology, history, ethics, and entertainment. It served to locate the individual within the concentric circles of the cosmos, nature, the community, and the family, and it provided a concrete account of what was expected of a man and what he might expect in that darkness which lies beyond death.

The centrality of storytelling in the formation of the identity and culture of preliterate man is well established, although it remains somewhat embarrassing to modern man. Since the enlightenment and the emergence of less dramatic but more scientific modes of thought, Western man has found great comfort in telling himself that he has come of age and passed beyond the primitive darkness of myth into the full light of reason. Therefore, in most accounts of the intellectual history of man, one may detect a sigh of relief when the narrative leaves the poetic-mythical thought of archaic man and focuses on the development of rational philosophical thought in the Greek city-state. The march toward the sun has begun! The education of the human race toward a world in which we no longer need to tell stories has progressed a step.

Unfortunately, this picture is more myth than fact. Although empirical science and philosophical reason had faint beginnings in classical Greece, the fundamental philosophical vision which animated Greek life was as solidly dramatic and mythological as that of archaic man.

Something of the Greek's estimate of the significance of storytelling may be gleaned from Hannah Arendt's suggestion that, symbolically, the *polis* was created by the heroes coming home from the Trojan Wars, who wanted an arena in which their deeds might be recounted and remembered. Democracy sprang from the need for an audience which would continue to applaud a hero after his death. Immortality was being included in a story which would be retold. Thus, the ultimate measure of a man was lost if his life was not lived in such a way that his deeds would fit into a broader story which future generations would preserve. Politics was to make the world safe for storytelling and, thus, for immortality.

The metaphor of the story goes even deeper into Greek thought. For the Greek mind, no less than the primitive, the key analogy by which human existence was interpreted was the seasonal rhythm of nature. The yearly vegetation cycle was a drama which provided the clue to the identity of the human soul. It was Dionysus, a god of vegetation, who gave birth to theatre. The soul, the cosmos, and the drama share a common structure:

Act One. Spring: Innocence, vitality, and promise. In the first green of life (which is gold), there is an announcement of intention. Birth contains a hidden promise of fulfillment; in the beginning is the end (the *telos*). The acorn promises the oak; the child, the man; potentiality looks forward to actuality. All life in its inception bears within it the promise of perfection. Thus, in the beginning there is no death. In childhood the promise of life is so overwhelming that knowledge of death is absent. Life begins with innocent immortality and humble omnipotence.

Act Two. Summer and Fall: Maturation and disillusionment. In actuality the promise is only partially fulfilled. The acorn grows into a stunted oak, and not every child matures into the essential humanity of a Socrates. By late summer it becomes obvious that maturation is always tragic, and the promise given in the beginning is doomed to be broken. The mature plant does not achieve the status of the ideal, and man is forever exiled from the perfection for which he longs. As summer passes into fall or as the verdant suppleness of life gives way to the brown brittleness of incipient decay, hope becomes strained, and the promise of life is transformed into the anxious question: The greenness of life is passing; will it ever return?

Act Three. Winter: Death and despair. Winter is always a crisis, both to the body and to the spirit. The disappearance of the vegetation raises to consciousness the suspicion and the lurking fear that the promise given in springtime was an illusion. Does not winter, perhaps, signify that life is ebbing away, that darkness triumphs over light, and that death has final dominion over life?

Act Four. Spring: Resurrection and return. Rebirth, although perennial, always comes as a surprise and a gift. As the sun gathers strength and impregnates the earth with the promise of green, the anxiety of winter is replaced by hope and the cosmos is reborn out of chaos.

It was this drama which was the structural warp upon which the diverse modes of Greek experience were woven. We find this same story celebrated in the myths of the simple and the philosophies of the sophisticated. For the literal-minded there were the stories of the vegetation dieties, such as Demeter, who lived half of the year in the underworld and the other half among mortals, or Dionysus, who was god of both ecstasy and death. For the intellectuals who had lost faith in the old myths there was the demythologized philosophy of Plato, which offered arguments to show the unity and immortality of the cosmos and the soul, or the more astringent philosophy of Aristotle, which presented the whole cosmos as a hierarchy of interrelated substances, all driven by the desire to actualize the potentiality with which they were pregnant. In Socrates the Greek world also had its incarnation of the vision of the man who knew his soul was as immortal as the cosmos. The ethics of Plato, Aristotle, and the Stoics are little more than theoretical commentaries on the type of life exemplified in Socrates. In the story of the death of Socrates it becomes clear why his biography could serve as the summary and ethical focus of the Greek vision of life. As the poison reaches his vital organs, Socrates lifts his head and says, "Crito, I owe a cock to Asclepius. Will you remember to pay the debt?" Strange and courageous words these are for a dying man! At the onset of death Socrates remembers he owes a debt to the god of healing. By this act he confesses his confidence in the dramatic unity of life and death and his belief that the promise of immortality which informs the soul is destined for fulfillment. Thus, the cosmic drama of life comes to be exemplified in a biography which became as normative for the Greek mind as the biography of Jesus was later to become for the Christian community.

In the Judeo-Christian tradition the drama which provides the structural meaning for human existence takes place on the stage of history rather than in the eternal cycle of nature. The whole of history is a story for which God has provided the script. Unlike the endlessly recurring drama of seasonal life, the story being told in history is once told; each moment is unique, even though it fits into the development of the plot. The drama of history may be summarized thusly:

Prelude. The Judeo-Christian story begins with the Storyteller—"In the beginning, God . . . ." The stage upon which the drama of history is played out is not eternal. Man and the cosmos had their beginning in the creative intention of a transcendent God. Thus, the stage and the actors are created for the drama. Why God chose to create the drama of history remains a mystery. Perhaps he was lonely and wanted to share his love. Or, as Wiesel suggests, it may be that he loved stories. At any rate, the reason is unimportant, or at least unknowable, and all man needs to know to orient himself in history is the outline of the drama which is being developed.

Act One. In the Garden. Like most good stories which undertake to explain human existence, this one begins its account of man with a picture of the innocence and harmony which ruled life in the mythical era of "once upon a time" (an era which is always present in the depth of the psyche). In the Garden of Eden there is finitude but no tragedy. In its ontological depths, life is good and has within itself the resources for its own fulfillment. In spite of the limitations which are represented by sexuality and the inevitability of death, there is no shame or estrangement in essential, or created, human life. The movement of life against death, the spirit against the flesh, or the id against the ego, which plays so large a part in the development of history, is alien to the intention of the Storyteller.

Act Two. The Fall. The biblical tradition does not explain the fall; it only describes it. Why history involves the tragic rupture of harmony between man and his environment (social, natural, and ultimate) remains a mystery. The story of Adam and the forbidden fruit merely illustrates the mystery of evil which is a part of the problem of historical human existence. The fall represents the moment when the story begins to develop in a manner not intended by the Storyteller. God experiences what every author does: having created a character to tell a story, he finds the character rebelling against the intention of the author and insisting upon telling his own story. Historical existence (the time lying between "once upon a time" and "someday") is the time of conflicting themes during which the Storyteller is forced to improvise, making use of the dialogue and action created by his recalcitrant characters, to salvage the story he intended to tell. His control over the development of the drama is real but tenuous as the agents of the snake, for the moment, remain powerful enough to destroy the intended artistic unity of the story. However, to those who have ears to hear, there is a promise hidden in the confused tale of history: the Storyteller will regain control of his creation and bring it to its intended fulfillment. There are the signs of the rainbow, the pillar of fire and the cloud of smoke, the old covenant sealed with commandments written in stone, and the new covenant which is written on the flesh. But here we are getting ahead of the story.

Act Three. In the End. Someday alienation will come to an end, and the story of history will reach the conclusion for which it is destined. In the end, as in the beginning, the intent of the Storyteller will be made manifest; the promises and possibilities with which history was pregnant in the Garden of Eden are brought to full birth in the kingdom of God. Judaism and Christianity have a fundamental disagreement about when the "sometime" is when history will reach its conclusion. For Christianity, spring has already begun in the cold midwinter of history; in the life, death, and resurrection of Jesus, the new era has its beginning. From this beginning it will grow rapidly, like a mustard seed, blotting out the estrangement and tragedy which have ruled history. For Judaism, the kingdom of God, which is both the *finis* and the *telos* of history, still lies in the future. The messiah, the herald of the end, has not yet come, but perhaps "next year in Jerusalem . . . ."

The different acts of the drama of history reflect also the movement of the life of the individual. Each man is Adam, bearing within himself a nostalgia for perfection which is a silent testimony that he is an exiled citizen of a country in which there is no estrangement. As Augustine stated the matter, "Thou hast made us for thyself, O God, and our hearts are restless till they rest in Thee." Thus, each individual repeats within himself the pilgrimage of history. As a wayfarer, man (*Homo viator*) is never totally lost, because he knows the story of the garden from which he came and the kingdom toward which he travels. If exile is difficult to bear, there is, at least, the comfort of the promise of homecoming; there is hope which is "a memory of the future" (Marcel). And for the Christian, there is, in the figure of Jesus, a biography which is revelatory of the ultimate intention of the creator of history which also provides a model for the conduct of life. For the pilgrim, authentic life lies in the imitation of Christ. Like the archaic man, both Jew and Christian belonged to a community in which the identity of the individual was shaped by shared stories and common models.

In a certain sense, we may date the birth of the modern world at the point when the Judeo-Christian story ceased to entertain and fascinate and new stories and ideologies were created which reflected man's growing love affair with the earth. Although the new stories no longer spoke of the gods or of God, the outline of the drama which Greek and Christian shared was still not changed. The costumes and the language changed, but the plot remained the same. In the new languages of politics, economics, philosophy, technology, and psychology, the drama of innocence/fall/recovery-of-innocence was retold. The enlightenment tried to replace the period of original innocence with the notion of the gradual education of the human race from the darkness of mytho-poetic thought into the full light of reason, but innocence returned in romanticism, socialism, and the ideology of American democracy. Once again, the various gospels proclaimed that man was born free, had fallen into chains, and was shortly to enter into a new birth of freedom. In romanticism the noble savage fell from nature into repressive civilization, but the redemption of spontaneity was shortly to be ushered in by poetry, or free love, or psychoanalysis. In socialism and communism the fall was from civility into class struggle, but the era of redemption, in a classless society without exploitation or alienation, was shortly to arrive by the inevitable logic of history and the devotion of the elect. In the ideology of American democracy, the inalienable rights of man had been compromised by adherents of monarchy and tradition but were soon to be restored and rendered safe by the emergence of a new nation which would make the world safe for democracy. On American soil Adam became the hero once again.

It is only within the present century that the metaphor of the story and the outline of the traditional drama which have been commonplace in Western civilization have been radically criticized and widely abandoned. For the contemporary intellectual the metaphysical myth has ceased to provide the context for identity. The conviction is gone that history tells a story or that reality may be appropriately known in dramatic terms. While we retain and share such political myths as those clustering around the labels "democracy" and "communism," we have lost the metamundane myths and even the confidence in their possible usefulness.

The new metaphor which reflects modern experience is *the happening*. Nature and history are governed by chance and probability. Luck is the only god, and crossing the fingers or knocking on wood is the only liturgy appropriate to a happenstance world. One thing happens after another, and, although there are causes for events, there are no reasons. Nowhere in nature or history does the modern intellectual find evidence of a guiding mind which gives coherence to what is still, erroneously, called the uni-verse. If history tells a tale, it is the tale of the idiot. It is up to the individual to give his own life meaning by creating a project to which he may give himself.

Antoine Roquentin, the hero of Sartre's novel *Nausea*, presents a vivid example of the man who has become a victim in a world where things just happen. He confesses that he always wanted to be able to see his own life develop with the form and symmetry of a character in a novel. It is precisely this demand which leads to his disillusionment.

This is what fools people: a man is always a teller of tales, he lives surrounded by his stories and the stories of others, he sees everything that happens to him through them; and he tries to live his own life as if he were telling a story.[4]

In real life there are no beginnings or endings; there are no moments of intrinsic significance which form a framework of meaning around experience. There are only days "tacked on to days without rhyme or reason, an interminable, monotonous addition." [5] The refrain that runs throughout *Nausea* is "anything can happen"; no universal reason sets limits to the possible and gives meaning to human history. In the face of the absurdity of existence, the only option for the lucid individual is to create a reason for existing by writing a book or joining a political movement, etc. Only by choosing some project, however arbitrary, can the individual fill the present moment and escape the nausea which results from awareness of the absolute contingency and absurdity of existence.

The existentialist hero who tries to live in the immediacy of the present moment is a figure who typifies our age. He is the stranger in Camus's novel, the beatnik of a generation ago who turned up in Kerouac's *On the Road*, and, most recently, he is the hippy who opts out of traditional culture and tunes in on the vibrations. Wherever he

4 Jean-Paul Sartre, *Nausea* (New York: New Directions Books, 1959), p. 56.
5 *Ibid.*, p. 57.

appears, one metaphysical assumption governs identity—there is no future, there is no past, so live in the moment. Marshall McLuhan tells us that this world of happenings, of "all-at-once-ness," is a product of the media. The linear, historical, storytelling mentality belonged to another age. In the tribal village of the electronic world no framework or perspective is possible—only total immersion. The perspective of the past, which has sometimes been called the wisdom of our fathers, is of no use to the existentialist hero. Indeed, anyone over thirty (unless he can sit in the lotus position) is already relegated to the scrapheap of the past.

The world defined as happening is merely the world from which God has departed. Over a century ago Dostoevski reduced the functional significance of the absence of God to one sentence: if God is dead, all things are possible. The concentration camps and the systematic use of what Marcel called "techniques of degradation" have demonstrated that all things are morally possible; the will-to-power makes it possible to violate all that past generations have considered sacred. As Richard Rubenstein has shown in *After Auschwitz,* the destruction of all moral limits roots in the desire to kill God and be rid of all restraint to pleasure. The metaphysical vision of a completely contingent world in which "anything can happen" has been explored by Sartre and by the Theater of the Absurd. Where chance is considered the ultimate metaphysical category, the world is reduced to radical pluralism, discontinuity, and chaos. If there is no overreaching principle of order or meaning, the order—moral and physical—which we have observed in the past cannot be projected into the future. Lacking any metamundane principle of unity, we can have no assurance of any continuity between past and future; thus, remembering and planning are equally futile. Spontaneity has replaced storytelling as the mode of authentic life.

By looking at the function the story served in traditional cultures and by contrasting the situation of the contemporary intellectual living in a happenstance world, we can get some notion of the implicit confession of faith involved in the act of telling a story and some measure of what has been lost.

In telling stories, traditional man was affirming the unity of reality. The individual, the tribe, nature, and the cosmos fit together in concentric circles of integrated meaning. All of the parts were necessary to form a coherent and artistic whole. Past, present, and future were, likewise, bound together in a thematic unity. Thus, the individual standing on the ever-disappearing point of present time could affirm that the meaning of his existence was not destroyed by the passing of time. He took courage from his knowledge that he had roots in what had been and that his memory and deeds would be preserved in what would be. In effect, the story affirmed that the reality of the individual was not reducible to the present moment of experience but belonged to a continuity of meaning that the flow of time could not erode. With this faith the individual could act with a sense of continuity and perspective; his spontaneity was tempered by memory and hope.

Another article of faith hidden in the act of storytelling is the confidence that the scale of Being is such that a human being can grasp the meaning of the whole. Personality is not an epiphenomenon in an alien world of matter ruled by chance and number but is the key to the cosmos. Man is a microcosm; thus, in telling his stories, he may have confidence that his warm, concrete, dramatic images are not unrelated to the forces that make for the unity of the macrocosm. While his images and stories may reduce the proportions of reality to a scale that is manageable by the human spirit, their distortion serves the cause of truth. Traditional man had every confidence that his symbols, myths, and stories were the most appropriate means to grasp reality and were not merely illusions projected out of his isolated, subjective brain.

It is too soon to evaluate the success of the modern effort to get along without the belief that history tells a story or that there is a meaningful continuity between past, present, and future. Whether a viable and creative identity can be formed where the ultimate symbol is the happening is questionable. Our knowledge of the dynamics of personality would suggest that it is psychologically impossible to attain the goal of spontaneous action except by an integration of all the modes of temporal experience. Genuine spontaneity is possible only to the person who has accepted the limits imposed upon him by his past experience and who is animated by some meaning he seeks to realize in his future. Gratuitous action is a parody of spontaneity in which unconscious motives drive a person to act in a manner totally discontinuous with his past. It is at least dubious whether any mature form of personality integration is conceivable in which the individual has not come to accept and relish his past and integrate it with his projects for the future. Nietzsche remarked that a man must come to love his wounds. To do this he must be able to weave his past and his hopes for the future into one coherent story. However this may be, without prejudging the modern experiment of forming an identity in the context of absurdity and discontinuity, we may ask a more modest question. Recognizing that the metaphor of the happening expresses the spiritual atmosphere of the contemporary world, we may ask whether we are forced to capitulate to this climate or whether it is permissible to change it. Are we condemned to live in a chaotic world of the happening with the view that our past is insignificant and our future nonexistent? Is there any intellectually respectable alternative to the view that God is dead and every man must give meaning to his personal existence? Is identity with continuity possible? Can there be any theology after the death of God or any account of a principle of metamundane unity and meaning operative in history.

II. A WAY BEYOND THE DEATH OF GOD— OR HOW TO TELL STORIES

We must begin our search with the realization that no form of neo-orthodoxy provides a viable starting point. The orthodox metamundane myths of religion are no longer supported by any authority strong enough to command the respect of an unprejudiced inquirer. Knowledge of comparative religions, textual criticism, and the dynamics of symbol formation and functioning has destroyed our ability to grant a priori authority to any religious tradition. For the moment, at least, we must put all orthodox stories in brackets and suspend whatever remains of our belief-ful attitude. Our starting point must be individual biography and history. If I am to discover the holy, it must be in *my* biography and not in the history of Israel. If there is a principle which gives unity and meaning to history it must be something I touch, feel, and experience. Our starting point must be radical.

We may use a series of questions to suggest a method which may lead us back to storytelling and theology. Is there anything on the native ground of my own experience—my biography, my history—which testifies to the reality of the holy? Since the word "holy" in this question is, itself, problematic, we may further translate it into functional terms. Thus, to restate our first question in operational terms: Is there anything in my experience which gives it unity, depth, density, dignity, meaning, and value—which makes graceful freedom possible? If we can discover such a principle at the foundation of personal identity, we have every right to use the ancient language of the holy, and, therefore, to mark out a domain for theological exploration.

Since I have shifted the ground of theology to the individual and the quotidian, I can proceed only by telling my story and then by inviting my reader to tell his.

Once upon a time when there were still Indians, Gypsies, bears, and bad men in the woods of Tennessee where I played and, more important still, there was no death, a promise was made to me. One endless summer afternoon my father sat in the eternal shade of a peach tree, carving on a seed he had picked up. With increasing excitement and covetousness I watched while, using a skill common to all omnipotent creators, he fashioned a small monkey out of the seed. All of my vagrant wishes and desires disciplined themselves and came to focus on that peach-seed monkey. If only I could have it, I would possess a treasure which could not be matched in the whole cosmopolitan town of Maryville! What status, what identity, I would achieve by owning such a curio! Finally I marshaled my nerve and asked if I might have the monkey when it was finished (on the sixth day of creation). My father replied, "This one is for your mother, but I will carve you one someday."

Days passed, and then weeks and, finally, years, and the someday on which I was to receive the monkey did not arrive. In truth, I forgot all about the peach-seed monkey. Life in the ambience of my father was exciting, secure, and colorful. He did all of those things for his children a father can do, not the least of which was merely delighting in their existence. One of the lasting tokens I retained of the measure of his dignity and courage was the manner in which, with emphysema sapping his energy and eroding his future, he continued to wonder, to struggle, and to grow.

In the pure air and dry heat of an Arizona afternoon on the summer before the death of God, my father and I sat under a juniper tree. I listened as he wrestled with the task of taking the measure of his success and failure in life. There came a moment of silence that cried out for testimony. Suddenly I remembered the peach-seed monkey, and I heard the right words coming from myself to fill the silence: "In all that is important you have never failed me. With one exception, you kept the promises you made to me—you never carved me that peach-seed monkey."

Not long after this conversation I received a small package in the mail. In it was a peach-seed monkey and a note which said: "Here is the monkey I promised you. You will notice that I broke one leg and had to repair it with glue. I am sorry I didn't have time to carve a perfect one."

Two weeks later my father died. He died only at the end of his life.

For me, a peach-seed monkey has become a symbol of all the promises which were made to me and the energy and care which nourished and created me as a human being. And, even more fundamentally, it is a symbol of that which is the foundation of all human personality and dignity. Each of us is redeemed from shallow and hostile life only by the sacrificial love and civility which we have gratuitously received. As Erik Erikson has pointed out in *Identity and the Life Cycle,* a secure and healthy identity is founded upon a sense of *basic trust* which is first mediated to a child by the trustworthiness of his parents. Identity has its roots in the dependability, orderliness, and nurturing responsiveness of the world of primal experience. That civility which separates men from the lower animals depends upon the making and keeping of promises, covenants, vows, and contracts. As Nietzsche so aptly put the matter, man is that animal who makes promises.

When I uncover the promises made and kept which are the hidden root of my sense of the basic trustworthiness of the world and my consequent freedom to commit myself to action, I discover my links with the past; I find the "once upon a time" which is the beginning of the story I must tell to be myself. In the same act of recovering the principle of my identity, I discover a task for my future; being the recipient of promises, I become the maker of promises. I seek to manifest that same faithfulness toward others which was gratuitously shown to me. In identifying myself as one who lives by promises and promising, I find the principle which gives unity to my life and binds together the past, the future, and the present. Without losing the spontaneity of significant action in the present, I transcend every dying moment toward my roots in the past and my end in the future. I have a story.

A series of questions arises at this point. Is the peach-seed monkey not of mere individual significance? While it may be of symbolic significance in the biography of Sam Keen, does it not lack the universal element which allowed the metamundane myths of former generation to be the shared property of a community? Does the intimate character of such a story merely point to the dilemma of the twentieth-century man, whose biography is not inserted into any shared mythological structure? And, finally, how can such a story lay claim to a theological meaning?

Two major discoveries of Freud may help us to see the universal dimension of what initially appears to be merely an incident in an individual biography.

First, the psychoanalytic method is based upon the assumption that each man has repressed crucial pages of his own history because they are too painful to remember. The path to health involves the de-repression of these hidden memories and the reconstruction of the individual's personal history. The implication of psychoanalytic theory is clear: the crucial history the individual must recover to be whole is familial rather than communal. Each individual must search out both the fidelities and the infidelities and both the wounds and the gifts which gave the unique character to his biography.

Second, although the Freudian path to salvation begins with the isolated individual's learning to tell his own story, it does not end here. Freud's second great discovery (which we usually associate with the name of Jung) was that once the individual recovers his own history, he finds it is the story of every man. For example, when shame and fear dissolve and I am able to confess that I hated as well as loved (or vice versa) the father who nurtured me, I discover that I am one with Oedipus. It is only a step from this insight to the realization that hating the father and rebelling against God are inseparable. Thus, being Oedipus, I am also Adam and Prometheus and all of the heroes and antiheroes of history. The more I know of myself, the more I recognize that nothing human is foreign to me. In the depth of each man's biography lies the story of all men.

The peach-seed monkey, thus, belongs as much to you as to me. Who can deny that his civility and humanity have been nurtured by a matrix of promise too rich and intricate to detail? To be minimally human involves the use of language and reason which can only be learned where there has been a modicum of civility and promise-keeping. He who reads or speaks confesses in that very act he has been succored, educated, and humanized in a social matrix. Psychological reflection shows that when the individual goes to the heart of his own biography unhampered by shame or repression, he finds there a universality of experience that binds him to all men.

If we look more deeply at the story of the peach-seed monkey, we discover that it has a theological as well as a universal significance. There is, of course, no way in which the existence, activity, or reality of God can be demonstrated from such a story. Therefore, if the criterion for theological significance is the use of God-language, the matter ends here. As we suggested earlier, however, theological language need not be limited to God-talk. Any language is authentically theological which points to what is experienced as holy and sacred. And we may now define the holy as "that irreducible principle, power, or presence which is the source and guarantor of unity, dignity, meaning, value, and wholeness." If such a phenomenological and functional definition of theological language is permissible, it becomes obvious that the peach-seed monkey points to a dimension of reality which is sacred. The sanctity of promises is the *sine qua non* of humanness; it is the principle upon which identity and community are founded.

Traditional theists and humanists alike will deny that any principle grounded in purely human commitment is a candidate for theological honors. Both will maintain that theology has to do with the extraordinary rather than the ordinary, the supernatural rather than the natural, or the transcendent source rather than the subterranean foundations of life. A phenomenological approach does not allow us the luxury of such a segregation of the holy. If we begin with a description of the functional significance of the encounter with the holy, we are forced to conclude that the power to give unity and meaning to life which was once mediated by metamundane myths is today experienced as present in the principles which are the foundation of identity and community.

By locating the holy in the spiritual depths rather than the heights—in the quotidian rather than the supernatural—the form and imagery, not the substance, of the religious consciousness is changed. If the promises that redeem us spring from mundane soil rather than from an authorized covenant with God, history is, nevertheless, experienced as the story of promise and fulfillment. Human existence is still sanctified by sacrifice, and we may appropriately face the mysterious givenness of life and personality with gratitude and reverence. This change in language from images of height to depth represents the religious response of the twentieth-century mind to the loss of the traditional metamundane myths. If God is gone from the sky, he must be found in the earth. Theology must concern itself not only with the Wholly Other God but with the sacred "Ground of Being" (Tillich)—not with a unique incarnation in past history but with the principles, powers, and persons which are presently operative to make and keep human life luminous and sacred.

Whether such a subterranean theology will allow us to weather the crisis in spiritual identity through which we are passing is still unknown. For those who no longer find in the stories and myths of orthodox religion the power to inform life with creative meaning, it may, at least, point to a locality and a method which may be useful in discovering a sacred dimension of life. And, perhaps, if each of us learns to tell his own story, even if we remain ignorant of the name of God or the form of religion, it will be sufficient.

THE GHOST IN THE COSMOS AND THE GHOST IN THE MACHINE

Norbert O. Schedler

NORBERT SCHEDLER is Chairman of the Philosophy Department at Purdue University—Fort Wayne. He is co-editor with James S. Churchill of *The Essential Writings of Martin Heidegger* (1973).

There has been a great deal of debate within analytic philosophy regarding religious assertions such as "God exists," "God is love," "God is all-powerful"—that is, statements about God himself. I will in this essay discuss a set of locutions that are more crucial to the theological enterprise; namely, locutions that speak about God's relation to the world. For as a matter of fact, many examples of religious language subjected to the scrutiny of the early analysts were not drawn from the mainstream of biblical theology. I have in mind locutions such as the following:

1. And they heard the *sound* of the Lord God *walking* in the garden.
2. God *led* Israel out of Egypt.
3. God *created* the world and all that is therein.
4. God *was in* Christ *reconciling* the world unto Himself.
5. God *spoke* through the burning bush.
6. God *appeared* in a rushing wind.
7. God *raised* Jesus Christ from the dead.
8. God *was revealed in* the person, words, deeds, death, and resurrection of Jesus.
9. In the Jesus of history, who is fully understood in the Christ of faith, we *encounter* God.
10. In Christ God *has found* me.

What these locutions have in common is their reference to God as a *person* (subject) who *acts* (agent) *in the world* (relation). They are locutions that are central to the school of theology I will call "Heilsgeschichte theology." [1] This theology requires a notion of God as agent in the world. Using this theology as our specimen for analysis has the advantage of employing material drawn from the God-talk that occurs in the churches.

If we consider the logic of these locutions, a number of puzzles immediately arise. There are, for example, a *number* of possible models or pictures [2] that could be used in understanding the logic of these locutions. Each picture has a different understanding of God as a subject of acting in the world.

I. LITERAL SUPERNATURALISM

This position takes the Bible literally in that what is recorded are reports of straightforward *events* (miraculous victories, resurrections from the read, manna from heaven, sun standing still, Yahweh appearing in a burning bush) and a voice that *speaks* and people *hear,* interpreting the event as a theophany (an appearance of God in space and time). In this picture God is a person of a special sort, but not discontinuous with human personhood, knowing, doing and speaking. That is, when we speak about God, our words are univocal—they have the same meaning as when referred to human actions and powers, only raised to a degree proper to God. When God makes the world it is not wholly unlike my son who takes muck and makes ducks, so God takes earth and makes Adam. This God intervenes in history when he chooses, though his proper abode is Mount Sinai, or the Temple, or the like. God can be directly known, in visions or a voice heard, by inhabitants of heaven and earth, and even under the earth. For this picture locutions 1–10 are what we today call empirical claims similar to "Dean Gilbert walked into my office today." These locutions are then known to be true or false on the basis of miracles witnessed, visions seen, prophecies fulfilled, or divine self-manifestations encountered. The logic of these locutions is the straightforward empirical claim that can be proven true or false in principle (I know what counts for or against it being true. See! He just caused the rain to fall.) And, the use of the words we employ to speak of God as a subject acting are not equivocal (i.e., they do not have totally

---

[1] Heilsgeschichte means "sacred history." Central to this position is the claim that God reveals himself in our history. Theology is remembrance of his past actions, alertness to his present presence in the events of our time, and anticipation of his future self-disclosures in the emerging future. Cf. earlier essays in this section.

[2] For a more detailed understanding of "picture" the reader should consult Chapter Four. For the purposes of this essay one need only see that language has meaning within a language game that is part of a form of life implicit in which is a fundamental picture.

different meanings as in the case of "bat" in baseball and "bat" flying around in my house), but are univocal.

I do not mean to imply that people who hold this position are empiricists in the contemporary sense of holding that all cognitive claims are reduced to analytic truths and claims confirmed in *sense* experience. But there is a similarity in that the literal supernaturalist believes God is known in a direct way, though he has a much larger range of experiences that he allows to count as evidence: dreams, visions, feelings, miracles, and so on. There was no need to distinguish empirical from transempirical or supernatural. The world of experience was big enough to include all these experiences. Nor do I claim that there are many who hold this position today. What I do want to show, however, is that contemporary biblical theologians who *deny* this literal position are logically committed to it, whether they admit it or not.

Literal supernaturalism, while it has the advantage of simplicity, is not viable for most contemporaries. It is to be guilty of anthropomorphism (seeing God in human form), failing to see the radical gap between God and man. And second, it involves prescientific views of the world that offend our current sensibilities.

In any case, the contemporary heilsgeschichte theologians do not accept locutions 1–10 as literally true. They *do say* that God reveals himself in the events of Israel's history and in the life, death, and resurrection of Jesus, but no longer in this straightforward empirical (now called naïve) way. Literal supernaturalism believed that when God was said to have "acted," he performed an observable act in space and time. And when he spoke, he was heard just as one hears a human voice. But heilsgeschichte theology denies this univocal use of theological words. To speak of God "acting," "working," "speaking," "revealing," no longer has univocal meaning with man "acting," and so on. Instead these words are to be understood in an *analogical*[3] sense. This claim is made, but little work has been done to show how the analogies work.

This is not an idle issue, for if we do not in some sense know what the analogy means and how it is used, the analogy is empty and unintelligible. If we must bracket everything we read about God's acts [not really an act like a human act], what does it then say? What did God *really* do? What *was* his mighty act if he did not literally lead Israel out of Egypt with a pillar of fire?

We have heard these stories of God's mighty deeds many times, but

---

[3] An analogy points to a similarity without maintaining an identity as in the case of a univocal predicate. And although an analogy shows a difference, the difference is not so great as to be equivocal. The way of analogy moves between these two extremes. Whether it can be successful in theology is a matter of much debate. Cf. Chapter Four for more materials on this topic. What is important here is that we *speak* in analogies, we do not *know* by analogies. Analogies presuppose we already know what the analogies refer to.

although we respond to them emotively, do they have any cognitive meaning? On the other hand, if these words are used as analogies (God speaks, but utters no sound; God loves, but his love is beyond our understanding), do we have any idea at all as to just what sort of deed or communication these analogies refer? It is no way out to let the Bible speak for itself if we cannot settle this issue. It is no good to call these analogies revealed, for we must know what they mean to acknowledge them as revelation. It is the essence of our faith to affirm "God has acted mightily and specially in history for our salvation, and so God is *known* in this self-revelation in historical events." But unless the logic of these analogies is made clear, all we can be sure of is that we believe this.

II. DUALISTIC SUPERNATURALISM (HEILSGESCHICHTE THEOLOGY)

The second interpretation of locutions 1–10 also claims to be biblical, arguing that even in the biblical witness there is a drive away from literalism, for example, "God no man hath seen at anytime" (John 1:18). After all, God is a *spirit*. As such, he is invisible and inaccessible to *ordinary* sense experience. Certainly God acts in the world in his providential care of the earth, in extra-ordinary events that define the meaning of existence. In other words, all the claims of literal supernaturalism without the literal understanding of "act," "speak," and so on. But notice the logical puzzle! The straightforward empirical claim is denied, but the content remains the same. If God is in principle not empirically known because he is a spirit, then what possible meaning can be attached to these locutions that seem to be modeled on empirical claims?

To put this in Wittgensteinian language, there are *two* pictures operating here. The assumption of literal supernaturalism is that the biblical picture corresponds *exactly* to the actual state of affairs. Just as a human being is known by his bodily behavior (literalism in theology is analogous to behaviorism in psychology and positivism in philosophy), so God is known by his actions that can be observed in a straightforward way.

The second picture (dualistic supernaturalism) has as its assumption that the biblical picture does *not* correspond exactly to actual states of affairs. The picture is an interpretation of the straightforward facts to a depth revealed through them, much on the model of a soul (spirit) using a body to reveal itself while not being identical with that body. So God (the infinite) reveals himself through the finite as I (my inner self) reveal myself through my body although I am not identical with my bodily behavior as God is not identical with the event.

The heilsgeschichte theologian stresses the *inner* meaning of an event or a person. He speaks of a self-disclosure, namely, a self disclosing itself *through* an action but not identical with that action. He speaks of the Christ of faith encountered through the Jesus of history. He speaks of God revealing himself through events that *by themselves are not revelatory*. My spirit is found by God's spirit mediated through the natural event. To articulate this found datum (not obviously there for everyone to see), the man of faith uses an image to point the hearer beyond the event to its depth meaning. Jesus (event) becomes the Christ (image) in faith. God remains hidden yet revealed in these events. Only faith "sees" the hidden meaning. The event *speaks* a word from God. God is addressing us through the events recorded in the Bible.

Now notice the similarity to psychological dualism (man is both body *and* something more, i.e., soul, spirit, self, mind, and so on), which argues that I am not identical with my bodily behavior. I reveal my "self" through my public action. But there is a hidden "me" which in principle only I can know fully, although I can give others "inklings" of who I am through my actions. I can also, through linguistic activity, interpret my actions to give the *inner* motivation for the external action. "I did that because I love you." So in heilsgeschichte theology we have the same kind of dualism—God *and* events through which he reveals himself plus words that give the inner meaning of the events.

This second picture is certainly a position to be entertained. Indeed, some form of dualism may be *required* if theism is to make any sense. But will psychological dualism of the kind developed above fulfill the task? I think not, at least as it is now understood. The whole mode of talking about a soul acting in a body is problematic for us today. The "ghost in the machine" theory developed above, and usually identified with Descartes, is widely considered to be illegitimate. Gilbert Ryle demythologized person-talk as Bultmann urged demythologizing of God-talk. To model God-talk on soul-talk, then, is to defend the logic of the Ghost in the cosmos with the logic of the Ghost in the machine, when the latter is bogged down in numerous puzzles.

For example, if one denies that God can be empirically known, then an appeal to empirical events as revelations of God requires something other than the event to determine its truth or falsity, for example, an act of faith. But this raises the question as to whether faith is not just a *subjective interpretation* of the event. For how could I, in principle, even check? Is *this* event really a revelation of the inner life of God? Why not *that* event? To make a judgment I would have to know God directly. Is this not the identical problem encountered by those who claim that the "self" cannot be known in one's external acts, the "self" being a mysterious "thou" which *can never* be known in a direct way? How can I ever then know *you*? For sure? For if only you know yourself then only you know for sure. The same problem arises in dualistic theology. For if God can never be known directly, how do we know this event is a true indication of his true self? Only God would know! Theology works only for God and presumably he does not need it.

One might argue that God reveals himself in the event in such a way that the event *is* identical with God. For example, Jesus is God in the flesh. God is known directly in the face of Jesus Christ.[4] But now we have a new set of problems. If the statement "Jesus *is* God" (putting aside the question of whether the New Testament would support this claim) is true then God sweats, spits, excretes, and so on. He also dies! Then who raised him from the dead? When Jesus prayed, was he talking to himself? No! God is more than Jesus! Fine! What more? Here an appeal to Jesus is of no help. As long as "Jesus" and "God" are exchangeable terms we have no problem. God was born in such and such a year and died in such and such a year, and so on. But I know of no Christian theologian who argues this. God is more! What more? Here the event cannot help us.

But, one might say, the event shows me what the "more" *must* be like. God in himself is like Jesus! But again, Jesus' actions, and so on, can be talked about because he was a *man*, but when we move to talk about God all the problems raised above and below emerge again. I can understand Jesus' love and Jesus' suffering for others, but what happens when I substitute "God" for "Jesus?" God loves us. God suffers for us. Even God suffers for us in Jesus Christ. All the problems raised earlier and in the following again present themselves. For how do I know Jesus' love is like God's love because I can never know God directly. We have the same problem here that psychological dualism has. How can I know that your bodily behavior is an external expression of your internal life? Only *you* would know! Only God would *know* if Jesus is an external expression of his internal life.

Another maneuver is often tried. The complete event of revelation includes the "acts" of God, plus an image or interpretation that illuminates the act. A particular calamity in national life is called the "avenging sword of the Lord," or the virgin birth of Jesus is an image (not a historical event) that interprets Jesus' origin as divinely ordained. The exodus of the Jewish people from Egypt is thought by many to have been a slow migration (event) that is mythologized (tales of miraculous crossings, manna from heaven, and so on) in order to relate the migration to God's inner plan for Israel. The event without the image is blind; the image without the event is empty.

But again, this raises more puzzles than it solves. For a beginner, what is the event and what is the image (myth) used to interpret the event? For example, is the resurrection of Jesus a myth (as many have argued) used to interpret the life and death of Jesus as to its *meaning for us*, or is it the event? How can we decide? Second, how do I know the interpretation is correct if I never directly know God? Analogously, how do I know your words express your inner intention if I never can know

4 As some interpret the incarnation.

you as you are inside? Or *are* you simply what you do and say? Or are the
events of the Bible all there is, plus the subjective interpretations of
people? As long as we believe in a mysterious Ghost in body and cosmos,
how will we ever know?

But the real problem is still to be marked out. For if God's acts are
not to be understood in a straightforward sense, we have no understanding of their new use without being given a logical map so that
we can find our way about. How can one call God a person if he does
not speak, hear, love, hate, move, intend, dream, imagine, and so on,
in ways that human persons do? How can God *act* without having a
body? How does one see or know without a brain? But you say, "God
is a person in a mysterious way that passes our understanding." Besides
being a conversation stopper, this is no answer but a restatement of the
problem. It is similar to believing that Igly boo is farkel! The sentence is
perfectly formed but unless I know *what* "Igly boo" is and what characteristic "farkel" describes, my sentence is nonsense. I cannot believe
or reject it! My only response can be, "What the heck are you talking
about?" And to claim revealed status for these locutions does not infuse
them with meaning, for I must *first* know what they mean before I can
accept or reject them. How does a "spirit" act, know, love, and so on?

The phrase "God acts" gets its meaning in situations where human
beings manipulate bodies and objects according to their intentions. Human beings are *in* space and time like the things they act on. But in
dualistic supernaturalism, God is not in the world. He is transcendent.
But then how can one also speak of him acting in the world without
explaining the logic of such locutions. One could say that God is both
transcendent (like my "self" is to my body) and immanent (like my
"self" is in a body). Or, these theologians like to say God is *wholly
Other* and yet as near as our breathing. These locutions elicit an
emotive response, "how mysterious!" but is this not a clear case of
equivocation (God is totally different in all his doings), then univoca-
tion (God is like us). Now you can't have it both ways without some
explanation of how the talk goes. My suspicion here is that while many
theologians reject literal supernaturalism as naïve, the meaning of what
they say is parasitic upon literal supernaturalism being true. Just as in the
case of psychological dualism I end up checking my knowledge about you
not against some mysterious you, but your public behavior.

To pursue this matter even further, what do we do with the preposi-
tions "in," "above," "beyond," "outside of," "ground of," "cause of," and
so on? Again, a literal supernaturalism is assumed where the world is
seen as a sphere with boundaries and God is *outside* this sphere, periodically popping in to do something as a human being enters and leaves a
room. But the dualistic supernaturalist agrees with Bultmann that this
way of looking at the world is mythical. Fine! What then do these prepo-
sitions mean?

This is an age-old problem in theology. On the one hand, God is not an object like finite objects in the world. He is so wholly Other that we cannot even speak of Him. He passes our understanding. But this desire to protect God from anthropomorphic descriptions leads to agnosticism, not knowing or being able to say anything about God. Theology ends in silence! But yet, the theologian wants to be true to the biblical witness that speaks of him acting in the world. After all, a God so removed from the human drama cannot call, elect, judge, or save people. But the more *this* side of God is stressed, the more like a human he becomes, and then we have a danger of making God into an object among other objects.

The similarity to "soul" talk is striking. Dualists want to argue that the soul is wholly other than a body, yet acts *in* a body and is *in* time. But if my "soul" or "mind" or "self" 'is not a physical entity, how can I *place* it anywhere?

What I have tried to show is that every language game has a logic. The logic of the above two games is clear, but based on two pictures that, for some, no longer work. I do not deny that these pictures did work at one time and may still work for some. What I am arguing is that pictures die, and with that death goes the whole language game.

The analysis I have given is a common one found in more detail in analytic literature.[5] A common criticism of this analysis is that it is reductionistic, assuming a positivistic empiricism. But note, I am not requiring the theologian to conform to my logic. I am raising questions within the games involved. If my analysis is correct I have not shown God-talk to be invalid, only unintelligible. Theologians are called upon to find new ways to talk about agents, actions, and relations that could be used to talk about God. If some form of dualism is necessary for God-talk, and I think it is because God is Other than man, then what model can we find to do the job? That is the task facing theology today. The Whiteheadian model seems the most promising.[6]

Another point I have made in this essay is that God-talk and self-talk are intimately related. Indeed, I would argue that as self-talk goes, so goes God-talk. I do not mean this in Feuerbach's sense that God is a projection of man's ideals. Rather, God-talk dies, at least in modern times, when the self loses transcendence over the body, i.e., when some form of dualism is denied. Theologians find themselves without models to use in talking about God. The current interest in levels of consciousness, peak experiences naturally and artificially induced, new talk of transcendence, oriental mysticism, have all contributed to a renewed interest in God-talk.[7]

Barring this, secular ways of talking about religious (peak) experiences will become more frequent if not necessary.

[5] Cf. Chapter Four.
[6] Cf. Chapter Six.
[7] Cf. Chapter Seven.

THE PSEUDONYMS OF GOD

Robert McAfee Brown

ROBERT MCAFEE BROWN is Professor of Religion in the Special Programs
in Humanities at Stanford University. His most recent book is *The
Pseudonyms of God* (1972).

The language about God these days tends to be a curious combination
of modesty and extravagance—modesty at how little some people claim
to know about Him, extravagance at the degree of assurance with which
others claim we can know little or nothing. To some, of course, God is
still totally and triumphantly *present,* and a noted evangelist can rebut
the charge that God is dead by countering, "I know that God is alive,
because I talked with Him this morning," a response that effectively
stops further pursuit of the point.

But the mood is generally more chastened. Ever since the time of
Isaiah, and probably before him, men have spoken of God as *hidden,*
and Pascal was not the only one to echo Isaiah's plaintive cry, "Truly,
thou art a God who hidest thyself." [1] Martin Buber has spoken of the
eclipse of God, another dramatic image, but has insisted that in spite
of this eclipse, brought about in part at least by man's sin, we must
seek to redeem the word that has fallen into such disrepute. "We cannot
cleanse the word 'God' and we cannot make it whole," he writes, "but,
defiled and mutilated as it is, we can raise it from the ground and set it
over an hour of great care." [2]

In our day the notion of the *absence* of God has gained much currency:
there may be a God, but if so, the evidence of His presence is so agonizingly slim that we must discount the possibility that He will reappear
in our time. Until He does, we must, in Gabriel Vahanian's words,
"Wait without idols." [3] This theme seems new and rather daring, but
it may in fact be little more than a refinement of the deistic notion, not
of the absent God, but of the absentee God, the one who was once
around but has now retired to the sidelines, leaving the universe to run
its own course, virtually independent of Him.

Even more extravagent than these images, of course, is the contemporary theme of the *death* of God, although it is not always clear what the
proponents of this theme mean. Sometimes they mean that the idea of

---

[1] Isaiah 45:15. Pascal picks up the theme in *Pensées,* #194, 242.

[2] Martin Buber, *Eclipse of God* (New York: Harper, 1952), p. 18.

[3] Cf. Gabriel Vahanian, *Wait Without Idols* (New York: Braziller, 1964). I have
explored the notion from a different perspective in "The Theme of Waiting in Modern
Literature," *Ramparts,* Summer 1964, 68–75, dealing with Beckett, Kafka, and Auden.

God, as a theme of human contemplation and commitment, has died, and that the term is thus a description of our cultural situation rather than a metaphysical or ontological statement.[4] Many of them find the news curiously liberating and seem unimpressed with Rabbi Richard Rubenstein's disavowal of such optimism: "The death of God as a cultural phenomenon is undeniable," he comments, "but this is no reason to dance at the funeral." Others, however, press beyond this phenomenological statement to the assertion that God really and truly has died, that this death is an historical event, and that it took a so-called Christian civilization about nineteen centuries to catch up with the truth. But even those who most buoyantly proclaim God's death go on to insist that there has been a kind of resurrection of God in a new form, as the epiphany of new possibilities for a humanity now liberated from false and outworn beliefs.[5]

In connection with this last position, I happen to be among those who believe that the reports of God's death, like the initial reports of Mark Twain's, have been somewhat exaggerated, and I agree with the editors of *New Theology No. 4* that the so-called "death of God theology" was a phenomenon already passing from the theological scene when it was belatedly discovered by *Time, Newsweek, Playboy,* and other representatives of the mass media.[6] I do not therefore intend in what follows to flail a dead horse, let alone a dead God. These modes of speech in our day which speak of God as present, hidden, eclipsed, absent or dead, are, I say, extravagant modes of speech. I do not use the term pejoratively, but descriptively, and partly as a means of setting off by contrast the more modest and less extravagant task in which I propose to engage. For I want to deal with the more circumscribed theme of God's pseudonyms, the "strange names" I believe him to be using in our time.

This theme suggests that to the degree that God is *present,* it may mean that He is present in a strange way, and that the usual criteria for measuring His presence may have to be revised. To the degree that God is *hidden,* it may mean that He has chosen to hide himself (as Isaiah suspected) so that we are forced to search Him out in unlikely places. To the degree that He is in *eclipse,* it may be that the shadows bringing about the eclipse can force us to survey the once-familiar terrain from new perspectives, and finally to see it with greater clarity than was possible for us when it was fully bathed in the sunshine of an undisturbed faith. To the degree that God is *absent,* it may be that such absence is His self-imposed catalyst to force us into acknowledging fresh modes

[4] Cf. Vahanian, *The Death of God* (New York: Braziller, 1961), and writings from William Hamilton's "middle period" such as *The New Essence of Christianity* (New York: Association Press, 1961).
[5] The literature is endless. Cf. inter alia, Altizer and Hamilton, *Radical Theology and the Death of God* (Indianapolis: Bobbs-Merrill, 1966), and Altizer, *The Gospel of Christian Atheism* (Philadelphia: Westminster, 1966), for first-hand expositions.
[6] Cf. Marty and Peerman, eds., *New Theology No. 4* (New York: Macmillan, 1967), esp. pp. 9–15.

for His apprehension. And to the degree that He is *dead*—but here, of course, the comparative mode of speech breaks down, for it is not possible to speak of degrees of "deadness" (though with some of the things theologians say these days, I would not put it past someone to try). The death of God as a description of a cultural phenomenon, however, can be so described, and to the degree that our notion of God has suffered mortal blows, this may in fact be precisely the prerequisite for a genuine resurrection in our experience of the true God, purged of at least some of the confining and distorting notions we have tried to attach to Him. And for this task of trying to make ourselves open once again to the reality of one whose dimensions we cannot measure, and whom eye cannot see nor ear hear, the imagery of the pseudonym may be of some use.

SILONE'S USE OF PSEUDONYMS

The theme was first suggested to me in the very moving novel of Ignazio Silone, called *Bread and Wine*.[7] The novel tells the story of Pietro Spina, a communist revolutionary in Italy in the 1930s during the rise of Italian fascism, the period in which Mussolini waged his savage war against Ethiopia. Spina is concerned to discern the signs of the times, and an elderly priest, Don Benedetto, who had been his teacher, makes the rather startling remark to him:

In times of conspiratorial and secret struggle, the Lord is obliged to hide Himself and assume pseudonyms. Besides, and you know it, He does not attach very much importance to His name. . . . Might not the ideal of social justice that animates the masses today be one of the pseudonyms the Lord is using to free Himself from the control of the churches and the banks?[8]

To get the full force of this statement, it must be realized that "the ideal of social justice that animates the masses" in Italy in the 1930s, to which the priest was referring, was communism. Don Benedetto was saying, in other words, that the hand of God might be more clearly discerned among the Italian communists than among the Italian priests or bankers.

Initially this seems a strange idea, perhaps even a demonic idea. It seems strange that a God who presumably wants to enter into fellowship

[7] Ignazio Silone, *Bread and Wine* (New York: Atheneum, 1962), a revision of an earlier form of the novel published in America by Penguin (New York, 1946). I have developed Silone's use of the theme more fully in "Ignazio Silone and the Pseudonyms of God," a contribution to a symposium to be published by the University of Pittsburgh Press.

[8] Silone, op. cit. (Penguin), pp. 247–248. Silone's later revision does not contain the quotation in this precise form.

with His children should show Himself not directly but indirectly, and it seems demonic that the vehicle through which He should indirectly show Himself—the pseudonym or false name He should use—would be something so apparently antithetical to His purposes as communism. But Don Benedetto, as he pursues his theme, makes clear that there is nothing new in this idea. It has, in fact, a long history.

This would not be the first time that the Eternal Father felt obligated to hide Himself and take a pseudonym. As you know, He has never taken the first name and the last name men have fastened on Him very seriously; quite to the contrary, He has warned men not to name Him in vain as His first commandment. And then, the Scriptures are full of clandestine life. Have you ever considered the real meaning of the flight into Egypt? And later, when he was an adult, was not Jesus forced several times to hide himself and flee from the Judeans? [9]

Don Benedetto also instances Elijah's experience in the desert, to which we shall presently turn, and Silone himself is so caught up with this theme that in his stage version of *Bread and Wine* he renames the story, *And He Did Hide Himself*,[10] developing even more prominently through the mouthpiece of Friar Giochinno the notion that Jesus Himself had to assume pseudonyms, another theme to which we shall presently turn. We may push the matter a bit further, therefore, not only in terms of Silone's use of the theme, but also in terms of his insistence that this is not a new theme but an old one, and that it is indeed a consistent Biblical theme as well.

BIBLICAL EXAMPLES OF THE PSEUDONYMOUS GOD

Three Old Testament examples of the theme of God's use of pseudonyms may be suggested as the foundation for a further consideration of its possible contemporary usefulness. The first of these occurs in Genesis 28:10–17. Jacob is *en route* from Beersheba to Haran. Night comes, and so he camps along the road, stopping at what is described as "a certain place" to spend the night. There is nothing special about this place at all. It is not a shrine, it is not a holy place, it is not the goal of the day's journey. It is simply where Jacob happens to be when the sun goes down. During the night he has a dream about a ladder from earth to heaven, upon which angels are ascending and descending.[11] What is important for our present purposes is neither the dream nor the content of the dream, but the comment that Jacob makes when he awakes, since it

[9] Silone, op. cit. (Atheneum), p. 274.
[10] Silone, *And He Did Hide Himself* (London: Jonathan Cape, 1946).
[11] I forego the tempting possibility of dealing with dreams as unlikely vehicles of the divine presence, enticing though that might be on another occasion.

becomes almost a paradigm of the experience of the pseudonymity of
God. The next morning Jacob makes two statements, both of which are
very true: first, "Surely the Lord is in this place," as indeed He was;
second, "I did not know it," as indeed he did not (cf. Genesis 28:16).
God's presence was not dependent upon Jacob's perception of that
presence—a fact from which we can derive some comfort when we today
too readily identify the reality or existence of God with our own degree
of perception of His reality or existence. But even more important, I
believe, was the fact that the reality of that presence came home to
Jacob in a quite unexpected place and set of circumstances. Jacob did
not discover God in a shrine or place of worship, but far from any such
place. He did not discover Him in the midst of any cultic exercise or act
of mercy. He did not suddenly in the midst of prayer experience the
healing reality of God's presence. No, it was in the totally unexpected
event of setting up camp in the desert, in the midst of a tedious journey,
that God manifested Himself in a strange way. How strange and irregular this was to Jacob's experience is rather perversely attested to by
the fact that Jacob's reaction was precisely to build a shrine on that
spot, to try to regularize the unexpected experience, to divest the experience of its pseudonymity and make it predictable, calculable and manageable.

A second Biblical example of God's use of pseudonyms is one to which
Don Benedetto himself makes oblique reference in his conversation with
Spina, and one that is recounted in 1 Kings 19:1–12. A little later in Israel's
history Elijah is also leaving Beersheba, only this time he is not making a
calculated journey: he is fleeing from that very domineering queen named
Jezebel who is after his neck. So Elijah flees to the wilderness. Yahweh
pursues him and orders him to stand upon the mount before the Lord.
"Before the Lord": but how will Elijah know the presence of the Lord?
The account continues:

And behold, the LORD passed by, and a great and strong wind rent the mountains, and broke in pieces the rocks before the LORD, but the LORD was not in
the wind; and after the wind an earthquake, but the LORD was not in the earthquake; and after the earthquake a fire, but the LORD was not in the fire; and
after the fire a still, small voice. . . .[12]

The Lord strong and mighty was not in the wind. The Lord of heaven
and earth was not in the earthquake. The Lord of all power was not in
the fire. Recall that these means—earthquake, wind and fire—were the
normal ways through which a man in Elijah's time would have expected
a theophany of the divine presence. But no, after these usual manifestations of the divine comes "a still, small voice," or as one translator has
put it, "the sound of a soft stillness." [13] And it was in "the sound of a soft

[12] 1 Kings 19:11–12.
[13] Cf. Brewer, *The Literature of the Old Testament* (New York: Columbia University Press, 1938), p. 48.

stillness" that the God of earthquake, wind and fire was present—the last place on earth in which Elijah would have expected to find Him. Once again, God is working through the unexpected, and confronting man not in the normal way but in a strange way, through pseudonymous activity.

A third example of this strange activity of God occurs still later in Israel's history, recounted in that curious and disturbing passage in Isaiah 10:5–19. Isaiah is rightly worried because Israel is paying no attention to Yahweh's demands. He feels that Yahweh is about to engage in a mighty manifestation of His sovereign power. And he links this with the fact that Assyria, a great pagan world power—today we would say a "secular" world power—is poised on the northern borders about to invade the land of God's people, the Jews. Isaiah feels that the power of Yahweh will be manifested in the ensuing battle. Now the customary thing to assume in such situations was that God would, of course, work through His chosen people. They who were to be a "light unto the Gentiles" would surely be the vehicle through which the strong right arm of Yahweh would be manifested to the Gentiles.

But Isaiah did not say that at all. Instead, he said the scandalous and shocking thing that God's instrument would be the pagan Assyria, and that it would be through Assyrian power that God would show forth His will. Assyria, of course, did not know that it was being used by God, and did not even acknowledge the existence of God. Indeed, Assyria would later claim that it had won the victory by the power of its own strong arm, and would scoff at the notion that it was the instrument of Yahweh. But nevertheless, so Isaiah asserts, it will be by means of Assyria that God will declare His will to His people Israel. Once again, God uses a strange name. He does not use the name of His people, Israel; He uses the name of a pagan people, Assyria. Assyria, not Israel, becomes "the rod of His anger, the staff of His fury," and the "godless people" against whom Assyria is sent, is paradoxically the very people of God.

There are three instances, taken almost at random, of a theme that could be reproduced many times over from the Old Testament. They illustrate that God can use whatever means He chooses, whatever means are to hand—a rest stop on a trip, the calm after a storm, the hosts of the pagans—in order to communicate His will to His people. His ways of working are not limited to the ways people expect Him to work, and He clearly refuses to be bound by man's ideas of how He ought to behave. Notice, too, one other thing about these examples. They illustrate three classic ways in which men have claimed to "find God"—through *personal experience* (in the case of Jacob), through *nature* (in the case of Elijah), and through *history* (in the case of Isaiah). In each case, indeed, a confrontation takes place between man and God, but in each case it takes place in an unexpected way. The personal experience is not the personal experience of worship or some other conventional means of encountering God. The confrontation in nature is through the vehicle of nature least expected to produce such a confrontation. The lesson read from history is the lesson least expected and the hardest to accept. In each case, God uses a pseudonym, a strange name, and upsets all human calculations.

THE PSEUDONYMS OF GOD TODAY

Let us accept, then, Don Benedetto's theme that God is sometimes obliged to hide Himself and assume pseudonyms, and that He does not attach very much importance to His name. The name men conventionally attach to Him may now be an empty name, the place men look for Him may now be the place He is not, and the places men fail to look may be precisely the locations in which His hidden activity is most apparent to those who look with eyes of faith. Where, then, do we find signs of His pseudonymous activity today? Are we to look for Him *only* in strange places? I do not believe so. To say that He acts pseudonymously does not mean He can never be found in His Church, but it will surely mean that He is not confined to His Church. To say that He acts pseudonymously does not mean that His light no longer shines through the saints, but it will surely mean that His saints are more numerous and found in more unlikely places than we are usually inclined to acknowledge. To say that He acts pseudonymously does not mean that Scripture is no longer useful in discerning His hidden ways (and the instances just cited should be supporting evidence enough for that), but it will surely mean that other literature as well is a vehicle for discerning His veiled presence, not only in Silone, who knows the lineaments of a Christian faith he cannot directly profess himself, but in a host of other writers who plumb the depths of the human predicament with a sensitivity not found in most contemporary pulpits.[14]

To try to discern the signs of the presence of pseudonymous God in the world today is surely a risky business, but the risk must be taken if we are not to leave our thesis irrelevantly suspended in mid-air. I therefore offer now two examples of places where I see signs of His activity more compelling to me than the conventional modes of His expression that theologians normally delight to trace, and to sharpen the issue I shall state these in deliberately provocative terms.

The first example of this pseudonymous activity of God in our present age is in the agitation and demonstration in which our country has been engaged in the field of civil rights for minority groups. The white churches, to their shame, have not been very active in this struggle. One

[14] On this theme, cf. inter alia such recent writings from diverse viewpoints as Scott, *The Broken Center* (New Haven: Yale University Press, 1965); TeSelle, *Literature and the Christian Life* (New Haven: Yale University Press, 1966); and Axthelm, *The Modern Confessional Novel* (New Haven: Yale University Press, 1967).

does not look to those who call themselves "God's own people" for leadership in this matter. There has been little significant indication that many white Christians have really been concerned about the indignities that they and other white people have visited upon the black people of this country for the last three hundred years. If we are to be honest, we must acknowledge that the real battle has been carried on by the secular groups, or by the Negro church groups, but not by the white church groups. Whatever advances have been won in the cause of social justice have been won either in the face of white Christian apathy or white Christian opposition. As the late Martin Luther King forcefully and correctly put it, "What is disturbing is not the appalling actions of the bad people, but the appalling silence of the good people." Such an indictment must be accepted not merely as a justifiable cry of outrage, but as a simple descriptive statement.

Now let us face it. We do not usually expect to see the hand of the Lord in secular groups, in mass meetings, in public demonstrations, in picket lines, in sit-ins, in civil disobedience, in people being herded off to jail, in court rooms, and all the rest. But can we escape the fact that those are the places and activities through which concern for the fact that *all* men are God's children is being expressed today? And that the same fact is not expressed, but denied, in the white communities with written or unwritten covenants of closed occupancy, or the white churches with the token Negro tenor prominently displayed in the choir? No, the Lord is in those strange places, and, like Jacob, we have not known it.

The tragedy has been that we have not learned it soon enough, and that, because of *our* blindness and callousness and indifference, the incredible patience of non-violent Negro discipline has turned to violence. The white community cannot blame the black community for the urban riots of the summer of 1967, and the fearful portent of more to come in succeeding summers. The white community, holding all the power, has done too little, too late, and forced the despairing outcry that finally has exhausted any hope of working through the white-dominated political process, and turns now in total frustration to all that is left—the brick, the stick, the fire, the bullet.[15] Is not a word of the Lord being spoken through all this, that the longer we flout the demand for justice and mercy, the heavier will be the penalties we have to pay? Let us learn to listen, through the anguished cries of the dispossessed in the ghettoes, to the insistent word, the ground bass theme of all the history of exploitation of one group by another, "Let my people go."

[15] These words were written before the release of the Presidential Advisory Commission's Report on Civil Disorders. This "secular" document insists, in hard-hitting terms, that the reason for the riots is not black conspiracy, but "white racism." Cf. *Report of the National Advisory Commission on Civil Disorders*, with an introduction by Tom Wicker (New York: Bantam Books, 1968). The document is a splendid example of the voice of the pseudonymous God speaking in our time.

To me the most haunting line in contemporary literature occurs in the exchange between Msimangu and Kumalo, the two black priests in Alan Paton's book. *Cry, the Beloved Country.* They are talking about the white man. And Msimangu says to Kumalo, "I have one great fear in my heart, that one day when they are turned to loving they will find that we are turned to hating." [16] So insistent is the theme that Paton has Kumalo recall it a second time at the very end of the book: "When they turn to loving they will find we are turned to hating." [17] It is already possible that this could become the epitaph of our nation. And the question is: can we hear this as the insistent clamor of the pseudonymous God in our day, addressed to us, warning us, "Do not look for me just in the sanctuaries, or in the precise words of theologians, or in the calm of the countryside; look for me in the place where men are struggling for their very survival as human beings, where they are heaving off the load of centuries of degradation, where they are insisting that the rights of the children of God are the rights of all my children and not just some; and if you will not find me there, expect to find me acting in more heavy-handed fashion elsewhere."

There is a second place where I see the pseudonymous God at work in our nation today. This is at the moment a more "controversial" issue, just as a few years ago civil rights was more controversial than it is now. But the fact that it is more controversial does not deter me, for I have a conviction that wherever God turns up, pseudonymously or not, He provokes controversy, since He challenges what is going on. (Let us not suppose that Isaiah's suggestion that Assyria, and not Israel, had become God's instrument went unchallenged; he was probably lucky to escape with his life.) I believe that God is using His "strange name" in trying to tell us something desperately important through the rising voice of protest about American involvement in Vietnam. I do not intend to turn this discussion into a treatment of the intricacies of American foreign policy, but it would be the height of hypocrisy as well as the expression of a lack of even minimal moral courage, to try to sidestep the issue, since it is the most burning moral issue of this decade.[18]

That there is something wrong about the most powerful nation on earth systematically destroying a tiny nation ought long ago to have been crystal clear to everyone, but it has not been. Dropping napalm on women and children and the aged, so that peoples' chins melt into their chests, ought long ago to have aroused in us the height of moral indignation, but it has not. That we justify our presence in Vietnam in the name of opposing a monolithic "world communism" that began to crumble

[16] Alan Paton, *Cry, the Beloved Country* (New York: Scribners, 1948), pp. 39–40.

[17] Ibid., p. 272.

[18] No one hopes more than the author that the material that follows will soon become dated. But this only underlines the central thesis of the chapter, that God must be looked for in contemporaneous events and not only in generalities.

over a decade ago, ought long ago to have made us demand a stern accounting of our leaders, but it has not. That we are entitled to impose our will wherever we wish in the world, supporting military dictatorships that do not represent their people, ought long ago to have made us cry out in protest, but it has not. "Destroying a city in order to save it," as an American officer described our destruction of Ben Tre, ought to impress us as a hideous example of Orwellian doublethink, but it does not.

Once more, we must concede that the churches have been relatively silent on this issue. After one has mentioned the late Archbishop Halliman, Bishop Shannon, Bishop Sheen, Bishop Doughterty and one or two others, he can count on the fingers of one hand the American Roman Catholic bishops who have publicly felt a sense of moral ambiguity about American presence in Vietnam. With a few individual exceptions, the top-brass leadership in Protestantism, Orthodoxy and Judaism has been similarly reticent about a real probe of the morality of mass killing in the name of the high-sounding ideals our State Department once avowed, and has now abandoned in the name of a tough-minded policy of national interest, which even on those terms can be rebutted as self-defeating. The churches, the "godly," have had an incredible timidity in this matter. Would that American Roman Catholic bishops went even as far as the South Vietnamese Roman Catholic bishops, who asked for a cessation of the bombing of North Vietnam even as the American military forces, with the implicit support of most churchmen, continued the senseless destruction around Hanoi which the former Secretary of Defense himself said did not succeed.

Where has the voice of moral outrage come from? Not from churches, not from business, not from labor. No, it has come from the students, who on this issue have displayed considerably greater moral sensitivity than their elders. They have helped to remind the rest of us that national pride and arrogance are things in which they take no pride, and for which their generation is not willing to kill dark-skinned peoples thousands of miles away. And we are witnessing an escalation of moral protest in response to the escalation of military power, as students across the land are trying to tell the older generation that the war we are fighting is both futile and immoral. Many from both generations may not like some of the stridency of voice and action that accompanies the protest, but it has been our deafness that has made the stridency necessary, and woe to those of any generation who do not hear in this anguished protest a strong note of moral urgency.

If in this situation, I look for a sign of the pseudonymous God at work, do I find it in an administration that has in fact committed itself to a policy that anything is permissible to achieve military victory? I do not. I find it much more in the words of dozens of young men I have talked to, and thousands more across the land, who say, "I will not kill my fellow man, even if it means five years in prison"; who say, "If America intends to police the world, it will first have to imprison its youth." I find it also in the commitment of those in public life who are willing to pay a great price to speak against the madness that has seized our nation's leaders. These voices are few indeed, in comparison to the rest who by silence or inactivity condone our slaughter of the Vietnamese, and there are times when I wonder whether human madness may not stifle and destroy the presence of God.

In such a mood, I turn back to Silone, and discover that Don Benedetto faced the same question himself, and that the analogies to the Italian war in Ethiopia, to which the aged priest refers, and the American war in Vietnam become more congruent with each passing hour. Don Bene-detto ruminates:

I, too, in the dregs of my affliction, have asked myself: Where is God and why has He abandoned us? Certainly the loud-speakers and bells announcing the new slaughter were not God. Nor were the cannon shots and the bombing of Ethiopian villages, of which we read every day in the newspapers. But if one poor man gets up in the middle of the night and writes on the walls of the village with a piece of charcoal or varnish, "Down with the War," the presence of God is undoubtedly behind that man. How can one not recognize the divine light in his scorn of danger and in his love for the so-called enemies? Thus, if some simple workmen are condemned for these reasons by a special tribunal, there's no need to hesitate to know where God stands.[19]

That the manner of contemporary protest against the war is disquieting is no sign that God is absent. Indeed, we can expect that God's presence, in whatever form, will be disquieting. We will find Him not just where there is peace, but where there is turmoil; not just where things are calm, but where things are stirred up.

The Supreme Pseudonym

It is a temptation to stop right there. One could surely argue that a case has been made: God can work in unexpected ways, employ pseudonyms, and we have now seen instances of this not only in biblical history but in our own contemporary history. Q.E.D. But one must not succumb to the temptation to stop right there. For out of a number of questions that could be raised, particularly about the immediately preceding para-graphes, there is one surely that must be faced, whatever others are to be omitted. This is the question: how can one be sure that it is *God* who is working in these various ways and not someone or something else? Is not this whole approach likely to make God simply capricious, not really trustworthy or knowable, to be looked for merely in the bizarre or the curious circumstances? Or to focus the question even more bluntly:

[19] Silone, *Bread and Wine*, pp. 275–276.

do we not simply pick our own pet social hobbies and try to invest them with ultimate moral worth by saying that they are the activities through which God is working? Are we not simply trying to enlist God on our side? How can we be so sure God is working through the pseudonyms that just happen to appeal to us?

That is a fair question. (It can be asked, I have discovered from personal experience, in considerably less genteel ways and with considerably more venom behind it.) Let me try to indicate the guidelines along which I think it can be answered. The answer involves, for me at any rate, a shift from the Old Testament material to the New Testament, though I think an answer congruent to the one I am suggesting is to a high degree possible on Old Testament terms as well.

If we want to find a criterion in terms of which to discern where God is or is not employing pseudonyms today, I think we find it in relation to the time and place where God did show us most clearly who He is and how He makes Himself known to us. Any other attempt to trace His activity must be tested against how adequately they reflect what we know of Him from that central event. The time, of course, is the first thirty years of what we now call the Christian era, though it presupposes the many generations of Jewish history preceding it. The place is that tiny little strip of land known as Palestine, tucked off in a corner of the Roman Empire. And the important thing for our present concern is that this event likewise underlines the unexpectedness of the divine activity, the sense in which here too God used a pseudonym, the sense in which here too His activity was just as strange and unexpected as in the case of Jacob, Elijah or Isaiah, the sense in which all that came to fulfillment in the life Jesus of Nazareth is simply contrary to the way any of us would have written the script.

Kierkegaard puts the theme most strongly when he reminds us that it is not possible to understand who Jesus of Nazareth is unless we have gone through the possibility of offense at the claims that center on Him. We must be offended at the notion that God would work through the son of a lower-class carpenter who may well have been illiterate. What else can we be but offended? Only if we have genuinely entertained the possibility, Kierkegaard insists, that God would work in such a strange way, with such a strange name as Jeshua bar-Josef, can we go beyond offense to affirmation.[20]

Let me seek, if possible, to drive the point home by the following device: Suppose, just for a moment, that we were waiting now for some tremendous manifestation of God's activity. Suppose that it had been promised that God would intervene in our human situation, and that it was now clear that the time was at hand. Where would we look for Him? Where would we expect that God would manifest Himself?

[20] Cf. further on this theme, Kierkegaard, *Training in Christianity* (Princeton: Princeton University Press, 1941), esp. Part II, pp. 79–144.

Surely, the answer would be, in one of the great nations, where as many people as possible would be exposed to this important fact; surely in a well-established family with much influence; surely in such a way that all the resources of public opinion and mass media could be used to acquaint people with what happened; surely it would be the most public and open and widely accessible event possible.

But in terms of the way the New Testament reports it happening back then, if it were to happen today, I think it would be more like this: A child would be born into a backward South African tribe, the child of poor parents with almost no education. He would grow up under a government that would not acknowledge his right to citizenship. During his entire lifetime he would travel no more than about fifty miles from the village of his birth, and would spend most of that lifetime simply following his father's trade—a hunter, perhaps, or a primitive farmer. He would, toward the end, begin to gather a few followers together, talking about things that sounded so dangerous to the authorities that the police would finally move in and arrest him, at which point his following would collapse and his friends would fade back into their former jobs and situations. After a short time in prison and a rigged trial he would be shot by the prison guards as an enemy of the state.

I submit that most of us would find it hard to take seriously the claim that such an event was the most important manifestation of God that men ever had, or were going to have in the future. That would indeed appear to be a pseudonymous act, with the emphasis on the "pseudo-," the false. And yet that is precisely what the attitude of almost any first-century person must have been to the assertion that the Son of God had been born in a cowstall in tiny Bethlehem and that he was, of all things, a lower-class Jew, whose parents became refugees, and who had Himself to go into hiding on several occasions. If on other occasions the common people heard Him gladly,[21] when it came to the showdown and there was a kind of first-century "demonstration" in the streets of Jerusalem, they quickly shifted their "hosannas" to cries of "crucify Him."[22]

And yet those episodes, and others like them, are the very stuff out of which the Christian claim is created. Jesus of Nazareth becomes God's unexpected way of acting, God's pseudonym, and He becomes the norm or pattern in terms of which we are to believe that God will continue to act. So if it strikes us as strange today that God should be working through Negroes in cities, or through students who for reasons of conscience defy a law, or through groups that are not part of the religious establishment, such assertions are at least consistent with the strange way God acted back then through One who was looked upon as a criminal, spat upon and despised, and finally strung up in the midst of the city dump heap.

21 Cf. Mark 12:37.
22 Cf. the shift between Matthew 21:9 and Matthew 27:22–23.

In different periods of history men emphasize different portions of those gospel accounts, and surely for our age, with its concern for the extension of justice to those to whom it has been denied, the Christological theme that Bonhoeffer stresses of Jesus as "the Man for others" is an inescapable theme.[23] Since He was an outcast, we must not be surprised to find contemporary reflections of His presence among the outcast. Since He was a servant, we must look for signs of His presence today among those who serve. Since He was part of an oppressed minority, we must expect to hear the echo of His voice today among those who are oppressed. In an era when many men have no place to call their own, we must expect a response of resonating concern from One who had nowhere to lay His head. Since two-thirds of the world goes to bed hungry each night, we must recall the One who made available not only spiritual comfort but solid and tangible loaves and fishes.

Since He became man, we must acknowledge that in every man there is one who can be served in His name, just as He served all men in His Father's name. Since He lived very much in the world, we will look for Him not only in holy places or by means of holy words, but will look for Him also in the very common, ordinary things of life for which He gave Himself: bread (whether broken around a kitchen table or at an altar), carpentry, men in need, even tax collectors. In a time when men suffer, we will not be surprised to discover that He suffered also, nor will we flinch when Bonhoeffer pronounces the initially disturbing words, "Only the suffering God can help." [24] And we will find also, in that strange paradox of which Bonhoeffer also speaks, that in the very midst of God-forsakenness, which Jesus too experienced, we thereby discover the presence of God even in the place that is defined as His absence.[25]

In one of her plays about the nativity, Dorothy Sayers sums up this theme. One of the three kings is describing what it would mean to him, if one could take seriously the staggering possibility that God deigns to stoop to identify Himself with man. And he goes on:

I do not mind being ignorant and unhappy—
All I ask is the assurance that I am not alone,
Some courage, some comfort against this burden of fear and pain.
. . . I look out between the strangling branches of the vine and see
Fear in the east, fear in the west; armies
And banners marching and garments rolled in blood.
Yet this is nothing, if only God will not be indifferent,
If He is beside me, bearing the weight of His own creation,
If I may hear His voice among the voices of the vanquished,
If I may feel His hand touch mine in the darkness,

23 Cf. Bonhoeffer, *Letters and Papers from Prison* (New York: Macmillan, 1967), esp. pp. 209–210, foreshadowed in his earlier lectures, *Christ the Center* (New York: Harper and Row, 1966).
24 Bonhoeffer, *Letters and Papers from Prison*, p. 197.
25 The theme is developed in ibid., pp. 196–197.

> If I may look upon the hidden face of God
> And read in the eyes of God
> That He is acquainted with grief.[26]

That, I suppose, is the ultimate in the pseudonymous activity of God—that He should be acquainted with grief. And yet that appears to be the place where we must look for Him today. In his parable of the King and the maiden, Kierkegaard makes response as follows, to the claim that in Jesus the God incarnate is present:

> The servant-form is no mere outer garment, and therefore the God must suffer all things, endure all things, make experience of all things. He must suffer hunger in the desert, he must thirst in the time of his agony, he must be forsaken in death, absolutely like the humblest—behold the man! His suffering is not that of his death, but this entire life is a story of suffering; and it is love that suffers, the love which gives all is itself in want.[27]

So the point of greatest clarity is the point of greatest incongruity and surprise. Jesus Himself is the grand pseudonym, the supreme instance of God acting in ways contrary to our expectation, the point at which we are offered the criterion in terms of which the action of God elsewhere can be measured. And if we miss His presence in the world, it will not be because He is not there, but simply because we have been looking for Him in the wrong places.

Suggested Readings

For a general introduction to biblical materials as well as translations and commentary on the text, see George A. Buttrick, et al., (eds.), * The Interpreter's Bible, 12 vols. (Nashville: Abingdon Press, 1951–57). Volumes I and VII contain excellent articles on background, history, and so on. The Heilsgeschichte approach to theology is developed by Oscar Cullmann, * Christ and Time (Philadelphia· Westminster Press, 1950) and * Salvation in History (New York: Harper & Row, 1967). For other volumes that deal with the issue of revelation, see Alan Richardson, * History: Sacred and Profane (Philadelphia: Westminster, 1964), H. R. Niebuhr, The Meaning of Revelation (New York: Macmillan, 1941p); John Baille, The Idea of Revelation in Recent Thought (New York: Columbia University Press, 1956p); Martin Buber, The Prophetic Faith (New York: Harper & Row, 1960p); G. Ernest Wright, God Who Acts (Naperville, Ill.: Alec R. Allenson, 1952p); and by the same with Reginald H. Fuller, * The Book of the Acts of God (New York: Doubleday Anchor, 1960p). A conservative approach is found in Carl Henry (ed.), * Revelation and the Bible (Grand Rapids, Mich.: Baker, 1958). Two new books that take new approaches are W. Pannenberg (ed.), Revelation as History (New York: Macmillan, 1968p) and

[26] Dorothy Sayers, Four Sacred Plays (London: Gollancz, 1948), p. 227. Reprinted by permission.

[27] Soren Kierkegaard, Philosophical Fragments (Princeton: Princeton University Press, 1962), p. 40.

F. Gerald Downing, *Has Christianity a Revelation?* (London, SCM Press, 1964). Perhaps the best short introduction to the issues of this chapter is Carl E. Braaten, ° *History and Hermeneutics* (New Directions in Theology Today, Vol. II) (Philadelphia: Westminster Press, 1966p).

The following books introduce the reader to the mass of material written on the issue of myth, history, and religion: Mircea Eliade, *Cosmos and History* (New York: Harper & Row, 1959p); *Myth and Reality* (New York: Harper & Row, 1963p) W. Taylor Stevenson, ° *History as Myth* (New York: Seabury Press, 1969). Two recent books that stress the importance of myth in all cultures are Henry A. Murray (ed.), ° *Myth and Mythmaking* (Boston: Beacon Press, 1968p) and Cornelius Loew, ° *Myth, Sacred History and Philosophy* (New York: Harcourt, Brace & World, 1967p). Two books that cover the field and introduce the reader to the importance of Heidegger and question of hermeneutics are Paul J. Achtemeier, ° *An Introduction to the New Hermeneutic* (Philadelphia: Westminster, 1969) and Robert W. Funk, *Language, Hermeneutic, and Word of God* (New York: Harper & Row, 1966). The latter is especially helpful in introducing the reader to the work of Fuchs and Ebeling who go beyond the position of Bultmann.

The following works of Bultmann are especially useful on the issue of faith and history: *Jesus Christ and Mythology* (New York: Scribner's Sons, 1958p); *History and Eschatology* (New York: Harper & Row, 1957p); and *Kerygma and Myth: A Theological Debate*, ed. by Hans W. Bartsch, Vol. 1 (New York: Harper & Row, 1961p). Two books by John Macquarrie serve as good introduction to Bultmann's theology: ° *An Existentialist Theology* (New York: Macmillan, 1955p) and ° *The Scope of Demythologizing* (New York: Harper & Row, 1960p). Other volumes of interest that merely constitute a beginning into the Bultmann legacy are S. Ogden, ° *Christ Without Myth* (New York: Harper & Row, 1961) Friedrich Gogarten, ° *Demythologizing and History* (London: SCM Press, 1955); James M. Robinson, ° *A New Quest of the Historical Jesus* (Naperville, Ill.: Alec R. Allenson, 1959p); Heinz Zahrnt, *The Historical Jesus* (New York: Harper & Row, 1963); and Ian Henderson, *Myth in the New Testament* (Naperville, Ill.: Alec R. Allenson, 1952). Bultmann's answers to his critics may be found in Charles W. Kegley (ed.), ° *The Theology of Rudolf Bultmann* (New York: Harper & Row, 1966). Footnotes and bibliographies in the above will lead the reader into the massive material generated by Bultmann's theology.

A key book that places the issue of faith and history into a large context is V. A. Harvey, ° *The Historian and the Believer* (New York: Macmillan, 1966p). Harvey's approach is broadly analytic.

And finally mention should be made of two anthologies that contain material in current debate, J. M. Robinson and J. B. Cobb, Jr. (eds.), *The Later Heidegger and Theology* (Harper & Row, 1963p) and by the same editors, *The New Hermeneutic* (New York: Harper & Row, 1964p).

CHAPTER THREE

Good-Luck Charm of Theism[1]
or New Humanism?

In an attempt to define existentialism one is met immediately by a host of difficulties. Although existentialism is a sophisticated movement in philosophy, the label "existentialist" has been vulgarized to the point of obscurity.[2] Also, if you find two philosophers classified as existentialists you cannot assume that they agree on anything. Although it is true that there is a family resemblance among these philosophers, giving a general description of these similarities requires the continual caveat—but this does not apply to the following. The best introduction to existentialism is to get right into the material. The first essay in this chapter, by Sartre, is such an introduction. I will restrict myself therefore to a few comments that provide a context for the following essays.

Existentialism for Sartre is a *protest* against any attempt to deny the uniqueness of human existence. This protest takes the form of a rejection of the use of nonhuman categories to define existence. Man is unique in that he alone stands out (meaning of "ex-ist") of what he is and is able, therefore, to question the meaning of his being. This transcendence is man's glory—he alone is free to choose his nature because he is not identical with what he is but is still becoming—but also the source

---

[1] Paul Tillich makes this claim for he sees existentialism as a "God-send" for theology which is in a perpetual search for languages in which to make its claims. R. Bultmann, in his essay, has already introduced the reader to the theological use of existential categories. See Chapter Two. See bibliography for other examples of religious existentialism.

[2] As someone put it, "No self-respecting existentialist would accept being called an existentialist."

of man's misery for he alone knows what he *must* choose who he is to become. This awareness of one's freedom ("condemned to freedom," as Sartre puts it) is the source of anxiety in man. This uniqueness is the starting point for philosophy.

Although each individual is unique, there are certain general descriptions of human existence that can be made.[3] For example, unlike natural objects, human beings do not have their essential nature given to them. Each human being is separated from what he is to become. He makes himself up as he goes along. It is through free choice that he becomes what he is to be. As Sartre states it, "existence precedes essence."

Most existentialists also protest against the positivist tradition that models knowing on the empirical sciences. Empirical science is useful for dealing with certain objects, to be sure, but one's method should be appropriate to the subject matter under investigation. A human subject's *existence* defies being known through laboratory techniques. The existential philosopher is also *involved* in the question and the answer as, for example, a scientist studying the sex life of fruit flies is not. The philosopher has *his own* existence as the subject of his thought. Philosophy is wrestling with the question of one's own identity. One cannot be a detached observer, for the question and the answer is who I am. I am the question and I am the answer.

Sartre begins then with *man* as a subject—not an object—and describes the conditions that make human existence what it is. For this reason he begins with very *personal* phenomena: freedom, decision responsibility, guilt, despair, awareness of being born to die, anxiety, boredom, and so on. Other existentialists have described the phenomena of hope, joy, faith, courage, and so on.

The above description of human phenomena is not known to be true because I can prove it. Truth for existentialism consists in knowing it *to be* true in one's existence.[4] We do not know truth by speculating, reflecting, thinking; we become the truth. This is not to deny that there is objective truth. But a great many questions (and the most important for my existence) do not allow for empirical or logical resolution. Many times I must *choose* and take a *risk*. Kierkegaard has made this point famous by his description of the "leap of faith." Thought only gives us *possibilities*. As long as we think about someone, something, or some action, we remain in the realm of possibility. "Truth as subjectivity" is choosing one possibility and making it actual in our existence. So while the possibility may be *objectively* uncertain, subjectively one is in the

---

[3] But remember the caveat—this is not necessarily true of all existentialists. Also, even if it is true that certain *general* structures are true of all men, this does not relieve the individual of his responsibility to become aware of these structures in existence.

[4] The truth of a description is not supported in the manner of proving a scientific truth. The description opens to view what is there. Truth (ἀ-λήθεια) is removing a veil, making un-hidden. The hearer must also experience this uncovering if he is to accept the description as true.

truth. Atheism or theism is just such an objective uncertainty. To choose either to be true is a leap of faith in which one becomes the truth of that choice. But there is always the doubt that one may be objectively wrong. But choose we must! For not to choose is itself a choice! Tillich develops these points in his notion of faith as "ultimate concern."

Existentialists further describe man in terms of two modes of being, authentic or inauthentic. Heidegger speaks of "inauthentic" existence as one in which a person flees from the responsibility for his own being into the mediocrity of the average, or by seeing himself as a universal rather than a particular [5] Tillich sees inauthentic existence as being estranged from God, world, others, and self. He sees authentic existence as living under the conditions of existence without estrangement. Authentic existence (new being) is living in love (overcoming estrangement), faith (grasp by the ground of being), courage (overcoming the threats of nonbeing), and so on. Camus sees authentic existence as living without appeal or hope in accepting the absurdity of existence. Only then is one free for the now and for humanity. While the details differ, they all agree that persons are either inauthentic or authentic.[6]

In the essays that follow I have selected two issues for consideration. The first issues deals with the meaning of existence with or without God. The atheistic existentialists (in this case, Sartre and Camus) claim that if God exists, man is robbed of his autonomy, dignity, and worth. If God exists, man is not free to create his own essence and his worth or dignity is judged in terms of this Perfect Being. As long as God exists man has an inferiority complex. But if God is dead, does everything then become possible? When God dies does man also die? No! say Sartre and Camus. Although it is true that God's death is a shock to man, it can provide the occasion for a new man to arise; for Sartre, a truly free man, and for Camus, the secular saint.

Sartre argues that man's freedom must be preserved at all costs. Man chooses who he is to become, for himself *and* for humanity. There is no God who gives man some essence that he simply fills out. Camus argues that our desire for an answer to the meaning of existence ends in dead silence. We must learn to live with this cosmic silence (no answer from God) by refusing any illusions (hopes); live in the lucid awareness of the absurdity of existence. This is the dignity and honesty of the authentic man: to know *and* accept absurdity. The struggle itself is enough to fill a man's heart as we see in Sisyphus, the secular saint.[7]

Although Sartre and Camus find man *thrust* into a world devoid of God and condemned to create what he is to become, others find that man does not fully exist without there being a God. When God dies, man dies.

[5] For example, the difference between saying, "All men must die," and, "I will die."
[6] Existentialism is not completed in a *description* of the modes of existence. It is also a call to *be* authentic.
[7] Camus does not stop here. For a description of the life-style he recommends, see *The Rebel* (New York: Random House), 1956.

Tillich argues that only God who is beyond the ambiguities of existence can ground our courage to be in the face of the ever-present threat of nonbeing. Man can overcome anxiety caused by 1) fate and death, 2) emptiness and meaninglessness, 3) guilt and self-condemnation, only as a gift from the Ground of Being, God. Buber, in his own way, agrees. Man is not fully human without the I-Thou dimension, without relationship with the Eternal Thou, God.

The second issue I've selected for this chapter is the cognitive problem. How do we check religious truth-claims? How do we determine what descriptions are appropriate for the object of faith, God. Tillich argues that all talk about God must be symbolic. Buber argues that our knowledge of God is analogous to I-Thou encounters. What is an I-Thou encounter? Are no checks possible? Hepburn and Edwards raise these issues.[8]

Appropriately, existentialism leaves us with a choice.[9] Is the humanism of Sartre or Camus what we must accept if we are to preserve our freedom? Or is the threat of anxiety overcome in God, the Ground of all that is? Either way the choice is a cruel and long-range affair. No man has seen God. We are all struggling in the darkness to live well. "The choice must be hard either way; for man, a problematic being to his depth, cannot lay hold of his ultimate commitments with smug and easy security." [10]

EXISTENTIALISM AS A HUMANISM

Jean-Paul Sartre

JEAN-PAUL SARTRE, a French thinker and writer, is a leading exponent of contemporary atheistic existentialism. In 1964 he was awarded the Nobel prize for literature, which he declined. His major philosophical work is *Being and Nothingness* (1956).

. . . there are two kinds of existentialist; first, those who are Christian, among whom I would include Jaspers and Gabriel Marcel, both Catholic; and on the other hand the atheistic existentialists, among whom I class Heidegger, and then the French existentialists and myself. What they have in common is that they think that existence precedes essence, or, if you prefer, that subjectivity must be the starting point.

Just what does that mean? Let us consider some object that is manu-

[8] The cognitive issue is central to Chapter Four. The claims of Buber and Tillich should be reviewed with that analytic material in mind.
[9] William Barrett, *Irrational Man* (Garden City: Doubleday & Co., 1958), p. 263. Chapter Five contains more material on the atheistic standpoint.
[10] Ibid. Existentialism not only describes what *is* the case, but recommends what *ought* to be the case.

factured, for example, a book or a paper-cutter: here is an object which has been made by an artisan whose inspiration came from a concept. He referred to the concept of what a paper-cutter is and likewise to a known method of production, which is part of the concept, something which is, by and large, a routine. Thus, the paper-cutter is at once an object produced in a certain way and, on the other hand, one having a specific use; and one can not postulate a man who produces a paper-cutter but does not know what it is used for. Therefore, let us say that, for the paper-cutter, essence—that is, the ensemble of both the production routines and the properties which enable it to be both produced and defined—precedes existence. Thus, the presence of the paper-cutter or book in front of me is determined. Therefore, we have here a technical view of the world whereby it can be said that production precedes existence.

When we conceive God as the Creator, He is generally thought of as a superior sort of artisan. Whatever doctrine we may be considering, whether one like that of Descartes or that of Leibnitz, we always grant that will more or less follows understanding or, at the very least, accompanies it, and that when God creates He knows exactly what He is creating. Thus, the concept of man in the mind of God is comparable to the concept of paper-cutter in the mind of the manufacturer, and, following certain techniques and a conception, God produces man, just as the artisan, following a definition and a technique, makes a paper-cutter. Thus, the individual man is the realization of a certain concept in the divine intelligence.

In the eighteenth century, the atheism of the *philosophes* discarded the idea of God, but not so much for the notion that essence precedes existence. To a certain extent, this idea is found everywhere; we find it in Diderot, in Voltaire, and even in Kant. Man has a human nature; this human nature, which is the concept of the human, is found in all men, which means that each man is a particular example of a universal concept, man. In Kant, the result of this universality is that the wild-man, the natural man, as well the bourgeois, are circumscribed by the same definition and have the same basic qualities. Thus, here too the essence of man precedes the historical existence that we find in nature.

Atheistic existentialism, which I represent, is more coherent. It states that if God does not exist, there is at least one being in whom existence precedes essence, a being who exists before he can be defined by any concept, and that this being is man, or, as Heidegger says, human reality. What is meant here by saying that existence precedes essence? It means that, first of all, man exists, turns up, appears on the scene, and, only afterwards, defines himself. If man, as the existentialist conceives him, is indefinable, it is because at first he is nothing. Only afterward will he be something, and he himself will have made what he will be. Thus, there is no human nature, since there is no God to conceive it. Not only is man what he conceives himself to be, but he is also only what he wills himself to be after this thrust toward existence.

Man is nothing else but what he makes of himself. Such is the first principle of existentialism. It is also what is called subjectivity, the name we are labeled with when charges are brought against us. But what do we mean by this, if not that man has a greater dignity than a stone or table? For we mean that man first exists, that is, that man first of all is the being who hurls himself toward a future and who is conscious of imagining himself as being in the future. Man is at the start a plan which is aware of itself, rather than a patch of moss, a piece of garbage, or a cauliflower; nothing exists prior to this plan; there is nothing in heaven; man will be what he will have planned to be. Not what he will want to be. Because by the word "will" we generally mean a conscious decision, which is subsequent to what we have already made of ourselves. I may want to belong to a political party, write a book, get married; but all that is only a manifestation of an earlier, more spontaneous choice that is called "will." But if existence really does precede essence, man is responsible for what he is. Thus, existentialism's first move is to make every man aware of what he is and to make the full responsibility of his existence rest on him. And when we say that a man is responsible for himself, we do not only mean that he is responsible for his own individuality, but that he is responsible for all men.

The word subjectivism has two meanings, and our opponents play on the two. Subjectivism means, on the one hand, that an individual chooses and makes himself; and, on the other, that it is impossible for man to transcend human subjectivity. The second of these is the essential meaning of existentialism. When we say that man chooses his own self, we mean that every one of us does likewise; but we also mean by that that in making this choice he also chooses all men. In fact, in creating the man that we want to be, there is not a single one of our acts which does not at the same time create an image of man as we think he ought to be. To choose to be this or that is to affirm at the same time the value of what we choose, because we can never choose evil. We always choose the good, and nothing can be good for us without being good for all.

If, on the other hand, existence precedes essence, and if we grant that we exist and fashion our image at one and the same time, the image is valid for everybody and for our whole age. Thus, our responsibility is much greater than we might have supposed, because it involves all mankind. If I am a workingman and choose to join a Christian trade-union rather than be a communist, and if by being a member I want to show that the best thing for man is resignation, that the kingdom of man is not of this world, I am not only involving my own case—I want to be resigned for everyone. As a result, my action has involved all humanity. To take a more individual matter, if I want to marry, to have children; even if this marriage depends solely on my own circumstances or passion or wish, I am involving all humanity in monogamy and not merely myself. Therefore, I am responsible for myself and for everyone else. I am

creating a certain image of man of my own choosing. In choosing myself,
I choose man.

This helps us understand what the actual content is of such rather
grandiloquent words as anguish, forlornness, despair. As you will see, it's
all quite simple.

First, what is meant by anguish? The existentialists say at once that
man is anguish. What that means is this: the man who involves himself
and who realizes that he is not only the person he chooses to be, but also
a lawmaker who is, at the same time, choosing all mankind as well as
himself, can not help escape the feeling of his total and deep responsibility. Of course, there are many people who are not anxious; but we
claim that they are hiding their anxiety, that they are fleeing from it.
Certainly, many people believe that when they do something, they themselves are the only ones involved, and when someone says to them, "What
if everyone acted that way?" they shrug their shoulders and answer,
"Everyone doesn't act that way." But really, one should always ask
himself, "What would happen if everybody looked at things that way?"
There is no escaping this disturbing thought except by a kind of double-
dealing. A man who lies and makes excuses for himself by saying "not
everybody does that," is someone with an uneasy conscience, because the
act of lying implies that a universal value is conferred upon the lie.

Anguish is evident even when it conceals itself. This is the anguish
that Kierkegaard called the anguish of Abraham. You know the story:
an angel has ordered Abraham to sacrifice his son; if it really were an
angel who has come and said, "You are Abraham, you shall sacrifice
your son," everything would be all right. But everyone might first
wonder, "Is it really an angel, and am I really Abraham? What proof do
I have?"

There was a madwoman who had hallucinations; someone used to
speak to her on the telephone and give her orders. Her doctor asked her,
"Who is it who talks to you?" She answered, "He says it's God." What
proof did she really have that it was God? If an angel comes to me,
what proof is there that it's an angel? And if I hear voices, what proof
is there that they come from heaven and not from hell, or from the subconscious, or a pathological condition? What proves that they are addressed to me? What proof is there that I have been appointed to impose
my choice and my conception of man on humanity? I'll never find any
proof or sign to convince me of that. If a voice addresses me, it is always
for me to decide that this is the angel's voice; if I consider that such an act
is a good one, it is I who will choose to say that it is good rather than bad.

Now, I'm not being singled out as an Abraham, and yet at every moment I'm obliged to perform exemplary acts. For every man, everything
happens as if all mankind had its eyes fixed on him and were guiding
itself by what he does. And every man ought to say to himself, "Am I
really the kind of man who has the right to act in such a way that hu-

manity might guide itself by my actions?" And if he does not say that to himself, he is masking his anguish.

There is no question here of the kind of anguish which would lead to quietism, to inaction. It is a matter of a simple sort of anguish that anybody who has had responsibilities is familiar with. For example, when a military officer takes the responsibility for an attack and sends a certain number of men to death, he chooses to do so, and in the main he alone makes the choice. Doubtless, orders come from above, but they are too broad; he interprets them, and on this interpretation depend the lives of ten or fourteen or twenty men. In making a decision he can not help having a certain anguish. All leaders know this anguish. That doesn't keep them from acting; on the contrary, it is the very condition of their action. For it implies that they envisage a number of possibilities, and when they choose one, they realize that it has value only because it is chosen. We shall see that this kind of anguish, which is the kind that existentialism describes, is explained, in addition, by a direct responsibility to the other men whom it involves. It is not a curtain separating us from action, but is part of action itself.

When we speak of forlornness, a term Heidegger was fond of, we mean only that God does not exist and that we have to face all the consequences of this. The existentialist is strongly opposed to a certain kind of secular ethics which would like to abolish God with the least possible expense. About 1880, some French teachers tried to set up a secular ethics which went something like this: God is a useless and costly hypothesis; we are discarding it; but, meanwhile, in order for there to be an ethics, a society, a civilization, it is essential that certain values be taken seriously and that they be considered as having an *a priori* existence. It must be obligatory, *a priori,* to be honest, not to lie, not to beat your wife, to have children, etc., etc. So we're going to try a little device which will make it possible to show that values exist all the same, inscribed in a heaven of ideas, though otherwise God does not exist. In other words—and this, I believe, is the tendency of everything called reformism in France—nothing will be changed if God does not exist. We shall find ourselves with the same norms of honesty, progress, and humanism, and we shall have made of God an outdated hypothesis which will peacefully die off by itself.

The existentialist, on the contrary, thinks it very distressing that God does not exist, because all possibility of finding values in a heaven of ideas disappears along with Him; there can no longer be an *a priori* Good, since there is no infinite and perfect consciousness to think it. Nowhere is it written that the Good exists, that we must be honest, that we must not lie; because the fact is we are on a plane where there are only men. Dostoievsky said, "If God didn't exist, everything would be possible." That is the very starting point of existentialism. Indeed, everything is permissible if God does not exist, and as a result man

is forlorn, because neither within him nor without does he find anything
to cling to. He can't start making excuses for himself.

If existence really does precede essence, there is no explaining things
away by reference to a fixed and given human nature. In other words,
there is no determinism, man is free, man is freedom. On the other
hand, if God does not exist, we find no values or commands to turn to
which legitimize our conduct. So, in the bright realm of values, we have
no excuse behind us, nor justification before us. We are alone, with no
excuses.

That is the idea I shall try to convey when I say that man is condemned to be free. Condemned, because he did not create himself, yet,
in other respects is free; because, once thrown into the world, he is
responsible for everything he does. The existentialist does not believe
in the power of passion. He will never agree that a sweeping passion is a
ravaging torrent which fatally leads a man to certain acts and is therefore an excuse. He thinks that man is responsible for his passion.

The existentialist does not think that man is going to help himself by
finding in the world some omen by which to orient himself. Because he
thinks that man will interpret the omen to suit himself. Therefore, he
thinks that man, with no support and no aid, is condemned every moment to invent man. Ponge, in a very fine article, has said, "Man is
the future of man." That's exactly it. But if it is taken to mean that this
future is recorded in heaven, that God sees it, then it is false, because it
would really no longer be a future. If it is taken to mean that, whatever
a man may be, there is a future to be forged, a virgin future before him,
then this remark is sound. But then we are forlorn.

To give you an example which will enable you to understand forlornness better, I shall cite the case of one of my students who came to see
me under the following circumstances: his father was on bad terms with
his mother, and, moreover, was inclined to be a collaborationist; his
older brother had been killed in the German offensive of 1940, and the
young man, with somewhat immature but generous feelings, wanted to
avenge him. His mother lived alone with him, very much upset by the
half-treason of her husband and the death of her older son; the boy was
her only consolation.

The boy was faced with the choice of leaving for England and joining
the Free French Forces—that is, leaving his mother behind—or remaining with his mother and helping her to carry on. He was fully aware
that the woman lived only for him and that his going off—and perhaps
his death—would plunge her into despair. He was also aware that every
act that he did for his mother's sake was a sure thing, in the sense that
it was helping her to carry on, whereas every effort he made toward
going off and fighting was an uncertain move which might run aground
and prove completely useless; for example, on his way to England he
might, while passing through Spain, be detained indefinitely in a Spanish

camp; he might reach England or Algiers and be stuck in an office at a desk job. As a result, he was faced with two very different kinds of action: one, concrete, immediate, but concerning only one individual; the other concerned an incomparably vaster group, a national collectivity, but for that very reason was dubious, and might be interrupted en route. And, at the same time, he was wavering between two kinds of ethics. On the one hand, an ethics of sympathy, of personal devotion; on the other, a broader ethics, but one whose efficacy was more dubious. He had to choose between the two.

Who could help him choose? Christian doctrine? No. Christian doctrine says, "Be charitable, love your neighbor, take the more rugged path, etc., etc." But which is the more rugged path? Whom should he love as a brother? The fighting man or his mother? Which does the greater good, the vague act of fighting in a group, or the concrete one of helping a particular human being to go on living? Who can decide a priori? Nobody. No book of ethics can tell him. The Kantian ethics says, "Never treat any person as a means, but as an end." Very well, if I stay with my mother, I'll treat her as an end and not as a means; but by virtue of this very fact, I'm running the risk of treating the people around me who are fighting, as means; and, conversely, if I go to join those who are fighting, I'll be treating them as an end, and, by doing that, I run the risk of treating my mother as a means.

If values are vague, and if they are always too broad for the concrete and specific case that we are considering, the only thing left for us is to trust our instincts. That's what this young man tried to do; and when I saw him, he said, "In the end, feeling is what counts. I ought to choose whichever pushes me in one direction. If I feel that I love my mother enough to sacrifice everything else for her—my desire for vengeance, for action, for adventure—then I'll stay with her. If, on the contrary, I feel that my love for my mother isn't enough, I'll leave."

But how is the value of a feeling determined? What gives his feeling for his mother value? Precisely the fact that he remained with her. I may say that I like so-and-so well enough to sacrifice a certain amount of money for him, but I may say so only if I've done it. I may say "I love my mother well enough to remain with her" if I have remained with her. The only way to determine the value of this affection is, precisely, to perform an act which confirms and defines it. But, since I require this affection to justify my act, I find myself caught in a vicious circle.

On the other hand, Gide has well said that a mock feeling and a true feeling are almost indistinguishable; to decide that I love my mother and will remain with her, or to remain with her by putting on an act, amounts somewhat to the same thing. In other words, the feeling is formed by the acts one performs; so, I can not refer to it in order to act upon it. Which means that I can neither seek within myself the true condition which will impel me to act, nor apply to a system of ethics for concepts which will permit me to act. You will say, "At least, he did go to a teacher for advice." But if you seek advice from a priest, for example, you have chosen this priest; you already know, more or less, just about what advice he was going to give you. In other words, choosing your adviser is involving yourself. The proof of this is that if you are a Christian, you will say, "Consult a priest." But some priests are collaborating, some are just marking time, some are resisting. Which to choose? If the young man chooses a priest who is resisting or collaborating, he has already decided on the kind of advice he's going to get. Therefore, in coming to see me he knew the answer I was going to give him, and I had only one answer to give: "You're free, choose, that is, invent." No general ethics can show you what is to be done; there are no omens in the world. The Catholics will reply, "But there are." Granted—but, in any case, I myself choose the meaning they have.

When I was a prisoner, I knew a rather remarkable young man who was a Jesuit. He had entered the Jesuit order in the following way: he had had a number of very bad breaks; in childhood, his father died, leaving him in poverty, and he was a scholarship student at a religious institution where he was constantly made to feel that he was being kept out of charity; then, he failed to get any of the honors and distinctions that children like; later on, at about eighteen, he bungled a love affair; finally, at twenty-two, he failed in military training, a childish enough matter, but it was the last straw.

This young fellow might well have felt that he had botched everything. It was a sign of something, but of what? He might have taken refuge in bitterness or despair. But he very wisely looked upon all this as a sign that he was not made for secular triumphs, and that only the triumphs of religion, holiness, and faith were open to him. He saw the hand of God in all this, and so he entered the order. Who can help seeing that he alone decided what the sign meant?

Some other interpretation might have been drawn from this series of setbacks; for example, that he might have done better to turn carpenter or revolutionist. Therefore, he is fully responsible for the interpretation. Forlornness implies that we ourselves choose our being. Forlornness and anguish go together.

As for despair, the term has a very simple meaning. It means that we shall confine ourselves to reckoning only with what depends upon our will, or on the ensemble of probabilities which make our action possible. When we want something, we always have to reckon with probabilities. I may be counting on the arrival of a friend. The friend is coming by rail or street-car; this supposes that the train will arrive on schedule, or that the street-car will not jump the track. I am left in the realm of possibility; but possibilities are to be reckoned with only to the point where my action comports with the ensemble of these possibilities, and no further. The moment the possibilities I am considering are not rigorously involved by my action, I ought to disengage myself from them, because no God, no scheme, can adapt the world and its possibilities to my will. When Descartes said, "Conquer yourself rather than the world," he meant essentially the same thing.

. . . .

Actually, things will be as man will have decided they are to be. Does that mean that I should abandon myself to quietism? No. First, I should involve myself; then, act on the old saw, "Nothing ventured, nothing gained." Nor does it mean that I shouldn't belong to a party, but rather that I shall have no illusions and shall do what I can. For example. suppose I ask myself, "Will socialization, as such, ever come about?" I know nothing about it. All I know is that I'm going to do everything in my power to bring it about. Beyond that, I can't count on anything. Quietism is the attitude of people who say, "Let others do what I can't do." The doctrine I am presenting is the very opposite of quietism, since it declares, "There is no reality except in action." Moreover, it goes further, since it adds, "Man is nothing else than his plan; he exists only to the extent that he fulfills himself; he is therefore nothing else than the ensemble of his acts, nothing else than his life."

According to this, we can understand why our doctrine horrifies certain people. Because often the only way they can bear their wretchedness is to think, "Circumstances have been against me. What I've been and done doesn't show my true worth. To be sure, I've had no great love, no great friendship, but that's because I haven't met a man or woman who was worthy. The books I've written haven't been very good because I haven't had the proper leisure. I haven't had children to devote myself to because I didn't find a man with whom I could have spent my life. So there remains within me, unused and quite viable, a host of propensities, inclinations, possiblities, that one wouldn't guess from the mere series of things I've done."

Now, for the existentialist there is really no love other than one which manifests itself in a person's being in love. There is no genius other than one which is expressed in works of art; the genius of Proust is the sum of Proust's works; the genius of Racine is his series of tragedies. Outside of that, there is nothing. Why say that Racine could have written another tragedy, when he didn't write it? A man is involved in life, leaves his impress on it, and outside of that there is nothing. To be sure, this may seem a harsh thought to someone whose life hasn't been a success. But, on the other hand, it prompts people to understand that reality alone is what counts, that dreams, expectations, and hopes warrant no more than to define a man as a disappointed dream, as miscarried hopes, as vain expectations. In other words, to define him negatively and not positively. However, when we say, "You are nothing else than your life," that does not imply that the artist will be judged solely on the basis of his works of art; a thousand other things will contribute toward summing him up. What we mean is that a man is nothing else than a series of undertakings, that he is the sum, the or-

ganization, the ensemble of the relationships which make up these
undertakings

When all is said and done, what we are accused of, at bottom, is not
our pessimism, but an optimistic toughness. If people throw up to us
our works of fiction in which we write about people who are soft, weak,
cowardly, and sometimes even downright bad, it's not because these
people are soft, weak, cowardly, or bad; because if we were to say, as
Zola did, that they are that way because of heredity, the workings of
environment, society, because of biological or psychological determinism, people would be reassured. They would say, "Well, that's what
we're like, no one can do anything about it." But when the existentialist
writes about a coward, he says that this coward is responsible for his
cowardice. He's not like that because he has a cowardly heart or lung
or brain; he's not like that on account of his physiological make-up; but
he's like that because he has made himself a coward by his acts. There's
no such thing as a cowardly constitution; there are nervous constitutions;
there is poor blood, as the common people say, or strong constitutions.
But the man whose blood is poor is not a coward on that account, for
what makes cowardice is the act of renouncing or yielding. A constitution is not an act; the coward is defined on the basis of the acts he performs. People feel, in a vague sort of way, that this coward we're talking
about is guilty of being a coward, and the thought frightens them.
What people would like is that a coward or a hero be born that way.

One of the complaints most frequently made about *The Ways of
Freedom* * can be summed up as follows: "After all, these people are
so spineless, how are you going to make heroes out of them?" This objection almost makes me laugh, for it assumes that people are born
heroes. That's what people really want to think. If you're born cowardly,
you may set your mind perfectly at rest; there's nothing you can do
about it; you'll be cowardly all your life, whatever you may do. If you're
born a hero, you may set your mind just as much at rest; you'll be a hero
all your life; you'll drink like a hero and eat like a hero. What the
existentialist says is that the coward makes himself cowardly, that the
hero makes himself heroic. There's always a possibility for the coward not
to be cowardly any more and for the hero to stop being heroic. What
counts is total involvement; some one particular action or set of circumstances is not total involvement.

Thus, I think we have answered a number of the charges concerning
existentialism. You see that it can not be taken for a philosophy of quietism, since it defines man in terms of action; nor for a pessimistic description of man—there is no doctrine more optimistic, since man's destiny
is within himself; nor for an attempt to discourage man from acting,

* *Les Chemins de la Liberté*, M. Sartre's projected trilogy of novels, two of which,
L'Age de Raison (*The Age of Reason*) and *Le Sursis* (*The Reprieve*) have already
appeared.—Translator's note.

since it tells him that the only hope is in his acting and that action is
the only thing that enables a man to live. Consequently, we are dealing
here with an ethics of action and involvement.

Nevertheless, on the basis of a few notions like these, we are still
charged with immuring man in his private subjectivity. There again
we're very much misunderstood. Subjectivity of the individual is indeed
our point of departure, and this for strictly philosophic reasons. Not
because we are bourgeois, but because we want a doctrine based on
truth and not a lot of fine theories, full of hope but with no real basis.
There can be no other truth to take off from than this: *I think; therefore,
I exist*. There we have the absolute truth of consciousness becoming
aware of itself. Every theory which takes man out of the moment in
which he becomes aware of himself is, at its very beginning, a theory
which confounds truth, for outside the Cartesian *cogito*, all views are
only probable, and a doctrine of probability which is not bound to a
truth dissolves into thin air. In order to describe the probable, you must
have a firm hold on the true. Therefore, before there can be any truth
whatsoever, there must be an absolute truth; and this one is simple and
easily arrived at; it's on everyone's doorstep; it's a matter of grasping
it directly.

Secondly, this theory is the only one which gives man dignity, the
only one which does not reduce him to an object. The effect of all
materialism is to treat all men, including the one philosophizing, as objects, that is, as an ensemble of determined reactions in no way distinguished from the ensemble of qualities and phenomena which constitute
a table or a chair or a stone. We definitely wish to establish the human
realm as an ensemble of values distinct from the material realm. But
the subjectivity that we have thus arrived at, and which we have claimed
to be truth, is not a strictly individual subjectivity, for we have demonstrated that one discovers in the *cogito* not only himself, but others
as well.

The philosophies of Descartes and Kant to the contrary, through the
I think we reach our own self in the presence of others, and the others
are just as real to us as our own self. Thus, the man who becomes aware
of himself through the *cogito* also perceives all others, and he perceives
them as the condition of his own existence. He realizes that he can not
be anything (in the sense that we say that someone is witty or nasty or
jealous) unless others recognize it as such. In order to get any truth
about myself, I must have contact with another person. The other is
indispensable to my own existence, as well as to my knowledge about
myself. This being so, in discovering my inner being I discover the other
person at the same time, like a freedom placed in front of me which
thinks and wills only for or against me. Hence, let us at once announce
the discovery of a world which we shall call intersubjectivity; this is the
world in which man decides what he is and what others are.

Besides, if it is impossible to find in every man some universal essence which would be human nature, yet there does exist a universal human condition. It's not by chance that today's thinkers speak more readily of man's condition than of his nature. By condition they mean, more or less definitely, the *a priori* limits which outline man's fundamental situation in the universe. Historical situations vary; a man may be born a slave in a pagan society or a feudal lord or a proletarian. What does not vary is the necessity for him to exist in the world, to be at work there, to be there in the midst of other people, and to be mortal there. The limits are neither subjective nor objective, or, rather, they have an objective and a subjective side. Objective because they are to be found everywhere and are recognizable everywhere; subjective because they are *lived* and are nothing if man does not live them, that is, freely determine his existence with reference to them. And though the configurations may differ, at least none of them are completely strange to me, because they all appear as attempts either to pass beyond these limits or recede from them or deny them or adapt to them. Consequently, every configuration, however individual it may be, has a universal value.

.   .   .   .

In this sense we may say that there is a universality of man, but it is not given, it is perpetually being made. I build the universal in choosing myself; I build it in understanding the configuration of every other man, whatever age he might have lived in. This absoluteness of choice does not do away with the relativeness of each epoch. At heart, what existentialism shows is the connection between the absolute character of free involvement, by virtue of which every man realizes himself in realizing a type of mankind, an involvement always comprehensible in any age whatsoever and by any person whosoever, and the relativeness of the cultural ensemble which may result from such a choice; it must be stressed that the relativity of Cartesianism and the absolute character of Cartesian involvement go together. In this sense, you may, if you like, say that each of us performs an absolute act in breathing, eating, sleeping, or behaving in any way whatever. There is no difference between being free, like a configuration, like an existence which chooses its essence, and being absolute. There is no difference between being an absolute temporarily localized, that is, localized in history, and being universally comprehensible.

This does not entirely settle the objection to subjectivism. In fact, the objection still takes several forms. First, there is the following: we are told, "So you're able to do anything, no matter what!" This is expressed in various ways. First we are accused of anarchy; then they say, "You're unable to pass judgment on others, because there's no reason to prefer one configuration to another"; finally they tell us, "Everything is arbitrary in this choosing of yours. You take something from one pocket and pretend you're putting it into the other."

These three objections aren't very serious. Take the first objection. "You're able to do anything, no matter what" is not to the point. In one sense choice is possible, but what is not possible is not to choose. I can always choose, but I ought to know that if I do not choose, I am still choosing. Though this may seem purely formal, it is highly important for keeping fantasy and caprice within bounds. If it is true that in facing a situation, for example, one in which, as a person capable of having sexual relations, of having children, I am obliged to choose an attitude, and if I in any way assume responsibility for a choice which, in involving myself, also involves all mankind, this has nothing to do with caprice, even if no *a priori* value determines my choice.

If anybody thinks that he recognizes here Gide's theory of the arbitrary act, he fails to see the enormous difference between this doctrine and Gide's. Gide does not know what a situation is. He acts out of pure caprice. For us, on the contrary, man is an organized situation in which he himself is involved. Through his choice, he involves all mankind, and he can not avoid making a choice: either he will remain chaste, or he will marry without having children, or he will marry and have children; anyhow, whatever he may do, it is impossible for him not to take full responsibility for the way he handles this problem. Doubtless, he chooses without referring to pre-established values, but it is unfair to accuse him of caprice. Instead, let us say that moral choice is to be compared to the making of a work of art. And before going any further, let it be said at once that we are not dealing here with an aesthetic ethics, because our opponents are so dishonest that they even accuse us of that. The example I've chosen is a comparison only.

Having said that, may I ask whether anyone has ever accused an artist who has painted a picture of not having drawn his inspiration from rules set up *a priori*? Has anyone ever asked, "What painting ought he to make?" It is clearly understood that there is no definite painting to be made, that the artist is engaged in the making of his painting, and that the painting to be made is precisely the painting he will have made. It is clearly understood that there are no *a priori* aesthetic values, but that there are values which appear subsequently in the coherence of the painting, in the correspondence between what the artist intended and the result. Nobody can tell what the painting of tomorrow will be like. Painting can be judged only after it has once been made. What connection does that have with ethics? We are in the same creative situation. We never say that a work of art is arbitrary. When we speak of a canvas of Picasso, we never say that it is arbitrary; we understand quite well that he was making himself what he is at the very time he was painting, that the ensemble of his work is embodied in his life.

The same holds on the ethical plane. What art and ethics have in common is that we have creation and invention in both cases. We can not decide *a priori* what there is to be done. I think that I pointed that out quite sufficiently when I mentioned the case of the student who came to see me, and who might have applied to all the ethical systems, Kantian or otherwise, without getting any sort of guidance. He was obliged to devise his law himself. Never let it be said by us that this man—who, taking affection, individual action, and kind-heartedness toward a specific person as his ethical first principle, chooses to remain with his mother, or who, preferring to make a sacrifice, chooses to go to England—has made an arbitrary choice. Man makes himself. He isn't ready made at the start. In choosing his ethics, he makes himself, and force of circumstances is such that he can not abstain from choosing one. We define man only in relationship to involvement. It is therefore absurd to charge us·with arbitrariness of choice.

In the second place, it is said that we are unable to pass judgment on others. In a way this is true, and in another way, false. It is true in this sense, that, whenever a man sanely and sincerely involves himself and chooses his configuration, it is impossible for him to prefer another configuration, regardless of what his own may be in other respects. It is true in this sense, that we do not believe in progress. Progress is better-ment. Man is always the same. The situation confronting him varies. Choice always remains a choice in a situation. The problem has not changed since the time one could choose between those for and those against slavery, for example, at the time of the Civil War, and the present time, when one can side with the Maquis Resistance Party, or with the Communists.

But, nevertheless, one can still pass judgment, for, as I have said, one makes a choice in relationship to others. First, one can judge (and this is perhaps not a judgment of value, but a logical judgment) that certain choices are based on error and others on truth. If we have defined man's situation as a free choice, with no excuses and no recourse, every man who takes refuge behind the excuse of his passions, every man who sets up a determinism, is a dishonest man.

The objection may be raised, "But why mayn't he choose himself dishonestly?" I reply that I am not obliged to pass moral judgment on him, but that I do define his dishonesty as an error. One can not help considering the truth of the matter. Dishonesty is obviously a falsehood because it belies the complete freedom of involvement. On the same grounds, I maintain that there is also dishonesty if I choose to state that certain values exist prior to me; it is self-contradictory for me to want them and at the same state that they are imposed on me. Suppose some-one says to me, "What if I want to be dishonest?" I'll answer, "There's no reason for you not to be, but I'm saying that that's what you are, and that the strictly coherent attitude is that of honesty."

Besides, I can bring moral judgment to bear. When I declare that freedom in every concrete circumstance can have no other aim than to want itself, if man has once become aware that in his forlornness he imposes values, he can no longer want but one thing, and that is free-dom, as the basis of all values. That doesn't mean that he wants it in the abstract. It means simply that the ultimate meaning of the acts of honest men is the quest for freedom as such. A man who belongs to a communist or revolutionary union wants concrete goals; these goals imply an abstract desire for freedom; but this freedom is wanted in something concrete. We want freedom for freedom's sake and in every particular circumstance. And in wanting freedom we discover that it depends entirely on the freedom of others, and that the freedom of others depends on ours. Of course, freedom as the definition of man does not depend on others, but as soon as there is involvement, I am obliged to want others to have freedom at the same time that I want my own freedom. I can take freedom as my goal only if I take that of others as a goal as well. Consequently, when, in all honesty, I've recognized that man is a being in whom existence precedes essence, that he is a free being who, in various circumstances, can want only his freedom, I have at the same time recognized that I can want only the freedom of others.

Therefore, in the name of this will for freedom, which freedom itself implies, I may pass judgment on those who seek to hide from themselves the complete arbitrariness and the complete freedom of their existence. Those who hide their complete freedom from themselves out of a spirit of seriousness or by means of deterministic excuses, I shall call cowards; those who try to show that their existence was necessary, when it is the very contingency of man's appearance on earth, I shall call stinkers. But cowards or stinkers can be judged only from a strictly unbiased point of view.

Therefore though the content of ethics is variable, a certain form of it is universal. Kant says that freedom desires both itself and the freedom of others. Granted. But he believes that the formal and the universal are enough to constitute an ethics. We, on the other hand, think that principles which are too abstract run aground in trying to decide action. Once again, take the case of the student. In the name of what, in the name of what great moral maxim do you think he could have decided, in perfect peace of mind, to abandon his mother or to stay with her? There is no way of judging. The content is always concrete and thereby unforeseeable; there is always the element of invention. The one thing that counts is knowing whether the inventing that has been done, has been done in the name of freedom.

For example, let us look at the following two cases. You will see to what extent they correspond, yet differ. Take *The Mill on the Floss*. We find a certain young girl, Maggie Tulliver, who is an embodiment of the value of passion and who is aware of it. She is in love with a young man, Stephen, who is engaged to an insignificant young girl. This Maggie Tulliver, instead of heedlessly preferring her own happiness, chooses, in the name of human solidarity, to sacrifice herself and give up the man she loves. On the other hand, Sanseverina, in *The Charterhouse of Parma*, believing that passion is man's true value, would say that a great love deserves sacrifices; that it is to be preferred to the banality of the conjugal love that would tie Stephen to the young ninny he had to marry. She would choose to sacrifice the girl and fulfill her happiness; and, as

Stendhal shows, she is even ready to sacrifice herself for the sake of passion, if this life demands it. Here we are in the presence of two strictly opposed moralities. I claim that they are much the same thing; in both cases what has been set up as the goal is freedom.

You can imagine two highly similar attitudes: one girl prefers to renounce her love out of resignation; another prefers to disregard the prior attachment of the man she loves out of sexual desire. On the surface these two actions resemble those we've just described. However, they are completely different. Sanseverina's attitude is much nearer that of Maggie Tulliver, one of heedless rapacity.

Thus, you see that the second charge is true and, at the same time, false. One may choose anything if it is on the grounds of free involvement.

The third objection is the following: "You take something from one pocket and put it into the other. That is, fundamentally, values aren't serious, since you choose them." My answer to this is that I'm quite vexed that that's the way it is; but if I've discarded God the Father, there has to be someone to invent values. You've got to take things as they are. Moreover, to say that we invent values means nothing else but this: life has no meaning *a priori*. Before you come alive, life is nothing; it's up to you to give it a meaning, and value is nothing else but the meaning that you choose. In that way, you see, there is a possibility of creating a human community.

I've been reproached for asking whether existentialism is humanistic. It's been said, "But you said in *Nausea* that the humanists were all wrong. You made fun of a certain kind of humanist. Why come back to it now?" Actually, the word humanism has two very different meanings. By humanism one can mean a theory which takes man as an end and as a higher value. Humanism in this sense can be found in Cocteau's tale *Around the World in Eighty Hours* when a character, because he is flying over some mountains in an airplane, declares, "Man is simply amazing." That means that I, who did not build the airplanes, shall personally benefit from these particular inventions, and that I, as man, shall personally consider myself responsible for, and honored by, acts of a few particular men. This would imply that we ascribe a value to man on the basis of the highest deeds of certain men. This humanism is absurd, because only the dog or the horse would be able to make such an overall judgment about man, which they are careful not to do, at least to my knowledge.

But it cannot be granted that a man may make a judgment about man. Existentialism spares him from any such judgment. The existentialist will never consider man as an end because he is always in the making. Nor should we believe that there is a mankind to which we might set up a cult in the manner of Auguste Comte. The cult of mankind ends in the self-enclosed humanism of Comte, and, let it be said, of fascism. This kind of humanism we can do without.

But there is another meaning of humanism. Fundamentally it is this:

man is constantly outside of himself; in projecting himself, in losing himself outside of himself, he makes for man's existing; and, on the other hand, it is by pursuing transcendent goals that he is able to exist; man, being this state of passing-beyond, and seizing upon things only as they bear upon this passing-beyond, is at the heart, at the center of this passing-beyond. There is no universe other than a human universe, the universe of human subjectivity. This connection between transcendency, as a constituent element of man—not in the sense that God is transcendent, but in the sense of passing beyond—and subjectivity, in the sense that man is not closed in on himself but is always present in a human universe, is what we call existentialism humanism. Humanism, because we remind man that there is no law-maker other than himself, and that in his forlornness he will decide by himself; because we point out that man will fulfill himself as man, not in turning toward himself, but in seeking outside of himself a goal which is just this liberation, just this particular fulfillment.

From these few reflections it is evident that nothing is more unjust than the objections that have been raised against us. Existentialism is nothing else than an attempt to draw all the consequences of a coherent atheistic position. It isn't trying to plunge man into despair at all. But if one calls every attitude of unbelief despair, like the Christians, then the word is not being used in its original sense. Existentialism isn't so atheistic that it wears itself out showing that God doesn't exist. Rather, it declares that even if God did exist, that would change nothing. There you've got our point of view. Not that we believe that God exists, but we think that the problem of His existence is not the issue. In this sense existentialism is optimistic, a doctrine of action, and it is plain dishonesty for Christians to make no distinction between their own despair and ours and then to call us despairing.

ABSURDITY AND THE MEANING OF LIFE

Albert Camus

ALBERT CAMUS was, with Sartre, one of the foremost existential thinkers. Before his death in 1960 he wrote many novels, plays, and essays for which he was awarded the Nobel prize for literature.

There is but one truly serious philosophical problem, and that is suicide. Judging whether life is or is not worth living amounts to answering the fundamental question of philosophy. All the rest—whether or not the world has three dimensions, whether the mind has nine or twelve categories—comes afterwards. . . .

A world that can be explained even with bad reasons is a familiar world. But, on the other hand, in a universe suddenly divested of illusions and lights, man feels an alien, a stranger. His exile is without remedy since he is deprived of the memory of a lost home or the hope of a promised land. This divorce between man and his life, the actor and his setting, is properly the feeling of absurdity. . . .

One must brush everything aside and go straight to the real problem. One kills oneself because life is not worth living, that is certainly a truth—yet an unfruitful one because it is a truism. But does that insult to existence, that flat denial in which it is plunged come from the fact that it has no meaning? Does its absurdity require one to escape it through hope or suicide—this is what must be clarified, hunted down, and lucidated while brushing aside all the rest. Does the Absurd dictate death? . . .

All great deeds and all great thoughts have a ridiculous beginning. Great works are often born on a streetcorner or in a restaurant's revolving door. So it is with absurdity. The absurd world more than others derives its nobility from that abject birth. In certain situations, replying "nothing" when asked what one is thinking about may be pretense in a man. Those who are loved are well aware of this. But if that reply is sincere, if it symbolizes that odd state of soul in which the void becomes eloquent, in which the chain of daily gestures is broken, in which the heart vainly seeks the link that will connect it again, then it is as it were the first sign of absurdity.

It happens that the stage sets collapse. Rising, streetcar, four hours in the office or the factory, meal, streetcar, four hours of work, meal, sleep, and Monday Tuesday Wednesday Thursday Friday and Saturday according to the same rhythm—this path is easily followed most of the time. But one day the "why" arises and everything begins in that weariness tinged with amazement. "Begins"—this is important. Weariness comes at the end of the acts of a mechanical life, but at the same time it inaugurates the impulse of consciousness. It awakens consciousness and provokes what follows. What follows is the gradual return into the chain or it is the definitive awakening. At the end of the awakening comes, in time, the consequence: suicide or recovery. In itself weariness has something sickening about it. Here, I must conclude that it is good. For everything begins with consciousness and nothing is worth anything except through it. There is nothing original about these remarks. But they are obvious; that is enough for a while, during a sketchy reconnaissance in the origins of the absurd. Mere "anxiety," as Heidegger says, is at the source of everything.

Likewise and during every day of an unillustrious life, time carries us. But a moment always comes when we have to carry it. We live on the future: "tomorrow," "later on," "when you have made your way," "you will understand when you are old enough." Such irrelevancies are wonderful, for, after all, it's a matter of dying. Yet a day comes when a man notices or says that he is thirty. Thus he asserts his youth. But simultaneously he situates himself in relation to time. He takes his place in it. He admits that he stands at a certain point on a curve that he acknowledges having to travel to its end. He belongs to time, and by the horror that seizes him, he recognizes his worst enemy. Tomorrow, he was longing for tomorrow, whereas everything in him ought to reject it. That revolt of the flesh is the absurd.[1]

A step lower and strangeness creeps in: perceiving that the world is "dense," sensing to what a degree a stone is foreign and irreducible to us, with what intensity nature or a landscape can negate us. At the heart of all beauty lies something inhuman, and these hills, the softness of the sky, the outline of these trees at this very minute lose the illusory meaning with which we had clothed them, henceforth more remote than a lost paradise. The primitive hostility of the world rises up to face us across millennia. For a second we cease to understand it because for centuries we have understood in it solely the images and designs that we had attributed to it beforehand, because henceforth we lack the power to make use of that artifice. The world evades us because it becomes itself again. That stage scenery masked by habit becomes again what it is. It withdraws at a distance from us. Just as there are days when under the familiar face of a woman, we see as a stranger her we had loved months or years ago, perhaps we shall come even to desire what suddenly leaves us so alone. But the time has not yet come. Just one thing: that denseness and that strangeness of the world is the absurd.

Men, too, secrete the inhuman. At certain moments of lucidity, the mechanical aspect of their gestures, their meaningless pantomime makes silly everything that surrounds them. A man is talking on the telephone behind a glass partition; you cannot hear him, but you see his incomprehensible dumb show: you wonder why he is alive. This discomfort in the face of man's own inhumanity, this incalculable tumble before the image of what we are, this "nausea," as a writer of today calls it, is also the absurd. Likewise the stranger who at certain seconds comes to meet us in a mirror, the familiar and yet alarming brother we encounter in our own photographs is also the absurd.

I come at last to death and to the attitude we have toward it. On this point everything has been said and it is only proper to avoid pathos. Yet one will never be sufficiently surprised that everyone lives as if no one "knew." This is because in reality there is no experience of death. Properly speaking, nothing has been experienced but what has been lived and made conscious. Here, it is barely possible to speak of the experience of others' deaths. It is a substitute, an illusion, and it never quite convinces us. That melancholy convention cannot be persuasive. The horror comes in reality from the mathematical aspect of the event. If time frightens us, this is because it works out the problem and the

---

[1] But not in the proper sense. This is not a definition, but rather an *enumeration* of the feelings that may admit of the absurd. Still, the enumeration finished, the absurd has nevertheless not been exhausted.

solution comes afterward. All the pretty speeches about the soul will have their contrary convincingly proved, at least for a time. From this inert body on which a slap makes no mark the soul has disappeared. This elementary and definitive aspect of the adventure constitutes the absurd feeling. Under the fatal lighting of that destiny, its uselessness becomes evident. No code of ethics and no effort are justifiable *a priori* in the face of the cruel mathematics that command our condition.

.   .   .   .

ABSURD FREEDOM

Now the main thing is done, I hold certain facts from which I cannot separate. What I know, what is certain, what I cannot deny, what I cannot reject—this is what counts. I can negate everything of that part of me that lives on vague nostalgias, except this desire for unity, this longing to solve, this need for clarity and cohesion. I can refute everything in this world surrounding me that offends or enraptures me, except this chaos, this sovereign chance and this divine equivalence which springs from anarchy. I don't know whether this world has a meaning that transcends it. But I know that I do not know that meaning and that it is impossible for me just now to know it. What can a meaning outside my condition mean to me? I can understand only in human terms. What I touch, what resists me—that is what I understand. And these two certainties—my appetite for the absolute and for unity and the impossibility of reducing this world to a rational and reasonable principle—I also know that I cannot reconcile them. What other truth can I admit without lying, without bringing in a hope I lack and which means nothing within the limits of my condition?

If I were a tree among trees, a cat among animals, this life would have a meaning, or rather this problem would not arise, for I should belong to this world. I should *be* this world to which I am now opposed by my whole consciousness and my whole insistence upon familiarity. This ridiculous reason is what sets me in opposition to all creation. I cannot cross it out with a stroke of the pen. What I believe to be true I must therefore preserve. What seems to me so obvious, even against me, I must support. And what constitutes the basis of that conflict, of that break between the world and my mind, but the awareness of it? If therefore I want to preserve it, I can through a constant awareness, ever revived, ever alert. This is what, for the moment, I must remember. At this moment the absurd, so obvious and yet so hard to win, returns to a man's life and finds its home there. At this moment, too, the mind can leave the arid, dried-up path of lucid effort. That path now emerges in daily life. It encounters the world of the anonymous impersonal pronoun "one," but henceforth man enters in with his revolt and his lucidity.

He has forgotten how to hope. This hell of the present is his Kingdom at last. All problems recover their sharp edge. Abstract evidence retreats before the poetry of forms and colors. Spiritual conflicts become embodied and return to the abject and magnificent shelter of man's heart. None of them is settled. But all are transfigured. Is one going to die, escape by the leap, rebuild a mansion of ideas and forms to one's own scale? Is one, on the contrary, going to take up the heart-rending and marvelous wager of the absurd? Let's make a final effort in this regard and draw all our conclusions. The body, affection, creation, action, human nobility will then resume their places in this mad world. At last man will again find there the wine of the absurd and the bread of indifference on which he feeds his greatness.

Let us insist again on the method: it is a matter of persisting. At a certain point on his path the absurd man is tempted. History is not lacking in either religions or prophets, even without gods. He is asked to leap. All he can reply is that he doesn't fully understand, that it is not obvious. Indeed, he does not want to do anything but what he fully understands. He is assured that this is the sin of pride, but he does not understand the notion of sin; that perhaps hell is in store, but he has not enough imagination to visualize that strange future; that he is losing immortal life, but that seems to him an idle consideration. An attempt is made to get him to admit his guilt. He feels innocent. To tell the truth, that is all he feels—his irreparable innocence. This is what allows him everything. Hence, what he demands of himself is to live *solely* with what he knows, to accommodate himself to what is, and to bring in nothing that is not certain. He is told that nothing is. But this at least is a certainty. And it is with this that he is concerned: he wants to find out if it is possible to live *without appeal*.

Now I can broach the notion of suicide. It has already been felt what solution might be given. At this point the problem is reversed. It was previously a question of finding out whether or not life had to have a meaning to be lived. It now becomes clear, on the contrary, that it will be lived all the better if it has no meaning. Living an experience, a particular fate, is accepting it fully. Now, no one will live this fate, knowing it to be absurd, unless he does everything to keep before him that absurd brought to light by consciousness. Negating one of the terms of the opposition on which he lives amounts to escaping it. To abolish conscious revolt is to elude the problem. The theme of permanent revolution is thus carried into individual experience. Living is keeping the absurd alive. Keeping it alive is, above all, contemplating it. Unlike Eurydice, the absurd dies only when we turn away from it. One of the only coherent philosophical positions is thus revolt. It is a constant confrontation between man and his own obscurity. It is an insistence upon an impossible transparency. It challenges the world anew every second. Just as danger provided man the unique opportunity of seizing awareness, so metaphysical revolt extends awareness to the whole of experience. It is that constant presence of man in his own eyes. It is not aspiration, for it is devoid of hope. That revolt is the certainty of a crushing fate, without the resignation that ought to accompany it.

This is where it is seen to what a degree absurd experience is remote from suicide. It may be thought that suicide follows revolt—but wrongly. For it does not represent the logical outcome of revolt. It is just the contrary by the consent it presupposes. Suicide, like the leap, is acceptance at its extreme. Everything is over and man returns to his essential history. His future, his unique and dreadful future—he sees and rushes toward it. In its way, suicide settles the absurd. It engulfs the absurd in the same death. But I know that in order to keep alive, the absurd cannot be settled. It escapes suicide to the extent that it is simultaneously awareness and rejection of death. It is, at the extreme limit of the condemned man's last thought, that shoelace that despite everything he sees a few yards away, on the very brink of his dizzying fall. The contrary of suicide, in fact, is the man condemned to death.

That revolt gives life its value. Spread out over the whole length of life, it restores its majesty to that life. To a man devoid of blinders, there is no finer sight than that of the intelligence at grips with a reality that transcends it. The sight of human pride is unequaled. No disparagement is of any use. That discipline that the mind imposes on itself, that will conjured up out of nothing, that face-to-face struggle have something exceptional about them. To impoverish that reality whose inhumanity constitutes man's majesty is tantamount to impoverishing him himself. I understand then why the doctrines that explain everything to me also debilitate me at the same time. They relieve me of the weight of my own life, and yet I must carry it alone. At this juncture, I cannot conceive that a skeptical metaphysics can be joined to an ethics of renunciation.

Consciousness and revolt, these rejections are the contrary of renunciation. Everything that is indomitable and passionate in a human heart quickens them, on the contrary, with its own life. It is essential to die unreconciled and not of one's own free will. Suicide is a repudiation. The absurd man can only drain everything to the bitter end, and deplete himself. The absurd is his extreme tension, which he maintains constantly by solitary effort, for he knows that in that consciousness and in that day-to-day revolt he gives proof of his only truth, which is defiance. This is a first consequence.

.   .   .   .

Losing oneself in that bottomless certainty, feeling henceforth sufficiently remote from one's own life to increase it and take a broad view of it—this involves the principle of a liberation. Such new independence has a definite time limit, like any freedom of action. It does not write a check on eternity. But it takes the place of the illusions of *freedom*, which all stopped with death. The divine availability of the condemned man before whom the prison doors open in a certain early dawn, that un-

believable disinterestedness with regard to everything except for the pure
flame of life—it is clear that death and the absurd are here the principles
of the only reasonable freedom: that which a human heart can experience
and live. This is a second consequence. The absurd man thus catches
sight of a burning and frigid, transparent and limited universe in which
nothing is possible but everything is given, and beyond which all is
collapse and nothingness. He can then decide to accept such a universe
and draw from it his strength, his refusal to hope, and the unyielding
evidence of a life without consolation.

But what does life mean in such a universe? Nothing else for the
moment but indifference to the future and a desire to use up everything
that is given. . . .

Knowing whether or not one can live *without appeal* is all that interests
me. I do not want to get out of my depth. This aspect of life being
given me, can I adapt myself to it? Now, faced with this particular
concern, belief in the absurd is tantamount to substituting the quantity
of experiences for the quality. If I convince myself that this life has no
other aspect than that of the absurd, if I feel that its whole equilibrium
depends on that perpetual opposition between my conscious revolt and
the darkness in which it struggles, if I admit that my freedom has no
meaning except in relation to its limited fate, then I must say that what
counts is not the best living but the most living. It is not up to me to wonder if this is vulgar or revolting, elegant or deplorable. Once and for all,
value judgments are discarded here in favor of factual judgments. I
have merely to draw the conclusions from what I can see and to risk
nothing that is hypothetical. Supposing that living in this way were
not honorable, then true propriety would command me to be dishonor-
able. . . .

The Myth of Sisyphus

The gods had condemned Sisyphus to ceaselessly rolling a rock to the
top of a mountain, whence the stone would fall back of its own weight.
They had thought with some reason that there is no more dreadful
punishment than futile and hopeless labor.

If one believes Homer, Sisyphus was the wisest and most prudent
of mortals. According to another tradition, however, he was disposed
to practice the profession of highwayman. I see no contradiction in this.
Opinions differ as to the reasons why he became the futile laborer of the
underworld. To begin with, he is accused of a certain levity in regard
to the gods. He stole their secrets. Ægina, the daughter of Æsopus, was
carried off by Jupiter. The father was shocked by that disappearance
and complained to Sisyphus. He, who knew of the abduction, offered to

tell about it on condition that Æsopus would give water to the citadel of Corinth. To the celestial thunderbolts he preferred the benediction of water. He was punished for this in the underworld. Homer tells us also that Sisyphus had put Death in chains. Pluto could not endure the sight of his deserted, silent empire. He dispatched the god of war, who liberated Death from the hands of her conqueror.

It is said also that Sisyphus, being near to death, rashly wanted to test his wife's love. He ordered her to cast his unburied body into the middle of the public square. Sisyphus woke up in the underworld. And there, annoyed by an obedience so contrary to human love, he obtained from Pluto permission to return to earth in order to chastise his wife. But when he had seen again the face of this world, enjoyed water and sun, warm stones and the sea, he no longer wanted to go back to the infernal darkness. Recalls, signs of anger, warnings were of no avail. Many years more he lived facing the curve of the gulf, the sparkling sea, and the smiles of earth. A decree of the gods was necessary. Mercury came and seized the impudent man by the collar and, snatching him from his joys, led him forcibly back to the underworld, where his rock was ready for him.

You have already grasped that Sisyphus is the absurd hero. He *is*, as much through his passions as through his torture. His scorn of the gods, his hatred of death, and his passion for life won him that unspeakable penalty in which the whole being is exerted toward accomplishing nothing. This is the price that must be paid for the passions of this earth. Nothing is told us about Sisyphus in the underworld. Myths are made for the imagination to breathe life into them. As for this myth, one sees merely the whole effort of a body straining to raise the huge stone, to roll it and push it up a slope a hundred times over; one sees the face screwed up, the cheek tight against the stone, the shoulder bracing the claycovered mass, the foot wedging it, the fresh start with arms outstretched, the wholly human security of two earth-clotted hands. At the very end of his long effort measured by skyless space and time without depth, the purpose is achieved. Then Sisyphus watches the stone rush down in a few moments toward that lower world whence he will have to push it up again toward the summit. He goes back down to the plain.

It is during that return, that pause, that Sisyphus interests me. A face that toils so close to stones is already stone itself! I see that man going back down with a heavy yet measured step toward the torment of which he will never know the end. That hour like a breathing-space which returns as surely as his suffering, that is the hour of consciousness. At each of those moments when he leaves the heights and gradually sinks toward the lairs of the gods, he is superior to his fate. He is stronger than his rock.

If this myth is tragic, that is because its hero is conscious. Where would his torture be, indeed, if at every step the hope of succeeding upheld him? The workman of today works every day in his life at the same tasks, and this fate is no less absurd. But it is tragic only at the rare moments when it becomes conscious. Sisyphus, proletarian of the gods, powerless and rebellious, knows the whole extent of his wretched condition: it is what he thinks of during his descent. The lucidity that was to constitute his torture at the same time crowns his victory. There is no fate that cannot be surmounted by scorn.

If the descent is thus sometimes performed in sorrow, it can also take place in joy. This word is not too much. Again I fancy Sisyphus returning toward his rock, and the sorrow was in the beginning. When the images of earth cling too tightly to memory, when the call of happiness becomes too insistent, it happens that melancholy rises in man's heart: this is the rock's victory, this is the rock itself. The boundless grief is too heavy to bear. These are our nights of Gethsemane. But crushing truths perish from being acknowledged. Thus, Œdipus at the outset obeys fate without knowing it. But from the moment he knows, his tragedy begins. Yet at the same moment, blind and desperate, he realizes that the only bond linking him to the world is the cool hand of a girl. Then a tremendous remark rings out: "Despite so many ordeals, my advanced age and the nobility of my soul make me conclude that all is well." Sophocles' Œdipus, like Dostoevsky's Kirilov, thus gives the recipe for the absurd victory. Ancient wisdom confirms modern heroism.

One does not discover the absurd without being tempted to write a manual of happiness. "What! by such narrow ways—?" There is but one world, however. Happiness and the absurd are two sons of the same earth. They are inseparable. It would be a mistake to say that happiness necessarily springs from the absurd discovery. It happens as well that the feeling of the absurd springs from happiness. "I conclude that all is well," says Œdipus, and that remark is sacred. It echoes in the wild and limited universe of man. It teaches that all is not, has not been, exhausted. It drives out of this world a god who had come into it with dissatisfaction and a preference for futile sufferings. It makes of fate a human matter, which must be settled among men.

All Sisyphus' silent joy is contained therein. His fate belongs to him. His rock is his thing. Likewise, the absurd man, when he contemplates his torment, silences all the idols. In the universe suddenly restored to its silence, the myriad wondering little voices of the earth rise up. Unconscious, secret calls, invitations from all the faces, they are the necessary reverse and price of victory. There is no sun without shadow, and it is essential to know the night. The absurd man says yes and his effort will henceforth be unceasing. If there is a personal fate, there is no higher destiny, or at least there is but one which he concludes is inevitable and despicable. For the rest, he knows himself to be the master of his days. At that subtle moment when man glances backward over his life, Sisyphus returning toward his rock, in that slight pivoting he contemplates that series of unrelated actions which becomes his fate, created by him, combined under his memory's eye and soon sealed by his death. Thus, convinced of the wholly human origin of all that is human, a blind man eager to see who knows that the night has no end, he is still on the go. The rock is still rolling.

I leave Sisyphus at the foot of the mountain! One always finds one's burden again. But Sisyphus teaches the higher fidelity that negates the gods and raises rocks. He too concludes that all is well. This universe henceforth without a master seems to him neither sterile nor futile. Each atom of that stone, each mineral flake of that night-filled mountain, in itself forms a world. The struggle itself toward the heights is enough to fill a man's heart. One must imagine Sisyphus happy.

DYNAMICS OF FAITH

Paul Tillich

PAUL TILLICH is one of the foremost theologians of this century. He taught at Union Theological Seminary, Harvard, and the University of Chicago. Of his many writings the following may be consulted in progressive order of difficulty, *Dynamics of Faith, The Courage to Be, Theology of Culture,* and his momentous three-volume *Systematic Theology.* He died in 1965.

What Faith Is

1. FAITH AS ULTIMATE CONCERN

Faith is the state of being ultimately concerned: the dynamics of faith are the dynamics of man's ultimate concern. Man, like every living being, is concerned about many things, above all about those which condition his very existence, such as food and shelter. But man, in contrast to other living beings, has spiritual concerns—cognitive, aesthetic, social, political. Some of them are urgent, often extremely urgent, and each of them as well as the vital concerns can claim ultimacy for a human life or the life of a social group. If it claims ultimacy it demands the total surrender of him who accepts this claim, and it promises total fulfillment even if all other claims have to be subjected to it or rejected in its name. If a national group makes the life and growth of the nation its ultimate concern, it demands that all other concerns, economic well-being, health and life, family, aesthetic and cognitive truth, justice and humanity, be sacrificed. The extreme nationalisms of our century are laboratories for the study of what ultimate concern means in all aspects of human existence, including the smallest concern of one's daily life. Everything is centered in the only god, the nation—a god who certainly proves to be a demon, but who shows clearly the unconditional character of an ultimate concern.

But it is not only the unconditional demand made by that which is one's ultimate concern, it is also the promise of ultimate fulfillment which is accepted in the act of faith. The content of this promise is not necessarily defined. It can be expressed in indefinite symbols or in concrete symbols which cannot be taken literally, like the "greatness" of one's nation in which one participates even if one has died for it, or the conquest of mankind by the "saving race," etc. In each of these cases it is "ultimate fulfillment" that is promised, and it is exclusion from such fulfillment which is threatened if the unconditional demand is not obeyed.

An example—and more than an example—is the faith manifest in the religion of the Old Testament. It also has the character of ultimate concern in demand, threat and promise. The content of this concern is not the nation—although Jewish nationalism has sometimes tried to distort it into that—but the content is the God of justice, who, because he represents justice for everybody and every nation, is called the universal God, the God of the universe. He is the ultimate concern of every pious Jew, and therefore in his name the great commandment is given: "You shall love the Lord your God with all your heart, and with all your soul, and with all your might" (Deut 6:5). This is what ultimate concern means and from these words the term "ultimate concern" is derived. They state unambiguously the character of genuine faith, the demand of total surrender to the subject of ultimate concern. The Old Testament is full of commands which make the nature of this surrender concrete, and it is full of promises and threats in relation to it. Here also are the promises of symbolic indefiniteness, although they center around fulfillment of the national and individual life, and the threat is the exclusion from such fulfillment through national extinction and individual catastrophe. Faith, for the men of the Old Testament, is the state of being ultimately and unconditionally concerned about Jahweh and about what he represents in demand, threat and promise.

Another example—almost a counter-example, yet nevertheless equally revealing—is the ultimate concern with "success" and with social standing and economic power. It is the god of many people in the highly competitive Western culture and it does what every ultimate concern must do: it demands unconditional surrender to its laws even if the price is the sacrifice of genuine human relations, personal conviction, and creative *eros*. Its threat is social and economic defeat, and its promise—indefinite as all such promises—the fulfillment of one's being. It is the breakdown of this kind of faith which characterizes and makes religiously important most contemporary literature. Not false calculations but a misplaced faith is revealed in novels like *Point of No Return*. When fulfilled, the promise of this faith proves to be empty.

Faith is the state of being ultimately concerned. The content matters infinitely for the life of the believer, but it does not matter for the formal definition of faith. And this is the first step we have to make in order to understand the dynamics of faith.

· ·

5. Faith and Doubt

We now return to a fuller description of faith as an act of the human personality, as its centered and total act. An act of faith is an act of a finite being who is grasped by and turned to the infinite. It is a finite act with all the limitations of a finite act, and it is an act in which the infinite participates beyond the limitations of a finite act. Faith is certain in so far as it is an experience of the holy. But faith is uncertain in so far as the infinite to which it is related is received by a finite being. This element of uncertainty in faith cannot be removed, it must be accepted. And the element in faith which accepts this is courage. Faith includes an element of immediate awareness which gives certainty and an element of uncertainty. To accept this is courage. In the courageous standing of uncertainty, faith shows most visibly its dynamic character.

If we try to describe the relation of faith and courage, we must use a larger concept of courage than that which is ordinarily used.[1] Courage as an element of faith is the daring self-affirmation of one's own being in spite of the powers of "nonbeing" which are the heritage of everything finite. Where there is daring and courage there is the possibility of failure. And in every act of faith this possibility is present. The risk must be taken. Whoever makes his nation his ultimate concern needs courage in order to maintain this concern. Only certain is the ultimacy as ultimacy, the infinite passion as infinite passion. This is a reality given to the self with his own nature. It is as immediate and as much beyond doubt as the self is to the self. It *is* the self in its self-transcending quality. But there is not certainty of this kind about the content of our ultimate concern, be it nation, success, a god, or the God of the Bible: They all are contents without immediate awareness. Their acceptance as matters of ultimate concern is a risk and therefore an act of courage. There is a risk if what was considered as a matter of ultimate concern proves to be a matter of preliminary and transitory concern—as, for example, the nation. The risk to faith in one's ultimate concern is indeed the greatest risk man can run. For if it proves to be a failure, the meaning of one's life breaks down; one surrenders oneself, including truth and justice, to something which is not worth it. One has given away one's personal center without having a chance to regain it. The reaction of despair in people who have experi-

[1] Cf. Paul Tillich, *The Courage to Be*. Yale University Press.

enced the breakdown of their national claims is an irrefutable proof of
the idolatrous character of their national concern. In the long run this is
the inescapable result of an ultimate concern, the subject matter of which
is not ultimate. And this is the risk faith must take; this is the risk which
is unavoidable if a finite being affirms itself. Ultimate concern is ultimate
risk and ultimate courage. It is not risk and needs no courage with respect
to ultimacy itself. But it is risk and demands courage if it affirms a concrete concern. And every faith has a concrete element in itself. It is
concerned about something or somebody. But this something or this somebody may prove to be not ultimate at all. Then faith is a failure in its
concrete expression, although it is not a failure in the experience of the
unconditional itself. A god disappears; divinity remains. Faith risks the
vanishing of the concrete god in whom it believes. It may well be that
with the vanishing of the god the believer breaks down without being
able to re-establish his centered self by a new content of his ultimate
concern. This risk cannot be taken away from any act of faith. There is
only one point which is a matter not of risk but of immediate certainty
and herein lies the greatness and the pain of being human; namely, one's
standing between one's finitude and one's potential infinity.

All this is sharply expressed in the relation of faith and doubt. If faith
is understood as belief that something is true, doubt is incompatible with
the act of faith. If faith is understood as being ultimately concerned, doubt
is a necessary element in it. It is a consequence of the risk of faith.

The doubt which is implicit in faith is not a doubt about facts or
conclusions. It is not the same doubt which is the lifeblood of scientific
research. Even the most orthodox theologian does not deny the right of
methodological doubt in matters of empirical inquiry or logical deduction.
A scientist who would say that a scientific theory is beyond doubt would
at that moment cease to be scientific. He may believe that the theory can
be trusted for all practical purposes. Without such belief no technical
application of a theory would be possible. One could attribute to this
kind of belief pragmatic certainty sufficient for action. Doubt in this case
points to the preliminary character of the underlying theory.

There is another kind of doubt, which we could call skeptical in contrast
to the scientific doubt which we could call methodological. The skeptical
doubt is an attitude toward all the beliefs of man, from sense experiences
to religious creeds. It is more an attitude than an assertion. For as an
assertion it would conflict with itself. Even the assertion that there is no
possible truth for man would be judged by the skeptical principle and
could not stand as an assertion. Genuine skeptical doubt does not use
the form of an assertion. It is an attitude of actually rejecting any certainty. Therefore, it can not be refuted logically. It does not transform its
attitude into a proposition. Such an attitude necessarily leads either to
despair or cynicism, or to both alternately. And often, if this alternative
becomes intolerable, it leads to indifference and the attempt to develop
an attitude of complete unconcern. But since man is that being who is

essentially concerned about his being, such an escape finally breaks down. This is the dynamics of skeptical doubt. It has an awakening and liberating function, but it also can prevent the development of a centered personality. For personality is not possible without faith. The despair about truth by the skeptic shows that truth is still his infinite passion. The cynical superiority over every concrete truth shows that truth is still taken seriously and that the impact of the question of an ultimate concern is strongly felt. The skeptic, so long as he is a serious skeptic, is not without faith, even though it has no concrete content.

The doubt which is implicit in every act of faith is neither the methodological nor the skeptical doubt. It is the doubt which accompanies every risk. It is not the permanent doubt of the scientist, and it is not the transitory doubt of the skeptic, but it is the doubt of him who is ultimately concerned about a concrete content. One could call it the existential doubt, in contrast to the methodological and the skeptical doubt. It does not question whether a special proposition is true or false. It does not reject every concrete truth, but it is aware of the element of insecurity in every existential truth. At the same time, the doubt which is implied in faith accepts this insecurity and takes it into itself in an act of courage. Faith includes courage. Therefore, it can include the doubt about itself. Certainly faith and courage are not identical. Faith has other elements besides courage and courage has other functions beyond affirming faith. Nevertheless, an act in which courage accepts risk belongs to the dynamics of faith.

This dynamic concept of faith seems to give no place to that restful affirmative confidence which we find in the documents of all great religions, including Christianity. But this is not the case. The dynamic concept of faith is the result of a conceptual analysis, both of the subjective and of the objective side of faith. It is by no means the description of an always actualized state of the mind. An analysis of structure is not the description of a state of things. The confusion of these two is a source of many misunderstandings and errors in all realms of life. An example, taken from the current discussion of anxiety, is typical of this confusion. The description of anxiety as the awareness of one's finitude is sometimes criticized as untrue from the point of view of the ordinary state of the mind. Anxiety, one says, appears under special conditions but is not an ever-present implication of man's finitude. Certainly anxiety as an acute experience appears under definite conditions. But the underlying structure of finite life is the universal condition which makes the appearance of anxiety under special conditions possible. In the same way doubt is not a permanent experience within the act of faith. But it is always present as an element in the structure of faith. This is the difference between faith and immediate evidence either of perceptual or of logical character. There is no faith without an intrinsic "in spite of" and the courageous affirmation of oneself in the state of ultimate concern. This intrinsic element of doubt breaks into the open under special individual and social conditions. If doubt appears, it should not be considered as the negation of faith, but as an element which was always and will always be present in the act of faith. Existential doubt and faith are poles of the same reality, the state of ultimate concern.

The insight into this structure of faith and doubt is of tremendous practical importance. Many Christians, as well as members of other religious groups, feel anxiety, guilt and despair about what they call "loss of faith." But serious doubt is confirmation of faith. It indicates the seriousness of the concern, its unconditional character. This also refers to those who as future or present ministers of a church experience not only scientific doubt about doctrinal statements—this is as necessary and perpetual as theology is a perpetual need—but also existential doubt about the message of their church, e.g., that Jesus can be called the Christ. The criterion according to which they should judge themselves is the seriousness and ultimacy of their concern about the content of both their faith and their doubt.

What Faith Is Not

1. THE INTELLECTUALISTIC DISTORTION OF THE MEANING OF FAITH

Our positive description of what faith is implies the rejection of interpretations that dangerously distort the meaning of faith. It is necessary to make these implicit rejections explicit, because the distortions exercise a tremendous power over popular thinking and have been largely responsible for alienating many from religion since the beginning of the scientific age. It is not only the popular mind which distorts the meaning of faith. Behind it lie philosophical and theological thoughts which in a more refined way also miss the meaning of faith.

The different distorted interpretations of the meaning of faith can be traced to one source. Faith as being ultimately concerned is a centered act of the whole personality. If one of the functions which constitute the totality of the personality is partly or completely identified with faith, the meaning of faith is distorted. Such interpretations are not altogether wrong because every function of the human mind participates in the act of faith. But the element of truth in them is embedded in a whole of error.

The most ordinary misinterpretation of faith is to consider it an act of knowledge that has a low degree of evidence. Something more or less probable or improbable is affirmed in spite of the insufficiency of its theoretical substantiation. This situation is very usual in daily life. If this is meant, one is speaking of *belief* rather than of faith. One believes that one's information is correct. One believes that records of past events are useful for the reconstruction of facts. One believes that a scientific theory is adequate for the understanding of a series of facts. One believes that a person will act in a specific way or that a political situation will change in a certain direction. In all these cases the belief is based on evidence sufficient to make the event probable. Sometimes, however, one believes something which has low probability or is strictly improbable, though not impossible. The causes for all these theoretical and practical beliefs are rather varied. Some things are believed because we have good though not complete evidence about them; many more things are believed because they are stated by good authorities. This is the case whenever we accept the evidence which others accepted as sufficient for belief, even if we cannot approach the evidence directly (for example, all events of the past). Here a new element comes into the picture, namely, the trust in the authority which makes a statement probable for us. Without such trust we could not believe anything except the objects of our immediate experience. The consequence would be that our world would be infinitely smaller than it actually is. It is rational to trust in authorities which enlarge our consciousness without forcing us into submission. If we use the word "faith" for this kind of trust we can say that most of our knowledge is based on faith. But it is not appropriate to do so. We believe the authorities, we trust their judgment, though never unconditionally, but we do not have faith in them. Faith is more than trust in authorities, although trust is an element of faith. This distinction is important in view of the fact that some earlier theologians tried to prove the unconditional authority of the Biblical writers by showing their trustworthiness as witnesses. The Christian may believe the Biblical writers, but not unconditionally. He does not have faith in them. He should not even have faith in the Bible. For faith is more than trust in even the most sacred authority. It is participation in the subject of one's ultimate concern with one's whole being. Therefore, the term "faith" should not be used in connection with theoretical knowledge, whether it is a knowledge on the basis of immediate, prescientific or scientific evidence, or whether it is on the basis of trust in authorities who themselves are dependent on direct or indirect evidence.

The terminological inquiry has led us into the material problem itself. Faith does not affirm or deny what belongs to the prescientific or scientific knowledge of our world, whether we know it by direct experience or through the experience of others. The knowledge of our world (including ourselves as a part of the world) is a matter of inquiry by ourselves or by those in whom we trust. It is not a matter of faith. The dimension of faith is not the dimension of science, history or psychology. The acceptance of a probable hypothesis in these realms is not faith, but preliminary belief, to be tested by scholarly methods and to be changed by every new discovery. Almost all the struggles between faith and knowledge are rooted in the wrong understanding of faith as a type of knowledge which has a low degree of evidence but is supported by

religious authority. It is, however, not only confusion of faith with knowledge that is responsible for the world historical conflicts between them;
it is also the fact that matters of faith in the sense of ultimate concern lie
hidden behind an assumedly scientific method. Whenever this happens,
faith stands against faith and not against knowledge.

The difference between faith and knowledge is also visible in the kind
of certitude each gives. There are two types of knowledge which are
based on complete evidence and give complete certitude. The one is
the immediate evidence of sense perception. He who sees a green color
sees a green color and is certain about it. He cannot be certain whether the
thing which seems to him green is really green. He may be under a
deception. But he cannot doubt that he sees green. The other complete
evidence is that of the logical and mathematical rules which are presupposed even if their formulation admits different and sometimes conflicting methods. One cannot discuss logic without presupposing those
implicit rules which make the discussion meaningful. Here we have
absolute certitude; but we have no reality, just as in the case of mere
sense perception. Nevertheless, this certitude is not without value. No
truth is possible without the material given by sense perception and without the form given by the logical and mathematical rules which express
the structure in which all reality stands. One of the worst errors of theology and popular religion is to make statements which intentionally or
unintentionally contradict the structure of reality. Such an attitude is
an expression not of faith but of the confusion of faith with belief.

Knowledge of reality has never the certitude of complete evidence.
The process of knowing is infinite. It never comes to an end except in a
state of knowledge of the whole. But such knowledge transcends infinitely
every finite mind and can be ascribed only to God. Every knowledge of
reality by the human mind has the character of higher or lower probability. The certitude about a physical law, a historical fact, or a psychological structure can be so high that, for all practical purposes, it is
certain. But theoretically the incomplete certitude of belief remains and
can be undercut at any moment by criticism and new experience. The
certitude of faith has not this character. Neither has it the character of
formal evidence. The certitude of faith is "existential," meaning that the
whole existence of man is involved. It has, as we indicated before, two
elements: the one, which is not a risk but a certainty about one's own
being, namely, on being related to something ultimate or unconditional;
the other, which is a risk and involves doubt and courage, namely, the
surrender to a concern which is not really ultimate and may be destructive
if taken as ultimate. This is not a theoretical problem of the kind of higher
or lower evidence, of probability or improbability, but it is an existential
problem of "to be or not to be." It belongs to a dimension other than any
theoretical judgment. Faith is not belief and it is not knowledge with a low
degree of probability. Its certitude is not the uncertain certitude of a
theoretical judgment.

2. The Voluntaristic Distortion of the Meaning of Faith

One can divide this form of the distorted interpretation of faith into a Catholic and a Protestant type. The Catholic type has a great tradition in the Roman Church. It goes back to Thomas Aquinas, who emphasized that the lack of evidence which faith has must be complemented by an act of will. This, first of all, presupposes that faith is understood as an act of knowledge with a limited evidence and that the lack of evidence is made up by an act of will. We have seen that this way of understanding faith does not do justice to the existential character of faith. Our criticism of the intellectualistic distortion of the meaning of faith hits basically also the voluntaristic distortion of the meaning of faith. The former is the basis of the latter. Without a theoretically formulated content the "will to believe" would be empty. But the content which is meant in the will to believe is given to the will by the intellect. For instance, someone has doubts about the so-called "immortality of the soul." He realizes that this assertion that the soul continues to live after the death of the body cannot be proved either by evidence or by trustworthy authority. It is a questionable proposition of theoretical character. But there are motives driving people to this assertion. They decide to believe, and make up in this way for the lack of evidence. If this belief is called "faith," it is a misnomer, even if much evidence were collected for the belief in a continuation of life after death. In classical Roman Catholic theology the "will to believe" is not an act which originates in man's striving, but it is given by grace to him whose will is moved by God to accept the truth of what the Church teaches. Even so, it is not the intellect which is determined by its content to believe, but it is the will which performs what the intellect alone cannot do. This kind of interpretation agrees with the authoritarian attitude of the Roman Church. For it is the authority of the Church which gives the contents, to be affirmed by the intellect under the impact of the will. If the idea of grace mediated by the Church and motivating the will is rejected, as in pragmatism, the will to believe becomes willfulness. It becomes an arbitrary decision which may be supported by some insufficient arguments but which could have gone in other directions with equal justification. Such belief as the basis of the will to believe is certainly not faith.

The Protestant form of the will to believe is connected with the moral interpretation of religion by Protestants. One demands "obedience of faith," following a Paulinian phrase. The term can mean two different things. It can mean the element of commitment which is implied in the state of ultimate concern. If this is meant, one simply says that in the state of ultimate concern all mental functions participate—which certainly is true. Or the term "obedience of faith" can mean subjection to the command to believe as it is given in prophetic and apostolic preaching. Certainly, if a prophetic word is accepted as prophetic, i.e., as coming from God, obedience of faith does not mean anything other than accepting a message as coming from God. But if there is doubt whether a "word" is prophetic, the term "obedience of faith" loses its meaning. It becomes an arbitrary "will to believe." Yet one may describe the situation in a more refined way and point to the fact that we are often grasped by something, e.g., Biblical passages, as expressions of the objectively ultimate concern, but we hesitate to accept them as our subjective ultimate concern for escapist reasons. In such cases, one says, the appeal to the will is justified and does not ask for a willful decision. This is true; but such an act of will does not produce faith—faith as ultimate concern is already given. The demand to be obedient is the demand to be what one already is, namely, committed to the ultimate concern from which one tries to escape. Only if this is the situation can obedience of faith be demanded; but then faith precedes the obedience and is not the product of it. No command to believe and no will to believe can create faith.

This is important for religious education, counseling and preaching. One should never convey the impression to those whom one wants to impress, that faith is a demand made upon them, the rejection of which is lack of good will. Finite man cannot produce infinite concern. Our oscillating will cannot produce the certainty which belongs to faith. This is in strict analogy to what we said about the impossibility of reaching the truth of faith by arguments and authorities, which in the best case give finite knowledge of a more or less probable character. Neither arguments for belief nor the will to believe can create faith.

3. THE EMOTIONALISTIC DISTORTION OF THE MEANING OF FAITH

The difficulty of understanding faith either as a matter of the intellect or as a matter of will, or of both in mutual support, has led to the interpretation of faith as emotion. This solution was, and partly is, supported from both the religious and the secular side. For the defenders of religion it was a retreat to a seemingly safe position after the battle about faith as a matter of knowledge or will had been lost. The father of all modern Protestant theology, Schleiermacher, has described religion as the feeling of unconditional dependence. Of course, feeling so defined does not mean in religion what it means in popular psychology. It is not vague and changing, but has a definite content: unconditional dependence, a phrase related to what we have called ultimate concern. Nevertheless, the word "feeling" has induced many people to believe that faith is a matter of merely subjective emotions, without a content to be known and a demand to be obeyed.

This interpretation of faith was readily accepted by representatives of science and ethics, because they took it as the best way to get rid of interference from the side of religion in the processes of scientific research and technical organization. If religion is mere feeling it is innocuous. The old conflicts between religion and culture are finished. Culture goes its way, directed by scientific knowledge, and religion is the private affair of every individual and a mere mirror of his emotional life. No claims for truth can be made by it. No competition with science, history, psychology, politics is possible. Religion, put safely into the corner of subjective feelings, has lost its danger for man's cultural activities.

Neither of the two sides, the religious and the cultural, could keep this well-defined covenant of peace. Faith as the state of ultimate concern claims the whole man and cannot be restricted to the subjectivity of mere feeling. It claims truth for its concern and commitment to it. It does not accept the situation "in the corner" of mere feeling. If the whole man is grasped, all his functions are grasped. If this claim of religion is denied, religion itself is denied. It was not only religion which could not accept the restriction of faith to feeling. It was also not accepted by those who were especially interested in pushing religion into the emotional corner. Scientists, artists, moralists showed clearly that they also were ultimately concerned. Their concern expressed itself even in those creations in which they wanted most radically to deny religion. A keen analysis of most philosophical, scientific and ethical systems shows how much ultimate concern is present in them, even if they are leading in the fight against what they call religion.

This shows the limits of the emotionalist definition of faith. Certainly faith as an act of the whole personality has strong emotional elements within it. Emotion always expresses the involvement of the whole personality in an act of life or spirit. But emotion is not the source of faith. Faith is definite in its direction and concrete in its content. Therefore, it claims truth and commitment. It is directed toward the unconditional, and appears in a concrete reality that demands and justifies such commitment.

Symbols of Faith

1. The Meaning of Symbol

Man's ultimate concern must be expressed symbolically, because symbolic language alone is able to express the ultimate. This statement demands explanation in several respects. In spite of the manifold research about the meaning and function of symbols which is going on in contemporary philosophy, every writer who uses the term "symbol" must explain his understanding of it.

Symbols have one characteristic in common with signs; they point beyond themselves to something else. The red sign at the street corner points to the order to stop the movements of cars at certain intervals. A red light and the stopping of cars have essentially no relation to each other, but conventionally they are united as long as the convention lasts. The same is true of letters and numbers and partly even words. They point beyond themselves to sounds and meanings. They are given this special function by convention within a nation or by international conventions, as the mathematical signs. Sometimes such signs are called symbols; but this is unfortunate because it makes the distinction between signs and symbols more difficult. Decisive is the fact that signs do not participate in the reality of that to which they point, while symbols do. Therefore, signs can be replaced for reasons of expediency or convention, while symbols cannot.

This leads to the second characteristic of the symbol: It participates in that to which it points: the flag participates in the power and dignity of the nation for which it stands. Therefore, it cannot be replaced except after an historic catastrophe that changes the reality of the nation which it symbolizes. An attack on the flag is felt as an attack on the majesty of the group in which it is acknowledged. Such an attack is considered blasphemy.

The third characteristic of a symbol is that it opens up levels of reality which otherwise are closed for us. All arts create symbols for a level of reality which cannot be reached in any other way. A picture and a poem reveal elements of reality which cannot be approached scientifically. In the creative work of art we encounter reality in a dimension which is closed for us without such works. The symbol's fourth characteristic not only opens up dimensions and elements of reality which otherwise would remain unapproachable but also unlocks dimensions and elements of our soul which correspond to the dimensions and elements of reality. A great play gives us not only a new vision of the human scene, but it opens up hidden depths of our own being. Thus we are able to receive what the play reveals to us in reality. There are within us dimensions of which we cannot become aware except through symbols, as melodies and rhythms in music.

Symbols cannot be produced intentionally—this is the fifth characteristic. They grow out of the individual or collective unconscious and cannot function without being accepted by the unconscious dimension of our being. Symbols which have an especially social function, as political and religious symbols, are created or at least accepted by the collective unconscious of the group in which they appear.

The sixth and last characteristic of the symbol is a consequence of the fact that symbols cannot be invented. Like living beings, they grow and they die. They grow when the situation is ripe for them, and they die when the situation changes. The symbol of the "king" grew in a special period of history, and it died in most parts of the world in our period. Symbols do not grow because people are longing for them, and they do not die because of scientific or practical criticism. They die because they can no longer produce response in the group where they originally found expression.

These are the main characteristics of every symbol. Genuine symbols are created in several spheres of man's cultural creativity. We have mentioned already the political and the artistic realm. We could add history and, above all, religion, whose symbols will be our particular concern.

2. Religious Symbols

We have discussed the meaning of symbols generally because, as we said, man's ultimate concern must be expressed symbolically! One may ask: Why can it not be expressed directly and properly? If money, success or the nation is someone's ultimate concern, can this not be said in a direct way without symbolic language? Is it not only in those cases in which the content of the ultimate concern is called "God" that we are in the realm of symbols? The answer is that everything which is a matter of unconditional concern is made into a god. If the nation is someone's ultimate concern, the name of the nation becomes a sacred name and the nation receives divine qualities which far surpass the reality of the being and functioning of the nation. The nation then stands for and symbolizes the true ultimate, but in an idolatrous way. Success as ultimate concern is not the natural desire of actualizing potentialities, but is readiness to sacrifice all other values of life for the sake of a position of power and social predominance. The anxiety about not being a success is an idolatrous form of the anxiety about divine condemnation. Success is grace; lack of success, ultimate judgment. In this way concepts designating ordinary realities become idolatrous symbols of ultimate concern.

The reason for this transformation of concepts into symbols is the character of ultimacy and the nature of faith. That which is the true ultimate transcends the realm of finite reality infinitely. Therefore, no finite reality can express it directly and properly. Religiously speaking, God transcends his own name. This is why the use of his name easily becomes an abuse or a blasphemy. Whatever we say about that which concerns us ultimately, whether or not we call it God, has a symbolic meaning. It points beyond itself while participating in that to which it points. In no other way can faith express itself adequately. The language of faith is the language of symbols. If faith were what we have shown that it is not, such an assertion could not be made. But faith, understood as the state of being ultimately concerned, has no language other than symbols. When saying this I always expect the question: Only a symbol?

He who asks this question shows that he has not understood the difference between signs and symbols nor the power of symbolic language, which surpasses in quality and strength the power of any nonsymbolic language. One should never say "only a symbol," but one should say "not less than a symbol." With this in mind we can now describe the different kinds of symbols of faith.

The fundamental symbol of our ultimate concern is God. It is always present in any act of faith, even if the act of faith includes the denial of God. Where there is ultimate concern, God can be denied only in the name of God. One God can deny the other one. Ultimate concern cannot deny its own character as ultimate. Therefore, it affirms what is meant by the word "God." Atheism, consequently, can only mean the attempt to remove any ultimate concern—to remain unconcerned about the meaning of one's existence. Indifference toward the ultimate question is the only imaginable form of atheism. Whether it is possible is a problem which must remain unsolved at this point. In any case, he who denies God as a matter of ultimate concern affirms God, because he affirms ultimacy in his concern. God is the fundamental symbol for what concerns us ultimately. Again it would be completely wrong to ask: So God is nothing but a symbol? Because the next question has to be: A symbol for what? And then the answer would be: For God! God is symbol for God. This means that in the notion of God we must distinguish two elements: the element of ultimacy, which is a matter of immediate experience and not symbolic in itself, and the element of concreteness, which is taken from our ordinary experience and symbolically applied to God. The man whose ultimate concern is a sacred tree has both the ultimacy of concern and the concreteness of the tree which symbolizes his relation to the ultimate. The man who adores Apollo is ultimately concerned, but not in an abstract way. His ultimate concern is symbolized in the divine figure of Apollo. The man who glorifies Jahweh, the God of the Old Testament, has both an ultimate concern and a concrete image of what concerns him ultimately. This is the meaning of the seemingly cryptic statement that God is the symbol of God. In this qualified sense God is the fundamental and universal content of faith.

It is obvious that such an understanding of the meaning of God makes the discussions about the existence or non-existence of God meaningless. It is meaningless to question the ultimacy of an ultimate concern. This element in the idea of God is in itself certain. The symbolic expression of this element varies endlessly through the whole history of mankind. Here again it would be meaningless to ask whether one or another of the figures in which an ultimate concern is symbolized does "exist." If "existence" refers to something which can be found within the whole of reality, no divine being exists. The question is not this, but: which of the innumerable symbols of faith is most adequate to the meaning of faith? In other words, which symbol of ultimacy expresses the ultimate without idolatrous elements? This is the problem, and not the so-called "existence of God"—which is in itself an impossible combination of words. God as the ultimate in man's ultimate concern is more certain than any other certainty, even that of oneself. God as symbolized in a divine figure is a matter of daring faith, of courage and risk.

God is the basic symbol of faith, but not the only one. All the qualities we attribute to him, power, love, justice, are taken from finite experiences and applied symbolically to that which is beyond finitude and infinity. If faith calls God "almighty," it uses the human experience of power in order to symbolize the content of its infinite concern, but it does not describe a highest being who can do as he pleases. So it is with all the other qualities and with all the actions, past, present and future, which men attribute to God. They are symbols taken from our daily experience, and not information about what God did once upon a time or will do sometime in the future. Faith is not the belief in such stories, but it is the acceptance of symbols that express our ultimate concern in terms of divine actions.

Another group of symbols of faith are manifestations of the divine in things and events, in persons and communities, in words and documents. This whole realm of sacred objects is a treasure of symbols. Holy things are not holy in themselves, but they point beyond themselves to the source of all holiness, that which is of ultimate concern.

3. Symbols and Myths

The symbols of faith do not appear in isolation. They are united in "stories of the gods," which is the meaning of the Greek word "mythos"— myth. The gods are individualized figures, analogous to human personalities, sexually differentiated, descending from each other, related to each other in love and struggle, producing world and man, acting in time and space. They participate in human greatness and misery, in creative and destructive works. They give to man cultural and religious traditions, and defend these sacred rites. They help and threaten the human race, especially some families, tribes or nations. They appear in epiphanies and incarnations, establish sacred places, rites and persons, and thus create a cult. But they themselves are under the command and threat of a fate which is beyond everything that is. This is mythology as developed most impressively in ancient Greece. But many of these characteristics can be found in every mythology. Usually the mythological gods are not equals. There is a hierarchy, at the top of which is a ruling god, as in Greece; or a trinity of them, as in India; or a duality of them, as in Persia. There are savior-gods who mediate between the highest gods and man, sometimes sharing the suffering and death of man in spite of their essential immortality. This is the world of the myth, great and strange, always changing but fundamentally the same: man's ultimate concern symbolized in divine figures and actions. Myths are symbols of faith combined in stories about divine-human encounters.

Myths are always present in every act of faith, because the language of faith is the symbol. They are also attacked, criticized and transcended in each of the great religions of mankind. The reason for this criticism is the very nature of the myth. It uses material from our ordinary experience. It puts the stories of the gods into the framework of time and space although it belongs to the nature of the ultimate to be beyond time and space. Above all, it divides the divine into several figures, removing ultimacy from each of them without removing their claim to ultimacy. This inescapably leads to conflicts of ultimate claims, able to destroy life, society, and consciousness.

The criticism of the myth first rejects the division of the divine and goes beyond it to one God, although in different ways according to the different types of religion. Even one God is an object of mythological language, and if spoken about is drawn into the framework of time and space. Even he loses his ultimacy if made to be the content of concrete concern. Consequently, the criticism of the myth does not end with the rejection of the polytheistic mythology.

Monotheism also falls under the criticism of the myth. It needs, as one says today, "demythologization." This word has been used in connection with the elaboration of the mythical elements in stories and symbols of the Bible, both of the Old and the New Testaments—stories like those of the Paradise, of the fall of Adam, of the great Flood, of the Exodus from Egypt, of the virgin birth of the Messiah, of many of his miracles, of his resurrection and ascension, of his expected return as the judge of the universe. In short, all the stories in which divine-human interactions are told are considered as mythological in character, and objects of demythologization. What does this negative and artificial term mean? It must be accepted and supported if it points to the necessity of recognizing a symbol as a symbol and a myth as a myth. It must be attacked and rejected if it means the removal of symbols and myths altogether. Such an attempt is the third step in the criticism of the myth. It is an attempt which never can be successful, because symbol and myth are forms of the human consciousness which are always present. One can replace one myth by another, but one cannot remove the myth from man's spiritual life. For the myth is the combination of symbols of our ultimate concern.

A myth which is understood as a myth, but not removed or replaced, can be called a "broken myth." Christianity denies by its very nature any unbroken myth, because its presupposition is the first commandment: the affirmation of the ultimate as ultimate and the rejection of any kind of idolatry. All mythological elements in the Bible, and doctrine and liturgy should be recognized as mythological, but they should be maintained in their symbolic form and not be replaced by scientific substitutes. For there is no substitute for the use of symbols and myths: they are the language of faith.

The radical criticism of the myth is due to the fact that the primitive mythological consciousness resists the attempt to interpret the myth of myth. It is afraid of every act of demythologization. It believes that the broken myth is deprived of its truth and of its convincing power. Those who live in an unbroken mythological world feel safe and certain. They resist, often fanatically, any attempt to introduce an element of uncertainty by "breaking the myth," namely, by making conscious its symbolic character. Such resistance is supported by authoritarian systems, religious or political, in order to give security to the people under their control and unchallenged power to those who exercise the control. The resistance against demythologization expresses itself in "literalism." The symbols and myths are understood in their immediate meaning. The material, taken from nature and history, is used in its proper sense. The character of the symbol to point beyond itself to something else is disregarded. Creation is taken as a magic act which happened once upon a time. The fall of Adam is localized on a special geographical point and attributed to a human individual. The virgin birth of the Messiah is understood in biological terms, resurrection and ascension as physical events, the second coming of the Christ as a telluric, or cosmic, catastrophe. The presupposition of such literalism is that God is a being, acting in time and space, dwelling in a special place, affecting the course of events and being affected by them like any other being in the universe. Literalism deprives God of his ultimacy and, religiously speaking, of his majesty. It draws him down to the level of that which is not ultimate, the finite and conditional. In the last analysis it is not rational criticism of the myth which is decisive but the inner religious criticism. Faith, if it takes its symbols literally, becomes idolatrous! It calls something ultimate which is less than ultimate. Faith, conscious of the symbolic character of its symbols, gives God the honor which is due him.

One should distinguish two stages of literalism, the natural and the reactive. The natural stage of literalism is that in which the mythical and the literal are indistinguishable. The primitive period of individuals and groups consists in the inability to separate the creations of symbolic imagination from the facts which can be verified through observation and experiment. This stage has a full right of its own and should not be disturbed, either in individuals or in groups, up to the moment when man's questioning mind breaks the natural acceptance of the mythological visions as literal. If, however, this moment has come, two ways are possible. The one is to replace the unbroken by the broken myth. It is the objectively demanded way, although it is impossible for many people who prefer the repression of their questions to the uncertainty which appears with the breaking of the myth. They are forced into the second stage of literalism, the conscious one, which is aware of the questions but represses them, half consciously, half unconsciously. The tool of repression is usually an acknowledged authority with sacred qualities like the Church or the Bible, to which one owes unconditional surrender. This stage is still justifiable, if the questioning power is very weak and can easily be answered. It is unjustifiable if a mature mind is broken in its personal center by political or psychological methods, split in his unity, and hurt in his integrity. The enemy of a critical theology is not natural literalism but conscious literalism with repression of and aggression toward autonomous thought.

Symbols of faith cannot be replaced by other symbols, such as artistic ones, and they cannot be removed by scientific criticism. They have a genuine standing in the human mind, just as science and art have. Their symbolic character is their truth and their power. Nothing less than symbols and myths can express our ultimate concern.

One more question arises, namely, whether myths are able to express every kind of ultimate concern. For example, Christian theologians argue that the word "myth" should be reserved for natural myths in which repetitive natural processes, such as the seasons, are understood in their ultimate meaning. They believe that if the world is seen as a historical process with beginning, end and center, as in Christianity and Judaism, the term "myth" should not be used. This would radically reduce the realm in which the term would be applicable. Myth could not be understood as the language of our ultimate concern, but only as a discarded idiom of this language. Yet history proves that there are not only natural myths but also historical myths. If the earth is seen as the battleground of two divine powers, as in ancient Persia, this is an historical myth. If the God of creation selects and guides a nation through history toward an end which transcends all history, this is an historical myth. If the Christ—a transcendent, divine being—appears in the fullness of time, lives, dies and is resurrected, this is an historical myth. Christianity is superior to those religions which are bound to a natural myth. But Christianity speaks the mythological language like every other religion. It is a broken myth, but it is a myth; otherwise Christianity would not be an expression of ultimate concern.

THE MEANING OF EXISTENCE

. . . The root meaning of "to exist," in Latin, *existere*, is to "stand out." Immediately one asks: "To stand out of what?" On the one hand, in English, we have the word "outstanding," which means standing out of the average level of things or men, being more than others in power and value. On the other hand, "standing out" in the sense of *existere* means that existence is a common characteristic of all things, of those which are outstanding and of those which are average. The general answer to the question of what we stand out of is that we stand out of non-being. "Things do exist" means they have being, they stand out of nothingness. But we have learned from the Greek philosophers (what they have learned from the lucidity and sensitivity of the Greek language) that non-being can be understood in two ways, namely, as *ouk on,* that is, absolute non-being, or as *me on,* that is, relative non-being. Existing, "to stand out," refers to both meanings of non-being. If we say that something exists, we assert that it can be found, directly or indirectly, within the corpus of reality. It stands out of the emptiness of absolute non-being. But the metaphor "to stand out" logically implies something like "to stand in." Only that which in some respect stands in can stand out. He who is outstanding rises above the average in which he stood and partly still stands. If we say that everything that exists stands out of absolute non-being, we say that it is in both being and non-being. It does not stand completely out of non-being. As we have said in the chapter on finitude (in the first volume), it is a finite, a mixture of being and non-being. To exist, then, would mean to stand out of one's own non-being.

But this is not sufficient because it does not take into consideration this question: How can something stand out of its own non-being? To this the answer is that everything participates in being, whether or not it exists. It participates in potential being before it can come into actual being. As potential being, it is in the state of relative non-being, it is not-yet-being. But it is not nothing. Potentiality is the state of real possibility, that is, it is more than a logical possibility. Potentiality is the power of being which, metaphysically speaking, has not yet realized its power. The power of being is still latent; it has not yet become manifest. Therefore, if we say that something exists, we say that it has left the state of mere potentiality and has become actual. It stands out of mere potentiality, out of relative non-being.

In order to become actual, it must overcome relative non-being, the state of *me on.* But, again, it cannot be completely out of it. It must stand out and stand in at the same time. An actual thing stands out of mere potentiality; but it also remains in it. It never pours its power of being completely into its state of existence. It never fully exhausts its potentialities. It remains not only in absolute non-being, as its finitude shows, but also in relative non-being, as the changing character of its existence shows. The Greeks symbolized this as the resistance of *me on,* of relative non-being, against the actualization of that which is potential in a thing.

Summarizing our etymological inquiry, we can say: Existing can mean standing out of absolute non-being, while remaining in it; it can mean finitude, the unity of being and non-being. And existing can mean standing out of relative non-being, while remaining in it; it can mean actuality, the unity of actual being and the resistance against it. But whether we use the one or the other meaning of non-being, existence means standing out of non-being. . . .

. . . The state of existence is the state of estrangement. Man is estranged from the ground of his being, from other beings, and from himself. The transition from essence to existence results in personal guilt and universal tragedy. It is now necessary to give a description of existential estrangement and its self-destructive implications. But, before doing so, we must answer the question which has already arisen: What is the relation of the concept of estrangement to the traditional concept of sin?

Man as he exists is not what he essentially is and ought to be. He is estranged from his true being. The profundity of the term "estrangement" lies in the implication that one belongs essentially to that from which one is estranged. Man is not a stranger to his true being, for he belongs to it. He is judged by it but cannot be completely separated, even if he is hostile to it. Man's hostility to God proves indisputably that he belongs to him. Where there is the possibility of hate, there and there alone is the possibility of love.

Estrangement is not a biblical term but is implied in most of the biblical descriptions of man's predicament. It is implied in the symbols of the expulsion from paradise, in the hostility between man and nature, in the deadly hostility of brother against brother, in the estrangement of nation from nation through the confusion of language, and in the continuous complaints of the prophets against their kings and people who turn to alien gods. Estrangement is implied in Paul's statement that man perverted the image of God into that of idols, in his classical description of "man against himself," in his vision of man's hostility against man as combined with his distorted desires. In all these interpretations of man's predicament, estrangement is implicitly asserted. Therefore, it is certainly not unbiblical to use the term "estrangement" in describing man's existential situation.

Nevertheless, "estrangement" cannot replace "sin." Yet the reasons for attempts to replace the word "sin" with another word are obvious. The term has been used in a way which has little to do with its genuine biblical meaning. Paul often spoke of "Sin" in the singular and without an article. He saw it as a quasi-personal power which ruled this world. But in the Christian churches, both Catholic and Protestant, sin has been used predominately in the plural, and "sins" are deviations from moral laws. This has little to do with "sin" as the state of estrangement from that to which one belongs—God, one's self, one's world. Therefore, the characteristics of sin are here considered under the heading of "estrangement." And the word "estrangement" itself implies a reinterpretation of sin from a religious point of view.

Nevertheless, the word "sin" cannot be overlooked. It expresses what is not implied in the term "estrangement," namely, the personal act of turning away from that to which one belongs. Sin expresses most sharply the personal character of estrangement over against its tragic side. It expresses personal freedom and guilt in contrast to tragic guilt and the universal destiny of estrangement. The word "sin" can and must be saved, not only because classical literature and liturgy continuously employ it but more particularly because the word has a sharpness which accusingly points to the element of personal responsibility in one's estrangement. Man's predicament is estrangement, but his estrangement is sin. It is not a state of things, like the laws of nature, but a matter of both personal freedom and universal destiny. For this reason the term "sin" must be used after it has been reinterpreted religiously. An important tool for this reinterpretation is the term "estrangement."

Reinterpretation is also needed for the terms "original" or "hereditary" with respect to sin. But in this case reinterpretation may demand the rejection of the terms. Both point to the universal character of estrangement, expressing the element of destiny in estrangement. But both words are so much burdened with literalistic absurdities that it is practically impossible to use them any longer.

If one speaks of "sins" and refers to special acts which are considered as sinful, one should always be conscious of the fact that "sins" are the expressions of "sin." It is not the disobedience to a law which makes an act sinful but the fact that it is an expression of man's estrangement from God, from men, from himself. Therefore, Paul calls everything sin which does not result from faith, from the unity with God. And in another context (following Jesus) all laws are summed up in the law of love by which estrangement is conquered. Love as the striving for the reunion of the separated is the opposite of estrangement. In faith and love, sin is conquered because estrangement is overcome by reunion. . . .

THE COURAGE TO BE

The Interdependence of Fear and Anxiety

Anxiety and fear have the same ontological root but they are not the same in actuality. This is common knowledge, but it has been emphasized and overemphasized to such a degree that a reaction against it may occur and wipe out not only the exaggerations but also the truth of the distinction. Fear, as opposed to anxiety has a definite object (as most authors agree), which can be faced, analyzed, attacked, endured. One can act upon it, and in acting upon it participate in it—even if in the form of struggle. In this way one can take it into one's self-affirmation. Courage can meet every object of fear, because it is an object and makes participation possible. Courage can take the fear produced by a definite object into itself, because this object, however frightful it may be, has a side with which it participates in us and we in it. One could say that as long as there is an *object* of fear love in the sense of participation can conquer fear.

But this is not so with anxiety, because anxiety has no object, or rather, in a paradoxical phrase, its object is the negation of every object. Therefore participation, struggle, and love with respect to it are impossible. He who is in anxiety is, insofar as it is mere anxiety, delivered to it without help. Helplessness in the state of anxiety can be observed in animals and humans alike. It expresses itself in loss of direction, inadequate reactions, lack of "intentionality" (the being related to meaningful contents of knowledge or will). The reason for this sometimes striking behavior is the lack of an object on which the subject (in the state of anxiety) can concentrate. The only object is the threat itself, but not the source of the threat, because the source of the threat is "nothingness."

One might ask whether this threatening "nothing" is not the unknown, the indefinite possibility of an actual threat? Does not anxiety cease in the moment in which a known object of fear appears? Anxiety then would be fear of the unknown. But this is an insufficient explanation of anxiety. For there are innumerable realms of the unknown, different for each subject, and faced without any anxiety. It is the unknown of a special type which is met with anxiety. It is the unknown which by its very nature cannot be known, because it is nonbeing.

Fear and anxiety are distinguished but not separated. They are immanent within each other: The sting of fear is anxiety, and anxiety strives toward fear. Fear is being afraid of something, a pain, the rejection by a person or a group, the loss of something or somebody, the moment of dying. But in the anticipation of the threat originating in these things, it is not the negativity itself which they will bring upon the subject that is frightening but the anxiety about the possible implications of this negativity. The outstanding example—and more than an example—is the fear of dying. Insofar as it is *fear* its object is the anticipated event of being killed by sickness or an accident and thereby suffering agony and the loss of everything. Insofar as it is *anxiety* its object is the absolutely unknown "after death," the nonbeing which remains nonbeing even if it is filled with images of our present experience. The dreams in Hamlet's soliloquy, "to be or not to be," which we may have after death and which make cowards of us all are frightful not because of their manifest content but because of their power to symbolize the threat of nothingness, in religious terms of "eternal death." The symbols of hell created by Dante produce anxiety not because of their objective imagery but because they express the "nothingness" whose power is experienced in the anxiety of guilt. Each of the situations described in the *Inferno* could be met by courage on the basis of participation and love. But of course the meaning is that this is impossible; in other words they are not real situations but symbols of the objectless, of nonbeing.

The fear of death determines the element of anxiety in every fear. Anxiety, if not modified by the fear of an object, anxiety in its nakedness, is always the anxiety of ultimate nonbeing. Immediately seen, anxiety is the painful feeling of not being able to deal with the threat of a special situation. But a more exact analysis shows that in the anxiety about any special situation anxiety about the human situation as such is implied. It is the anxiety of not being able to preserve one's own being which underlies every fear and is the frightening element in it. In the moment, therefore, in which "naked anxiety" lays hold of the mind, the previous objects of fear cease to be definite objects. They appear as what they always were in part, symptoms of man's basic anxiety. As such they are beyond the reach of even the most courageous attack upon them.

This situation drives the anxious subject to establish objects of fear. Anxiety strives to become fear, because fear can be met by courage. It is impossible for a finite being to stand naked anxiety for more than a flash of time. People who have experienced these moments, as for instance some mystics in their visions of the "night of the soul," or Luther under the despair of the demonic assaults, or Nietzsche-Zarathustra in the experience of the "great disgust," have told of the unimaginable horror of it. This horror is ordinarily avoided by the transformation of anxiety into fear of something, no matter what. The human mind is not only, as Calvin has said, a permanent factory of idols, it is also a permanent factory of fears—the first in order to escape God, the second in order to escape anxiety; and there is a relation between the two. For facing the God who is really God means facing also the absolute threat of nonbeing. The "naked absolute" (to use a phrase of Luther's) produces "naked anxiety"; for it is the extinction of every finite self-affirmation, and not a possible object of fear and courage. But ultimately the attempts to transform anxiety into fear are vain. The basic anxiety, the anxiety of a finite being about the threat of nonbeing, cannot be eliminated. It belongs to existence itself.

TYPES OF ANXIETY

The Three Types of Anxiety and the Nature of Man

Nonbeing is dependent on the being it negates. "Dependent" means two things. It points first of all to the ontological priority of being over nonbeing. The term nonbeing itself indicates this, and it is logically necessary. There could be no negation if there were no preceding affirmation to be negated. Certainly one can describe being in terms of non-nonbeing; and one can justify such a description by pointing to the astonishing prerational fact that there is something and not nothing. One could say that "being is the negation of the primordial night of nothingness." But in doing so one must realize that such an aboriginal nothing would be neither nothing nor something, that it becomes nothing only in contrast to something; in other words, that the ontological status of nonbeing as nonbeing is dependent on being. Secondly, nonbeing is dependent on the special qualities of being. In itself nonbeing has no quality and no difference of qualities. But it gets them in relation to being. The character of the negation of being is determined by that in being which is negated. This makes it possible to speak of qualities of nonbeing and, consequently, of types of anxiety.

Up to now we have used the term nonbeing without differentiation, while in the discussion of courage several forms of self-affirmation were mentioned. They correspond to different forms of anxiety and are understandable only in correlation with them. I suggest that we distinguish three types of anxiety according to the three directions in which nonbeing threatens being. Nonbeing threatens man's ontic self-affirmation, relatively in terms of fate, absolutely in terms of death. It threatens man's spiritual self-affirmation, relatively in terms of emptiness, absolutely in terms of meaningfulness. It threatens man's moral self-affirmation, relatively in terms of guilt, absolutely in terms of condemnation. The awareness of this threefold threat is anxiety appearing in three forms, that of fate and death (briefly, the anxiety of death), that of emptiness and loss of meaning (briefly, the anxiety of meaninglessness), that of guilt and condemnation (briefly, the anxiety of condemnation). In all three forms anxiety is existential in the sense that it belongs to existence as such and not to an abnormal state of mind as in neurotic (and psychotic) anxiety. . . .

The Anxiety of Fate and Death

Fate and death are the way in which our ontic self-affirmation is threatened by nonbeing. "Ontic," from the Greek *on,* "being," means here the basic self-affirmation of a being in its simple existence. (Ontological designates the philosophical analysis of the nature of being.) The anxiety of fate and death is most basic, most universal, and inescapable. All attempts to argue it away are futile. Even if the so-called arguments for the "immortality of the soul" had argumentative power (which they do not have) they would not convince existentially. For existentially everybody is aware of the complete loss of self which biological extinction implies. The unsophisticated mind knows instinctively what sophisticated ontology formulates: that reality has the basic structure of self-world correlation and that with the disappearance of the one side the world, the other side, the self, also disappears, and what remains is their common ground but not their structural correlation. It has been observed that the anxiety of death increases with the increase of individualization and that people in collectivistic cultures are less open to this type of anxiety. The observation is correct yet the explanation that there is no basic anxiety about death in collectivist cultures is wrong. The reason for the difference from more individualized civilizations is that the special type of courage which characterizes collectivism, as long as it is unshaken, allays the anxiety of death. But the very fact that courage has to be created through many internal and external (psychological and ritual) activities and symbols shows that basic anxiety has to be overcome even in collectivism. Without its at least potential presence neither war nor the criminal law in these societies would be understandable. If there were no fear of death, the threat of the law or of a superior enemy would be without effect—which it obviously is not. Man as man in every civilization is anxiously aware of the threat of nonbeing and needs the courage to affirm himself in spite of it.

The anxiety of death is the permanent horizon within which the anxiety of fate is at work. For the threat against man's ontic self-affirmation is not only the absolute threat of death but also the relative threat of fate. Certainly the anxiety of death overshadows all concrete anxieties and gives them their ultimate seriousness. They have, however, a certain independence and, ordinarily, a more immediate impact than the anxiety of death. The term "fate" for this whole group of anxieties stresses one element which is common to all of them: their contingent character, their unpredictability, the impossibility of showing their meaning and purpose. One can describe this in terms of the categorical structure of our experience. One can show the contingency of our temporal being, the fact that we exist in this and no other period of time, beginning in a contingent moment, ending in a contingent moment, filled with experiences which are contingent themselves with respect to quality and quantity. One can show the contingency of our spatial being (our finding ourselves in this and no other place, and the strangeness of this place in spite of its familiarity); the contingent character of ourselves and the place from which we look at our world; and the contingent character of the reality at which we look, that is, our world. Both could be different: this is their contingency and this produces the anxiety about our spatial existence. One can show the contingency of the causal interdependence of which one is a part, both with respect to the past and to the present, the vicissitudes coming from our world and the hidden forces in the depths of our own self. Contingent does not mean causally undetermined but it means that the determining causes of our existence have no ultimate necessity. They are given, and they cannot be logically derived. Contingently we are put into the whole web of causal relations. Contingently we are determined by them in every moment and thrown out by them in the last moment.

Fate is the rule of contingency, and the anxiety about fate is based on the finite being's awareness of being contingent in every respect, of having no ultimate necessity. Fate is usually identified with necessity in the sense of an inescapable causal determination. Yet it is not causal necessity that makes fate a matter of anxiety but the lack of ultimate necessity, the irrationality, the impenetrable darkness of fate.

The threat of nonbeing to man's ontic self-affirmation is absolute in the threat of death, relative in the threat of fate. But the relative threat is a threat only because in its background stands the absolute threat.

Fate would not produce inescapable anxiety without death behind it. And death stands behind fate and its contingencies not only in the last moment when one is thrown out of existence but in every moment within existence. Nonbeing is omnipresent and produces anxiety even where an immediate threat of death is absent. It stands behind the experience that we are driven, together with everything else, from the past toward the future without a moment of time which does not vanish immediately. It stands behind the insecurity and homelessness of our social and individual existence. It stands behind the attacks on our power of being in body and soul by weakness, disease, and accidents. In all these forms fate actualizes itself, and through them the anxiety of nonbeing takes hold of us. We try to transform the anxiety into fear and to meet courageously the objects in which the threat is embodied. We succeed partly, but somehow we are aware of the fact that it is not these objects with which we struggle that produce the anxiety but the human situation as such. Out of this the question arises: Is there a courage to be, a courage to affirm oneself in spite of the threat against man's ontic self-affirmation?

The Anxiety of Emptiness and Meaninglessness

Nonbeing threatens man as a whole, and therefore threatens his spiritual as well as his ontic self-affirmation. Spiritual self-affirmation occurs in every moment in which man lives creatively in the various spheres of meaning. Creative, in this context, has the sense not of original creativity as performed by the genius but of living spontaneously, in action and reaction, with the contents of one's cultural life. In order to be spiritually creative one need not be what is called a creative artist or scientist or statesman, but one must be able to participate meaningfully in their original creations. Such a participation is creative insofar as it changes that in which one participates, even if in very small ways. The creative transformation of a language by the interdependence of the creative poet or writer and the many who are influenced by him directly or indirectly and react spontaneously to him is an outstanding example. Everyone who lives creatively in meanings affirms himself as a participant in these meanings. He affirms himself as receiving and transforming reality creatively. He loves himself as participating in the spiritual life and as loving its contents. He loves them because they are his own fulfillment and because they are actualized through him. The scientist loves both the truth he discovers and himself insofar as he discovers it. He is held by the content of his discovery. This is what one can call "spiritual self-affirmation." And if he has not discovered but only participates in the discovery, it is equally spiritual self-affirmation.

Such an experience presupposes that the spiritual life is taken seriously, that it is a matter of ultimate concern. And this again presupposes that in it and through it ultimate reality becomes manifest. A spiritual life

in which this is not experienced is threatened by nonbeing in the two
forms in which it attacks spiritual self-affirmation: emptiness and meaninglessness.

We use the term meaninglessness for the absolute threat of nonbeing
to spiritual self-affirmation, and the term emptiness for the relative
threat to it. They are no more identical than are the threat of death and
fate. But in the background of emptiness lies meaninglessness as death
lies in the background of the vicissitudes of fate.

The anxiety of meaninglessness is anxiety about the loss of an ultimate
concern, of a meaning which gives meaning to all meanings. This anxiety
is aroused by the loss of a spiritual center, of an answer, however symbolic and indirect, to the question of the meaning of existence.

The anxiety of emptiness is aroused by the threat of nonbeing to the
special contents of the spiritual life. A belief breaks down through
external events or inner processes: one is cut off from creative participation in a sphere of culture, one feels frustrated about something which
one had passionately affirmed, one is driven from devotion to one object
to devotion to another and again on to another, because the meaning of
each of them vanishes and the creative eros is transformed into indifference or aversion. Everything is tried and nothing satisfies. The contents of the tradition, however excellent, however praised, however
loved once, lose their power to give content *today*. And present culture
is even less able to provide the content. Anxiously one turns away from
all concrete contents and looks for an ultimate meaning, only to discover
that it was precisely the loss of a spiritual center which took away the
meaning from the special contents of the spiritual life. But a spiritual
center cannot be produced intentionally, and the attempt to produce it
only produces deeper anxiety. The anxiety of emptiness drives us to the
abyss of meaninglessness.

Emptiness and loss of meaning are expressions of the threat of nonbeing to the spiritual life. This threat is implied in man's finitude and
actualized by man's estrangement. It can be described in terms of doubt,
its creative and its destructive function in man's spiritual life. Man
is able to ask because he is separated *from*, while participating *in*, what
he is asking about. In every question an element of doubt, the awareness
of not having, is implied. In systematic questioning systematic doubt is
effective; e.g. of the Cartesian type. This element of doubt is a condition
of all spiritual life. The threat to spiritual life is not doubt as an element
but the total doubt. If the awareness of not having has swallowed the
awareness of having, doubt has ceased to be methodological asking and
has become existential despair. On the way to this situation the spiritual
life tries to maintain itself as long as possible by clinging to affirmations
which are not yet undercut, be they traditions, autonomous convictions,
or emotional preferences. And if it is impossible to remove the doubt, one
courageously accepts it without surrendering one's convictions. One takes

the risk of going astray and the anxiety of this risk upon oneself. In this way one avoids the extreme situation—till it becomes unavoidable and the despair of truth becomes complete.

Then man tries another way out: Doubt is based on man's separation from the whole of reality, on his lack of universal participation, on the isolation of his individual self. So he tries to break out of this situation, to identify himself with something transindividual, to surrender his separation and self-relatedness. He flees from his freedom of asking and answering for himself to a situation in which no further questions can be asked and the answers to previous questions are imposed on him authoritatively. In order to avoid the risk of asking and doubting he surrenders the right to ask and to doubt. He surrenders himself in order to save his spiritual life. He "escapes from his freedom" (Fromm) in order to escape the anxiety of meaninglessness. Now he is no longer lonely, not in existential doubt, not in despair. He "participates" and affirms by participation the contents of his spiritual life. Meaning is saved, but the self is sacrificed. And since the conquest of doubt was a matter of sacrifice, the sacrifice of the freedom of the self, it leaves a mark on the regained certitude: a fanatical self-assertiveness. Fanaticism is the correlate to spiritual self-surrender: it shows the anxiety which it was supposed to conquer, by attacking with disproportionate violence those who disagree and who demonstrate by their disagreement elements in the spiritual life of the fanatic which he must suppress in himself. Because he must suppress them in himself he must suppress them in others. His anxiety forces him to persecute dissenters. The weakness of the fanatic is that those whom he fights have a secret hold upon him; and to this weakness he and his group finally succumb.

It is not always personal doubt that undermines and empties a system of ideas and values. It can be the fact that they are no longer understood in their original power of expressing the human situation and of answering existential human questions. (This is largely the case with the doctrinal symbols of Christianity.) Or they lose their meaning because the actual conditions of the present period are so different from those in which the spiritual contents were created that new creations are needed. (This was largely the case with artistic expression before the industrial revolution.) In such circumstances a slow process of waste of the spiritual contents occurs, unnoticeable in the beginning, realized with a shock as it progresses, producing the anxiety of meaninglessness at its end.

Ontic and spiritual self-affirmation must be distinguished but they cannot be separated. Man's being includes his relation to meanings. He is human only by understanding and shaping reality, both his world and himself, according to meanings and values. His being is spiritual even in the most primitive expressions of the most primitive human being. In the "first" meaningful sentence all the richness of man's spiritual life is potentially present. Therefore the threat to his spiritual being is a threat to his whole being. The most revealing expression of this fact is the desire to throw away one's ontic existence rather than stand the despair of emptiness and meaninglessness. The death instinct is not an ontic but a spiritual phenomenon. Freud identified this reaction to the meaninglessness of the never-ceasing and never-satisfied libido with man's essential nature. But it is only an expression of his existential self-estrangement and of the disintegration of his spiritual life into meaninglessness. If, on the other hand, the ontic self-affirmation is weakened by nonbeing, spiritual indifference and emptiness can be the consequence, producing a circle of ontic and spiritual negativity. Nonbeing threatens from both sides, the ontic and the spiritual; if it threatens the one side it also threatens the other.

The Anxiety of Guilt and Condemnation

Nonbeing threatens from a third side; it threatens man's moral self-affirmation. Man's being, ontic as well as spiritual, is not only given to him but also demanded of him. He is responsible for it; literally, he is required to answer, if he is asked, what he has made of himself. He who asks him is his judge, namely he himself, who, at the same time, stands against him. This situation produces the anxiety which, in relative terms, is the anxiety of guilt; in absolute terms, the anxiety of self-rejection or condemnation. Man is essentially "finite freedom"; freedom not in the sense of indeterminacy but in the sense of being able to determine himself through decisions in the center of his being. Man, as finite freedom, is free within the contingencies of his finitude. But within these limits he is asked to make of himself what he is supposed to become, to fulfill his destiny. In every act of moral self-affirmation man contributes to the fulfillment of his destiny, to the actualization of what he potentially is. It is the task of· ethics to describe the nature of this fulfillment, in philosophical or theological terms. But however the norm is formulated man has the power of acting against it, of contradicting his essential being, of losing his destiny. And under the conditions of man's estrangement from himself this is an actuality. Even in what he considers his best deed nonbeing is present and prevents it from being perfect. A profound ambiguity between good and evil permeates everything he does, because it permeates his personal being as such. Nonbeing is mixed with being in his moral self-affirmation as it is in his spiritual and ontic self-affirmation. The awareness of this ambiguity is the feeling of guilt. The judge who is oneself and who stands against oneself, he who "knows with" (conscience) everything we do and are, gives a negative judgment, experienced by us as guilt. The anxiety of guilt shows the same complex characteristics as the anxiety about ontic and spiritual nonbeing. It is present in every moment of moral self-awareness and can drive us toward complete self-rejection, to the feeling of being condemned—not to an external punishment but to the despair of having lost our destiny.

To avoid this extreme situation man tries to transform the anxiety of guilt into moral action regardless of its imperfection and ambiguity. Courageously he takes nonbeing into his moral self-affirmation. This can happen in two ways, according to the duality of the tragic and the personal in man's situation, the first based on the contingencies of fate, the second on the responsibility of freedom. The first way can lead to a defiance of negative judgments and the moral demands on which they are based; the second way can lead to a moral rigor and the self-satisfaction derived from it. In both of them—usually called anomism and legalism—the anxiety of guilt lies in the background and breaks again and again into the open, producing the extreme situation of moral despair.

Nonbeing in a moral respect must be distinguished but cannot be separated from ontic and spiritual nonbeing. The anxiety of the one type is immanent in the anxieties of the other types. The famous words of Paul about "sin as the sting of death" point to the immanence of the anxiety of guilt within the fear of death. And the threat of fate and death has always awakened and increased the consciousness of guilt. The threat of moral nonbeing was experienced in and through the threat of ontic nonbeing. The contingencies of fate received moral interpretation: fate executes the negative moral judgment by attacking and perhaps destroying the ontic foundation of the morally rejected personality. The two forms of anxiety provoke and agument each other. In the same way spiritual and moral nonbeing are interdependent. Obedience to the moral norm, i.e. to one's own essential being, excludes emptiness and meaninglessness in their radical forms. If the spiritual contents have lost their power the self-affirmation of the moral personality is a way in which meaning can be rediscovered. The simple call to duty can save from emptiness, while the disintegration of the moral consciousness is an almost irresistible basis for the attack of spiritual nonbeing. On the other hand, existential doubt can undermine moral self-affirmation by throwing into the abyss of skepticism not only every moral principle but the meaning of moral self-affirmation as such. In this case the doubt is felt as guilt, while at the same time guilt is undermined by doubt.

. . . .

Absolute Faith and the Courage to Be

We have avoided the concept of faith in our description of the courage to be which is based on mystical union with the ground of being as well as in our description of the courage to be which is based on the personal encounter with God. This is partly because the concept of faith has lost its genuine meaning and has received the connotation of "belief in something unbelievable." But this is not the only reason for the use of terms other than faith. The decisive reason is that I do not think either mystical union or personal encounter fulfills the idea of faith. Certainly there is faith in the elevation of the soul above the finite to the infinite, leading to its union with the ground of being. But more than this is

included in the concept of faith. And there is faith in the personal encounter with the personal God. But more than this is included in the
concept of faith. Faith is the state of being grasped by the power of being-
itself. The courage to be is an expression of faith and what "faith" means
must be understood through the courage to be. We have defined courage
as the self-affirmation of being in spite of nonbeing. The power of this
self-affirmation is the power of being which is effective in every act of
courage. Faith is the experience of this power.

But it is an experience which has a paradoxical character, the character
of accepting acceptance. Being-itself transcends every finite being infinitely; God in the divine-human encounter transcends man unconDitionally. Faith bridges this infinite gap by accepting the fact that in spite of
it the power of being is present, that he who is separated is accepted.
Faith accepts "in spite of"; and out of the "in spite of" of faith the "in
spite of" of courage is born. Faith is not a theoretical affirmation of
something uncertain, it is the existential acceptance of something transcending ordinary experience. Faith is not an opinion but a state. It is the
state of being grasped by the power of being which transcends everything that is and in which everything that is participates. He who is
grasped by this power is able to affirm himself because he knows that he
is affirmed by the power of being-itself. In this point mystical experience
and personal encounter are identical. In both of them faith is the basis of
the courage to be.

This is decisive for a period in which, as in our own, the anxiety of
doubt and meaninglessness is dominant. Certainly the anxiety of fate and
death is not lacking in our time. The anxiety of fate has increased with
the degree to which the schizophrenic split of our world has removed the
last remnants of former security. And the anxiety of guilt and condemnation is not lacking either. It is surprising how much anxiety of guilt comes
to the surface in psychoanalysis and personal counseling. The centuries
of puritan and bourgeois repression of vital strivings have produced
almost as many guilt feelings as the preaching of hell and purgatory in
the Middle Ages.

But in spite of these restricting considerations one must say that the
anxiety which determines our period is the anxiety of doubt and meaninglessness. One is afraid of having lost or of having to lose the meaning
of one's existence. The expression of this situation is the Existentialism
of today.

Which courage is able to take nonbeing into itself in the form of
doubt and meaninglessness? This is the most important and most disturbing question in the quest for the courage to be. For the anxiety of
meaninglessness undermines what is still unshaken in the anxiety of fate
and death and of guilt and condemnation. In the anxiety of guilt and
condemnation doubt has not yet undermined the certainty of an ultimate
responsibility. We are threatened but we are not destroyed. If, however,
doubt and meaninglessness prevail one experiences an abyss in which the

meaning of life and the truth of ultimate responsibility disappear. Both the Stoic who conquers the anxiety of fate with the Socratic courage of wisdom and the Christian who conquers the anxiety of guilt with the Protestant courage of accepting forgiveness are in a different situation. Even in the despair of having to die and the despair of self-condemnation meaning is affirmed and certitude preserved. But in the despair of doubt and meaninglessness both are swallowed by nonbeing.

The question then is this: Is there a courage which can conquer the anxiety of meaninglessness and doubt? Or in other words, can the faith which accepts acceptance resist the power of nonbeing in its most radical form? Can faith resist meaninglessness? Is there a kind of faith which can exist together with doubt and meaninglessness? These questions lead to the last aspect of the problem discussed in these lectures and the one most relevant to our time: How is the courage to be possible if all the ways to create it are barred by the experience of their ultimate insufficiency? If life is as meaningless as death, if guilt is as questionable as perfection, if being is no more meaningful than nonbeing, on what can one base the courage to be?

There is an inclination in some Existentialists to answer these questions by a leap from doubt to dogmatic certitude, from meaninglessness to a set of symbols in which the meaning of a special ecclesiastical or political group is embodied. This leap can be interpreted in different ways. It may be the expression of a desire for safety; it may be as arbitrary as, according to Existentialist principles, every decision is; it may be the feeling that the Christian message is the answer to the questions raised by an analysis of human existence; it may be a genuine conversion, independent of the theoretical situation. In any case it is not a solution of the problem of radical doubt. It gives the courage to be to those who are converted but it does not answer the question as to how such a courage is possible in itself. The answer must accept, as its precondition, the state of meaninglessness. It is not an answer if it demands the removal of this state; for that is just what cannot be done. He who is in the grip of doubt and meaninglessness cannot liberate himself from this grip; but he asks for an answer which is valid within and not outside the situation of his despair. He asks for the ultimate foundation of what we have called the "courage of despair." There is only one possible answer, if one does not try to escape the question: namely that the acceptance of despair is in itself faith and on the boundary line of the courage to be. In this situation the meaning of life is reduced to despair about the meaning of life. But as long as this despair is an act of life it is positive in its negativity. Cynically speaking, one could say that it is true to life to be cynical about it. Religiously speaking, one would say that one accepts oneself as accepted in spite of one's despair about the meaning of this acceptance. The paradox of every radical negativity, as long as it is an active negativity, is that it must affirm itself in order to be able to negate itself. No actual negation can be without an implicit affirmation. The hidden pleasure

produced by despair witnesses to the paradoxical character of self-negation. The negative lives from the positive it negates.

The faith which makes the courage of despair possible is the acceptance
of the power of being, even in the grip of nonbeing. Even in the despair
about meaning being affirms itself through us. The act of accepting
meaninglessness is in itself a meaningful act. It is an act of faith. We
have seen that he who has the courage to affirm his being in spite of fate
and guilt has not removed them. He remains theatened and hit by them.
But he accepts his acceptance by the power of being-itself in which he
participates and which gives him the courage to take the anxieties of fate
and guilt upon himself. The same is true of doubt and meaninglessness.
The faith which creates the courage to take them into itself has no special
content. It is simply faith, undirected, absolute. It is undefinable, since
everything defined is dissolved by doubt and meaninglessness. Nevertheless, even absolute faith is not an eruption of subjective emotions or a
mood without objective foundation.

An analysis of the nature of absolute faith reveals the following elements in it. The first is the experience of the power of being which is
present even in face of the most radical manifestation of nonbeing. If
one says that in this experience vitality resists despair one must add
that vitality in man is proportional to intentionality. The vitality that can
stand the abyss of meaninglessness is aware of a hidden meaning within
the destruction of meaning. The second element in absolute faith is the
dependence of the experience of nonbeing on the experience of being
and the dependence of the experience of meaninglessness on the experience of meaning. Even in the state of despair one has enough being to make
despair possible. There is a third element in absolute faith, the acceptance
of being accepted. Of course, in the state of despair there is nobody
and nothing that accepts. But there is the power of acceptance itself
which is experienced. Meaninglessness, as long as it is experienced,
includes an experience of the "power of acceptance." To accept this
power of acceptance consciously is the religious answer of absolute faith,
of a faith which has been deprived by doubt of any concrete content,
which nevertheless is faith and the source of the most paradoxical manifestation of the courage to be.

This faith transcends both the mystical experience and the divine-
human encounter. The mystical experience seems to be nearer to absolute
faith but it is not. Absolute faith includes an element of skepticism
which one cannot find in the mystical experience. Certainly mysticism
also transcends all specific contents, but not because it doubts them or
has found them meaningless; rather it deems them to be preliminary.
Mysticism uses the specific contents as grades, stepping on them after
having used them. The experience of meaninglessness, however, denies
them (and everything that goes with them) without having used them.
The experience of meaninglessness is more radical than mysticism.
Therefore it transcends the mystical experience.

Absolute faith also transcends the divine-human encounter. In this encounter the subject-object scheme is valid: a definite subject (man) meets a definite object (God). One can reverse this statement and say that a definite subject (God) meets a definite object (man). But in both cases the attack of doubt undercuts the subject-object structure. The theologians who speak so strongly and with such self-certainty about the divine-human encounter should be aware of a situation in which this encounter is prevented by radical doubt and nothing is left but absolute faith. The acceptance of such a situation as religiously valid has, however, the consequence that the concrete contents of ordinary faith must be subjected to criticism and transformation. The courage to be in its radical form is a key to an idea of God which transcends both mysticism and the person-to-person encounter.

. . . .

Theism Transcended

The courage to take meaninglessness into itself presupposes a relation to the ground of being which we have called "absolute faith." It is without a *special* content, yet it is not without content. The content of absolute faith is the "God above God." Absolute faith and its consequence, the courage that takes the radical doubt, the doubt about God, into itself, transcends the theistic idea of God.

Theism can mean the unspecified affirmation of God. Theism in this sense does not say what it means if it uses the name of God. Because of the traditional and psychological connotations of the word God such an empty theism can produce a reverent mood if it speaks of God. Politicians, dictators, and other people who wish to use rhetoric to make an impression on their audience like to use the word God in this sense. It produces the feeling in their listeners that the speaker is serious and morally trustworthy. This is especially successful if they can brand their foes as atheistic. On a higher level people without a definite religious commitment like to call themselves theistic, not for special purposes but because they cannot stand a world without God, whatever this God may be. They need some of the connotations of the word God and they are afraid of what they call atheism. On the highest level of this kind of theism the name of God is used as a poetic or practical symbol, expressing a profound emotional state or the highest ethical idea. It is a theism which stands on the boundary line between the second type of theism and what we call "theism transcended." But it is still too indefinite to cross this boundary line. The atheistic negation of this whole type of theism is as vague as the theism itself. It may produce an irreverent mood and angry reaction of those who take their theistic affirmation seriously. It may even be felt as justified against the rhetorical-political abuse of the name of God, but it is ultimately as irrelevant as the theism which it negates. It cannot reach the state of despair any more than the theism against which it fights can reach the state of faith.

Theism can have another meaning, quite contrary to the first one: it can be the name of what we have called the divine-human encounter. In this case it points to those elements in the Jewish-Christian tradition which emphasize the person-to-person relationship with God. Theism in this sense emphasizes the personalistic passages in the Bible and the Protestant creeds, the personalistic image of God, the word as the tool of creation and revelation, the ethical and social character of the kingdom of God, the personal nature of human faith and divine forgiveness, the historical vision of the universe, the idea of a divine purpose, the infinite distance between creator and creature, the absolute separation between God and the world, the conflict between holy God and sinful man, the person-to-person character of prayer and practical devotion. Theism in this sense is the nonmystical side of biblical religion and historical Christianity. Atheism from the point of view of this theism is the human attempt to escape the divine-human encounter. It is an existential—not a theoretical—problem.

Theism has a third meaning, a strictly theological one. Theological theism is, like every theology, dependent on the religious substance which it conceptualizes. It is dependent on theism in the first sense insofar as it tries to prove the necessity of affirming God in some way; it usually develops the so-called arguments for the "existence" of God. But it is more dependent on theism in the second sense insofar as it tries to establish a doctrine of God which transforms the person-to-person encounter with God into a doctrine about two persons who may or may not meet but who have a reality independent of each other.

Now theism in the first sense must be transcended because it is irrelevant, and theism in the second sense must be transcended because it is one-sided. But theism in the third sense must be transcended because it is wrong. It is bad theology. This can be shown by a more penetrating analysis. The God of theological theism is a being beside others and as such a part of the whole of reality. He certainly is considered its most important part, but as a part and therefore as subjected to the structure of the whole. He is supposed to be beyond the ontological elements and categories which constitute reality. But every statement subjects him to them. He is seen as a self which has a world, as an ego which is related to a thou, as a cause which is separated from its effect, as having a definite space and an endless time. He is a being, not being-itself. As such he is bound to the subject-object structure of reality, he is an object for us as subjects. At the same time we are objects for him as a subject. And this is decisive for the necessity of transcending theological theism. For God as a subject makes me into an object which is nothing more than an object. He deprives me of my subjectivity because he is all-powerful and all-knowing. I revolt and try to make *him* into an object, but the revolt fails and becomes desperate. God appears as the invincible tyrant, the being in contrast with whom all other beings are without freedom and subjectivity. He is equated with the recent tyrants who with the help of terror try to transform everything into a mere object, a thing among things, a cog in the machine they control. He becomes the model of everything against which Existentialism revolted. This is the God Nietzsche said had to be killed because nobody can tolerate being made into a mere object of absolute knowledge and absolute control. This is the deepest root of atheism. It is an atheism which is justified as the reaction against theological theism and its disturbing implications. It is also the deepest root of the Existentialist despair and the widespread anxiety of meaninglessness in our period.

Theism in all its forms is transcended in the experience we have called absolute faith. It is the accepting of the acceptance without somebody or something that accepts. It is the power of being-itself that accepts and gives the courage to be. This is the highest point to which our analysis has brought us. It cannot be described in the way the God of all forms of theism can be described. It cannot be described in mystical terms either. It transcends both mysticism and personal encounter, as it transcends both the courage to be as a part and the courage to be as oneself.

The God Above God and the Courage to Be

The ultimate source of the courage to be is the "God above God"; this is the result of our demand to transcend theism. Only if the God of theism is transcended can the anxiety of doubt and meaninglessness be taken into the courage to be. The God above God is the object of all mystical longing, but mysticism also must be transcended in order to reach him. Mysticism does not take seriously the concrete and the doubt concerning the concrete. It plunges directly into the ground of being and meaning, and leaves the concrete, the world of finite values and meanings, behind. Therefore it does not solve the problem of meaninglessness. In terms of the present religious situation this means that Eastern mysticism is not the solution of the problems of Western Existentialism, although many people attempt this solution. The God above the God of theism is not the devaluation of the meanings which doubt has thrown into the abyss of meaninglessness; he is their potential restitution. Nevertheless absolute faith agrees with the faith implied in mysticism in that both transcend the theistic objectivation of a God who is a being. For mysticism such a God is not more real than any finite being, for the courage to be such a God has disappeared in the abyss of meaninglessness with every other value and meaning.

The God above the God of theism is present, although hidden, in every divine-human encounter. Biblical religion as well as Protestant theology are aware of the paradoxical character of this encounter. They are aware that if God encounters man God is neither object nor subject and is therefore above the scheme into which theism has forced him. They are aware that personalism with respect to God is balanced by a transpersonal presence of the divine. They are aware that forgiveness can be accepted only if the power of acceptance is effective in man—biblically speaking, if the power of grace is effective in man. They are aware of the paradoxical character of every prayer, of speaking to somebody to whom you cannot speak because he is not "somebody," of asking somebody of whom you cannot ask anything because he gives or gives not before you ask, of saying "thou" to somebody who is nearer to the I than the I is to itelf. Each of these paradoxes drives the religious consciousness toward a God above the God of theism.

The courage to be which is rooted in the experience of the God above the God of theism units and transcends the courage to be as a part and the courage to be as oneself. It avoids both the loss of oneself by participation and the loss of one's world by individualization. The acceptance of the God above the God of theism makes us a part of that which is not also a part but is the ground of the whole. Therefore our self is not lost in a larger whole, which submerges it in the life of a limited group. If the self participates in the power of being-itself it receives itself back. For the power of being acts through the power of the individual selves. It does not swallow them as every limited whole, every collectivism, and every conformism does. This is why the Church, which stands for the power of being-itself or for the God who transcends the God of the religions, claims to be the mediator of the courage to be. A church which is based on the authority of the God of theism cannot make such a claim. It inescapably develops into a collectivist or semicollectivist system itself.

But a church which raises itself in its message and its devotion to the God above the God of theism without sacrificing its concrete symbols can mediate a courage which takes doubt and meaninglessness into itself. It is the Church under the Cross which alone can do this, the Church which preaches the Crucified who cried to God who remained his God after the God of confidence had left him in the darkness of doubt and meaninglessness. To be as a part in such a church is to receive a courage to be in which one cannot lose one's self and in which one receives one's world.

Absolute faith, or the state of being grasped by the God beyond God, is not a state which appears beside other states of the mind. It never is something separated and definite, an event which could be isolated and described. It is always a movement in, with, and under other states of the mind. It is the situation on the boundary of man's possibilities. It *is* this boundary. Therefore it is both the courage of despair and the courage in and above every courage. It is not a place where one can live, it is without the safety of words and concepts, it is without a name, a church, a cult, a theology. But it is moving in the depth of all of them. It is the power of being, in which they participate and of which they are fragmentary expressions.

One can become aware of it in the anxiety of fate and death when the traditional symbols, which enable men to stand the vicissitudes of fate and the horror of death have lost their power. When "providence" has become a superstition and "immortality" something imaginary that which once was the power in these symbols can still be present and create the courage to be in spite of the experience of a chaotic world and a finite existence. The Stoic courage returns but not as the faith in universal reason. It returns as the absolute faith which says Yes to being without seeing anything concrete which could conquer the nonbeing in fate and death.

And one can become aware of the God above the God of theism in the anxiety of guilt and condemnation when the traditional symbols that enable men to withstand the anxiety of guilt and condemnation have lost their power. When "divine judgment" is interpreted as a psychological complex and forgiveness as a remnant of the "father-image," what once was the power in those symbols can still be present and create the courage to be in spite of the experience of an infinite gap between what we are and what we ought to be. The Lutheran courage returns but not supported by the faith in a judging and forgiving God. It returns in terms of the absolute faith which says Yes although there is no special power that conquers guilt. The courage to take the anxiety of meaning-lessness upon oneself is the boundary line up to which the courage to be can go. Beyond it is mere non-being. Within it all forms of courage are re-established in the power of the God above the God of theism. *The courage to be is rooted in the God who appears when God has disappeared in the anxiety of doubt.*

PROFESSOR TILLICH'S CONFUSIONS

Paul Edwards

PAUL EDWARDS is Professor of Philosophy at Brooklyn College. He is the author of *The Logic of Mortal Discourse* (1955), and co-editor of *A Modern Introduction to Philosophy* (1973, with Pap). He is also editor-in-chief of the eight-volume *Encyclopedia of Philosophy* (1967).

1. ANTHROPOMORPHIC AND METAPHYSICAL CONCEPTIONS OF GOD

There is a tendency among believers, especially those who are professional philosophers, to make God as unlike human beings as possible. The opposite tendency, of regarding God as very much like a human being, only wiser, kinder, juster, and more powerful, is also, of course, quite common. In Hume's *Dialogues Concerning Natural Religion*, the believers in God, Demea and Cleanthes, are spokesmen for these two positions respectively. "His ways," remarks Demea, "are not our ways. His attributes are perfect, but incomprehensible." "When we mention the supreme Being," it may indeed be "more pious and respectful" to retain various of the terms which we apply to human beings, but in that case we "ought to acknowledge, that their meaning is totally incomprehensible; and that the infirmities of our nature do not permit us to reach any ideas, which in the least correspond to the ineffable sublimity of the divine attributes." [1] Cleanthes denounces Demea and those who share his views as "atheists without knowing it" (ibid., p. 159). He maintains that the divine mind must be regarded as a mind in the sense in which we speak of human minds, and when we apply such words as "rational" and "good" and "powerful" to the deity we are using them in one or other of their familiar senses—what we say is by no means incomprehensible.

I shall refer to views like Demea's as "metaphysical" and to those typified by Cleantheseas "anthropomorphic" theology. If this terminology is adopted then Professor Tillich has to be classified as a metaphysical believer. He is quite emphatic in his rejection of the anthropomorphic position to which he disdainfully applies such labels as "monarchic monotheism." The God of the anthropomorphic believers, Tillich writes, "is a being beside others and as such a part of the whole of reality. He certainly is considered its most important part, but as a part and therefore as subjected to the structure of the whole. He is supposed to be beyond the ontological elements and categories which constitute reality. But every statement subjects him to them. He is seen as a self which has a world, as an ego which is related to a thou, as a cause which is separated from its effect, as having a definite space and an endless time. He is a being, not being itself." [2] No, God is not "*a being*." "The being of God is being-itself. . . . If God is *a* being, he is subject to the categories of finitude, especially to space and substance. Even if he is called the 'highest being' in the sense of the 'most perfect' and the 'most powerful' being this situation is not changed. When applied to God, superlatives become diminutives. . . . Whenever infinite or unconditional power and meaning are attributed to the highest being, it has ceased to be *a* being and has become being-itself." [3] God is that "which transcends the world infinitely." The idea of God is not the idea of "some*thing* or some*one* who might not exist" (*ST*, p. 205, Tillich's italics).

Like Demea, Tillich maintains that the words which we apply to human beings cannot be applied to God in their literal senses since God is so very far removed from anything finite. "As the power of being, God transcends every being and also the totality of beings—the world. . . .

---

[1] *Dialogues Concerning Natural Religion*, Kemp Smith ed., p. 156.
[2] *The Courage to Be* (from now on referred to as *CB*), p. 184.
[3] *Systematic Theology*, Vol. 1 (to be referred to as *ST*), p. 235.

Being-itself infinitely transcends every finite being. There is no proportion or graduation between the finite and infinite. There is an absolute break, an infinite 'jump' " (ST, p. 237).

There is only one statement that we can make about God in which we use words "directly and properly," i.e. literally, and that is the statement that "God is being-itself." This statement, it is true, can be elaborated to mean that "God as being-itself is the ground of the ontological structure of being without being subject to this structure himself. He *is* the structure; that is, he has the power of determining the structure of everything that has being. . . . If anything beyond this bare assertion is said about God, it no longer is a direct and proper statement" (ST, p. 239). Tillich does indeed in various places say such things as that God is Love or that God is living. But these, as well as any other statements ascribing characteristics to God, must be treated as "metaphorical or symbolic" [4] utterances. "Any concrete assertion about God," Tillich makes it clear, "must be symbolic, for a concrete assertion is one which uses a segment of finite experience in order to say something about him" (ST, p. 239).

God, as Being-itself, so far transcends any separate, conditioned, finite being that we cannot even properly assert his existence. God is indeed "the creative ground of essence and existence," but it is "wrong . . . to speak of him as existing." "God does not exist." God is "above existence" and "it is as atheistic to affirm the existence of God as it is to deny it" (ST, pp. 204–205, 236, 237).

It may at first seem pointless for an unbeliever (like myself) to take issue with a philosopher who concedes that "God does not exist." But Tillich does make other remarks which unbelievers would or should oppose. Thus he speaks of the "actuality of God" (ST, p. 239) and he also holds that unlike any contingent, finite entity, Being-itself possesses necessary being (it is not, as we saw, something or someone who might or might not exist) so that, as Sidney Hook has pointed out, "despite Tillich's denial, Being is endowed with a certain kind of existence—that which cannot not be." [5] But in any event, I do not wish to argue that Being-itself does not exist. To do so would presuppose that Tillich's talk about Being-itself is intelligible and this is what I wish to deny.

When I say, with certain reservations to be explained below, that Tillich's assertions about Being-itself are unintelligible, I am not merely applying the general positivistic condemnation of metaphysics to this particular system. The war-cry of the early logical positivists that "metaphysics is nonsense" does seem to be open to serious objections. For one

---

[4] CB, p. 179. When making admissions of this kind, Tillich seems to use "symbolic," "metaphorical," and "analogous" interchangeably and I shall also follow this practice. It is fair to add that in discussing the history of religion Tillich uses "symbol" in other ways also. For a critical discussion of Tillich's various uses of this word, see W. Alston's "Tillich's Conception of the Religious Symbol," in S. Hook (ed.), *Religious Experience and Language*, New York University Press, 1961.

[5] "The Quest for 'Being,' " *Journal of Philosophy*, 1953, p. 719.

thing, it is notoriously difficult to formulate a criterion of meaning which does not rule out either too much or too little and which does not have the appearance of being, in certain respects, arbitrary and question-begging. There can also be no doubt that metaphysical systems are much more complex than some of the enemies of metaphysics believed—frequently they have all kinds of interesting and curious "links" to experience and they are only on the rarest occasions purely "transcendent." Granting this, it seems to me that the logical positivists nevertheless deserve great credit for helping to call attention to certain features of many sentences (and systems) commonly called "metaphysical." The metaphysicians are sometimes obscurely, but never, to my knowledge, clearly aware of these features. On the contrary, they manage by various stratagems to hide these features both from themselves and others. When, in non-philosophical contexts, it is found that a sentence possesses one or more of these characteristics, we do not hesitate to call it meaningless. We do not hesitate to say that it fails to assert anything.

I propose to show now that many of the most important sentences of Tillich's metaphysical system do possess certain of these features. Since they are put forward not merely as expressions of devout feeling or as vehicles of edifying pictures but as truth-claims, it would be interesting to know why, if they really possess the features in question, they should not be rejected as meaningless.

Throughout this article I am using "meaningless," "unintelligible," "devoid of cognitive content," "failing to make an assertion," "saying nothing at all," and "lacking referential meaning" interchangeably. I am aware that, as widely used, not all these expressions have the same meaning or the same force. For example, if I say to a taxi driver, "Go to Amsterdam Avenue and 82nd Street!" this is "intelligible," it is "meaningful," it "says something," but it would not be said to possess "cognitive content" by those who use this expression at all, we would not say that I used the sentence to make an assertion and most of those who used the word "referent" would say that this sentence, like imperatives generally, was without referential meaning. I do not think that this departure from widespread uses is of any consequence for the purposes of this article, but in any event I would be willing to argue that Tillich's theology is all of the things mentioned—meaningless, unintelligible, and all the rest.

2. TILLICH'S THEOLOGY IS COMPATIBLE WITH ANYTHING WHATSOEVER

We normally regard as empty, as devoid of (cognitive) meaning or content a sentence which, while pretending to assert something, is on further examination found to be compatible with any state of affairs. If, for example, I say "Bomba is going to wear a red tie tonight" and if I do not withdraw my statement even if he shows up wearing a brown or a black or a grey tie, and if it further becomes clear that I will not consider my statement refuted even if Bomba wears no tie at all and in fact that I will consider it "true," no matter what happens anywhere, then it would be generally agreed that I have really said nothing at all. I have in this context deprived the expression "red tie" of any meaning. I have excluded no conceivable state of affairs and this, in the context in which people are attempting to make factual assertions, is generally considered a sufficient ground for condemning the sentence in question as empty or devoid of content.

Now, unless I have misunderstood Tillich, exactly the same is true of *his* belief in God. However, before showing this, it would be well to bring out as forcibly as possible the enormous difference between Tillich's position and the anthropomorphic theology of Cleanthes and of most ordinary believers. Cleanthes at one stage produces what he calls the "illustration" of the "heavenly voice." Suppose, he says, that an articulate voice were heard in the clouds, much louder and more melodious than any which human art could ever reach: Suppose that this voice were extended in the same instant over all nations, and spoke to each nation in its own language and dialect: Suppose, that the words delivered not only contain a just sense and meaning, but convey some instruction altogether worthy of a benevolent Being, superior to mankind." We can make this more definite by supposing that the voice made statements about the cure and prevention of all kinds of illnesses, such as cancer, which are as yet very imperfectly understood, as well as about a large number of other unsolved scientific problems and that upon examination every one of these statements turned out to be true. It is clear that if such a voice were heard, Cleanthes would regard this as confirmation of the existence of God in the sense in which he asserted it. I think it is equally clear that most ordinary believers would be jubilant if such events occurred and that they too would regard their belief confirmed. I do not know how Tillich would in fact react to such events, but I know how he *should* react. The only attitude consistent with his position would be to be (theoretically) wholly indifferent to what happened. The heavenly voice would in no way whatever be a confirmation of *his* theology.

Since heavenly voices do not actually exist, this departure from anthropomorphic theology may not seem to be to Tillich's disadvantage. His position, moreover, may seem to possess a considerable advantage over that of believers in an anthropomorphic God who is declared to be *all*-powerful and *perfectly* good. It has often been shown that the existence of evil falsifies the belief in such a God, and it is generally admitted, even by those who stick to this belief, that the fact of evil presents a ticklish problem. Tillich's theology, however, is immune to any such attack. Since he does not maintain either that God is all-powerful, in the literal sense, or that he is all-good, in the literal sense, Tillich's theology does not imply that there is no evil in the world, in any of the ordinary senses

of the word. In fact, even if the world were immensely more full of evil
than it is, if it were such a frightful place that Nazi concentration camps
and cancer hospitals would be regarded, by comparison, as utopian
places of health and happiness and justice—even such a state of affairs
would in no way falsify Tillich's view. Being-itself, i.e. God, would still
be "actual."

The same would hold for any other aspect of the world. Whether human beings discover more and more order in the world or not, whether
future scientific developments show space to be finite or infinite or
neither, whether new observations confirm the steady-state theory of
Hoyle and Bondi or the "bing-bang" cosmology of Gamow and Lemaitre
—it all makes no difference: Being-itself would still be actual. Being-itself,
as we noted, is not "something or someone who might or might not be."
This may be true of the anthropomorphic deity, but not of Being-itself.

I hope that my point is clear now. Tillich's theology is indeed safe from
anti-theological arguments based on the existence of evil, but only at the
expense of *being compatible with anything whatever*. All of us normally
regard this, as I tried to show, as a reason for calling a sentence meaningless or devoid of cognitive content.

3. BEING-ITSELF AND IRREDUCIBLE METAPHORS

As we saw, Tillich readily admits that only in the basic statement of
his system are all words used in their literal senses. All other statements
about Being-itself are "symbolic" or "metaphorical." Tillich not only
repeatedly makes general statements to this effect, he also tells us on
many, though *not* on all, occasions when he discusses the characteristics
of Being-itself that the words he uses in characterizing the Ultimate
Reality are not to be understood literally. Thus he writes, "If one is
asked how nonbeing is related to being-itself, one can only answer metaphorically: being 'embraces' itself and nonbeing. Being has nonbeing
'within' itself as that which is eternally present and eternally overcome in
the process of the divine life" (*CB*, p. 34). Again: "In a metaphorical
statement (and every assertion about being-itself is either metaphorical or
symbolic) one could say that being includes nonbeing but nonbeing does
not prevail against it. 'Including' is a spatial metaphor which indicates
that being embraces itself and that which is opposed to it, nonbeing.
Nonbeing belongs to being; it cannot be separated from it" (*CB*, p. 179).
Again: "The divine life participates in every life as its ground and aim.
God participates in everything that is; he has community with it; he
shares in its destiny. Certainly such statements are highly symbolic. . . .
God's participation is not a spatial or temporal presence. It is meant not
categorically but symbolically. It is the parousia, the 'being with' of
that which is neither here nor there. If applied to God, participation

and community are not less symbolic than individualization and personality" (*ST*, p. 245). And again: "But in God as God there is no distinction
between potentiality and actuality. Therefore, we cannot speak of God as
living in the proper or nonsymbolic sense of the word 'life' " (*ST*, p. 242).

Tillich sees nothing at all wrong in his constant employment of metaphors. On the contrary, he stresses the fact that without employing terms
taken from "segments of finite experience," theological sentences would
have little or no emotional force. "Anthropomorphic symbols," he writes,
"are adequate for speaking of God religiously. Only in this way can he be
the living God for man" (*ST*, p. 242). Tillich is indeed aware of the
objection of certain philosophers that it is illegitimate to use terms which
have a reasonably well-defined meaning in everyday contexts to make
assertions about a reality that is infinitely removed from the contexts in
which these expressions were originally introduced. He dismisses this
objection without much ado. Such "accusations are mistaken," Tillich
replies, "they miss the meaning of ontological concepts. . . . It is the
function of an ontological concept to use some realm of experience to
point to characteristics of being-itself which lie above the split between
subjectivity and objectivity and which therefore cannot be expressed
literally in terms taken from the subjective or the objective side. They
must be understood not literally but analogously." This, however, Tillich
insists, "does not mean that they have been produced arbitrarily and can
easily be replaced by other concepts. Their choice is a matter of experience and thought, and subject to criteria which determine the adequacy
or inadequacy of each of them" (*CB*, p. 25).

The rejoinder that "of course" the terms in question are used "analogously," "symbolically" or "merely as metaphors" exercises the same
hypnotic spell over Tillich as it has on metaphysicians in the past. He
seems to think that it is a solution of the problem. In fact, however, it is
nothing of the sort. It is an implicit admission that a problem exists. The
concession by an author that he is using a certain word metaphorically is
tantamount to admitting that, in a very important sense and a sense
relevant to the questions at issue between metaphysicians and their
critics, he does not mean what he says. It does not automatically tell us
what he does mean or whether in fact he means anything at all. When
Bradley, for example, wrote that "the Absolute enters into . . . evolution
and progress" it is clear that the word "enter" is used in a metaphorical
and not a literal sense. But realizing this does not at once tell us what, if
anything, Bradley asserted.

Often indeed when words are used metaphorically, the context or
certain special conventions make it clear what is asserted. Thus, when a
certain historian wrote that "the Monroe Doctrine has always rested on
the broad back of the British navy," it would have been pedantic and
foolish to comment "what on earth does he mean—doesn't he know that
navies don't have backs?" Or if a man, who has been involved in a scandal
and is advised to flee his country, rejects the advice and says, "No, I

think I'll stay and face the music," it would be absurd to object to his statement on the ground that it is not exactly music that he is going to hear. In these cases we know perfectly well what the authors mean although they are using certain words metaphorically. But we know this because we can eliminate the metaphorical expression, because we can specify the content of the assertion in non-metaphorical language, because we can supply the literal equivalent.

The examples just cited are what I shall call "reducible metaphors." I prefer this to the phrase "translatable metaphor" because of certain ambiguities in the use of "translatable." We sometimes say of the English version of a foreign original—e.g. of the Kalisch version of the *Rosen-kavalier*—that it is a bad or inadequate translation although it does in fact reproduce all the truth-claims contained in the original. Conversely we sometimes, as in the case of the Blitzstein version of the *Dreigrosche-noper*, speak of a magnificent translation although we know that *not* all truth-claims of the original have been reproduced. In the present context, however, we are exclusively concerned with reproduction of truth-claims and in calling a metaphor "reducible" all I mean is that the truth-claims made by the sentence in which it occurs can be reproduced by one or more sentences all of whose components are used in literal senses.

Now, Tillich and many other metaphysicians fail to notice the difference between metaphors which are reducible in the sense just explained and those which are not. When a sentence contains an irreducible metaphor, it follows at once that the sentence is devoid of cognitive meaning, that it is unintelligible, that it fails to make a genuine assertion. For what has happened is that the sentence has been deprived of the referent it would have had, assuming that certain other conditions had also been fulfilled, if the expression in question had been used in its literal sense. To say that the metaphor is irreducible is to say in effect that no new referent can be supplied.

It will be instructive to look at an actual case in which a philosopher gave this very reason for his accusation that certain statements by another philosopher were devoid of meaning. I am referring to Berkeley's attack on Locke's claim that the material substratum "supports" the sense-qualities. Berkeley first pointed to the original context in which the word "support" is introduced, as when we say that pillars support a building. He then pointed out that since, according to Locke, the material substratum is a "something, x, I know not what" whose characteristics are unknown and indeed unknowable, and, since, therefore, it is not known to resemble pillars in any way, Locke could not possibly have been using the word "support" in its "usual or literal sense." "In what sense therefore," Berkeley went on, "must it be taken? . . . What that is they (Locke and those who share his view) do not explain." Berkeley then concluded that the sentences in question have "no distinct meaning annexed" [6] to them.

[6] *Principles of Human Knowledge*, §§ 16–17.

Let us consider some possible answers to Berkeley's criticism without in any way implying that Locke himself would have approved of any of them. Perhaps the most obvious answer would be that Locke should never have spoken of the material substratum as an unknowable entity. It should really be understood as an aggregate of material particles to which certain adjectives like mass- and velocity-predicates can be applied in their literal senses. Locke's statement that the material substratum supports the sense-qualities can then be translated into some such statement as that the particular "gross" sense-qualities perceived at any moment are, in part, causally dependent on the distribution and velocities of, the particles in question. On this view there would be no irreducible metaphors in the original sentence.

A second line of defence would begin by admitting that the material substratum *would* be completely unknowable, if sensory observation were the only method of becoming acquainted with objective realities. In fact, however, it would be said, we possess a "super-sensuous" faculty with which we "experience" such realities as material and spiritual substances. We could, if we wanted, introduce a set of terms as the symbols literally referring to the data disclosed by this super-sensuous faculty and we could exchange information about these with all who share in the possession of the faculty. If we call this the "intellectual language," then, so this defence of Locke would run, sentences with metaphors when containing terms from the "sensory level," can be translated into sentences in the intellectual language which will be free from metaphors.

Finally, in view of our later discussion, it is worth looking at a particularly naïve and lame answer to Berkeley. A defender of Locke, when confronted with the question "You do not mean 'support' in its literal sense, what then do you mean?" might say, "I mean that the material substratum holds the sense qualities together." The answer to this is obvious. "Hold together" is no more used in its literal sense than "support" and hence the difficulty has in no way been removed.

Turning now to Tillich metaphysical theology, it seems perfectly clear from numerous of his general observations that Being-itself is, even in principle, inaccessible to anybody's observation. In this respect it is exactly like Locke's material substratum. We do not and cannot have a stock of literally meaningful statements about it at our disposal which would serve as the equivalents of Tillich's "symbolic" statements. The metaphors in Tillich's sentences are, in other words, irreducible and hence, if my general argument has been correct, the sentences are unintelligible. If Tillich's statements are not to become propositions of physics or psychology or history no way out corresponding to the first of the defences of Locke is feasible. And unlike certain contemporary writers, Tillich does not avail himself of an appeal to mystical experience which would correspond to the second defence. For, if I understand Tillich correctly, he denies that even the mystic experiences Being-itself. The (true) "idea of God," Tillich writes, "transcends both mysticism and

the person-to-person encounter." [7] As I shall show in a moment, Tillich
does avail himself of a line of defence corresponding to the third of the
defences of Locke. We already saw, however, that such a defence is
altogether futile.

It may be said that I have not been fair to Tillich and other metaphysicians who defend themselves by insisting that they are using cetrain
expressions metaphorically or analogously. It may be said that I have
emphasized the negative implications of this admission—that the words in
question are not used in their literal senses—without doing justice to its
positive implications. For, it may be argued, when it is said that a certain
word is used "analogously," it *is* implied that the term has a referent,
namely a referent which is in some important respect similar to the
referent it has when used literally.

This objection rests on a confusion. We must here distinguish two
possible meanings of the assertion that a certain word is used "analogously." This may, firstly, mean no more than that the word in question is
not used literally. But it may also amount to the much stronger claim
that the word *has a referent* and hence that the sentence in which it
occurs is, if certain other conditions are fulfilled, cognitively significant.
If "analogously" is used in the former sense, then of course I would not
for a moment deny that the relevant words are used analogously in
Tillich's sentences and in the sentences of other metaphysicians. But this
is an innocuous admission. For to say that the words are used analogously
in this sense has no tendency whatever to imply that the sentences in
which they occur possess cognitive meaning. "If "analogously" is used in
the second sense, then, as just observed, it would automatically follow that
the sentences are, if other conditions are also fulfilled, cognitively significant; but in that event I would deny that the terms we have discussed are
used analogously in Tillich's sentences or in the sentences of other metaphysicians. To put the matter very simply: merely saying that a sentence,
or any part of it, has meaning does not by itself give it meaning. Such
a claim does not assure us that the sentence is intelligible. Similarly the
claim that a sentence has an "analogous" referent is a claim and no more
—it may be false. If I say, to use an example given by Sidney Hook,[8]
that the sea is angry, the word "angry" really has a referent which is
analogous to its referent when used literally. I can in this case specify
the features of the sea to which I am referring when I call it angry and I
can also specify the similarities between these features and the anger of
human beings. If, however, I say that Being-itself is angry, I could not
independently identify the features of Being-itself to which I am supposedly referring. Nor of course could I specify the similarities between

---

[7] *CB,* p. 178. I am not sure that I have here correctly understood Tillich. He also
seems to be saying the opposite at times—that mystics do have "direct access" to
Being-itself. If that is Tillich's position then some of the criticisms which follow
would not apply, but it would then be open to a number of other objections.

[8] "The Quest for Being," op. cit., p. 715.

the anger of human beings and the putative anger of Being-itself. My claim that "angry" is used analogously in this sentence in a sense in which this implies that it has a referent would be false or at any rate baseless.

The narcotic effect of such phrases as "symbolic language" or "analogous sense" is only a partial explanation of Tillich's failure to be clear about the irreducibility of his metaphors. To tell the whole story one has to take notice of an aspect of Tillich's philosophizing which I have so far ignored. What I have so far brought out may be called Tillich's "modest" side—"modest" because he does not in the passages in question claim any literal knowledge about Being-itself. But there is also what may be called Tillich's "dogmatic" side. He then seems to be jotting down in a matter-of-fact way the characteristics of Being-itself, much as a doctor might jot down descriptions of the symptoms displayed by a patient. He then writes as if he had a completely unobstructed view of the Ultimate Reality. Thus we are told as a plain matter of fact and without the use of any quotation marks that "God is infinite because he has the finite (and with it that element of non-being which belongs to finitude) within himself united with his infinity." The expression "divine life," we are told, points to "this *situation*" (*ST*, p. 252, my italics). "The divine life," Tillich admits, "is infinite mystery," but we can nevertheless say that "it is not infinite emptiness. It is the ground of all abundance, and it is abundant itself" (*ST*, p. 251). Again, we are told, without the use of any quotation marks, and I do not think their absence is a mere oversight, that God "is the eternal process in which separation is posited and is overcome by reunion" (*ST*, p. 242). In one place, to give one more illustration of the dogmatic side of his philosophy, Tillich discusses the question of whether will or intellect are dominant "in God." He quotes the rival views of Aquinas and Duns Scotus and he notes that Protestants have tended to favour the latter position which subordinates the intellect. Tillich easily resolves this dispute as if he were reading off the truth by a quick glance at God. "Theology," he writes, "must balance the new with the old (predominantly Catholic) emphasis on the form character of the divine life" (*ST*, p. 248), i.e. it must assign equal rank to will and intellect in God. The divine life, we are assured, "inescapably unites possibility with fulfillment. Neither side threatens the other nor is there a threat of disruption" (*ST*, p. 247).

Tillich, the dogmatist, does not hesitate to offer translations or what I have called reductions of his "symbolic" statements about God. We can also express literally, for example, what we mean "symbolically" when we say that God is living. "God lives," the reduction runs, "insofar as he is the ground of life" (*ST*, p. 242). Again, our symbolic statement that God is personal "does not mean that God is *a* person. It means that God is the ground of everything personal and that he carries within himself the ontological power of personality" (*ST*, p. 245). And if we symbolically say God is "his own destiny" we thereby "point to . . . the participation of God in becoming and in history" (*ST*, p. 249).

· I wish to make two observations concerning all this. Firstly, although Tillich gives the impression that the metaphors have been eliminated in these and similar cases, this is not so.: He never seems to have noticed that even in his basic statement, when elaborated in terms of "ground" and "structure," these words are used metaphorically and not literally. When Tillich writes that God or Being-itself "is the ground of the ontological structure of being and has the power of determining the structure of everything that has being," the word "ground," for example, is clearly not used in any of its literal senses. Being-itself is surely not claimed to be the ground of the ontological structure in the sense in which the earth is the ground beneath our feet or in the sense in which the premises of a valid argument may be said to be the ground for accepting the conclusion. Similar remarks apply to the use of "structure," "power," and "determine." Hence when we are told that "God lives insofar as he is the ground of life" or that "God is personal" means "God is the ground of everything personal and . . . carries within himself the ontological power of personality," expressions like "ground" and "carry within himself" and even "power" are not used literally. Tillich is here in no better a position than the supporter of Locke who substituted "hold together" for "support." That Tillich does not succeed in breaking through the circle of expressions *lacking* literal significance, i.e. lacking referential meaning, is particularly clear in the case of the "translation" of the sentence "God is his own destiny." By this "symbolic characterization, as we just saw, we "point" among other things to "the participation of God in becoming and in history." But a little earlier, in a passage which I also reproduced, we were informed that "God's participation is not a spatial or temporal presence" and twice in the same paragraph we were given to understand that when "applied to God," participation "is meant not categorically but symbolically." In other words, one metaphorical statement is replaced by another but literal significance is never achieved.

Tillich constantly engages in "circular" translations of this sort. Again and again he "explains" the meaning of one "symbolically" used expression in terms of another which is really no less symbolic. Thus in a passage reproduced at the beginning of section 3 of this article the sentence "being includes nonbeing" which contains the admittedly symbolic word "include" is translated into "nonbeing belongs to being, it cannot be separated from it." "Belong" and "separate" are no longer put inside quotation marks and one is apt to suppose that some progress has been made. Countless other illustrations of this practice could be given.

Secondly, I have the impression that, in spite of his distaste for "monarchic monotheism," Tillich occasionally relapses into something not too different from it. When offering translations such as those just quoted and generally when assessing the adequacy of certain symbols as "pointers" to the "divine life" Tillich seems to think that he has at his disposal a stock of literal truths about God not too different from those asserted by anthropomorphic believers. There is a remarkable passage in which this is strikingly evident:

Religious symbols are double-edged. They are directed toward the infinite which they symbolize *and* toward the finite through which they symbolize it. They force the infinite down to finitude and the finite up to infinity. They open the divine for the human and the human for the divine. For instance, if God is symbolized as 'Father,' he is brought down to the human relationship of father and child. But at the same time this human relationship is consecrated into a pattern of the divine-human relationship. If 'Father' is employed as a symbol for God, fatherhood is seen in its theonomous, sacramental depth. . . . If God is called the 'king,' something is said not only about God but also about the holy character of kinghood. If God's work is called 'making whole' or 'healing,' this not only says something about God but also emphasizes the theonomous character of all healing. . . . The list could be continued (*ST*, pp. 240–241).

Now, if it were known or believed that God is "majestic" in the same sense in which human beings have sometimes been called that, it would make sense to call God a "king" and it would be right to prefer this symbol to symbols like "slave" or "waiter" or "street-cleaner." Similarly, if it were known or believed that God is "concerned with the welfare" of all human beings in the literal sense of this expression, then it would make sense to speak of him as our "father" and it would be right to prefer this symbol to symbols like "daughter" or "soprano" or "carpenter." An anthropomorphic believer has criteria at his disposal in such cases, but Tillich's non-anthropomorphic theology necessarily deprives him of it. Tillich says very correctly that this list of adjectives "could be continued." Since the "comparison" between fathers and kings on the one hand and the infinitely transcending, infinitely mysterious, indescribable Being-itself, on the other, is a bogus comparison, God may no less appropriately be said to be a soprano, a slave, a street-cleaner, a daughter, or even a fascist and a hater than a father or a king.

4. Bombastic Redescriptions of Empirical Facts

Readers who were less critical than Berkeley did not realize the meaninglessness of the sentence "the material substance supports the sense-qualities" or its equivalents chiefly because of the presence of words like "support" which automatically call up certain images. Similarly, I have no doubt that the presence of such words as "embrace" and "resist" and the mental picture connected with them prevents many a reader from realizing the meaninglessness of Tillich's talk about being and nonbeing and their mutual relations. But there is also another reason why this unintelligibility is not always obvious. The reason is that, *in a certain sense,* some of Tillich's sentences are *not* unintelligible. In this connection I wish to call attention to a technique which is employed by Tillich as well as by many other metaphysicians and certainly by all other existentialists with whose writings I am familiar. I will call it the technique of "bombastic redescription" and I think that one simple illustration will make quite clear what I am referring to. Some well-known chronological facts about Freud may be stated in the following words:

Freud was born in 1856 and died in 1939   (1)

The very same facts may also be expressed in a much more bombastic fashion:

In 1856 Freud migrated from nonbeing to being and then in 1939 he returned from being to nonbeing   (2)

Now, let us assume for a moment that the author of (2) is not a metaphysician and does not in fact claim that (2) asserts anything over and above what is asserted by (1). In that event we cannot accuse him of uttering either a meaningless sentence or a falsehood, since what he says is perfectly intelligible and moreover true, or of performing an illegitimate inference; (2) does follow from (1) no less than for example "some mortal beings are men" follows from "some men are mortal." We can, however, point out that our author is employing needlessly high-sounding language to express a truth which can be stated much more simply and that (2) does not embody any grand new "insight" into anything whatever.

Let us next assume that the author of (2) is a metaphysician who assures us that (2) is not a set of simple biographical statements but belongs to "ontology"—the study of "being" and "non-being." He assures us that (2) asserts a great deal more than (1). In that event we would be entitled to reply, first, that it is not at all clear what, if anything, (2) means now, and secondly, that if it does mean more than (1), the step from (1) to (2) is not warranted. Our ontologist is thus either guilty of making a meaningless pronouncement and of performing an invalid inference or at the very least of the latter.

Let us finally assume that we are dealing with an exceedingly nebulous ontologist whose writings hardly ever contain anything that can be dignified as an "argument" or a "definition." Among his many observations about being and nonbeing he on one occasion includes sentence (2) and somewhere, not too remote in space, there also occurs sentence (1). This nebulous ontologist, unlike the other two people we considered, has not committed himself to any view about the relations between (2) and (1) and, because of this omission, he enjoys the best of two worlds. To certain uncritical readers, (2) will appear to be a profound metaphysical utterance—surely not just a redescription of the familiar facts asserted by (1). At the same time, however, (1) does remain in the background and the picture aroused by it will tend to be vaguely associated also with (2). It will be felt that it is unfair to accuse the author of "wild speculation" since his ontological statement is "firmly rooted" in experience: after all, Freud was born in 1856 and he did die in 1939.

A more critical reader could, however, confront our nebulous ontologist with the following dilemma: either (2) merely asserts what is already asserted by (1)—in that event it is nothing but a bombastic redescription of familiar facts which hardly needed an ontologist or a metaphysician for their discovery, and in that event, furthermore, it is an *empirical* proposition and its truth is in no way incompatible with empiricism or positivism or any of the doctrines despised by ontologists; or else (2) does assert more—in that event it is not at all clear what, if anything, it does assert and secondly, as already pointed out, in that event it does not follow from (1).

In much of what he is doing, Tillich, no less than other existentialists, closely resembles this nebulous ontologist. Like that ontologist he talks grandiloquently about being and nonbeing and he goes even one better in talking about "not-yet-being." Tillich's observations about being and nonbeing and not-yet-being correspond to sentence (2). Like the ontologist, Tillich also either explicitly mentions certain well-known empirical facts in conjunction with his ontological pronouncements or, when he does not actually mention them, the language chosen nevertheless very strongly tends to call these facts to the reader's mind and, I am pretty certain, to Tillich's mind also. This would correspond to sentence (1). Finally, like our nebulous ontologist, Tillich leaves the relation between his ontological remarks and the background empirical facts suitably vague. In this way what he says simultaneously enjoys the appearance of being profound, of revealing to us special insights into superempirical facts—facts about transcendent realms to which science and ordinary observation have no access but to which "existential analysis" holds the clue—and of being quite intelligible and indeed "firmly rooted" in human experience, in the "existential situation." Tillich is of course open to the same objection as our nebulous ontologist. He cannot, logically, have it both ways: either his ontological talk is merely a bombastic redescription of certain empirical facts which are often trivial and in no instance new; or it is not clear what, if anything, his sentences assert and in any event they are not then warranted by any of the empirical facts presented to the reader.

I will now give a few illustrations of this procedure. In each case, I will first summarize, in bald and untarnished language, the empirical facts of the case whether they are openly mentioned by Tillich or whether they merely hover discreetly in the background. We might refer to this as the cash-value of the doctrine in question. I will then state the corresponding ontological doctrine and whenever possible I will reproduce Tillich's own words. The reader can judge for himself whether one is justified in confronting Tillich with the dilemma mentioned in the last paragraph.

Let us begin with the subject of man's most heroic deeds.

Cash-value: Selfishness and other unadmirable motives are involved in even the best human actions.

Ontological doctrine: "Even in what he considers his best deed nonbeing is present and prevents it from being perfect. . . . Nonbeing is mixed with being in his moral self-affirmation as it is in his spiritual and ontic self-affirmation (*CB*, p. 52).

Let us turn next to man's "creatureliness."

Cash-value: Human beings have not always existed; all of them are born and before they were born or rather before they were conceived they did not exist; all of them also eventually die, and after they die they are dead, they are not then alive.

Ontological doctrine: Nonbeing in man has a dialectical character.

Full statement of ontological doctrine: "The doctrine of man's creatureliness is another point in the doctrine of man where nonbeing has a dialectical character. Being created out of nothing means having to return to nothing. The stigma of having originated out of nothing is impressed on every creature. . . . Being, limited by nonbeing, is finitude. Nonbeing appears as the 'not yet' of being and as the 'no more' of being . . . everything which participates in the power of being is 'mixed' with nonbeing. It is being in process of coming from and going toward nonbeing. It is finite" (*ST*, pp. 188–189).

Nonbeing, as we just found, appears at times as the "not-yet" of being. Ontologists can therefore hardly neglect the question of man's relation to "not-yet-being" and Tillich promptly addresses himself to this problem.

Cash-value: Human beings frequently fail to have attributes which they may or will possess at a later time—for example, babies sometimes don't have hair, but later on their heads are covered with hair; a person may at one time know only his native language, but several years later he may have mastered other languages as well, etc. etc.

Ontological doctrine: "Being and not-yet-being are 'mixed' in him (man), as they are in everything finite" (*ST*, p. 236).

5. BEING, NONBEING AND "SOME LOGICIANS"

Tillich is much irked by "some logicians" who "deny that nonbeing has conceptual character and try to remove it from the philosophical scene except in the form of negative judgments" (*CB*, p. 34). As against the logicians, Tillich insists on "the mystery of non-being" and he recommends that the "fascinating" and "exasperating" question, "What kind of being must we attribute to non-being?" should be taken seriously. His answer to the logicians is worth reproducing in full:

There are two possible ways of trying to avoid the question of nonbeing, the one logical. . . . One can assert that nonbeing is a negative judgment devoid of ontological significance. To this we must reply that every logical structure which is more than merely a play with possible relations is rooted in an ontological structure. The very fact of logical denial presupposes a type of being which can transcend the immediate given situation by means of expectations which may be disappointed. An anticipated event does not occur. This means that the judgment concerning the situation has been mistaken, the necessary conditions for the occurrence of the expected event have been non-existent. Thus disappointed, expectation creates the distinction between being and nonbeing. But how is such an expectation possible in the first place? What is the structure of this being which is able to transcend the given situation and to fall into error? The answer is that man, who is this being, must be separated from his being in a way which enables him to look at it as something strange and questionable. And such a separation is actual because man participates not only in being but also in nonbeing. Therefore, the very structure which makes negative judgements possible proves the ontological character of nonbeing. Unless man participates in non-being, no negative judgements are possible. The mystery of nonbeing cannot be solved by transforming it into a type of logical judgement (*ST*, p. 187).

Elsewhere, if I understand him correctly, Tillich repeatedly quotes, as support of his view concerning the reality of nonbeing, the existence of such "negativities" as "the transitoriness of everything created and the power of the 'demonic' in the human soul and history" (*CB*, pp. 33–34). I am certain that Tillich would also endorse Heidegger's appeal to such a "negative" phenomena as loathing, refusal, mercilessness, and renunciation [9] and William Barrett's discussion of the effects of blindness [10] as evidence for the same position.

There are so many confusions here that it is difficult to know where to begin. Probably the most serious defect of Tillich's discussion is his failure to be clear about the real point at issue between himself and the "logicians." By the "logicians" Tillich presumably means philosophers like Russell, Carnap and Ayer [11] who deny that such words as "nothing" and "nobody" and "not" are names of descriptions. Although they deny *this*, there are two other things which the "logicians" do not deny. Firstly, they do not deny the existence of the various phenomena to

---

[9] *Existence and Being*, p. 373.

[10] *Irrational Man*, pp. 256–257.

[11] Russell discusses the subject of negation in "The Philosophy of Logical Atomism," which is reprinted in *Logic and Knowledge*, in *An Enquiry Meaning and Truth* and in *Human Knowledge—Its Scope and Limits;* Carnap in "The Elimination of Metaphysics Through Logical Analysis of Language," which is reprinted in Ayer's *Logical Positivism;* Ayer discusses the subject in "Jean-Paul Sartre," *Horizon*, 1945, in "Some Aspects of Existentialism," *Rationalist Annual*, 1948 and in "Negation," reprinted in his *Philosophical Essays*. It is perhaps worth adding that the "logicians" are divided among themselves on the question of whether, in Russell's words, "there are facts which can only be asserted in sentences containing the word 'not'." William Barrett, who is the most lucid of the existentialist defenders of Nothingness, seems to think that their case would be helped if it could be shown, to use Russell's words once more, that "the world cannot be completely described without the employment of logical words like 'not'." This, however is a confusion. From the admission that "not" or "nothing" are indispensable it in no way follows that these words are names or descriptions since it is anything but obvious that only names and descriptions are indispensable.

which Tillich refers as "negatives." They do not deny that human beings quite often behave destructively, that they feel disgust, hatred, or what have you. Nor do they deny that human beings sometimes become blind or crippled in various ways and that the loss of eyes, limbs, or other parts of their bodies produces vast amounts of grief. Not only do the logicians not deny any of these phenomena, but it is difficult to see how anybody could believe or argue that such denials are logically implied by the view that "nothing" is not a name or a description. Yet, unless such denials are implied by this view, references to phenomena like hatred or blindness are completely beside the point.

The logicians, furthermore, do not deny that "not" and "nothing" are words in the "object-language" and that sentences in which they occur are frequently just as "descriptive of reality" as affirmative sentences. I do not know of any "logician" who has ever denied, for example, that the sentence "there is no butter in the refrigerator" is as descriptive of the world as the sentence "there is butter in the refrigerator" or that the sentence "I know nothing about Chinese grammar" is just as descriptive as the sentence "I know a good deal about German grammar." It is again not easy to see how it could be argued that such denials are logically implied in the view that "nothing" is not a description. I for one also see nothing objectionable in saying that while sentences like "there is butter in the refrigerator" refer to "positive" facts, sentences like "there is no butter in the refrigerator" refer to "negative" facts, that the former sentence refers to the *presence,* while the latter refers to the *absence* of butter in the refrigerator. Whatever misgivings I have about this way of talking concern the use of "fact" and not the use of "positive" and "negative" as qualifying adjectives.[12]

Once the ground is cleared in this way and no appeal is made to such totally irrelevant matters as the existence of hatred and blindness or to the fact that "not" and "nothing" occur in descriptive sentences it is easily seen that the "logicians" are right and that Tillich and other believers in nothingness are wrong. It becomes plain that Tillich and his fellow-existentialists are wrong, not necessarily in believing in some mysterious realm or mode of being which they call "nonbeing" or "nothingness," but in holding that, if there is such a realm, it is named by the word "nothing," *as that word is normally used.* They are wrong, further, in believing that the existence of such "logical structures" as negative judgements implies any transcendent ontological truths. I need not waste much time over showing that words like "nobody" or "nothing" are not names or descriptions. If somebody asks me, "Who is outside?" and I say "Bomba is outside" and on a second occasion I answer "Mrs. Bomba is outside," "Bomba" and "Mrs. Bomba" function as names— they refer to unmysterious human beings. If on a third occasion I answer "Nobody is outside," the word "nobody" is not the name of a mysterious

---

[12] For an innocuous use of "unreality" similar to my use of "negative facts," see R. L. Cartwright, "Negative Existentials," *Journal of Philosophy,* 1960.

shadowy human being. It functions as a sign of denial. To say that no-body is outside is to say that it is false to maintain that anybody is out-side. Similarly, if I say that Germany is separated from Russia by Poland or that New Jersey and New York are separated by the Hudson River, "Poland" and "the Hudson River" are names of certain things or areas. But to say about two objects or areas, the boroughs of Queens and Brooklyn, for example, that they are separated by nothing, is to say, in Ayer's words, "that they are *not* separated; and that is all that it amounts to." [13] One is not asserting here that the two areas are separated by a mysterious area which is named by the word "nothing." "Nothing," like "nobody," functions as a sign of denial and not as a name—either of something familiar or of something mysterious in a realm to which only specially gifted persons have access.

It is perhaps worth adding that the dispute is not, as Tillich suggests, between himself and existentialists on one side and "some logicians" on the other. It is between the former group and practically the whole of mankind. Ordinary people do *not* believe that "nothing" is a name. I do not suppose that ordinary people hold any explicit view on this subject, but any occasion on which the existentialist theory is presented to them, they regard it as a joke. They simply do not believe that anybody seriously advocates such a position. This surely is the only possible in-terpretation of the mirth provoked by such exchanges as those between the Messenger and the King of *Alice Through the Looking Glass*.

> "Who did you pass on the road?" the King went on, holding out his hand to the Messenger for some more hay.
> "Nobody," said the Messenger.
> "Quite right,". said the King: this young lady saw him too. So of course Nobody walks slower than you."
> "I do my best," said the Messenger in a sullen tone. "I'm sure nobody walks much faster than I do."
> "He can't do that," said the King, "or else he'd have been here first."

I have often wondered why existential ontologists pay so little atten-tion to caves, hollow tubes and holes in general. These are clear in-stances of nonbeing which should silence any sceptic. In certain table-cloths, for example, it is the number and the position of the holes which determines the excellence of the tablecloths. This surely shows that holes are real negativities. I was pleased to come across a discussion of this subject in an essay entitled "On the Social Psychology of Holes" by the unjustly forgotten German writer, Kurt Tucholsky. "When a hole is filled," Tucholsky asks, "where does it go? . . . If an object occupies a place, this place cannot also be occupied by another object but what about holes? If there is a hole in a given place can that place be occupied by other holes as well? And why aren't there halves of holes?" In short: what kind of being must we attribute to holes? I hope that Tillich or

---

[13]"Jean-Paul Sartre," op. cit., p. 18.

some other existentialist will before long address himself to this question.

To my knowledge the only people who have believed that "nothing" is a name are certain metaphysicians (including, it is true, some of the most famous like Hegel) and *some* beginning students of philosophy who in their first gropings tend to assume that all words are names.

Tillich is right in regarding disappointed expectations and the erroneous beliefs connected with them, as one of the motives for the introduction of various negative terms. He is wrong, incidentally, if he thinks that it is only the motive—such phenomena as disagreement, refusal to give information, ignorance, rejection, in a sense in which this is not simply disagreement, have also made it necessary to employ these expressions. His statement that "every logical structure is rooted in an ontological structure" is true in the case of negation if it means no more than, firstly, that negative terms would not have been introduced into our various languages if it were not for disappointed expectations, disagreement, ignorance and other phenomena of the kinds just mentioned and, secondly, that they frequently occur in sentences which are descriptive of reality. His statement is not true if it means that the word "nothing" names a special reality which needs existentialists or some rival group of ontologists for its exploration. Tillich's error becomes very evident when we reflect that words like "or" and "and" also have "existential roots." We would not have introduced them if we never hesitated, if our knowledge in a given field were always complete, if we never felt the need to enumerate our possessions, etc. Again, there is no doubt that sentences containing "or" and "and" are frequently descriptive of reality. Yet not even Tillich has had the heart to add and-being or or-being to his ontological inventory.

BUBER AND ENCOUNTER THEOLOGY

Ronald Hepburn

R. W. HEPBURN is Professor of Philosophy at Edinburgh. He is the author of *Christianity and Paradox* (1958) and, with S. E. Toulmin and Alasdair MacIntyre, of *Metaphysical Beliefs* (1957).

1

Theologians who believe that it is possible to encounter God directly, and so to offer, as we have been saying, some kind of ostensive definition of him, have recently been arguing along the following lines.

If God were an object like a hidden vein of gold or a heavenly body,

206 Good-Luck Charm of Theism or New Humanism?

too small or too remote for the telescope, then observation and argument, verifying procedures and speculation might be adequate for searching him out. But if he is no object, if instead he is a *person*, the whole situation is changed, and quite another approach to him is demanded. We approach *things* in detachment, confident that they will passively suffer our scrutiny, that our discoveries about them can be corroborated by others. Persons, on the other hand, reveal themselves fully only if we renounce our detachment and enter into reciprocal relations with them. The impact a person makes upon me may be unique to the point of being incommunicable to anyone else. The abstractness of speculation or systems of ideas is quite hostile to the immediacy and concreteness of personal encounters. Even if apologists successfully demonstrated by argument that God exists, such speculation could lead only to a 'God of the philosophers,' to an impersonal, remote First Principle. The living God, the God of Abraham, can be authentically known only to the man who addresses him as *Thou*, who finds him in the unique directness of personal contact.

Of course, a human being is not distinctively personal in all circumstances or forever. He weighs so many stones, occupies so many cubic feet; he stumbles or sits on his hat when wishing to be most thoroughly poised and personal. He also dies. God, however, never becomes an *It*, an object: he is eternally a *Thou* only. There is no detecting *his* presence by bumps on the stair or even a whispered word or the glimpse of a face. We cannot, with *him*, point or glance in this or that direction, and say, 'There, he is coming now.' We have only that felt sense of personal meeting, a sense of addressing and being addressed. He leaves no marks of his presence such that we might say—'This proves he is with us.' There is nothing for the camera or the tape-recorder. For all these and the like evidences involve the degrading of God from being a pure *Thou* to an *It*, passively at our disposal.

We should therefore be advised to cease demanding the impossible, that the existence of God should be verifiable like the presence of a chair or a table, or leave traces like a burglar who drops his jemmy. We have no right to expect the ostensive definition of 'God' to be in every respect parallel to that of 'light' (in our original example). The one appropriate procedure is to entrust ourselves in prayer to the being who is properly only talked *to*, not theorized *about*. There need be no fear of rendering our faith irrational or unsupported through this exchange. Instead of depending on uncertain chains of reasoning, we should depend on a self-authenticating direct awareness of God; a knowledge by acquaintance, from which all fallible inference-steps are absent. If the philosopher declares himself unhappy about this exchange, and suspects that it disguises a retreat to a pietistic concern with feelings and attitudes only, then he can be accused of shirking the venture of faith, a venture not of swallowing hard doctrine, but of self-commitment to the divine *Thou*, a commitment without which God's being remains veiled from us. Or if he tries but fails to have any sense of encounter with God, we must conclude that he is insensitive to the divine *Thou*, much as a colour-blind man is insensitive to certain colour-distinctions or a tone-deaf man to musical intervals. Only, *this* insensitivity, unlike the others, may be ultimately rooted in sin.

.   .   .   .

Buber's analysis of personal relations, given classical expression in his short but difficult book *I and Thou*, has provided not only the central thesis—that knowledge of God is irreducibly personal, but also much of the vocabulary, the distinctions, the either/or's, which the discussion of that thesis continues to employ. To Buber, the two 'primary words' *I-Thou* and *I-It*, describe two fundamentally different, mutually exclusive forms of our relation to our world. A being is an *It* to us when we study it with a view to manipulating it, mastering it, classifying it, comparing it with other things. Human beings also are *Its* (or what comes to the same thing, *He*s and *She*s) when regarded in these ways, treated as objects of our curiosity, sources of useful information, or exploitable means to our pleasure. In these cases we are not, in Buber's language, properly in relation with persons *as* persons: their personal being eludes us entirely. *I-It* relations must inevitably dominate many aspects of our living; but the man or woman who knows only *I-It* and is a stranger to *I-Thou* is excluded both from freedom and from 'real life'.

As the *I-It* relation can span both things *and* people, so too can the *I-Thou* relation. A natural object, say a mountain, can cease to be seen as an obstacle to the road-builder or as the stance for a fine view or a likely haunt for the eagle, and become for me a *Thou* in Buber's sense, something with which I am directly related, aware of its individuality, its uniqueness. I am not in this case concerned with this or that *aspect* of it, but I simply contemplate it as it is in itself, 'bodied over against me.' [1] There is here even a faint sense of reciprocity. The mountain or lake or tree 'has to do with me, as I with it—only in a different way . . . Relation is mutual.' [2]

With human beings naturally, the reciprocity is much more explicit. To know a person is not merely to know that his eyes are grey, his hair brown, his patience inexhaustible. It is not to know any list of characteristics, however long a list. If what we are out to do is take note of characteristics, we are still in the relation of *I-It*, the spectator *vis-à-vis* the *object* of his scrutiny. In sharp contrast,

I do not experience the man to whom I say *Thou*. But I take my stand in relation to him, in the sanctity of the primary word. . . . in the act of experience *Thou* is far away.
All real living is meeting.[3]

[1] Martin Buber, *I and Thou* (Edinburgh: T. & T. Clark, 1937), p. 8.
[2] Ibid., loc. cit.
[3] Ibid., pp. 9, 11.

All human *I-Thou* encounters pave the way for the encounter with the eternal *Thou*. Conviction of God's existence is not the result of any process of argument, for God is 'the Being that is directly, most nearly, and lastingly, over against us, that may properly only be addressed, not expressed'.[4] The moment a person begins to make an inventory of the features of the person who has been *Thou* to him, that person becomes *It* instead. But when someone detaches himself from the *divine* encounter and tries to give *it* objectivity by listing whatever half-glimpsed features he can recall of *that* meeting, he finds the original situation is being far *more* radically warped in the very describing of it. He sets out to speak of God, but finds he has spoken of something else, or discovers with dismay that he has nothing to speak of at all. But from the poverty of our descriptions nothing follows about the fact of the encounter itself. Indeed, the *I-Thou* relation is consummated, becomes fully pure, only in the encounter with God as 'absolute person'.

All this is the merest paraphrase of Buber's central teaching. Further aspects of it will emerge during the comments and criticisms I am going on to make. But first it may be helpful to substantiate the claim that the Jewish thinker, Buber, has profoundly influenced many of the best-known *Christian* theologians. The new emphasis on *meeting* rather than thinking *about* is nowhere clearer than in Emil Brunner's *The Divine-Human Encounter*. Brunner aims to return to 'Reformation principles' by rejecting both what he calls 'objectivist' and 'subjectivist' standpoints with regard to our knowledge of God. Knowing God, Brunner believes, is not receiving revealed information about him (the objective view): but it is no truer to say that God is known through the devout feelings of worshipers (the subjective option). Denying both alternatives, Brunner says he is known only through encountering him in faith. This is not the communicating of information, but an 'event . . . an act.' Faith is no simple 'believing *that*' such and such is the case, but is 'the single "answering" acceptance of the Word of God.' Knowing God is not analogous to making a scientific discovery, but is much more clearly analogous to our encounters with human beings.[5]

.   .   .   .

Karl Barth is equally sure that God does not present himself to us as an object for verification. God is the 'Subject that remains indissolubly Subject.' He sees, however, as some theologians seem (oddly) to forget, that a person who loves someone may well choose to put himself in some sense 'at the disposal' of the other. To remain hidden and elusive would tend to thwart rather than further their love. In the Incarnation God does exactly this: puts himself at man's disposal; permits man to touch and handle, even to kill. But Barth's position is a complex one.

4 Ibid., pp. 80 ff.
5 Emil Brunner, *The Divine–Human Encounter* (London: S.C.M., 1944), pp. 15, 20, 28, 34, 49, 59.

He denies that through successful historical research, say, belief could be forced on someone. For knowledge of Christ also must remain *personal* knowledge. He cannot be known like an object at the mercy of the researcher, but only in encounter.

In numerous Christian theologies (including the ones just mentioned) Buber's views are not simply reproduced, but are often considerably transformed. Perhaps the most frequent change is the intensifying of Buber's already dramatic contrast between the standpoints of *I-Thou* and *I-It*. Sin comes to be regarded as a kind of imprisonment in the world of *I-It;* that is to say, an inability to respond as a person to others. But our immediate purpose is not greatly complicated by variations on the main *I-Thou* theme: for that purpose is to appraise critically the whole attempt to argue for an immediate, self-authenticating encounter with God.

2

The main features of this approach can only be welcomed by the philosopher of religion. If the methods of verification that philosophers bring to religious statements are suitable for confirming the existence of *objects,* and if God is 'irreducibly *Subject,*' irreducibly *personal,* the application of these methods will quite misleadingly (perhaps falsely) proclaim that God does not exist. This warning is salutary, not only to the traditional 'rational theologian' with his speculative arguments for God's existence, but equally to the linguistic philosopher whose 'hangover' from positivism tempts him to think of verification as *par excellence* the confirmation of scientific hypotheses.

The religious person is always on edge, and rightly so, lest talk *about* God should for some reflective people replace prayer and self-committal *to* God, lest these people should exchange the all-important encounter with God for the (far less important) entertaining of more or less adequate ideas about him. The theology of *I* and *Thou* certainly ensures that the language of prayer is given priority over the language of reflection.

Yet we have to ask if the strongest claims of this theology are justified: if knowledge of God as personal can be entirely self-authenticating, or whether there is room here for (and even likelihood of) error and illusion. Can we accept that sharp division—either arguments for God *or* personal encounter; nothing in between? Are there no checking-procedures relevant to the encounter of person with person? Or does all 'checking' necessarily degrade persons to the status of things? If the vital analogy here is that between meeting people and meeting God, have the theologians established this analogy firmly enough to bear the weighty superstructure that they have reared upon it?

It is most unlikely that any conclusive argument could be brought

against someone's claim to have met God in personal encounter. The
great problem, we shall see, is to fathom how far this claim is in fact
a bare record of the *immediate* encounter, as it purports to be, and
how far that experience has been interpreted (and perhaps *mis*interpreted) by the subject in his very attempt to 'make sense' of it. Whom
or what was he aware of directly meeting—'the God of our Lord Jesus
Christ', God as 'Creator of heaven and earth,' a Supernatural being, or a
'numinous,' awful Presence? The question, which of these or other possible answers he will give, is of the first importance; for if the original
direct encounter was with a being known in the last-mentioned way—
as a holy and dreadful Presence—then one could *not* claim to have
been aware, directly and immediately, of (say) God as Father of Jesus
Christ. The judgement, 'I encountered the God revealed uniquely in
the New Testament' would be an indirect, not a direct judgement. It would
depend on inferences that could not themselves claim 'self-authentication'.
We shall also have to consider the objection that such certainty as the
Christian claims for his encounters with God can be had only by 'subjective' or 'psychological' statements: statements *not* to the effect that
such and such exists or is the case, but that I have such and such sensations and feelings, and no more. And from statements as cautious as those
one may *not* infer any equally certain statements about the world, about
things or persons other than the speaker.

In the encounter between man and God, Brunner says:

An exchange takes place . . . which is wholly without analogy in the sphere
of thinking. The sole analogy is in the encounter between human beings, the
meeting of person with person.

Human encounters, however, are unstable and impure. They alternate
between genuine *I-Thou* relations and degraded *I-It* relations. But they
can still serve as a guide to what *pure I-Thou* encounter with God must be.

When I stand opposite to God, I am face to face with him who unconditionally
is no 'something,' who in the unconditional sense is pure 'Thou.' [6]

That is to say, human encounters provide the classical analogy with
divine-human encounters. We can move, in thought, away from the
imperfections of our *human*-encounter examples towards an idea of the
perfection of the meeting with God. This we do by thinking away all
that remains of *I-It,* all vacillating between experiencing the other as
personal and as object, until there remains nothing at all of object-
knowledge, only pure encounter with a *Thou.*

The use of the words 'pure' and 'mixed' or 'impure' of encounters
implies that we could construct a scale of relative purity (within our
experience of human meetings) and then project it to its limiting, extreme case in the encounter with God. If we cannot give meaning to

[6] *The Divine–Human Encounter*, pp. 59 f.

this movement of thought, then we shall not be able to understand exactly what 'pure' and 'impure' signify here. But that breakdown in meaning would have serious consequences. We should not know what elements in the analogy direct us towards understanding the encounter with God, and what elements do not. We want above all to know whether the rails of analogy on which Brunner sets us run smoothly in the direction he points. And it is exactly this that begins to look uncertain. Consider three situations:

(*a*) Suppose I am talking to someone, and suddenly notice that he is looking at me in an odd and disquieting way. What, I ask myself, is he up to? I decide he is simply and literally looking *at* me, observing carefully my hand and arm movements, taking note of what I do with my eyes, how I modulate my voice. I feel as if I were in a shop-window on show, not engaged in what is meant to be mutual conversation.

This situation would pass as radically 'impure.' I am being treated as an *It*. (Perhaps the other man is studying me in order to be able to imitate me at a party.)   ·

(*b*) I have known Tom for a short time only, but our relations are rapidly becoming friendly and relaxed. He sits opposite me now, and he watches my hand, arm, and eyes, listens to my voice. But I should want to say that he does not use these as objects of curiosity, but uses them in order to enter into living relation with me. In this case, the impurity is much lessened.

(*c*) John is my fast and long-established friend. He is walking with me, and it is half-dark. We do not mind not being able to see hands, arms, eyes very clearly. There are long pauses between our remarks. But the silences are not wastes of time or embarrassing failures in *rapport*. We are still nearer Brunner's 'purity'.

In view of these illustrations, does it not look as if there *is* a scale here of, first, diminishing concern with human beings as objects; and, second, increasing purity of *I-Thou* relationship? Why should this *not* be projectible quite meaningfully and helpfully to its limit in man's meeting with God, alone 'purely personal'? It is tempting to say 'Why not indeed?': but we should be most incautious, if we did. Is it true that in moving from (*a*) to (*c*) the physical events (hands, eyes, voice, in movement and sound) have become progressively less essential; or have they remained quite essential in each case, although approached, used, attended to, in different ways, or checked up on less and less frequently because of the increasing intimacy of the people concerned? If the second alternative were correct, then purification would *not* have been shown to run parallel to dwindling reliance on 'knowing facts *about*' the other man, and the movement of thought which the analogy demands would not manage even to start.

Before we examine this possibility, we have to distinguish three different questions, which often become woefully confused. They refer to three different situations in which verification-problems may arise quite naturally in human relations.

(i) We may ask, 'Is there someone in the room, or is that a heap of clothes, a bolster in the bed, the shadow of a suitcase?' This sort of question may be answered without any need to enter into *I-Thou* relations with the person, if person there be. We turn up the light, pull back the bedclothes, look in the corner, and so on.

(ii) We may ask, 'Is James really unhappy, or does he show all the signs of misery, while being inwardly light of heart?' This is a problem about our knowledge of other people's minds. In practice, we may have to become a close friend of James before we can be sure in all circumstances, if *ever* we can be sure. But still we are dealing with what Buber would insist was an *I-It* relation; concerned with the discovery of facts about a person, facts that we can express in general terms—he really is sad, he really is a practical joker, he really is insane. As in the other case, we are quite dependent on the evidence of our senses, or on what James does, says, or betrays of his state of mind.

(iii) We may ask, 'How can I describe my personal relations with John, the peculiar impact his personality makes on me?" Any list, however extended, of his characteristics allows the all-important thing, the uniqueness, to slip through unexpressed. To do justice to it, I should have to add an account of all I have done with John, places visited together, the thousand chats and discussions, exchanges of letters: for all these more or less determine the *timbre* of our relationship. But how could anyone else sense the exact flavour these give it for me? General terms here seem to break down; and, significantly, they fail us just when a relationship appears most definitely to become *I-Thou*.

Yet notice that when we are in an *I-Thou* situation, talking with John, say, by firelight, we may quite easily make mistakes on each of the three levels we have just spoken of.

(i) I may speak to John, 'sensing' his presence with me, although unknown to me John may have quietly slipped out of the room, thinking that I had fallen asleep.

(ii) I may some day mistakenly interpret John's excitement as indicating a piece of good fortune; whereas it really is a sign of nervous tension over some personal crisis that I have not heard about.

(iii) Something John tells me one day about himself, or something I see him do, convinces me that I have never really known his 'centre' or his true personality. The kaleidoscope is suddenly reshuffled, a quite *new* 'uniqueness' is given to my relation with him. The impression I had formerly had of his personality was a highly particular one, concrete and impossible to generalize about (like all good *I-Thou* instances)—yet in some way it was fraught with illusion. What I believed was the *Thou* over against me, directly apprehended, has proved to have been my (false) interpretation of, or construction out of, what John seemed to me to be. I realize with a jolt what a crucial role is played by knowledge *about* John even in my *I* and *Thou* relation with him. He is now quite different to me; and it was the glimpse of an act or hearing a word that has brought about the change.

The fact that we can make occasional mistakes about encounters with human beings (as in these examples) would not necessarily make nonsense of the scale of 'purity.' What *does* upset it is a fact brought out by the same examples—namely, the continuing importance of 'knowledge about' or 'knowledge *that*' in even the most intimate relationships. Only the unexpected disappointment brings home to us that although we rarely or never *list* the characteristics our friend displays, we presuppose them nevertheless during every moment of our relationship. My ease of mind during John's silences is inductively justified by my memory of the countless times he has ended such a silence with words that showed he had been meditating on something I had said to him, and not with a yawn of boredom and a glance at the clock. The longer one has known somebody, and the more experience one has gathered of him, the longer the gaps that one can allow between checking in various ways upon his reaction to what is being said and done. In *this* sense one is not so dependent on information *about* him, on facts about what he is *like*, as in less intimate relationhips. But again, this is so only because we assume consistency in our friend's personality. Whereas, the actual forms that his consistent behaviour takes we have had to learn by watching, asking, and listening.

On the occasions when I sit opposite a friend and observe his gestures and expression, I am neither looking *at* these as at so many objects, nor in the belief that his entire personal being consists in such overt actions (behaviourism), nor am I looking 'through' these to the *hidden* personality, as I might look through the glass of a window, concerned only with the view beyond. His behaviour is not being taken as a 'window' into his immaterial, ghostly 'mind.' I admit that his inner life, like mine, is more than gestures, speech, smiles; but I doubt if we know what we are saying when we declare that personality and knowledge of personality are possible without these; I doubt if anything recognizably personal can be left over, once we have mentally stripped all such behaviour away.

I think I am saying more than that all human *I-Thou* encounters remain full of 'impurities' through their dependence on 'knowledge about.' The peculiar difficulty is to know how even theoretically the situation could be improved. If we seriously try to conceive circumstances in which we might claim to have done away with all behavioural checks in communing with someone, we will find either that we have in a peculiar way failed to maintain the separate identities of the two people concerned, or that we have no means of knowing whether we are in *rapport* with someone or not, which do not ultimately rely upon the behavioural checks themselves.[7] For consider the possibilities.

I might imagine that the ideal here would be a state where I did not have to see John flush, hear him slam doors, and shout, to know that he was angry: but simply knew it as John knows it himself. I should feel the ascent of blood to the head, the kinæsthetic feelings that go with cry-uttering and door-slamming, the tension and temptation to lose control. But how could this be distinguished from temporarily *becoming John?* This would be not to *encounter* some other personality, but to *assume* another personality. Or, if that sounds too fantastic, one could describe the situation in quite another way: by saying that instead of encountering an angry John (which was my original aim), I now merely become angry myself—a very different thing.

Alternatively, I might not reproduce John's sensations, but instead (by telepathy) see a red circle in the air when John was angry, a blue cross when he felt happy, and so on. But how could I ever know that this was a dependable 'code'? Only by checking up systematically with John himself (speaking to him, listening to him, watching him), and finding if my circles and crosses did correspond with his angers and delights. Unless I was prepared to trust such checks, i.e. to rely on the *normal* ways of discovering other people's states of mind, I would have no grounds at all for saying that my mental diagrams gave me knowledge of his mind.

Notice too that these fantasies have been operating only at what we have called level (ii)—where the question is an *I-It* question about what someone is thinking or feeling. If we ask what reciprocal, truly personal relations would be like when 'purified' to the point where no 'knowledge about' or 'memory that' or behavioural check was involved, the difficulties are enormously magnified.

In face of these reflections, the theologian might well decide that the analogy between meeting human beings and meeting God is too weak to carry any apologetic weight. But, rather than capitulate, he may choose to make a last-ditch stand. He could make it by staking all on that sense of utter uniqueness that is involved in all genuine *I-Thou* relations. If in all fact description using general terms fails to capture that uniqueness, surely the pith of personal-encounter experiences cannot be certain complexes of memories and present sensations: surely, that is, it is

---

[7] Readers of John Wisdom's *Other Minds* (Oxford: Blackwell, 1952) will recognize my occasional borrowings from the illustrations in that book in the present chapter. They will also need no telling that I am not attempting to reproduce Wisdom's own argument faithfully.

possible for the *I-Thou* situation to survive the pruning away of all these impurities?

This might be plausible, if it were true that individuality and uniqueness *cannot* depend on a complex interrelation of general factors. But we are in a position only to say that it often is hard to see what all the factors are and how their interrelating could produce precisely the effect it *does* produce. This is a recurrent and familiar situation in art or literary criticism. At first sight it is simply inexplicable how, say, a simple-looking stanza makes its wholly individual impact on the reader. It seems incredible that it could be only a matter of the interrelation of the senses and sounds of the everyday words that compose it. Thorough examination may begin to show just *how* the various suggestions, associations, near and remote, of these ingredients fuse together; and even though the analysis failed to account *completely* for the effect of the stanza, it might dispel our initial incredulity. Yes, we say, the effect is due to a subtle combination of meanings, overlaying one another, intensifying, qualifying one another. And so with the impact of one human being on another. Those factors mentioned earlier—the strata of memories of all the meetings, all the shared experiences—all far too numerous and complex to analyse exhaustively—may well fuse in a closely parallel way, and generate a similar sense of utter individuality. But to ask for the strikingness of that stanza without the words, to expect that there could be impact of personality without memories and sensations, would be like demanding the grin of the Cheshire cat without the cat itself.

To ask someone to think analogically is to ask him (*a*) to imagine some familiar item of experience, which is to afford a clue to the nature of what is unknown; and (*b*) to give him directions how to *modify* this item of experience so as to increase its resemblance to the unknown and diminish its inadequacy. For example, I may give a child some idea of the solar system by constructing an arrangement of table-lamps and tennis-balls; directing him to imagine the originals as so many thousand times larger than the models, and different in other, specified ways. But if we are not able to give clear indication of how to modify the familiar, no analogical thinking is possible. It is of no avail to insist nonetheless that there *is* an analogy somewhere, though we cannot say quite where. Now, we have been examining the claimed analogy between meeting human beings and meeting God as a pure person. We have seen that although different sorts of human relationship make different sorts of use of bodily features, sounds, and appearances, there is still nothing to suggest that these become progressively less and less necessary as the relationship becomes purer: nothing therefore to imply that there is a purest of all relationships, in which they are quite superfluous. We have . *not* been given the clear directions for modifying the familiar that we must have for safe analogical thinking. This analogy is like a car that stalls at the very start of a race.

·   ·   ·   ·   ·   ·   ·   ·   ·   ·   ·   ·   ·

This inquiry could not justly be accused of treating persons as objects, and blasphemously reducing God to a thing-at-our-disposal. It does not interpose any systems of ideas between the *I* and the *Thou*. Thus, I cannot follow Buber in declaring that 'cognitive truth means making the absolute into an object . . .',[8] provided that cogitation is simply concerned to answer the preliminary but important question, 'Am I or am I not in personal contact with someone?' For here cogitation is very much in place. We have seen that to be aware of someone as a personal subject involves knowing *about* that person (perhaps a great deal about him), although it does not entail giving our minds to the detailed *entertaining* of that knowledge. Totally dismissing all ideas about the person would lead not to 'purification' of personal relations but to their elimination: hence the misleadingness of Buber's either/or—'What the philosophers describe by the name of God cannot be more than an idea. But God, "the God of Abraham," is not an idea'.[9]

Suggested Readings

The following volumes are suggested as good surveys of the existential perspective: W. Barrett, *Irrational Man* (New York: Anchor Books, 1962p); R. C. Solomon, * *From Rationalism to Existentialism* (New York: Harper & Row, 1972p); G. A. Schrader (ed.), * *Existential Philosophers: Kierkegaard to Merleau-Ponty* (New York: McGraw-Hill, 1967p); Collins, * *The Existentialists* (New York: Regnery Co., 1952p); H. J. Blackham, * *Six Existentialist Thinkers* (New York: Harper & Row, 1959p); John Wild, * *The Challenge of Existentialism* (Bloomington: Indiana University Press, 1955p); C. Schrag, *Existence and Freedom* (Evanston: Northwestern University Press, 1961p). Two surveys in hardback that deserve mention are John Macquarrie, * *Existentialism* (Philadelphia: Westminster, 1972) and R. Grimsley, *Existentialist Thought* (Cardiff: University of Wales Press, 1955).

A number of anthologies that contain basic existential texts are Nino Langiulli (ed.), * *The Existentialist Tradition* (Garden City, N.Y.: Anchor Books, 1971p); W. Kaufmann (ed.), *Existentialism from Dostoevsky to Sartre* (New York: Meridian Books, 1956p); H. J. Blackham (ed.), *Reality, Man and Existence* (New York: Bantam Books, 1965p); Barrett and Aiken (eds.), *Philosophy in the Twentieth Century*, Vol. 3 (New York: Harper & Row, 1962p), and Will Herberg (ed.), *Four Existentialist Theologians* (New York: Doubleday, 1958p).

A number of introductions that deal more specifically with the relationship between Judeo-Christian tradition and existentialism are Carl Michaelson, *Christianity and the Existentialists* (New York: Scribner's, 1956); D. E. Roberts, *Existentialism and Religious Belief* (New York: Oxford University Press, 1957p); J. Macquarrie, *Studies in Christian Existentialism* (Philadelphia: Westminster, 1966); J. Rodman Williams, * *Contemporary Existentialism and Christian Faith* (Englewood Cliffs, N. J.: Prentice-Hall, 1956p); and Roger

[8] Martin Buber, *Eclipse of God* (London: Gollancz, 1953), pp. 44 f.
[9] Ibid., p. 67.

Troisfontaines, *Existentialism and Christian Thought* (London: Dacre Press, 1949).

The following works of Sartre may serve as an introduction: *Being and Nothingness* (New York: Philosophical Library, 1956p); *Existentialism* (New York: Philosophical Library, 1947p); *No Exit and Three Other Plays* (New York: Vintage Books, 1955p); *The Wall and Other Stories* (New York: New Directions, 1948p); *Nausea* (New York: New Directions, 1949). A great number of secondary works on Sartre are available of which the following are suggested for commentary and criticism: W. Desan, * *The Tragic Finale* (New York: Harper & Row, 1960p); Klaus Hartmann, * *Sartre's Ontology* (Evanston: Northwestern University Press, 1966); Edith Kern, *Sartre: A Collection of Clinical Essays* (Englewood Cliffs, N. J.: Prentice-Hall, 1962p); A. Mauser, *Sartre: A Philosophic Study* (London: Othlone, 1966); M. A. Natanson, * *A Critique of Jean-Paul Sartre's Ontology* (Lincoln, Neb.: University of Nebraska Press, 1951); J. Fell, *Emotion in the Thought of Sartre*, 3rd ed. (New York: Columbia University Press, 1965); Alfred Stern, *Sartre* (New York: Dell Publishing Co., 1967p). For two analytic criitques see A. J. Ayer, "Sartre," *Horizon* XII, No. 67 (July 1945) and P. Heath, "Nothing," *Encyclopedia of Philosophy*, P. Edwards, ed., op. cit.

The following works of Camus are suggested: *The Myth of Sisyphus* (New York: Vintage Books, 1959p); *The Rebel: An Essay on Man in Revolt* (New York: Vintage Books, 1956p); *Resistance, Rebellion and Death* (New York: Knopf, 1961); *The Stranger* (New York: Vintage Book, 1954p); *The Plague* (New York: Vintage Books, 1972p); and *The Fall* (New York: Vintage Books, 1957p).

The following studies of Camus should be consulted: G. Bree, *Camus* (New Brunswick: Rutgers University Press, 1959); also by Bree (ed.), *Camus: A Collection of Critical Essays* (Englewood Cliffs, N. J.: Prentice-Hall, 1962p); J. Cruicksshank, * *Albert Camus and the Literature of Revolt* (London: Oxford, 1959); T. Hanna, * *The Thought and Art of Albert Camus* (Chicago: Regnery, 1958p); Phillip Rhein, * *Albert Camus* (New York: Hippocrene Books, 1972p); P. Thody, * *Albert Camus, 1913–1960* (London: Hamish Hamilton, 1961); and Fred Willhoite, * *Beyond Nihilism* (Baton Rouge: Louisiana State University Press, 1968)

Tillich was a prolific writer. The student will find the following, in order of difficulty, important to understanding his thought: *The Dynamics of Faith* (New York: Harper & Row, 1958p); *Theology of Culture* (New York: Oxford University Press, 1959p); *Biblical Religion and the Search for Ultimate Reality* (Chicago: University of Chicago Press, 1955p); *The Courage To Be* (New Haven: Yale University Press, 1952p); *Systematic Theology*, 3 Vols. (Chicago: University of Chicago Press, 1953–64). A helpful survey of Tillich's works and criticism from Barthian position, see A. J. McKelway, *The Systematic Theology of Paul Tillich* (Richmond: John Knox Press, 1964p). A Roman Catholic critique can be found in G. H. Tavard, *Paul Tillich and the Christian Message* (New York: Scribners, 1962). J. H. Thomas, *Paul Tillich: An Appraisal* (Philadelphia: Westminster Press, 1963) gives a critique from an analytic point of view. Other important critiques and commentaries are C. W. Kegley and R. W. Bretall (eds.), * *The Theology of Paul Tillich* (New York: Macmillan, 1952p); D. H. Kelsey, * *The Fabric of Paul Tillich's Theology* (New Haven: Yale University Press, 1967); J. L. Adams, * *Paul Tillich's Philosophy of Culture, Science and Religion* (New York: Harper & Row, 1965p); and

W. L. Rowe's excellent critique of Tillich's Theory of Symbol, *Religious Symbols and God* (Chicago: University of Chicago Press, 1968).

Martin Buber has written a number of very influential books among which are the following: *I and Thou,* trans. Kaufmann (New York: Scribner's, 1970p); *The Prophetic Faith* (New York: Harper & Row, 1960p); *Between Man and Man* (Boston: Beacon Press, 1955p); and *Eclipse of God* (New York: Harper & Row, 1952p). Critical appraisals of Buber include the following: M. Diamond, *Martin Buber, Jewish Existentialist* (New York: Oxford University Press, 1960p); M. Friedman, *Martin Buber: The Life of Dialogue* (New York: Harper & Row, 1960p); R. E. Wood, ° *Martin Buber's Ontology* (Evanston: Northwestern University Press, 1969); and more difficult is P. A. Schilpp and M. Friedman (eds.), ° *The Philosophy of Martin Buber* (La Salle, Illinois: Open Court, 1967). For a critical discussion see P. Edwards, *Buber and Buberism—A Critical Evaluation* (Lawrence: University of Kansas Press, 1970p). A clear, short introduction can be found in M. Wyschogrod's article on Buber in the *Encyclopedia of Philosophy* (ed. P. Edwards). Maurice Friedman, *Touchstones of Reality: Existential Trust and the Community of Peace* (New York: E. P. Dutton, 1972) develops on the themes of Buber in a new way.

There are a great number of other existentialists that one might study with profit. See the above surveys for more details.

CHAPTER FOUR

Analytic Philosophy:
Linguistic Veto?

Analytic philosophy, although it has its roots deep in the past, marks a revolution in philosophy. This revolution began at the turn of the century with the activities of G. E. Moore and Bertrand Russell. These two philosophers were still concerned about giving a comprehensive description of the whole of reality (i.e., they were not antimetaphysical), but their attention focused more and more on the tool of philosophy—language.

The meaning of language has indeed been the occupational concern of philosophy in the English speaking world in this century. The revolution begun by Moore and Russell consists in seeing that the activity of the philosopher is primarily analysis, not giving information about God, humankind, and the world. "The result of philosophy is not a number of philosophical propositions, but to make propositions clear" (Wittgenstein). Philosophy is an activity whose goal is clarification. There are no facts that philosophers discover and announce to the world, though the analyst hopes that his analysis of language will shed light on philosophical problems.

The early analysts were concerned with analysis so as to state their position clearly and unambiguously. A great deal of their analysis was directed to typically *philosophical* language. The second stage in analysis was concerned with developing an *ideal language* because ordinary language seemed imprecise. Just as science developed its own special language to achieve precision, so philosophy developed symbolic logic as its tool for precision in dealing with philosophical problems. The third stage in analytic philosophy marked a return to ordinary language.[1] Rather than criticize ordinary language, these philosophers tended to leave it as it is. More often than philosophers like to admit, philosophical puzzles arise just because philosophers go beyond ordinary language. Philosophy in this stage was seen as a kind of linguistic therapy that removed the linguistic traps *philosophers* had fallen into.

As Wittgenstein said, "What we do is to bring words back from their metaphysical to their everyday use." But there was more to do than just remove traps. The philosopher was also to show the diversity of language and help catalogue its rules; for example, construct a logical map of different kinds of languages—scientific language, religious language, and so on. This often involved intricate detailing of specific words and the many shades of meaning these words had in different contexts. And so although these philosophers disagreed on a number of items, they all agreed that the primary concern of philosophy was with language.[2]

The last stage in the development of analytic philosophy is the most important for our purposes because it is still practiced. Perhaps the essential difference between the first two stages and the third is this: although the first two stages analyzed to get at *clarity* (*reduction* to clear and simple items) or *precision* (*translation* of every problem into an artificial language such as symbolic logic), the third stage, when it had completed its work, left everything just where it was. Philosophy simply *described* actual use; it did not *prescribe* how it ought to be used.

Although analytic philosophers tend to look at themselves as neutral (presuppositionless), the student should be alert to finding hidden metaphysical tenets. Recent analytic philosophers have been more open to metaphysics. Indeed, a revolution may be beginning within analytic philosophy itself, moving from seeing philosophy as simply a description of the workings of language to proposals of how we *ought* to use language based on certain metaphysical claims.[3]

Still another crucial difference between the last stage and the first two was that practitioners of the first two stages were concerned with finding the *essence* of language. Generally, this essence was seen as *picturing* or *mirroring* reality. Words *name* or *refer* to realities. They are word pictures. The philosophers in the last stage repudiate this view of language. They see that language does many different jobs, granting that ordinary language does not need translation into other languages.

The student may find it trying to read analytic philosophers because they do not make many first-order statements. By this I mean analytic philosophers do not talk about God, humankind, or the world (a first-order activity), but talk *about* the talk of God, humankind, and the world.

---

[1] And so is often referred to as "ordinary language philosophy." Late Wittgenstein, Ryle, and Austin are the chief exponents of this position.

[2] See bibliography for volumes that trace the revolution in detail.

[3] See Richard Rorty, "Introduction" in *The Linguistic Turn* (Chicago: The University of Chicago Press, 1967).

This may seem to be a failure of nerve. But it is the contention of these philosophers that in throwing light on the workings of our language, we can be more articulate about our standpoint.

Because analytic philosophy has dominated the English speaking world in this century, the reader would be right in thinking that the material written by analysts on religious language is voluminous. Most students have been introduced to some of this material in introductory philosophy courses. Rather than repeat this material in detail, I have written a historical introduction that surveys the basic issues. Footnotes in this article and in the bibliography will lead the reader to the basic materials. The remaining essays in this chapter typify the current debate. Kai Nielsen presents a challenge to theism from an analytic standpoint. Is his position presuppositionless? John Hick is perhaps the foremost theistic analyst currently writing. His essay is a defense of God-talk. What are the issues between Nielsen and Hick? Ludwig Wittgenstein's essay on religion gave rise to what we call "Wittgensteinian fideism." Can we be satisfied with this *description?* Donald Evans contrasts religious language with scientific language, drawing on the insights of Martin Buber (existentialist) and John Austin (analyst). Can we avoid the questions raised by Schedler and Nielsen?

TALK ABOUT GOD-TALK:
A HISTORICAL INTRODUCTION

Norbert O. Schedler

NORBERT SCHEDLER is Chairman of the Philosophy Department at Purdue University—Fort Wayne. He is co-editor with James S. Churchill of *The Essential Writings of Martin Heidegger* (1973).

In this essay I trace the changing attitude of empirical-linguistic [1] philosophy toward religious language.[2] My concern in this essay is with the broad issue of what religious words mean, how religious truth-claims are justified, and so on. This is not an essay in theology but meta-theology. By this I mean, I will talk about 'talk about God,' not talk about God. My concern is not with whether the claims of the theologian are true, but what a theological truth *claim* is. My concern is not with what re-

---

[1] I'm unhappy with this term but will use it to cover a loosely knit family of philosophers. The family begins with the empiricists. I will use David Hume as my example. Logical positivism (empiricism) represents the youthful exuberance of the family. I will use A. J. Ayer as my example. The family matures into ordinary language philosophy (linguistic analysis). I will use Ludwig Wittgenstein as my example.

[2] The singular does not imply that religious language has only one use. This awareness is part of the maturing process in the empirical-linguistic family.

ligious words are proper, but how religious people order what they mean
by 'proper' or 'apt.' My concern is with the logic of 'God is love,' not with
the proclamation of "God is love." [3]

The Three Stages

Stage	Attitude	Concern
1. David Hume	Attack	Theological arguments
2. A. J. Ayer	Attack	All theological statements
3. Ludwig Wittgenstein	Neutral	Logical mapping of God-talk

THE FIRST STAGE—DAVID HUME

It is possible to discern three stages in the attitude of empirical-linguistic philosophy to religious language. The first stage, represented by
David Hume, took the form of an attack upon traditional *metaphysical
arguments,* including, of course the traditional proofs for the existence
of God. This latter activity was called *natural* (as opposed to revealed)
theology in which the theologian attempted to demonstrate the existence
of God from either the cosmos, moral experience, or the idea of God
intuitively known. He made no appeal to revelation. Each of the arguments began with some fact readily known and argued to its *necessary*
condition—God.

Against this sort of approach Hume used what is called "Hume's
Fork." Any argument or proof was either empirical (inductive) or
analytic (deductive). A deductive argument could lead to a conclusion
that was necessarily true, but as analytic arguments they prove nothing
about the *existence* of anything. An inductive argument could lead to a
conclusion that asserted something about what exists, but could never
be more than *probable.*

Analytic arguments do not increase our knowledge and for this reason
they are called tautologies. Their truth does not depend upon experience,
only upon the consistent use of clearly defined terms. If words with
clearly defined meanings are used inconsistently, the result is contradiction. If words with clearly defined meanings are used consistently, the
result is necessary truth. The truth or falsity of an analytic argument rests
solely on the meaning of the terms used. Analytic proofs lead to either
necessary truths or contradictions.

Empirical arguments are never true by definition. Their truth or falsity
can be discovered only by reference to some nonlinguistic element, a fact.

---

[3] The word *logic* has a special use here. It means the rules governing the use of a
linguistic element, i.e., a sentence. This kind of concern is also called a second-order
activity. A first-order activity is saying something; a second-order activity is describing the logic of the first-order activity. Note: single quotation marks indicate
that the enclosure is being talked out; double quotation marks indicate a quotation.

Empirical arguments are based on sense experience, moving from a claim about something to the confirmation of that claim in future experience. Notice that the movement in empirical arguments is not from definitions to necessary conclusions, a totally linguistic activity. Synthetic arguments require sense experience for their confirmation. If I claim that it is raining outside, no amount of thinking about it will confirm the claim. Looking out the window will. Analytic argument, however, only requires the careful manipulation of clearly defined terms, for instance, many examples in mathematics and logic.

If "bachelor" is defined as "unmarried man" then it is analytically true that if there is a bachelor he is unmarried. But this statement cannot prove that there *is* a bachelor. If God is defined as a being whose existence is necessary (as opposed to contingent) then it is true by definition that if there is a God he must necessarily exist, but it does not prove *that there is such a being.* So the ontological argument defines God as having necessary existence, which only shows that *if* there is a God he necessarily exists; it cannot prove *that* he exists. Another version of the ontological argument starts with the definition of God as a perfect being and argues that a being so defined *must* exist. For if he did not exist, he would be less than perfect. But again, all this argument shows is that *if* a perfect being does exist his existence cannot be accidental; he must have necessary existence.

If, on the other hand, the existence of God is argued for inductively, his existence is not capable of strict demonstration, for inductive arguments give us only a high degree of *probability.* The cosmological arguments all start with some empirically known item and then argue that, given the existence of that item, God *necessarily* exists as its cause. If anything exists, God *must* exist as its cause. You cannot deny this without contradiction. But from empirical premises one can only draw empirical conclusions. The cosmological argument starts with empirical premises and arrives at necessary conclusions. But one cannot get more out of a conclusion than is already contained in the premises. If the premises are empirical, the conclusion must be empirical, therefore only probable. If the premises are analytic, the conclusion must be analytic, therefore an uninformative (about the existence of anything in the world) tautology. Hume's fork divides strictly deductive and inductive arguments. The former sort of argument is appropriate in logic and mathematics and does not prove the existence of anything in the world. The latter is appropriate to the experimental sciences. While the inductive arguments can prove the existence of something, they cannot prove the *necessary* existence of anything. The traditional arguments are a mixture of the two kinds of arguments. The result is "illusion." As Hume puts it:

When we run over libraries, persuaded of these principles, what havoc must we make! If we take in our hand any volume of divinity or school metaphysics, for instance; let us ask, "Does it contain any abstract reasoning concerning quantity or number?" No. "Does it contain any experimental reasoning concerning matter of fact and existence?" No. Commit it then to the flames, for it can contain nothing but sophistry and illusion.[4]

Although there is a great deal more to Hume's criticism of the arguments, I want here to make only two points. First, Hume is analyzing types of *arguments*. Second, Hume is not attacking all theology but *natural* theology. Hume's attack upon *natural* theology was a serious one and is still widely accepted as decisive by both philosophers *and* theologians. Hume himself suggested (perhaps tongue-in-cheek), "The truths of our religion find their best and most solid foundation in Faith and Divine Revelation." Many theologians have taken this approach and declare that theology begins not with reason and proof but faith and revelation. Faith *precedes* understanding and is necessary prior to a full understanding.[5] I will discuss the viability of this position later.

Although there is a continuing debate about the 'proofs' for the existence of God, Hume's criticisms have generally held the day.[6] This does not mean, however, that the 'proofs' have no use. One can catalogue a number of uses. 1. The 'proofs' are really *confessions* of faith. See Barth's analysis of Anselm.[7] 2. The 'proofs' are really man's asking of the God-*question*. I'm finite; is there anything infinite? I'm contingent; is there anything necessary? The 'proofs' express man's estrangement from the "Ground of Being" and his longing for reunion with the divine. Paul Tillich develops this approach. "The arguments for the existence of God neither are arguments nor are they proof of the existence of God. They are expressions of the *question* of God that is implied in human finitude. This question is their truth; every answer they give is untrue.[8] 3. The 'proofs' are really *definitions* of how a theist intends to use the word 'God'. 4. The 'proofs' lead one to an "apprehension" or "discernment" of God. The 'proofs' evoke God in a moment of illumination. They are not

[4] David Hume, *An Enquiry Concerning Human Understanding*, ed. L. A. Selby-Bigge (Oxford: Clarendon Press, 1902), p. 165.
[5] *Credo ut intelligam* (I believe in order that I might understand). This fideist position has had a long history in Christian theology. It is strongly represented on the contemporary scene by the followers of Kierkegaard and Barth.
[6] See Wallace I. Matson, *The Existence of God* (Ithaca: Cornell University Press, 1966) for a more detailed discussion of the arguments. In spite of my remark about *most* philosophers, some have revived interest in both the ontological and cosmological arguments. See Arthur McGill and John Hick, *The Many-Faced Argument* (New York: Macmillan, 1967); Donald Burrill, *The Cosomological Arguments* (Garden City, N.Y.: Anchor Books, 1967); essays by J. F. Ross and W. L. Rowe in *Logical Analysis and Contemporary Theism*, edited by John Donnelly (New York: Fordham University Press, 1972); and numerous articles in philosophical and theological journals, for example, Robert C. Coburn, "Recent Work in Metaphysics," *American Philosophical Quarterly*, Vol. I (1964); Steven M. Cahn, "The Irrelevance to Religion of Philosophic Proofs for the Existence of God," *American Philosophical Quarterly*, 6 (1969).
[7] Karl Barth, *Anselm: Fides Quaerens Intellectum* (London: SCM Press, 1961).
[8] Paul Tillich, *Systematic Theology*, Vol. I (Chicago: University Press, 1951), p. 205.

"knock down" proofs, but thought-starters that lead one to God at the end of an intuitive leap.[9]

THE SECOND STAGE—A. J. AYER AND A. FLEW

The second stage in the attitude of empirical-linguistic philosophy to religious language centered around a group of philosophers, scientists, and mathematicians who met in Vienna in the late 1920s.[10] The position of this group, called the Logical Positivists (they preferred Logical Empiricists), is classically expressed in the youthful polemic of A. J. Ayer.[11] Ayer's *bulldozer* is different from Hume's fork in that it distinguishes two basic types of significant *statements* (not arguments)—analytic and empirical. "Cognitively significant statements" (i.e., statements that assert what we claim to *know* as opposed to sentences that express attitudes, emotions, and so on) are reduced without remainder to analytic and empirical statements. This bulldozer allows Ayer to clear out discourse that is not cognitively significant, for example, metaphysics, ethics, and religion.

Analytic statements are definitions prescribing the use of certain terms: formal definitions, tautologies, and linguistic conventions (for example, "A triangle has three sides." "A bachelor is an unmarried man.") The function of analytic statements is to give information about linguistic use, *not* information about the world. Analytic statements are true by definition. Logic and mathematics are disciplines that contain analytic statements.

Empirical statements are those that can be verified by reference to the facts of sense experience. The Verification Principle comes down to this: for a sentence to qualify as a cognitively (literally, factually, descriptively) significant statement, one must *in principle* be able to show what would count for its being true. If this condition cannot be met then the sentence is cognitively meaningless.

The bulldozer comes to this: we will call "cognitively significant" any statement to which we can assign procedures for verification. In mathematics and logic we can assign such procedures, derivations from definitions and axioms. In empirical sciences we can assign such procedures by reference to sense-experience. If a sentence does not test out by the above rule, it is declared to be "emotive," "non-sense," or "meaningless."

Driving this buldozer, the positivists attempted to clear out of philoso-

---

[9] See especially Ian Ramsey, *Models and Mystery* (London: Oxford University Press, 1964), Ch. 3 and other writings of Ramsey.

[10] Victor Kraft, *The Vienna Circle* (New York: Philosophical Library, 1953); Julius Weinberg, *An Examination of Logical Positivism* (Patterson, N.J.: Littlefield, Adams and Co., 1960).

[11] A. J. Ayer, *Language, Truth and Logic* (New York: Dover Publications, Rev. ed., 1946).

phy the propositions of metaphysics, ethics, and religion which, because they were devoid of cognitive significance, were forthwith declared to be vacuous. Ayer was not arguing that the statements 'God exists,' or 'God is love' were false, but *meaningless*. Indeed, even the atheists who claimed that these two assertions were false were uttering nonsense. The proper response to a theological utterance was not, "You are wrong," but "I don't know what you mean! I do not know what is being claimed!"

The theologian, in response to this position, *cannot* follow the same maneuver recommended in the case of David Hume, i.e., appealing to faith and revelation. Why? Because Ayer is not attacking theological arguments. He is not asking whether theological statements are true. But he is asking whether theological statements have any meaning.

All theological statements are meaningless because they are not meant to be analytic, for they would then simply be definitions, i.e., tautologies. They are also not empirical because an empirical statement is so only if the speaker can give means for its verification. But, for example, there is no way to test the truth or falsity of the statement, "God is in this room." There is no evidence you could imagine that would enable us to determine the truth or falsity of the claim. Therefore, because theological statements (pseudo-statements) are neither analytic nor empirical, they are meaningless.

Many criticisms were raised of Ayer's position and many attempts to salvage the bulldozer were made. Let me just summarize a few of the more important criticisms. First, every attempt to formulate the principle was either too *strong* so that it eliminated many statements the positivists themselves accepted as meaningful, or too *weak* so that the very statements the positivists wished to exclude (ethics, metaphysics, theology) weren't eliminated at all. Second, the principle seemed to be a "persuasive definition" that arbitrarily set up a standard of meaning. 'Meaningful' is not synonomous with 'empirically verifiable.' The pejorative terms *meaningless, non-sense, unintelligible, emotive,* and *vacuous,* were used to lead one to a conclusion when all that was really being argued was a distinction between 'empirical' and 'nonempirical.' Certainly there are other uses of 'meaningful.' Third, the verification principle itself must be subject to Ayer's bulldozer. Is it analytic? Then it is only a recommendation for a definition. Is it empirically verifiable? No. The meaningfulness of the principle itself is then in question. Fourth, the whole issue of the meaning of sentences was too narrowly conceived. Language does many more jobs than the two that Ayer seems to allow. Ayer took the 'logic' of mathematical and scientific assertions and ruthlessly applied it to all language games. The later analysts, following Wittgenstein, argued that we must look into the logic of each game itself and *describe* its logic, *not prescribe* to it a logic from without. Fifth, does not Ayer himself have an implied metaphysics? Does not Ayer assume that experience is restricted to what we can see and touch? Does he not have a phenomenalistic metaphysics (i.e., all statements can be reduced to statements about sense-data)? Sixth, the verification principle seems to eliminate from philosophical discussion all the really significant questions by ruling them out from the start.[12]

Pause for Some Comments

1. It is interesting to note that many philosophers in this stage came to philosophy from science and mathematics. Both these disciplines have clear models for making truth-claims. In the hands of the positivists these *models* became *dogmas*. Other disciplines were judged by models not appropriate to them. The recommendation of Aristotle that one should apportion his method to the subject under consideration was not heeded. This dogmatism was not new in philosophy for the drive for simplicity tends philosophers (and theologians) to bring every area of experience under one model.

2. The simplicity of the dogma accounted for much of its appeal. An issue (problem or question) was legitimate only if one could in principle show the lines for its solution. No permanent "mystery" was allowed. "What red is to a bull, mystery is to Ayer." We have only 'problems' and 'puzzles.' Problems can be defined and require only more information or more sophisticated tools for their solution. Puzzles are verbal problems that arise from lack of clarity. Once we clear up the logic of the language then the puzzle disappears. Many theological problems are really *puzzles* [The debate between the atheist and the theist is a puzzle which once one sees that the two are only expressing their feelings about the world, the puzzle as to which is true evaporates, for the issue between them is *not* about what is true or false.] It is a matter of attitudes. A world then of problems that *in principle* can be solved by data and inventive skills with computers, and so on and puzzles to be removed by linguistic analysis. A neat, tidy, world. Whatever can be said must be said clearly and precisely, and the method for its solutions defined; otherwise it is a pseudo-problem.

3. But this seems too neat! This standpoint led philosophers to classify as non-sense all sorts of things people were constantly saying and thereby meaning. "Just who do you philosophers think you are to *prescribe* what I can or cannot say? I utter moral and religious words all the time, and both I and the hearer know what they mean."

4. The positivism of Ayer became a kind of *preaching*. He not only wished to distinguish science from metaphysics, theology, and ethics, but he also wished to *eliminate* the latter three. Ayer and his followers (also in psychology, sociology, and so on) became missionaries in a holy war against the worst sin possible, "to utter non-sense." The worst name you could call one philosophically was "Metaphysician!" The religious fervor

---

[12] See bibliography for more detailed account of the history of the verification principle and its use in theological discussion.

was revealing. I lived through these days and attended many "services." It was hard not to be a believer.

5. Positivism, on the popular level, drew its recruits from the growing number of secular, scientific, tough-minded young rebels who affirmed the earth. In fact, the movement was more a reaction *against* than it was *for* anything.[13] And when metaphysics faded and theology retreated from the game (warning all about vain philosophy), the slogan became, "Why continue to stab a dead *bull?*" Philosophy would have to find something else to do.

Beyond Positivism(?)

While Ayer's position has been left behind in philosophy, even by Ayer himself, it is surprising how tenaciously it has held on in the area of philosophy of religion. The "ghost of positivism" is still very much with us. It is important, therefore, to see exactly what is at issue and consider some options.

Although it is true that very few, if any, philosophers would now call themselves 'positivists,' when it comes to 'factual meaning' the criterion has remained the same for many. There are many different kinds of meaning, to be sure. 'Meaningful' is not restricted to analytic and empirical as in the case of Positivism. But 'factually meaningful' still means that one can in principle give what would count for or against the assertion. So although most analytic philosophers recognize different sorts of meaning, for many 'factually meaningful' still requires coming under the rules laid down by positivism. What then is at issue?

A sentence expresses an assertion (as distinct from a command, exclamation, attitude, and so on) if and only if it can be verified in sense experience; or rather, because very few statements can be conclusively verified, if and only if it can be conclusively falsified. Thus, the typical example, "all swans are white" cannot be conclusively verified because we in principle cannot observe all swans. But we know what would count against it being true, as it was in fact conclusively falsified when black swans were found in Australia.

But even this formulation is too simple because there are statements that are assertions but which cannot be conclusively falsified; for example, "There are three successive sevens in the decimal determination of pi." The final loose formulation came down to this: a sentence expresses an assertion if and only if some possible sense experience could constitute evidence for or against it. If a statement fails to pass this test, it will not be dismissed as non-sense in Positivistic fashion, but it also will not be classified as an assertion.

For many analytic philosophers, statements about God do not pass this test. They complain that theists, when asked what would count as evi-

---

13 Atheism of protest. See Chapter Five.

dence against their belief in God, protest that nothing could (logically) count as evidence against it. As Flew relates it, when someone tells us that God loves us as a father loves his children, we are reassured. But when we see a child dying of cancer and his earthly father is frantically trying to do something about it, where is the love of the heavenly father? The priest says, "God's love is *not* a human love" or "God's love is a love that *passes* our understanding." What this amounts to is that this fact of the innocent child dying is compatible with God's love. But if everything that happens is compatible with God's love, how does God's love differ from God's hate? Has not the assertion that 'God loves us as a father' died the death of 1,000 qualifications? What difference is there experientially between saying 'God loves me' and 'God hates me?' 'God loves me' seems to be compatible with anything that happens. It cannot be falsified. No matter what happens it is called an act of God's love! If something is being asserted, then something is being denied. If God's love is compatible with *any* amount of pain, *any* amount of unrelieved disaster, then nothing is being asserted. No difference; no meaning. "He who keeps Israel never slumbers nor sleeps." Israel is reassured. But what about Auschwitz? As Richard Rubinstein says, "Of one thing I am convinced: more than the bodies of my people went up in smoke at Auschwitz. The God of the covenant died there." [14] Or, take the example, 'Everything happens because of God's will.' If nothing counts against this, then are we not just saying that 'God's will' simply means 'Everything that happens?' As such, this is *not* an *assertion*, but a definition. Some prefer one term to the other; that is all. Examples of this erosion of meaning in theology are legion; so argue some analysts. The classical formulation of this challenge to the *factual* meaningfulness of religious assertions comes in the form of a parable told by Flew.

Once upon a time two explorers came upon a clearing in the jungle. In this clearing they noticed many *flowers* and *weeds*. Explorer A said, "There must be someone about, a gardener who cares for this plot!" The other explorer B said, "There is no gardener. Look at the weeds!" So they pitched their tents and watched. No gardener appeared! Explorer A said, "Perhaps he is an invisible gardener." So they built a fence, electrified it, and patrolled with bloodhounds. (They remembered how H. G. Wells's *The Invisible Man* could be both smelt and touched though he could not be seen.) But there were no shrieks or other evidence that anyone was about! Just weeds and flowers growing and dying. But the Believer was not convinced. "There is a gardener, invisible, intangible, insensible to electric shocks, who moves in mysterious ways to care for his flowers, in spite of the weeds and blight that infects some of the flowers. He comes to look after a garden which he loves." The sceptic gave up, "Just what remains of your original assertion that there is a gardener? How does an invisible, intangible, mysterious, eternally elusive gardener differ from an *imaginary* gardener or better, from no gardener at all? The difference between us is not a *factual* one. The plot is the same, but our *attitudes* toward the plot differ." [15]

If the meaning of a factual statement is identical with the experiences relevant to the possibility of its falsification, then to move the assertion out of the domain of verification or falsification is to re-move its factual meaning. What we have here is a theory of *truth* determining a theory of *meaning*. As Ayer says, "Surely from empirical premises nothing whatsoever concerning the properties, or even the existence, of anything superempirical can legitimately be inferred." (Theory of truth.) But what follows? It is not that the statement "There is a gardener" is false (this could not *in principle* be shown) but rather, it has no *meaning*. Therefore, if one should ask Flew, "Does God exist? Is God loving?" he would not reply with, "There is no God of Love." He would say, "I not only don't know, I don't even know what you mean and I suspect you don't either." When any state of affairs is compatible with an assertion, then it is either analytic or factually meaningless! (Theory of meaning.)

It is the challenge of Flew that many analytic philosophers feel causes a theological flu (Flew) for which there is no known inoculation. The rest of this essay will deal with this challenge. At first glance we seem to be faced with three options. [16]

1. Accept the criterion of falsification and show that theological statements satisfy it, i.e. are assertions. Blackstone calls this the "right-wing" position.
2. Accept the criterion of falsification and argue that theological statements are *not* statements, but something else, i.e. attitudes, bliks, policies for living, and so on. Blackstone calls this the left-wing" position.
3. Reject the criterion and develop new criteria.

Pause to Deal with Fideism [17] and the Way of Analogy

FIDEISM

But before I go on to discuss these options I must pause to deal with one approach that has had a long history in theology. It may even have

[15] A. Flew, "Theology and Falsification," in *New Essays in Philosophical Theology,* edited by A. Flew and A. MacIntyre (New York: Macmillan, 1955). Flew is making use of a parable originally told by John Wisdom in an essay, "Gods," *Philosophy and Psycho-Analysis* (London: Basil Blackwell, 1953), pp. 149–159.

[16] I am following Blackstone's distinctions. For his discussion of the issues raised in this essay see William T. Blackstone, *The Problem of Religious Knowledge* (Englewood Cliffs, N.J.: Prentice-Hall, 1963).

[17] I am indebted here to Kai Nielsen and F. Ferre. See especially Kai Nielsen, "Can Faith Validate God-Talk?" *New Theology No. 1,* Martin Marty and Dean Peerman, eds. (New York: Macmillan, 1964), and F. Ferre, "Is Language About God Fraudulent?" *The Scottish Journal of Theology,* Vol. 12, No. 4, (December 1959).

gone through your mind as you read the first part of this essay. The approach goes like this. My religious beliefs rest solely on faith. A fallen man cannot know God without the aid of God's Grace. The existence of God is not a matter of proof or demonstration. Our natural experience is not sufficient to answer the God-question. God is not found at the end of a syllogism or by the astronauts up in the sky. It is the feelings of despair and the absurdity of it all that drive us to God. Without God, life would be meaningless. Faith gives life meaning and hope; unbelief leads to the experience of nothingness. The man of faith must take a Kierkegaardian "leap of faith," not knowing if his risk is based on objective truth. But the risk is worth the benefit for faith provides a total solution to a total dilemma. This is the purple prose version.

The more sophisticated thrust of the above version is that the content of the Judeo-Christian tradition is discontinuous with *ordinary experience* and *ordinary language*. Theology is *extra*-ordinary because its object is literally not of this world. Theologians must be obedient to their Object (Subject) just as any science must apportion itself to its object. Because, the theological Object is extra-ordinary, theology involves a break with ordinary ways of thinking and speaking. This extra-ordinary Object can only be known as being *given*, a self-revelation in event [18] or encounter.[19]

Now notice! The model for knowing is the empiricist's model of perception in which one *has* a perception, i.e., God. The theologians who argue the above are theological *positivists*. Something is *given* and faith simply is the act of reception. Just as in sense experience, something is *given;* even the *response is given*, faith.

Though this position is widely held, is it really tenable? Simply because a sentence has a correct grammatical form and evokes a response does not necessarily mean that it has meaning. And what is even more important, simply because a sentence has meaning does not mean it has factual meaning. "Igly boo is farkel! I firmly believe that!" These sentences have correct grammatical form and, let us say, evoke feelings of awe in me. But what factual meaning does the first sentence have? If I say that I accept the above on faith and that its meaning passes my understanding, can I accept or reject it? Does not the assertion have to be understandable to someone? If I do not understand what 'Igly' ('God') means, then 'believe' also becomes meaningless. For what does 'belief' in 'Igly' mean? At this point faith cannot exist prior to understanding. Faith presupposes that the assertion is meaningful. We may have faith in something without having evidence for it, but we cannot have faith in what we do not understand.

Consider an example drawn from Ferre. Imagine someone asking you, "Would you lend me your largest ramafuge?" The sentence is grammatically correct, but unintelligible unless I know what 'ramafuge' means.

[18] See Chapter Two for examples of those who make this claim.
[19] For example, Martin Buber. See in Chapter Three the essay by Hepburn and in this chapter the essay by Donald Evans.

But it is not only the last word whose intelligibility is questioned, for the other words in the sentence are also in doubt. If I do not know what a 'ramafuge' is, I do not know what 'largest' or 'lend' means. For example, we know what 'lend' means in cases where the object to be loaned is known, but what does 'lend' mean when the object is unknown? "Lend me your largest X I know not what!" The *whole* sentence is unintelligible! If the religious believer claims to have faith in God, but 'God' stands for something beyond our comprehension then the word *faith* also becomes unintelligible. If someone asked you to lend him your largest ramafuge your only response could be, "Before I say 'yes' or 'no' I must know what a ramafuge is." So, before one can accept *or* reject faith in God one must know what the word *God* means. (Compare the following remark by Van Buren: "Today, we cannot even understand the Nietzschian claim that 'God is dead!' for if it were so, how could we know? No, the problem now is that the *word God* is dead." [20]) The fideist position, it would seem, is therefore untenable.

THE WAY OF ANALOGY

The way of analogy is probably the most widely held theory of talk about God. My discussion will be restricted to a brief account of this theory as found in the *followers* of St. Thomas.[21]

In finding an appropriate way to talk about a reality that seems to be infinitely beyond us, St. Thomas proposed the *via negativa* and the *via affimativa*. The way of negation is a procedure of removing predicates of God that are inappropriate. Although we cannot know God's nature as it is in itself, we can know what it is not. Mystics are fond of this particular maneuver. God is infinite (*not* finite), immutable (*not* changeable), incorporeal (*not* material), and so on. So although nothing is being affirmed of God, we have made an advance because we know what God is not.[22] The *via affimativa* moves us further by showing how certain predicates can be predicated of God positively, i.e., goodness, wisdom, existence, and so on. But again, because we cannot know *what* God is directly, our language about what God is must have a special logic. The logic of analogy is one such logic.

[20] Paul Van Buren, *The Secular Meaning of the Gospel* (New York: Macmillan, 1963), p. 103.

[21] There is a great deal of debate about exactly what St. Thomas held about analogy. Current interest in analogy finds expression in three excellent interpreters: Victor Preller, *Divine Science and the Science of God* (Princeton: Princeton University Press, 1967); Ralph McInerny, *The Logic of Analogy* (The Hague: Martinus Nijhoff, 1961); and James F. Ross, "Analogy as a Rule of Meaning for Religious Language," *International Philosophical Quarterly*, I (1961), pp. 468–502. For a traditional account see F. Copleston, *Aquinas* (London: Penguin Books, 1955); and "The Doctrine of Analogy," from E. L. Mascall, *Existence and Analogy* (London: Longmans, Green & Co., Ltd., 1949).

[22] Is there not a problem with this claim? If I describe something that I do not know in itself, say X, can I deny any predicate of it without knowing *what* it is?

The way of analogy recognizes that one cannot appeal to revelation unless one knows what the words of revelation mean. For revelation is received in human language. It is the task of the theologian to map out how these words signify God. For example, we know what it would mean to call John good, but what about calling God good? How is God's goodness related to man's goodness? Is there an infinite qualitative difference? Is there a likeness? We know what it means to call John a person, but what does it mean to call God a person? Being a person involves bodily states, attitudes, dispositions, drives, being burdened by one's past and confronted by an open future. How is God a person in any of these ways? It is these questions that the defender of the way of analogy attempts to answer. He grants the necessity of natural theology, i.e., that before the words of revelation can be believed or rejected the theologian must show the logic of his words. But how do the words go across the *gap* between creator and creature? Is the gap infinite? If so, then how can human language—creature talk—be used to talk about the creator. Is the gap overcome in the *relation* of creator to creature? If so, what is this relation? Is it likeness? So much for the purpose of the way of analogy.

In developing the middle way (via media) there are two extremes to be avoided, anthropomorphism and agnosticism. These extremes are *natural* movements in theology and therefore are avoided only by effort. The drive toward agnosticism is theologically motivated to protect God from being compared to anything created. God is infinite, transcendent, wholly other, inconceivable. God as He is in Himself is beyond our knowing and speaking. Praise lies silent on our lips! Reverence for God as an object worthy of worship requires this move away from comparing God to anything in this world. God is literally out of this world.

What follows from this maneuver is that the predicates we apply to God are *equivocal*, i.e., two totally different meanings. God's love is totally different from human love. God's love passes our understanding. Our talk about God must be "cleansed" of all reference to human love. But where does this maneuver leave us? With an unknowable God! How does this position differ from agnosticism?

But there is a contrasting movement in theology with equal religious motivation to stress God's presence *in* the world and involvement in the happenings of world history and individual's histories. A God totally transcended is not available religiously. Who can worship, pray to, preach about that which is totally other?! Such a God is irrelevant to our life and our world. This contrasting movement stresses God's involvement, God's humanity, God's immanence, God's agency in our world to seek and to save. God gets angry, changes his mind, appears, acts, loves, hates, and in Christ is incarnated in the world. But if God speaks, hears, loves, and so on, and these terms are used *univocally* (have the same meaning when used of God as of man), then God seems to lose his "Godness."

What then is the *difference* between God and man? God seems to be human (anthropomorphism).

The way of analogy moves between the extremes of anthropomorphism (univocal predication) and agnosticism (equivocal predication). When we talk about goodness, wisdom, love, personhood, these predicates cannot mean exactly the same when used in reference to both God and humans. Nor can they be used in totally different senses. These predicates must be used *analogically*. We must also remember that because we are creatures we cannot know God as He is in Himself, at least outside revelation. We know God only through His effects in the world that bear a resemblance to their maker; at least, so say the defenders of the way of analogy.

Without going into great detail, let me briefly indicate the basic form of analogy, the analogy of proportion. The analogy of proportion *assumes* the analogy of being, that is, everything is on a scale of being with God at the top. Since God is Being itself, everything that *is* bears some resemblance to his Being. Why? Because God is the *cause* of the being of everything that is. Now the *relation* between cause and effect is such that the effect bears a resemblance to that which is its cause. Because God is the *cause* of all being, all beings bear a resemblance to Him as an *effect* of his creative act. As St. Thomas says,

Sensible things, from which the human reason takes the origin of its knowledge, retain within themselves some sort of trace of a likeness to God. This is so imperfect, however, that it is absolutely inadequate to manifest the substance of God. For effects bear within themselves, in their own way, the likeness of their causes, since an agent produces its like; yet an effect does not always reach to the full likeness of its cause.[23]

Given the fact that creatures *are,* they bear a resemblance to God because there is assumed the relation of creature to Creator; effect to Cause; being to Being.

The analogy of proportion states specifically that there is a relation between two analogates such that one analogate possesses the attribute predicated of it in a formal sense while the other analogate possesses the predicate in a virtual sense. For example, we may call men and mountain resorts 'healthy.' Men are formally 'healthy,' whereas mountain resorts are called 'healthy' in the virtual sense in that they *cause* health. So, because God is the cause of goodness, wisdom, and existence in humans, He can be called 'good,' 'wise,' and 'existence' in the virtual sense.

But there are several difficulties with this position. The analogy of proportion does not tell us anything about God formally, only virtually, i.e., that He is the *cause* of goodness, wisdom, and so on. But He may not

[23] St. Thomas Aquinas, *Summa Contra Gentiles,* I, 14, trans. Anton C. Pegis (Garden City, N.Y.: Image Books, 1955), p. 8.

have these characteristics *formally.* The mountain resort has health virtually but not formally. Might this not also be true of God? To answer this question we would have to know God as He is in Himself. But this is denied us as creatures. But if we do not know God in Himself then these predicates are not helpful in talking *about God.*

This theory is also too permissive. If God is the cause of everything there is, then all kinds of predicates can be applied to God virtually. He must be virtually 'hot,' 'cold,' 'colored,' and so on. There is no control over the predicates without knowing some predicates that define God's nature *formally.* This definition would then serve as a criterion for excluding and including predicates. But to do so we would again have to know God's nature in a nonanalogical sense.

But even more crucial to this position is the assumption that causes resemble effects. Is this true? Not always. To answer we would have to know the cause outside of the effect, not through the effect. And what is more, this theory assumes the *relation* of cause and effect. But how are we to understand this relation? When we speak of God as a 'creator' or 'cause' we do not mean this in a literal sense. In what sense then? In an analogical sense? But this analogy would have to be grounded in yet another relation. But how is that relation to be understood? Analogically? But somewhere the analogies must stop, otherwise we have an infinite regression. This analogy explains this analogy which explains this analogy which. . . . Somewhere the analogies must stop and be grounded in some statement that is nonanalogous.

In summary, for the way of analogy to work, some direct, nonanalogous statement about God's nature must be made, or we can never know that to which our analogies point, which analogies are appropriate, and which ones are not appropriate. An analogy *by itself* is not illuminating. Some *prior* knowledge of that to which the analogy points is necessary. Another way of putting this is that "we don't . . . claim to *know* by analogy, but only to argue by analogy." [24] What this means is that when someone asks you how you know that God is loving, you do not argue by analogy. You are expected to provide some justification for your claim based on some evidence. Given this evidence I can then show the analogy between His love and my love. But notice! This presupposes that the similarity is already known. We do not come to know by analogy. Yet this is exactly what the defense of the way of analogy tries to argue. We can use analogies only if we already know in a nonanalogical sense.

The Left-Wing Response. (Early defenders [25] of this position include R. M. Hare, R. B. Braithwaite, and Ronald Hepburn. A contemporary exponent is Paul Van Buren.)

[24] J. L. Austin, "Other Minds." *Proceedings of the Aristotelian Society,* Suppl., Vol. 20 (1946), p. 148.

[25] See bibliography for books and articles that depict this response.

The left-wing response to Ayer-Flew is composed of those philosophers who argue that religious language, although meaningful, is not *factually* meaningful. I will briefly summarize two of the most influential exponents of this position, Hare and Braithwaite, and give my criticisms of their standpoints.

Hare and 'Bliks' [26]

Hare agrees with Flew that religious language is neither verifiable nor falsifiable. Religious language is not a series of assertions about the world and God, but a "blik," or attitude toward the world. A "blik" is not an assertion but a pervasive attitude of mind that determines how one *interprets* facts. The "blik" is not drawn from the facts, but is brought to the facts. As such, a blik is not falsifiable. Bliks are not true or false. To make his point, Hare tells a parable about an undergraduate lunatic who is convinced that all professors are out to get him. No matter how many gentle, loving, considerate professors he meets he continues in his blik. "These latter dons are just more cunning and are plotting my ultimate downfall." The undergraduate will accept no state of affairs as counting against his blik about dons. His assertion is, therefore, unfalsifiable. Although it *appears* to be an assertion, it really asserts nothing at all about dons. It is an attitude, standpoint, or blik about dons.

This does not mean, however, that because bliks are not assertions that they are unimportant. We all have bliks—*perspectives* through which we see the world—and it is important to have the "right" blik or a "sane" blik. Hare himself believes, that the religious blik is the right blik.[27] A 'right' blik is known by the effect it has on one's actions. A 'right' blik entails a policy for acting in the world whose anticipation may be right or wrong. But then reasons can be given, evidence cited.

But what then is the logic of 'right' and 'sane'? It would seem that these locutions are possible only if one counts evidence for and/or against bliks. If this is so then bliks are *assertions* and come under the logic of assertions. Hare countered Flew's challenge by denying the assertive character of religious language, only to resurrect the same logic (of assertions) when he speaks of 'sane' or 'right' bliks. We will come back to this issue when we discuss Wittgenstein's notion of 'pictures' and Hick's discussion of 'seeing as.' [28]

[26] Flew and MacIntyre, op. cit., pp. 99–103.

[27] Other examples of right bliks are confidence in the rigidity of the steel in one's car; the assumption that physical objects have a stable character so that they do not pop in and out of existence. Note similarity to Hume's notion of natural belief. See Blackstone, op. cit., pp. 78–81.

[28] See essays by Wittgenstein and Hick in this chapter.

R. B. Braithwaite and the Conative Theory of Religious Language [29]

Braithwaite represents another left-wing response to the challenge of Ayer-Flew. He agrees with the latter two that religious assertions are not empirical claims testable by experience. But it does not follow that they are meaningless non-sense. For if a sentence has a 'use' then it has a meaning. In other words, he is arguing over against Ayer that the meaning of a sentence is not its verification but its use. He is echoing here the *popular* Wittgenstein point: "Don't ask for the meaning; look at the use." If we look at the *use* of religious language we find a definite use, therefore a meaning. The use of religious language, Braithwaite argues, is moral. The function of moral language is not as Ayer argued, simply emotive, but to express the speaker's commitment to a certain policy of action. Moral language is *conative* rather than purely emotive. Moral language expresses the speaker's *intention* to act in a certain way. Religious language is also used in this way; to express and recommend a commitment to a certain general policy or way of life. A Christian's assertion that God is love (agape) is the announcement of his "intention to follow an agapeistic way of life."

When two religions seem to involve the same *intention* to act in a particular way (e.g., Christianity and some forms of Buddhism), what is the difference? The significant difference is in the stories (myths, parables, legends, and so on.) that are told. Christianity is made up of the company of those who *intend* to act in a certain way in the world and tell a collection of stories that back up their way of life.

These stories *need not be true or even need be believed to be true*. The function of the story is not to tell the truth about a state of affairs; its function is a psychological one, to motivate people to act in a certain way. Stories are judged in terms of these consequences and continue to be told as long as they motivate people to certain actions. Many fables are known to be false, but continue to be used because of their importance in this motivational respect, for example, Peter Rabbit and Farmer MacGregor. (I cite this fable because it seems to have had quite an effect on my son, David.)

Summary

"A religious assertion, for me, is the assertion of an intention to carry out a certain behavior policy, subsumable under a sufficiently general

---

[29] *An Empiricist's View of the Nature of Religious Belief* (Cambridge: Cambridge University Press, 1955). This position is also defended with variations by Peter Munz, *Problems of Religious Knowledge* (London: SCM Press, 1959); T. R. Miles, *Religion and the Scientific Outlook* (London: George Allen & Unwin, 1959); Ronald Hepburn, *Christianity and Paradox* (London: Watts, 1958); Paul F. Schmidt, *Religious Knowledge* (Glencoe: The Free Press, 1961); Paul Van Buren, *Secular Meaning of the Gospel* (New York: Macmillan, 1965).

principle to be a moral one, together with the implicit or explicit statement, but not the assertion, of certain stories." (Braithwaite)

Some Comments

1. If Braithwaite is using 'use' as his criterion for meaning, religious
people generally would not restrict their use of religious language in this
way. Religious people use religious language to *assert* something about
God, persons, and the world. As a description of actual use, Braithwaite
is wrong; as a *recommendation* for how religious people ought to use their
language in light of the Ayer-Flew challenge, his position has a rightful
place on the list of options.[30]

2. Braithwaite also commits a common error made by many early
analysts, i.e., they assume religious language has *one* use. Religious language does many different jobs. Even stories have diverse uses: historical
accounts, mythological stories, legends, and so on. He assumes that all
stories are modeled on the logic of *parables*. Christianity includes parables, but is much more.

Right-Wing Response

While the left-wing response searches for some 'use' for religious language other than the factual or assertive, the right-wing philosophers
accept the criterion of Ayer-Flew and argue that religious language can
be used to make assertions so defined. John Hick is perhaps the best known
philosopher taking this tack.

John Hick and Eschatological Verification [31]

Although Hick has written extensively on the logic of religious language, I will deal only with his analysis of the cognitive issue vis-a-vis
Ayer-Flew. For Hick faith is a total *interpretation* of the universe. An
interpretation of the universe is a *way of looking* at the world that determines what we consider significant and prescribes a life-style to be followed. There are a great number of possible interpretations, no one of
which seems to be the more probable. This latter impasse has led some to
say that interpretations, because they are incapable of being verified, are
simply subjective 'bliks.' This is also true of atheism which is as unverifiable as a theism. The issue between atheist and theist is not a
cognitive one, but simply a difference in onlooks. Hick denies that this

---

[30] Van Buren makes the same mistake. See essay by L. Gilkey in Chapter Five.

[31] John Hick, "Theology and Verification," *Theology Today*, XVII, No. 1 (April
1960). This essay has been reprinted in numerous volumes on God-talk. For criticism
of this position see Kai Nielsen, "Eschatological Verification," *Canadian Journal of
Theology*, Vol. IX, No. 4 (1963); Terence Penelhum, *Problems of Religious Knowledge* (New York: Herder and Herder, 1972). Footnotes in the latter book provide
information on the extensive material written on this issue.

is the case, arguing that the *future* expectations of a life beyond death as described in the Christian onlook would verify the theist's claim thereby showing that the choice between theism and atheism is a *real* choice. In making out his case he develops the conception of eschatological verification.

The verification of a factual assertion, for Hick, involves the *removal of rational doubt*. Note, what is demanded for verification is not knock-down perception, but removal of rational doubt. This is especially true in the case of religious experience where knowledge of God is not direct but mediated. As an interpretation, Christian theism is verified if the predicated state ensues in which all rational doubt is removed. Hick uses a parable to make his point:

Two men are walking down the road of life. One of them is a believer. He believes that the road leads to the Celestial City. Everything that happens to him is *interpreted* in terms of the end. Good happenings are interpreted as encouragement. Bad happenings are interpreted as trials of his faith. The unbeliever does not see life as a pilgrimage to the Celestial City, but as an aimless succession of events. He accepts the good and the bad as they come, for that is all there is.

Both men accept what happens to them. They do not disagree about *what happens*. As to their differing interpretations, there is no way on the way to determine which one is right. But, and this is Hick's point, *one man proves to be right all along* if they turn a corner and there is the Celestial City as described by the believer. Life, to the Christian, is presently ambiguous. But he claims that there is a future unambiguous state that will show that he has been right all along.

What are the points Hick seeks to make with this parable? One, theism and atheism are interpretations that have cognitive significance. Two, on Ayer's own grounds, the Christian vision is cognitively significant because it can in principle be verifiable (all rational doubt removed).

What would this unambiguous state be like? First, the fulfillment of God's purpose for ourselves and, second, communion with God mediated through the person of Christ. What this means is that the individual experiences great joy and peace; he acts in a loving way; he always resists temptation, and so on. He also relates to a person who is recognizable as Jesus of Nazareth. These conditions, Hick argues, would be sufficient to remove all rational doubt as to the truth of the Christian interpretation.

Hick's position has been criticized on a number of points. Let me review some of the more important ones. First, eschatological verification makes almost any claim factually meaningful. "Igly boo is farkel! Wait and see!" Then the question becomes, *in via*, how do I choose if the evidence comes only at the end? But perhaps this is unfair to Hick. He is not trying to prove the Christian interpretation is true, only that it is a *meaningful claim*. Second, the traditional problem of evil arises in a different way. If God can remove rational doubt *in patria*, why not now?

Because he does not want us to be forced to accept Him? The believer says, "God protects our freedom by allowing us to choose against him! If God forced us to do only the good, then we would be robots, not humans." God *cannot* create a person who is free, yet always chooses the good. But what is the force of 'cannot'? Is it not claimed in the Christian vision that in heaven we will be *confirmed* in our *bliss?* Does this not mean that we will always do good; be happy; be fully human? But if God can do this at the end, why not at the beginning? Most reasons given to these question make God morally repugnant.[32]

Third, does talk of life after death make sense? What is a *spiritual* body? How would I know that I had survived my death if my body and environment were totally different? [33]

Fourth, even if life after death can be meaningfully talked about and discovered to be what Christians say it will be, does this verify their claim? Could it not be *interpreted* differently, for example, by the Buddhist or humanist? One could imagine debate, even in heaven, as to what interpretation is correct. Might not the same problem arise that came up with Hare's bliks? A person might interpret his experience in heaven as the act of an evil god who was setting us all up for a terror-filled hell in contrast to heaven. And this could be eschatologically verified. It would be a meaningful claim a la Hick's own analysis. Present facts allow room for a number of interpretations. Logically, that will still be the case in heaven.

My fifth criticism deals with Hick's thesis that faith or belief is an *interpretation* of experience; that is a "seeing as." But if *all* seeing is really 'seeing as,' this would make nonsense of the very notion of 'seeing as.' For 'seeing as' implies something known that you see as such and such. But if this is true then not all seeing is 'seeing as.' The same is true if all experience is an *interpretation* of some independent existing world. For the notion of interpretation implies an experience that is not an interpretation. If every experience is an interpretation then it is not an interpretation!

My sixth criticism deals with the circular nature of Hick's position. He *assumes* the meaning of God-talk for eschatological verification, but that is exactly what is in doubt. If I can never know God directly, even in the future life, then the *facts* that I use to verify God-talk are open to various interpretations, even then. For unless I already knew what 'God's grace' meant, I would not recognize it when it occurred. All I would know is that I had survived my death, that people loved one another, and so on. What would it mean to call these events examples of the 'reign of God?' What event or series of events would confirm or infirm the claim? What

[32] For discussion of this and related issues see Nelson Pike (ed.) *God and Evil* (Englewood Cliffs, N.J.: Prentice-Hall, 1965); Alvin Plantinga *God and Other Minds* (Ithaca, N.Y.: Cornell University Press, 1967).
[33] See Terence Penelhum, *Survival and Disembodied Existence* (New York: Humanities Press, 1970).

facts point unambiguously to the claim that our experience in heaven is an example of God's reign? The difference still seems to be a difference in *interpretation*. Which one is right? How would we know? Flew's challenge still seems valid even in heaven.[34]

THE THIRD STAGE—THE LATE WITTGENSTEIN

Ludwig Wittgenstein is probably the most influential philosopher in the English speaking world in this century. Consequently, the material involved in any discussion of his philosophy is voluminous. An added complication is that he repudiates some of his early position after going through a philosophical conversion. To compound the problem, Wittgenstein's style is to use aphorisms and countless puzzles and examples without drawing systematic conclusions (part of his philosophical position). This has led to a myriad of interpretations. His followers dominate the philosophical scene in the English speaking world.[35]

I will summarize Wittgenstein's description of how language works under six topic sentences or aphorisms (Part One) and then show how this description sheds light on the workings of religious language (Part Two). I will also weave in some suggestion by John Austin.[36]

Part One

1. Attack upon *essentialism!* Wittgenstein's conversion consisted primarily in his realization that words do not have essential meanings to which they point. Words do not stand for meanings or ideas that we have in our minds. Words are not external signs for internal meanings. Therefore, for example, it is ridiculous to look for the essential meaning of 'good' or 'know' or 'true.' Their meanings are determined by their *use* in public language games. There may be a family resemblance among the uses, but no essential meaning by which all the uses are judged. For example, the word 'good' may do a great variety of jobs: A. Grading. "That's

[34] For an in-depth discussion of this point see Kai Nielsen, *Contemporary Critiques of Religion,* op. cit., pp. 71–79 and Terence Penelhum, *Problems of Religious Knowledge,* op. cit., pp. 66–86.

[35] The "Bible" of the movement is Wittgenstein's *Philosophical Investigations,* 3rd Edition (New York: Macmillan, 1958). It is notoriously difficult to read if you do not know what he is up to. One should begin with N. Malcolm, *Ludwig Wittgenstein: A Memoir* (London: Oxford University Press, 1958). This paperback is not only about his philosophy, but the strangely fascinating *man.* Reading this book should help prevent some from saying that linguistic philosophy is only a word game. For an excellent introduction to his philosophy and an extensive bibliography, see K. T. Fann, *Wittgenstein's Conception of Philosophy* (Berkeley: University of California Press, 1971).

[36] John Austin is also very influential in ordinary language philosophy. Donald Evans has made extensive use of Austin's philosophy of language, vis-a-vis religious language. See especially, Donald Evans, *The Logic of Self-Involvement* (London: SCM Press, 1963).

good; that's bad"; B. Exclamation. "Good God!"; C. Expressive of feelings:
"Good grief, Charlie Brown!"; D. Expressing agreement as when one says
'good' after someone makes a proposal. Notice, there is no essential
meaning to 'good' and the quest for such, while it has had a long history,
is ill-advised.

What Wittgenstein is attacking is the so-called 'Fido'—Fido theory of
meaning, i.e., words refer to things, relations, qualities, or meanings that
one has in his mind. When I say a word, for example, you may *believe* it
stands for a meaning that you have in your mind. But is this actually so? If
words referred to private meanings one had in a mind, how would we ever
know if we were understood? This view of language leads to linguistic so-
lipsism, i.e., the view that only the user knows what the words mean. But
we do know what others mean and the ways of checking are *public,* not
private.

2. "Language is a varied as the tools in your tool-box." By this Wittgenstein means that language does many jobs, i.e., naming, describing,
praising, commanding, and so on. The positivist was mainly concerned
with only one language job, i.e., asserting facts. And the model he used
was that of language picturing states of affairs. The statement referred
to or pictured a fact that made it true. "The cat is on the mat!" refers
to the cat on the mat. But language does many more jobs than name
things or facts. In fact, even a *statement* such as "John made it" may be
used to say *who* made it; how well it was made (an evaluation); how
poorly it was made; who it belongs to, "so keep your dirty hands off it"
(a command); a commitment to a certain pattern of behavior, for example, if John made it then treat it with loving care.[37] Wittgenstein hints
that creation talk *may* be like this latter example. "God made the earth
and all that is therein," means "Treat the earth kindly because God
made it."

If this analysis is correct, then it is nonsense to ask, what does religious
language do? There is no such animal as 'religious language'! We may
use it as a shorthand term but religious expressions do *many* different
jobs. To try to find *one* model for religious language is to allow one's mind
to be bewitched by simplicity. Positivism made this mistake by viewing
religious language on the single model of factual statements. Therefore,
the one who makes the statement must show what would count for their
truth or falsity. But religious language does many differing jobs. The
philosopher should describe how in fact individual expressions are used.
He will find that religious expressions are not used as a mirror of reality
as the positivist seemed to understand scientific statements.[38] This does

[37] See Donald Evans, op. cit.

[38] Using the model of a mirror for understanding scientific language has been
shown to be very naïve. Scientific language does not *re-present* the way things are
in reality. Scientific language does not picture in words the way things are in reality.
See Ian Ramsey, *Models and Mystery* (London: Oxford University Press, 1964)
and Max Black, *Models and Metaphors: Studies in Language and Philosophy* (Ithaca:
Cornell University Press, 1962).

not mean that the cognitive issue does not arise. It does, but it arises in its own unique context. The philosopher must *look* and *see* how *religious* people raise and settle the issue. "Religious expressions are as varied as the tools in your tool box."

3. The meaning of a word is determined by *seeing* how it is *used*. Positivism made the mistake of modeling all language on mathematics and science (understood in the naïve sense of picturing facts). Ayer legislated on these models as to how all cognitively significant language *must* be used. Wittgenstein is arguing here that the philosopher should *describe*, not *prescribe*.

4. The use of words or sentences is determined within language games, that is, public ways in which two or more people agree to use words or sentences. For example, think how many different games the word 'cool' has come to be used in. Take the word 'true' as another example. It has *many* uses in a *variety* of language games. "He is true blue!" "It is true that 2 + 2 = 4." "That's true!" "I truly believe that." "His poetry rings true." "It is true that this paper is yellow." "I am the Truth, the Way and the Life." Knowing the meaning of a word is knowing the rules for its use in particular language games.

5. The *nonverbal context* must be included in any thorough analysis of an expression. Why? Because learning a language involves learning *when* to use it and what *behavior* is appropriate before and/or after the utterance. Language is a way of life, a form of life. As Wittgenstein says, "If a lion could talk we could not understand him." Why? Imagine a lion saying, "Hello, how are you?" and instead of shaking your hand, eating it. The lion obviously does not understand, nor do I understand him, if his nonverbal behavior does not fit with his verbal behavior. Certain expressions are proper in certain nonverbal contexts and find meaning *there* not elsewhere. Although "Jump over the puddle!" is a perfectly formed sentence, it does not make sense if you utter it to your professor as you hand him your paper.

Let's take another example, "I know Merlin Rehm!" When would it be proper to utter this locution? First, one does not generally use the word *know* unless there is an element of doubt in the situation. I would say "I know Merlin Rehm" if someone *asked* me if I knew the Hebrew professor who wears that awful red academic gown from some second-rate eastern school. "Oh, you mean Merlin Rehm from Harvard? I know him!" Second, if one uses the locution 'know' it is what we call a *speech-act* in which you not only say words but you do something in the saying of the words. In this case you give a person a promissory note that you can perform an appropriate action for this case of knowing. For example, I should be able to ask "How tall is he? Where does he live?" and so on. If you can not perform, then you only thought you knew him. To say "I believe I know him," for example, is like the preceding with respect to the element of doubt but is different in the sense that saying "I believe I know him" is almost asking to be let off the hook of performing. You can say "I believe I know him" but are not expected to perform in the rigorous way that "I know what" or "I know how" would require.

The above discussion is important for understanding religious language since ritualistic and confessional language requires certain nonverbal behavior to complete it. For example, to say that one believes "God is love" is not only to say something *about* God, it is also to say something about how one should act, what one should expect in the cosmic process, and so on. Evans argues, to cite another example, that 'knowing' God is a *self*-involving act. To say one knows God is to involve one's self in a pattern of behavior, i.e., to announce one's intention to act in a certain way. We have taken 'know' on the model of 'sight' or 'proof' and, therefore, missed the other uses of 'know.' When the prophets issued the imperative, "Know the Lord, your God!" he was not saying something like, "Learn your math tables." To know God is not to be able to describe him, but to do his will. Those who know God are those who love one another. To know God is to know what he requires. If you say that you know God but do not act as He demands then you do *not* know him.

6. Philosophy helps one see things in a new way such that once one *pictures* the world in a certain way, now in a new way, just as one can look at

DUCK-RABBIT [39]
                                    and change his picture
(interpretation) from duck to rabbit. Notice, the world remains what it is; philosophy only changes how one sees it. Notice too that the question of whether that *really* is a rabbit or duck is ridiculous (cf. points 1 & 2) except within specified contexts.

Wittgenstein says the following about problems in philosophy (think theology):

These are, of course, not empirical problems; they are solved, rather, by looking into the workings of our language, and that in such a way as to make us recognize those workings: *in despite of* an urge to misunderstand them. The problems are solved, not by giving new information, but by arranging what we have always known. Philosophy is a battle against the bewitchment of our intelligence by means of language. (Investigations #109).

Religious language is a picture or seeing the world as ——————.
The language has meaning within the community that uses it; it follows its

[39] Adapted from L. Wittgenstein, *Philosophical Investigations*, p. 194.

own rules as well as *shares* rules with other games, crisscrossing. And it is the philosopher's job to show that logic, how it is shared with other games and what special rules are unique to a particular game.

Part Two Religious Application [40]

1. *Training* is extremely important in learning the rules which form our language games. Learning what words mean in particular games is like learning what job chess pieces do in the game of chess. The meaning of a word is the role it plays just as the meaning of a pawn is the role it plays in the game of chess. "Every sign *by itself* seems dead. *What* gives it life?—In use it is *alive.* Is life breathed into it there?—Or is the *use* its life?" [41] Words acquire meaning in use and use is taught. Understanding a religious person is not understanding some esoteric meaning (a thing?) that one has in one's mind; understanding a person is seeing how he uses his words in specific contexts. This understanding requires 'training.'

2. To speak a word or sentence, then, is part of an activity, a form of life. Wittgenstein means that training in the uses of certain words is not sufficient for understanding. For, as we saw earlier, we could not understand the lion because his behavior would be too radically at variance with ours. (Don't think of Snoopy because his behavior is not doglike but human.)

3. What we do in our language game always rests on a picture. What Wittgenstein seemed to have meant by this is that all language games involve a "depth grammar," i.e., a picture or "seeing as" which cannot be supported except within that game. What constitutes a 'fact' or a 'reason' or a 'justification' is determined within the language game following from the picture. (Hare's blik?)

If we take these three summary points and apply them to specifically religious contexts, we get the following description.

1. Religious *belief* involves *training* in the technique of using the appropriate picture. This means learning what conclusions are drawn from the picture and what conclusions are not drawn. For example, "God's eye sees everything." One should not ask of this assertion, if one understands the depth grammar, "What color are his eyes?" "Does he have 20-20 vision?" On the surface these questions would seem appropriate.

[40] See in particular Dallas High, *Language, Persons and Belief* (New York: Oxford University Press, 1967); *Donald Evans, The Logic of Self-Involvement, op. cit.;* W. D. Hudson, *Ludwig Wittgenstein: The Bearing of His Philosophy Upon Religious Belief* (Richmond, Va.: John Knox Press, 1968) and Ludwig Wittgenstein, *Lectures and Conversations on Aesthetics, Psychology and Religious Belief* (Berkeley: University of California Press, 1967). The latter volume has given rise to what is called Wittgensteinian fideism. My concern in this section is to put before the reader the main tenets of that faith. I have followed a prominent Wittgensteinian fideist in my exposition, W. D. Hudson. See also Peter Winch and D. Z. Phillips.

[41] L. Wittgenstein, *Philosophical Investigation,* op. cit., sec. 432.

But if one *understands* the depth grammar of the picture, he learns that we are not in the context of discussing shaggy eyebrows, but rather God's providential care of the earth, God's knowledge of the intentions behind our acts, and so on. One *learns* what questions are appropriate, as any Sunday School teacher knows. Children frequently have the wrong picture and draw the wrong conclusions. For example, "Johnny, God made the world." Johnny: "And who made God?" He is not understanding the picture and, therefore, asking the wrong question.

It follows from this that *saying* and *doing* by themselves do not constitute religious belief. Religious belief also includes understanding. What does this involve? If I taught one the right words to say at the altar and when to kneel for the sacrament, this would not constitute *understanding*. Understanding involves drawing consequences of the picture for each new situation. Theological debate is about the *understanding* of the picture. Heresy is *mis-understanding* (mis-using) the picture, i.e., drawing the wrong conclusions. "And hearing they do not understand." We can determine if a child understands 'God is the Father of all mankind' if he uses this as his reason for loving his black neighbor. If he debates how God, as a physical progenitor, could father all mankind he obviously has not understood the picture.

'Understanding,' it seems to me, involves a. *Seeing* the connection between what is said and the picture itself. b. Drawing conclusions from the picture for new situations. c. Understanding *ordinary* uses of words from which religious uses may *differ*. To understand the religious use one must understand the ordinary use. 'The eye of God' or 'God the father' have meaning in the context of knowing (1) nonreligious uses, and (2) how religious use differs.

2. To learn the religious language game involves learning, for example, what the meaning is of 'reasonable' and 'unreasonable' in the game. It is a *mistake* to use 'reasonable' and 'unreasonable' from other games and apply them to religious belief. Wittgenstein calls it "ludicrous" to attempt to corroborate or refute religion on the basis of scientific evidence. What constitutes a 'reason' or a 'proof' in religion will differ from 'reason' or 'proof' in mathematics or science.

Religious belief involves *using a picture with understanding* to regulate your whole life, having it constantly in the foreground of your thought and action. The basic disagreement between believer and unbeliever is *not about facts* but a difference of *pictures*. If, for example, an unbeliever is asked what he *means* by 'I don't believe in a Last Judgment,' his answer is that on the basis of empirical evidence I do not think it probable that this event will occur, i.e., Christ will come again to judge the quick and the dead. But the believer when he says, "I believe in a Last Judgment" does not mean that he thinks there is empirical evidence for this event occurring in the future. He believes it because Christ said that He would come again. As such, Wittgenstein says the believer and unbeliever cannot contradict one another because contradiction occurs only within accepted presuppositions. If a believer says, 'I believe X' and an unbeliever says, 'I do not believe X,' they can only contradict one another If they mean the same by 'believe' and 'X.' Religious believers and unbelievers do not mean the same thing, therefore, the disagreement is *more fundamental.* It goes back to the use of *different pictures.* As Wittgenstein puts it: "Suppose someone is ill and he says, 'This is a punishment' and I say, 'If I'm ill, I don't think of punishment at all.' If you say, 'Do you believe the opposite?' you can call it believing the opposite, but it is entirely different from what we would normally call believing the opposite. I think differently, in a different way. I have different pictures." [42]

3. 'Belief.' There is an enormous gulf between believer and unbeliever in religion which is not paralleled in science, says Wittgenstein. Suppose someone said that he believed in the Last Judgment and I said, 'Well, I'm not so sure. *Possibly.*' You would say there is an enormous gulf between us. If he said, 'It is going to rain today'; and I said, 'Possibly' you would not say there is an enormous gulf between us. Religious controversies involve enormous gulfs. As Wittgenstein puts it, ". . . you don't get in religious controversies, the form of controversy where one person is *sure* of the thing, and the other says: 'Well, possibly'." [43]

And why is this the case? Because 'belief' in religion means something quite different from ordinary contexts. There is "this extraordinary use of the word 'believe.' One talks of believing and at the same time one doesn't use 'believe' as one does ordinarily. You might say (in the normal use) 'You only believe—oh well . . .' Here (in religion) it is used entirely differently: on the other hand it is not used as we generally use the word 'know'." [44]

What does Wittgenstein mean by these cryptic remarks? The religious use of 'believe' is not as I analyzed 'believe' earlier in the context of 'know.' In this context 'believe' would mean a. I don't have sufficient evidence, b. I would not stake my existence on its truth. But in religion 'belief' is an all-or-nothing commitment in spite of the lack of evidence or, on the basis of evidence that seems *unreasonable.* Wittgenstein argues that religious belief is not a matter of being reasonable or unreasonable. Religious belief is not to be judged by 'reasonable' or 'unreasonable' from our ordinary context. Religious belief does not even *pretend* to be 'reasonable' or 'unreasonable' in those senses. [45]

This position developed by Wittgenstein particularly in his lectures on religion is called "Wittgensteinian fideism." Prominent among those who defend and develop this viewpoint are Peter Winch, W. D. Hudson, and D. Z. Phillips. Although I agree that understanding a religious language

---

[42] Wittgenstein, *Lectures,* op. cit., p. 55.

[43] Ibid., p. 56.

[44] Ibid., pp. 59–60.

[45] Ibid., p. 58. For criticism of this position see Kai Nielsen, "Wittgensteinian Fideism," *Philosophy, 42:* 1967. More bibliography on this issue can be found on pp. 563–564 of Paul Edwards and Arthur Pap, editors, *A Modern Introduction to Philosophy,* 3rd Edition (New York: The Free Press, 1973).

game requires understanding it in terms of itself; although I agree that there is no standpoint outside all standpoints that would provide a place from which to judge the pictures (standpoints); I do find that people *within* the game have *doubts* about the truth or falsity of the game. Being in the game is compatible with doubting it. But on what grounds?

My position is that we are more polymorphic (many forms) than these Wittgensteinian fideists would admit. We play *many* different games; are involved in many forms of life. *And*, the religious game is being played with less and less seriousness by a significant number of people. More and more students talk of Christianity as they would of a poem or a painting than as an assertion about what is the case. It is ugly or beautiful, good or bad, a bad trip or in the groove; but it is not true or false.

Wittgenstein himself said that forms of life may die from dis-use. Although the reasons for this are complex, one reason seems predominant— the religious form of life or picture is no longer our *ordinary* form of life. It requires a *special look* to see the world religiously, whereas the reverse was true just a few generations ago. If our dominant picture is not the religious one, we judge the religious one in terms of the secular one. Witness the whole move in the churches toward the secular.[46] The duck is now a rabbit! To see it as a duck requires more strain than many are willing to endure.

A Start at a Meta-Theology

A *meta-theology:* a partial list of the uses of religious language and the meaning of religious belief. The list is not meant to be exhaustive or clean, but to give the student some idea of how an analytic philosopher of religion might do a logical map of God-talk.

1. *Commissive Use* (Hudson, Evans, Hick and Hare)

Every language game has a tacit presupposition (Collingwood) or picture (Wittgenstein) that rules over the game. There is a basic *seeing-as* that determines for that perspective how the world is to be interpreted. We do not see the world but through perspectives. One cannot always determine why one sees in this particular way rather than that. New perspectives are strikingly similar to conversions. Wittgenstein points this out with his duck-rabbit as we have already seen.

2. *Tautological Use*

Many sentences in the Bible and particularly in theology are *definitions* which legislate for the community how certain words are to be used, for example, 'God is necessary being,' 'Sin is disobeying the will of God.' These sentences are true by definition within the game. *Note*, these sentences may do other jobs as well; remember my earlier remarks about diverse uses for single expressions.

3. *Emotive Use* (Ayer)

---

[46] See essays in Chapters One, Five, and Seven.

Although the positivists reduced *all* religious language to emotive language, I see emotive as one among many uses. For example, hymns, religious poetry, ritualistic expressions in some contexts have the sole purpose of arousing and giving vent to religious sentiments. This should not be surprising if religion concerns the whole man. "Praise the Lord!" is like ˙ shouting out, "Three cheers for God!" Or, "I feel at one with God" may express a feeling as well as *assert* something about the character of God.

4. *Performatory Use* (Austin and Evans)

This analysis stresses the self-involving character of some speech-acts. When a religious man says, "God created the universe and all that is therein," he is not simply making an assertion such as "made in Japan." The *saying* of this means that one intends to act in a certain way in the world. The *saying* of the expressions *involves* my self in a prescribed behavior, i.e., to respect the world as 'creation,' not simply as 'nature.' Braithwaite's comments about the conative use of religious language would be similar to this analysis, but leaves out the self-involving character of these utterances.

5. *Paradoxical Use* (Myth, analogy, symbol, and so on.)

The purpose of paradoxical language is not to confuse but to illuminate, i.e., to call attention to something one might not otherwise have noticed. Paradoxical language shows how religious language *differs* from ordinary language, goes beyond ordinary ways of knowing and meaning. John Wisdom has shown that paradox may be a case of linguistic penetration rather than linguistic confusion. What we must determine is "when a contradiction is not a mere contradiction, but a sublime Paradox, a mystery." (Wisdom)

Paradoxical language is *unavoidable* in theology because theologians must talk about "what's seen and more" in terms of a language suited to observables. As Ian Ramsey argues, if one is to a. understand what theologians actually do, b. defend religious language as *cognitive*, then paradoxical language must be used. Since the 'facts' that ground religious assertions go beyond ordinary facts, religious language *is odd* (paradoxical) with respect to other games.[47]

6. *Constative Use* (Austin)

Although performatives are self-involving in that my saying of it (speech-act) is the doing of it (for example, 'Thank God the Almighty!' is to *have* thanked Him), constatives are used to make *descriptions;* make cognitive claims. It is this use that becomes crucial, for it seems to me that religious people use 'God loves mankind,' or 'God created the universe,' to make *factual* claims. If religious people are making cognitive claims, then some set of 'facts' must be relevant to their truth or falsity.

Religion cannot survive the abandonment of this claim that religious

---

[47] Ian Ramsey, *Religious Language* (New York: Macmillan, 1963); "Paradox in Religion," *Proceedings of the Aristotelian Society,* Suppl. Vol. XXXIII (1959).

people witness religious facts. If there are not some religious assertions
that describe uniquely religious facts, then the reductionistic analyses
of philosophers like Ayer, Braithwaite and Van Buren have won the
day. Too many Christian linguistic philosophers fail to see this. To show
that religious language has a use is not enough. Why? Because we also
want to know if the claims are *true!* How would I know if they are true?
The fact that a word has meaning does not show that it *refers* to anything. The fact that a word has a use does not show that use is *justified*.

A Final Word

Theology, it seems, is involved in the technique of using the Christian
picture. Although many of us have learned the game from our youth,
the theologian gives us lessons in its grammar just as we learn English
before Professor Schramm teaches us English grammar in school. The
theologian is a grammarian of the Christian language game. He draws
out the consequences of the picture for each new situation; he teaches
us what can and cannot be said; he balances models (parables, symbols,
myths) against one another when we try to take them literally (ordinary
use); looks for *new* languages that develop out of the primitive picture.

The philosopher's job is critical, that is, testing for consistency; revealing the 'depth grammar'; logically mapping the uses of religious language;
comparing religious language games with other games, and so on.

But the question of the *grounding* of any one picture is the crucial
task. This question must be asked and some help given, although I find
a solution to this issue is beyond my wit. How, for example, can I show
my son David that his belief in Superman is a fantasy, whereas my
belief in God is not? The rules seem so much the same! Or, how do I
handle the contention of many that the Christian language game is
obsolete, remembering Wittgenstein's point that language games can
become "obsolete and get forgotten." The Christian language game is not
dying the "death of a thousand qualifications," but a death from dis-use.
Our children are learning new and different language games that are
taking over for the religious language game. If *meaning* is in *use* in
games with dominant *pictures* that are the results of *training*, then part
of the crisis in religion is education. For, if I have been *taught* that this
is a rabbit, how do I come to see it as a duck, except by training or a
conversion?

IN DEFENSE OF ATHEISM

Kai Nielsen

KAI NIELSEN is Professor of Philosophy at the University of Calgary.
He is the author of many articles and books on religion. See especially,
Contemporary Critiques of Religion (1971), *Reason and Practice*
(1971), and *Scepticism* (1973).

I

Jews, Christians and Moslems do not and cannot take their religion to
be simply their fundamental conceptual framework or metaphysical system. Fundamental human commitments and attitudes are an essential
part of being religious. The feeling of gratitude for one's very existence
no matter what the quality or condition of that existence is at the very
heart of religion. To be religious consists fundamentally in living in a
certain way, in holding a certain set of convictions, in the having of certain attitudes and in being a member of a distinctive confessional group.

Religious discourse reflects this. Religious utterances express our
basic sense of security in life and our gratitude for being alive. Jews,
Christians and Moslems pray, and engage in rituals and ceremonies in
the doing of which they use language in a distinctive way. In religious
discourse, we give voice to our deepest and most pervasive hopes, ideals
and wishes concerning what we should try to be and what expectations
we may entertain. If we really are religious and do not regard religion
simply as "moral poetry" but use religious discourse seriously to make
distinctively religious claims, we commit ourselves to what we as believers take to be a certain general view about "the ultimate basis of the
universe." This is exhibited in the very use of certain religious utterances.

(1) God is my Creator to whom everything is owed.
     and
(2) God is the God of mercy of Whose forgiveness I stand in need.

are paradigms of the above mentioned use of religious discourse; they
presumably are fact-stating uses of discourse, though this is not all they
are, and they are closely linked with other uses of religious discourse.
Such ceremonial and evocative talk as we find in Christianity could
hardly exist if it were not for such uses of language as exhibited in (1)
and (2). (1) and (2) are not theologians' talk about God but are
sample bits of living religious discourse. Yet for believer and nonbeliever
alike they are perplexing bits of discourse.

Wittgenstein and others have taught the importance of context. We must not examine religious utterances—especially those which appear to have a statement-making function—in isolation, but we should examine them on location as part of that complex activity we call "religion." To understand a religious utterance properly we must come to understand the topic or topics of our discourse and the purposes for which it is used.

Indeed, in using language we must not forget what Strawson has called the Principle of the Presumption of Knowledge or the Principle of Relevance. Of all speech functions to which this applies, it applies most appositely to the making of statements, which is indeed a central speech function if anything is. That is to say, when "an empirically assertive utterance is made with an informative intention" there is the standing presumption on the part of the speaker that "those who hear him have knowledge of empirical facts revelant to the particular point to be imparted in the utterance." [1] Moreover, statements have topics, they are in that sense about something, and reflect what Strawson calls a "centre of interest." To understand a statement we must understand the topic or center of interest involved in its assertion. We must not forget that we do not characteristically give out information or give voice to utterances in an isolated, unconnected manner; but only as part of some connected discourses. We need a Principle of Relevance to pick out, in terms of the topic in question, the proper kind of answer to what a statement is about. This is integral to our understanding of how to take (understand) the statement in question.

Take the classic example "The King of France is bald." We need a context, an application of the Principles of Relevance and the Presumption of Knowledge, to know how to take it. If our context is the present, and the relevant questions are "What is the King of France like?" or "Is he bald?" then neither "The King of France is bald" nor "The King of France is not bald" would be a correct answer, for the above questions in the above context are not to be answered, but are to be replied to by being rejected. The proper reply—a reply which rejects such questions—is: (De Gaulle notwithstanding) "There is no King of France." But if our topic is historical and, with some specific period in mind, we are asking, "What bald notables are there?"; "The King of France is bald" in such a changed context is an appropriate answer. And here it is a true or false statement.

"God," like "the King of France," is what Strawson calls a referring expression, though this shouldn't be taken to imply that it is *simply* a referring expression. In asserting that they are referring expressions, I am giving you to understand that presumably both expressions make identifying reference. Referring expressions may be names, pronouns,

[1] P. F. Strawson, "Identifying Reference and Truth-Values," *Theoria*, Vol. XXX (1964, Part 2), p. 115.

definite descriptions or demonstrative descriptions. In using referring expressions in identifying descriptions to make identifying references, e.g., "The Point Judith Ferry is White" or "Block Island is windy," we do not, Strawson points out, inform the audience of the *existence* of what our referring expressions refer to. Rather the very task of identifying reference can be undertaken "only by a speaker who knows or presumes his audience to be already in possession of such knowledge of existence. . . ." [2]

Similarly, when a religious man utters (1) or (2)—our paradigm religious utterances quoted above—there is the presumption that the speaker understands "God" and knows or believes in the reality of what is being talked about. The acceptance of the truth of (1) and (2) is partially definitive of what it is to be a Jew or Christian. In asserting (1) and (2), the religious man *presupposes* that there is a God and that this God has a certain character. The atheist, on the other hand, does not believe that (1) and (2) are true because he does not accept the presupposition on which they are made, namely that there is a God. He either does not accept such a presupposition because he believes it to be false or because he believes the concept of God to be an incoherent concept. If he believes that the concept of God is incoherent then he must also believe that the presupposition on which (1) and (2) are based could not possibly be true. The agnostic, in turn, does not accept the presupposition on which (1) and (2) are built because he feels that he does not have sufficient grounds for accepting it even on faith, and yet he is not convinced that we have sufficiently good grounds to be justified in dismissing it as false or utterly incoherent.

As I remarked initially, Judaism, Christianity and Islam are not by any means constituted by the making and accepting of certain statements. Rather the making of religious statements like (1) and (2) are the cornerstones on which all the other types of religious utterances in such religions depend; and they in return presuppose that the statement "There is a God" is true, and that in turn presupposes that "There is a God" is a genuine statement and that the concept of God is a viable concept. The most crucial question we can ask about Judaism, Christianity and Islam is whether these religious presuppositions are justified.

It might be felt that I have already too much ignored context. In live religious discourse, it is sometimes maintained, questions about the existence of God or the coherence of the concept of God do not arise. It is only by ignoring the context of religious talk that I can even make them seem like real questions.

There are multiple confusions involved in this objection. First, believers characteristically have doubts; even the man in "the circle of faith" is threatened with disbelief. Tormenting religious doubts arise in the religious life itself and they are often engendered by some first-order

[2] Ibid., p. 101.

uses of God-talk. "All my life I have lived under an illusion. There is no
Divine Reality at all" is first-order God-talk and not talk about talk, e.g.,
"The word 'God' only has emotive meaning." The above first-order religious utterance has a natural context and topic for a religious man
locked in a religious crisis. Most atheists and agnostics were once believers—in our traditions they were once Jews, Christians or Moslems—
and they have a participant's understanding of these forms of life. Many
of them, like Hägerström, Joyce or Sartre, have been caught up and
immersed in such forms of life. They are not like anthropologists who in
trying to gain an understanding that approximates a participant's understanding are trying to grasp how the discourses hang together. Moreover
—to zero in on the critical objection about context—people who have a
participant's grasp of the form of life in which (1) and (2) are embedded know how to use them and can, readily, for certain purposes
prescind in reflecting about them from the context in which they are at
home; for they know in what sort of linguistic environment they belong
and to what sort of topics, centers of interest, they are directed. Reflecting about them in their religious context, we say that they presuppose
the intelligibility and truth of "There is a God." Context or not, it is
this traditional and central question that we need to face in asking fundamental questions about the Judeo-Christian tradition, though if we
do not understand the environment in which the utterances which presuppose it are at home, we will not understand what is involved in such
a question.

II

In pursuing this question let us start quite simply but centrally by
asking: Why should anyone be an agnostic or an atheist? Why should
this question about God be such a biting one? Formerly skeptical philosophers could not bring themselves to accept religious beliefs because
they felt the proofs all failed, the problem of evil was intractable and
the evidence offered for believing in the existence of God was inadequate. But contemporary philosophical disbelief cuts deeper and poses
more fundamental problems, problems which challenge even the fideist
who, à la Kierkegaard, would claim that the last thing a genuine knight
of faith would want or should have is a proof of God's existence.[3] Ronald Hepburn succinctly states the sort of considerations that are involved in that "deeper ground":

Where one gives an account of an expression in our language, and where that
expression is one that refers to an existent of some kind, one needs to provide

[3] This view is well expressed by Alasdair MacIntyre in his *Difficulties in Christian
Belief.*

not only a set of rules for the use of the expression, but also an indication of how the referring is to be done—through direct pointing perhaps, or through giving instructions for an indirect method of identifying the entity. Can this be done in the case of God? Pointing, clearly, is inappropriate, God being no finite object in the world. The theologian may suggest a number of options at this point. He may say: God can be identified as that being upon whom the world can be felt as utterly dependent, who is the completion of its incompletenesses, whose presence is faintly adumbrated in experience of the awesome and the numinous. Clear direction-giving has here broken down; the theologian may well admit that his language is less descriptive or argumentative than obliquely evocative. Does this language succeed in establishing that statements about God have a reference? To persons susceptible to religious experience but at the same time logically and critically alert, it may seem just barely to succeed, or it may seem just barely to fail. Some may even oscillate uneasily between these alternatives without finding a definite procedure of decision to help them discriminate once for all.[4]

An agnostic, abreast of contemporary philosophical developments, will indeed oscillate in this fashion. "God" is a referring expression whose referent obviously cannot be indicated by ostension. The agnostic clearly recognizes this and he also recognizes the need to exhibit an adequate nonanthropomorphic extralinguistic referent for "God." In essence his doubt comes to this: is the concept of God sufficiently coherent to make belief possible for a reasonable, nonevasive man? He knows that philosophically sophisticated, reflective Jews and Christians do not deny that the concept of God is a difficult, illusive, paradoxical concept. They stress that it could not be otherwise, but believe that it is not so illusive, not so ill-conceived, as to fail to make an intelligible and yet a religiously appropriate reference. In talking about God, a believer is committed to the belief that we are talking about a mystery, but while God, by common reflective consent, is indeed in large measure incomprehensible, the concept of God is not so utterly incoherent as to vitiate religious belief. This is the minimal commitment of a religious man; he may share much with the agnostic but this much he does believe; he *must* take his stand here.

I shall argue that both the agnostic and the believer are mistaken. Careful reflection on the use of "God" in the stream of Jewish and Christian life is enough to justify an atheism which asserts that the concept of God is so incoherent that there could not possibly be a referent for the word "God." I take it here that we are speaking of Jews and Christians who have advanced beyond anthropomorphism; Jews and Christians, who as MacQuarrie puts it, have revolted decisively "against the idea that the divine can be objectified, so as to manifest itself in sensible phenomena."[5] The Jew, Christian or Moslem who remains an anthropomorphite simply has false, superstitious beliefs. But I am con-

[4] Ronald Hepburn, "Agnosticism," Vol. I, *Encyclopedia of Philosophy,* Paul Edwards, ed. (New York: Macmillan & Co. and The Free Press, 1967), pp. 58–59.

[5] John MacQuarrie, *God-Talk* (New York: Harper & Row, Publishers, Inc., 1967), p. 176.

cerned here with the Jew, Christian or Moslem who, consciously at
least, is beyond anthropomorphism. I am maintaining against him that
his belief in God is so incoherent that it could not possibly be true. If
this controversial philosophical thesis is correct, it would have quite concrete normative consequences, for if it is correct, the rational thing to do
is to reject belief in the God of the Jews, Christians and Moslems.

III

In arguing that the concept of God is incoherent, I am not claiming that "God" is utterly meaningless. Surely "God" has a use in the
language; there are deviant and nondeviant bits of God-talk. If I say
"God is a ride in a yellow submarine" or "God brews good coffee" or
even "God died," I have not said something that is false; I have not
even succeeded in saying something blasphemous; I have rather indicated, if I make such utterances with a serious intent, that I do not
understand God-talk. In saying something such as "God is a ride in a yellow submarine" I have said something closer to "Quite grounds calculated
carefully" or "Elope sea with trigonometry." In short, my utterances are
without a literal meaning. "God is a ride in a yellow submarine" could
indeed be a metaphor. In the context of a poem or song, it might be
given a meaning, but taken just like that it does not have a meaning.
But even out of context—say in the middle of a commencement address
—"Pass me a peanut butter sandwich" would be perfectly meaningful,
would have a literal meaning, though the point, if any, of uttering it
would remain obscure. However, "God brews good coffee," like "Elope
sea with trigonometry," are immediately recognized as not even being
absurdly false like "Humphrey walked on water" but as being without
any literal meaning. "God is a ride in a yellow submarine" or "God
brews good coffee" is immediately and unequivocally recognized as deviant by people with a participant's grasp of God-talk, while other bits
of God-talk are immediately recognized to be nondeviant and do in fact
have a use in the language, e.g., "Oh God be my Sword and my
strength" or "God so loved mankind that he gave to the world his only
son." Even agnostics and atheists who understand how to use Jewish
and Christian religious talk do not balk at such nondeviant utterances.
If they are reading a religious novel or sermon, they keep right on going
and do not balk at these nondeviant sentences, e.g., "God protect me in
my need," as they would at "God lost weight last week." Philosophically
perplexed as they are about nondeviant God-talk, they do not balk at it,
while they do in a quite ordinary way balk at "Procrastination drinks
grief" or "God brews good coffee." There are absurdities and absurdities.
Thus it is plainly a mistake to say that God-talk is meaningless.

However, in saying that the concept of God is incoherent, I am saying that where "God" is used nonanthropomorphically, as it is at least officially in developed Jewish and Christian God talk, there occur sentences such as (1) and (2) which purportedly have a statement-making function, yet no identifiable state of affairs can be characterized which would make such putative religious statements true and no intelligible directions have been given for identifying the supposed referent for the word "God." Religious believers speak of religious truth but "religious truth" is a Holmesless Watson.

God, as Hepburn points out, cannot be pointed to but must be identified intralinguistically through certain descriptions, if He can be identified at all. But the putative descriptions Hepburn mentions will not do. If in trying to identify God we speak of "that being upon whom the world can be felt to be utterly dependent," nothing has been accomplished, for what does it *mean* to speak of "the world (the universe) as being utterly dependent" or even dependent at all? (And if we do not understand this, we do not know what it would be like to *feel* that the world is utterly dependent.) If we are puzzled by "God," we will be equally puzzled by such phrases. We know what it means to say a child, an adult, a nation, a species, a lake is dependent on something. We could even give sense to the earth's being dependent on something, but no sense has been given to the universe's being dependent on anything. What are the sufficient conditions for the universe? What would make it true or false or what would even count for the truth or falsity of the putative statement "The universe is dependent" or "The universe is not dependent"? To answer by speaking of "God," e.g., the universe is dependent because God is its final cause, is to pull oneself up by one's own bootstraps, for talk of the dependency of the universe was appealed to in the first place in order to enable us to identify the alleged referent of "God." And to speak of a *logically* necessary being upon whom the universe depends is to appeal to a self-contradictory conception, for only propositions or statements, not beings, can either be *logically* necessary or fail to be logically necessary. Yet to speak of a "factually necessary being" upon whom the universe depends is again to pull oneself up by one's own bootstraps; for what would count toward establishing the truth or falsity of a statement asserting or denying the existence of such an alleged reality? Nothing has been specified and no directions have been given for identifying "a self-existent being" or "a self-caused being" or "a necessary being" or "a totally independent being." All these expressions purport to be referring expressions, but no rules (implicit or explicit) or regulations have been discovered for identifying their putative referents. With them we are in at least as much trouble as we are with "God," and unlike "God," they do not even have an established use in the language. It is indeed true that Jews and Christians do not think of God as something or someone who might or might not exist. If God exists, He somehow exists necessarily. But given the self-contradictoriness of the concept of a logically necessary being or existent, it cannot be true that there can be anything which must exist simply because its existence is logically possible. Moreover, no sense has been given to the claim that there is something—some given reality—which categorically must exist.

It may well be that when believers use "God" in sentences like (1) and (2) they *feel* à la Otto as if they were in the presence of a reality which is awesome and numinous—an "ultimate reality" whose presence is but faintly adumbrated in experience. Yet if this numinosity is taken to be the God of the developed Judeo-Christian tradition, it is taken to be "transcendent to the world." But, while "transcendent to the world" is at best an obscure phrase, it should still be evident that "a transcendent X" could not be "an X whose presence was given in experience." Something given in experience would *eo ipso* be nontranscendent, for it would automatically be part of the spatio-temporal world. Believers, who in defending the coherence of this belief appeal to their experience of God, are pinned by a Morton's fork: on the one hand, it is not logically possible to encounter a "reality transcendent to the world" and, on the other, if our numinosity is not thought to be transcendent, we are no longer talking of the God of developed Judeo-Christianity.[6]

IV

The central beliefs of Judaism, Christianity and Islam are indeed metaphysical beliefs since their scope purports to transcend the empirical world. If we are to come to grips with Judaism or Christianity there is no avoiding what Hägerström labelled "metaphysical religiosity." Such a metaphysical religiosity remains in even a minimal characterization of the common core of Judaism, Christianity and Islam, for they all affirm the reality of one and only one God who is said to have created the universe out of nothing, and man, regarded as a sinful, creaturely being, is taken to be utterly dependent on this creator in whose purpose man is said to discover his own reason for living. To be a Jew, Christian or Moslem is to believe much more than that but it is to believe that, and it is here that we find, so to say, the basic propositions of faith upon which the whole edifice of western religiosity stands or falls. If in these religions there is to be religious truth, the statements expressing these core religious beliefs must be true, but, it should be objected, their meaning is so indeterminate, so problematical, that it is doubtful whether we have in them anything sufficiently coherent to constitute true or false statements.

To understand what it is to speak of the reality of God essentially involves understanding the phrase "creator of the universe out of noth-

6 See John Hick, "Christianity," Vol. II, *Encyclopedia of Philosophy*.

ing." Theologians characteristically do not mean by this that the universe was created at a moment in time. To speak of such a creator is to speak not of an *efficient* cause but of a *final* cause of the universe. It involves making the putative existential claim that there is an eternal, ever present creative source and sustainer of the universe. But do we really understand such talk? We understand what it is for a lake to be a source of a river, for oxygen to be necessary to sustain life, for the winning of the game to be the end for which it is played and for good health to be the reason why we exercise. But "the universe" is not a label for some gigantic thing or process or activity. It is not a name for a determinate reality whose existence can be sustained or not sustained. Moreover, what would we have to discern or fail to discern to discover or to "see" even darkly the end, the purpose or the meaning of the universe? *A* asserts the universe has a source or a sustainer and *B* denies it, but no conceivable recognizable turn of events counts for or against either of their claims; we have no idea what would have to obtain for either *A*'s or *B*'s claim to be so or even probably so. Yet both believe they are making assertions which are true or false. Plainly, language has gone on a holiday. We have bits of discourse which purport to be fact-stating but in reality they fail to come off as factual statements; that is to say, they do not function as fact-stating utterances. They purport to be fact-stating but they are not. But with a failure to make sense here, much more talk essential to the Judeo-Christian picture becomes plainly incoherent. Consider such key bits of God-talk as:

(3) God is wholly other than the world He made.
(4) God is the creator of the moral order of the universe.
(5) The universe is absolutely dependent on God.

In reflecting on them, we should not forget that "the world" ("the universe") does not denote a thing, an entity, process or even an aggregate which might be made or brought into existence. Moreover there is the ancient point that "to make something" presupposes that there already is something out of which it is made. If it is replied that I am forgetting my previous remark that God is taken to be the *final* cause and not the efficient cause of the universe and that "make" here means "sustain" or "order," then it should be noted that this still presupposes something to be sustained or ordered; there is no use for "ordering or sustaining out of nothing." Even if we try to give it a use by saying that the universe was chaotic until ordered by God or that unless the universe is a reality ordered by God the universe would be chaotic, we are still lost, for both "the universe is chaotic" and "the universe is not chaotic" are without a coherent use. Since the universe is not an entity or even a totality, there is no sense in talking of its being ordered or not ordered and thus, while we might speak coherently of "the moral order of his life" or "the morality of a culture or ethos," there is no coherent use for "the moral order of the universe," so (4) as well as (3) is nugatory. And again, considering (5), we have seen that no sense has been given to "the universe is dependent" so (5), to put it conservatively, is also conceptually unhappy, i.e., it purports to make a factual statement but we have no idea of what, if anything, could count for or against its truth or falsity.

Some theologians with an antimetaphysical bias would try to avoid treating (3), (4) or (5) as part of the corpus of Judaism or Christianity. If my argument has been correct, this is indeed an inadequate and evasive defense against skeptical criticism, but allowing it for the sake of the discussion and returning to (1) and (2), which are surely part of that corpus, with respect to those utterances, we still have overwhelming conceptual difficulties. Consider (2) "God is the God of mercy of Whose forgiveness I stand in need." This statement entails the further statement that God does or can do something, that God acts or can act in a certain way, for it is utterly senseless to speak of being merciful if one could not even in principle act, do or fail to do merciful acts. To recognize and accept this is not to be committed to reductionism or materialism. One might even argue, as Strawson does, that the concept of a person is a primitive notion not fully analyzable in behavioristic terms, but it does not follow from this that there can be "bodiless action," that we can understand what it would be like for a person to do something without making at least a tacit reference to his body, to a living, moving being with a spatio-temporal location. But God in developed Judeo-Christianity is supposed to be conceptualized as Pure Spirit; at the very least. He cannot be taken to be a reality with a body or as something with a spatio-temporal location. God is not a being existing in space. Some theologians have even wanted to deny that God is *a* being at all. Rather He is Being, but Being or a being, it is certainly evident that God is not conceptualized as a being existing in space. As the above arguments make clear, only something with a body could act, could do something, and thus trivially could act mercifully or fail to act mercifully. But if it is *logically* impossible for X to act or fail to act mercifully then it is also logically impossible for X to be merciful or fail to be merciful. Thus (2), a key bit of God-talk, is also seen to be an incoherent utterance.

To arguments of this sort it has been replied:

Theists . . . are not people who misconceive action in applying it to God; they are simply people who employ this concept of action or agency in contexts where the nontheistic, or nonreligious do not. Which is to say no more than that they believe in God, while others do not. It is certainly not to say that their employment of the concept must be nonsensical.[7]

What is the argument for this? It is pointed out 1) that the language of action is logically distinct from that of bodily movement and that agency is logically distinct from spatio-temporal causation, 2) that there

---

. [7] W. D. Hudson, "Transcendence," *Theology*, Vol. LXIX (March, 1966), p. 104.

is no sharp distinction between the agent's body and the rest of his physical situation, and 3) that God is an agent without being a person.[8] I think all three of these claims are quite questionable to say the least. But even if we accept them, the argument can still be seen to be defective.

Consider how the argument runs: no matter how detailed our account of bodily movement, alternative descriptions of what an agent did would still always be possible. If my fist bangs against Jones' jaw in the water, this is quite compatible with any of the following three action descriptions (descriptions which in turn are arbitrarily selected from an indefinitely large number of apposite action descriptions of that bodily motion): I was trying to save his life, I was paying him back for an injury, I was trying to kill him. The conclusion which is drawn is that "an account of what is going on in terms of bodily movement, i.e. of spatio-temporal events causally connected, never tells us what the agent is doing." [9] But the acceptance of this argument does nothing at all to show that someone could possibly do anything without making bodily movements or without having a body. But this is what must be shown. A similar thing holds for both the claim that causal talk is not applicable to the language of agency and for the claim that no sharp distinction can be made between the agent and his physical environment. These claims might be accepted and it would still do nothing at all to show that it makes sense to say "action A occurred but nobody or nothing did it." To say "that was a merciful action," implies that some agent acted, but even though agency is hard to isolate from the rest of its physical situation and even if we cannot properly speak of the cause of an action, still an agent is a person and there can be no identifying a person and hence an agent except by reference to their bodies. A necessary condition for understanding the concept of action is the understanding of bodily movement.

However, in trying to resist such a conclusion it has been argued that God is not a person. We indeed, so the argument runs, cannot conceive of a person without a body, but we can, though characteristically we do not, think of agency without some idea of a bodily movement being involved. God, we are told, is to be thought of as an agent without a body; this "bodiless agent" acts without a body; he does merciful things without a body.[10]

I would counter that even when using a term such as "chemical agent"—where we refer to an active force or substance producing an effect—there is still a physically specifiable something which reacts in a determinate physically specifiable way. We have no idea of what it would be like for something to be done, for something to *do* something, for an action to occur, without there being a body in motion. In this connection we need to consider again "God is the God of mercy"

8 Ibid., pp. 103–4.
9 Ibid., p. 103.
10 Ibid.

("God is love" would work as well); this means He (it) is conceived of as doing something or being able to do something, but we can only understand the doing of something if there is something identifiable which is said to do it. Moreover, X is only identifiable as an agent, and thus X can only be intelligibly said to be an agent if X has a body. For agency to be logically possible, we must have a discrete something specifiable in spatio-temporal terms. But the transcendent God of Judaism and Christianity is thought to be a wholly independent reality, wholly other than the world which is utterly dependent on this "ultimate reality" and is said to be ultimately unintelligible without reference to this nonphysical *mysterium tremendum et fascinans.* But then it is senseless to speak, as Jews and Christians do, of God as the God of mercy of Whose forgiveness man stands in need. Yet if this is so, it would appear to be the case that Judaism, Christianity and Islam are incoherent *Weltanschauungen.*

V

A standard ploy at this point in the dialectic is to maintain that utterances like "God is all merciful," "God is the Creator of the heavens and the earth" or "God loves all His creation," are symbolic or metaphorical utterances which manifest the Ultimate or Unconditioned Transcendent but are themselves not literal statements which could be true or false. They hint at an ineffable metaphysical ultimate which is, as Tillich put it, "unconditionally beyond the conceptual sphere." [11] The only thing nonsymbolic we can say about God is:

(6) God is being-itself, the ineffable ultimate.
(7) God is the Unconditioned Transcendent on which everything else is dependent.

On the remarkable assumption that such verbosities are helpful explications, some theologians, addicted to this obscure manner of speaking, have gone on to make remarks like (8) or (9).

(8) Being-itself is not another being but the *transcendens* or *the comprehensive,* the incomparable and wholly other source and unity of all beings.
(9) God is not a being, but Being-itself that wider Being within which all particular beings have their being.

Here "Being"—as well as "Being-itself" in (6)—purportedly functions as a name or referring expression; that is to say, as a word which sup-

[11] Paul Tillich, "The Religious Symbol," in *Religious Experience and Truth,* Sidney Hook, ed., p. 303.

posedly denotes or stands for something. But to do this, that is, to function descriptively or designatively, "being" and being-itself" must have
an intelligible opposite. But in the above sentences it has no intelligible
opposite. When we use "being," "being-itself," or "being-as-such," in
sentences like (6) through (9) we are trying to catch the cognitive import of "God." We are trying to say that there is a realm of being as
such over and above the being of individual objects. (The sense of "over
and above" remains problematic. It is not a spacial sense, of course, but
in what way it is "over and above" remains utterly mysterious.)

Such being is said to be neither a genus nor a property. But then we
can scarcely avoid severe philosophical perplexity concerning its character and how, if at all, being is to be identified. To discover this, we
would have to discover what it is not; we would have to discover its intelligible opposite; yet the opposite of "being" is "nothing." But "nothing," in ordinary discourse, does not function as a name or referring
expression and if we try to regiment discourse and make "nothing"
function as a referring expression then we are led to the absurdities that
Lewis Carroll satirized in *Through the Looking Glass* when the Red
King thought that if Nobody passed the messenger on the road then
Nobody would have arrived first. To try to treat "nothing" as a name or
referring expression is to get involved in the absurdity of asking what
kind of a something, what kind of *a* being or what kind of being is nothing. It involves the incoherent reifying of nothing into a kind of opposed power to being and, at the same time, spoiling its supposed
contrast with "being" by treating "nothing" as the name of a mysterious
something, which makes it either identical with Being-itself or a being
which has its being in Being. In either case we have an absurdity. But
unless "Nothing" is treated as a referring expression, "Being," where we
try to construe it as a referring expression, has no intelligible opposite
and without an intelligible opposite "being" lacks descriptive or desig-
native significance and thus it is not, after all, as the Being-talk-man requires, a referring expression. Superficially it appears to have that role
but actually has no such use in the language. For (6), (8) or (9) to
come off as intelligible factual assertions, "being" and being-itself"
must be genuine referring expressions with intelligible opposites. Unfortunately, for the theologian committed to such an approach, these expressions do not so function, and thus our sample sentences are not
sentences with which we can make factual statements.

Basically the same difficulties apply to the terms in the above sentences which presumably are taken to be elucidations of "being-itself" or
"being-as-such" by people who like to talk in this obscure and, I suspect,
obscurantist manner. Consider such phrases as "ineffable ultimate,"
"Unconditioned Transcendent," *"transcendens,"* or "the Comprehensive." They are not ordinary language expressions with fixed uses; that is,
in order to understand them we must be given some coherent directions
concerning their use. But we are hardly given any directions here. Pre-

sumably they are putative referring expressions, but how even in principle could we identify their referents? *A* says "There is really the
Comprehensive" and *B* replies "It's a myth, there is no such reality." *C*
wonders whether there really is an Unconditioned Transcendent, the *transcendens* or an ineffable ultimate and *D* reassures him that actually
there are no such realities. Actually those who are hip on Being-talk
never take such a matter-of-fact tone, but even if they did, it is evident
that there is not only no way at all of deciding who is right where such
matter-of-fact-*sounding* questions are raised, but there is also no way of
deciding which putative factual claim is the more probable. Nothing
that we could experience now or hereafter, even assuming the intelligibility of "hereafter," helps us out vis-à-vis such "questions." But what
then are we talking about if we try to question, affirm or deny that
there really is an Unconditioned Transcendent? If, as it certainly
seems to be, it is impossible to give an answer, then "being-talk" is only
a less familiar and less evocative species of incoherence than God-
talk.

At this point we are likely to hear talk about ineffability. To be so
analytic, it will be contended, is appropriate to an examination of scientific discourse, but it is not appropriate to religious discourse. Such an
analytic approach, it will be proclaimed in certain circles, ignores the
existential dimension of man. Suffering from cultural lag, such an analytic approach, still too much in the temper of positivism, fails to take to
heart man's existential encounter with Being, when the dread of nonbeing gives him a sense, scarcely characterizable in words, of his "total
existence." Being-talk may indeed be so paradoxical as to be scarcely intelligible, but such concrete human experiences do lead to a confrontation with Being. And being-itself is indeed the Ineffable: that which is
beyond all conceptualization. In our despair and estrangement we are
led to an ineffable but supremely Holy something which can be experienced in a compelling manner but it can never be more than obliquely
and metaphorically hinted at in words, symbols and images. To gain
insight here, we need to transcend our pedestrian literalness and acknowledge that there are some things which are literally unsayable or inexpressible but are nonetheless given in those experiences of depth where man
must confront his own existence.

What is involved here is the claim that there are "ineffable truths"
which cannot be put into words; religious truths—so the argument
runs—are species of that genus. Men with the proper experience and attitudes understand them; that is, they in a sense understand the concept
of God, but what they know to be true cannot in any way be literally
expressed. Our samples of being-talk haltingly and falteringly suggest
these truths; they can awake in us the experience of such "ineffable
truths" but they do not make true or false statements themselves. Instead they function evocatively to give rise to such experiences or ex-
pressively to suggest what cannot be literally stated. Given the proper

experience, the reality they obliquely attest to will, while remaining irreducibly mysterious, be humanely speaking undeniable.

Such doctrines of the Ineffable are incoherent and will not enable us to meet or resolve religious quandries legitimately. To hold such a doctrine is to be committed to the thesis that, though there may be something appropriately called "God," "Being-itself" or "the Unconditioned Transcendent," in reality nothing literal, or at least nothing affirmative, can be said about God. That is to say, no sentences about God or sentences in which "God" occurs literally express a fact or make a true or false assertion. Thus, on such a reading of God-talk, "The world is dependent on God" or any other God-sentence cannot literally make a true or false statement, assert something that is so or is not so, though such sentences are not without sense for they have a metaphorical or symbolic use. But if an utterance P is metaphorical, this entails that it is *logically* possible for there to be some literal statement G which has the same conceptual content. "Metaphorical," or for that matter "symbolic" or "analogical," gets its meaning by being contrastable with "literal." There can be intelligible metaphorical or symbolic or analogical God-talk if there can be no literal God-talk. Thus the ineffability thesis is internally incoherent.

However, it might be replied that the above argument does not touch the most fundamental core of the ineffability thesis, namely that the man of faith can know what he means by "God" though he cannot, literally or even obliquely, say what he means and what he means cannot in any way be expressed, even if it is given in an ecstatic encounter or confrontation with Being or an Unconditioned Transcendent. The latter part of this is nonsense, for, as I have already pointed out, a reality transcendent to the universe could not be encountered or confronted; only some being in the world could, logically could, be encountered or confronted.

We are, however, still on slightly peripheral ground, for the major claim in the ineffability thesis is that one can know what P means even though P cannot even in principle be expressed or publicly exhibited. One can know that there is a God though the concept of God is inexpressible and our talk of God is nonsensical.

What makes this maneuver seem more plausible than it actually is, is its easy confusion with the rather ordinary experience of knowing very well what something is (say a bird one sees) and yet being at that time quite unable to *say* what it is. One looks at the bird and recognizes it but one cannot remember its name. In this context we should also call to mind that we have a whole range of "aha!-experiences." But the ineffability thesis under examination maintains something far more radical than would be encompassed by a theory which took into account, as it indeed should take into account, the above straightforwardly empirical phenomena. The ineffability thesis commits one to the belief that there are things one can know which are *in principle* impossible, that is, logically impossible, to express or to exhibit in any system of notation. In this way "a true religious statement" or "an expressed religious truth" would be self-contradictory.

It is tempting to take the short way with such a thesis and to reject it on the following grounds: 1) If one knows P then P is true, since "I know it but it isn't true" is a contradiction. Thus, since only statements are literally true, there could be no inexpressible knowledge. 2) Reflection on "means" also establishes that there could be no such "ineffable understanding." For something to have a meaning or to have meaning, it must have a use in a language or in some system of notation. This partially specifies what it means for something to have a meaning or have meaning even when we speak of the meaning of a concept, for we use "concept" to signify what is expressed by synonymous expressions in the same or different languages or systems of notation. But only if something has meaning or has a meaning can we understand what it means, so we cannot understand something which is inexpressible *in principle;* there would be nothing to be understood, for there would be nothing that is meaningful.

However, some might think, mistakenly I believe, that some of these premises make unjustified and question-begging assumptions. Rather than extending my argument for them here or entering into complicated questions about so-called "private languages" and the like, I shall see if there are still simpler considerations that can probably be utilized to refute or render implausible the ineffability thesis. (Keep in mind that the job of challenging premises can always go on and on; the most we can hope for in philosophy is to give from the alternatives available the most plausible perspicacious representation of the conceptual area in question.) [12] First, take note of the platitude that if you know something that is literally in principle unsayable, inexpressible, incapable of being shown or in any way exhibited, then there trivially can be no communicating it. You cannot justifiably say it is *God* you experience, know, encounter, love or commit yourself to in utter trust; you, on your own thesis, cannot significantly say that if you do such and such and have such and such experiences, you will come to know God or come to be grasped by God. "What is unsayable is unsayable," is a significant tautology. Only if one could at least obliquely or metaphorically express one's experience of the Divine could one's God-talk have any significance, but on the present *radical* ineffability thesis even the possibility of obliquely expressing one's knowledge or belief is ruled out. So, given such a thesis, there could be no confessional community or circle of

[12] This conception of philosophy as resting on considerations of plausibility is well expressed by J. J. C. Smart in his *Philosophy and Scientific Realism* (New York: Humanities Press, 1963), pp. 12–13, and in more detail in his "Philosophy and Scientific Plausibility," in Feyerabend, Paul K. and Maxwell, G. E. (eds.) *Mind, Matter, and Method, Essays in Honor of Herbert Feigl* (Minneapolis, Minn.: U. of Minn. Press, 1966).

faith; in fine, the thesis is reduced to the absurd by making it impossible for those who accept such a thesis to acknowledge the manifest truth that the Judeo-Christian religion is a social reality. On this simple consideration alone, we should surely rule out the ineffability thesis. Thus Dom Illyd Trethowan is wide of the mark when he remarks: "Flew and Nielsen . . . are asking for a description of God. And the believer, again if he knows his business will reply . . . that God cannot be described. God is the Other." [13] If we try to take this claim of Trethowan's literally, then the word "God" is surely not just the vehicle for an incoherent concept, but "God" is *meaningless* for we cannot even say *that* something is if it is indescribable. What is indescribable is also unintelligible.

Three reminders here: 1) In asserting that nonanthropomorphic concepts of God are incoherent and according to some theological construals of "God" even meaningless, I am not merely giving you to understand that skeptics (atheists and agnostics) do not understand God-talk. Rather, I have been contending that, the believer's beliefs *about* his beliefs notwithstanding, the concept of God in developed Judaism and Christianity is an incoherent one and neither believer nor nonbeliever understands what they are talking about when they talk about God or attempt to talk to God. I am not simply urging that the believer make his beliefs meaningful to the skeptic, I am asking that he show how God-talk is a coherent form of language, period.[14] 2) I do not accept either the Wittgensteinian assumption that every form of discourse is all right as it is and that the only thing that could be out of order is the philosophical talk about the talk or the further and related Wittgensteinian claim that philosophy can only relatively display the forms of life and not relevantly criticize them or assess them. Not only God-talk but also Witch-talk and talk of fairies have their own distinctive uses and even within our culture once constituted a discourse and were embedded in a form of life. But all the same such forms of life were open to criticism and came gradually to be discredited as they were recognized to be incoherent. Indeed in *many cases* first-order discourse and the beliefs embedded in them are beyond philosophical reproach and it is merely the characterization, the second-order discourse, that is troublesome. Thus if someone tells you that you never see tables or chairs and that you do not have a mind, that is a bad joke, but if someone tells you that you do not have a soul, you just think you do, it may very well engender a live dispute or a live worry if you are a tradi-

[13] Illyd Trethowan, "In Defense of Theism—A Reply to Professor Kai Nielsen," Vol. 2, *Religious Studies*, No. 1 (1966), p. 39.

[14] So Trethowan is again wide of the mark when he remarks: "Nielsen will be entitled to say that he can make nothing of it, but (I submit) he will not be entitled to say that there is anything logically the matter with it. He seems to think that a believer is not logically entitled to regard his beliefs as meaningful unless he can make them meaningful to an unbeliever." Ibid., pp. 38–39. Generally, it seems to me, Trethowan's defense of theism and criticisms of my arguments are ineffective.

tional Christian. Where God-talk is involved, both the first-order and the second-order discourse are problematical.[15] 3) The acceptance of even a thorough-going fideistic point of view will not protect the believer from my critique. If we understood what it *meant* to assert or deny "And God shall raise the quick and the dead" or "God is the Creator of the Heavens and the earth," we might accept them humbly on faith. We might, out of our desperate need to make sense of our lives, accept them *de fide*. But we can only do that if we have some understanding of what they *mean*. If I ask you to believe in Irglig, you cannot believe in Irglig no matter how deep your need because you do not know *what* to take on faith (on trust). Faith presupposes a *minimal understanding* of what you take on faith, and if my arguments are correct, we do not have that understanding of a nonanthropomorphic concept of God.[16]

VI

It might be contended that I have so far ignored the major and most obvious objection to my procedure. I am, it is natural to say, being a philosophical Neanderthal, for my arguments rest too exclusively on verificationist principles and by now it is well known that the verifiability principle is plainly untenable.[17]

I, of course, agree that it is certainly plainly evident that it is not true that a sentence is meaningful only if it is verifiable. In fact, I would go further and claim that such a claim is itself incoherent. It is sentences, not statements, which are meaningful or meaningless and it is statements, not sentences, which are confirmable or infirmable, true or false. Questions of meaning are logically prior to questions of verification; in order to verify or confirm a statement we must already know what it means. Moreover, many sentences which are plainly meaningful, e.g., "Pass the butter," "Oh, if this agony would only end," "Will the weather change?" do not even purport to make statements, let alone

[15] I have stated this rather bruskly and perhaps in a dogmatic sounding way. I have argued for it in some detail in my "Wittgensteinian Fideism," *Philosophy*, Vol. XLII (July, 1967), in "Language and the Concept of God," *Question 2* (January, 1969), pp. 36–40, in "God and the Forms of Life," *Indian Review of Philosophy*, forthcoming, and in my book *The Quest for God*, forthcoming.

[16] I have argued the ins and outs of this in my "Can Faith Validate God-Talk?" *New Theology No. 1*, Martin Marty and Dean Peerman, eds. (New York, Macmillan & Co. and The Free Press, 1964) and in my "Religious Perplexity and Faith," *The Crane Review*, Vol. VIII (Fall, 1965).

[17] The application of these considerations to religious discourse have been succinctly stated by Alvin Plantinga, "Analytic Philosophy and Christianity," *Christianity Today* (October 25, 1963), pp. 75–78, and by George L. Mavrodes, "God and Verification," *Canadian Journal of Theology*, Vol. 10 (1964) pp. 187–191. But see my response "God and Verification Again," *Canadian Journal of Theology*, Vol. XI (1965), pp. 135–141.

statements of fact which are confirmable or infirmable. It is by now
crystal clear that the verifiability principle will never do as a general
criterion of meaningful discourse.[18]

There are two points, however, that should be made here: 1) it is
less evident that some form of the verifiability criterion is not correct as
a criterion of *factual* significance and 2) that many of my key arguments
do not even depend on or presuppose such a criterion of factual significance. The second point alone is enough to free me from the charge
that I am entangled in a thoroughly discredited "logical empiricist
metaphysics" but I would like, in what I fear is too brief and too brusk a
manner, to defend my first point, for it may seem obscurantist.

Do we have, for the many and varied types of meaningful utterance, a criterion in virtue of which we can decide which of them are fact-
stating? I maintain that we do, for a statement has factual content only
if it is in principle testable or, to put it differently, for a sentence to
function in a discourse as a factual assertion, it must make a statement
which it is logically possible to confirm or infirm. If anything can give us
"some insight into the ultimate nature of things"—to utter a tantalizing
obscurity—it will be factually informative statements, i.e., statements
which give us knowledge of what is the case. To have insight into "the
ultimate nature of things" would be at least to have some reliable
beliefs about what *in fact* the universe is like. That is, we would gain
some information about some very fundamental facts. I do not say this
is all we would need but we would at least have to have that. But *factually* informative utterances must, in principle, be verifiable. To put the
point more exactly, a statement has factual significance only if it is at
least logically possible to indicate the conditions or set of conditions
under which it could be to some degree confirmed or infirmed, i.e., that
it is logically possible to state evidence for or against its truth.[19]

Certainly my claim here is a controversial one—a claim that many
analytic philosophers would reject on the grounds that it blurs too many
distinctions and relies on too many vague claims. I have already voided
some of the usual criticisms through the very specification of its actual
scope. Beyond that, all I can do in the space available here is to use
Hume's method of challenge and to ask you if you can think of a single

[18] These and other closely related points have been decisively argued by G. J.
Warnock, "Verification and the Use of Language," *Revue Internationale de Philosophie,* Vol. 17 (1951); J. L. Evans, "On Meaning and Verification," *Mind,* Vol.
LXII (1953) and *The Foundations of Empiricism* (Cardiff, 1965); Paul Marhenke,
"The Criterion of Significance," *Proceedings and Addresses of the American Philosophical Association,* 1950; and R. W. Ashby, "Verifiability Principle," Vol. 8, *The
Encyclopedia of Philosophy.*
[19] Some contemporary philosophers have tried to take up this challenge and show
how certain key religious utterances are verifiable. I examine their arguments and
attempt to show *that* they fail and *how* they fail in my "Christian Positivism and
the Appeal to Religious Experience," *The Journal of Religion,* Vol. XLII (October,
1962); "Eschatological Verification," *Canadian Journal of Theology,* Vol. IX (1962)
and "On Fixing the Reference Range of 'God'," *Religious Studies* (October, 1966).

unequivocally factual statement—a statement that all parties would agree had factual content—that is not in the sense specified above verifiable (confirmable or infirmable) in principle. If you cannot—and I do not think you can—is it not reasonable to believe that my demarcation line for a statement of fact is justified? [20]

Indeed this gauntlet has been taken up, but the most usual and sophisticated of the alleged counter examples to my claim are of the following two sorts, neither of which seem to me genuine counter examples: 1) "Every human being has some neurotic traits," and 2) "My head aches." As Hempel and Rynin have pointed out, statements of unrestricted generality with mixed quantification are not decisively confirmable or infirmable and we cannot even state a precise probability weight for their confirmation or disconfirmation.[21] But this does not mean that in a weaker and less precise sense we could not give perfectly empirical evidence for or against their truth. Since language is not like a calculus, we should not continue to believe that it will function like one. If we continue to discover neurotic traits in all the people who are so examined and if some independently testable personality theory gives us reason to believe, say, that the very growing up in a family always leads to some neurotic stress, the generalization has some confirmation. On the other hand, if we find a human being who does not, so far as we can determine, behave neurotically at all, the generalization is slightly weakened. The same thing is true for other statements involving mixed quantification which might be plainly thought to have factual content, e.g., "Every substance has some solvent" or "Every planet has some form of life."

"My head aches," or "I have a headache," poses different problems. From the period of *The Blue Book* on, Wittgenstein thought that such utterances do not have a verification. Malcolm points out that in his *Philosophische Bemerkungen* Wittgenstein thought that they could be verified, but after 1932 his recognition that they were avowals rather than statements of fact led to his "turning away from the full-blown verification theory of meaning." [22] However, it is just this conception of avowals that is important for my case. I do not verify, "My head aches," or "I have a headache." After all, in normal circumstances I could not doubt it. I could not inquire into whether my head aches, or check up on whether my head aches or wonder whether my head aches. "My head seems to ache," or "Perhaps my head aches," has no straightforward use. In normal circumstances, I, by my very utterance, simply avow that my head aches. I am not, Wittgenstein argued, trying to state a fact but to give expression to how I feel.

[20] I argue for this in detail in my *Quest for God,* forthcoming.
[21] Carl Hempel, *Aspects of Scientific Explanation,* Chapter IV (New York, The Free Press, 1965) and David Rynin, "Vindication of L°G°C°L°P°S°T°V°SM," *Proceedings and Addresses of the American Philosophical Association,* 1957.
[22] Norman Malcolm, "Wittgenstein's *Philosophische Bemerkungen,*" *The Philosophical Review,* Vol. LXXVI (April, 1967), p. 225.

If you reply—and I for one have considerable sympathy with that reply—that this is too extreme, for "head aches," in "My head aches," when uttered by Nielsen, has factual content, note that it has the same factual content as "Nielsen's head aches" and that this statement is perfectly open to confirmation by what I say and do. What makes "Nielsen's head aches" true or false is exactly what makes "My head aches" true or false, where the utterer of this last utterance is Nielsen. So we still have no genuine example of a factual statement which is not verifiable. Either we drop the claim that "My head aches" is true or false in which case no issue arises about its being a factual statement or about how we could come to know that it is so, or we allow it is true or false, in which case we come to know that it is true or false, that it is verified, in the same way that we come to know or verify that "Nielsen's head aches" is true or false. When I utter "My head aches" and Jones utters "Nielsen's head aches," both these claims are, to use a slightly outmoded and pleonastic terminology, intersubjectively verified in the same way, to the extent they are verified or are known to be true or false at all.

There are those who think that behind my talk of "factual significance" and the verifiability principle there lurks a series of false dichotomies such as "factual meaning"/"emotive meaning," "cognitive meaning"/"metaphorical meaning," "literal meaning"/"nonliteral meaning," and the like. I do not think any such "multiplication of meanings beyond need," is involved in what I have argued, but for those who remain unconvinced and suffer from the anxieties described above, I want to stress that what is most essential to my argument about fact-stating discourse can be put in this way: If a sentence is used to make what is thought to be a factual statement and yet the statement made by its use is neither confirmable nor infirmable even in principle, then the statement in question actually fails to come off as a factual statement, i.e., it fails to assert a fact and thus is not a genuine bit of fact-stating discourse. An utterance that comes off as a statement of fact must be verifiable in principle.

To sum up. Judaism and Christianity are thought by Jews and Christians to involve an entry into a relationship with a being transcendent to the world or at least with a creative and gracious "world ground" which is distinct from the world and upon which the world is dependent. Thus we face what for the Jew or Christian is an awkward fact, namely that while being a Jew or Christian consists in much more than believing that certain allegedly factual statements are true, it does, in an utterly irreducible manner, involve the acceptance of what are taken by the faithful to be certain factual beliefs. And these purportedly factual beliefs are often of vast scope; they are not only ordinary empirical beliefs such as Jesus was born in Bethlehem. The expression of such "cosmic factual beliefs" results in the making of religious or, if you will, theological statements, e.g., "There is an infinite, eternal Creator of the world" or "There is an ultimate loving reality in which all men find their being," and these statements are taken by the faithful to be factual statements. Yet they are neither directly nor indirectly confirmable or infirmable even in principle and thus are in reality, as many nonbelievers have suspected, devoid of factual content.[23] They purport to be factual but fail to behave as factual statements. We have no idea of how to establish their truth or probable truth, or their falsity or probable falsity. We have no conception of what it would be like for them to be true (or probably true) or false (or probably false). Yet they are supposedly expressive of factual beliefs. But a statement which is in no way confirmable or infirmable even in principle is not a factual statement. To make sense of such utterances on their own terms, and not just the sense a Santayana or Feuerbach would make of them, believers must believe that these key bits of God-talk are fact-stating, but these utterances fail to come off as bits of fact-stating discourse. So here we have at the very foundation of such faiths a radical incoherence which vitiates such religious claims.[24]

It might be countered that "Every human being is dependent on an infinite 'world ground' transcendent to the universe," is factually intelligible because it is after all weakly confirmable or infirmable in a manner similar to the way "Every human being has some neurotic traits," is confirmable or infirmable. There is weak verification in each case. Feeling dependent and morally insufficient counts weakly for the truth of the putative theological assertion; making sense of one's life and of morality independent of any reference to religion and overcoming feelings of utter dependency counts against its truth. But this is deceiving for atheists can, and *some* do, agree that human beings pervasively have these feelings of dependency and moral insufficiency and still these atheists can make nothing of nonanthropomorphic talk of God or an infinite "world ground" transcendent to the universe. The believer cannot legitimately respond that he is simply talking about such feelings and *nothing more* for then his belief would be indistinguishable from atheism. But it is his alleged "something more" that does not make a verifiable difference even in the weak sense. "God is wholly Other," is, taken by itself, nonsense for it is an incomplete sentence: in order to understand it, we need to know "a wholly other *what*." The alleged

[23] This cannot be taken as evidence that we have statements which are plainly factual but still not verifiable, for the examples themselves do not have an undisputed factual status. Many nonbelievers and even some who call themselves believers (Hare, Braithwaite, and Miles) do not regard them as factual statements. Moreover, they do not all make this assumption because they assume the verifiability criterion of factual significance but some do so because they think an examination of the use, the depth grammar, of key religious utterances will show that they have a very different function than do statements of fact.

[24] I am not asking that religion become what it plainly is not, i.e., science. There are plenty of fact-stating discourses which are not scientific. Man did not have to wait for the rise of science before he could start stating facts. I am also not ignoring context, for these presuppositions operate in religious contexts. See Crombie's remarks on this in the opening pages of his "The Possibility of Theological Statements," in *Faith and Logic*, Basil Mitchell, ed. (London, Allen & Unwin, 1957), pp. 31–33.

answer frequently comes by talk of "Being-in-itself," "Unconditioned Transcendent," "Being transcendent to the world" and the like, but, as we have seen, though they are purportedly referring expressions, no intelligible directions have been given as to how to identify the supposed referents of such referring expressions. The affirmation and denial that there are such "realities" is equally compatible with anything and everything that could conceivably be experienced. Such nonanthropomorphic God-talk does not make verifiable sense.

VII

Such is my argument about God-talk. There are three morals I wish to draw from this, one religious and ideological and the other two about philosophical methodology.

To put the religious or ideological point bluntly: If my central arguments are essentially correct, one should not be a Jew, Christian, Moslem or any kind of theist. To be any of these things involves having beliefs "whose scope transcends the empirical world." More specifically, in involves believing in the reality of God as a creator of the universe. But, if my arguments are near to their mark, such a belief is utterly incoherent. That is to say, with nonanthropomorphic conceptions of God there is nothing intelligible to be believed, so atheism (a reasoned rejection of belief in God) becomes the most reasonable form of life. If beliefs are persisted in where there are no *reasons* for holding them, we should look for the *causes:* look for what makes people believe as they do; belief in God is absurd, but, as Feuerbach, Santayana and Freud have shown, the psychological need for this construct of the human heart is so great that in cultures like ours many people must believe in spite of the manifest absurdity of their belief. They can see and accept this absurdity in the religious beliefs of other tribes and sometimes, as with Hamman and Kierkegaard, they can partially see it and accept it in their own tribe, but the acceptance is not unequivocal and the full absurdity of their own belief remains hidden from them.

It is sometimes objected that no such normative conclusions could follow from purely non-normative premises, and that atheism, as it plainly is for Sartre, ultimately, as John Courtney Murray puts it in his *The Problem of God,* is "a total option made by free decision rather than an intellectual position reached by argument." [25]

There are multiple confusions here. I am philosophically conservative enough to believe, Searle and Black to the contrary notwithstanding, that categorical normative conclusions are not entailed by any set of purely non-normative premises. But even if I am right about this and

[25] John Courtney Murray, *The Problem of God,* p. 84.

there is such an is/ought divide, it does not at all follow that normative claims are not supported or justified or at least weakened or strengthened by non-normative claims. After all, entailments are not the only conceptual connections.[26] And this is all I am maintaining. In other words, I am only maintaining that, if my arguments about the concept of God are accepted, it would be unreasonable for those who accept them to remain Jews, Christians or Moslems. Moreover, in such a circumstance it would be more reasonable to be an atheist than an agnostic. There are in such considerations crucial normative implications about how to live and die. The clickety-clack of linguistic analysis has human implications.

I want to turn for a moment to Murray's dichotomy for it is a false dichotomy. Atheism, like Christianity or any other way of life, does, of course, involve a normative stance, an option about how to live. But it is by no means a matter of the godless man of the academy or the marketplace simply willing or opting "to understand the world without God." Any way of acting which reflects deliberation involves the decision to act in a certain way; and to act deliberately in a certain way is part of what it is to live in accordance with norms. That is to say, my remarks here are conceptual remarks or what Wittgenstein, with a considerable stretch of "grammatical," called "grammatical remarks." Between men of God and atheists there is indeed the clash of affirmations. But it is not *simply* a clash of affirmations or even in *the last analysis* simply a clash of affirmations. Atheism involves a decision about how to live, but it also involves an intellectual understanding of what our world is like; and the decision to reject religious belief would not be made without a certain intellectual understanding of the situation.

My concluding remarks about philosophical methodology are not unrelated to what I have just maintained. For anyone at all knowledgeable about philosophical analysis, for anyone touched by the work of Moore, Wittgenstein, and Austin, it is natural, when faced with my arguments, to assert that something must have gone wrong somewhere. Philosophical analysis is normatively and, if you will, ideologically or metaphysically neutral. It is tempting to maintain that when anyone claims to have drawn such vast ideological conclusions as I claim to have drawn from philosophical analysis, you can be quite confident that he is unwittingly sneaking some nonanalytical element into his philosophical analysis—that somewhere, somehow some special pleading has occurred —for philosophical analyses are ideologically neutral.

There is an ambiguity in the phrase "philosophical analysis is neutral" which once exposed will undermine this argument. Philosophical analysis is neutral in the sense that, *independently* of one's normative, ideological, or metaphysical view of the world, it either does or does not follow that

---

[26] Stephen Toulmin argues this point very effectively in his *The Uses of Argument* (Cambridge, Cambridge University Press, 1964).

to say X ought to do Y presupposes X can do Y, or to say that X knows God is to give one to understand that X loves God, or to say that X believes *in* God presupposes that X believes *that* God exists. These relationships are logical or conceptual, and they either hold or fail to hold, and what in this way holds or fails to hold here is not a factor of one's ideological commitments. In this important sense philosophical analysis is ideologically neutral. If this were not so, philosophical dispute would degenerate into a clash of rival unarguable affirmations. In a very important sense it would cease being *philosophical* and philosophy would itself be impossible.

However, there is another sense in which philosophical analysis is not normatively or ideologically neutral. In carrying out a philosophical analysis, we attempt, through a description of the uses and the unscheduled inferences of philosophically perplexing terms and utterances, to gain a perspicuous representation of the discourse in question. If, after a careful analysis of "can," one concluded that "I can," in moral contexts typically and irreducibly functioned categorically and that these uses of discourse were essential to the understanding of human action, it would be unreasonable to be a soft determinist; if, after a careful analysis of "good," "right," and "ought" in moral contexts, it became apparent that "good" was never equivalent to any term or set of terms standing for purely empirical characteristics or relations, it would be unreasonable to be an ethical naturalist; similarly it would not be reasonable to remain a Jew or a Christian if careful elucidation of "God" and God-talk indicated that, while believers took "God" to be a referring expression, "God" actually functions neither as a name nor as a definite or indefinite description and that there are no directions in the discourse concerning how to identify God so that we could have some idea of what we are talking about when we speak of God.

It is evident in such a situation vis-à-vis soft determinism, ethical naturalism and theism, that certain results of philosophical analysis indicate that a given ideological position is not tenable.[27] In this respect philosophical analysis is not ideologically neutral. But if it were not philosophically neutral in the way I first characterized, analysis itself would be impossible and there could be no philosophically relevant grounds for accepting or rejecting any of these ideological positions.

This leads me to my last point which is a general one about the nature of philosophy. It is tempting to remark that in proceeding as I

---

[27] It might be objected that this does not hold for ethical naturalism, for ethical naturalism is itself a meta-ethical theory and not a normative ethical theory. That it is a meta-ethical theory is indeed so, and I would further agree that this distinction in ethical theory is an important one. But meta-ethical theories themselves have normative implications. It would be unreasonable for a man not to take the dictates of his own society as normative for his behavior within that society, *if* he believed that "One ought to do Y" *meant* "Y is a dictate of one's society." For a discussion of the normative implications of meta-ethics see my "Problem of Ethics," Vol. 3, *The Encyclopedia of Philosophy*, pp. 119–124.

have in this essay, I have been trying to do something that cannot be done: I have in effect tried to give philosophy a task which cannot be its own; I have implicitly prescribed what activities, what forms of life, are legitimate or rational and what usages, reflecting these forms of life, are coherent, when in actuality philosophy can only legitimately clearly display the actual structure of the discourse embedded in these activities. Again we are back to a very Wittgensteinian point. The claim is that the philosopher's sole legitimate function is to describe our discourse so as to dispel conceptual perplexities engendered by a failure properly to understand the workings of our language.

Certainly such a Wittgensteinian stress is an understandable and justified reaction to the kind of *prescriptivism* which would persuasively redefine "knowledge," "proof," "explanation," "evidence," and the like in such a way that most of the things commonly called such are not *real* knowledge, proof, explanation, evidence and the like. Moore, Wittgenstein and ordinary language philosophers have amply demonstrated the barrenness of such philosophical rationalism. But such a descriptivism can throw out the baby with the bath and utterly lose one of the deepest rationales for doing philosophy, namely that of criticizing received opinions and more generally and uniquely of providing a critical discussion of critical discussions and forms of life.

These are grand old phrases, it might be replied, but they remain empty: what exactly is this critical discussion of critical discussions and what Archimedian point can the philosopher possibly attain which would enable him legitimately to criticize whole forms of life; the very concept of rationality is itself a deeply contested and context-dependent concept.

In considering this, let us start with one of the less contested points first. "Rational" and "rationality" are indeed used eulogistically, but we should beware of concluding that they are just emotive labels or that they are so essentially contested as to be thoroughly subjective. Translation into the concrete should make this evident, though it will not, of course, provide us with an elucidation of the concept of rationality. A man who never listens to others and always shouts others down is not rational; it is also irrational to persist in a practice which gives rise to vast human suffering when this could be avoided by adopting another practice that would achieve much the same thing as the first practice but would cause much less suffering; finally, to point to a specific kind of behavior, to believe in witches or fairies is also irrational if one is a tolerably well-informed Westerner living in the twentieth century. "Rational," whatever its precise analysis, is not so vague that it does not have an established use and evident paradigm cases. Moreover, activities or forms of life are not neatly isolated activities with their own distinctive criteria. There is, for example, no such thing as "religious language," though there are religious discourses carried on in English, Swedish, German, French, etc. And even in these discourses the criteria of relevance, the use of "evidence," "rationality," and the like are not utterly unique to the discourse in question. It is just not so that God-talk is a self-contained form of language or form of life, though it does have its distinctive topics and centers of interest.

The very criticisms I have made of religious beliefs, if they are on the whole correct, constitute a *reductio* of the Wittgensteinian thesis that philosophy can only be descriptive. To this it might be replied that since philosophy can only be descriptive there must be something basically wrong with my arguments about religious belief. Forms of life are immune from anything but piecemeal criticism; there can be no incoherent forms of language or irrational forms of life. But remembering the very different things that philosophy has been throughout its long history, and keeping in mind the immense variety of types of investigation that have gone on under the name of "philosophy," and the precariousness and contested nature of generalizations about the nature of philosophy, is it not—I put it to your reflective consideration—more reasonable to doubt the descriptivist thesis as a completely adequate account of the proper office of philosophy, than to reject my arguments *simply on the grounds that they fail to square with a thesis in the philosophy of philosophy?*

Wittgenstein generalized primarily from reflecting on epistemology, the philosophy of mind, and mathematics. There his descriptivist thesis seems to me thoroughly plausible; but he may, to turn his own phrase against him, have suffered from a one-sided diet. Religion is a form of life that may indeed be given, but it is still not beyond the pale of relevant philosophical criticism.

This essay might have been entitled "A refutation of Theism" or "A Refutation of Judeo-Christianity." Until and unless specific arguments can be provided to show that my criticisms fail, it is more reasonable to accept them and reject such a form of life than to maintain, on the basis of a general and disputed thesis in the philosophy of philosophy, that such arguments must be mistaken. Even if some—or worse still all—of my criticisms fail, unless criticisms of such *a general type* can be shown to be irrelevant, there is no reason to assume that the descriptivist thesis must be so and that "A Philosophical Refutation of Theism" is a conceptual anomaly.

I admit that the concept of such a type of critical assessment (a "criticism of criticisms" or "a critical discussion of forms of life and of critical discussion") is itself a disputed concept expressive of a controversial thesis in the philosophy of philosophy and that it is in need of a careful elucidation and defense.[28] But *ambulando* what I have done here vis-à-vis religion and what Ronald Hepburn did in *Christianity and*

[28] What I have said in the last few pages has been influenced by the views of John Passmore; see his essay "Philosophy" in Vol. 6, *The Encyclopedia of Philosophy*, pp. 216–226. I have tried to say something about philosophy as a criticism of criticisms in my "John Dewey's Conception of Philosophy," *The University of Massachusetts Review*, Vol. II, No. 1 (Autumn, 1960).

Paradox and Antony Flew did in *God and Philosophy* are examples of what I have in mind. We have learned from Moore and Ryle that we can typically do with words what we may not in fact be able on demand to characterize adequately.

It is also well known that "What is philosophy?" is itself a deeply contested philosophical problem and many men—past and present—who considered themselves philosophers and who are generally considered philosophers have thought they could provide disciplined, rational criticism of ways-of-life. Moreover, they thought they were doing this in the course of philosophizing and not as an activity that was ancillary to their philosophizing.[29] I have tried to do just that for a family of ways-of-life, namely Judaism, Christianity and Islam, by exhibiting the incoherence of absolutely central beliefs they hold in common. Most of my arguments are fairly specific exercises in philosophical analysis. Unless they and arguments like them fail, we have good grounds for believing that it is not the case that philosophy properly done must always be purely descriptive. So my exercise gives rise to two important general claims: it challenges Judeo-Christian belief at its very heart and it also challenges a fashionable thesis about the nature of philosophy.

One final salvo of I hope not too homiletic a nature. People who try to apply the techniques of linguistic analysis are still frequently accused of engaging in trivial endeavors and with what has been called "an abdication of philosophy." But note this: whatever else may be wrong with what I have argued here, it remains one example of analytic philosophy that cannot be so criticized. What the critic must do is to show that my arguments are mistaken and not complain that they are trivial because they do not touch fundamental problems of human existence.

RELIGIOUS FAITH AS EXPERIENCING-AS

John Hick

JOHN HICK is Professor of Theology at the University of Birmingham. He is the author of *Faith and Knowledge* (1957), *Evil and the God of Love* (1966), *Philosophy of Religion* (1973), and others.

The particular sense or use of the word 'faith' that I am seeking to understand is that which occurs when the religious man, and more specifically the Christian believer, speaks of 'knowing God' and goes on to explain

[29] A powerful case for such ideological considerations being ancillary has been made by Anthony Quinton in "Philosophy and Beliefs," but in line with the point I have been making, note the powerful counter thrusts of Stuart Hampshire and Isaiah Berlin. See A. Quinton, S. Hampshire, S. Murdoch and I. Berlin, "Philosophy and Beliefs," *The Twentieth Century*, Vol. CLVII (1955), pp. 495–521.

that this is a knowing of God by faith. Or again, when asked how he professes to know that God, as spoken about in Christianity, is real, his answer is 'by faith'. Our question is: what does 'faith' mean in these contexts? And what I should like to be able to do is to make a descriptive (or if you like phenomenological) analysis that could be acceptable to both believers and non-believers. A Christian and an atheist or agnostic should equally be able to say, Yes, that is what, phenomenologically, faith is—though they would of course then go on to say radically different things about its value.

The modes of cognition have been classified in various ways. But the distinction that is most relevant to our present purpose is that between what I shall call cognition in presence and cognition in absence; or acquaintance (using this term less restrictedly than it was used by Russell) and holding beliefs-about. We cognise things that are present before us, this being called perception; and we also cognise things in their absence, this being a matter of holding beliefs about them. And the astonishing fact is that while our religious literature—the Bible, and prayers, hymns, sermons, devotional meditations and so on—confidently presupposes a cognition of God by acquaintance, our theological literature in contrast recognises for the most part only cognition in absence. That is to say, whereas the Bible itself, and other writings directly expressing the life of faith, are full of men's encounters with God and men's personal dealings with the divine Thou, the dominant systems of Christian theology nevertheless treat faith as belief, as a propositional attitude. In the Catholic tradition deriving from St. Thomas, and no less in the Protestant Orthodoxy that supervened upon the Reformation movement, faith has been quite explicitly defined as believing on God's authority certain truths, i.e. propositional truths, that he has revealed. Thus faith, instead of being seen as a religious response to God's redemptive action in the life of Jesus of Nazareth, has been seen instead as primarily an assent to theological truths. For good or ill this was a very major and radical step, taken early on in the Church's history and displaying its implications over the centuries in many different aspects of the life of Christendom. I believe that it was a wrong step, which the Reformers of the sixteenth century sought to correct. If this is so, we want to find a viable way, or perhaps even ways (in the plural), of thinking of faith as a form of cognition by acquaintance or cognition in presence. Instead of assimilating faith to propositional belief—whether such belief be produced by reasoning or act of will or both—we must assimilate it to perception. I therefore want to explore the possibility that the cognition of God by faith is more like perceiving something, even perceiving a physical object, that is present before us than it is like believing a statement about some absent object, whether because the statement has been proved to us or because we want to believe it.

But surely—if I may myself at once voice an inevitable protest—the cognition of God can no more be like sense perception than God is like a physical object. It is true that Christian tradition tells of an ultimate beatific vision of God, but we are not now speaking of this but of the ordinary believer's awareness of God in our present earthly life. And this is not a matter of perceiving him, but of believing, without being able to perceive him, that he nevertheless exists. It is in fact, as it has traditionally been held to be, a case of cognition in absence, or of holding beliefs-about.

However the hypothesis that we want to consider is not that religious faith *is* sense perception, but that as a form of cognition by acquaintance it is *more like* sense perception than like propositional belief. That propositions may be validly founded upon the awareness of God, and that they then play an indispensable and immensely valuable part in the religious life, is not in question. But what we are interested in now is the awareness of God itself; for this is faith—that is to say, distinctively religious cognition—in its primary sense.

It is today hardly a contentious doctrine requiring elaborate argumentation that seeing—to confine ourselves for the moment to this one mode of perceiving—is not a simple straightforward matter of physical objects registering themselves on our retinas and thence in our conscious visual fields. There are complexities, and indeed a complex variety of complexities. The particular complexity that concerns us now was brought to the attention of philosophers by Wittgenstein's discussion of seeing-as in the *Philosophical Investigations*. Wittgenstein pointed to puzzle pictures and ambiguous diagrams of the kind that are found in abundance in some of the psychological texts—for instance the Necker cube, Jastrow's duck-rabbit, and Köhler's goblet-faces. The cube diagram, for instance, can be seen as a cube viewed either from below or from above, and the perceiving mind tends to alternate between these two perspectives. The goblet-faces diagram can be seen as the outline of a goblet or vase or as the outlines of two faces looking straight into each other's eyes. The duck-rabbit can be seen as the presentation of a rabbit's head facing to the left or of a duck's head facing to the right. In these cases every line of the diagram plays its part in both aspects (as Wittgenstein called them) and has equal weight in each: these may accordingly be called cases of total ambiguity. Another sort, artistically more complex, might be called cases of emergent pattern; for example, those puzzle pictures in which you are presented with what at first seems to be a random and meaningless scattering of lines and dots, but in which as you look at it you come to see, say, a face; or again, as another example, the well-known 'Christ in the snow' picture. And in between there are various other sorts of intermediate cases which we need not however take account of here. We speak of seeing-as when that which is objectively there, in the sense of that which affects the retina, can be consciously perceived in two different ways as having two different characters or natures or meanings or significances; and very often, in these two-dimensional instances, we find that the mind switches back and forth between the alternative ways of seeing-as.

Let us at this point expand the notion of seeing-as into that of experiencing-as. The elements of experiencing-as are the purely visual seeing-as which we have thus far been discussing, plus its equivalents for the other senses. For as well as seeing a bird as a bird, we may hear it as a bird— hear the bird's song as a bird's song, hear the rustle of its wings as a bird in flight, hear the rapping of the woodpecker as just that; and so on. Again, a carpenter may not only see the wood as mahogany but also feel it as mahogany; he may recognise it tactually as well as visually. Or again, we may taste the wine as Burgundy and smell the cheese as Gorgonzola. Not of course that the different senses normally function in isolation. We perceive and recognise by means of all the relevant senses co-operating as a single complex means of perception; and I suggest that we use the term 'experiencing-as' to refer to the end-product of this in consciousness.

The next step is from these two-dimensional pictures and diagrams to experiencing-as in real life—for example, seeing the tuft of grass over there in the field as a rabbit, or the shadows in the corner of the room as someone standing there. And the analogy to be explored is with two contrasting ways of experiencing the events of our lives and of human history, on the one hand as purely natural events and on the other hand as mediating the presence and activity of God. For there is a sense in which the religious man and the atheist both live in the same world and another sense in which they live consciously in different worlds. They inhabit the same physical environment and are confronted by the same changes occurring within it. But in its actual concrete character in their respective 'streams of consciousness' it has for each a different nature and quality, a different meaning and significance; for one does and the other does not experience life as a continual interaction with the transcendent God. Is there then any true analogy or parallel between, on the one hand, these two ways of experiencing human life, *as* an encounter with God or *as* an encounter only with a natural order, and on the other hand the two ways of seeing the distant shape, *as* a rabbit or *as* a tuft of grass?

An immediate comment might be: if there is any such analogy, so much the worse for religious cognition! For does not the analogy between seeing a puzzle picture in a certain way and experiencing human life in a certain way underline once again the purely subjective and gratuitous character of religious knowledge-claims in contrast with the compelling objectivity of ordinary sense perception?

So far as the argument has thus far gone, perhaps it does. But the next point to be introduced must considerably affect the upshot of what has gone before. This is the thesis that *all* experiencing is experiencing-as— not only, for example, seeing the tuft of grass, erroneously, as a rabbit, but also seeing it correctly as a tuft of grass. On the face of it this sounds paradoxical. One might put the difficulty in this way: we may if we like speak of seeing the tuft of grass *as* a tuft of grass because it is evidently possible to misperceive it as a sitting rabbit. But what about something utterly familiar and unmistakable? What about the fork on the table? Would it not be absurd to say that you are seeing it *as* a fork? It must be granted that this particular locution would be distinctly odd in most circumstances. However we have more acceptable names for ordinary seeing-as in real life; we call it 'recognising' or 'identifying.' Of course we are so familiar with forks that normally we recognise one without encountering even enough difficulty to make us notice that we are in fact performing an act of recognition. But if the fork were sufficiently exotic in design I might have occasion to say that I can recognise the thing before me on the table as a fork—that is, as a man-made instrument for conveying food into the mouth. And, going further afield, a Stone-Age savage would not be able to recognise it at all. He might identify it instead as a marvellously shining object which must be full of *mana* and must not be touched; or as a small but deadly weapon; or as a tool for digging; or just as something utterly baffling and unidentifiable. But he would not have the concept of a fork with which to identify it as a fork. Indeed to say that he does not have this concept and that he cannot perform this act of recognition are two ways of saying the same thing. That there is no ambiguity or mystery about forks for you or me is simply due to the contingent circumstance that forks are familiar parts of the apparatus of our culture. For the original nature or meaning of an artefact is determined by the purpose for which it has been made, and this purpose necessarily operates within a particular cultural context. But simply as a physical object of a certain size and shape an artefact does not bear its meaning stamped upon it. To recognise or identify is to experience-as in terms of a concept; and our concepts are social products having their life within a particular linguistic environment.

Further, this is as true of natural objects as it is of artefacts. Here, too, to recognise is to apply a concept; and this is always to cognise the thing as being much more than is currently perceptible. For example, to identify a moving object in the sky as a bird is not only to make implicit claims about its present shape, size, and structure beyond what we immediately observe but also about its past (for instance, that it came out of an egg, not a factory) about its future (for instance, that it will one day die), and about its behaviour in various hypothetical circumstances (for instance, that it will tend to be frightened by loud noises). When we thus equate experiencing-as with recognising it is I think no longer a paradoxical doctrine that all conscious experiencing is experiencing-as.

But—if I may raise a possible objection—is it not the case that 'He recognises *x*' entails that the thing recognised is indeed *x*, while 'He is experiencing *a* as *x*' does not entail that *a* is indeed *x*: and must we not therefore acknowledge a distinction between recognising and experiencing-as? As a matter of the ordinary use of these words the objection is, I think, in order. But what it indicates is that we lack a term to cover both recognition and misrecognition. We are accordingly driven to use 'recognition' generically, as 'knowledge' in 'theory of knowledge' is used to cover error as well as knowledge, or as 'morality' in 'theory of morality' is used to cover immorality also. I have been using 'recognition' here in an analogous way to include unjustified as well as justified identification assertions.

I proceed, then, from the proposition that all conscious experiencing involves recognitions which go beyond what is given to the senses and is thus a matter of experiencing-as. This means that ordinary secular perceiving shares a common epistemological character with religious experiencing. We must accordingly abandon the view—if we ever held it—that sense perception at the highly sophisticated human level is a mere automatic registering by the mind of what is on the retina, while religious perception is, in contrast, a subjective response which gratuitously projects meanings into the world. We find instead that all conscious perceiving goes beyond what the senses report to a significance which has not as such been given to the senses. And the religious experience of life as a sphere in which we have continually to do with God and he with us is likewise an awareness in our experience as a whole of a significance which transcends the scope of the senses. In both cases, in a classic statement of John Oman's, 'knowing is not knowledge as an effect of an unknown external cause, but is knowledge as we so interpret that our meaning is the actual meaning of our environment'.[1] And, as Oman also taught, the claim of the religious believer is that in his religious commitment he is relating himself to his total environment in its most ultimate meaning.

The conclusion that *all* experiencing is experiencing-as enables us to meet a fundamental objection that might be made against the analogy between experiencing-as in ordinary life and in religious awareness. It might be pointed out that it is only possible to see, let us say, a tuft of grass as a rabbit if one has previously seen real rabbits; and that in general to see A as a B presupposes acquaintance with Bs. Analogously, in order to experience some event, say a striking escape from danger or a healing, as an act of God it would seem that we must first know by direct acquaintance what an act of God is like. However all that has ever been witnessed in the way of divine actions are earthly events which the religious mind has seen as acts of God but which a sceptical observer could see as having a purely natural explanation. In other words, we never have before us unambiguously divine acts, but only ambiguous events which are capable of taking on religious significance to the eyes of faith. But in that case, it will be said, we have no unproblematic cases of divine actions available to us, as we have in abundance unproblematic instances of rabbits and forks; and consequently we can never be in a position to recognise any of these ambiguous events *as* acts of God. Just as it would be impossible for one who had never seen rabbits to see anything *as* a

[1] *The Natural and the Supernatural* (Cambridge, 1931), p. 175.

rabbit, so it must be impossible for us who have never seen an undeniable act of God, to see an event *as* an act of God. This seems on the face of it to be a conclusive objection.

However the objection collapses if, as I have been arguing, *all* experiencing, involving as it does the activity of recognising, is to be construed as experiencing-as. For although the process of recognising is mysterious, there is no doubt that we do continually recognise things, and further that we can learn to recognise. We have learned, starting from scratch, to identify rabbits and forks and innumerable other kinds of things. And so there is thus far in principle no difficulty about the claim that we may learn to use the concept 'act of God', as we have learned to use other concepts, and acquire the capacity to recognise exemplifying instances.

But of course—let it at once be granted—there are very obvious and indeed immense differences between the concept of a divine act and such concepts as rabbit and fork. For one thing, rabbits and forks are objects—substances, if you like—whereas a divine act is an event. This is already a considerable conceptual contrast. And we must proceed to enlarge it still further. For the cognition of God recorded in the Bible is much wider in scope than an awareness of particular isolated events as being acts of God. Such divine acts are but points of peculiarly intense focus within a much wider awareness of existing in the presence of God. Indeed the biblical cognition of God is typically mediated through the whole experience of the prophet or apostle after his call or conversion, even though within this totality there are specially vivid moments of awareness of God, some of which are evoked by striking or numinous events which thereby become miracles or theophanies. However, we are primarily concerned here with the wider and more continuous awareness of living within the ambience of the unseen God—with the sense of the presence of God—and this is surely something very unlike the awareness of forks and rabbits.

But although the sense of the presence of God is indeed very far removed from the recognition of forks and rabbits, it is already, I think, clear that there are connecting links in virtue of which the religious awareness need not be completely unintelligible to us. In its epistemological structure it exhibits a continuity with our awareness in other fields.

In seeking further to uncover and investigate this continuity we must now take note of another feature of experiencing-as, namely the fact that it occurs at various levels of awareness. By this I mean that as well as there being values of x and y such that to experience A as x is incompatible with experiencing it as y, because x and y are mutually exclusive alternatives, there are also values of x and y such that it is possible to experience A as simultaneously x and y. Here y is supplementary to x, but on a different level. What is meant by 'levels' in this context? That y is on a higher level than x means that the experiencing of A as y presupposes but goes beyond the experiencing of it a x. One or two examples may be useful at this point. As an example, first, of mutually exclusive experiencing-as, one cannot see the tuft of grass simultaneously as a tuft of grass and as a rabbit; or the person whose face we are watching as both furiously angry and profoundly delighted. On the other hand, as an example of supplementary experiencings-as, we may see what is moving above us in the sky as a bird; we may further see it as a hawk; and we may further see it as a hawk engaged in searching for prey; and if we are extremely expert bird watchers we may even see it as a hawk about to swoop down on something on the far side of that low hump of ground. These are successively higher-level recognitions in the sense that each later member of the list presupposes and goes beyond the previous one.

Now let us call the correlate of experiencing-as 'significance', defining this by means of the notion of appropriate response. That is to say, to recognise what is before us as an *x* involves being in a dispositional state to act in relation to it in a certain distinctive way or range of ways. For example, to recognise the object on the table as a fork is to be in a different dispositional state from that in which one is if one recognises it as a fountain pen. One is prepared in the two cases for the object to display different characteristics, and to be surprised if it doesn't; and one is prepared to use it in different ways and on different occasions, and so on; and in general to recognise something *as* a this or a that (i.e. as significant in this way or in that way) involves being in a certain dispositional state in relation to it.

Our next step must be to shift attention from isolated objects as units of significance to larger and more complex units, namely situations.

A situation is composed of objects; but it is not simply any random collection of objects. It is a group of objects which, when attended to as a group, has its own distinctive significance over and above the individual significances of its constituent members. That is to say, the situation evokes its own appropriate dispositional response.

As in the case of object-significance there can be different levels of situational significance, with higher levels presupposing lower. An example that is directly relevant is the relation between the ethical significance of a human situation and its purely natural or physical significance. Think of any situation involving an element of moral obligation. Suppose, for example, that someone is caught at the foot of a steep cliff by an incoming tide and I at the top hear his cries for help. He asks me to run to the nearest telephone, ring the police and ask them to call out the lifeboat to rescue him. Consider this first at the purely natural or physical level. There are the cliff and the sea, a human creature liable in due course to be submerged by the rising tide, and his shouted appeals for help. And, morality apart, that is all that there is—just this particular pattern of physical events. However as moral beings we are aware of more than that. As well as experiencing the physical events as physical events we also experience them as constituting a situation of moral claim upon ourselves. We experience the physical pattern as having ethical significance; and the dispositional response that it renders appropriate is

to seek to help the trapped person in whatever way seems most prac-
ticable. We can, however, conceive of someone with no moral sense at all,
who simply fails to be aware of the ethical significance of this situation.
He would be interpreting or recognising or experiencing-as only at the
physical level of significance. And there would be no way of proving to
someone who was thus morally defective that there is any such thing as
moral obligation. No doubt an amoral creature could be induced by
threats and promises to conform to a socially desirable pattern of behaviour, but he could never be turned by these means into a moral being.
In the end we can only say, tautologously, that a person is aware of the
ethical significance of situations because he is a moral being; he experiences in moral terms because he is built that way.

The ethical is experienced as an order of significance which supervenes
upon, interpenetrates, and is mediated through the physical significance
which it presupposes. And if on some occasion the moral character of a
situation is not at first apparent to us, but dawns upon us as we contemplate it, something happens that is comparable to the discovery of an
emergent pattern in a puzzle picture. As the same lines and marks are
there, but we have now come to see them as constituting an importantly
new pattern, so the social situation is there with the same describable
features, but we have now come to be aware of it as laying upon us an
inescapable moral claim.

Now consider religious significance as a yet higher level of significance.
It is a higher level of significance, adding a new dimension which both
includes and transcends that of moral judgement, and yet on the other
hand it does not form a simple continuation of the pattern we have
already noted. As between natural and ethical significance it is safe to
say that every instance of the latter presupposes some instance of the
former; for there could be no moral situations if there were no physical
situations to have moral significance. But as between ethical and religious
significance the relationship is more complex. Not every moment of religious awareness is superimposed upon some occasion of moral obligation.
Very often—and especially in the prophetic type of religion that we know
in Judaism and Christianity—the sense of the presence of God does carry
with it some specific or general moral demand. But we may also be
conscious of God in solitude, surrounded only by the natural world, when
the divine presence is borne in upon us by the vastness of the starry
heavens above or the majestic beauty of a sunrise or a mountain range
or some lake or forest scene, or other aspect of earth's marvellously varied
face. Again, the sense of the presence of God may occur without any
specific environmental context, when the mind is wrapt in prayer or
meditation; for there is a contemplative and mystical awareness of God
which is relatively independent of external circumstances. And indeed
even within the prophetic type of religious experience there are also
moments of encounter with God in nature and through solitary prayer as
well as in the claims of the personal world. But on the other hand even

when the sense of the presence of God has dawned upon us in solitude it is still normally true that it leads us back to our neighbours and often deepens the ethical significance of our relations with them. Thus the dispositional response which is part of the awareness of God is a response in terms of our involvement with our neighbours within our common environment. Even the awareness of God through nature and mystical contemplation leads eventually back to the service of God in the world.

Let us then continue to think here primarily of the prophetic awareness of God, since although this is not the only form of religious cognition it is the typically Judaic-Christian form. And let us test the notion of faith as religious experiencing-as by applying it to the particular history of faith which is reflected in the biblical records.

The Old Testament prophets were vividly conscious of Jahweh as acting in relation to the people of Israel in certain of the events of their time. Through the writings which recall their words and deeds we feel their overwhelmingly vivid consciousness of God as actively present in their contemporary history. It was God who, in the experience of Amos, was threatening selfish and complacent Israel with Assyrian conquest, while also offering mercy to such as should repent. It was God in his holy anger who, in the experience of Jeremiah, was bringing up the Babylonian army against Jerusalem and summoning his people to turn from their greed and wickedness. It is equally true of the other great prophets of the Old Testament that they were experiencing history, as it was taking place around them, as having a distinctively religious significance. Humanly explicable events were experienced as also acts of God, embodying his wrath or his mercy or his calling of the Jewish nation into covenant with him. The prophets experienced the religious significance of these events and declared it to the people; and this religious significance was always such that to see it meant being conscious of a sacred demand to behave in a new way toward one's neighbours.

It is, I think, important to realise that this prophetic interpretation of Hebrew history was not in the first place a philosophy of history, a theoretical pattern imposed retrospectively upon remembered or recorded events. It was in the first place the way in which the great prophets actually experienced and participated in these events at the time. Hosea did not *infer* Jahwah's mercy; second Isaiah did not *infer* his universal sovereignty; Jeremiah did not *infer* his holy righteousness—rather they were conscious of the Eternal as acting towards them, and towards their nation, in his mercy, in his holy righteousness, in his absolute sovereignty. They were, in other words, experiencing-as.

Again, in the New Testament, the primary instance of faith, the rock on which Christianity is based, consisted in seeing Jesus as the Christ. This was the faith of the disciples, epitomised in Peter's confession at Caesarea Philippi, whereby their experience of following Jesus was also an experience of being in the presence of God's personal purpose and claim and love. They may or may not at the time have used any of the terms that were later used in the New Testament writings to express this awareness—Messiah, Son of God, divine Logos. However, these terms point back to that original response, and the faith which they came to express must have been implicit within it. And once again this primary response of the first disciples to Jesus as Lord and Christ was not a theory about him which they adopted, but an experience out of which Christian language and theory later grew. That he was their Lord was a fact of experience given in their personal dealings with him. And the special character of their way of seeing and responding to him, in contrast to that of others who never found him to be their Lord, is precisely the distinctive essence of Christian faith.

The experiencing of Jesus of Nazareth as Lord—Jesus of Nazareth, that is to say, not as a theological symbol but in his historical concreteness, including his teaching concerning God and man—meant coming to share in some degree both his experiencing of life as the sphere of God's re-demptive activity and his practical response to God's purposes in the world. What that involved for Jesus himself, as the one in whom men were to see the divine Logos made flesh, is spelled out in his life, and especially in the drama of his death. What it involves for Christians—for those who have begun to share Jesus' vision of the world in its relation to God,—is indicated in his moral teaching. For this is simply a general description, with concrete examples drawn from the life of first-century Palestine, of the way in which someone tends spontaneously to behave who is consciously living in the presence of God as Jesus has revealed him.

I have now, I hope, offered at least a very rough outline of a conception of faith as the interpretative element within our cognitive religious experience. How is one to test such a theory, and how decide whether to accept or reject it? All that can be done is to spell out its consequences as fully as possible in the hope that the theory will then either flounder under a weight of implausible corollaries, or else show its viability as it proceeds and float triumphantly on to acceptance. I have already tried to indicate its epistemological basis in the thesis that all experiencing is experiencing-as, and the way in which this thesis is relevant to the stream of distinctively religious experience recorded in the Bible. Let me now in conclusion sketch some of its lines of implication in other directions.

It suggests, as I have already mentioned, a view of the Christian ethic as the practical corollary of the distinctively Christian vision of the world. Taking a hint from the modern dispositional analysis of belief we may say that to experience the world as having a certain character is, among other things, to be in a dispositional state to live in it in the manner which such a character in our environment renders appropriate. And to experience it in a way derived from Christ's own experience is accordingly to tend to live in the kind of way that he both taught and showed forth in his own life.

Another implication of this theory of faith concerns the nature of revelation. For in Christian theology revelation and faith are correlative concepts, faith being a human response to the divine activity of self-revelation. If faith is construed as a distinctively religious experiencing of life as mediating God's presence and activity, this clearly fits and even demands a *heilsgeschichtliche* conception of revelation as consisting in divine actions in human history. God is self-revealingly active within the world that he has made. But his actions are not overwhelmingly manifest and unmistakable; for then men would have no cognitive freedom in relation to their Maker. Instead God always acts in such a way that man is free to see or fail to see the events in question as divine acts. The prophets were conscious of God at work in the happenings of their time; but many of their contemporaries were not. Again, the disciples were conscious of Jesus as the Christ; but the scribes and pharisees and the Romans were not. Thus revelation, as communication between God and man, only becomes actual when it meets an answering human response of faith; and the necessity for this response, making possible an uncompelled cognition of God's presence and activity, preserves the freedom and responsibility of the finite creature in relation to the infinite Creator.

This in turn suggests an understanding of the special character of the Bible and of its inspiration. The Bible is a record of the stream of revelatory events that culminated in the coming of the Christ. But it differs from a secular account of the same strand of history in that the Bible is written throughout from the standpoint of faith. It describes this history as it was experienced from within by the prophets and then by the apostles. And the faith of the writers, whereby they saw the revelatory events *as* revelatory, is their inspiration. The uniqueness of the Bible is not due to any unique mode or quality of its writing but to the unique significance of the events of which it is the original documentary expression, which became revelatory through the faith of the biblical writers. As such the Bible mediates the same revelation to subsequent generations and is thus itself revelatory in a secondary sense, calling in its own turn for a response of faith.

This theory of faith can also be used to throw light on the nature of the miraculous. For a miracle, whatever else it may be, is an event through which we become vividly and immediately conscious of God as acting towards us. A startling happening, even if it should involve a suspension of natural law, does not constitute for us a miracle in the religious sense of the word if it fails to make us intensely aware of being in God's presence. In order to be miraculous, an event must be experienced as religiously significant. Indeed we may say that a miracle is any event that is experienced as a miracle; and this particular mode of experiencing-as is accordingly an essential element in the miraculous.

Finally, yet another application of this theory of faith is to the sacraments. In the sacraments some ordinary material object, bread or wine or water, is experienced as a vehicle of God's grace and becomes a focus of specially intense consciousness of God's overshadowing presence and purpose. A sacrament has in fact the same religious quality as a miracle but differs from other miracles in that it occurs within a liturgical context and is a product of ritual. In themselves, apart from the sacramental context of worshipping faith, the bread and wine or the water are ordinary material things; they have no magical properties. What happens in the sacramental event is that they are experienced as channels of divine grace. They thus invite a peculiarly direct moment of religious experiencing-as, fulfilling for subsequent believers the faith-eliciting and faith-nourishing function of the person of Christ in the experience of the first disciples.

Now in conclusion may I repeat something that I said near the beginning. What I have been attempting to formulate is an epistemological analysis of religious faith, not an argument for the validity of that faith. Faith, I have been suggesting, is the interpretative element within what the religious man reports as his experience of living in the presence of God. But whether that experience is veridical or illusory is another question. My own view is that it is as rational for the religious man to treat his experience of God as veridical as it is for him and others to treat their experience of the physical world as veridical. But that requires another argument, which I have not attempted to supply here.

LECTURES ON RELIGIOUS BELIEF

Ludwig Wittgenstein

LUDWIG WITTGENSTEIN (1889–1951) is perhaps the most influential philosopher in the analytic tradition. His most influential work is the *Philosophical Investigations* (1958).

An Austrian general said to someone: "I shall think of you after my death, if that should be possible." We can imagine one group who would find this ludicrous, another who wouldn't.

(During the war, Wittgenstein saw consecrated bread being carried in chromium steel. This struck him as ludicrous.)

Suppose that someone believed in the Last Judgement, and I don't, does this mean that I believe the opposite to him, just that there won't be such a thing? I would say: "not at all, or not always."

Suppose I say that the body will rot, and another says "No. Particles will rejoin in a thousand years, and there will be a Resurrection of you."

If some said: "Wittgenstein, do you believe in this?" I'd say: "No." "Do you contradict the man?" I'd say: "No."

If you say this, the contradiction already lies in this.

Would you say: "I believe the opposite," or "There is no reason to suppose such a thing"? I'd say neither.

Suppose someone were a believer and said: "I believe in a Last Judgement," and I said: "Well, I'm not so sure. Possibly." You would say that
there is an enormous gulf between us. If he said "There is a German
aeroplane overhead," and I said "Possibly I'm not so sure," you'd say we
were fairly near.

It isn't a question of my being anywhere near him, but on an entirely
different plane, which you could express by saying: "You mean something
altogether different, Wittgenstein."

The difference might not show up at all in any explanation of the
meaning.

Why is it that in this case I seem to be missing the entire point?

Suppose somebody made this guidance for this life: believing in the
Last Judgement. Whenever he does anything, this is before his mind. In
a way, how are we to know whether to say he believes this will happen
or not?

Asking him is not enough. He will probably say he has proof. But he
has what you might call an unshakeable belief. It will show, not by
reasoning or by appeal to ordinary grounds for belief, but rather by
regulating for in all his life.

This is a very much stronger fact—foregoing pleasures, always appealing to this picture. This in one sense must be called the firmest of all
beliefs, because the man risks things on account of it which he would not
do on things which are by far better established for him. Although he
distinguishes between things well-established and not well-established.

Lewy: Surely, he would say it is extremely well-established.

First, he may use "well-established" or not use it at all. He will treat
this belief as extremely well-established, and in another way as not well-
established at all.

If we have a belief, in certain cases we appeal again and again to
certain grounds, and at the same time we risk pretty little—if it came to
risking our lives on the ground of this belief.

There are instances where you have a faith—where you say "I believe"
—and on the other hand this belief does not rest on the fact on which
our ordinary everyday beliefs normally do rest.

How should we compare beliefs with each other? What would it mean
to compare them?

You might say: "We compare the states of mind."

How do we compare states of mind? This obviously won't do for all
occasions. First, what you say won't be taken as the measure for the firm-
ness of a belief? But, for instance, what risks you would take?

The strength of a belief is not comparable with the intensity of a pain.
An entirely different way of comparing beliefs is seeing what sorts of
grounds he will give.

A belief isn't like a momentary state of mind. "At 5 o'clock he had very
bad toothache."

Suppose you had two people, and one of them, when he had to decide which course to take, thought of retribution, and the other did not. One person might, for instance, be inclined to take everything that happened to him as a reward or punishment, and another person doesn't think of this at all.

If he is ill, he may think: "What have I done to deserve this?" This is one way of thinking of retribution. Another way is, he thinks in a general way whenever he is ashamed of himself: "This will be punished."

Take two people, one of whom talks of his behaviour and of what happens to him in terms of retribution, the other one does not. These people think entirely differently. Yet, so far, you can't say they believe different things.

Suppose someone is ill and he says: "This is a punishment," and I say: "If I'm ill, I don't think of punishment at all." If you say: "Do you believe the opposite?"—you can call it believing the opposite, but it is entirely different from what we would normally call believing the opposite.

I think differently, in a different way. I say different things to myself. I have different pictures.

It is this way: if someone said: "Wittgenstein, you don't take illness as punishment, so what do you believe?"—I'd say: "I don't have any thoughts of punishment."

There are, for instance, these entirely different ways of thinking first of all—which needn't be expressed by one person saying one thing, another person another thing.

What we call believing in a Judgement Day or not believing in a Judgement Day—The expression of belief may play an absolutely minor role.

If you ask me whether or not I believe in a Judgement Day, in the sense in which religious people have belief in it, I wouldn't say: "No. I don't believe there will be such a thing." It would seem to me utterly crazy to say this.

And then I give an explanation: "I don't believe in . . .," but then the religious person never believes what I describe.

I can't say. I can't contradict that person.

In one sense, I understand all he says—the English words "God," "separate," etc. I understand. I could say: "I don't believe in this," and this would be true, meaning I haven't got these thoughts or anything that hangs together with them. But not that I could contradict the thing.

You might say: "Well, if you can't contradict him, that means you don't understand him. If you did understand him, then you might." That again is Greek to me. My normal technique of language leaves me. I don't know whether to say they understand one another or not.

These controversies look quite different from any normal controversies. Reasons look entirely different from normal reasons.

They are, in a way, quite inconclusive.

The point is that if there were evidence, this would in fact destroy the whole business.

Anything that I normally call evidence wouldn't in the slightest influence me.

Suppose, for instance, we knew people who foresaw the future; make forecasts for years and years ahead; and they described some sort of a Judgement Day. Queerly enough, even if there were such a thing, and even if it were more convincing than I have described but, belief in this happening wouldn't be at all a religious belief.

Suppose that I would have to forego all pleasures because of such a forecast. If I do so and so, someone will put me in fires in a thousand years, etc. I wouldn't budge. The best scientific evidence is just nothing.

A religious belief might in fact fly in the face of such a forecast, and say "No. There it will break down."

As it were, the belief as formulated on the evidence can only be the last result—in which a number of ways of thinking and acting crystallize and come together.

A man would fight for his life not to be dragged into the fire. No induction. Terror. That is, as it were, part of the substance of the belief.

That is partly why you don't get in religious controversies, the form of controversy where one person is *sure* of the thing, and the other says: 'Well, possibly.'

You might be surprised that there hasn't been opposed to those who believe in Resurrection those who say "Well, possibly."

Here believing obviously plays much more this role: suppose we said that a certain picture might play the role of constantly admonishing me, or I always think of it. Here, an enormous difference would be between those people for whom the picture is constantly in the foreground, and the others who just didn't use it at all.

Those who said: "Well, possibly it may happen and possibly not" would be on an entirely different plane.

This is partly why one would be reluctant to say: "These people rigorously hold the opinion (or view) that there is a Last Judgement." "Opinion" sounds queer.

It is for this reason that different words are used: 'dogma,' 'faith.'

We don't talk about hypothesis, or about high probability. Nor about knowing.

In a religious discourse we use such expressions as: "I believe that so and so will happen," and use them differently to the way in which we use them in science.

Although, there is a great temptation to think we do. Because we do talk of evidence, and do talk of evidence by experience.

We could even talk of historic events.

It has been said that Christianity rests on an historic basis.

It has been said a thousand times by intelligent people that indubitability is not enough in this case. Even if there is as much evidence as for Napoleon. Because the indubitability wouldn't be enough to make me change my whole life.

It doesn't rest on an historic basis in the sense that the ordinary belief in historic facts could serve as a foundation.

Here we have a belief in historic facts different from a belief in ordinary historic facts. Even, they are not treated as historical, empirical, propositions.

Those people who had faith didn't apply the doubt which would ordinarily apply to *any* historical propositions. Especially propositions of a time long past, etc.

What is the criterion of reliability, dependability? Suppose you give a general description as to when you say a proposition has a reasonable weight of probability. When you call it reasonable, is this *only* to say that for it you have such and such evidence, and for others you haven't?

For instance, we don't trust the account given of an event by a drunk man.

Father O'Hara [1] is one of those people who make it a question of science.

Here we have people who treat this evidence in a different way. They base things on evidence which taken in one way would seem exceedingly flimsy. They base enormous things on this evidence. Am I to say they are unreasonable? I wouldn't call them unreasonable.

I would say, they are certainly not *reasonable*, that's obvious.

'Unreasonable' implies, with everyone, rebuke.

I want to say: they don't treat this as a matter of reasonability.

Anyone who reads the Epistles will find it said: not only that it is not reasonable, but that it is folly.

Not only is it not reasonable, but it doesn't pretend to be.

What seems to me ludicrous about O'Hara is his making it appear to be *reasonable*.

Why shouldn't one form of life culminate in an utterance of belief in a Last Judgement? But I couldn't either say "Yes" or "No" to the statement that there will be such a thing. Nor "Perhaps," nor "I'm not sure."

It is a statement which may not allow of any such answer.

If Mr. Lewy is religious and says he believes in a Judgement Day, I won't even know whether to say I understand him or not. I've read the same things as he's read. In a most important sense, I know what he means.

If an atheist says: "There won't be a Judgement Day and another person says there will," do they mean the same?—Not clear what criterion of meaning the same is. They might describe the same things. You might say, this already shows that they mean the same.

We come to an island and we find beliefs there, and certain beliefs we are inclined to call religious. What I'm driving at is, that religious beliefs will not . . . They have sentences, and there are also religious statements.

[1] Contribution to a Symposium on *Science and Religion* (London: Gerald Howe, 1931, pp. 107–116).

These statements would not just differ in respect to what they are about. Entirely different connections would make them into religious beliefs, and there can easily be imagined transitions where we wouldn't know for our life whether to call them religious beliefs or scientific beliefs.

You may say they reason wrongly.

In certain cases you would say they reason wrongly, meaning they contradict us. In other cases you would say they don't reason at all, or "It is an entirely different kind of reasoning." The first, you would say in the case in which they reason in a similar way to us, and make something corresponding to our blunders.

Whether a thing is a blunder or not—it is a blunder in a particular system. Just as something is a blunder in a particular game and not in another.

You could also say that where we are reasonable, they are not reasonable—meaning they don't use *reason* here.

If they do something very like one of our blunders, I would say, I don't know. It depends on further surroundings of it.

It is difficult to see, in cases in which it has all the appearances of trying to be reasonable.

I would definitely call O'Hara unreasonable. I would say, if this is religious belief, then it's all superstition.

But I would ridicule it, not by saying it is based on insufficient evidence. I would say: here is a man who is cheating himself. You can say: this man is ridiculous because he believes, and bases it on weak reasons.

II

The word 'God' is amongst the earliest learnt—pictures and catechisms, etc. But not the same consequences as with pictures of aunts. I wasn't shown [that which the picture pictured].

The word is used like a word representing a person. God sees, rewards, etc.

"Being shown all these things, did you understand what this word meant?" I'd say: "Yes and no. I did learn what it didn't mean. I made myself understand. I could answer questions, understand questions when they were put in different ways—and in that sense could be said to understand."

If the question arises as to the existence of a god or God, it plays an entirely different role to that of the existence of any person or object I ever heard of. One said, had to say, that one *believed* in the existence, and if one did not believe, this was regarded as something bad. Normally if I did not believe in the existence of something no one would think there was anything wrong in this.

Also, there is this extraordinary use of the word 'believe.' One talks of believing and at the same time one doesn't use 'believe' as one does ordinarily. You might say (in the normal use): "You only believe—oh well. . . ." Here it is used entirely differently; on the other hand it is not used as we generally use the word 'know'.

If I even vaguely remember what I was taught about God, I might say: "Whatever believing in God may be, it can't be believing in something we can test, or find means of testing." You might say: "This is nonsense, because people say they believe on *evidence* or say they believe on religious experiences." I would say: "The mere fact that someone says they believe on evidence doesn't tell me enough for me to be able to say now whether I can say of a sentence 'God exists' that your evidence is unsatisfactory or insufficient."

Suppose I know someone, Smith. I've heard that he has been killed in a battle in this war. One day you come to me and say: "Smith is in Cambridge." I inquire, and find you stood at Guildhall and saw at the other end a man and said: "That was Smith." I'd say: "Listen. This isn't sufficient evidence." If we had a fair amount of evidence he was killed I would try to make you say that you're being credulous. Suppose he was never heard of again. Needless to say, it is quite impossible to make inquiries. "Who at 12.05 passed Market Place into Rose Crescent?" Suppose you say: "He was there." I would be extremely puzzled.

Suppose there is a feast on Mid-Summer Common. A lot of people stand in a ring. Suppose this is done every year and then everyone says he has seen one of his dead relatives on the other side of the ring. In this case, we could ask everyone in the ring. "Who did you hold by the hand?" Nevertheless, we'd all say that on that day we see our dead relatives. You could in this case say: "I had an extraordinary experience. I had the experience I can express by saying: 'I saw my dead cousin'." Would we say you are saying this on insufficient evidence? Under certain circumstances I would say this, under other circumstances I wouldn't. Where what is said sounds a bit absurd I would say: "Yes, in this case insufficient evidence." If altogether absurd, then I wouldn't.

Suppose I went to somewhere like Lourdes in France. Suppose I went with a very credulous person. There we see blood coming out of something. He says: "There you are, Wittgenstein, how can you doubt?" I'd say: "Can it only be explained one way? Can't it be this or that?" I'd try to convince him that he'd seen nothing of any consequence. I wonder whether I would do that under all circumstances. I certainly know that I would under normal circumstances.

"Oughtn't one after all to consider this?" I'd say: "Come on. Come on." I would treat the phenomenon in this case just as I would treat an experiment in a laboratory which I thought badly executed.

"The balance moves when I will it to move." I point out it is not covered up, a draught can move it, etc.

I could imagine that someone showed an extremely passionate belief in such a phenomenon, and I couldn't approach his belief at all by saying: "This could just as well have been brought about by so and so" because he could think this blasphemy on my side. Or he might say: "It is possible that these priests cheat, but nevertheless in a different sense a miraculous phenomenon takes place there."

I have a statue which bleeds on such and such a day in the year. I have red ink, etc. "You are a cheat, but nevertheless the Deity uses you. Red ink in a sense, but not red ink in a sense."

Cf. Flowers at seance with label. People said: "Yes, flowers are materialized with label." What kind of circumstances must there be to make this kind of story not ridiculous?

I have a moderate education, as all of you have, and therefore know what is meant by insufficient evidence for a forecast. Suppose someone dreamt of the Last Judgement, and said he now knew what it would be like. Suppose someone said: "This is poor evidence." I would say: "If you want to compare it with the evidence for it's raining to-morrow it is no evidence at all." He may make it sound as if by stretching the point you may call it evidence. But it may be more than ridiculous as evidence. But now, would I be prepared to say: "You are basing your belief on extremely slender evidence, to put it mildly." Why should I regard this dream as evidence—measuring its validity as though I were measuring the validity of the evidence for meteorological events?

If you compare it with anything in Science which we call evidence, you can't credit that anyone could soberly argue: "Well, I had this dream . . . therefore . . . Last Judgement." You might say: "For a blunder, that's too big." If you suddenly wrote numbers down on the blackboard, and then said: "Now, I'm going to add," and then said: "2 and 21 is 13," etc. I'd say: "This is no blunder."

There are cases where I'd say he's mad, or he's making fun. Then there might be cases where I look for an entirely different interpretation altogether. In order to see what the explanation is I should have to see the sum, to see in what way it is done, what he makes follow from it, what are the different circumstances under which he does it, etc.

I mean, if a man said to me after a dream that he believed in the Last Judgement, I'd try to find what sort of impression it gave him. One attitude: "It will be in about 2,000 years. It will be bad for so and so and so, etc." Or it may be one of terror. In the case where there is hope, terror, etc., would I say there is insufficient evidence if he says: "I believe . . ."? I can't treat these words as I normally treat 'I believe so and so'. It would be entirely beside the point, and also if he said his friend so and so and his grandfather had had the dream and believed, it would be entirely beside the point.

I would not say: "If a man said he dreamt it would happen to-morrow," would he take his coat?, etc.

Case where Lewy has visions of his dead friend. Cases where you don't try to locate him. And case where you try to locate him in a business-like way. Another case where I'd say: "We can pre-suppose we have a broad basis on which we agree."

In general, if you say: "He is dead" and I say: "He is not dead" no-one would say: "Do they mean the same thing by 'dead'?" In the case where a man has visions I wouldn't offhand say: "He means something different."

Cf. A person having persecution mania.

What is the criterion for meaning something different? Not only what he takes as evidence for it, but also how he reacts, that he is in terror, etc.

How am I to find out whether this proposition is to be regarded as an empirical proposition—'You'll see your dead friend again?' Would I say: "He is a bit superstitious?" Not a bit.

He might have been apologetic. (The man who stated it categorically was more intelligent than the man who was apologetic about it.)

'Seeing a dead friend,' again means nothing much to me at all. I don't think in these terms. I don't say to myself: "I shall see so and so again" ever.

He always says it, but he doesn't make any search. He puts on a queer smile. "His story had that dreamlike quality." My answer would be in this case "Yes," and a particular explanation.

Take "God created man." Pictures of Michelangelo showing the creation of the world. In general, there is nothing which explains the meanings of words as well as a picture, and I take it that Michelangelo was as good as anyone can be and did his best, and here is the picture of the Deity creating Adam.

If we ever saw this, we certainly wouldn't think this the Deity. The picture has to be used in an entirely different way if we are to call the man in that queer blanket 'God', and so on. You could imagine that religion was taught by means of these pictures. "Of course, we can only express ourselves by means of picture." This is rather queer . . . I could show Moore the pictures of a tropical plant. There is a technique of comparison between picture and plant. If I showed him the picture of Michelangelo and said: "Of course, I can't show you the real thing, only the picture" . . . . The absurdity is, I've never taught him the technique of using this picture.

It is quite clear that the role of pictures of Biblical subjects and rôle of the picture of God creating Adam are totally different ones. You might ask this question: "Did Michelangelo think that Noah in the ark looked like this, and that God creating Adam looked like this?" He wouldn't have said that God or Adam looked as they look in this picture.

It might seem as though, if we asked such a question as: "Does Lewy *really* mean what so and so means when he says so and so is alive?"—it might seem as though there were two sharply divided cases, one in which he would say he didn't mean it literally. I want to say this is not so. There will be cases where we will differ, and where it won't be a question at all of more or less knowledge, so that we can come together. Sometimes it will be a question of experience, so you can say: "Wait another 10 years."

And I would say: "I would disencourage this kind of reasoning" and Moore would say: "I wouldn't disencourage it." That is, one would *do* something. We would take sides, and that goes so far that there would really be great differences between us, which might come out in Mr. Lewy saying: "Wittgenstein is trying to undermine reason", and this wouldn't be false. This is actually where such questions rise.

III

Today I saw a poster saying: " 'Dead' Undergraduate speaks."

The inverted commas mean: "He isn't really dead." "He isn't what people call dead. They call it 'dead' not quite correctly."

We don't speak of "door" in quotes.

It suddenly struck me: "If someone said 'He isn't really dead, although by the ordinary criteria he is dead' "—couldn't I say "He is not only dead by the ordinary criteria; he is what we all call 'dead'."

If you now call him 'alive', you're using language in a queer way, because you're almost deliberately preparing misunderstandings. Why don't you use some other word, and let "dead" have the meaning it already has?

Suppose someone said: "It didn't always have this meaning. He's not dead according to the old meaning" or "He's not dead according to the old idea".

What is it, to have different ideas of death? Suppose you say: "I have the idea of myself being a chair after death" or "I have the idea of myself being a chair in half-an-hour"—you all know under what circumstances we say of something that it has become a chair.

C.f. (1) "This shadow will cease to exist."

(2) "This chair will cease to exist." You say that you know what this chair ceasing to exist is like. But you have to think. You may find that there isn't a use for this sentence. You think of the use.

I imagine myself on the death-bed. I imagine you all looking at the air above me. You say "You have an idea".

Are you clear when you'd say you had ceased to exist?

You have six different ideas [of 'ceasing to exist'] at different times.

If you say: "I can imagine myself being a disembodied spirit. Wittgenstein, can you imagine yourself as a disembodied spirit?"—I'd say: "I'm sorry. I [so far] connect nothing with these words."

I connect all sorts of complicated things with these words. I think of what people have said of sufferings after death, etc.

"I have two different ideas, one of ceasing to exist after death, the other of being a disembodied spirit."

What's it like to have two different ideas? What is the criterion for one man having one idea, another man having another idea?

You gave me two phrases, "ceasing to exist", "being a disembodied spirit". "When I say this, I think of myself having a certain set of experiences." What is it like to think of this?

If you think of your brother in America, how do you know that what you think is, that the thought inside you is, of your brother being in America? Is this an experiential business?

Cf. How do you know that what you want is an apple? [Russell].

How do you know that you believe that your brother is in America?

A pear might be what satisfied you. But you wouldn't say: "What I wanted was an apple."

Suppose we say that the thought is some sort of process in his mind, or his saying something, etc.—then I could say: "All right, you call this a thought of your brother in America, well, what is the connection between this and your brother in America?"

Lewy: You might say that this is a question of convention.

Why is it that you don't doubt that it is a thought of your brother in America?

One process [the thought] seems to be a shadow or a picture of something else.

How do I know that a picture is a picture of Lewy?—Normally by its likeness to Lewy, or, under certain circumstances, a picture of Lewy may not be like him, but like Smith. If I give up the business of being like [as a criterion], I get into an awful mess, because anything may be his portrait, given a certain method of projection.

If you said that the thought was in some way a picture of his brother in America—Yes, but by what method of projection is it a picture of this? How queer it is that there should be no doubt what it's a picture of.

If you're asked: "How do you know it is a thought of such and such?" the thought that immediately comes to your mind is one of a shadow, a picture. You don't think of a causal relation. The kind of relation you think of is best expressed by "picture", "shadow," etc.

The word "picture" is even quite all right—in many cases it is even in the most ordinary sense, a picture. You might translate my very words into a picture.

But the point is this, suppose you drew this, how do I know it is my brother in America? Who says it is him—unless it is here ordinary similarity?

What is the connection between these words, or anything substitutable for them, with my brother in America?

The first idea [you have] is that you are looking at your own thought, and are absolutely sure that it is a thought that so and so. You are looking at some mental phenomenon, and you say to yourself "obviously this is a thought of my brother being in America". It seems to be a super-picture. It seems, with thought, that there is no doubt whatever. With a picture, it still depends on the method of projection, whereas here it seems that you get rid of the projecting relation, and are absolutely certain that this is thought of that.

Smythies's muddle is based on the idea of a super-picture.

We once talked about how the idea of certain superlatives came about in Logic. The idea of a super-necessity, etc.

"How do I know that this is the thought of my brother in America?"—that *what* is the thought?

Suppose my thought consists of my *saying* "My brother is in America"—how do I know that I *say* my brother is in America?

How is the connection made?—We imagine at first a connection like strings.

Lewy: The connection is a convention. The word designates.

You must explain "designates" by examples. We have learnt a rule, a practice, etc.

Is thinking of something like painting or shooting at something?

It seems like a projection connection, which seems to make it indubitable, although there is not a projection relation at all.

If I said "My brother is in America"—I could imagine there being rays projecting from my words to my brother in America. But what if my brother isn't in America?—then the rays don't hit anything.

[If you say that the words refer to my brother by expressing the proposition that my brother is in America—the proposition being a middle link between the words and what they refer to]—What has the proposition, the mediate link, got to do with America?

The most important point is this—if you talk of painting, etc. your idea is that the connection exists *now*, so that it seem as though as long as I do this thinking, this connection exists.

Whereas, if we said it is a connection of convention, there would be no point in saying it exists while we think. There is a connection by convention—What do we mean?—This connection refers to events happening at various times. Most of all, it refers to a technique.

["Is thinking something going on at a particular time, or is it spread over the words?" "It comes in a flash." "Always?—it sometimes does come in a flash, although this may be all sorts of different things.]

If it does refer to a technique, then it can't be enough, in certain cases, to explain what you mean in a few words; because there is something which might be thought to be in conflict with the idea going on from 7 to 7.5, namely the practice of using it [the phrase].

When we talked of: "So and so is an automaton", the strong hold of that view was [due to the idea] that you could say: "Well, I know what I mean" . . . , as though you were looking at something happening while you said the thing, entirely independent of what came before and after, the application [of the phrase]. It looked as though you could talk of understanding a word, without any reference to the technique of its usage. It looked as though Smythies said he could understand the sentence, and that we then had nothing to say.

What was it like to have different ideas of death?—What I meant was—Is having an idea of death something like having a certain picture, so that you can say "I have an idea of death from 5 to 5.1 etc."? "In whatever way anyone will use this word, I have now a certain idea"—if you call this "having an idea", then it is not what is commonly called "having an idea", because what is commonly called "having an idea", has a reference to the technique of the word, etc.

We are all here using the word "death", which is a public instrument, which has a whole technique [of usage]. Then someone says he has an idea of death. Something queer; because you might say "You are using the word 'death', which is an instrument functioning in a certain way."

If you treat this [your idea] as something private, with what right are you calling it an idea of death?—I say this, because we, also, have a right to say what is an idea of death.

He might say "I have my own private idea of death"—why call this an 'idea of death' unless it is something you connect with death. Although this [your 'idea'] might not interest us at all. [In this case,] it does not belong on the game played with 'death', which we all know and understand.

If what he calls his "idea of death" is to become relevant, it must become part of our game.

'My idea of death is the separation of the soul from the body'—if we know what to do with these words. He can also say: "I connect with the word 'death' a certain picture—a woman lying in her bed"—that may or may not be of some interest.

If he connects

with death, and this was his idea, this might be interesting psychologically.

"The separation of soul from body" [only had a public interest.] This may act like black curtains or it may not act like black curtains. I'd have to find out what the consequences [of your saying it] are. I am not, at least, at present at all clear. [You say this]—"So what?"—I know these words, I have certain pictures. All sorts of things go along with these words.

If he says this, I won't know yet what consequences he will draw. I don't know what he opposes this to.

Lewy: "You oppose it to being extinguished."

If you say to me—"Do you cease to exist?"—I should be bewildered, and would not know what exactly this is to mean. "If you don't cease to exist, you will suffer after death", there I begin to attach ideas, perhaps ethical ideas of responsibility. The point is, that although these are well-known words, and although I can go from one sentence to another sentence, or to pictures [I don't know what consequences you draw from this statement],

Suppose someone said: "What do you believe, Wittgenstein? Are you a sceptic? Do you know whether you will survive death?" I would really, this is a fact, say "I can't say. I don't know", because I haven't any clear idea what I'm saying when I'm saying "I don't cease to exist," etc.

Spiritualists make one kind of connection.

A Spiritualist says "Apparition" etc. Although he gives me a picture I don't like, I do get a clear idea. I know that much, that some people connect this phrase with a particular kind of verification. I know that some people don't—religious people e.g.—they don't refer to a verification, but have entirely different ideas.

A great writer said that, when he was a boy, his father set him a task, and he suddenly felt that nothing, not even death, could take away the responsibility [in doing this task]; this was his duty to do, and that even death couldn't stop it being his duty. He said that this was, in a way, a proof of the immortality of the soul—because if this lives on [the responsibility won't die]. The idea is given by what we call the proof. Well, if this is the idea, [all right].

If a Spiritualist wishes to give *me* an idea of what he means or doesn't mean by 'survival', he can say all sorts of things—

[If I ask what idea he has, I may be given what the Spiritualists say or I may be given what the man I quoted said, etc., etc.]

I would at least [in the case of the Spiritualist] have an idea of what this sentence is connected up with, and get more and more of an idea as I see what he does with it.

As it is, I hardly connect anything with it at all.

Suppose someone, before going to China, when he might never see me again, said to me: "We might see one another after death"—would I necessarily say that I don't understand him? I might say [want to say] simply, "Yes. I *understand* him entirely."

Lewy: "In this case, you might only mean that he expressed a certain attitude."

I would say "No, it isn't the same as saying 'I'm very fond of you' "— and it may not be the same as saying anything else. It says what it says. Why should you be able to substitute anything else?

Suppose I say: "The man used a picture."

"Perhaps now he sees he was wrong." What sort of remark is this?

"God's eye sees everything"—I want to say of this that it uses a picture.

I don't want to belittle him [the person who says it].

Suppose I said to him "You've been using a picture", and he said "No, this is not all"—mightn't he have misunderstood me? What do I want to do [by saying this]? What would be the real sign of disagreement? What might be the real criterion of his disagreeing with me?

Lewy: "If he said: 'I've been making preparations [for death].'"

Yes, this might be a disagreement—if he himself were to use the word in a way in which I did not expect, or were to draw conclusions I did not expect him to draw. I wanted only to draw attention to a particular technique of usage. We should disagree, if he was using a technique I didn't expect.

We associate a particular use with a picture.

Smythies: 'This isn't all he does—associate a use with a picture.'

Wittgenstein: Rubbish. I meant: what conclusions are you going to draw? etc. Are eyebrows going to be talked of, in connection with the Eye of God?

"He could just as well have said so and so"—this [remark] is fore-shadowed by the word "attitude". He couldn't just as well have said something else.

If I say he used a picture, I don't want to say anything he himself wouldn't say. I want to say that he draws these conclusions.

Isn't it as important as anything else, what picture he does use?

Of certain pictures we say that they might just as well be replaced by another—e.g. we could, under certain circumstances, have one projection of an ellipse drawn instead of another.

[He *may* say]: "I would have been prepared to use another picture, it would have had the same effect. . . ."

The whole *weight* may be in the picture.

We can say in chess that the exact shape of the chess-men plays no rôle. Suppose that the main pleasure was, to see people ride; then, playing it in writing wouldn't be playing the same game. Someone might say: "All he's done is change the shape of the head"—what more could he do?

When I say he's using a picture I'm merely making a *grammatical* remark: [What I say] can only be verified by the consequences he does or does not draw.

If Smythies disagrees, I don't take notice of this disagreement.

All I wished to characterize was the conventions he wished to draw. If I wished to say anything more I was merely being philosophically arrogant.

Normally, if you say "He is an automaton" you draw consequences, if you stab him, [he'll feel pain]. On the other hand, you may not wish to draw any such consequences, and this is all there is to it—except further muddles.

DIFFERENCES BETWEEN SCIENTIFIC
AND RELIGIOUS ASSERTIONS

Donald D. Evans

DONALD D. EVANS is a member of the Department of Philosophy at the University of Toronto. He is the author of *The Logic of Self-Involvement* (1963) and numerous articles on religious language.

Two conflicting views concerning comparisons between religion and science are current today. On the one hand, both existentialist theologians and positivist critics of religion maintain that religious assertions and scientific assertions are radically *different*. On the other hand, some scientific thinkers who are keen to humanize science or to legitimize religion maintain that religion and science are essentially *similar,* and that they differ mainly in subject matter rather than in method. It seems to me that although there are a few genuine similarities between religious theory (theology) and scientific theory, there are fundamental differences between religion and science which the second view fails to acknowledge. The first view, properly qualified in response to cogent criticisms from the second, seems closer to the truth.

This paper has four parts. I shall discuss religion, then science, and then their similarities and differences. Finally, I shall summarize my conclusions.

I. RELIGIOUS FAITH AND DEPTH-EXPERIENCES

There are many varieties of religion. Some, such as classical Buddhism, are not theistic. Others, such as the modern so-called "religionless Christianity," attempt a theism without religion. The kind of religion which we shall consider is one in the Judeo-Christian tradition which equates *religious* faith with faith in *God.* Faith in God is best understood, it seems to me, by reference to "depth-experiences." This term will become clear as we look at five different kinds of depth-experience.

1. Depth-Experiences

a. Personal encounter. I encounter John Brown. He has an I-Thou attitude toward me, as Martin Buber would say.[1] That is, he is outgoing,

---

[1] My debt to Martin Buber will be evident in this section. Similarly my account of numinous experience is partly derived from Rudolph Otto, moral responsibility from John Baillie, radical despair from Paul Tillich, and indignant compassion from D. M. Mackinnon and Dietrich Bonhoeffer. In each case, however, my own account differs somewhat from theirs.

open, available, and responsive. He focuses his whole self exclusively on me in my uniqueness, involving himself in my world and committing himself to me. If I respond in kind, even though less profoundly, something mysterious flashes between us, changing both of us so that we become more truly human, more real as persons. I emerge from the encounter aware of a new meaning in life, a meaning which is expressed more in a new mode of life than in any words.

This personal encounter is a depth-experience. If an agnostic or an atheist has had a similar experience and agrees with me that it is real and important, he does not thereby agree that there is a God. He only agrees that there are mysterious depths in human relations. But he does enter a context in which I can begin to explain part of what I mean by "God." God is, in part, a hidden being whose unlimited and perfect I-Thou attitude toward me is revealed in the limited and imperfect I-Thou attitude which John Brown and others have toward me. That is, I interpret the I-Thou encounter with John Brown as a revelation of God. I look on John Brown's "presence with a meaning" as a revelation of a divine presence, an eternal meaning. I see in his I-Thou attitude toward me a revelation of God, the Eternal Thou whose I-Thou attitude toward me is complete and constant and utterly trustworthy. A believer looks on a depth-experience of personal encounter as a revelation of God and tries to live accordingly; that is, he is open to the "address" of the Eternal Thou, which comes through the words and deeds of men whom he meets in personal encounter. An agnostic or atheist interprets the depth-experience in purely human terms: "Yes, human beings are mysterious; there are depths in man which can only be known in personal encounters; but why bring in God?"

In general, depth-experiences are interpreted in one of two ways: as revelations concerning *man* or as revelations concerning both *man* and *God*. Faith involves the latter interpretation. Faith is an ongoing practical commitment to an interpretation of some depth-experiences as revelations not only of man but also of God. Sometimes a depth-experience "hits" the believer as a divine revelation, so that he is aware of no alternative interpretation at the time; but honest reflection afterwards should lead him to acknowledge the possibility of interpreting his depth-experience in purely human terms. His faith presupposes a belief that there is a hidden personal being called "God" who sometimes reveals Himself in depth-experiences. Note that his faith thus involves both commitment and belief.

Let us consider another kind of depth-experience.

b. Numinous experience. I look at a sunset or a waterfall. I have an overwhelming feeling of awe, a sense of my own littleness coupled with a joy in being so much alive and a dumfounded wonder at the mystery of beauty. Or I meet a man whom religious people call a "saint," and I have similar feelings of reverence, self-abasement, exhilaration, and bewilderment.

Such "numinous" feelings need not be interpreted in a religious way. An agnostic or atheist who is profoundly impressed by sunset or saint is not being illogical if he refrains from bringing in God. On the other hand, it is not unreasonable for a man of faith to look on the impressive features of sunset or saint as expressions of a hidden numinous being.[2] An unbeliever can understand part of what is meant by "God" in this context. God is the numinous, worshipful being who expresses Himself, reveals Himself, in such a way as to evoke numinous feelings. The man of faith interprets the depth-experience as a revelation concerning both man and God. Like many unbelievers he sometimes finds in men a mysterious depth, a capacity for awe, self-abasement, exaltation, and wonder; and in a few men he finds a mysterious impressiveness which evokes such responses in their fellows. For the man of faith, however, the depth-experience is also a revelation of God, the hidden personal being who reveals His inner nature through the numinous sunset or saint. Each element in the numinous depth-experience is correlated in meaning with an attribute of God: awe with "holiness," self-abasement with "majesty," exaltation with "spirit," and wonder with "glory." In each case the transcendence of a divine attribute is correlated with the unlimited character of the appropriate numinous response.

c. *Moral responsibility.* Some men have a strong sense of moral responsibility. Moral obligations come, as it were, from outside oneself, imperiously subordinating one's own inclinations and interests, urgently demanding acknowledgment and action.

Such moral seriousness is common to both unbelief and belief at their best. A believer differs in that he looks on his own sense of moral responsibility as a revelation of a hidden moral Sovereign who has a rightful and righteous authority over his life. He looks on the unconditional and awesome demands of the moral imperative as divine imperatives. Such faith does not equate conscience with the voice of God, for no infallibility is assumed or assured. The question, "What ought I to do?" is the same question for a believer as the question, "What does God require me to do?"—but he has no infallible method for answering his question, and his certainty and uncertainty concerning particular moral obligations may be the same as that of an unbeliever. Rather, he differs in having a sobering sense of being responsible and answerable not merely to himself or to society or to an impersonal moral law, but to a hidden personal being who is a moral Sovereign, whose wisdom is perfect, and whose demand for obedience is unqualified.

An unbeliever, however, may interpret his own moral seriousness and that of others as an indication of something profound and mysterious in human nature, without going on to interpret it as a revelation of God as well. For the believer, it reveals both man and God. Note that the morally

---

[2] For a detailed analysis of "impressive" and "expressive," see Donald Evans, *The Logic of Self-Involvement* (London: SCM Press, 1963), chaps. 2, 4.

serious unbeliever is in a position to understand part of what the believer
means by "God" because they share a common sense of moral responsibility. Here again the depth-experience provides a context for meaningful language concerning God. On the other hand, to the extent to which
a man lacks depth-experience he will be unable to understand such language.

We have considered three depth-experiences: personal encounter, numinous experience, moral responsibility. We now turn to a fourth.

d. Radical despair. A man is in a state of radical despair. Life seems
meaningless and pointless—not only life around him, but his own life.
Nevertheless he protests passionately against this meaninglessness. His
despair is not a state of apathy or indifference, although he finds no basis
for deciding between life and death, between right and wrong; his despair
is vital and vehement; meaninglessness is for him a matter of ultimate
concern.

Such radical despair is sometimes paradoxical. In such cases, the more
the man protests against the meaninglessness of life, the more meaning
he gives to life by his very protest. The more ultimate his concern about
meaninglessness, the more meaning he gives to life by his very concern.
The more vehement his rejection of this supposed meaning and that supposed meaning, the more transcendent his own sense of what a meaningful
existence would be. The more profound and vital his anxiety in the face
of meaninglessness, the more profound and vital his own courage in facing
this anxiety.

Radical despair, like other depth-experiences, is open to alternative
interpretations. The man of faith interprets his own concern for meaning
as a revelation of a being who is the source of meaning in life. He
interprets his own existential courage as a revelation of a being who is its
source, and his own passionate yearning for an ultimate as itself a revelation of the ultimate. The man of faith believes that Pascal was right when
he put those famous words into the mouth of God: "You would not be
seeking me unless you had already found me." The unbeliever, however,
interprets his radical despair in terms of man alone. His concern for
meaning, his existential courage, and his passionate yearning for an ultimate may reveal mysterious depths in human personality. But the unbeliever does not share the believer's conviction that there is also a
revelation of God, that both God and man are active in the depth-
experience.

e. Indignant compassion. Some believers and unbelievers have this in
common: they identify themselves compassionately with other human
beings in their suffering, sharing in it, but also grieving and rebelling
against it. Like Dostoievsky's atheist Ivan Karamazov, or Camus' atheist
Dr. Rieux, their compassion is compounded with a sense of outrage and
revulsion that nature and men should inflict mental and physical torture
on human beings. Karamazov and Rieux focus their revolt on the alleged
God who made a world in which children can be torn to pieces by hunting

dogs as a sport, or in which children writhe helplessly in the pains of the plague.

This atheistic protest is, for some believers, supreme blasphemy; but for other believers it is an admirable attitude which can be a profound revelation of God. For example, D. M. Mackinnon of Cambridge says, "The man who revolts, determined somehow to affirm in this most desperate situation that God did not so make the world, is met by the mystery of God's own revolt against the world He made." [3] On such a view, a man interprets his own indignant compassion as a revelation of the infinite indignant compassion of a hidden personal being, as well as an indication of mysterious depths in human nature. For the unbeliever, however, it is only the latter.

Belief in a God of indignant compassion involves a belief in a God who suffers, God as depicted by Bonhoeffer when he wrote "Christians stand by God in his hour of grieving." Bonhoeffer's image is vivid and daring. In a Nazi prison, he interprets his own grieving for humanity as a participation in God's grieving. It is as if he were standing by a friend who grieves over the sufferings of the friend's child. His own grieving is as nothing compared to his friend's. His own compassion for the child is a sharing in his friend's compassion. Similarly a man's finite concern for others is a way of sharing in the infinite divine concern.

We have considered five kinds of depth-experience. There are others which might have been included, but I shall not discuss them in this paper. Let us now examine depth-experiences more closely in relation to religious faith.

2. Religious Faith

Religious faith is a practical commitment to an interpretation of depth-experiences as divine revelations. Such faith presupposes a belief that there exists a hidden personal being who reveals himself in these ways. This being, who has the proper name "God," reveals Himself as the Eternal Thou, the awesome numinous, the moral Sovereign, the source of meaning, and the grieving friend. The believer holds that in each case the depth-experience has limitations and imperfections, but that the God who is thereby revealed does not. For example, the I-Thou attitude of the Eternal Thou is *perfect* in its constancy and openness. Although I am far from being clear as to what I mean when I describe God in these ways, and although I assume that any attempted description will be inadequate, and although the meaning of the descriptions cannot be understood in abstraction from elusive and mysterious depth-experiences, my faith does involve a *"belief-that."* I stress this, because I want to make clear my disagreement with those religious philosophers who rightly stress the

---

[3] D. M. Mackinnon, *Christian Faith and Communist Faith* (London: Macmillan & Co., 1953), pp. 247–48.

element of commitment in faith, but who wrongly deny that the commitment presupposes a *belief-that*.

I also wish to distinguish my account of religious faith from some which resemble it in taking a depth-experience seriously and in finding common ground between believers and some unbelievers, but which differ in *equating* a depth-experience with faith or with God. Paul Tillich, for example, says that faith *is* the state of being ultimately concerned.[4] He also says, in a passage made famous by being quoted in *Honest to God,* "If you know that God means depth, you know much about him. . . . You can not think or say: Life has no depth! Life is shallow. Being itself is surface only. If you could say this in complete seriousness, you would be an atheist; but otherwise you are not. He who knows about depth knows about God." [5] Elsewhere Tillich seems to equate faith (his "absolute faith") with the radical despair which protests against meaninglessness.[6] I reject Tillich's equation.[7] God is not the same as the depths in man, and faith is not the same as an experience of these depths. If Tillich wants to use the words "God" and "faith" in a peculiar way which abolishes any radical distinction between belief and unbelief he is free to do so, but both believers and unbelievers have a right to protest, indeed to protest with Tillichian passion! Similarly it is a mistake to equate faith with numinous experience or personal encounter or moral responsibility or indignant compassion. Faith involves an interpretation of a depth-experience as a revelation of God.

The various descriptions of God are indirect. God is a being such that various unlimited depth-experiences are appropriate responses to Him. This does not mean that God *is* a depth-experience. Such an account would be an unwarranted reductionism, similar to a reduction of material objects to sense-data or a reduction of other minds to observable public behavior. The meaning of a statement is linked with its method of verification, but the two need not be equivalent. Nor is an indirect description of God a matter of *acting-as-if*. Religious faith is not an *acting-as-if* there were a God to whom various responses would be appropriate if He really did exist. No, there really does exist such a God, though what is meant by talk about Him cannot be understood in abstraction from human depth-experiences.

3. Christian Faith

Thus far in this paper I have talked about a religious faith which is not specifically Christian. A Christian faith differs in that depth-experiences

4 Paul Tillich, *Dynamics of Faith* (New York: Harper & Row, 1958), p. 1.
5 J. A. T. Robinson, *Honest to God* (London: SCM Press, 1963), p. 22.
6 Paul Tillich, *The Courage To Be* (London: Nisbet & Co., 1952), esp. p. 167.
7 Sometimes Tillich does not equate God with a depth-experience or a depth in man; God is the "ground" or even the "source" of these. This strand in Tillich's thought is not in conflict with my approach.

are interpreted in relation to Jesus, the man of Nazareth whom Christians believe to be now alive and present in the depth-experience. For example, in the case of personal encounters, the Christian looks on another man's "presence with a meaning" as a revelation of Jesus Christ. In the words of Hopkins:

> [The just man]
> Acts in God's eye what in God's eye he is—
> Christ—for Christ plays in ten thousand places,
> Lovely in limbs, and lovely in eyes not his
> To the Father through the features of men's faces.[8]

Also, the Cross of Christ transforms our ordinary notions of what is supremely *numinous*. A Christian looks on the Cross as the normative expression of divine glory: transcendence revealed in humility, majesty revealed in sacrifice, life and spirit revealed in death, mystery revealed in agony. Others, both believers and unbelievers, may look on the Cross as the unfortunate death of a good man; but the Christian looks on the Cross in such a way that, more than sunsets and saints, it arouses his awe, his self-abasement, his exultation, and his wonder. In other words, the Christian worships Christ crucified.

The Christian also interprets his moral experience in relation to Jesus Christ. His sense of moral responsibility to the divine sovereign is modified in various ways because of this. For example, in so far as a man is a Christian, he looks on his status before God as something which he cannot earn, something which he receives as a gift from God through Christ. He is justified by grace, and so his moral seriousness has an underlying joy and an absence of anxious strain.

I shall not try to indicate the specifically Christian interpretation of radical despair and indignant compassion. Perhaps I have said enough to show that the Christian reinterpretation of a depth-experience may involve a more or less radical revision of a man's religious interpretation. We should also note two additional points. On the one hand, my conviction concerning Jesus of Nazareth may reinforce an original decision of faith. Indeed, some elements in a step from agnosticism to faith may seem implausible unless the Christian claims for Jesus are true; for example, the interpretation of one's own grieving as a revelation of God's grieving may seem implausible unless one believes that Jesus was divine, so that the Cross reveals God's grieving. On the other hand, my conviction concerning Jesus is in some respects not a basis for faith but rather something which itself requires a basis. It is only rational to interpret depth-experiences today in terms of Jesus if there is an adequate basis for believing two things about him: that as an historical figure he was a normative medium for God's self-revelation, and that he conquered death in such a way as to become a living presence in the depth-experiences of multitudes

[8] *Poems of Gerard Manley Hopkins,* ed. W. H. Gardner (New York: Oxford University Press, 1948), p. 95. Reprinted by permission.

of men. These beliefs concerning the character and the resurrection of Jesus depend, in turn, partly on historical evidence. But this cannot be explored further here.

II. Scientific Language and Objectivity

Some writers have claimed not only that some science is nonobjective but that objectivity is not even a tenable ideal for science. Such a claim may contain many valid objections against popular notions of scientific objectivity, but it is far too extreme. There are three important ways in which scientists actively, and often successfully, seek for objectivity. In each of these ways, as we shall see, science differs radically from religion. A scientific assertion should be *logically neutral, comprehensible impersonally,* and *testable by observations.* The first requirement has to do with the logic of scientific assertions, the second with conditions for understanding them, and the third with their method of verification.

Before we consider each requirement in turn, I should indicate how I am using two terms: "assertion" and "objective." "Assertion" will be used in a very loose and general way so that it covers scientific observation-reports, laws, hypotheses, or theories; the differences between these will be noted only when necessary. An "objective" assertion is one whose truth or falsity can in principle be established on the basis of maximal inter-subjective agreement.

1. Scientific Assertions Are Logically Neutral

The term "neutral" can mean a great many different things. The meaning which I shall select and refine is one which makes "neutral" the opposite of *"self-involving."* A self-involving assertion is one which commits the person who asserts it or accepts it to further action, or which implies that he has an attitude for or against whatever the assertion is about, or which expresses such an attitude. For example, in saying "I promise to return this book tomorrow," I commit myself, logically, to a specific future action. In saying, "I commend Jones for his restraint," I imply that I approve of Jones' restraint. In saying, "I look on you as a father," I express an attitude toward you. In each case I *cannot* deny the self-involvement. I cannot deny that "I promise . . ." commits me, or that "I command . . ." implies a favorable attitude, or that "I look on you as a father" expresses an attitude. The "cannot" is a *logical* one. It is based on part of the *meaning* of the utterance, namely its performative force: what one is doing in saying such-an-such.[9] This meaning or force depends

___
[9] See *The Logic of Self-Involvement,* pp. 27–46, which depends on J. L. Austin's account of "illocutionary force" in *How To Do Things with Words* (Oxford: Clarendon Press, 1962).

on public linguistic and institutional conventions, though it sometimes also depends on special contexts of meaning or on the special intentions of the speaker (what *he* means in saying such-and-such).

Of course a man may be deceitful when he promises or commends or expresses an attitude. Although he implies that he intends to return the book or that he has a favorable attitude toward Jones, he may have no such intention or attitude. Similarly an utterance which expresses an attitude may be quite insincere. But deceit or insincerity does not affect the meaning of the utterance. Although the speaker does not "mean what he says," what he says *has* a meaning; his deceit or insincerity depends on this linguistic fact. As I propose to use the terms "self-involvement" and its opposite "neutrality," they have to do with matters of logic and meaning rather than introspective psychology.

Let us now consider scientific assertions. It is a requirement of science that scientific language should be *neutral*. In asserting or accepting a scientific theory, law, or observation-report, I give assent to it without committing myself to future conduct (other than verbal consistency), and without implying or expressing any personal attitude for or against what is asserted. If the scientific assertion were not neutral, agreement between scientists would depend partly on each one's personal commitments and attitudes, especially his moral commitments and attitudes. For example, if the Kinsey report says, "Such-and-such sexual behavior is normal," and the word "normal" here does not mean "average" or "usual" but "normative," a scientist's assent to the assertion would depend partly on whether or not he approves of the behavior. Scientists rightly seek a language which is as neutral as possible in order to minimize any dependence on such considerations. The objectivity which can be achieved through intersubjective testing in science depends partly on the logical neutrality of scientific assertions. Science can discover what *is* the case, what *is* being done, only if scientists do not have to agree concerning what *ought* to be the case, what *ought* to be done.

Logical neutrality must not be confused with *psychological neutrality*. A particular scientist may be a bitter opponent or an enthusiastic practitioner of the sexual conduct which he is reporting; or he may be very detached and disinterested. In each case, however, his report can and ought to be logically neutral if it is to be a scientific report. Which attitude tends to promote scientific progress, scientific "detachment" or scientific "passion"? Whatever the answer to this question (my own answer is "both, but in different ways and different contexts"), the issue has nothing to do with the requirement that scientific language be neutral in its public meaning. Nor does the logical neutrality of scientific language mean that science is doomed to be existentially trivial. A scientific report (for example, the results of a test for cancer) may be both logically neutral and profoundly important.

Logical neutrality must also not be confused with *absence of belief*. In making a scientific assertion, a speaker usually implies that he believes it.

The strength of the belief implied varies according to the type of assertion. Where a scientific hypothesis is presented, no belief need be implied at all. But where a belief is implied, this belief is not itself an attitude for or against something, nor is it a commitment to a future pattern of conduct. The belief may provide a basis for such an attitude or commitment, but it is not itself an attitude or commitment. Furthermore, whether or not a speaker actually *has* the belief which he implies is an empirical or psychological matter. He may be sweating with conviction or inwardly sneering with scepticism, but the kind of belief which he *implies* depends on conventions of language concerning the meaning (performative force) of what he says. If a scientist is testing a new hypothesis, will his work be better if he passionately believes in it or if he cautiously entertains it as a mere possibility? Whatever the answer to this question—and there are conflicting answers given—the issue has nothing to do with the requirement that scientific language be logically neutral.

One final clarification concerning logical neutrality. Critics of objectivity-claims for science often point out that all investigations involve a *selection* of subject matter and that these involve implicit *judgments concerning importance.* This seems to me to be a legitimate point. No investigation, whether scientific or nonscientific, deals with everything or with every aspect of an event, and what is included is presumably regarded as being more important for the investigation than what is omitted. But this point does not show that logical neutrality is impossible. When I say, "The litmus paper has turned red," my assertion may involve some implicit judgments concerning the importance of such color changes, but I do not imply that I have a pro-attitude or a con-attitude. The term "implicit" may mislead us here, for I do not *imply* a judgment (or attitude) concerning importance in the way that I *imply* a pro-attitude when I say, "I commend you for your restraint." The so-called "implicit judgment" is one which a speaker might make in giving a *reason* for having selected changes in *color* rather than, say, changes in *shape.* Furthermore, any implicit judgment concerning importance—assuming there are such judgments—could itself be logically neutral. In saying, "X is important" I imply no pro-attitude or con-attitude toward X. We should also notice that the scientific importance of X lies in its relation to other matters in science. X may *also* be of profound personal relevance to the investigator, but this is not necessary.

2. Scientific Assertions Are Comprehensible Impersonally

Obviously *all* comprehension or understanding, including scientific understanding, is "personal" rather than "impersonal" in the sense that it is *persons* who understand. But we also say, "He's an unusual person, he deals with every problem so impersonally." In a somewhat similar way we can say, "Scientific assertions are understood by persons, but they are understood impersonally." That is, if a man has sufficient intelligence and scientific training, he should be able to understand a particular scientific assertion regardless of his personal attitudes concerning what the assertion is about, and regardless of his moral, aesthetic, or spiritual appreciation of what the assertion is about. The conditions for understanding are scientific, not intimately personal. For example, let us suppose that John Brown does not understand what is meant by "Light travels in straight lines." If he has enough brain power and if he studies enough physics he should be able to understand the assertion. This understanding should be possible whether or not light is something that matters tremendously to him, whether or not he is a self-centered or an altruistic person, whether or not he has ever contemplated a beam of light with the eye of an artist. The conditions for understanding a particular scientific assertion are independent of these variable personal factors. It is a matter of intelligence and scientific training.

Scientific training, however, involves a good deal of *attitudinal* training, especially for people who have not grown up in a scientific culture. There are various scientific virtues to be inculcated if a student is to become a scientist: industry, patience, curiosity, open-mindedness, detachment, self-discipline, rigorous and orderly thinking, scrupulous honesty in reporting results, etc. These virtues are conditions for understanding science. If too many are lacking, a student will not make any progress in understanding. Thus he may fail to understand "Light travels in straight lines," not because of his attitudes toward light or his failure to appreciate light aesthetically, but because he is lazy—or more generally, because he has not been sufficiently interested in science to continue his studies. When I say that scientific assertions are "comprehensible impersonally" I am not denying that the understanding of a particular scientific assertion depends *indirectly* on the fulfillment of prior personal conditions.

Science does differ from many other disciplines in that its indirect dependence on personal conditions is, on the whole, less; and the conditions themselves are less profoundly and intimately personal than those in some other disciplines; obviously they differ from basic conditions in aesthetics, morality, or religion. But the main point is that the understanding of a particular scientific assertion does not depend *directly* on personal conditions. There is no direct relation between the meaning of a particular scientific term and a particular scientific virtue or attitude. The meaning of "electron" is not correlated with an attitude of detachment, or with any other attitude. The meaning of "holy," however, *is* correlated with an attitude of reverence; that is, "X is holy" means (in part) "X is such that an attitude of reverence is an appropriate response." More generally, the meaning of "God" is correlated with various attitudinal depth-experiences.

The requirement of impersonal comprehensibility (like that of logical neutrality) is rightly designed to minimize the relevance of personal factors in science. It is an attempt at maximal mutual understanding in spite of the profound and numerous personal differences which exist among men, especially differences in aesthetic, moral, and spiritual attitudes. There are limits, of course, not only because of variations in degree of intelligence and kind of scientific training, but also because of variations in *kind* of intelligence. Also, the more theoretical and frontier-exploratory the nature of the scientific work, the fewer the scientists who can, at the time, understand one another fully.

We should also notice that there are a great many different levels of understanding; a man only gradually gets to "know his way around" in a field, grasping more and more of the significance of various terms or theories. Nor is all scientific language easily intelligible because precisely defined; the fertility of some theoretical concepts depends partly on their open texture. In short, the requirement that scientific assertions be comprehensible impersonally does not mean that all science should be like a ten-year-old's scientific textbook! It does nevertheless mean three things. First, the indirect dependence on personal conditions is less than in many other disciplines. Second, these conditions are less profoundly personal than those in many other disciplines. Third (most important), the comprehensibility of a particular scientific assertion is not directly dependent on profoundly personal conditions.

We have considered two requirements of scientific assertions, each of which in a different way is designed to promote the objectivity of science: logical neutrality and impersonal comprehensibility. The first is a matter of logic, and can be stated with precision. The second is a matter of conditions for understanding, and is much less clearly statable. The third requirement, which also is designed to promote objectivity, has to do with methodology; it is fairly clear, but complex.

3. Scientific Assertions Are Testable by Observations

A scientific assertion should be, in principle, testable by observations. That is, a scientist should be able to specify the observable states of affairs which would verify his assertion—or at least help to support it. And he should also be able to specify the observable states of affairs which would falsify his assertion—or at least help to undermine it. He may not be able to test his assertion at the moment; he may have to wait until further evidence comes in, or until technicians build an apparatus. But he must be able to say what observable states of affairs *would* verify or support his assertion, and what *would* falsify or undermine his assertion; his assertion must be testable in principle. It must not be compatible with any and every possible state of affairs.

In the early days of positivism, the requirement that scientific assertions be testable by observations was mistakenly regarded as the key to the whole of science. Today, however, philosophers of science set forth many qualifications and objections concerning it, so much so that there is considerable danger of its being ignored in comparisons between science and religion. Let us consider some of the qualifications and objections

which have been propounded, looking successively at four different kinds
of scientific assertion: observation-reports, theories, paradigms, and presuppositions.

a. Observation-reports. The claim that scientific assertions are testable
by observations needs to be qualified, since all observation involves
interpretation. There are no "pure" observations, "given" perceptions, or
"raw" experiences. Human minds impose various conceptual frameworks
on all observations, perceptions, or experiences. What we "observe" depends on the conceptual framework which we bring to the observations;
we can never disentangle observations completely from interpretations so
as to "test" interpretations by reference to "pure" observations. Scientific
observations, moreover, involve a special kind of interpretation. They are
"theory-laden"; that is, what one observes as a scientist is already interpreted in terms of concepts drawn from scientific theory. Where common sense observes a swinging stick, the scientist observes a pendulum.
Where common sense observes a flash, the scientist observes an electrical
discharge.

Does this mean that scientific assertions are not testable by observations? Surely not. It means that there are differing levels of interpretation
of experience, and that "higher" levels cannot be reduced to lower ones.
That is, if we consider a common-sense observation-report ("The stick is
swinging") this involves terms such as "stick" which are not reducible to
lower-level talk about sense–impressions. Above the common-sense level,
a scientific observation-report ("The pendulum is swinging") involves
terms such as "pendulum" which are not reducible to lower-level common-
sense talk about sticks. At a still higher level, a scientific theory will use
terms like "gravity," which are not reducible to terms used in scientific
observations.

At each level, including the "bottom" level of sense-impression reports,
there is an element of interpretation. Yet the different levels are linked.
Although a higher-level assertion is not reducible to a lower-level one
since it is *not equivalent in meaning*, the *truth* of the higher-level one
depends partly on the *truth* of the lower-level one. This hierarchical picture of language is an oversimplification; however, it does seem to me to
provide a way to avoid a possible misunderstanding of the testability
requirement. The requirement need involve neither reductionism nor a
belief in an uninterpreted basis for all knowledge. It does not depend on a
crudely empiricist epistemology.

More important, the testability requirement is part of scientific practice as this is described even by such antipositivists as Harold Schilling.[10]
There is an accumulation of established scientific knowledge which has
been tested by observation and which is permanent (or virtually so)
because of this testing. Such knowledge includes experimental (that is,

[10] Harold Schilling, *Science and Religion* (New York: Charles Scribner's Sons,
1962), esp. chaps. 5–8.

observational) laws which are not undermined by changes in scientific
theory.[11] It is true that the laws may be reinterpreted by being explained
in relation to new theories, so that the newly interpreted law is not
equivalent in meaning to the old one; nevertheless the law also has a
relatively uninterpreted meaning, and its truth in this form has been
established by reference to observations. Probably the observations would
not have been made were it not for the existence of a scientific theory,
but this does not show that the testability requirement is unnecessary.
It is also true that the observations are usually reported in a language
which includes scientific terms that are relatively theoretical or interpretive as compared with the everyday language of common sense. But the
scientific terms are linked to common-sense terms, though they are not
reducible to common-sense terms. If a nonscientist in the laboratory sees
no spark or feels no tingling pain on touching a wire, the scientist's report
concerning an electrical discharge may be undermined or even falsified.

b. Theories. Someone might concede that perhaps experimental laws
are testable by observations, but insist that theories are not. It is clear that
the evaluation of a theory involves various criteria which are not observational.[12] There are *formal* criteria: internal consistency, coherent conceptual relations, and simplicity or relative independence from *ad hoc*
assumptions. There is an *aesthetic* criterion of "elegance"; although minimized by some scientists, it is stressed by others. Then there is the
explanatory power of the theory in displaying a pattern in many previously unrelated states of affairs. Some would stress the role of scientific
models in this respect. Then there is the *"fertility"* of the theory in stimulating the invention or discovery of new theories, concepts, and experimental laws, and its consistency and coherence with other highly rated
theories. Since there are many different criteria, there is no such thing as
a "knockdown" falsification or a "conclusive" verification of a theory by
reference to observations.

This objection is extremely important in destroying crude positivist
conceptions of scientific "verification." But with reference to the testability
requirement, all it shows is that the requirement is only one among many.
A theory may pass observational tests as well as its rival does, and yet be
rejected because it is inferior when appraised by reference to its fertility,
say, or its internal coherence. If, as some experts claim, it is true that *no*
theory ever fits *all* the relevant observations, then obviously the testability
requirement is not as strict as one might imagine. Also, if it is true that
no theory is ever "falsified" by observations, this is an important point in
understanding the requirement properly. But none of this shows that no
theory is ever *undermined* by observations. A theory is not compatible

---

[11] Cf. Schilling, op. cit., and Ernest Nagel, *The Structure of Science* (New York:
Harcourt, Brace & Co., 1961), chap. 5.

[12] Most of these are outlined in Ian Barbour, *Issues in Science and Religion* (Englewood Cliffs, N.J.: Prentice-Hall, 1966), pp. 144–50. I am greatly indebted to Dr.
Barbour for his balanced and lucid discussions of various issues throughout his book.

with any and every conceivable state of affairs that might be observed. Finally, however many philosophers of science may insist that scientific theories are not evaluated *solely* in terms of whether or not they enable scientists to make precise and specific *predictions* of observable states of affairs, or to *produce* these at will; surely these features of science are important, and surely they mark important differences between scientific theories and theories in metaphysics or in theistic religion.

A different, but related, objection to the testability requirement is that scientific theories are not representations of the real world at all, but are merely useful fictions or regulative maxims. A theory can be neither true nor false, it is said, so it can be neither verified nor falsified; indeed, observations can neither support nor undermine the alleged truth of a theory, for a theory cannot be "true." This objection is relevant only if we accept a nonrealist view of scientific theories. Yet even if we do, we need not reject the testability requirement. Rather, we understand the "test" of a theory to be a test of usefulness rather than of truth.

c. Paradigms. The term "paradigm," as used by Thomas Kuhn,[13] refers to a type of scientific theory which has a special role in science. The paradigm theory, together with certain laws which it explains and perhaps an exemplary application and instrumentation, dominates a whole area of scientific investigation. It not only provides solutions to scientific problems; it largely determines what *counts* as a scientific problem and what *counts* as a scientific solution. It provides a framework of presumptions within which detailed scientific investigation can flourish. When a paradigm is replaced by another paradigm, this is no minor change; it is a scientific revolution. An established paradigm is scarcely affected at all by some of the observations which do not fit in with it. In the overthrow of a paradigm, nonobservational criteria play a major role, and these criteria themselves may be modified or reinterpreted.

It is clear that in the paradigm we find science in a form most remote from observational testing, from "knockdown" falsification or "conclusive" verification by means of specific observations. Paradigms are very different from restricted generalizations such as "All the boys in this room right now have blue eyes." Nevertheless, even Kuhn says that "observation and experience can and must drastically restrict the range of admissible scientific belief, else there would be no science." [14] More specifically, in his account of the "anomalies" which force scientific revolutions he notes that a paradigm makes possible a precision of observational expectations which renders it specially sensitive to possible undermining by anomalous observational findings.[15] Without the paradigm, one would not notice that such-and-such an observed state of affairs is anomalous, yet the paradigm is put in question by this observed state of affairs. When Kuhn says that

[13] Thomas Kuhn, *The Structure of Scientific Revolutions* (Chicago: University of Chicago Press, 1962).
[14] Thomas Kuhn, op. cit., p. 4.
[15] Ibid., p. 65.

paradigms "provide all phenomena except anomalies with a theory-determined place in the scientist's field of vision," [16] he is indicating both a way in which paradigms are relatively *immune* from being undermined by observations and a way in which they are peculiarly *sensitive* to such undermining. Indeed, his account of paradigm sensitivity helps to explain a fact noted by Nagel:

Prescientific beliefs are frequently incapable of being put to definite experiential tests, simply because those beliefs may be vaguely compatible with an indeterminate class of unanalyzed facts. Scientific statements, because they are required to be in agreement with more closely specified materials of observation, face greater risks of being refuted by such data.[17]

d. Presuppositions. Antipositivist writings on science, especially those which stress alleged similarities between science and religion, often maintain that science involves unfalsifiable presuppositions which constitute the "faith" of a scientist. The argument goes as follows: a scientist believes that the world has an order, that it has regularity, that it is dependable. No observable state of affairs could falsify this claim. His faith is not testable by observations. So if a religious faith is not testable by observations, this is not a feature of religion which distinguishes it from science.

Later I shall indicate the one strength and the many weaknesses of this argument. Here I shall distinguish between two different kinds of scientific presupposition. First, there is the paradigm, which we have already considered. A paradigm involves belief in a specific kind of order, regularity, and dependability within a specific area to be investigated by a subcommunity of scientists. Investigations which are carried out within the framework of a paradigm involve a great many implicit or explicit presuppositions. We have seen that paradigms are remote from "knockdown" falsifiability by observations, but nevertheless have not only a resistance but also a *sensitivity* to possible undermining by observations. It would be misleading to say that paradigms are in principle unfalsifiable, for old paradigms *are* replaced by new ones, and this happens partly because of anomalous observations.

Although I suspect that most of what practicing scientists might mean by "scientific faith" arises from paradigms, there is a second type of presupposition which also has a role to play. It has the general form, *"Every X has a Y,"* where it is possible to verify "This X has a Y," but not to falsify it. Consider, for example, *"Every event has a sufficient condition."* Whenever scientists discover an experimental law and apply it to a particular event which is covered by the law, the proposition "This event has a sufficient condition" is verified. But what if scientists cannot find a sufficient condition for an event, for example, the particular movement of a particular electron? They may go on looking, but they may abandon the search. The proposition "Every event has a sufficient condition" is

---

[16] Ibid., p. 96.
[17] Ernest Nagel, op. cit., p. 9.

not falsifiable, yet it may be so undermined by failure to verify that it is abandoned—at least in a specific area of science. In so far as scientists believe in a world "order" or a "regularity," where these terms have a definite sense, the belief is not immune from being undermined by observations, though observations alone do not suffice to overthrow it.

In this section we have examined the requirement that scientific assertions be testable by observations, and we have noted various ways in which it needs to be qualified. Observation involves interpretation. Theories are not tested solely by reference to observations. Paradigms and presuppositions are not falsifiable by observations. In previous sections we considered two other requirements of scientific assertions: logical neutrality and impersonal comprehensibility. Before we move on to see whether religious assertions fulfill any of the three requirements, I should note one important omission in my account: I have not considered the requirements in relation to *social* science. My own view is that special difficulties arise only in relation to the second requirement. Some assertions in social studies, though logically neutral and testable by observation, are not comprehensible impersonally. In that respect, they are not "scientific," though they are nevertheless respectable and important. I am referring to assertions concerning how an agent views his situation, where the agent's views may be very difficult for an investigator to understand unless there is some affinity or rapport between the two men. But I cannot discuss this matter further here.

III. Religious Language and Objectivity

1. Religious Assertions Are Not Logically Neutral

Religious faith, as it was described in Part I, is expressed in such assertions as the following:

"I look on this man's I-Thou attitude toward me as a revelation of a hidden being whose I-Thou attitude is complete and constant."

"I look on the impressive beauty of this sunset as an artistic expression of a hidden numinous being."

"I look on this unconditional moral demand as a command from a hidden being who has rightful authority over my life."

"I look on my concern for meaning in life as a revelation of a being who is the source of the concern and of ultimate meaning."

"I look on my indignant compassion as a revelation of a hidden being whose compassion is infinite."

These assertions are not neutral, but *self-involving*. Each is an expression of attitude, a commitment to interpret a depth-experience as a revelation.

In religious assertions where the word "God" occurs, the meaning of the word "God" is roughly "the hidden being who is such that various attitudinal depth-experiences are appropriate responses." God is the hidden being who is worthy of worship. In using the word "God," a member of a religious community is using self-involving language. He may, of course, be insincere. He may be, as a matter of fact, psychologically neutral. But his language is not logically neutral. It is a requirement of the religious community that his language be self-involving in its meaning.

There are two important exceptions to this. First, many *theological* assertions are second-order statements *about* religious assertions, and are not themselves self-involving. Talk about self-involving assertions need not itself be self-involving. In saying, "I promise . . . ," I do promise; my utterance is self-involving. But in saying, "I promised . . . ," or "He is promising . . . ," or "Promises are self-involving," I do not promise; nor are my utterances in any other way self-involving. Similarly if a theologian says "What Christians mean by 'God' is 'the being worthy of worship,'" the assertion is not self-involving. And even when he says "God is the being worthy of worship," although his assertion is not *explicitly* a second-order statement about religious assertions, it may be second-order implicitly, especially if the context is descriptive.

This leads us to the second exception. The context in which self-involving language is used may be artificially made a "descriptive" one. That is, there may be an implicit agreement among speakers or writers that self-involving elements are to be set aside. A man can use the word "God" to mean, say, "the [alleged] being whom [some] people believe to be worthy of worship," without implying or expressing any religious attitudes himself. In this way it is possible for unbelievers or wavering members of the religious community (or theologians!) to talk about God without insincerity.[18]

Neither of these exceptions detracts from the self-involving character of primary religious assertions. The secondary theological or descriptive uses of religious language are parasitic on the primary use; that is, they depend on the primary use for their meaning. Similarly second-order talk about promises depends on the existence of first-order promise-making, and descriptive uses of the word "good" depend on self-involving uses of the word "good."

2. Religious Assertions Are Not Comprehensible Impersonally

The main point can be dealt with briefly. The account of religious faith in Part I and of this requirement in Part II have already indicated my conclusion. Religious assertions require special personal conditions for understanding. Each depth-experience is an elusive and mysterious ex-

---

[18] For a further discussion of "descriptive" contexts see *The Logic of Self-Involvement,* pp. 50–51, 160–62, 183–85.

perience which a man will not have had unless he has fulfilled various personal conditions. In order to understand what an I-Thou attitude is, one must be responsive to it in others, and this depends on one's own basic life-experience and attitudes to people. Similar conditions apply in the case of other depth-experiences. There are intelligent men, well-trained men, for whom some or all of the descriptions of depth-experiences have little meaning. Yet one can understand the meaning of talk about "God" only to the extent that one understands talk about the depth-experiences. Religious language is directly correlated to depth-experiences in its meaning. So religious assertions are not comprehensible impersonally.

This conclusion, however, needs some clarification and qualification. What constitutes an "understanding" of an assertion? A man may be able to use the words of the assertion without making any gross mistakes concerning its relations with other words. A psychopath, for example, might pick up much of what Wittgenstein calls the "logical grammar" of the word "conscience" by listening to other people talk. Yet in terms of his own experiences he does not understand what a conscience is. Similarly a deprived but intelligent child might learn how to use the word "love," without having had any deep experience of what it is to love and to be loved. Similarly a man of no depth-experiences might learn how to use religious language, for example, that "God" is connected with "worship"; he need not have had a personal experience of worship in order to do this. We seem to need a distinction between *"verbal"* and *"experiential"* understanding or comprehension of language. I cannot explore this further here, but some such distinction is required if the comprehensible-impersonally requirement is to be properly clarified. A man needs depth-experiences for *experiential* understanding of religious language.

3. Religious Assertions Are Not Testable by Observations

In Part II we saw that scientific assertions should be testable by observations. We also noted that science has a presupposition, "Every event has a sufficient condition," which is unfalsifiable. Are religious assertions testable by observations? Are there any unfalsifiable religious presuppositions of the form "Every X has a Y"?

My answer to the second question is, "Maybe." Some believers do hold, for example, that every event has a divine purpose. But religious faith is fundamentally a conviction that *some* depth-experiences are divine revelations. The word "faith" is appropriate for two different reasons. First, "This depth-experience is a revelation" is *unfalsifiable*, like "This event has a sufficient condition." Second, "This depth-experience is a revelation" is *"verified"* only by presupposing the existence of God. The second reason is what distinguishes religious faith from so-called scientific faith.

Do religious assertions resemble scientific assertions in being testable by observations? In four important ways they do not. We shall consider these ways in turn, considering scientific assertions first in each case.

First, although scientific presuppositions, paradigms, and theories are evaluated in terms of various nonobservational criteria, they are also open to support or undermining by *observational tests*. And although scientific observation-reports are not reducible to common-sense observation-reports, they can be supported or undermined by common-sense observation-reports, which thus provide a base on which the whole hierarchical superstructure of science is built. The superstructure of religious and theological assertions, however, is based on reports of elusive and mysterious depth-experiences rather than on common-sense observations. Although talk about God is not reducible to talk about depth-experiences, the former cannot be understood in abstraction from the latter; and if there had never been any depth-experiences, there would be no empirical basis for religion.

Second, scientific observation-reports are in the principle open to *intersubjective testing* by anyone with the requisite intelligence and scientific training. If I think I observe an electrical discharge, but no other scientist does, my observation-report is radically undermined. The intersubjective element in religion, however, is very different. Suppose that other people report fewer depth-experiences or very different ones, or that other people stop having depth-experiences which seem to them to be divine revelations. As a believer I am committed to go on believing in spite of this. I may, as a matter of fact, falter, especially if my own spiritual life has gone dry. But I ought not to falter, for this runs contrary to my religious commitment. Depth-experiences depend on elusive personal conditions, and those which are divine revelations also depend on the free action of God. Men ought not to try to test God; it is God who "tests" men by sometimes withdrawing His presence. There is, to be sure, an intersubjective element in religious faith. The believer holds that God has revealed Himself to other members of the religious community in the *past*. Moreover, the believer's convictions concerning what counts as revelation are derived mainly from the religious community. Faith is a trust in God which is based partly on a trust in intersubjective testimony. But it is not a matter of intersubjective testing or experimenting similar to that in science, for there are two open "variables" in the venture of faith: God and human sin. If God seems to be absent (or dead!) this is either because He has chosen to withhold His presence or because men are not responsive to it.

Third, the interpretive move from common-sense descriptions of events to scientific descriptions is so designed as to enable men to make *precise predictions of observables*. Covering laws are discovered: whenever conditions *C1 to C5* hold, an event of type *T1* occurs. And if men can produce conditions *C1 to C5*, they can thereby produce events of type *T1*. (They can explode an H-bomb.) Scientific theories work not only in that they make the world more intelligible, but also in that they make possible such prediction and control. In religion, however, the interpretive move from depth-experiences to divine revelations does not enable men to make predictions on the basis of covering laws, and still less to produce divine revelations at will.

Fourth, the move from common sense to scientific observation-reports begins with an ontological assumption that there is a real external world which we can observe. A *realist* view of scientific theories may involve some further ontological conviction concerning the nature of the world. No further ontology, however, is entailed. In religion a further ontology *is* entailed. The move from reports of depth-experiences to religious assertions involves an assumption that there exists a hidden divine being, distinct from the world but revealing Himself through the world, a being such that various human attitudes are appropriate responses. This assumption differs even from the scientific realist's assumption concerning the world, a world such that various scientific theories "work." Religious theory, for those who make the crucial assumption that God exists, works in two ways. On the one hand it meets *intellectual needs* by making more intelligible the various depth-experiences-interpreted-as-divine-revelations; for example, it might link the numinous aspect of God with the moral aspect. On the other hand, it meets *spiritual needs* by helping to promote those depth-experiences and interpretations which are believed to bring men into right relation with God; that is, it promotes faith.

In four important ways the testable-by-observations requirement in science thus differentiates science from religion. We should note, however, that religious theory (theology) *may* resemble scientific theory in so far as various nonobservational criteria are used to evaluate it. I say may, because theologians disagree moderately concerning the extent to which theology should be appraised in terms of consistency, internal coherence, and simplicity, and they disagree greatly concerning the attempt to fit theology into a consistent and coherent relation with other disciplines. Even more generally, the spiritual-need emphasis in theology may become more and more dominant in contrast with an intellectual interest in producing a system. The more this happens, the more remote becomes the analogy between theology and scientific theory.

Before I close this section of the paper, I should expose a major weakness. I have failed to grapple with one way in which religious faith *is* in principle testable by observations.[19] Since revelation is a divine *action*, it should make a difference to what happens. A depth-experience must be partially *caused* by God if it is to be a *revelation* of God. Of course some convictions concerning God might be true even though God did not produce them. A critic of religion is committing the "genetic fallacy" if he attacks the truth of some religious convictions by exposing their non-

[19] *Christian* faith, as we saw at the end of Part I, is also testable by observation (i.e., historical investigation) in so far as it depends on beliefs concerning the man Jesus.

divine causal origin. It is possible that a Freudian explanation of my belief
that God is like a father could be correct, yet my belief might nevertheless
be true, by a happy coincidence. Or perhaps it is not a coincidence; perhaps God the Creator made the world in such a way that natural causation would lead to my having this true religious belief. But if my religious
conviction is that *God sometimes actively reveals Himself* in depth-
experiences, this specific conviction involves a causal claim concerning
God. If *all* religious convictions of this specific kind could be accounted
for by reference to nondivine sufficient conditions, then faith in an actively
self-revealing God would be falsified. Such falsification is not possible
in practice, only in principle. But a substantial and rightful undermining
of religious faith is a possibility. If this were not so, the religious believer
would not be making any claim concerning a God who *acts* in the world.
Nothing ventured, nothing claimed.

What kind of *causal claim* is involved? The nearest analogy, I think, is
something like "Without your encouragement, John, I could not have
done it" (or "would not have done it" or "would not have felt it"). Such
a claim can be undermined by behavioral evidence, yet the basis for the
claim is not simply a Humean constant conjunction. The recipient of the
action is in a privileged position to back his claim by referring to his own
private experience. Yet his claim may become untenable in the face of
overwhelming contrary evidence. Similar issues arise when a man claims
that God actively revealed Himself in a depth-experience, so that a human
action or a human feeling was partially caused by God. The recipient of
the divine action is in a privileged position to back his claim, yet it may
become untenable in the face of overwhelming contrary evidence.

For some philosophers no problems arise concerning the need to test
claims concerning divine action by reference to observations. These men
hold that there are two complementary and nonconflicting ways to talk
about some events: as the action of a personal agent (human or divine)
and as an effect of a set of nonpersonal sufficient conditions. I do not think
that this account will stand up to scrutiny. I do not think that we can
have our cake of agent causality if we eat it up with a determinism of
natural causality. Perhaps I am mistaken concerning this, but if I am
not, then my faith in a God who sometimes acts by revealing Himself
in depth-experiences is a faith which is open to undermining by reference
to observations.

IV. CONCLUSIONS

Three conclusions can be drawn concerning differences between religious and scientific assertions. *First,* religious assertions are self-involving,
though second-order theological assertions may be logically neutral, and
there may be special descriptive contexts in which self-involving elements

are set aside. Scientific assertions are logically neutral. *Second,* religious
assertions are understood experientially only to the extent that men have
had various depth-experiences. Scientific assertions are not directly or
indirectly dependent on such conditions for their comprehensibility, and
they are indirectly dependent on different and less personal conditions.
Third, religious assertions are not testable by observations, except where
they involve causal claims concerning divine actions (or where they
depend on historical claims concerning the man Jesus). Scientific assertions are testable by observations, although many are evaluated by reference to nonobservational criteria as well, and many are not falsifiable
solely by observations.

SUGGESTED READINGS

A good history of analytic philosophy can be found in G. J. Warnock, ° *English
Philosophy Since 1900* (London: Oxford University Press, 1969p); J. Passmore,
° *A Hundred Years of Philosophy* (Harmondsworth: Pelican Books, 2nd ed.,
1968p) and J. O. Urmson, *Philosophical Analysis: Its Development Between
the Two World Wars* (Oxford: Clarendon Press, 1956). Three anthologies that
contain much of the important analytic material and good bibliographies: A. J.
Ayer (ed.), ° *Logical Positivism* (New York: Free Press, 1959p); Robert R.
Ammerman (ed.), ° *Classics of Analytic Philosophy* (New York: McGraw-Hill,
1965); Richard Rorty (ed.), ° *The Linguistic Turn* (Chicago: University of
Chicago Press, 1967p). An extensive bibliography on the whole analytic family
of philosophies can be found in Edwards & Pap (eds.), ° *A Modern Introduction to Philosophy* (New York: Free Press, 1973, 3rd ed.), pp. 810–817.

Two good introductions to Wittgenstein are K. T. Fann, ° *Wittgenstein's Con-
ception of Philosophy* (Berkeley: University of California Press, 1969p) and
David Pears, ° *Ludwig Wittgenstein* (New York: Viking Press, 1971p). For a
look at Wittgenstein's life by two admirers see *Norman Malcolm: A Memoir*
(London: Oxford University Press, 1968, rev. ed., p). The following works of
Wittgenstein may also be consulted: *The Blue and Brown Books* (New York:
Harper & Row, 1965p); *Lectures and Conversations on Aesthetics, Psychology
and Religious Belief* (Berkeley: University of California Press, 1966p);
Philosophical Investigations (New York: Macmillan, 3rd edition, 1967); and
Zettel (Berkeley: University of California Press, 1967p).

The basic materials on the current debate surrounding God-talk may be found
in the following anthologies: A. Flew and A. C. MacIntyre (eds.), *New Essays
in Philosophical Theology* (New York: Macmillan, 1955p), Royal Institute of
Philosophy Lectures, Vol. 2, *Talk of God* (New York: St. Martin's Press,
1969p); Robert H. Ayers & William T. Blackstone (eds.), *Religious Language
and Knowledge* (Athens: University of Georgia Press, 1972p); Ian Ramsey
(ed.), *Words About God* (New York: Harper & Row, 1971p); Basil Mitchell
(ed.), *The Philosophy of Religion* (London: Oxford University Press, 1971p);
Ronald E. Santoni (ed.), *Religious Language and the Problem of Religious
Knowledge* (Bloomington: Indiana University Press, 1968p); John Hick (ed.),
Faith and the Philosophers (New York: St. Martin's Press, 1964); Steven M.

Cahn (ed.), *Philosophy of Religion* (New York: Harper & Row, 1970p); and John Donnelly (ed.), *Logical Analysis and Contemporary Theism* (New York: Fordham University Press, 1972). This is just a good start at a complete list.

Some of the better philosophies of religion written from an analytic point of view are Terence Penelhum, *Religion and Rationality* (New York: Random House, 1971); also his ° *Survival and Disembodied Existence* (New York: Humanities Press, 1970) and *Problems of Religious Knowledge* (New York: Herder and Herder, 1972). Penelhum should be read along with John Hick, *Faith and Knowledge* (Ithaca, N.Y.: Cornell University Press, 2nd ed., 1966); *Evil and the God of Love* (New York: St. Maritn's Press, 1966); and his numerous articles out of which the following are selected: "Theology and Verification" reprint in his *Existence of God* (New York: Macmillan, 1964p); "The Justification of Religious Belief" in *Theology*, 1968, pp. 100–107, and numerous articles in *Encyclopedia of Philosophy*. Hick's defense of "eschatological verification" is criticized by Kai Nielsen, "Eschatological Verification" in *Canadian Journal of Theology*, Vol. 9 (1963), pp. 271–281. See Edwards and Pap, op. cit., p. 563, Penelhum, op. cit., and Nielsen, *Contemporary Critiques of Religion* (New York: Herder and Herder, 1971) for more extensive bibliography on this issue.

"Wittgensteinian Fideism" is defended by W. D. Hudson, *Ludwig Wittgenstein —The Bearing of His Philosophy Upon Religious Belief* (Richmond: John Knox Press, 1968p) and "Some Remarks on Wittgenstein's Account of Religious Belief," in *Talk of God*, op. cit. Also see D. Z. Phillips (ed.), *Religion and Understanding* (Oxford: Blackwell, 1967) and D. M. High (ed.), *New Essays on Religious Language* (New York: Oxford University Press, 1969p) which contain papers by "Wittgensteinian Fideists." For a critical discussion see the following articles that also contain bibliographies: Kai Nielsen, "Wittgensteinian Fideism," *Philosophy* (1967); Patrick Sherry, "Truth and the 'Religious Language-Game'," *Philosophy* (1972); F. Gerald Downing, "Games, Families, the Public, and Religion," in the same issue as Sherry; and an article by the latter in *American Philosophical Quarterly*, April 1972, "Is Religion a 'Form of Life'?"; and finally, James Kellenberger, "The Language-Game View of Religion and Religious Certainty," *Canadian Journal of Philosophy*, December 1972.

The following are volumes the student may consult for further study on the issue of God-talk. E. Cell, ° *Language, Existence and God* (Nashville: Abingdon Press, 1971); W. T. Blackstone, ° *The Problem of Religious Knowledge* (Englewood Cliffs, N.J.: Prentice-Hall, 1963p); F. Ferre, ° *Language, Logic and God* (New York: Harper, 1961p); R. Hepburn, *Christianity and Paradox* (London: Watts, 1958p); P. Schmidt, *Religious Knowledge* (New York: Free Press, 1961); T. R. Miles, *Religion and the Scientific Outlook* (London: Allen & Unwin, 1959); A. C. Ewing, *Non-Linguistic Philosophy* (London: Allen & Unwin, 1968); and the many books and articles of H. D. Lewis which argue against the linguistic tide. See the latter's *Experience of God* (London: Allen & Unwin, 1959). Other important attempts to defend God-talk are A. Plantinga, *God and Other Minds* (Ithaca, N.Y.: Cornell University Press, 1967) and Dallas High, *Language, Persons, and Belief* (New York: Oxford University Press, 1967). Ian T. Ramsey has made important contributions to the current discussion. See his *Religious Language* (New York: Macmillan, 1957) and *Christian Discourse* (London: Oxford University Press, 1965). John Macquarrie in his *God-Talk* (New York: Harper & Row, 1967) makes a defense of God-talk out of the existential tradition. Donald Evans has written an important contribution that makes use of insights from John Austin. See his *The Logic of Self-*

Involvement (London: SCM, 1963). See also W. Zuurdeeg, *An Analytical Philosophy of Religion* (Nashville: Abingdon Press, 1958).

And finally these volumes deserve mention as they try to break new ground: R. S. Heimbeck, ° *Theology and Meaning* (Stanford: Stanford University Press, 1969); James Richmond, *Theology and Metaphysics* (New York: SCM Press, 1970); and J. Ross, *Philosophical Theology* (Indianapolis: Bobbs-Merrill, 1969), the latter by drawing on the Thomistic tradition; Jerry Gill, ° *The Possibility of Religious Knowledge* (Grand Rapids: Erdmans, 1971p); Langdon Gilkey, *Naming the Whirlwind: The Renewal of God-Language* (Indianapolis: Bobbs-Merrill, 1969p); John E. Smith, *The Analogy of Experience* (New York: Harper & Row, 1972); and James Kellenberger, *Religious Discovery, Faith and Knowledge* (New York: Prentice-Hall, 1972).

CHAPTER FIVE

Atheism: Failure of Nerve
or Rational Belief?

In our generation atheism has achieved the status of a viable standpoint with a consequent life-style for a great many people. The atheist is no longer the "odd" character in the village who, while being singled out for ridicule by the morally upright, is cherished because he serves as an example of what one ought not be. To be an atheist is not to be a deviate; for it is now the *religious* who are looked upon as being less than what one ought to be. To be religious has come to mean, at least for some, that one is dogmatic, uptight, uninformed, superstitious, and so on. The contemporary atheist [1] is not an atheist because he is hesitant to adopt the rigors of a religious discipline that demands too much, but rather because religion has come to demand too little. It is on *moral* and *rational* grounds that contemporary atheists make their stand; belief in God is immoral and irrational.

Contemporary atheism is rooted in man's sense of autonomy. *I* am responsible for my own acts, whether good or bad. Religion is an escape from my responsibility for my creation of my essence. Religion destroys human freedom and dignity. One finds this argument particularly in Sartre and Camus. [2]

---

[1] I do not mean to imply that what follows was not also true of past atheists. My point is that our general opinion of atheism has shifted from condemnation to respect. Atheists also have their values and their life-style is a demanding one. See M. Novak, "The Christian and the Atheist," *A Time to Build* (New York: Macmillan, 1967), pp. 51–59.

[2] See essays by Sartre and Camus in Chapter Three and Camus, *The Rebel* (New York: Random House, 1956), especially pp. 55–104.

In this chapter the reader confronts *reasons* for being an atheist. These reasons can be classified under four headings.[3] First, religion is *patho-logical;* it is a sign of a sick person. Religion is a universal neurosis that must now be cured. A variant on this theme is the claim that religion is simply society's goals idealized and reinforced by divine sanctions and threats.

Second, theism belongs to a world-view that is no longer viable; it is *superstitious.* Religion belongs to the childhood of mankind and we have outgrown it. We no longer have need of spirits and demons to understand our experience. The scientific view of the world makes belief in God obsolete. The obsolescence of religion is not simply its conceptual frame-work, which can be updated by translation into, for example, existential [4] or process [5] language. Religion is at its *core* a throwback to childhood and must be outgrown.

The third reason for atheism, and the reason most widely adopted today by many analytically oriented philosophers, is that religious assertions are *unintelligible.* The "unintelligibility" of religious language has been in-vestigated in Chapter Four. The argument, briefly stated, is that religious assertions have no cognitive value because the user cannot give adequate criteria for establishing the truth or falsity of such assertions. If one responds by claiming that these assertions still have *emotive* meaning, then the atheist either raises reason one above or asserts that no elaborate critique is necessary. After all, religious "assertions"(?) are *merely* emo-tive or ideological.

The fourth reason for adopting atheism as a standpoint is that theism is *contradictory.* Although a number of such critiques are current, this chapter will deal primarily with the *problem of evil.* It is the contention of many atheists that the fact of evil contradicts the claims of theism that God is all-powerful and all-good (loving). "Is he willing to prevent evil, but not able? Then is he impotent? Is he able, but not willing? Then is he malevolent? Is he both able and willing? Whence then is evil?" [6] Judged on the scale of justice, God comes out to be unjust. As the poem on a gravestone has it,

> Here lies Martin Elginbrode
> Have mercy on me Lawd Gawd
> As I would have on you
> If I was Lawd Gawd
> And you were Martin Elginbrode

---

[3] I have followed Stenson here but have developed the classifications my own way. Sten Stenson, *Sense and Nonsense in Religion* (New York: Abingdon Press, 1969), pp. 16–21.

[4] See essays by R. Bultmann and P. Tillich.

[5] See essays in Chapter Six.

[6] David Hume, *Dialogues Concerning Natural Religion* (New York: Hafner Pub-lishing Co., 1959), p. 66. In Chapter Six this issue is raised within the context of process-theology.

Based on the experience of evil in the world God does not show a morality higher than man but less than man.

H. W. Richardson has distinguished three types of atheism: atheism of protest, atheism of boredom, and atheism of concern.[7] Atheism of *protest* exists only because the traditional theistic position continues to be affirmed. This atheism derives its vitality from the affirmations it opposes. If the affirmation dies so does the protest. "You can rebel only as long as Mother and Father are there." Atheism of protest, not surprisingly then, is found within the churches; it is theologians (?) who are proclaiming "God is dead" in our time. The essay by L. Gilkey surveys these Death-of-God theologies. And it should be noted that these theologians are not claiming that God is dead because people believe in some outmoded *conception of God*. They are saying that the God proclaimed by the churches is dead.

But there is another form of atheism widespread among those whom James Pike has called the "Church Alumni." Richardson calls this type of atheism the atheism of *boredom*. The traditional problems that gave rise to belief or disbelief in God no longer appear to be live issues. Many today are simply not interested in questions about the virgin birth, the historicity of the resurrection of Jesus, and so on, or even the very existence and nature of God. They have simply learned to live without these concerns. The debate between the theist *and* the antheist is a bore. Who could care less? As Herman Tennessen states it, "Atheism is extinct in the more advanced parts of the world—for lack of opposites. A serious atheist is considered in Scandinavia a slightly ludicrous bore. The myths are neither pompously condemned nor solemnly repudiated, but rather conceived as sweet and charming subjects for art and poetry—like old-fashioned steam engines and antique hot-water bottles." [8]

And finally, there is an atheism of *concern*. The problems that traditional theism dealt with are no longer primary. New *concerns* and life-styles have resulted in a whole new set of problems for contemporary thinkers. This position is not strictly atheistic or theistic. Concerned people are experimenting with all kinds of standpoints and life–styles.[9] We do not know yet what will emerge. What is certain is that the *future* is open and we must be concerned about creating standpoints and life-styles that make possible a responsive, sensitive, gentle, self-fulfilled, trusting, celebrating *human* being. As Toffler has reminded us: "If we do not learn from history, we shall be compelled to relive it. True. But if we do not change the future, we shall be compelled to endure it. And that could be worse." [10]

[7] Herbert W. Richardson, *Toward an American Theology* (New York: Harper & Row, 1967), pp. 7–8. The whole volume can be read with profit.

[8] Quoted by Kai Nielson, *Reason and Practice* (New York: Harper & Row, 1971), p. 257.

[9] See the essays in Chapter One and Chapter Seven which exhibit the polymorphus diversity (perversity?) of many today.

[10] Alvin Toffler (ed.), *The Futurists* (New York: Random House, 1972), p. 3.

In the essays that follow, Langdon Gilkey reports on the antheism of protest currently found in theology itself. Edward H. Maddon evaluates the typical solutions to the problem of evil put forward by theists. John Hick's essay defends theism by arguing that the reasons usually given for atheism (reasons 1, 2 and 4 mentioned previously) are not conclusive. Kai Nielsen's careful analysis not only gives reasons for atheism but defends atheism against the charges of moral bankruptcy. Erich Fromm argues that we must move beyond atheism or theism to humanism.

THE RADICAL THEOLOGIES

Langdon Gilkey

LANGDON GILKEY is Professor of Theology at the University of Chicago Divinity School. He is the author of *Maker of Heaven and Earth* (1959) and *Naming the Whirlwind: The Renewal of God-Language* (1969), among others.

The first striking trait of the present situation in theology is its sharp reversal of all that characterized the neoorthodox period that preceded it. For the latter, as we have seen, religious existence and so theological language were based solely on the certainty of faith in the transcendent divine Word and were separated as fully as possible from the ambiguities of secular experience in the world. In the present situation, on the other hand, religious existence and theological discourse are in part immobilized and in part energized by the secular in all of its aspects. On the one hand, because of that secular spirit, a sense of doubt, of emptiness, and at best of preliminary and tentative steps forward pervades the theological enterprise. On the other hand, whatever elements of creative life and power exist in our churches are to be found precisely in the identity of Christian existence with the suffering, problems, and hopes of the world. Instead of blocking out the world and centering itself on the relation to the transcendent, the contemporary religious and theological mood blocks out the transcendent dimension of religion and concentrates its energies on being "secular" and "worldly" in both thought and practice, theology and behavior.

This movement toward the world characterizes every aspect of the Church's present situation. As we shall see, it dominates all its most recent theologies; it has led within the last few years to an almost total rethinking and potential restructuring of the task of the Church in relation to the world and of the understanding of the ministry of the Church; and it has resulted both in a new awareness of the responsibility of the Christian to and for the world, and in a new view of the Christian style of life as one characterized by worldly action rather than by inward obedience and faith. Thus has the Urban Training Center for ministers in the midst of the city rightly become the symbol of present creative movements within Christianity, as formerly the theological classrooms in the seminary, and the pulpit in the church, were the symbols of a theology based on the inward reception of the divine Word in faith. In the midst of such a sudden and sharp reversal as this—it manifested itself clearly only as recently as 1963—theological concepts as well as ecclesiastical forms are bound to be in ferment, with new methods of both theology and ministry being tried, old doctrines and attitudes torn down, rejected, or radically reformulated, and a wide variety of untested positions and approaches appearing on the scene. Theoretically, practically, and institutionally, wherever one looks, in Protestantism, Catholicism, or Judaism, things are radically fluid, nothing is certain, and all oracles or prophecies are suspect.

It was Dietrich Bonhoeffer, martyred by the Nazis, who became the main instigator and so creator of this radical movement toward the world, and his influence has correspondingly been immense. Although this writer believes that Bonhoeffer himself probably retained the centrality of the vertical dimension of faith in relation to God—and therefore remained fundamentally neoorthodox—nevertheless, some of the things he *said* in his latest writings could be interpreted as a rejection of this whole religious or vertical dimension of Christianity in favor of action in and for the world.[1] Man has, he wrote, come of age; he no longer needs God to solve his problems, and the symbol God has long since become meaningless to the world's important questions.[2] Thus real Christianity is "religionless."[3] It does not seek God to fulfill a need in us; it turns its face from the religious and so from God, and toward the world, which it serves in love and self-giving. A creative Christianity is not religious, dependent on God, but worldly, being in the world as Jesus had been.

When this religionless and worldly form of neoorthodox Lutheranism crossed both English Channel and Atlantic Ocean, and there met a form of theology and Church life much more closely related to the secular

---

[1] Dietrich Bonhoeffer, *Letters and Papers from Prison* (London: Fontana Books, 1963), especially pp. 88–125.

[2] "Man has learned to cope with all questions of importance without recourse to God as a working hypothesis. . . . It is becoming evident that everything goes along without 'God' and just as well as before." Ibid., pp. 106–107.

[3] The word "religionless" has, like many important theological words, a recently ambiguous history. The present author can think of three quite distinct meanings or connotations theologically of the word: (1) that of Barth, where "religionless" means a faith founded on special revelation, and so solely on the initiative of God, rather than on "human religion," and thus on the initiative of man; (2) a form of Christian faith in God which realizes itself, not in "religious" action (worship, prayer, and so on) directed at God or the Church, but "secular action" in the world, suffering and serving there—this is, we take it, Bonhoeffer's meaning; (3) a form of "religionless faith" which is not only "worldly" in its arena of action, but unrelated to God at all and so related only to the human Jesus—which we take it is the understanding of "religionless" in the radical theologians, which understanding we will be discussing in this chapter. On the whole, this author thinks the whole category "religionless" applied to what is patently and in ordinary usage a form of religion, whether we speak of definitions (1), (2), or (3) above, creates more confusion than clarity in theology.

world than is any Continental religiosity, its radical implications were actualized. For as we have noted, the internal dissolution of neoorthodoxy had been proceeding apace in empiricist and secular America, its language had become arduous and unreal, and its experiences elusive—the whole superstructure of neoorthodoxy, with its transcendent realities, its unobservable events, and its esoteric forms of word and sacrament, had in the new, postwar world gradually become a burden rather than a refuge from chaos, as it had been before. In this American mood, Bonhoeffer exploded: his words functioned now in a context of secularity rather than in that of Lutheranism, and the "God is dead" theology appeared. The key to understanding the ferment, therefore, is to comprehend (1) the dissolution of neoorthodox theology, (2) the character, scope, and power of the secular spirit in the American cultural and so Church scene, and (3) to see the resulting radical theology as an effort to interpret Christianity, as Bonhoeffer said, in worldly terms, where "worldly" is defined and limited by the secular spirit as we have sought to describe it.

The radical or "God is dead" theology, which has captured so much of our attention in the last two or three years, is therefore an attempt to understand Christianity from a secular point of view, within terms of the world view of secular man. It is, as we said in Chapter I, immensely important for two reasons: (1) because it expresses the secular mind of modern religious and Christian man, and thus is in much closer touch than was neoorthodoxy with the actual spiritual situation of both clergy and laity in the second half of the twentieth century; (2) because radical theology forces theological attention on the primary rather than the secondary theological problems of our age. By raising radically the question of the reality of God, by asserting that modern man has inwardly lost God, and by denying that Christian man has any need of God or that Christian faith has any essential relation to him, this theology has forced theological reflection to deal directly, for the first time in this century, with the question of God. Is there anything beyond the secular to talk about; is any sort of religious language meaningful, is there any Word beyond human words, any reality beyond the contingent, relative realities around us—or is the whole traditional transcendent reference of Christian faith irrelevant, empty, or meaningless in our age? These are the questions which express contemporary Christian doubts—and such doubts are universally prevalent—and therefore should exercise contemporary theological reflection. To this writer, other current options in theology are to be understood and judged with regard to their relevance in the light of this primary question of the reality of God and the meaningfulness of language about him in our secular age and for us secular men—who aim to be Christians. Without some answer to this question of God, all talk about Word and sacrament, about scripture and hermeneutic, about the covenant community of the Church, about a Christ who is Lord of our life and of history, and about an eschatological interpretation of history in God's action, is vain and empty—for without God these do not exist as theological concerns. Let us, therefore, turn to the radical theologians and see the way in which they have raised these problems with which all religious thought must now deal. We shall confine ourselves to the movement as it has appeared in America, because here it is, I believe, more radical than in England or on the Continent, and thus focuses the central issues for theology more sharply. [4]

The central theme that unites the radical theologians is well expressed in the enigmatic slogan "God is dead." [5] Although each of them means by this phrase something slightly different, its general import for all is that, first, the God who has been the center of faith and theological reflection for the Judeo-Christian tradition is now seen to be nonexistent, unreal, and an illusion; and, secondly, that Christianity (or Judaism)[6] must henceforth understand itself without him. In slightly different ways, therefore, this group accepts as the truth the naturalistic viewpoint characteristic of the secular spirit as we have described it: we live in a cosmos without God, without an ultimate coherence or meaning on which we can depend and to which we should in faith, worship, and obedience relate

---

[4] This is the reason, as we noted above, that we shall not discuss the most widely read of the general group of radical theologians, namely Bishop John Robinson. However, such writers as R. B. Braithwaite and John Wren-Lewis in England have, as lay theologians, represented positions similar to those discussed below. Generally speaking, however, the debate in England has not taken as radical a form as it has here.

We shall also not discuss various Continental representatives of the "absence of God" movement, such as Herbert Braun and Arnold Metzger. The reason is that, to this writer at least, while these men are very much aware of our present inability to speak of God or to experience him, they do not seem to conclude from this that God is *unreal* and that consequently we live in a naturalistic universe devoid of all deity. The problem for them is, therefore, to find some experienced aspect of life: the Word, the relations of men to men, our ordinary life of hope, and so on, in which the hiddenness of God may become presence, and so in which God and language about him may be found. It is not, therefore, the problem of constructing a form of Christianity which has within it no relation at all to deity. The ontological framework for the experience of the "absence of God" in Continental theology remains the reality of a God now hidden, veiled, or absent; the ontological framework for the experience of the "absence of God" in the American movement is a naturalistic universe, which makes it a much more radical movement. The Continentals agree that, in our *experienced world*, God is absent, but as children of the Word of God theology, this does not mean to them that God is unreal; the Americans, being more empirical and less "Word of God" in their theological approach, conclude from the absence of God in our experienced world that he is unreal, and that therefore the cosmos is merely "blind nature." The Continental position, that God is absent from secular experience, but still there in his Word, is in America best represented by Gabriel Vahanian in his many searching and yet lively books.

[5] Ironically, all the strange linguistic puzzles and weird entailments that arise when we speak of God's existence—e.g., how it can be that *he* exists, how *he*, being God, must exist *necessarily,* etc.—crop up again when we try "to say that he is dead. For, we ask, how can *God* die? If he be God, surely he is eternal by definition and so cannot be contingent and mortal. Thus if he ever has been at all—and he must have been "alive" in order to be able to "die"—then how could *he* ever cease to be?

[6] In these remarks, I refer to Judaism as well as to Christianity because (*a*) secularism has had many of the same effects on Judaism, and (*b*) one of the most powerful expressions of this movement has come from Rabbi Richard Rubenstein, whose thought we will summarize briefly below.

ourselves. And as a consequence, what meaning we can find in life must come from our own autonomous human powers, and what religion we can affirm must be one structured alone on our own worldly obligations and possibilities.

For all of them, moreover, it is the *authentic* God of Christian (or Jewish) faith who is gone. They are *not* attacking an idol, a misunderstanding of God, a wrong sort of theological conception of God—perhaps philosophical or mythological. It is the God to which our symbols seek to point who is dead, not our own faulty interpretation of him. What they are saying is that there is no God anywhere; the cosmos is stripped bare of such a divine being, or of such a divine source of being. It is not that God is hiding, or beyond our experience; it is that the total universe is made up of rocks, stars, and beetles, and nothing at all like God is there or ever has been there. Thus for most of them the strange word "death" in the phrase "death of God," implying as it does that what is now said to be "dead" was once alive, refers only to a *cultural* event, the death of *belief* in God, which they accept as a fact of our time. In the same way one might speak meaningfully of the "death of the witches" in the eighteenth and nineteenth centuries, and not imply thereby that witches had been really existent in the seventeenth century, when they were believed in. Obviously this disbelief in the reality of God has for some time been characteristic of the atheist and humanist traditions in Western culture. What is new in this movement is the acceptance by a group of theologians of this secular spirit as true, and the attempt to formulate an interpretation of Christianity or of Judaism on its basis.

When we scrutinize in more detail the positive content of radical theology, we find, I think, six guiding principles that characterize most of its present forms. The way in which all thought takes its shape in reaction to what preceded it is here vividly illustrated: these six principles are almost the exact inverse of the corresponding principles of neoorthodoxy we have noted. One qualification must be made: while, as we shall see, Altizer shares the three most important of these principles, nevertheless his thought deviates importantly from the last three. Let us now review these basic affirmations of radical theology, and then show how each of the three men interprets them in his own unique way.

(1) The unreality of God for our age; his absence from our current experience; the irrelevance and meaninglessness of all talk about him; the emptiness and actual harmfulness of any so-called relation to him; the difficulty of understanding our experience of evil if we try to believe in him. Above all, the impossibility of being contemporary and secular, that is, of being *ourselves*, if we as Christians try to believe and speak of God—all of these leading to the one central assertion: God is dead in our time. (2) The principle of the "coming of age of man," that is, that man does not need God as the center of his existence. This means, in terms of a doctrine of man, the denial of the *imago dei,* or of any religious *a priori* or religious dimension as basic to man. Here man is in his essential

nature viewed as autonomous and not theonomous; and as autonomous he is thoroughly capable through his own rational, moral, and social powers of "getting along." There follows as a consequence the affirmation of the world and so of secular culture, created by autonomous man, as providing the sole relevant environment, spiritual as well as physical, in which modern man and so the modern Christian can live. Thus the standards that the world recognizes as normative for inquiry are accepted as valid totally in theology; the attitudes accepted in that world determine what Christians can believe; and, presumably, the goals of the world's life are regarded as normative for our moral life—though there appears to be real ambiguity with regard to this latter point.

(3) With the loss of the divine, and so any possibility of a category of revelation or of religious experience, there is in Christian faith no longer any "religious mode of knowing" and thus no possibility of a deposit of sacred truth, held in either scripture or tradition and received by faith. The Divine Word and faith, therefore, cease to be authorities for valid theological statements. Consequently a new principle appears: the restriction of theological statements to what I can actually believe and accept myself, and so to what makes sense in my cultural context, whose principles I share in my thinking. This may be called, as it was in the Enlightenment, the principle of personal intellectual honesty, a refusal to accept any statement as true on a merely authoritative or traditional ground [7] (for example, because it is "the Biblical view," or because "the Church has always said that . . ."). There is here, then, no bias toward saving or even reinterpreting any elements of Christian belief that are not immediately commensurate with the modern understanding. (4) The centrality of the *historical* Jesus as our sole Lord, as he who ethically claims and guides us into the new worldly life, and as the sole subject of contemporary theological discourse. (5) The tendency to dispense with all mythological, suprahistorical, divine, eschatological, or otherwise nonvisible and merely "theological" entities or categories because they are meaningless in a secular age; and the consequent confining of attention to this world and to what is directly visible, experienceable, and verifiable within it.

(6) Finally, this is an action-centered view of human existence. It repudiates the neoorthodox view that one must have one's faith and one's theology in hand before one enters the world to act creatively—how many people in the civil rights or the peace movements have read Barth, Niebuhr, or even Luther? Rather, if man does not "need" God to do good —and the evidence seems to indicate that he does not—then why waste time on the abstract theological matters of faith before one plunges into

---

[7] John Locke stated this same principle in 1700: "I think there is one unerring mark of it [a love of truth] viz. The not entertaining any Proposition with greater assurance than the proofs it is built on will warrant. Whoever goes beyond this measure of Assent, 'tis plain receives not Truth in the love of it; loves not Truth for Truth's sake, but for some other bye end." "Of Enthusiasm," from *Essay Concerning Human Understanding*.

the busy life of the world? Is there any legitimate role that religion, understood as the relation to God of the individual soul, plays in being a Christian, which surely means simply and solely "standing by the neighbor in the world"? Has not this sort of "religion," this emphasis on an impractical faith and theology centered in the parish church, become merely a way of justifying the religious establishments of the middle class which shun creative worldliness in the cities? No, says the modern man, to be a Christian is to act, to become involved, to enter the worldly scene in love and service, and *there* to be like "Jesus to the world." In doing this, such theology as is relevant, that is, such experience of the divine as might help a real Christian faith, will be discovered and then fashioned. Theology does not precede and condition action in the world; insofar as it exists and is relevant at all, it follows it and formulates what is experienced of the divine there; and faith is merely one's inner response to what one discovers of God by being a good neighbor within the worldly scene, or perhaps by being involved in revolutionary action. As Aristotle might have said to Luther: "One becomes good, and so becomes a believer, by doing good actions—not by believing first and then acting afterwards." [8] Needless to say, in this way the radical theology challenged at its deepest level the predominance of faith and of theology as prerequisites to active life in the Church and tended to make life in the academic seminaries of our land even more frustrated than it was before!

William Hamilton was the earliest, and perhaps remains the most influential, of the radical theologians.[9] He found himself, he says, unable as a theologian to speak of God for two main reasons: (1) the evil of the world made it impossible for him honestly to believe in, or even to wish to believe in, a God who ruled over nature and history; (2) the absence of God in his own experience, his inability to encounter God through faith, Word, or prayer, meant that there was, when he was honest with himself, no basis for either believing in God or speaking about him any longer. As he put this, doubt had so permeated faith as to take away all of the latter's certainty and so its power to give us knowledge of God. "Perhaps we ought to conclude that the special Christian burden of our time is the situation of being without God. There is for some reason no possession of God for us, but only a hope, only a waiting. . . . To be a Christian today is to stand, somehow, as a man without God, but with hope." [10]

Thus any theological language which presupposes either the gift or the present possession of faith is, if we are honest, neither valid nor authoritative. We cannot easily say "faith declares," or "faith assures us," or "faith

[8] Cf. Martin Luther, *The Treatise on Christian Liberty*.

[9] The best expression of the early stages of Hamilton's "radical" thought is found in his book *The New Essence of Christianity* (New York: Association Press, 1961); later developments of Hamilton's theology can be seen in his essays in the book, written with Thomas Altizer, *Radical Theology and the Death of God* (Indianapolis: Bobbs-Merrill, 1966).

[10] Hamilton, *The New Essence*, pp. 63–64.

knows" [11] when we speak of God, for in fact our faith, being not a present possession but only a hope, has no cognitive powers and thus is not able to say any of these things, and so neither should we.[12] Theology cannot, therefore, begin with faith as if it were a cognitively certain starting point. For we are personally not at all *at* that starting point, and in reality our faith is not at all certain that it knows God. Consequently, since Hamilton has neither interest nor confidence in natural theology or metaphysical analysis, he finds no grounds for saying anything whatsoever about God.

This weakening of the cognitive certainty of personal faith is, I think, the crucial element in the movement we have been tracing from neo-orthodoxy to the radical theology, and Hamilton has been the most helpful in documenting it in his writings. In neoorthodoxy, as we saw, all knowledge of God and so all language about him developed from the faith encounter. The intelligibility and so certainty of its God-language were, therefore, directly dependent on the cognitive power, that is, the definiteness, the authenticity, and the certainty involved in the faith relationship to God. Outside of that relation to the "Wholly Other," experience in general was devoid of God, the world was secular, and no theological language was possible. When, therefore, that relation itself seemed to dissolve through the acids of secularity, the sole touch to God in neo-orthodoxy vanished as well. It is, says Hamilton, "a short step, but a critical one, to move from the otherness of God to the absence of God." [13]

Since the publication of this earlier book, Hamilton's thought with regard to God has become a good deal more radical. He has dropped his

[11] See the following from H. Richard Niebuhr as a particularly clear and persuasive example of the way the older theology regarded (1) *faith* as a direct and relatively autonomous cognitive relation to God in which God is "known" as objective reality, and (2) *theology,* therefore, as the rational explication of what is known of God in "religious faith"; "It [theos] is the name for that objective being, that other-than-the-self, which men have before them as they *believe* rather than as they see, hear, feel, or even as they reason. This objective reality—God or the gods—is acknowledged or known in faith we say. . . . Theology must attend to the God of faith if it is to understand faith no less than it must attend to faith in God if it would understand God. Faith is at least as much an unavoidable counterpart of the presence of God as sense experience is an unavoidable counterpart of the presence of natural entities or powers . . . but faith and God belong together somewhat as sense experience and physical reality do." H. Richard Niebuhr, *Radical Monotheism and Western Culture* (New York: Harper & Bros., 1943), pp. 12 and 13.

[12] "Those of us who are trying to make the Christian faith intelligible to ourselves and to others have probably spent too much time and too many words saying that we saw and believed what we did not truly see and believe, and we did not like the experience of having deceived ourselves, even if we deceived no one else." Hamilton, *The New Essence,* pp. 28–29. Here is a clear expression not only of the paucity of present faith, but also of what we have called the "principle of radical personal honesty," and so the rejection of theological statements on the sole basis of either scripture or tradition. It is surely also significant of our wider spiritual situation that close on the heels of the linguistic philosophers' denial of the cognitive powers of speculative reason comes the radical theologians' equally vehement denial of the cognitive powers of religious faith. Perhaps the main question of this book is, when all such transimmediate cognitive powers are culturally denied, how *does* the Church know "God"?

[13] Ibid., p. 55.

earlier categories of "waiting" for God, and of "enjoying God" instead of "needing Him." Thus the absence or removal of God have been replaced by "the death of God," "My Protestant has no God, has no faith in God, and affirms both the death of God and all forms of theism," and, now "the death of God radical theologians . . . are men without God who do not anticipate his return." [14]

This death, moreover, is not merely an individual matter, says Hamilton, but a fact for our whole culture, for everyone. It represents a historic, cultural event that signifies an irrevocable change in fundamental attitudes and so the virtual impossibility for men now to believe in God, if, of course, they are real participants in our contemporary cultural life. He and his group, he says, witness to this event [the death of the experience and so the symbol of God] as happening objectively in our time,[15] that is, as a cultural event of universal, contemporary scope. In speaking, then, of the death of God, Hamilton does not seem to envision any change in the ontological structure of the universe as does Altizer, but he does imply a change in the character of our cultural mood or spirit, a change so fundamental as to make belief in God impossible in our age.

How is it possible to be a Christian in this time of the death of God; can there be a religionless and godless Christian theology? Hamilton answers this question, and so distinguishes himself from atheistic humanism, in terms of a continuing and, to him, essential relationship to Jesus and to the community formed around and through him. Jesus retains, in his view, a central and necessary role in the Christian's life, even if God be gone. It is he who, in effect, gives us a model of who we are and what we should be and do, and so who shapes that style of life which characterizes Christian existence. He loved the world, served it, stood beside the neighbor in need, and finally suffered in its hands out of love; this pattern is our pattern, so we should "become like Jesus in and to the world." [16] Christian faith, then, is not a relation to God or a basis of knowing God, surrendering to him or serving him; it is, rather, "a place to be," namely being in the world alongside the neighbor in love. Thus human beings, in their acts of love through community, can do for one another all that "God" was once supposed to have done, and all the problems that can be solved are removable by such loving communal action.[17]

As these last comments indicate, a second important shift in Hamilton's theology has been his gradually growing optimism about man and about the possibility of historical progress. This optimism, to be sure, has always been implicit: to relinquish God and to retain a pessimistic view of man's capabilities is to invite despair. Furthermore, one of Hamilton's main themes has been the affirmation of man's autonomy. By this he means that man does not need God at all; if man has problems, and of course he does,

[14] Altizer and Hamilton, *Radical Theology*, pp. 37 and 6.
[15] Cf. Ibid., pp. 27–28 and 46–47.
[16] Ibid., p. 49.
[17] Ibid., p. 116, and especially "The New Optimism," pp. 157–169.

solutions to these problems must come from man himself: "There are thus no places in the self or the world . . . where problems emerge that only God can solve. There are problems and needs, to be sure, but the world itself is the source of the solutions, not God." [18] In such a situation, where there are no intractable human dilemmas but only "problems" solvable by man's capacities, religion, which proclaims man's religious dependence on God for the resolution of his basic difficulties, can be only a useless and distracting "crutch." [19] By implication, then, even in his darker earlier writings, Hamilton implied that, if men were free of religion and committed with Jesus to serving the world, man's major problems might be solved.

Now, however, this optimism has become explicit: the world is no longer cruel, and our godlessness is no tragic fate. Rather, the world is a place of joy, of creative discovery, of developing reform, and of expanding values. If we Christians can catch this mood—from the social sciences, our developing technology, creative and innocent social protest, former President Johnson himself, contemporary poetry, song, the dance, and the Beatles—we can be relieved of our theological gloom and learn to play, to be vital, creative, and good. Secular progress on all front—especially in civil rights and the peace movement—in our democratic, pluralistic, and idealistic society assures us that man in community can make a better life for himself, and the Christian should join in—though what the

[18] Ibid., p. 116. In these remarks, and in his acceptance of Bonhoeffer's description of God as a "problem-solver," Hamilton has indicated clearly from the beginning his fundamentally optimistic or autonomous view of man. For "problems" are by nature solvable by human brains and application: like mending a roof, solving an equation, or dealing with a recalcitrant germ, mountainside, or even neighbor. They are soluble, to be mastered by a better technique, a more considered approach, a more energetic and dedicated application of will, i.e., they are to be solved by human powers in human ways. Classically, theology has dealt not with such "problems" but with real "dilemmas," where human powers are not effective, where precisely man finds himself unable to cope, either by intelligence or by will, with what confronts him: namely sin, fate, and death. To call God a "problem solver" is, therefore, first of all to misinterpret the main thrust of the classical tradition *vis à vis* the *kind* of need fulfilled by God, but even more it is *ipso facto* to declare that such dilemmas do not in fact exist, and so that everything that confronts man is a problem which human will and intelligence can resolve. In other words, it is to enunciate a very optimistic view of the human condition as subject to neither sin nor fate, and so as capable, in concert if not individually, of solving all the problems of life that can in any way be resolved.

[19] Clearly Hamilton more and more reflects the fundamental concepts of the great atheistic humanist, Ludwig Feuerbach: for Feuerbach, (1) belief in God is a diversion from man's real work for man, making him think that without his effort the good can be accomplished; religion provides, that is, an unreal and futile *deus ex machina* that keeps man from active service; (2) what people once thought that only God could do, the community can do: judging, forgiving, supporting in time of individual need, providing ethical ideals, and so on. As Feuerbach says, the worship and dependence given to God should be directed at the species; and the love man thinks he owes to God, he should owe to his neighbor. The only significant difference between Feuerbach's thought and Hamilton's present position is the centrality of Jesus in the theology of the latter. Whether Hamilton can accept so much of Feuerbach and not go all the way to humanism with him is a question we shall further discuss in Chapter 5. Cf. Ludwig Feuerbach, *The Essence of Christianity* (New York: Harper Torchbooks, 1957).

Christian (or Jesus) adds to the game is not so easy any longer to discover. It seems unquestionable to this observer that more and more
Hamilton's thought is taking on the lineaments of liberal humanistic faith
in man at the very moment when, ironically, the most "with it" movements
in secularism, the hippies, the New Left, and the black power movement
have precisely lost this faith in the possibilities of our democratic society.
Only the continuing centering of this ethical humanism on the figure of
Jesus as inspiration and model and Hamilton's personal sense of identification with the Christian community keep this thought in touch with any
elements of the classical Christian tradition.[20]

One of the continuing dilemmas of radical theology, well illustrated by
Hamilton, is the problem of method, that is, of the sources, content, and
criteria of theology as a form of thought. In line with the "secular spirit"
in both its antimetaphysical and its antitheological aspects, radical theology has rejected both metaphysical speculation and special religious
sources, such as revelation or religious experience, for theological reflection, and it has embraced the secular as providing the materials, insights,
and criteria for its thinking. Thus theology has relinquished any "home
ground," so to speak, for its thought, and must find its place among the
specialized and unconnected disciplines of secular life. If, like van Buren,
the theologian is also a philosopher by training, nature, and inclination,
he can, of course, move onto the ground of linguistic philosophy and
carry on in the general field of analytic philosophy of religion. But if he
is not, he is driven to depend on various other secular disciplines to
supplement his own personal experience of life. Thus, as in Hamilton's
case, literature becomes one central source for reflective theological insight, and we find theological ideas being developed out of the analyses
of such literary figures as Dostoevski and Shakespeare, and categories
such as "a Hamlet theology" and "an Orestes theology" appearing prominently in his writings. A second source is provided by studies of culture
by social scientists and other experts;[21] here, too, Hamilton finds ideas
about man, his prospects, and his destiny which are useful to the new
theology.

There are, however, several serious problems for theological method
and so for the theologian as a craftsman involved in this inevitable shift
to the secular. In the first place, the theologian has no special competence
in literary criticism or in social science. As a theologian, he carries no

[20] See Altizer and Hamilton, *Radical Theology*, pp. 48–49. In this place, Hamilton
denies that his position is "sheer atheistic humanism" on two grounds: (1) the category of "waiting" (i.e., agnosticism) and (2) the relation to Jesus as Lord. Since the
first category has been removed in his later thought, our analysis seems fair: this is
ontologically atheistic, but inwardly it is a "religion" in the sense of involving an
ultimate commitment to follow Jesus.

[21] Cf. Hamilton, ibid., "Banished from the Land of Unity," pp. 53–84, and for the
other references, cf. "Thursday's Child" for a brief discussion of his sources, pp. 89–
90; "The Death of God Theologies Today," pp. 42–46; and "The New Optimism—
from Prufrock to Ringo," pp. 157–69.

authority in these fields, and thus the truth of what he says must depend entirely either on his own personal insight as an amateur critic or else on the competence of others who are specialists, which tends in the long run to weaken both the creativity and the persuasiveness of his thought. Secondly, what he draws from the other disciplines, say from the social sciences, are not those elements of their thought in which these scientists are most competent, for Hamilton is not writing social science. What he can use in his theological reflection are only their convictions, guesses, hopes, conclusions, and prophecies about the ultimate nature and destiny of man and of the human story; not the scientific content of the social sciences but what Stephen Toulmin would call their mythical or "religious" meanings are grist to his mill. But it is obvious that, on this level, social science, and literary or cultural criticism as well, are at their weakest. In speaking of man's nature and destiny, that is, in providing us with either an optimistic or a pessimistic view of man, they have moved out of their field of special competence, where they contribute to our knowledge, into the realms of philosophy, religion, and myth. Here, like all of us, they are amateurs, and as often as not, like many physical scientists on this level, they merely reflect the unexamined and quite often naïve faiths and myths of our wider cultural context. The radical theologian, in sum, has no *Fach* or profession of his own. He tends to be an amateur in cultural analysis, and what he can elicit from specialized studies is precisely what is least authoritative in these fields. One wonders how long theology itself can live after the death of its traditional object and the consequent loss of its own indigenous methods.

Despite this criticism, what Hamilton is saying has important theological implications. These concern, I believe, the subtle and honest way in which he has explored the relation of doubt to personal faith in a secular time, and the very significant results that this has for Christian faith and theological method. First of all, he has asked us to examine honestly not the doubt that permeates the world outside, but that which is there in both our personal and our corporate Christian existence: is there here either in our individual experience or in the communal life of worship anything resembling a sure possessed faith, an actual experience of "encounter" with God that can be regarded as so certain and filled with cognitive content as to base thereon a *knowledge* of God sufficient for theological discourse? Is not faith *actually*, in ourselves and in our concrete communities, an unrealized hope rather than a realized possession; and therefore can we really say we "know God in faith," as neo-orthodox and hermeneutical theological methods have assumed?

Secondly, he has, I think, called the bluff involved in our usual answer to the question of the relation of doubt to faith. Far too often we have, either on Biblical or existential grounds, accepted doubt as one of the "normal" elements of vital faith—which it probably is. Thus we have said in effect, "However much I doubt, this does not touch my faith, for does not (*a*) Biblical faith always include doubt, or (*b*) does not the existential passion of doubt imply the stronger possession of faith?" Hamilton points out quite realistically that there comes a point where doubt ceases to reassure faith of its Biblical and/or its existential authenticity; rather, at that point it simply demolishes faith. If I *really* doubt that God is there, or that I have heard or encountered his Word in faith, this does not buttress my faith in him or in his revelation. What it does, in fact, is to replace it. It may indicate the death of God rather than the elusive hiddenness of the real God. In one of his best passages, Hamilton says:

> Let us continue to say that doubt is a necessary way for many of us to faith; that faith never overcomes doubt finally and completely; that lively faith can bear a good deal of doubt around the edges. But the depth of doubt is not the depth of faith; these are two places, not one, and a choice must finally be made between them. We cannot evade such a problem by a trick of redefinition.[22]

In an age where secular *existence* has cast deep doubt on the possibility of an encounter in faith with God, and so on both the meaning and the validity of theological language, this honest appraisal of the relation of doubt to faith inside Christian experience itself has great significance for Christian existence and not least for the viability of a "faith" starting point for theology.

Despite his very different bent of mind and quite different perspective, Paul van Buren, in his book *The Secular Meaning of the Gospel*,[23] nevertheless presented much the same picture of a contemporary secular Christianity. He shares with Bonhoeffer and Hamilton the acceptance of the world as the center and goal of Christian life, the consequent repudiation of "religion" as a false, individualistic withdrawal from real life and duty, and the assertion that a Christianity devoted to the life of the world is thus both secular and Biblical. Instead, however, of beginning with a personal and existential experience of doubt, van Buren found himself questioning, on philosophical grounds, the meaningfulness of language about God, of any language about ultimate reality and ultimate meaning. Although he had been a Barthian, finally he had to admit to himself that he was too much a thoroughly secular man to find meaning in this esoteric Biblical language, and thus that any faith that was to be credible to him must accord with the principles of his own secularity. This meant that any viable faith must be empirical, for, said he, empiricism is the essence of our modern spirit, and empirical means "verifiable or falsifiable," much as A. J. Ayer and Antony Flew had insisted.[24] But no statement about God

[22] Hamilton, *The New Essence,* op. cit., p. 61.

[23] Paul van Buren, *The Secular Meaning of the Gospel* (New York: Macmillan Company, 1963).

[24] For the former, see the important but now quite dated book, A. J. Ayer, *Language, Truth, and Logic* (London: Victor Gollancz, Ltd., 1946), pp. 35 and 41, and for the latter, Antony Flew, ed., *New Essays in Philosophical Theology* (London: SCM Press, 1955), especially Chapter 6, "Theology and Falsification." For Ayer's own repudiation of the stringent uses of this verification principle, and the admission of the meaningfulness of limited metaphysical investigation, cf. A. J. Ayer, *The Concept of a Person and Other Essays* (London: Macmillan & Company, 1963), especially the essay "Philosophy and Language."

fits this standard of meaningful discourse. It is, for example, impossible to specify the objective conditions which could either verify or falsify, establish or disprove, the proposition that God is love. Thus language about God is literally meaningless to the modern empirical mood, and the *word* "God" is dead in our age. As van Buren puts this strongly: "Today we cannot even understand the Nietzschian cry that 'God is dead!', for if it were so, how could we know? No, the problem now is that the *word* 'God' is dead." [25]

Like Hamilton, however, van Buren does not feel that Christianity has died with its God. The loss of words about God should, he says, be no more serious for theology than were similar losses of words about divine forces in the movement from astrology to astronomy or from alchemy to chemistry.[26] Christians still have the Jesus of history, a man remarkable in his freedom, in his love, and in the authenticity and creativity of his life. The "contagion" of his freedom uniquely affected his followers after Easter and continues to challenge, grasp, and even transform our own freedom into a similar form of authentic life.[27] Jesus thus remains our Lord, and theological statements are statements about him, his effects on us, the character of his life, and the perspective on ourselves and our behavior which he gives to us. Van Buren unfortunately adds that this is what the New Testament "really" said, and what (even more strangely) the Council and the Creed of Chalcedon "really meant," showing that, while an Episcopalian can dispense with God, he has a harder time relieving himself of ecclesiastical tradition!

When, later, van Buren was pressed about the empirical verifiability and thus meaning of his crucial word "contagion" (that is, "How does Jesus' contagion *work?*" "How can such an influence, whatever it is, be verified?" "How does or could *Jesus* grasp us?" "What does contagion *mean* here?" and so on), he admitted the dubious meaningfulness of this seemingly unverifiable or unfalsifiable usage of words. There being no possible physical virus with which the long-deceased Jesus could infect us today, use of the word "contagion" clearly illustrated no ordinary, univocal medical usage. If this language is to have any analogical meaning

[25] Van Buren, *The Secular Meaning of the Gospel*, p. 103.

[26] "Theology cannot escape this tendency [i.e., to reduce its language from a God-centered language to a secular language] if it is to be a serious mode of contemporary thought, and such a 'reduction' of content [i.e., eliminating God] need no more be regretted in theology than in astronomy, chemistry, or painting" (i.e., when, in the case of the first two, astrology was reduced to astronomy and alchemy to chemistry). Van Buren, ibid., p. 198. One may note, however, that the move from alchemy to chemistry was not a move *within* a given science, but a move from one dubious discipline to another, quite different, "scientific" one, whereas van Buren envisages this as a continuous progression within theology.

[27] Ibid., pp. 128, 132, 141, 155, 169. For example, ". . . on Easter they [the disciples] found that Jesus had a new power which he had not had, or had not exercised, before: the power to awaken freedom also in them," p. 132; and "The Christian has seen a man of remarkable and particular freedom, and this freedom has become contagious for him, as it was for the apostles at Easter," p. 155.

at all, therefore, propositions containing the word "contagion" must point to some sort of transnatural divine power or virus which links us with Jesus and so, seemingly, to imply the traditional (and exceedingly non-verifiable) God-language of the concept of grace! Thus it soon appeared that the category of the "contagion of Jesus" which grasps and transforms us is supernatural in its reference, and so must vanish along with deity from the secular theology. But this relation between our freedom in the present and the dead Jesus in the distant past is precisely the gospel as van Buren pictures it: "The Christian gospel is the news of a free man who did not merely challenge men to become free; he set men free." [28] And with the inability to speak intelligibly of this influence of Jesus on us, this relation becomes a great deal more tenuous than van Buren had at first proposed. Clearly the "Jesus-centric" character of this theology and thus its dependence upon scripture, the last carryover from the historic Christian tradition, becomes percarious without some semblance of God-language—even when the Lordship of Christ has been reduced to the "contagion" of the historical Jesus.[29]

In *The Secular Meaning of the Gospel,* van Buren had used a rather strict interpretation of the verification principle of meaning as the instrument with which he attacked God-language. As is well known, philosophical criticism of this principle by language analysts themselves has not only challenged such usage but has begun to admit the possibility of meaningful metaphysical discourse. Following this general trend in language philosophy, van Buren, too, has recently tended to focus his critical attention on our ordinary usage of words, reflecting as they do our ordinary experience of things, of people and their finite, relative, and contingent interrelationships. Thus his current philosophical viewpoint comes out to look very much like the naturalistic pluralism that preceded positivism in this country (and most probably always functioned as its "metaphysical presupposition"), especially that of John Dewey.[30] Man is

---

[28] Ibid., p. 169; cf. also pp. 128, 141.

[29] By far the best criticism of the philosophical foundations of this book to have appeared is that of Professor Harmon Holcomb in "Christology without God," *Foundations,* January 1965. For a poor second (if that), see the author's review in the *Journal of Religion,* July 1964, reprinted as "A New Linguistic Madness" in *New Theology II,* ed. Martin E. Marty and Dean G. Peerman (New York: Macmillan Company, 1965).

[30] In a paper delivered in the spring of 1964 at Drew University, and subsequently published in a new series of essays called *Theological Explorations* (New York: Macmillan Company, 1968), van Buren admitted some quite significant changes in his own position: (1) meaningful language is no longer defined by a verification principle but by usage; (2) that usage can vary widely in correlation with its emotional content and its communal and cultural context; (3) the way is open, therefore, for metaphysical language as giving proposals as to "how things are"—not as providing information but as a proposal regarding the structure or gestalt of things. Personally, he said, this must be "naturalistic" to be meaningful for him, but that this is a more open position *vis à vis* traditional theology he fully agreed. For some of the background of this general viewpoint *vis à vis* religious language, see John Dewey's *Experience and Nature* (Chicago: Open Court Press, 1925), *A Common Faith* (New Haven: Yale University Press, 1934).

here set within a shifting context of natural forces and of people in society with which he has innumerable transactions and which make up what he ordinarily calls "reality." Any attempt by thought to move beyond this reality to an absolute or to pull it all together into a rational, harmonious, unified system is unwarranted and slightly arrogant. Man can study it through science, and he can seek to control these factors through his projected ideals; but to confuse the realm of the real with that of the ideal, to identify the ideal which man envisions with the real which he seeks to shape, is a very serious error. The symbol "God" may be useful as a symbol of man's own ideals and dreams; but this symbol is only misleading and false if taken as a way of thinking about the contingent and blind reality of natural life with which man has ultimately to deal. This is, to be sure, an admission both that metaphysical propositions about the contingent realities of ordinary experience are now possible and that God-language may have some valid if strictly limited usage. Nevertheless, since van Buren envisions nothing remotely resembling either an "ultimate reality" or a permanent source of order in the plural and purposeless cosmos he believes to be the case, no substantial change with regard to the issue of the reality of God has occurred in this change of his own view.

Van Buren has been widely criticized for his "tardy" use of the verification principle after that principle had been somewhat thoroughly falsified in the course of philosophical discussion. For this reason, there has been a tendency among defenders of God-language to think that the problem of meaninglessness that he had raised by means of this principle has likewise been laid to rest—as if by showing positivism to be wrong, one had shown with relief that metaphysical and/or theological language was thereby meaningful to our age! As we have tried to argue, positivism is merely *one* expression, a particularly rough one to be sure, of the inability of our age to speak meaningfully about the wider environment of man's existence. The same hesitancy to embark on language about the ultimate nature of things appears in empirical naturalism, existentialism, and linguistic philosophy—and the same sense of the meaninglessness of religious discourse is all to evident in our Christian life, both individual and communal. This problem was not created by positivism's rigors, nor will it end with the death of the verification principle: it is *there* embedded deeply in the fundamental *Geist* of our age. Van Buren is important for having raised it so pointedly. In so doing, he has challenged the easy assumptions of *both* revelational and philosophical theology that their forms of language—the one Biblical and founded on faith, the other metaphyiscal and founded on speculative generalizations—were meaningful to their age. Further, he has cogently implied that, in carrying on these sorts of language, these two types of theology were in fact removing themselves into a world of unreal and empty symbols and using in that world a currency that was not negotiable in the life that men of the

twentieth century—and therefore theologians, too—are really living.[31]
What he has forced upon theology, therefore, is the important task of
investigating how religious language (God-language)—whether in Biblical
or metaphyiscal form—is possible, and what sorts of meanings it in fact
possesses. If, in other words, Hamilton has asked us, "How can we speak
of God if he eludes our personal experience and if our personal faith is
submerged in doubt?" Van Buren has asked us, "How can any talk of
God be meaningful if we live in a culture that knows nothing transcendent or ultimate at all?" And just as it is no answer to the first to appeal
to the authority of the Word, of faith, or of the Church, so it is no answer
to the second to insist that, since positivism is dead, a translation from
mythical to metaphysical categories answers the modern question of
meaningful discourse.

In many ways the most intriguing and certainly the most original of the
Christian radical theologians is Thomas J. J. Altizer. Initially he impresses
the reader as the most unabashedly atheistic of the trio. The cry "God is
dead" is here voiced with increased vehemence: "It is precisely the acceptance of Nietzsche's proclamation of the death of God that is the real
test of a contemporary form of faith." [32] "Furthermore, we shall simply
assume the truth of Nietzsche's proclamation of the death of God. . . .
This means we shall understand the death of God as an historical event:
God has died in *our* time, in *our* history, in *our* existence." [33] And as if
this were not enough: "Nor will it suffice for theology merely to accept
the death of God. If theology is truly to die, it must *will* the death of God,
must *will* the death of Christendom, must freely chose the destiny before
it, and therefore must cease to be itself. Everything that theology has
thus far become must now be negated." [34] "Never before has faith been
called upon to negate all *religious* meaning." [35]

[31] Schubert Ogden seems to recognize van Buren's fundamental point, as we have
formulated it here, in his new book, *The Reality of God* (New York: Harper & Row,
1966). Although there he still maintains (officially, might one say?) that the question
of the meaningfulness of theological categories is resolved in the translation of Biblical
words into the concepts of neoclassical speculative metaphysics (Chapters 2, 3, and
6), nevertheless, when he really conducts an argument on his own to establish the
possibility and even the necessity of God-language, it is not to the method of
speculative metaphysics that he turns, but to a combination of linguistic and phenomenological analysis of man's existential and moral problems (see pp. 22ff., 110ff.).
Apparently, just as fideistic theologians are less and less able merely to appeal to "the
Word received in faith," to ground the meaning and validity of their discourse, so the
metaphysical thinker, despite himself, turns away from these forms of abstraction to
other, more concrete and immediate forms of argument.
[32] T. J. J. Altizer, "America and the Future of Theology," *Radical Theology*,
op. cit., p. 11. Cf. also the following: "A theology that chooses to meet our times, a
theology that accepts the destiny of history, must first assess the theological significance of the death of God." Ibid.
[33] Altizer and Hamilton, *Radical Theology*, p. 95. For other writings of Altizer,
cf. *Mircea Eliade and the Dialectic of the Sacred* (Philadelphia: Westminster Press,
1963) and *Oriental Mysticism and Biblical Eschatology* (Philadelphia: Westminster
Press, 1961).
[34] Altizer and Hamilton, *Radical Theology*, p. 15.
[35] Ibid., p. 13.

When one reads these strident sentences, it seems at first that all touch with what has traditionally been called Christianity has been relinquished, and one wonders what sort of "Christian theology," which is what Altizer purports to be writing, is now possible. This is revolutionary fare, but still it claims to be Christian: "No, the radical Christian is a revolutionary, he is given to a total transformation of Christianity, a rebirth of the Christian Word in a new and final form." [36] But a further study of these oracular, often brilliant, and certainly original writings gradually unveils a quite new vision of Christianity which, while accepting most of the principles of radical theology, in the end differs almost as much from that of van Buren and Hamilton as it does from traditional Christian theology. In fact, as we shall see, while the most vehement in proclamaing the death of God, Altizer is the one member of the trio who does not believe for a moment that the divine is unreal or nonexistent. By no means a naturalistic, humanistic theologian, Altizer is inspired by a mystical awareness of, dependence on, and waiting for the divine power that manifests itself in current life and in history.

In order to understand this paradoxical theology, we have to move back into the nineteenth century, especially to the thought of Hegel, Nietzsche, Blake, Melville, and Freud, and above all we must bring to mind the radical polemic in the early Hegel against any form of transcendence and any attempt to freeze or render static that which is real. Following this tradition, then, Altizer's is a process, immanentist theology with a vengeance, the divine is life, flesh and world; and it despises any God separated in transcendence from flesh, life, and history. It is, then, precisely that transcendent, separated God who has died for Altizer. But that every aspect of the divine "principle" of this theology is dead, or that Altizer's ecstatic theological style follows van Buren's cool advice to eschew all forms of religious mystical, or metaphysical God-language (unverifiable and unempirical) would be a vast overstatement! This theology is saturated with a consciousness of the dynamic, redemptive power of the sacred; and in fact, the word "God" forms the active subject of most of the important theological statements in his most recent book. This is, then, a reformulation, not a denial of God-language in theology. Admittedly, God acts here in a very "queer" sort of way, but that the divine is for Altizer real, significant, and alive, there can be no doubt.[37]

---

[36] Ibid., p. 26.

[37] To take random samples of this affirmation of the reality and existence of God— at least as a very active subject of theological sentences: "God has negated and transcended himself in the incarnation, and thereby he has fully and finally ceased to exist in his original or primordial form. To know that God *is* Jesus is to know that God himself has become flesh; no longer does God exist as transcendent spirit or sovereign Lord, now God *is* love." *The Gospel of Christian Atheism* (Philadelphia: Westminster Press, 1966), p. 67. "The forward movement of the Incarnate Word is from God to Jesus, and the Word continues its kenotic movement and direction by moving from the historical Jesus to the universal body of humanity." Ibid., p. 83. "Obviously the relation between man and God must undergo genuine transformations as this process unfolds. Yet if this process is actual and real, that is to say, if it is a

How, then, are we to understand his proclamation of the death of God side by side with his continual assertions of the divine activity? The key to Altizer's thought is his concept of the living Christian Word. It is in the terms of this symbol that he interprets the other Christian symbols which he finds helpful, namely the Incarnation, eschatology, the Kingdom of God, and, of course, the real nature of the divine or God. This Word is for him, as for Hegel, now radically immanent, in process, forward moving and dynamic; implicitly it is the source of life, of meaning, and so of all culture creativity.

Apparently, however, this total immanence of the divine was not always the case. God himself, for Altizer as for Hegel, is in dynamic process, and this process consists in going out from himself in negation into an Other (the finite, the fleshly, and the historical), identifying himself dialectically with that Other, and forming a new dialectical synthesis out of the prior thesis of the transcendent, separate God, and the prior antithesis of the dynamic, finite, and contingent world. This dynamic process of self-alienation, self-negation, and final synthesis is for Altizer *historical;* it happens in *temporal* stages (whereas, one suspects, it was logical and ontological for Hegel). That is to say, the stages of this dialectic represent definite historical moments or periods within the development of process, and changes from stage to stage occurred as definite historical events. There was *once* the transcendent deity who was creator and lord of creation; but *then*, in the moment of historical time Christian faith calls the Incarnation, he negated himself, entered the Other in kenosis, and became radically immanent within that Other. The meaning of the symbols of the Incarnation and of the Atonement, therefore, is precisely that here in this total event the transcendent Lord came into the finite and identified himself totally with it. At the Incarnation, then, it was not only Christ the Son who entered flesh and died; rather the transcendent, separate God himself entered history and died as *transcendent,* through an act of self-negation.[38]

---

historical process occurring in the concrete contingencies of time and space, then God himself must act and exist in such a manner as to negate his primordial mode of Being," Ibid., p. 87.

While these quotations surely prove that this is a theology with a dynamic, immanentist deity, they certainly *also* establish that the divine here is a real, active, significant factor in the objective process of things, and that therefore this vision is anything but "naturalistic," "empirical," or even "humanistic" in the sense upheld by the theologies of Hamilton and van Buren. For this reason, I do not agree with Rubenstein's estimates of Altizer's thought as being radically humanistic and optimistic (see Richard L. Rubenstein, Jr., *After Auschwitz* [Indianapolis: Bobbs-Merrill, 1966], pp. 247ff.). It is the transcendent, separated deity that Altizer rejects with such vehemence; however, an imminent deity or principle of the sacred, incarnated in human flesh in the processes of history rather than the "autonomous" natural powers of human life, is for him the source and ground of salvation.

[38] Students of historical theology may possibly be able to place Altizer's thought by recalling the early Christian view (or heresy) called "modalism" or "patripassion-ism," a view associated with the name of Sabellius, and influential in Roman circles in the later second and early third centuries. There, too, a transcendent Lord changed

This is a new and quite unique meaning to the phrase "death of God," entirely different from anything Hamilton or van Buren had envisioned. It means, apparently, an ontological-historical event, not alone in man's culture but in the development of reality itself.[39] For Altizer, moreover, it is to this event of the divine self-negation that an authentic Christianity witnesses. And it is this new, dynamic, divine-finite synthesis of God and the historical to which Altizer refers when he speaks of "the Christian Word." This is not a changeless Word spoken and established by a God who otherwise still remains transcendent; on the contrary, it is a dynamic Word established precisely by the death or self-negation of the transcendent God.[40] It is this dynamic Word, passing from God to Jesus and thence in immanence out into history and into humanity, that can renew life, mankind, and all things. In this Word lies the principle of salvation, a salvation of and by God, through Jesus and realized in history, but pointing ever toward a future culmination, when "God will be all in all." [41] This future epiphany is that to which the Kingdom of God and all the other crucial eschatological symbols of the tradition refer. It is to this possibility, namely of a new age of the spirit in which the dialectical

---

his status, identified himself in kenotic self-giving in the Incarnation with the figure of Jesus, and so "died" on the cross, initiating thereby a third and final mode of his own existence, namely one of radical immanence in the Spirit. Strangely, Moltmann's view, as he admitted at a colloquium at Duke University, could *also* be described as a modern form of Sabellianism, except that there the roles of father, son, and spirit are reversed, and the father comes last, as the culminating eschatological event, not at creation!

[39] References affirming the ontological-cosmic character of the event of the "death of God" are legion in Altizer's later works. Here are two samples: "At no point in this process is God uniquely himself: each point or moment in the process embodies a metamorphosis of God, as God remains himself even while estranged from himself, for it is precisely God's self-estrangement or self-negation that actualizes his forward movement and process. . . . Yet the Christian confesses that it is God who has become Christ; and the God who became Christ was once manifest and real as Creator and Lord. . . . Therefore to speak of God as a dialectical process rather than as an existent Being is to speak of the God who has emptied himself of God in Christ." *The Gospel of Christian Atheism,* p. 90. "The radical Christian proclaims that God has actually died in Christ, that this death is both a historical and a cosmic event, and as such, it is a final and irrevocable event, which cannot be reversed by a subsequent religious or cosmic movement." Ibid., p. 103.

[40] "Before the Incarnation can be understood as a decisive and real event, it must be known as effecting a real change or movement in God himself: God becomes incarnate in the Word, and he becomes fully incarnate, thereby ceasing to exist or to be present in his primordial form." Ibid., p. 44. "As one who is called to witness to the dynamic presence and the forward movement of the Word, the Christian must always be open to the transfiguring power of the Incarnate Word, knowing that the Word is in process of renewing all things, not by recalling them to their pristine form in the Beginning, but rather by making them new so that they can pass into the End." Ibid., p. 18. "For the Christian *Word* is an evolving Word, a forward moving Word, a Word that only exists and is real only in the concrete life of history." Ibid., p. 45.

[41] "The forward movement of the Incarnate Word is from God to Jesus, and the Word continues its kenotic movement and direction by moving from the historical Jesus to the universal body of humanity, thereby undergoing an epiphany in every human hand and face." Ibid., p. 83.

oppositions of the sacred and the profane, of the God who has died and thus entered life, are known and proclaimed, that the living Christian faith witnesses—not to a "religious" return to an original, transcendent being, separated from concrete existence, repressive of it, and finally now, in our time, dead from emptiness, exhaustion, and just sheer satanic evil!

In its strange way, this remarkable and highly original vision reflects many elements of the classical structure of Christian orthodox faith: dependence throughout on God's dynamic activity, the centrality of the Incarnation, a relation to salvation through the continuing activity of the Spirit, all moving forward into the future to an eschatological end. And, as we noted, the central Christian symbols of God, creation, fall, Incarnation, Word, Spirit, Kingdom of God, etc., form the symbolic foundation on which this thought is constructed. From this point of view, this theology is much more conservative than are those of Hamilton and van Buren. There is no hint of materialistic naturalism, of an optimistic dependence on human autonomy alone,[42] or of a drastic reduction in modes of theological language, and this viewpoint could hardly be called "atheistic," despite the title of Altizer's main work.

On the other hand, Altizer's theology is in other respects more radical than that of the others. The central principle of the dynamic, forward-moving, ever-changing Word gives to his thought an essentially revolutionary character that the thought of the other two, with their present concern for the historical Jesus, cannot have. For Altizer insists repeatedly that the forms of the Word have continually changed and will always do so, often actually "negating" former forms and even negating the original form of the Word in Jesus himself. Thus no traditional theological categories, whether those of the Bible generally, of the New Testament gospels, or of ecclesiastical history have any real authority at all for the present Christian.[43] The theologian must speak of the living Word in the present, and the forms of his thought are determined alone by that present and not by the dead and heavy hand of the past.[44] The concept of the

___

[42] "Yet now the Christian God is dead! The transcendence of Being has been transformed into the radical immanence of Eternal Recurrence: to exist in our time is to exist in a chaos freed of every semblance of cosmological meaning or order." Altizer and Hamilton, *Radical Theology*, p. 102.

[43] As opposed to the other "radicals," Altizer rejects completely the authority for faith and life of the *historical* Jesus: "But by opening ourselves to the immediate actuality of the moment before us, we can know the Jesus who is present in the fullness of time itself, even if that time should prove to be a negation or reversal of the past event of Jesus of Nazareth." *The Gospel of Christian Atheism*, op. cit., p. 61. For other assertions of the irrelevance of the historical Jesus as a criterion of the present Word—as well as the impossibility of establishing what he was like—see ibid., pp. 48–54 and *Radical Theology*, op. cit., pp. 104 and 123–125.

[44] "Each historical expression of the Word will bear its own peculiar and distinct reality, and while no clear path may be seen to lie between one and another, faith must ever seek that particular form of the Word which acts in its own presence." *Gospel of Christian Atheism*, op. cit., p. 46. "A Word must be judged to be non-Christian if it cannot appear and become real in a present and human act of faith,

dynamic Word, therefore, provides the theological basis for Altizer's insistence that theology must be a *contemporary* witness to the cultural mood of its present and must "accept the destiny of its time"—and so, in our godless age, theology must affirm the death of God. This is, then, a revolutionary theology of the Spirit, as Altizer realizes, for the Word is not a Word of the past, nor even a Word once and finally shaped by the authority of Jesus.[45] It is present, alive, moving, changing—and so, presumably, is the theology that speaks of it.

For Altizer, therefore, there are no recognizable criteria for what the Christian theologian should say, as there are in a Biblical theology, a confessional or a philosophical theology, or even as in theologies based, as were those of van Buren and Hamilton, on contemporary reflection on the life and death of Jesus. Having heard Altizer say on occasion that *everything* that theology has been must now be negated,[46] and that we have lost *all* our Christian images, the reader wonders to what criteria, besides the formulations made explicit in his own theology, Altizer could point if he wished to say of a given form of thought, "No, that is not Christian," or to claim for his own thought that it is. And then one wonders, too, what conceivable principles can allow Altizer to appeal, as he frequently does, to an "authentic Christian faith" or to "the fundamental if underlying meaning of the earliest expressions of the Christian faith," [47] and use as authorities for his own theology such "authentic" symbols, as he calls them, from the past as the Incarnation, the Fall, and eschatology.

Perhaps, as these remarks hint, the main difficulty with this theology is the apparent impossibility of arguing with it; and the correlative difficulty for its proponent that it fails to convince. That is to say, it is hard to know, on the one hand, on what common ground we can disagree with Altizer and, on the other, what grounds *he* can appeal to to persuade us that what he says is true. The appeal to some agreed "authority" (whether of sense experience, scripture, "science," logic or custom) is, let us note, inescapable in the enterprise of rational discourse or argu-

---

and it is non-Christian to the extent it cannot become incarnate in the immediate horizon of faith." *Radical Theology,* op. cit., p. 122. See the remarkably similar assertion from the nineteenth-century liberal Auguste Sabatier: "Every divine revelation, every religious experience fit to nourish and sustain your soul, must be able to repeat and continue itself as an actual revelation and an individual experience in your own consciousness." *Outline of a Philosophy of Religion Based on Psychology and History* (London: Hodder & Stoughton, 1906), pp. 62–63.

[45] As he had disputed the authority of the *historical* Jesus, for faith, so one of the traditional Christian themes most frequently rejected by Altizer is the ultimacy, the *Einmaligkeit,* of the total Christ-event, so central to all forms of neoorthodox theology as a final revelation of the character of the Word of God: "At no point in this process does the incarnate Word or Spirit assume a final and definitive form." *Gospel of Christian Atheism,* op. cit., p. 104; cf. also ibid., p. 58 and *Radical Theology,* op. cit., pp. 18–19.

[46] Altizer and Hamilton, *Radical Theology,* p. 15.

[47] Altizer, *The Gospel of Christian Atheism,* p. 105.

mentation. For such appeal is the basis both of disproof or rejection of ideas, on the one hand and, on the other hand, of persuasion, of eliciting from the hearer agreement and conviction of the truth of what is said because it agrees with this commonly accepted authority. In inquiry some mode of "authority" provides the ground, or is the ground, for the verification or falsification of any hypothesis, and so the question "What is the authority to which you appeal?" is in effect the question "On what basis do you claim your statements to be true?"

Now, the point is that this theology seems to have rejected at one time or another all the familiar theological authorities: the Biblical Word in any of its forms; the historical facts of Jesus' life; classical, traditional, or modern Church doctrine; the consensus of the Church in the present; an analysis of religious experience, Christian or universal; philosophical inquiry into general experience, metaphysical, phenomenological, or linguistic; and certainly "science" in all its forms—all of these possible grounds for theological assertions are upset, overturned, or rendered irrelevant by the principle of the fast-moving Word. Even present culture in its specific philosophical forms is disregarded according to the dialectical principle that the "truth" of the present always negates the "surface" of the present.[48] This makes it impossible to argue with Altizer, for no common ground with his reader is presented—except for the authority of such figures as Hegel, Nietzsche, Blake, and Melville. And certainly it is useless to argue whether or not this theology is "contemporary," perhaps the one available criterion Altizer seems to recognize. For if there was ever a unique and "unsecular" form of thought, "far out" in relation to the contemporary mood of an empirical, scientific culture, it is this latter-day Hegelian, dialectical, and mystical vision of a dynamic, self-negating, divine immanence.

Correspondingly, however, one also does not know how one might be persuaded of its truth. Hegel argued laboriously by means of philosophical, logical, and historical analyses for a version of the same position; other theologians have argued for their positions on the grounds of the authority of scripture, tradition, "religious experience," or have carried on some sort of intelligible analysis of general human experience, individual and social. Altizer argues in none of these ways. He seems to appeal only to the thematic characteristics of Christian faith to persuade us: to the meanings implicit in such symbols as the Incarnation, the Word, eschatology, saying, in effect, "If you take these symbols seriously, you must understand them in such and such a way." This is not an impossible form of theological argument, as the Swedish school of *Motiv-forschung* has shown; but the *theological* force of their argument lay ultimately in the authority of scripture and tradition where these themes were discovered, and Altizer has already repudiated the validity of these two authorities. In the end, therefore, bereft of scripture, of tradition, of

[48] Altizer and Hamilton, *Radical Theology*, pp. 140–141.

philosophical method, of an appeal to personal experience, or of social analysis, this theology presents us as its sole authority the brilliant but quite particular vision of the author and of the literary tradition he represents. Because he provides us with no "place," besides his own thought itself, where we can look for the validation of his thought, we close his book with a feeling that, while he can proclaim powerfully to us and interest us masterfully, in the end he cannot persuade us that what he says is true.

Besides its inherent interest and stimulating power, what does this unique vision of Christianity offer us? For this writer, the most valuable contribution of Altizer is that through him—and through no other theologian of whom I am aware—the powerful polemic of nineteenth-century Romanticism, especially that of Hegel, Nietzsche, and Freud, against the transcendent, separated deity of orthodoxy, has entered and challenged the theological consciousness. This is a tradition which exulted in life, in joy, in the strength and courage to bear pain, in freedom, in the spontaneous, in the creative—that found living being a veritable spring of the only real values that there are. It was a tradition, therefore, that saw plainly that the *transcendent* as well as the "idolatrous" could function in a demonic manner in human life; that, to use Tillich's terms, emphasized the creativity of *autonomy* because it saw so clearly the dangers of the heteronomous.[49] To be sure, elements of the neoorthodox movement felt traces of this inheritance of Romanticism—or discovered it on the couch!—and so tried, not unsuccessfully, to establish these values of *life* and the joyous living of it through its doctrines of creation, Incarnation, and the reevaluation of most ethical problems. Having thus given a nod to this tradition of immanence, it tended then, however, to talk for the next four hundred pages about transcendence, judgment, external grace, and obedience. With the exception of Paul Tillich, dialectical theology had, in other words, far too little sense of the demonic possibilities of transcendence as well as of immanence, possibly because (having been reared by liberals and not by orthodox), its proponents were conscious only of the dangers of immanence and conceived of only the *prophetic* rather than the *repressive* possibilities of transcendence. But historically, psychologically, and theoretically, transcendence has often warred with joy in life, with human creativity, and with freedom—

---

[49] By "heteronomy" is meant an external divine power, separated from the essential nature and so creativity of the creature, which by its power and authority crushes and ultimately destroys the freedom and the autonomous powers of the creature. The concept goes back to Hegel in his criticism of the transcendent principle of Judaism and of historical Christian theology. In Hegel's own view, the Absolute works in and through the creature and so does not destroy it. The same point was made by Tillich in his defense of a theonomous religious principle. For this whole tradition, therefore, the supernatural that is separated, "above" and "over against" the creature, is essentially destructive of the natural life and powers of the creature, once the latter has experienced the infinite power of its own rational and moral freedom—and thus can no transcendent principle be borne or tolerated by modern man.

with the free exultant realization of one's own potentialities as a finite
being. It is no accident that the symbol of transcendence and the symbol
of the father figure have always been historically identified. This proclamation of autonomy, and of its joys and its possibilities, free now from
the transcendent that sets for it given rules, or carves out for it an *a priori*
niche, is one of the most creative elements of our modern secularity, and
it is this that Altizer's thought has brought into theology. From now on,
everyone will be more wary than before of any categories of transcendence that theology might be able to muster. Altizer argues that transcendence and life are essentially irreconcilable. To counter this as
erroneous, and to assert that the creative joy in life is not only consistent
with but ultimately dependent on a sense of the transcendent depths and
inexhaustible mystery of God, will be one of the main burdens of the
second part of this volume.

The most compelling of the radical theologians in our view is Rabbi
Richard L. Rubenstein, whose book *After Auschwitz* [50] appeared late in
1966. To Rubenstein, the experience of the death of six million Jews has
made forever incredible the two cardinal beliefs of historic Judaism: that
there is a God who is Lord of history, and that this God has a special
relation to the Jewish people. If these two assertions are true, says Rubenstein, then the murder of the Jews must have been a part of God's
purposes, and "I would rather live in an absurd, indifferent cosmos than
believe that." The cosmos, therefore, for Rubenstein, is blind, unfeeling,
indifferent—unrelated to any human meanings and projects except that it
has produced us and will claim us in the end, in death. Meanwhile, our
task is to find, create, and enjoy what meanings there are and can be in
this ultimately hopeless situation, and to be able to live the one life we
have with as much creativity, joy, and shared community as is possible.
Three quotations give the primary substance of his position:

> He [Camus in *The Plague*] would rather live in an absurd, indifferent cosmos
> in which men suffer and die meaninglessly but still retain a measure of tragic
> integrity than see every last human event encased in a pitiless framework of
> meaning which deprives man of even the consolation that suffering, though
> inevitable, is not entirely merited or earned. . . . We concur with this choice
> of an absurd and ultimately tragic cosmos. We do so because we share with
> Camus a greater feeling for human solidarity than the prophetic-Deuteronomic
> view of God and of history can possibly allow. . . . We have turned away
> from the God of history to share the tragic fatalities of the God of nature. . . .
> After the experiences of our time, we can neither affirm the myth of the
> omnipotent God of History nor can we maintain its corollary, the election of
> Israel. . . . Jews do not need these doctrines to remain a religious commu-
> nity.[51]
>
> If there is a God of history, he is the ultimate author of Auschwitz. I am
> willing to believe in God, the holy nothingness who is our source and our final

[50] For details of *After Auschwitz*, see note 37.
[51] Ibid., pp. 67–69.

destiny, but never again in a God of history. . . . What the existentialists do
mean is that there is no *ultimate* meaning to existence. They call upon men to
create with lucidity their own private meanings and purposes in the knowledge
that no power in the cosmos will ultimately sustain or validate them. . . .
What the death of God theologians depict is an undoubted *cultural fact* in our
time: God is totally unavailable as a source of meaning or value. There is no
vertical transcendence. Our problem is not how we shall think of God in a
secular way. It is how men can best share the decisive crises of life, given the
cold, unfeeling, indifferent cosmos that surrounds us and given the fact that
God, the Holy Nothingness, offers us only disillusion and death as the way out
of earthly existence. It is in this situation that the traditional church and synagogue are most meaningful.[52]

There is only one Messiah who redeems us from the irony, the travail and the
limitations of human existence. Surely he will come. He is the Angel of Death.
Death is the true Messiah and the land of the dead the place of God's true
kingdom. Only in death are we redeemed from the vicissitudes of human
existence. We enter God's kingdom only when we enter His holy Nothingness.[53]

We are called, then, to create with our own human powers and projects
a creative life in the midst of this nothingness. Such a creative human life
is for Rubenstein, therefore, no easy task: technology, "goods," "progress,"
and even better political, social, and economic structures make little real
difference to the character of human existence. Man's life is difficult and
tragic in every age, and his fundamental problems of loving and being
loved, of loneliness, guilt, aging, and death are much the same from
generation to generation. What is necessary in order to bear these tragic
aspects of life and so to become a "decent human animal," is that we are
aware of and know who we are, what our stage of life is, how our acts
are suffused with guilt, how lonely and isolated we often feel, and how
death is to borne. To know this in a community that shares with us in
lucidity and honesty this awareness of fragmentariness and mortality is
essential. For this, a religious community is necessary, and especially one
structured by traditional rituals which allow us communally to express
and so to relieve these recurrent, cyclical crises of human existence. "In
a world without God religion is more necessary than ever," a religion
that is man-made, priestly in form, ritualistic in practice, communal—and
of psychological validity only.[54] As Rubenstein puts this, we must relinquish the God of history and return to the gods of nature—of life, birth,
family, passage, and death—a pagan form of Judaism is the only viable

---

[52] Ibid., pp. 204–205.

[53] Ibid., p. 198.

[54] An ironical aspect for Christian theology of Rubenstein's thought is that this
"psychological, man-made, ritualistic" *religion*, unrelated to any divine activity or
revelation at all, is precisely the picture of "religion" that neoorthodoxy found so
appalling. That Rubenstein should find this "demonic" (to neoorthodoxy) human
creation the sole form of "faith" possible to modern man shows the vast shift of
theological temper that has taken place. We should also note that it marks a turn
away even from Bonhoeffer, who wished to "speak about God without religion,"
whereas Rubenstein seeks to speak of religion without God.

form of modern Jewish existence.[55] In Rubenstein, the sense of the death of God in a tragic and meaningless world has led to possibly the most violent upheaval of established theological concepts of all. For a rabbi to defend the pagan gods against the Lord of history is in truth something new under the sun!

One must, however, posit a fundamental question about this interpretation, profound as it is. First, can ritual ever be separated as fully as Rubenstein wishes, from its accompanying myth, without losing the strength and meaningfulness of the ritual acts themselves? Rubenstein is right that consciously held doctrines and consciously determined deeds are not the substance of religion and do not touch the subconscious depths of personality where both destruction and health originate. But surely it is obvious that ritual without *any* accompanying conscious elements, in this case some deeply affirmed religious myth or doctrine, is equally vapid and meaningless, done by rote for traditional reasons and so incapable of generating precisely the psychological forces of release, self-acceptance, and identity that Rubenstein feels we need so desperately. Ritual alone, the sacrament without the Word, the Jewish liturgy without any inward belief at all in the divine relation to history, is as barren as is the Word alone. Rubenstein has dispensed with the traditional "myths" of Judaism in which this ritualistic scheme of atonement, sacrifice, membership in the community, and death has found its meaning for conscious awareness; he cannot hope to reinstate these ritual forms today in terms of whatever pagan mythos preceded Sinai. One wonders, therefore, how stable is this complex ritualistic edifice in the naturalistic-existential universe Rubenstein affirms, and so whether, with the demise of the Lord of history, his gods of nature and of earth will not also weaken and die. Especially is this the case, an outsider feels, in Judaism, where the very depth of the understanding through its ritual of the anxieties of finitude and guilt, as well as the strength of its communal sense, both of which Rubenstein extols, depend on the very concepts of the Lord of history and of the covenant people which he has rejected. One suspects that real paganism, untouched by the covenant and by prophetic insight, would not help Rubenstein with his life's problems much more than would the busy optimism of our current secular world. It was, after all, the Teutonic, pagan gods of earth, place, and of race and blood, resurrected in the new technological world, that played at least a partial role in the events he deplores. Perhaps the same Canaanite deities in sunny Israel will prove more benevolent, though that itself is possibly dubious. But in the one case as in the other, some prophetic transcendence over the meanings and loyalties generated by community and racial ties seems necessary if the quietly creative humanity for which Rubenstein yearns is to be preserved—and not least when these religious communities reach political autonomy, as in Israel.

[55] Ibid., pp. 93–111, p. 240.

Among the many powerful themes in Rubenstein's thought, the one that carries the most force in his denial of God is surely his dealing with the problem of evil. The reality of tragedy in history has, as we noted in an earlier chapter, been a strong ally of recent neoorthodox apologetics in an age where secular humanism was "optimistic" and theology "realistic." Thus theologians could argue effectively, "*If* life is to have meaning as its necessary presupposition, that meaning must be affirmed by faith, and God must be affirmed as its sole source." A good many people in the twentieth century have believed in God *because* history was tragic, and they knew no other way to understand that tragedy creatively. Now Rubenstein—with the help of Camus, to be sure—has uncovered some of the deep problems of this ground for faith if it be the sole ground. Evil in history can reveal itself as so great that there is more existential meaning to life without belief in God than there is with it. As he argues, at a certain level of tragedy, it is surely easier to understand and to bear evil in a meaningless world than in one in which God rules. This potent argument poses a challenge very near to the heart of Biblical faith, which has always offered itself as the fullest answer in any existential situation to the problems of fate, sin, and death, and it represents the profoundest aspect of the mood of secular rebellion against the ancient sense of an ultimate order and goodness in the structure of being. Any theological answer to this revolt against God must incorporate this modern sensitivity to evil at its deepest point and never relinquish it—rather than simply using evil to lead thought to the God who can resolve it away.

In the radical theologians, therefore, we have protest against God-language on four related but significantly different grounds: the weakness of faith and the experience of the absence of God; the meaninglessness of all speech about reality as such, whether that speech be based on revelation or on metaphysical inquiry; the demonic character of the transcendent as a challenge to the joy and creativity of life; and, finally, the impossibility, nay the destructive immorality, of understanding historical evil on any other but naturalistic, radically secular terms. These protests are not by any means new to secular thought, but their appearance together as determinants of theological reflection create the new situation theologically.

THE MANY FACES OF EVIL

Edward H. Madden

EDWARD H. MADDEN is Professor of Philosophy at the State University
of New York at Amherst. Among his works are *Evil and the Concept
of God* (1968, with Hare), and *The Idea of God* (1968, with Handy
and Farber).

1

The formal way of presenting the problem of evil is this: If God is all-
powerful and all-good, why is there so much *prima facie* gratuitous and
unnecessary evil in the world? If he is all-powerful he should be able to
remove unnecessary evil, and if he is all-good he should want to remove
it; but he does not. Why? Must we assume that he is either not all-
powerful or not all-good? Theists want to avoid this conclusion at all
costs; they see the problem as one of logical compatibility: they must
have an answer which squares God's all-powerfulness, all-goodness, and
the existence, *prima facie* at least, of gratuitous evil. The qualification
"prima facie" is important and not to be taken lightly, for to speak of evil
as absolutely unnecessary would beg the question at issue and rule out
in advance certain attempted solutions to the problem as inadequate.

Theists offer numerous solutions to their problem of evil, and I cannot
hope to attend exhaustively to each one. I shall make every effort, however, to analyze carefully the most significant and historically influential
ones. In two of them, the free will and ultimate harmony views, I shall
be most interested, and to them I shall devote most analysis. However, I
shall be explicit enough about the other alleged solutions also, so that it
should be quite clear why I think none of them succeeds. I shall conclude, then, that the problem of evil is insoluble and that this insolubility
is a sufficient reason for not believing in any type of theistic god whatever.

2

(i) Theistic solutions to the problem vary a great deal in merit. Two
terribly flimsy ones, yet ones that are prevalent in the literature and in
everyday life, are the "contrast" and the "nonintervention" solutions. Evil,
so the first argument goes, is necessary as a contrast so that we shall be
able properly to understand and appreciate the good of life. Evil, according

to the second argument, is a by-product of the operation of the laws of the universe. Evil events like earthquakes, floods, famines, and plagues are simply natural events in a world which is, overall, a good one. One can look elsewhere for detailed criticisms of these views.[1] I shall be content with one simple criticism of each. (a) We need little evil by way of contrast to get the point; one should be allowed to bite his lip rather than go through life with a harelip. (b) Even if acceptable, which it is not, the second "solution" would account only for physical evil and leave moral evil untouched.

(ii) For a better try at the problem there is a cluster of related scriptural views. To the question "What does God have in mind by allowing gratuitous evil in his world?" students of Christian Scripture have replied variously: (a) evil is punishment for sin; (b) evil tests man's faith; and (c) evil is God's warning to man.

(a) Jobs, comforters, it is well-known, held this view. We know, of course, from the very structure of the Book of Job that this interpretation of evil is wrong from the Christian standpoint. Job, as God knew, had *not* done anything to merit his misery; the point of his suffering lay elsewhere. Indeed, Christ himself apparently rejected this view.[2] Scriptural argument aside, this retribution solution is quite untenable on any ground, Christian or otherwise. Consider the Peru landslides which annihilated many men, women, and children of several valley villages. If evil is punishment for sin, it is difficult to believe that only the inhabitants of these villages deserved such reprimands. Moreover, as Voltaire said, it is difficult to believe that just the sinners get singled out for destruction in such catastrophes.

(b) The notion that evil tests man's faith is not entirely clear. What precisely does it mean? It might mean that God inflicts pain on man to discover whether he will keep his faith in time of adversity or whether he is simply a summer Christian or a fair-weather believer. This interpretation will not do, however, for if God is all-powerful and hence all-knowing, he should already know the outcome.

However, this view might be interpreted quite differently. God tests people like Job, it is said, precisely because he knows they will be steadfast in their faith and thus act as a salutary example to other people. Unfortunately, this interpretation is even more vulnerable than the first one. Not everyone is a Job, and when affliction causes renunciation of God this makes a very bad example for fellow Christians. Moreover, such an interpretation could not account for mass disasters and catastrophes; the price would be too high to pay for an example, even if it were effective.

(c) The view that evil is God's "warning" to man is a clear and straightforward one, and it is particularly dear to the heart of a practical theist. Men are sunk, he says, in religious indifference and they need to be

[1] Cf. H. J. McCloskey, "God and Evil," in *The Philosophical Quarterly*, Vol. 10 (1960), pp. 102, 103–04.
[2] Luke, 13:1–5.

shocked into realization of God's presence by some awesome display of his power. When natural catastrophes like earthquakes, floods, and tornadoes occur, men become aware of God's great power, and their own littleness in the face of it, and they take on, as a result, the proper reverential awe of the Creator and a fear of violating his laws. These moral and religious results, in short, justify the physical pain resulting from natural causes. But do they? I think it is clear enough to anyone except a practical theist that they do not. Even if there were no objections to this view whatever, it would account for physical evil only and not moral evil, and hence leave the problem half-unsolved. Moreover, the demonstration of power need not be so deadly to achieve its aim, if this aim could be achieved at all. But it is certain that its aim, in fact, is not achieved. Indeed, rather than bringing man to God, these natural calamities frequently turn men against him. Such calamities forcefully bring to man's attention the whole problem of evil, and this problem, so difficult to solve, causes many people to give up their religious beliefs rather than strengthening them. According to a recent commentator, ". . . if God's object in bringing about natural calamities is to inspire reverence and awe, He is a bungler." Moreover,

. . . the use of physical evil to achieve this object is hardly the course one would expect a benevolent God to adopt when other, more effective, less evil methods are available to Him, for example, miracles, special revelation, etc.[3]

(iii) An even stronger try at solving the problem is the character-building theory. On this view evil is a necessary part of our world because the experience of it yields such virtues as courage, endurance, charity, and sympathy. People are born into the world as base metal, which has many impurities. The experience of evil is the fire that burns away the impurities and leaves the base metal, the spiritually significant self, free and unencumbered.

One must admit that this view is an attractive one. Who has not had the experience of wishing fervently to avoid some painful or even harrowing event and yet, after the event, having to admit that he is a better person for having undergone it? The difficulty with this view, of course, is clear and utterly damaging: it could only account for a small amount of evil, in any case, and could not account at all for the maiming of character which too much evil often produces (consider the brainwashing cases) or the mass annihilation of character (recall the Peru landslides). And it is difficult to see how the knowledge of such events could have an uplifting influence on people who witness or hear about them. Even if there were such an influence, the price would be much too high to pay for it. I would be the first one to insist on having *some* evil in the world for I, too, believe, it is impossible that a race "ignorant of suffering and unacquainted with grief should also achieve the heights and sound the

[3] McCloskey, op. cit., p. 103.

depths of intellectual and spiritual life." [4] But this view of spiritual ennoblement is not only deficient in ways already pointed out, but also cannot account for any moral evil at all. If someone does me a cruel wrong I may grow spiritually through the agony, but the evildoer's character is thereby being depraved at the expense of my spiritual growth. Moreover, it is not clear why God, if he is all-powerful, could not have created spiritually significant people in the first place. Finally, this solution is simply inapplicable to some physical evils, insanity being perhaps the best example.

(iv) The philosophical optimist claims that this is the best of all possible worlds even though evil is a necessary ingredient of it. The world, it is claimed, has just the right amount of pain to cultivate patience, the right amount of danger to cultivate courage, *etc.* "If there were any less evil, it would be a worse world, rather than a better one." [5] Optimists like Leibniz did not claim that evil was only an appearance or an illusion, as he is so often interpreted. He readily admitted that the world contained evil in a positive, real way, but his point was that it contained just exactly the right amount of evil. Hence it is the best of all possible worlds.

Arguments against this view are rather obvious. It seems oddly omniscient to announce that we have precisely the right amount of evil in the world. Much of it seems utterly gratuitous and does not lead to patience, courage, or anything else desirable; rather it crushes, shrivels, and annihilates the hapless ones it falls upon. Moreover, the distribution of evil presents a difficulty for the Optimist. That some people live in daily agony while others prosper hardly seems like just the right amount of evil to achieve the highest good. Indeed, "the theory seems to be most earnestly espoused by fairly comfortable people who point out to others how much worse their lives would be if they had less to combat." [6] Finally, it seems that God, if he were all-powerful, ought to be able to achieve the desirable ends without the evil means.

Leibniz, of course, had an answer to the last criticism.[7] Only God is infinite and perfect. Anything other than God of necessity is limited, imperfect, or—what is the same—evil. Hence, if God were to create anything at all, it had to exhibit some evil. God created the world which had the least amount; hence it is the best of all possible worlds. Leibniz called the imperfection inherent in all created things "metaphysical evil." However, this reply will not do. One willingly admits that the orthodox theistic God is not all-powerful in the sense that he can do what is logically self-contradictory. Such a limitation on omnipotence is not damaging. But Leibniz insisted that God could not create a finite thing that was perfect. But why not? The theistic God, after all, is supposed to be omnipotent not only *within* nature but *over* nature as well. *Thus,* God

[4] Alfred Noyes in *The Unknown God.*
[5] David Elton Trueblood, *The Logic of Belief,* p. 288.
[6] Ibid., p. 289.
[7] Cf. C. J. Ducasse, *A Philosophical Scrutiny of Religion,* pp. 357–61.

could have created *any world he pleased*—and he could have pleased to create a perfect one, or at least a better one! Moreover—and this point is fundamental—if metaphysical evil *were* ineluctable, then he should not have created any world at all, as any moral god would have refrained from doing.

The remaining two efforts to solve the problem, I believe, are the strongest ones—the most difficult ones to criticize effectively—and also the most influential ones historically. They are the free-will solution and the ultimate harmony viewpoint. Theism, I believe, depends for its very life on the success of one or the other of these notions.

(v) The free-will argument often is presented in the following way. God granted men free will, and man, unhappily, frequently misuses this gift, producing evil. Thus man, not God, is responsible for evil. This formulation is not satisfactory, however, because God, since he is all-knowing, would have foreseen this evil consequence of granting men free will and hence avoided it. It must be shown, therefore, why God gave man free will, even though he knew evil consequences would occur.

Theists have refurbished the argument in the following way. Free will is an inestimably important gift. Without it man would be a mere automaton, marching through life without significance or dignity. It is free will which makes him a human being and thus set apart from all the other creatures in the world. But it is not only the intrinsic value of free will which justifies God's granting it, but also its consequences; the claim being, that it leads more often than not to good works, moral endeavor, and beatitude. After these deliberations, God granted man free will, in spite of certain evil consequences, for not to do so would have been far more evil.

There are still numerous difficulties with this strengthened view. (a) Even if there were no objections whatever to this solution, it would explain the occurrence only of moral evil and would leave the problem of physical evil untouched. Man's free will had nothing to do with the Lisbon earthquake, the Peru landslides, the China famines, or with leprosy, cancer, and muscular dystrophy. To be sure, if one believes that free will accounts for moral evil, then he need only to find another solution for physical evil, and the whole problem will be solved. However, we have not yet encountered an adequate solution to the problem of physical evil, nor will we encounter one.

(b) God could have granted men free will but nevertheless still have prevented or avoided some of the moral evil in the world. He could do this in various ways: being all-powerful, God could have created man with a *disposition* to act decently, even though, to account for freedom, he *could* choose to do evil; God could have created a world in which men's wrong choices did not lead to quite such disastrous consequences; and God could, upon occasion, intervene to prevent a particularly hideous result.

The theist counterargues in the following way. God should *not* reduce the amount of evil in the world by giving men a disposition to do good, intervening, *etc.*, because the proper use of free will has moral significance only if it is done in the face of great odds and is the result of strenuous effort and struggle. However, this view leads to odd consequences.[8] On this view it becomes my duty to throw evil in the paths of my fellow men so that their struggle, and hence their beatitude, may grow! Unhappily, however, great evil, rather than causing growth, often stunts and destroys the free human soul. God, on this view, is doing this dreadful thing apparently: He creates human beings with free will, some of whom will grow spiritually through great evil, and some of whom will be destroyed completely. How can the former justify God's way in view of the latter? The price is too high to pay. Indeed, this whole view goes contrary to ordinary moral standards. We would consider it brazenly immoral to tempt a reformed alcoholic by drinking in his presence or by daring a person we know to be reckless to do some impossible feat. Such behavior would increase their struggle, to be sure, but might well cause their utter downfall. A human being who acted in such a way would be called immoral; if God acts that way, why should we call his behavior a "higher" morality?

(c) The claim is made that more often than not free will results in desirable consequences rather than undesirable ones. But this claim is an empirical one, and it is difficult indeed to see how anyone could have adequate evidence to establish its truth. It might *possibly* be the case, but we do not know that it is. Hence it might be a possible justification for God's granting free will, but we do not know that it is.

(d) This traditional criticism is well-known: God's omniscience and man's free will are incompatible notions. Jonathan Edwards was a brilliant advocate of this criticism. This question is fantastically complicated in its own right, and I could not hope to do justice to it within the scope of this paper. Suffice it to say here that if one means by 'free will' an 'uncaused will,' then I think one can show that the concepts of omniscience and free will are incompatible. However, if one carefully analyzes the notion of free will and concludes that it is not only compatible with determinism but in some sense implies it, then he may be able to show the consistency of omniscience and free will. In this case, however, one still has sufficient grounds in the previous criticisms to reject the free will solution to the problem of evil.

3

(vi) The ultimate harmony solution has been, perhaps, the most historically influential one of all, and many theists believe it to be their

8 Cf. McCloskey, op. cit., p. 113.

soundest answer. The view is usually presented in a metaphorical way, and the favorite metaphor is a musical one. A chord heard in isolation may sound dissonant and ugly, but when heard in context blends into a perfect whole or an ultimate harmony. So it is with evil. What human beings call evil is an event seen out of context, in isolation, and since man has only a fragmentary view of events, this is the only way he can see it. God, however, who has an overall view of events, sees how such events are good in the long run or good from an overall viewpoint. (For our purposes the notions of "good in the long run" and "good from an overall viewpoint" need not be separated, because any criticisms of the ultimate harmony view will apply equally well to both.) The ultimate harmony view has the important consequence that evil is only an appearance, an illusion; what appears to be evil is, after all, good.

What can be said against this view? There are numerous objections, as we shall see, but we might well begin by asking for an example of how apparent evil is really an ultimate good. I have been astounded through the years by the examples I have been offered: indeed, I have become convinced there is nothing that someone cannot find to be a good in disguise. I once mentioned Buchenwald as an example of great moral evil. But it was not really an evil, someone suggested, because it had helped immeasurably in solving the problem of population explosion. I confess that I was greatly agitated: I offered to shovel the speaker into my furnace as an added good. The important point here is this: if one holds the ultimate harmony view and honestly goes into detail trying to discover the ultimate good, he gets really bizarre results. Hence, the person who holds this view wisely refrains from offering detailed analyses. He contents himself by saying simply that in all cases there is an ultimate good, known to God, which human beings, with their limited powers, are unable to fathom. They say, in effect, that the ways of God pass understanding.

There are at least four serious objections to the present view. (a) To be sure, we are all aware of cases in our own experience where an apparent evil led to good. But what right do I have to assert that they always do, when I am equally aware of cases of apparent good leading to evil? If it be asserted that in the latter case I have not waited long enough for ultimate consequences, I must inquire how long the "long run" must be and must further inquire why the same argument does not apply equally well to the former case: perhaps I have not waited long enough either in cases where apparent evil leads to good consequences. In any case, even if apparent evil sometimes leads to good, and we neglect the opposite circumstances, it does not follow that we have proved it always will do so. This fact would only establish that it is *possible* that all cases of apparent evil lead to good, not that it is *probable*. But many events are possible for which we have, however, no warrant whatever to believe likely to happen. Moreover, in view of the enormous amount of apparent evil in the world, it seems *prima facie* unlikely that it could all be explained away as leading to good.[9]

(b) The ultimate harmony view has this outlandish consequence: if evil is really good in disguise, then we are wrong in thinking it is our moral duty to eliminate or mitigate evil circumstances. Rather, it apparently becomes our duty to aid and abet them. Moreover, if whatever is, is right, then we should not interfere in the slightest with the way things are in our world. Reform movements, on this view, must be viewed as positively immoral and pernicious. They are a kind of practical atheism which, in effect, say to the creation fresh from God's hands, 'Lo,—you are a miserable business; I will make you fairer!'' [10]

(c) The price that is paid for ultimate harmony is too great; ultimate harmony is not worth its cost in human misery. The end does not justify the means. The notion "all's well that ends well" is too simple-minded, particularly in this case, where we do not even know what the end is. Ivan makes this point forcefully in *The Brothers Karamazov*, in the section "Pro and Contra," where Ivan and Alyosha are discussing the problem of evil. The way he makes the point carries a person far beyond a simple understanding of it to a profound *feeling* for it. Let me paraphrase Ivan's great speech, however imperfectly, since it is too long to quote in full.

Take the suffering of children, Ivan tells Alyosha; there the point becomes very clear. Here is one example: a Russian general, retired on his great estate, treats his serfs like fools and buffoons. He is a great hunter and has many fine dogs. One day a serf boy of eight throws a stone in play and hurts the paw of the general's favorite dog. The general asks about his dog—what happened? After he is told, he has the boy locked in a shed overnight. Early the next morning the serfs, including the child's mother, are assembled for their edification. The child is stripped naked and told to run. The general sets the hounds after him, shouting "Get him, get him!" The dogs quickly overtake the boy and tear him to pieces in front of his mother's eyes. Did the general deserve to be shot? No doubt, but the atrocity already had been committed. If such an atrocity is needed to manure the soil for some future harmony, Ivan says, then such harmony is not worth the price. Then he asks, if *you* were God, Alyosha, could *you* consent to create a world in which everything turned out well in the end, but to achieve this end you had to see just one child tortured to death, beating its breast in a stinking outhouse, crying to "dear, kind God." No, it is not worth it. No doubt, God sees things differently from men. No doubt, on the day of resurrection, Ivan says, I too will join in the chorus, "Hallelujah, God, thy ways are just!" I too shall sing, as the mother embraces her son's murderer, "Praise God, I see why it had to be!" But, he

---

[9] Ibid., p. 105.

[10] Cf. E. H. Madden, "G. W. Curtis: Practical Transcendentalist," *The Personalist,* Vol. XL (1959), p. 373.

concludes, I loathe myself now for the very thought of doing that then. I renounce the "higher" morality, the ultimate harmony, altogether, while I still can, while there is still time. For the love of humanity I now renounce it altogether.

(d) The renunciation of the "higher" morality implied by the ultimate harmony theory requires further comment. J. S. Mill renounced it in the following way. He said, in effect: In everyday life I know what to call right or wrong, because I can plainly see its rightness or its wrongness. Now if a god requires that what I ordinarily call wrong in human behavior I must call right when he does it; or that what I ordinarily call wrong I must call right because he does, even though I do not see the point of it; and if by refusing to do so, he can sentence me to hell, to hell I will gladly go.

Theists have argued against Mill in the following way. Consider the moral relations between a father and son. Certainly a father knows moral principles of action that are unknown to his son. Now would it not be presumptuous for a son to say to his father that he could not accept as right anything of which he did not plainly see the rightness. Would it not be presumptuous to say, "Father, rather than call right what you call right—which I cannot, since this is not what I mean by right—I would be willing to go to—" —but theists do not repeat Mr. Mill's alternative. They ask, however, is it not just possible that there may be as much difference between man and God as there is between a child and his father.

This analogy, I believe, is not very convincing. We need to make the parallel more exact.[11] The child rightly has faith in his father's wisdom about things unknown to him. But the point is this: the child infers this wisdom from the wisdom and goodness of his father which he has seen and understood. He is, in short, as in all areas of thought, reasoning from the known to the unknown. With God, however, the case is quite otherwise. We are asked to accept a "higher" morality out of devotion and total ignorance. Indeed, the only thing we do know about it is that it runs counter to all that we *have* seen and understood about right and wrong. We are asked, in effect, to forget the little we know of right and wrong, abdicate our intelligence, submit ourselves to something we know not of, and all this out of blind devotion to the God about whom we wish to raise serious questions! If a child followed such a course of action toward his father, we would not think it an act of deep filial piety at all, but one of abject submission. The same attitude ought to exist, I submit, in the case of God and man.

At this point, the theist introduces a new gambit that is designed to cut off philosophical argument and discussion altogether. Belief in God, a higher morality, and ultimate harmony, they tell us, is a matter of faith—not blind faith, to be sure, but faith built on deep feeling and mystical

[11] Cf. Chauncey Wright, *Philosophical Discussions*, pp. 358–59.

experience.[12] About mystical experience and faith, presumably, there can be no philosophical argument. We have come, they say, to the moment of silence where nothing more can be said. I profoundly dislike this maneuver, so I have constructed a whimsical argument which staves off the moment of silence a while longer. That it is a whimsical argument will become evident by and by, but this quality, I hope, will not obscure the dead earnestness and significant points it contains.

The usual naturalistic way of explaining mystical experiences is well known. They are explained away by the concepts of abnormal psychology; they are results, some say, of hallucination, delusion, hypnosis, paranoia, *etc.* Indeed, if Saint Joan were alive today, hearing voices as she did, she would be committed immediately to a state mental hospital. However, I find it difficult to look at Saint Joan, Saint Therese, and Saint John of the Cross in this way. Rather, I shall accept all Christian mystical experiences at face value—assuming that they have significant religious meaning for those who experience them. Christian mysticism, however, is not the only kind. I have a friend who reported having a mystical experience with an all-powerful, all-evil god—"It was ghastly," he said, shaking even at the recollection of it. (If you do not choose to believe this, no matter; just consider that it is still a logical possibility.)

What, now, can the theists say to my friend? How can they show him to be wrong, for his sake and for their own peace of mind? They might, of course, explain the experience away by various hypotheses: he was drunk, he has a persecution complex, or whatever. But this tactic will not do; we have agreed that we would not explain away the Christian mystic's experience in such ways, but would accept it at face value. So, too, must the Christian accept my friend's experience at face value.

The theists, of course, still want mightily to show that my friend is mistaken. What can they say by way of rational argument to show that he is wrong? Why, they can point out to him that he has an insoluble problem of good on his hands. If God is all-powerful and all-evil, how can you explain the enormous amount of apparently unnecessary physical and moral good in the world? Consider, *e.g.*, how the soil, rain, and sunshine produce our crops and how many men have sacrificed themselves for the good of others. My friend sees that he has a problem but replies in the following way: yes, but I can square God's character with good by a contrast theory. Good is necessary as a contrast so that we shall be able properly to understand and feel the horror of evil. The theist objects that we do not need so much good to achieve this goal. My friend agrees, but offers another theory: it is man's free will, he says, which solves his problem. God granted man free will, knowing full well how he would use it to produce enormous evil. Unhappily, of course, if he is to have free will, he must be capable of doing good also. The theist objects that God's

---

[12] At this point the ultimate harmony view and the notion that God's ways simply "pass understanding" are indistinguishable.

omniscience and man's free will are incompatible concepts. My friend is forced to agree, but offers another theory: It Is, he says, the ultimate disharmony theory. What human beings call good is an event seen out of context, in isolation, and since man has only a fragmentary view of events, this is the only way he can see it. God, however, who has an overall view of events, sees how such events are evil in the long run or evil from an overall viewpoint. The theist objects that if one is not competent to know how good leads to evil, then he is not competent to judge evil either; for all he knows it might lead to good eventually. My friend retreats before this argument, but he has another—but it is not necessary to go further! The point should be perfectly clear by now that the problems of evil and good are completely isomorphic; what can be said about the one can be said about the other in reverse. For any solution to one problem, there is a parallel solution to the other, and for every counterargument in the one there is a parallel counterargument in the other.

There are two conclusions, or morals, to be drawn from my whimsical discussion of the problem of good. (a) All I ask the theist is to let others do unto him as he would do unto them. If people hold a position opposed to him and buttressed on the same ground of mysticism, he would wish to dissuade them from their view by rational argument in spite of their basing it on mystical experience. I simply wish to do the same to the theist. I do not say that he should ignore his mysticism and rely on rational argument alone, but I do suggest that he temper his mystical thought with a good dose of thought about his problem of evil, and check finally to see which way it goes.

(b) It is an interesting and ironic consequence of the problem of good that the theist cannot have what he wants both ways. He would like the problem of evil to be soluble, since he would dispose of the strongest anti-theistic argument thereby. On the other hand, he would like the problem of good to be insoluble, because this insolubility would be the best reason possible for giving up belief in an all-powerful, all-evil god. (By the way, the notion of an evil god is not all whimsey. It is difficult indeed to dispose of such a concept.) Unfortunately for the theist, he cannot have it both ways. Since the two problems are entirely isomorphic, if one is soluble so is the other, and if one is insoluble so is the other. The theist must choose one way or the other and lose something important either way he chooses.

GROUNDS FOR DISBELIEF IN GOD

John Hick

JOHN HICK is Professor of Theology at the University of Birmingham.
He is the author of *Faith and Knowledge* (1957), *Evil and the God
of Love* (1966), *Philosophy of Religion* (1973), among others.

The responsible skeptic, whether agnostic or atheist, is not concerned
with denying that religious people have had certain experiences as a result
of which they have become convinced of the reality of God. The skeptic
believes, however, that these experiences can be adequately accounted for
without postulating a God, by adopting instead a naturalistic interpretation of religion. Two of the most influential such interpretations will now
be discussed.

THE SOCIOLOGICAL THEORY OF RELIGION

Developed mainly by French sociologists, principally Emile Durkheim,[1]
earlier in the present century, this type of analysis appeals today to a
generation which is acutely conscious of the power of society to mold
for good or ill the minds of its members.

The sociological theory refers to this power when it suggests that the
gods whom men worship are imaginary beings unconsciously fabricated
by society as instruments whereby it exercises control over the thought
and behavior of the individual.

The theory claims that when men have the religious feeling of standing
before a higher power which transcends their personal lives and impresses its will upon them as a moral imperative, they are indeed in the
presence of a greater environing reality. This reality is not, however, a
supernatural Being; it is the natural fact of society. The encompassing
human group exercises the attributes of deity in relation to its members,
and gives rise in their minds to the idea of God, which, in effect, is thus
a symbol for society.

The sense of the holy and of God as the source of sacred demand,
claiming the total allegiance of the worshipper, is thus accounted for as
a reflection of society's absolute claim upon the loyalty of its members.
In primitive societies (in relation to which Durkheim's theory was originally worked out) this sense of the group's right to unquestioning

[1] *The Elementary Forms of the Religious Life*, 1912 (London: George Allen &
Unwin, Ltd., 1915).

obedience and loyalty is very strong. The tribe or clan is a psychic organism, within which the human members live as cells, not yet fully separated as individuals from the group mind. The tribal customs, beliefs, requirements, and taboos, are sovereign and bear collectively the awesome aspect of the holy. In advanced societies, this primitive unity enjoys a partial revival in time of war, when the national spirit is able to assert an almost unlimited authority over the citizens.

The key to the complementary sense of God as man's final succour and security is found in the way in which the individual is carried and supported in all the major crises of his life by the society to which he belongs. Man is social to the roots of his being, is deeply dependent upon his group, and is unhappy when isolated from it. It is the chief source of his psychic vitality, and he draws strength and reinforcement from it, when as a worshipper he celebrates with his fellows the religion which binds them together ("religion" derives from the Latin *ligare*, to bind or bind together).

It is, then, society as a greater environing reality standing over against the individual, a veritable "ancient of days" existing long before his little life and destined to persist long after his disappearance, that constitutes the concrete reality which has become symbolized as God. This theory accounts for the symbolization which transforms the natural pressures of society in to the supernatural presence of God by referring to a universal tendency of the human mind to create mental images and symbols.

Here, in brief, is an interpretation of the observable facts of religion that involves no reference to God as a supernatural Being who has created man and this world in which he lives. According to this interpretation, it is the human animal who has created God in order to preserve his own social existence.

Religious thinkers have offered various criticisms of this theory, perhaps the most comprehensive critique being that of H. H. Farmer.[2] The following difficulties have been stressed.

1. It is claimed that the theory fails to account for the universal reach of the religiously informed conscience, which on occasion goes beyond the boundaries of any empirical society and acknowledges a moral relationship to human beings as such. In the teaching of the great prophets and rabbis, and in the teaching of Jesus and of his church at its best, the corollary of monotheism has been pressed home: God loves *all* mankind and summons *all* men to care for one another as brothers.

How is this striking phenomenon to be brought within the scope of the sociological theory? If the call of God is only society imposing upon its members forms of conduct which are in the interest of that society, what is the origin of the obligation to be concerned equally for *all* men? Mankind as a whole is not a society as the term is used in the sociological theory. How, then, can the voice of God be equated with that of the

[2] See H. H. Farmer, *Towards Belief in God* (London: The Student Christian Movement Press, 1942), chap. 9, to which the present discussion is indebted.

group if this voice impels a man to extend to outsiders the jealously
guarded privileges of the group?

2. It is claimed that the sociological theory fails to account for the
moral creativity of the prophetic mind. The moral prophet is characteristically an innovator who goes beyond the established ethical code and
summons his fellows to acknowledge new and more far-reaching claims
of morality upon their lives. How is this to be accounted for if there is no
other source of moral obligation than the experience of the organized
group intent upon its own preservation and enhancement? The sociological theory fits a static "closed society"; but how can it explain the
ethical progress which has come about through the insights of pioneers
morally in advance of their groups?

3. It is claimed that the sociological theory fails to explain the socially
detaching power of conscience. Again the criticism focuses upon the
individual who is set at variance with his society because he "marches
to a different drum," for example, an Amos denouncing the Hebrew
society of his time or, to span the centuries, an Alan Paton or a Father
Huddleston rejecting the hegemony of his own race in South Africa. If
the sociological theory is correct, the sense of divine support should
be at a minimum or even altogether absent in such cases. The prophet
cannot have the support of God against society, if God is simply society
in disguise. The record shows, however, that the sense of divine backing
and support is often at a maximum in these situations. These men are
sustained by a vivid sense of the call and leadership of the Eternal. It is
striking that in one instance after another the Old Testament prophets
express a sense of closeness to God as they are rejected by their own
people; yet they belonged to an intensely self-conscious and nationalistic
society of the kind that, according to the sociological theory, ought to be
best able to impress its will upon its members.

It seems, therefore, that a verdict of "not proven" is indicated concerning this attempt to establish a purely natural explanation of religion.

THE FREUDIAN THEORY OF RELIGION

Sigmund Freud (1856–1939), the originator of psychoanalysis and a
figure comparable in importance with Galileo, Darwin, or Einstein, devoted a good deal of attention to the nature of religion.[3] He regarded
religious beliefs as ". . . illusions, fulfilments of the oldest, strongest and
most insistent wishes of mankind."[4] Religion, as Freud saw it, is a mental

[3] See his *Totem and Taboo* (1913), *The Future of an Illusion* (1927), *Moses and
Monotheism* (1939), *The Ego and the Id* (1923), and *Civilization and its Discontents* (1930).

[4] *The Future of an Illusion. The Complete Psychological Works of Sigmund Freud*,
newly translated and edited by James Strachey (New York: Liveright Publishing
Corporation and London: The Hogarth Press, 1961), XXI, 30.

defense against the more threatening aspects of nature—earthquake, flood, storm, disease, and inevitable death According to Freud, "With these forces nature rises up against us, majestic, cruel and inexorable." [5] But the human imagination transforms these forces into mysterious personal powers. "Impersonal forces and destinies [Freud said] cannot be approached; they remain eternally remote. But if the elements have passions that rage as they do in our own souls, if death itself is not something spontaneous but the violent act of an evil Will, if everywhere in nature there are Beings around us of a kind that we know in our own society, then we can breathe freely, can feel at home in the uncanny and can deal by psychical means with our senseless anxiety. We are still defenceless, perhaps, but we are no longer helplessly paralyzed; we can at least react. Perhaps, indeed, we are not even defenceless. We can apply the same methods against these violent supermen outside that we employ in our own society; we can try to adjure them, to appease them, to bribe them, and, by so influencing them, we may rob them of part of their power." [6] The solution adopted in Judaic-Christian religion is to project upon the universe the buried memory of our father as a great protecting power. The face which smiled at us in the cradle, now magnified to infinity, smiles down upon us from heaven. Thus, religion is ". . . the universal obsessional neurosis of humanity" [7] which may be left behind when at last men learn to face the world relying no longer upon illusions but upon scientifically authenticated knowledge.

In *Totem and Taboo*, Freud uses his distinctive concept of the Oedipus complex [8] (which rests on concurrent ambivalent feelings) to account for the tremendous emotional intensity of man's religious life and the associated feelings of guilt and of obligation to obey the behests of the deity. He postulates a stage of human pre-history in which the unit was the "primal horde" consisting of father, mother, and offspring. The father, as the dominant male, retained to himself exclusive rights over the females and drove away or killed any of the sons who challenged his position. Finding that individually they could not defeat the father-leader, the sons eventually banded together to kill (and also, being cannibals, to eat) him. This was the primal crime, the parricide which has set up tensions within the human psyche out of which have developed moral inhibitions, totemism, and the other phenomena of religion. Having slain their father, the band of brothers are struck with remorse, at least of a prudential kind. They also find that they cannot all succeed to his position and that there is a restraint. The dead father's prohibition accordingly takes on a new ("moral") authority as a taboo against incest. This association of religion with the Oedipus complex, which is renewed in each individual (for Freud

[5] Freud, *Complete Psychological Works*, XXI, 16.

[6] Freud, *Complete Psychological Works*, XXI, 16–17.

[7] Freud, *Complete Psychological Works*, XXI, 44.

[8] Oedipus is a figure in Greek mythology who unknowingly murdered his father and married his mother; the Oedipus complex of Freudian theory is the child's unconscious jealousy of his father and desire for his mother.

believed the Oedipus complex to be universal), is held to account for the mysterious authority of God in the human mind and the powerful guilt feelings which make men submit to such a phantasy. Religion is thus a "return of the repressed."

There is an extensive literature discussing the Freudian treatment of religion, which cannot be summarized here.[9] The "primal horde" hypothesis, which Freud took over from Darwin and Robertson Smith, is now generally rejected by anthropologists,[10] and the Oedipus complex itself is no longer regarded, even by many of Freud's disciples, as the key which unlocks all doors. Philosophical critics have further pointed out that Freud's psychic atomism and determinism have the status not of observational reports but of philosophical theories.

Although Freud's account of religion, taken as a whole, is highly speculative, and will probably be the least enduring aspect of his thought, his general view that faith is a kind of "psychological crutch" and has the quality of phantasy thinking is endorsed by many internal as well as external critics as applying to much that is popularly called religion. Empirical religion is a bewildering mixture of elements, and undoubtedly wish fulfillment enters in and is a major factor in the minds of many devotees.

Perhaps the most interesting theological comment to be made upon Freud's theory is that in his work on the father-image he may have uncovered the mechanism by which God creates an idea of himself in the human mind. For if the relation of a human father to his children is, as the Judaic-Christian tradition teaches, analogous to God's relationship to man, it is not surprising that human beings should think of God as their heavenly Father and should come to know him through the infant's experience of utter dependence and the growing child's experience of being loved, cared for, and disciplined within a family. Clearly, to the mind which is not committed in advance to a naturalistic explanation there may be a religious as well as a naturalistic interpretation of the psychological facts.

[9] Some of the discussions from the side of theology are: R. S. Lee, *Freud and Christianity* (London: James Clarke, 1948); H. L. Philip, *Freud and Religious Belief* (London: Rockliff, 1956); Arthur Guirdham, *Christ and Freud* (London: George Allen & Unwin, Ltd., 1959); and from the side of psychoanalytic theory, T. Reik, *Dogma and Compulsion* (New York: International Universities Press, 1951); M. Ostow and B. Scharfstein, *The Need to Believe* (New York: International Universities Press, 1954); J. C. Flugel, *Man, Morals and Society* (New York: International Universities Press, 1947).

[10] A. L. Kroeber, *Anthropology*, revised ed. (New York: Harcourt, Brace & World, Inc., 1948), p. 616. Kroeber describes the psychoanalytic explanation of culture as "intuitive, dogmatic, and wholly unhistorical." Bronislaw Malinowski remarks in the course of a careful examination of Freud's theory, "It is easy to perceive that the primeval horde has been equipped with all the bias, maladjustments and ill-tempers of a middle-class European family, and then let loose in a prehistoric jungle to run riot in a most attractive but fantastic hypothesis." Bronislaw Malinowski, *Sex and Repression in Savage Society* (London: Routledge & Kegan Paul, Ltd., 1927), p. 165.

Again, it seems that the verdict must be "not proven"; like the socio-logical theory, the Freudian theory of religion may be true, but has not been shown to be so.

THE CHALLENGE OF MODERN SCIENCE

The tremendous expansion of scientific knowledge in the modern era has had a profound influence upon religious belief. Further, this influence has been at a maximum within the Judaic-Christian tradition, with which we are concerned in this book. There has been a series of specific juris-dictional disputes between the claims of scientific and religious knowl-edge, and also a more general cumulative effect which constitutes a major element, critical of religion, in the contemporary intellectual climate.

Since the Renaissance, scientific information about the world has steadily expanded in fields such as astronomy, geology, zoology, chemistry, and physics; and contradicting assertions in the same fields, derived from the Bible rather than from direct observation and experiment, have increasingly been discarded. In each of the great battles between scien-tists and churchmen, the validity of the scientific method was vindicated by its practical fruitfulness. Necessary adjustments were eventually made in the aspects of religious belief which had conflicted with the scientists' discoveries. As a result of this long debate, it has become apparent that the biblical writers, recording their experience of God's activity in human history, inevitably clothed their testimony with their own contemporary pre-scientific understanding of the world. Advancing knowledge has made it possible and necessary to distinguish between their record of the divine presence and calling, and the primitive world-view which formed the framework of their thinking. Having made this distinction, the modern reader can learn to recognize the aspects of the Scriptures which reflect the pre-scientific culture prevailing at the human end of the divine-human encounter. Accordingly, we find that the three-storied universe of biblical cosmology, with heaven in the sky above our heads, hell in the ground beneath our feet, and the sun circling the earth but halting in its course at Joshua's command, is no longer credible in the light of modern knowl-edge. That the world was created some 6,000 years ago and that man and the other animal species came into being at that time in their present forms can no longer be regarded as a reasonable belief. Again, the expectation that at some future date the decomposed corpses of mankind through the ages will rise from the earth in pristine health for judgment has largely ceased to be entertained. Yet, in all of these cases, churchmen initially resisted, often with great vehemence and passion, scientific evi-dence which conflicted with their customary beliefs.[11] In part, this re-

[11] The classic history of these battles is found in A. D. White, *A History of the Warfare of Science with Theology* (1896), 2 vols. This history has recently been reprinted in a paperback edition by Dover Publications of New York.

sistance represented the natural reaction of conservative-minded men preferring established and familiar scientific theories to new and disturbing ones. But this reaction was supported and reinforced by an unquestioning acceptance of the propositional conception of revelation (see pp. 61–62). This conception assumes that all statements in the scriptures are God's statements; consequently, to question any of them is either to accuse God of being a liar or to deny that the Bible is divinely inspired.

The more general legacy of this long history of interlocking scientific advance and theological retreat is the assumption, which is part of the characteristic climate of thought in our twentieth-century Western world, that even though the sciences have not specifically disproved the claims of religion, they have thrown such a flood of light upon the world (without at any point encountering that of which religion speaks) that faith can now be regarded only as a harmless private phantasy. Religion is seen as a losing cause, destined to be ousted from more and more areas of man's knowledge until at last it arrives at a status precisely akin to that of astrology—a cultural "fifth wheel," persisting only as a survival from previous ages in which our empirical knowledge was much less extensive.

The sciences have cumulatively established the autonomy of the natural order. From the galaxies whose vastness numbs the mind to the unimaginably small events and entities of the sub-atomic universe, and throughout the endless complexities of our own world, which lies between these virtual infinities, nature can be studied without any reference to God. The universe investigated by the sciences proceeds exactly as though no God exists.

Does it follow from this fact that there is, indeed, no God?

There are forms of theistic belief from which this negative conclusion follows and others from which it does not.

If belief in the reality of God is tied to the cultural presuppositions of a pre-scientific era, this set of beliefs, taken as a whole, is no longer valid. But the situation is otherwise if we suppose (with much contemporary theology) that God has created this universe, in so far as its creation relates to man, as a neutral sphere in which his creatures are endowed with a sufficient degree of autonomy to be able to enter into a freely accepted relationship with their Maker. From this point of view, God maintains a certain distance from man, a certain margin for a creaturely independence which, although always relative and conditioned, is nevertheless adequate for man's existence as a responsible personal being. This "distance" is epistemic, rather than spatial. It consists in the circumstance that God, not being inescapably evident to the human mind, is known only by means of an uncompelled response of faith. (For a further elaboration of this idea, see pp. 70–71.) This circumstance requires that man's environment have the kind of autonomy which, in fact, we find it to have. The environment must constitute a working system capable of being investigated indefinitely without the investigator being driven to postulate God as an element within it or behind it. From the point of view of this conception of God, the autonomy of nature, as it is increasingly confirmed by the sciences, offers no contradiction to religious faith. The sciences are exploring a universe which is divinely created and sustained, but which has its own God-given autonomy and integrity. Such an understanding of God and of his purpose for the world is able to absorb scientific discoveries, both accomplished and projected, which have seemed to many religious believers to be profoundly threatening. The tracing back of man's continuity with the animal kingdom; the locating of the origin of organic life in natural chemical reactions taking place on the earth's surface, with the consequent prospect of reproducing these reactions in the laboratory; the exploration of outer space and the possibility of encountering advanced forms of life on other planets; the probing of the chemistry of personality and the perfecting of the sinister techniques of "brain-washing"; the harnessing of nuclear energy and the dread possibility of man's self-destruction in nuclear war—all of these facts and possibilities, with their immense potentialities for good or evil, are aspects of a natural order which possesses its own autonomous structure. According to religious faith, God created this order as an environment in which human beings, living as free and responsible agents, might enter into a relationship with God. All that can be said about the bearing of scientific knowledge upon this religious claim is that the claim does not fall within the province of any of the special sciences: science can neither confirm nor deny it.

From this theological point of view, what is the status of the miracle stories and the accounts of answered prayer which abound in the scriptures and in church records from the earliest to the present time? Must these be considered incompatible with a recognition that an autonomous natural order is the proper province of the sciences?

The answer to this question depends upon the way in which we define "miracle." It is possible to define the term in either purely physical and non-religious terms, as a breach or suspension of natural law, or in religious terms, as an unusual and striking event which evokes and mediates a vivid awareness of God. If miracle is defined as a breach of natural law, one can declare a priori that there are no miracles. It does not follow, however, that there are no miracles in the religious sense of the term. For the principle which states that nothing happens in conflict with natural law does not entail that there are no unusual and striking events which evoke and mediate a vivid awareness of God. Natural law consists of generalizations formulated retrospectively to cover whatever has, in fact, happened. When events take place which are not covered by the generalizations accepted thus far, the properly scientific response is not to deny that they occurred but to seek to revise and extend the current understanding of nature in order to include them. Without regard to the relevant evidence, it cannot be said that the story, for example, of Jesus healing the man with the withered hand (Luke 6:6–11) is untrue, or that comparable stories from later ages or from the present day are untrue. It is not scientifically impossible that unusual and striking events of this kind have occurred. Events which have religious significance that evoked and mediated a vivid sense of the presence and activity of God may have occurred, even though their continuity with the general course of nature cannot be traced in our present very limited state of human knowledge.

In the Protestant apologetic systems of former centuries, as in the official apologetic of Roman Catholicism today, miracles have played an important part. They have been supposed to empower religion to demand and compel belief. In opposition to this traditional view, many theologians today believe that far from providing the original foundation of religious faith, miracles presuppose such faith. The religious response, which senses the purpose of God in the inexplicable coincidence or the improbable and unexpected occurrence, makes an event a miracle. Thus, miracles belong to the internal life of a community of faith; they are not the means by which the religious community can seek to evangelize the world outside.[12]

The Problem of Evil

To many, the most powerful positive objection to belief in God is the fact of evil. Probably for most agnostics it is the appalling depth and extent of human suffering, more than anything else, that makes the idea of a loving Creator seem so implausible and disposes them toward one or another of the various naturalistic theories of religion.

As a challenge to theism, the problem of evil has traditionally been posed in the form of a dilemma: if God is perfectly loving, he must wish to abolish evil; and if he is all-powerful, he must be able to abolish evil. But evil exists; therefore God cannot be both omnipotent and perfectly loving.

Certain solutions, which at once suggest themselves, have to be ruled out so far as the Judaic-Christian faith is concerned.

To say, for example (with contemporary Christian Science), that evil is an illusion of the human mind, is impossible within a religion based upon the stark realism of the Bible. Its pages faithfully reflect the characteristic mixture of good and evil in human experience. They record every kind of sorrow and suffering, every mode of man's inhumanity to man and of his painfully insecure existence in the world.

---

[12] One of the best modern treatments of miracles is found in H. H. Farmer, *The World and God: A Study of Prayer, Providence and Miracle in Christian Experience*, 2nd ed. (London: Nisbet & Co., 1936). See also C. S. Lewis, *Miracles* (London: The Centenary Press, 1947).

There is no attempt to regard evil as anything but dark, menacingly ugly, heart-rending, and crushing. In the Christian scriptures, the climax of this history of evil is the crucifixion of Jesus, which is presented not only as a case of utterly unjust suffering, but as the violent and murderous rejection of God's Messiah. There can be no doubt, then, that for biblical faith, evil is unambiguously evil, and stands in direct opposition to God's will.

Again, to solve the problem of evil by means of the theory (sponsored, for example, by the Boston "Personalist" School) [13] of a finite deity who does the best he can with a material, intractable and co-eternal with himself, is to have abandoned the basic premise of Hebrew-Christian monotheism; for the theory amounts to rejecting belief in the infinity and sovereignty of God.

Indeed, any theory which would avoid the problem of the origin of evil by depicting it as an ultimate constituent of the universe, co-ordinate with good, has been repudiated in advance by the classic Christian teaching, first developed by Augustine, that evil represents the going wrong of something which in itself is good.[14] Augustine holds firmly to the Hebrew-Christian conviction that the universe is *good*—that is to say, it is the creation of a good God for a good purpose. He completely rejects the ancient prejudice, widespread in his day, that matter is evil. There are, according to Augustine, higher and lower, greater and lesser goods in immense abundance and variety; but everything which has being is good in its own way and degree, except in so far as it may have become spoiled or corrupted. Evil—whether it be an evil will, an instance of pain, or some disorder or decay in nature—has not been set there by God, but represents the distortion of something that is inherently valuable. Whatever exists is, as such, and in its proper place, good; evil is essentially parasitic upon good, being disorder and perversion in a fundamentally good creation. This understanding of evil as something negative means that it is not willed and created by God; but it does not mean (as some have supposed) that evil is unreal and can be disregarded. On the contrary, the first effect of this doctrine is to accentuate even more the question of the origin of evil.

Theodicy,[15] as many modern Christian thinkers see it, is a modest enterprise, negative rather than positive in its conclusions. It does not claim to explain, nor to explain away, every instance of evil in human experience, but only to point to certain considerations which prevent the fact of evil (largely incomprehensible though it remains) from constituting a final and insuperable bar to rational belief in God.

[13] Edgar Brightman's *A Philosophy of Religion* (Englewood Cliffs, N.J.: Prentice-Hall, Inc., 1940), chaps. 8–10, is a classic exposition of one form of this view.

[14] See Augustine's *Confessions*, Book VII, chap. 12; *City of God*, Book XII, chap. 3; *Enchiridion*, chap. 4.

[15] The word "theodicy," from the Greek *theos* (God) and *dike* (righteous), means the justification of God's goodness in the face of the fact of evil.

In indicating these considerations it will be useful to follow the traditional division of the subject. There is the problem of *moral evil* or wickedness: why does an all-good and all-powerful God permit this? And there is the problem of the *non-moral evil* of suffering or pain, both physical and mental: why has an all-good and all-powerful God created a world in which this occurs?

Christian thought has always considered moral evil in its relation to human freedom and responsibility. To be a person is to be a finite center of freedom, a (relatively) free and self-directing agent responsible for one's own decisions. This involves being free to act wrongly as well as to act rightly. The idea of a person who can be infallibly guaranteed always to act rightly is self-contradictory. There can be no guarantee in advance that a genuinely free moral agent will never choose amiss. Consequently, the possibility of wrongdoing or sin is logically inseparable from the creation of finite persons, and to say that God should not have created beings who might sin amounts to saying that he should not have created people.

This thesis has been challenged in some recent philosophical discussions of the problem of evil, in which it is claimed that no contradiction is involved in saying that God might have made people who would be genuinely free and who could yet be guaranteed always to act rightly. A quote from one of these discussions follows:

If there is no logical impossibility in a man's freely choosing the good on one, or on several occasions, there cannot be a logical impossibility in his freely choosing the good on every occasion. God was not, then, faced with a choice between making innocent automata and making beings who, in acting freely, would sometimes go wrong: there was open to him the obviously better possibility of making beings who would act freely but always go right. Clearly, his failure to avail himself of this possibility is inconsistent with his being both omnipotent and wholly good.[16]

A reply to this argument is suggested in another recent contribution to the discussion.[17] If by a free action we mean an action which is not externally compelled but which flows from the nature of the agent as he reacts to the circumstances in which he finds himself, there is, indeed, no contradiction between our being free and our actions being "caused" (by our own nature) and therefore being in principle predictable. There is a contradiction, however, in saying that God is the cause of our acting as we do but that we are free beings in relation to God. There is, in other words, a contradiction in saying that God has

[16] J. L. Mackie, "Evil and Omnipotence," *Mind* (April, 1955), 209. A similar point is made by Antony Flew in "Divine Omnipotence and Human Freedom," *New Essays in Philosophical Theology.* An important critical comment on these arguments is offered by Ninian Smart in "Omnipotence, Evil and Supermen," *Philosophy* (April, 1961), with replies by Flew (January, 1962) and Mackie (April, 1962).

[17] Flew, in *New Essays in Philosophical Theology.*

made us so that we shall of necessity act in a certain way, and that we are genuinely independent persons in relation to him. If all our thoughts and actions are divinely predestined, however free and morally responsible we may seem to be to ourselves, we cannot be free and morally responsible in the sight of God, but must instead be his helpless puppets. Such "freedom" is like that of a patient acting out a series of post-hypnotic suggestions: he appears, even to himself, to be free, but his volitions have actually been pre-determined by another will, that of the hypnotist, in relation to whom the patient is not a free agent.

A different objector might raise the question of whether or not we deny God's omnipotence if we admit that he is unable to create persons who are free from the risks inherent in personal freedom. The answer that has always been given is that to create such beings is logically impossible. It is no limitation upon God's power that he cannot accomplish the logically impossible, since there is nothing here to accomplish, but only a meaningless conjunction of words [18]—in this case "person who is not a person." God is able to create beings of any and every conceivable kind; but creatures who lack moral freedom, however superior they might be to human beings in other respects, would not be what we mean by persons. They would constitute a different form of life which God might have brought into existence instead of persons. When we ask why God did not create such beings in place of persons, the traditional answer is that only persons could, in any meaningful sense, become "children of God," capable of entering into a personal relationship with their Creator by a free and uncompelled response to his love.

When we turn from the possibility of moral evil as a correlate of man's personal freedom to its actuality, we face something which must remain inexplicable even when it can be seen to be possible. For we can never provide a complete causal explanation of a free act; if we could, it would not be a free act. The origin of moral evil lies forever concealed within the mystery of human freedom.

The necessary connection between moral freedom and the possibility, now actualized, of sin throws light upon a great deal of the suffering which afflicts mankind. For an enormous amount of human pain arises either from the inhumanity or the culpable incompetence of mankind. This includes such major scourges as poverty, oppression and persecution, war, and all the injustice, indignity, and inequity which occur even in the most advanced societies. These evils are manifestations of human sin. Even disease is fostered to an extent, the limits of which have not yet been determined by psychosomatic medicine, by moral and emotional factors seated both in the individual and in his social environment. To the extent that all of these evils stem from hu-

[18] As Aquinas said, ". . . nothing that implies a contradiction falls under the scope of God's omnipotence." *Summa Theologica*, Part I, Question 25, article 4.

man failures and wrong decisions, their possibility is inherent in the
creation of free persons inhabiting a world which presents them with
real choices which are followed by real consequences.

We may now turn more directly to the problem of suffering. Even
though the major bulk of actual human pain is traceable to man's mis-
used freedom as a sole or part cause, there remain other sources of pain
which are entirely independent of the human will, for example, earthquake, hurricane, storm, flood, drought, and blight. In practice, it is
often impossible to trace a boundary between the suffering which results
from human wickedness and folly and that which falls upon mankind
from without. Both kinds of suffering are inextricably mingled together
in human experience. For our present purpose, however, it is important
to note that the latter category does exist and that it seems to be built
into the very structure of our world. In response to it, theodicy, if it is
wisely conducted, follows a negative path. It is not possible to show
positively that each item of human pain serves the divine purpose of
good; but, on the other hand, it does seem possible to show that the
divine purpose as it is understood in Judaism and Christianity could
not be forwarded in a world which was designed as a permanent hedonistic paradise.[19]

An essential premise of this argument concerns the nature of the
divine purpose in creating the world. The skeptic's assumption is that
man is to be viewed as a completed creation and that God's purpose in
making the world was to provide a suitable dwelling-place for this fully-
formed creature. Since God is good and loving, the environment which
he has created for human life to inhabit is naturally as pleasant and
comfortable as possible. The problem is essentially similar to that of a
man who builds a cage for some pet animal. Since our world, in fact,
contains sources of hardship, inconvenience, and danger of innumerable
kinds, the conclusion follows that this world cannot have been created
by a perfectly benevolent and all-powerful deity.[20]

Christianity, however, has never supposed that God's purpose in the
creation of the world was to construct a paradise whose inhabitants
would experience a maximum of pleasure and a minimum of pain. The
world is seen, instead, as a place of "soul-making" in which free beings,
grappling with the tasks and challenges of their existence in a common
environment, may become "children of God" and "heirs of eternal life."
A way of thinking theologically of God's continuing creative purpose
for man was suggested by some of the early Hellenistic Fathers of the
Christian Church, especially Irenaeus. Following hints from St. Paul,
Irenaeus taught that man has been made as a person in the image of
God but has not yet been brought as a free and responsible agent into

---

[19] From the Greek *hedone,* pleasure.
[20] This is the nature of David Hume's argument in his discussion of the problem
of evil in his *Dialogues,* Part XI.

the finite likeness of God, which is revealed in Christ.[21] Our world, with
all its rough edges, is the sphere in which this second and harder stage
of the creative process is taking place.

This conception of the world (whether or not set in Irenaeus' theological framework) can be supported by the method of negative theodicy.
Suppose, contrary to fact, that this world were a paradise from which
all possibility of pain and suffering were excluded. The consequences
would be very far-reaching. For example, no one could ever injure
anyone else: the murderer's knife would turn to paper or his bullets
to thin air; the bank safe, robbed of a million dollars, would miracuously
become filled with another million dollars (without this device, on
however large a scale, proving inflationary); fraud, deceit, conspiracy,
and treason would somehow always leave the fabric of society undamaged.
Again, no one would ever be injured by accident: the mountain-climber,
steeplejack, or playing child falling from a height would float unharmed
to the ground; the reckless driver would never meet with disaster. There
would be no need to work, since no harm could result from avoiding
work; there would be no call to be concerned for others in time of need
or danger, for in such a world there could be no real needs or dangers.

To make possible this continual series of individual adjustments,
nature would have to work by "special providences" instead of running
according to general laws which men must learn to respect on penalty of
pain or death. The laws of nature would have to be extremely flexible:
sometimes gravity would operate, sometimes not; sometimes an object
would be hard and solid, sometimes soft. There could be no sciences,
for there would be no enduring world structure to investigate. In eliminating the problems and hardships of an objective environment, with
its own laws, life would become like a dream in which, delightfully but
aimlessly, we would float and drift at ease.[22]

One can at least begin to imagine such a world. It is evident that
our present ethical concepts would have no meaning in it. If, for example, the notion of harming someone is an essential element in the
concept of a wrong action, in our hedonistic paradise there could be no
wrong actions— nor any right actions in distinction from wrong. Courage and fortitude would have no point in an environment in which
there is, by definition, no danger or difficulty. Generosity, kindness, the
agape aspect of love, prudence, unselfishness, and all other ethical notions which presuppose life in a stable environment, could not even be
formed. Consequently, such a world, however well it might promote
pleasure, would be very ill adapted for the development of the moral
qualities of human personality. In relation to this purpose it would be
the worst of all possible worlds.

[21] See Irenaeus' *Against Heresies,* Book IV, chaps. 37 and 38.
[22] Tennyson's poem *The Lotus-Eaters,* well expresses the desire (analyzed by
Freud as a wish to return to the peace of the womb) for such "dreamful ease."

It would seem, then, that an environment intended to make possible the growth in free beings of the finest characteristics of personal
life, must have a good deal in common with our present world. It must
operate according to general and dependable laws; and it must involve
real dangers, difficulties, problems, obstacles, and possibilities of pain,
failure, sorrow, frustration, and defeat. If it did not contain the particular trials and perils which—subtracting man's own very considerable
contribution—our world contains, it would have to contain others instead.

To realize this is not, by any means, to be in possession of a detailed theodicy. It is to understand that this world, with all its "heart-
aches and the thousand natural shocks that flesh is heir to," an
environment so manifestly not designed for the maximization of human
pleasure and the minimization of human pain, may be rather well
adapted to the quite different purpose of "soul-making." [23]

These considerations are related to theism as such. Specifically,
Christian theism goes further in the light of the death of Christ, which
is seen paradoxically both (as the murder of the divine Son) as the worst
thing that has ever happened and (as the occasion of man's salvation)
as the best thing that has ever happened. As the supreme evil turned to
supreme good, it provides the paradigm for the distinctively Christian
reaction to evil. Viewed from the standpoint of Christian faith, evils do
not cease to be evils; and certainly, in view of Christ's healing work,
they cannot be said to have been sent by God. Yet, it has been the
persistent claim of those seriously and wholeheartedly committed to
Christian discipleship that tragedy, though truly tragic, may nevertheless be turned, through a man's reaction to it, from a cause of despair
and alienation from God to a stage in the fulfillment of God's loving
purpose for that individual. As the greatest of all evils, the crucifixion of
Christ, was made the occasion of man's redemption, so good can be
won from other evils. As Jesus saw his execution by the Romans as an
experience which God desired him to accept, an experience which was
to be brought within the sphere of the divine purpose and made to serve
the divine ends, so the Christian response to calamity is to accept the
adversities, pains, and afflictions which life brings, in order that they
can be turned to a positive spiritual use.[24]

At this point, theodicy points forward in two ways to the subject
of life after death, which is to be discussed in the following chapter.

First, although there are many striking instances of good being

[23] This brief discussion has been confined to the problem of human suffering. The
large and intractable problem of animal pain is not taken up here. For a discussion
of it see, for example, Nels Ferré, *Evil and the Christian Faith* (New York: Harper
and Row, Publishers, Inc., 1947), chap. 7; and Austin Farrer, *Love Almighty and
Ills Unlimited* (New York: Doubleday & Company, Inc., 1961), chap. 5.

[24] This conception of providence is stated more fully in John Hick, *Faith and
Knowledge* (Ithaca: Cornell University Press, 1957), chap. 7, some sentences from
which are incorporated in this paragraph.

triumphantly brought out of evil through a man's or woman's reaction to it, there are many other cases in which the opposite has happened. Sometimes obstacles breed strength of character, dangers evoke courage and unselfishness, and calamities produce patience and moral steadfastness. But sometimes they lead, instead, to resentment, fear, grasping selfishness, and disintegration of character. Therefore, it would seem that any divine purpose of soul-making which is at work in earthy history must continue beyond this life if it is ever to achieve more than a very partial and fragmentary success.

Second, if we ask whether the business of soul-making is worth all the toil and sorrow of human life, the Christian answer must be in terms of a future good which is great enough to justify all that has happened on the way to it.

The conclusion of this chapter is thus parallel to the conclusion of the preceding one. There it appeared that we cannot decisively prove the existence of God; here it appears that neither can we decisively disprove his existence.

RELIGION AND COMMITMENT

Kai Nielsen

KAI NIELSEN is Professor of Philosophy at the University of Calgary. He is the author of many articles and books on religion. See especially, *Contemporary Critiques of Religion* (1971), *Reason and Practice* (1971), and *Scepticism* (1973).

The end of ideology has been proclaimed. Whether or not it will come to an end is hard to predict. We do not know whether with our present understanding of ideology intellectuals will finally cease making claims that in reality are only empty rhetorical flourishes but are intended by their authors and taken by some of their hearers—hearers taken in by the ideology—to be grand cosmological claims about the nature and destiny of man.[1] But it is plain enough that a *philosopher ought not* as a philosopher to be an ideologist. Many think that philosophy, as conceptual analysis, should place itself quite modestly with the rest of the academic disciplines and renounce all claim to giving us reasoned insight into the human condition. Philosophers should not even seek to discover certain general principles, as Aristotle, Descartes and Hegel did, but they should limit themselves to conceptual analysis or, if you will, pure description

[1] These remarks about ideology were occasioned by a reading of Henry Aiken's perceptive essay "The Revolt Against Ideology," *Commentary* 37, no. 4 (1964): 29–30. For an exact account of the nature of ideological statements see my "On Speaking of God," *Theoria* 28 (1962): 118–125.

of those fundamental concepts that perplex us. It is often maintained that it is *not* a philosopher's job to propose general theses, to discover general principles, and above all it most certainly is not his job to be a sage or an ideologist. That is to say, it is not his job to tell his fellowman what his nature and destiny is or give him a blueprint of the good life. Any such attempt would be both absurd and unbelievably pretentious; his proper scholarly niche is to clear up the confusions that arise when we do not properly understand the workings of our language in certain very crucial areas, e.g., in talk about "time," "good," "God," "cause," "freedom," "truth," and the like.

Now I am ambivalent about this. I most certainly do not want, as a philosopher, to be an ideologist and I don't want other philosophers to be ideologists either. Ever since I was a graduate student, I have been distressed at the hollowness and the ideological character of traditional philosophers' talk about the nature and destiny of man. Much of what they have said about the nature of the good life has seemed to me ideological—empty obscurantist rhetoric passed off as statements of general principles about the ultimate nature of reality. Philosophers from Plato to Royce, and even down to such obscurantist mystagogues as Heidegger and Tillich, have indeed upon occasion said penetrating things about life. But, as John Passmore has perceptively noted, exactly the same thing can be found in the great novelists and dramatists.[2] The difference presumably is that the philosopher, unlike the sage, has *thought through* his principles; he doesn't *simply rely on insight* but also upon argument and reason. He doesn't seek simply to be perceptive but to give grounds for his insights. But the arguments one finds such philosophers using to support their insights are very obscure and often incoherent, and the metaphysical machinery is not infrequently scarcely intelligible. Increasingly with philosophers such as Heidegger, Sartre, and Jaspers, one gets what is in effect a contempt for closely reasoned argument. They dish out the dark, yet sometimes insightful sayings and you can either take them or leave them. They are not to be argued about and no serious attempt is made to reason for them. I expect what attracts nonphilosophers to Plato, Spinoza, or Sartre is not their towering metaphysical systems but their sage remarks about life. The strictly philosophical superstructure is not understood by them, but they feel that in some way—which they as neophytes do not understand—these philosophers' insights are supported by their obscure metaphysical superstructures and that people with a thorough training in philosophy can and do, if they are wise and deep men, understand this obscure talk and that perhaps they too could come to understand it, if only they would study it hard enough and long enough. But if even a little bit of what we have learned from analytic or linguistic philosophy is correct, these philosophical

2 These remarks were made by Professor Passmore in a lecture "What Is Philosophy?" given to the New York University Philosophy Club during the spring semester of 1964.

superstructures are in Wittgenstein's celebrated phrase "houses of cards."
Such philosophy is ideology and a good philosopher should oppose it
for what it is, e.g., he should show how disguised nonsense is patent
nonsense.

Rightly or wrongly, I believe that this low estimate of the metaphysical
claims and systematizings of much of traditional philosophy and contemporary continental philosophy is on the whole just. Yet, as I have said,
I am ambivalent, for while I want nothing of such metaphysics or such
philosophical systems, I am also unhappy with just doing analysis, *if*
this somehow is taken to *deny* that the *end* of a philosopher's activity
should be to give insight into the problems of life, though most certainly
insight supported by argument. I very much feel the force of Austin's
remark that we don't yet have enough clarity in philosophy and that
it will be time enough to say that clarity is not enough *in philosophy*
when we have achieved a tolerable degree of that. But I remain obsti-
nately concerned with the question *"Clarity for what?"* and, like Wittgenstein, I am concerned to "assemble reminders for a particular purpose."
I remain, if I dare put it so naively, concerned with trying to understand
the concept of truth and the concept of knowledge; and I find I am
interested in them because I am vitally interested in trying to know
what, if anything, it is possible to know about what sort of life a man
ought to lead, what would be a good life and what would be an ideal
society; and I very much want to know what, if anything, this has to do
with God, freedom and immortality. My activities as a philosopher
center around this enterprise, but I most certainly do not want to be
simply a sage, simply an undisciplined, free-floating intellectual, journalist
or publicist and most certainly I do not want simply to be an ideologist.
But I am prepared to argue for philosophical theses, though I am not
concerned to construct a philosophical system; but as a philosopher I am
concerned with the soundness of these theses and the necessity of giving
clear and convincing arguments for them. If I can bring this off, I should
hope and expect that it would have an important bearing, directly or
indirectly, on how a man should live his life and how we should order
society. I remain ambivalent about this; the fox in me warns me how
difficult it is and how pretentious it is. Yet it seems to me a task that
people should, though with fear and trembling, address themselves to.

But enough of such program constructing, enough of such grandiose
talk. Let me tie what I am trying to say to an example by saying something of religion. I shall also illustrate, by way of examples, (1) what I
mean by holding philosophical theses, for which I am prepared to give
arguments, and (2) to illustrate how these theses, if sound, would be
of considerable importance for our lives. It has long been a conviction
of mine—a conviction that has survived several changes in philosophical
orientation—that there is no reason, no intellectual justification or moral
need to believe in God. I am convinced that religious beliefs should

belong to the tribal folklore of mankind and there is no more need to believe in God than there is to believe in Santa Claus or the Easter Bunny. We do not need such beliefs to give our lives meaning or to undergird the moral life, and such beliefs are not essential for an understanding of the nature and destiny of man. The great religions do indeed contain bits which can serve as aspirational ideals, but in this respect there is nothing there that is not perfectly available to the atheist. That is to say, for *some* people religion may be of value as a kind of "moral poetry," but even in this way, it is not something essential to the human animal. Some people can get on very well without it. Man, I believe, should prize truth and should try to live according to what Freud called "the reality principle." But if he is to do this, he must reject the claims of religion. Here is my commitment. Let us have a look at how I can support it.

Let me state this conviction a little more fully and a little more exactly in the form of three philosophical theses. I shall then defend them and illustrate how I use philosophical analysis in their defense.

1. The ultimate basis or rationale of our morality cannot be grounded in our belief in God or in our belief that ultimate reality is being itself (whatever that may mean) or in anything of that order. In fact, just the reverse is the case, only if we already have some moral understanding, some *knowledge* of good and evil, could we ever come to believe that there is a God or properly understand what people are talking about when they speak of God.

2. When religious people talk of the love, mercy, and the omnipotence of God or even of His reality, they make statements which are either patently false, most probably false, or are, in a significant sense, unintelligible. Furthermore, modern theologians such as Buber, Tillich, Robinson, and Bultmann are no improvement on the traditional supernaturalists, for they either say, in extravagant Hegeloid jargon, something that is identical with what an atheist would or could consistently say or they engage in a kind of obscurantist gobbledygook that is as unintelligible as anything traditional supernaturalists tried to say. "There is a God" like "There is a Santa Claus" is a bit of mythology for it is either patently false, grossly improbable, or without the significant factual content it purports to have.

3. The claim, so characteristic of modern apologetics, that atheists are really believers in disguise, is not correct. Furthermore, there need be nothing either shallow, confused, or back-woodsy about atheism, and atheism is not itself, as such apologists claim, another religion. It is not even an *Ersatz*-religion.

Let us, in examining my first thesis, have a look at a fairly orthodox characterization of God. I take it from Pope Pius xi's Encyclical *Mit brennender Sorge*. In 1937, addressing himself to German Catholics, Pius xi first tells us what God is not:

Take care, Venerable Brethren, that above all, faith in God, the first and irreplaceable foundation of all religion, be preserved in Germany pure and unstained. The believer in God is not he who utters the name in his speech, but he for whom this sacred word stands for a true and worthy concept of the Divinity. Whoever identifies, by pantheistic confusion, God and the universe, by either lowering God to the dimensions of the world, or raising the world to the dimensions of God, is not a believer in God. Whoever follows that so-called pre-Christian Germanic conception of substituting a dark and impersonal destiny for the personal God, denies thereby the Wisdom and Providence of God. . . .

Whoever exalts race, or the people, or the State, or a particular form of State, or the depositories of power, or any other fundamental value of the human community—however necessary and honorable be their function in worldly things—whoever raises these notions above their standard value and divinizes them to an idolatrous level, distorts and perverts an order of the world planned and created by God: he is far from the true faith in God and from the concept of life which that faith upholds.[3]

Then Pius goes on to tell us what God really is. "Our God is the Personal God, supernatural, omnipotent, infinitely perfect, one in the Trinity of Persons, tri-personal in the unity of divine essence, the Creator of all existence, Lord, King and ultimate Consummator of the history of the world, who will not, and cannot, tolerate a rival god by His side." Orthodox Christians—Catholics and Protestants alike—have, until recently at least, all been asked to believe in such a God; and if we delete the part about the trinity of persons, we have a concept of Deity that is also integral to Judaism and Islam. There is much more to these religions than the asserting of certain dogmas, but one thing integral to these religions is just such a belief in God. It is presupposed in all the rest that a Christian and Jew does; it is presupposed in the rest of their religious activities. The core notion of such a Deity can be brefly put as follows: "God is the sole, supernatural, omnipotent, infinitely perfect creator and director of all finite existence." Now, in order to examine my first thesis, let us assume—what surely is to assume a lot—that such a statement is perfectly intelligible and a tolerably adequate characterization of God and let us also assume that there in fact is such a reality. In order to appraise my first thesis, let us now consider the relations between this God and morality. For a bit let us neglect, in asking this question, the phrase "infinitely perfect" in this characterization of God. Just consider (1) "There is a single, supernatural, omnipotent creator and director of all finite existence." What follows from this about what we *ought* to do and what would be good to do and what things, actions or attitudes, if any, are of *ultimate value?* The answer is nothing: (1) purports to be a factual statement and from a purely factual statement or from a set of factual statements no normative conclusions can be deduced. One cannot get a normative statement, directive of human behavior and/or attitudes, from purely non-normative statements.

[3] Anne Fremantle, ed., *The Papal Encyclicals* (New York: New American Library, 1956), p. 25.

To this it may be replied that while we cannot derive an *ought* from an *is*, we can and do all the time use factual statements to support our normative judgments. This is indeed true. Furthermore the existence of a single, supernatural, omnipotent creator and director of all finite existence would be a fact of great relevance to a believer. Given that fact (assuming now that it is a fact) and given the further fact that this Being commands a certain thing, a believer would most certainly judge that he ought to do what this being commands. But why, we might very well ask? His being creator of man and all finite existence, his being the omnipotent director of all finite existence does not *prove* or in any way establish his goodness, does not show that He is *worthy* of being obeyed. He might, with those attributes, even be a malevolent deity. After all, what did Job learn when God spoke to him out of the whirlwind but that God was marvelously powerful, that God was his creator and the like? Given God's behavior to Job and given God's pact with Satan, it would have been more reasonable for Job to have concluded with Schopenhauer that God is evil. How does power, intelligence, and creativity by itself show goodness?

If the Christians' picture of the world is true, we ultimately owe our existence to God and, given that we *prize* our existence, we should be glad of that. But this surely does not exhibit His goodness any more than the fact that we proximately owe our existence to the hot night of our father's desire exhibits our father's goodness. Given God's power and intelligence, it is certainly prudent to follow the commandments and directives of God. No one wants to suffer. But, in the heyday of their power, it would also have been prudent to follow the directives of a Hitler or a Stalin if you were under their hegemony. But these are prudential reasons for acting in one way rather than another. We have not yet found any *moral* reason for doing as God commands.

Well, we should do what God commands for God is all wise and perfectly good. It is only by dropping part of the Pope's characterization of God that we made difficulties for ourselves here. The Pope, as all believers do, conceives of God as being infinitely perfect.

Granting this conception, as surely we must, let us now ask: how do they or how can we come to *know* that God is infinitely perfect. Granted that a believer assumes it or presupposes it, why does he? What reasons does he have for his presupposition? And how could the man without faith come to know that God is infinitely perfect or even good?

Suppose we say: "Here is where we need Revelation, the Bible and an awareness of the concrete actions of God. Here is where our knowledge of Jesus is essential. Jesus the mediator through his moral perfection teaches us something of the infinite perfection of God. We see in gentle Jesus wisdom and goodness and thus we come to know the little we can know of the infinite goodness of God."

Now one might dispute about Jesus' perfection: one might wonder why *this* Bible, *this* putative revelation rather than that? Why the Bible rather than the *Koran* or the *Upanishads,* the *Kalevala,* the *Bhagavadgita* or the *Lotus of the Good Law?* But all such questions aside, let us for the sake of the argument assume that Jesus is perfect and The Old and New Testaments are the sole ultimate source of genuine revelation, still it is we finite creatures who saw in Jesus' behavior perfection and goodness. Using our own finite moral powers, we recognized that Jesus was this moral exemplar pointing to the infinite perfection of God; beyond that we also recognized that the parables of the Bible were so *noble* and *inspiring* that the Bible *ought* to be taken as our model in moral matters. But these things show, as clearly as can be, that in making these moral assessments we already have a moral criterion, quite independent of the Bible, God, and Jesus, in virtue of which we make these moral judgments.

The believer should say, I think, if he has his wits about him, that he doesn't have and can't have *reasons* for his assertion, anymore than I can have reasons for my assertion that all bachelors are males for, "God is infinitely perfect" is true by definition. It is, in the language of modern philosophy, analytic and this is why it is not open for the believer to question the goodness or perfection of God. Nothing within Christian and Jewish discourse would be called "God" unless it were also called "all good" and "infinitely perfect." This requirement is built into the very logic of God-talk and thus there can be no justification of it or no question of giving evidence for it. Believer and non-believer alike must recognize that within such religious discourse "God is *not* infinitely perfect" is a contradiction.

But doesn't this show, as clearly as anything could, that my first thesis is unsound? Not in the slightest. I can most economically show this in the following way: "God" in such discourses functions as a proper name, though indeed, like "Churchill" and "Mussolini" and unlike your names and mine, a name that takes certain fixed descriptions. Now as a proper name it must make reference, it must denote, it must stand for something that at least conceivably could exist. Now when we say something is good or bad, perfect or imperfect, we are not simply applying a certain descriptive predicate to it. We are not just characterizing it as having a certain property that could, directly or indirectly, be discovered by observation. What we are doing when we ascribe value to something is very difficult to say; sometimes we are expressing our approval of it, taking some interest in it, commending it and the like, but one thing is clear: "good" or "perfect" are not property words like "red" or "hard." We could not discover some action or person to be good by simply observing it quite independently of any attitudes we might take toward it. Now in considering the concept of God think for a moment only of what the term "God" purports to refer to. From what we observe in the world what could be given in an encounter with God or what could be postulated as actual characteristics of the deity? That is, we note our finitude and dependency and this leads us to conceive of a non-dependent, infinite being. Considering only this—considering that infinite but unique non-spatio-temporal individual that is supposed to be the *denotatum* of our word "God"—how do you know, from simply in some way being aware of the reality of that entity, that this individual is good or infinitely perfect? How can you know, except through your own limited, finite, fallible moral judgments concerning any X whatsoever that it is infinitely perfect or for that matter even perfect or good, where X is simply a force, creator, first cause, ground of being, whether spatio-temporal or non-spatio-temporal, finite or infinite? The answer is that you can't and thus in the most fundamental respect your moral judgments can't be derived from or based upon the fact that there is or is not a reality, some force or supernatural being or ground of being, whom some people call "God." "X is a powerful creator of everything other than himself, a director and sustainer of the universe but all the same X is evil" is perfectly possible. That such a Being *says* he is good, *says* he is infinitely perfect does not prove that he is, even if he is omniscient and omnipotent. How can we know or have reason to believe, except by making up our own minds that he or it is perfect or good? Fallible though our insight is, we must rely on it here.

When we decide to use the label "God" for this alleged Power or, if you will, this ground of being, we imply that this reality is infinitely perfect, but we are able to do this only because we have a prior and logically independent moral understanding that could *not* have been derived simply from discovering that there is a reality transcendent to the world, a reality that created man and sustains him, or from discovering that there is some being *as such*, some ground of being, that is the dimension of depth in the natural. In this crucial way morality, even Christian morality, must be independent of religion. In fact just the reverse is the case, for before we can intelligibly decide that some reality is worthy of worship and thus properly called "God" or some reality is ultimately gracious, to use the obscure talk of Macquarrie and Robinson, and thus our God, we must have some independently arrived at concept of worthiness or graciousness. Thus in a very crucial sense religion presupposes a moral understanding that is logically independent of religion and not, as Brunner, Kierkegaard, and Barth would have it, just the reverse. To say this is not an expression of human hubris, but simply a matter of logic.

Someone might very well accept this *logical* point and still insist that I miss an important *psychological* point about how religions reinforce the moral beliefs of many people. I recall a psychiatrist once saying to me, after I had given a lecture on psychoanalysis and religion, that while he didn't need religion, while many people didn't need religion, a significant number of people who came to him for help very much needed their religion to attain psychological stability. Their chance of finding any significance in their lives, and no doubt their ability to hold onto any effective moral orientation, was tied for all practical purposes to their holding onto their religious beliefs. But he also agreed that if they had been differently indoctrinated, soberly educated without these religious myths, they would not need this religious crutch. Yet his central point was that if we look at the actual, concrete situation, it is manifest that many people need their religion to give meaning to their lives. Many men know what they should do, but can't bring themselves to do it, many need the moral imagery, the parables, the stories of their religions; and they very much need the solidarity, the sense of belonging, that religion gives them. Without their religion they would as a matter of fact lose their aspirational ideals; their capacity for moral endeavor would be blighted. In a word, they need religion to put their heart into virtue.

Nothing I have said was calculated to deny this or even underplay it, though I should not like to see it apologetically overplayed into the Pascalian theme that *all* men need religion to give significance and moral orientation to their lives. But a recognition of this psychological truth does nothing to show how our knowledge of good and evil does or even can rest on our belief in God or in our knowledge that such a reality exists. It only shows how some men with an understanding of good and evil need a *prod* and *crutch* to continue to act as moral agents.

No doubt most people, in point of origin, get their moral beliefs from their religion in the sense that moral talk for many is first introduced in the context of religious talk, and later, psychologically speaking, they need to associate difficult moral endeavours with these religious pictures. But questions of *validity* are independent of *origin*. Such a psychological account says nothing whatsoever about how we can justify moral beliefs or about our *knowledge* of good and evil. This, as I have shown, is independent of religion. Furthermore, it does not show that all people need such images or that moral belief and significant moral endeavour could not survive and would not have a point in the twilight or even in the complete absence of the gods.

I shall now support my second thesis. Religion, as Hepburn has wisely reminded us, should not be identified with its doctrinal formulae; furthermore the great religions of the world have a unity, amidst a very considerable internal complexity, that makes it difficult to understand their central doctrinal claims in isolation.[4] Yet in stressing this, one must not make a new "myth of the whole," one must not neglect the fact that presupposed in these religions are certain very mysterious allegedly factual claims. And if they are truly factual claims, as they appear to be, they must have a certain logical character. For any statement p to be a bona fide factual statement the assertion and denial of p must *not* be equally compatible with any conceivable observation that might be made. If p and not-p have exactly the same empirical consequences, if everything that is logically possible for us to experience is equally com-

---

[4] Ronald Hepburn, "A Critique of Humanist Theology," in *Objections to Humanism*, ed. H. J. Blackham (Philadelphia: Lippincott, 1963), pp. 52–54.

patible with the truth and falsity, or the probable truth and falsity, of p and not-p then p and not-p are *not* factual statements, whatever p and not-p may be. This, of course, does not mean that in every respect they are meaningless. (In fact the ability to deny p implies that in *some sense p* is intelligible.) But what I have said above does show that p and not-p are devoid of factual significance or intelligibility if such conditions obtain. In short they could not be statements of fact.

Religious people, however, do believe that certain of their very central religious doctrines are statements of fact. They presuppose "there is a God"—that they do not utter it very often is logically irrelevant—and they believe "God created the world." Both of these statements they take to be factual statements.

A sufficiently anthropomorphic believer—someone who thinks that in *some way* it is literally possible to see God—might well use these statements as bona fide factual statements. For him God would be very much like the Homeric gods except that his monotheism commits him to taking God to be a loner and not the head of a clan of gods. But it is simply superstitious to believe in *such* a god. What evidence do we have for such a god up there or out there? [5] Who has observed him under controlled conditions? Why is it that the Eskimos see Sedena, a female God, who lives in the sea and not on the land and who controls the storms, the weather, and the sea mammals, while the Israelites with a very different family structure and very different problems see Yahweh, a God of the desert and a ferocious male God who protects the Israelites from alien peoples? The Alaskan Eskimos by contrast have their risks in the winter sea mammal hunting; here they meet some of the crucial crises of their lives. The anthropomorphic deities of the various cultures are tailor-made projectively to meet the anxieties and emotional needs of their members. [6] It isn't a question of first seeing or somehow apprehending Sedena or Yahweh and then making certain claims. It is rather a matter of projecting certain needs onto the universe and then making up stories about the deifications. Our divinities are fashioned projectively to fit our cultural preoccupations.

Even more fundamentally—all questions of origin apart—who has seen or in any way apprehended Sedena, Yahweh, Zeus, Wotan or Fricka? We have no good evidence for their existence. Belief in such anthropomorphic deities is intelligible enough. "Fricka exists" or "there is a God" are in such a context something we can understand. But to believe that there are such anthropomorphic divinities is just a bald superstition. To believe that there are such gods is like believing that there is a Santa Claus or that there are fairies.

---

[5] Some of the difficulties, evasions, and obscurities are brought out in Robinson's somewhat sensational book *Honest to God* and in the subsequent volume *The Honest to God Debate*.

[6] Weston LaBarre, "Religions, Rorschachs, and Tranquilizers," *The American Journal of Orthopsychiatry* 29 (1959): 688–698.

But sophisticated believers and, I believe, even most plain believers for a long time have ceased believing in such anthropomorphic gods. God is neither up there, down there or out there in any literal sense. God is not a reality you can see or even apprehend. God is thought to be transcendent to the whole cosmos, the creator and sustainer of this cosmos, but He is still somehow a person, an individual—though an infinite individual—who is non-identifiable, non-spatio-temporal, and in no spatio-temporal relation with the world.[7] The object of our discourse when we discourse of God—when we talk *to* as well as *about* God—is taken to be an infinite, non-spatio-temporal particular named by the name "God." But given this sophisticated use, "There is a God" or "God created the world" are not false but unfalsifiable statements, completely incapable of being confirmed or disconfirmed. No matter how much order we see in the world, the non-believer can deny what the believer affirms with as much and with as little plausibility. He can quite consistently, after taking note of this order, assert that there is no God and that the observed order is just a natural part of the world; likewise no matter how much evil and disorder there is, the believer can speak of man's corruption and God's inscrutable grace. The believer can and does go on making his affirmations, no matter what happens and the non-believer can and does make his denials no matter what happens. Try this little experiment for yourselves: if you think of yourselves as believers, what *conceivable* turn of observable events would make you say you were mistaken or probably mistaken in holding that belief; and if you think of yourself as an atheist or as an agnostic try this experiment on yourself: what *conceivable* turn of observable events, if only you were to observe them, would make you say you were mistaken or probably mistaken in denying or doubting that it is true or probably true that there is a God? If the God you believe in, deny, or doubt, is anything like the non-anthropomorphic God I have just characterized, I predict you will not be able to answer that question. But if this is so, and I think it is, then your alleged God-statements "there is a God" or "God created the world" are devoid of *factual* significance. They are then equally compatible with anything and everything that the believer and non-believer alike can conceive as being experienceable. This being the case, they are no more saying anything that is in reality incompatible, than the American is asserting anything that the Englishman is not when the American calls all those things and only those things elevators that the Englishman calls lifts. The man, in such a circumstance, who says "there is a God" is not asserting anything incompatible with or even different from the statement of a man who says "there is no God." But this shows that neither statement has factual content; neither succeeds in asserting nor denying the existence of the peculiar reality that they were

[7] This is most clearly put by I. M. Crombie in his "The Possibility of Theological Statements," in *Faith and Logic,* ed. Basil Mitchell (London: George Allen and Unwin, Ltd., 1957), pp. 31–83.

meant to assert or deny. Belief, paradoxically enough, becomes indistinguishable from atheism. But this, in effect, shows that such a believer has not succeeded in showing how he can make a claim to reveal a reality or reveal some level of reality that the non-believer does not grasp. The realm of the supernatural remains unrecognizable.

We are no better off, if like Tillich and Robinson, we reject supernaturalism and claim that to speak of God being transcendent to the cosmos is to speak metaphorically or that to speak of the creation of the world by God is to speak metaphorically, for we are still saddled with very similar difficulties. Consider the following sentences, sentences that are used to make central claims within their theologies.

1. There is being itself.
2. There is a creative ground of being and meaning.
3. The *agape* of the cross is the last word about Reality.
4. Reality is not ultimately impersonal or neutral; it is ultimately gracious.
5. God is the beyond in the midst of our lives.

Apply the same tests to these statements. What conceivable experiences would lend probability to any of these statements, would make it more or less reasonable to believe them to be true? What would confirm or disconfirm them where they are taken to affirm something incompatible with what a non-believer could say? These obscurantist statements are no more capable of supporting belief than are the familiar claims of traditional theism. You are being deluded if you think people like Tillich, Bultmann or Robinson will take you beyond the chains of illusion. All you are doing is substituting an unfamiliar absurdity for a familiar one.

There is an important objection to my arguments that deserves careful attention. Such an objector agrees "there is a God," is intended, when believers use it in typical contexts, to assert a fact.[8] He would stress, as I would, that it most certainly is not intended simply to express a person's attitude toward the world or simply to guide conduct or alter behaviour. But, he would add, we must not forget there are all kinds of assertions and many kinds of factual statements. By taking "there is a God" to be a contingent factual statement asserting a contingent fact or a "contingent state-of-affairs" one distorts the actual logic of God-talk. We must not violate the integrity of God-talk by forcing upon it alien rules or alien criteria. If we, as we should, consider how "God" and "there is a God" are actually used in religious contexts, we will come to see that the existence of God cannot be taken to be a "contingent fact," and if "there is a God" cannot be taken to be "a contingent fact" then the proposition

[8] The views I have in mind are clearly expressed by Bowman L. Clarke in his "Linguistic Analysis and the Philosophy of Religion," *The Monist* 47 (Spring 1963): 365–386; and Charles Hartshorne, *The Logic of Perfection* (LaSalle, Illinois: The Open Court Publishing Co., 1962).

which asserts the existence of God cannot, it is argued, be a contingent proposition. "There is a God" must be taken to be logically or necessarily true.

This being so, it, of course, makes no sense to ask how "there is a God" can be verified or falsified, confirmed or disconfirmed, for it is a mark of a logical or necessary truth that it is true a priori. The man who asks for some contingent, empirical state of affairs to verify an a priori or logical statement merely shows that he does not understand the statement in question.[9] He shows by his very request, that he doesn't understand what an a priori statement is. Given that "there is a God" is logically and thus necessarily true and that God, the superlatively good and only adequate object of worship, necessarily exists, my request for confirmation or disconfirmation is utterly inappropriate.

But why say God's existence is necessary and that "there is a God" is a logical truth or necessarily true? A crucial and typical employment of "there is a God" is to assert that there is a being, superlatively worthy of worship, who is the sole adequate object of the religious attitude of worship. But an adequate object of such an attitude could not be a being who just happens to exist, or might come to exist or cease to exist or upon whom other beings just happen to depend.[10] Such an object of worship, that is God, must be a being whose nonexistence is wholly unthinkable in any circumstance. There must be no conceivable alternative to such a reality. Since, by definition, God is said to be that reality upon which all other things depend for their very existence, we could not, of course, state even a conceivable state of affairs that would be incompatible with His existence for, for any X if some conceivable state of affairs Y is incompatible with the existence of X, then X by definition could not be God, for Y would attest to the fact that there was something whose existence did not depend on X. Similarly since God's nonexistence is unthinkable under any circumstance (including any conceivable circumstance), God's existence is necessary and "there is a God" is logically true and asserts a "logical fact."

There are a host of objections that can and have been made to arguments of this sort, but I shall here, so as to not go too far afield, limit myself to one.[11] The crucial point I want to make here is just this: in asserting that in calling something "God" we must also say about that object of our discourse that its existence is necessary, its nonexistence

[9] J. N. Findlay, "Can God's Existence Be Disproved?" in *New Essays in Philosophical Theology* (New York: The Macmillan Co., 1955), pp. 47–57.

[10] Ibid., p. 52.

[11] Terrence Penelhum's essay "Divine Necessity," *Mind* 69 (1960): 175–186, the essays in response to Malcolm's defense of the ontological argument by Allen, Abelson and Penelhum, *The Philosophical Review* (January 1961): pp. 56–92; Robert C. Coburn's, "Professor Malcolm on God," *Australasian Journal of Philosophy* 41 (1963); John O. Nelson, "Modal Logic and the Ontological Proof for God's Existence," *The Review of Metaphysics* 17 (1963); and Adel Daher, "God and Logical Necessity," *Philosophical Studies* (Dublin, Ireland) 18 (1969) all raise effective arguments against some facets of such a position.

wholly unthinkable, it is not at all necessary to construe "necessary" or "the necessity" here as "logically necessary" or "logical necessity." [12] The modal term "necessary" has many uses. As Anscombe and Geach point out "since what is 'necessary' is what 'cannot' not be, to say that 'necessary' can only refer to logical necessity is equivalent to saying that whatever cannot be so, logically cannot be so—e.g., that since I cannot speak Russian, my speaking Russian is logically impossible: which is absurd." [13]

It is true that if something is appropriately designated by the word "God," it cannot not-exist. But it doesn't at all follow from this, what is prima facie implausible, that "there is no God" is a contradiction and "there is a God" is a logical truth. This would only follow if the "cannot" in "cannot not-exist" were a logical cannot, but what evidence do we have that this is so? Surely it looks as if we could significantly deny that there is a God.

That God couldn't just happen to exist, come to exist, cease to exist, if He exists at all, establishes that we conceive of God as an eternal being, but that "God is eternal" is analytic does not at all prove that an eternal being exists or that there are eternal beings. God couldn't come to exist or cease to exist, but it might be the case that there is no God.

That "God" is so defined that other beings are said to be completely dependent on God and that this dependence is not merely fortuitous does not prove that "there is a God" is logically necessary. "There is no completely independent being upon whom all beings depend" or "there is a reality whose existence is necessary for all other being" can be significantly denied.

God's existence is thought to be necessary; but there is no good reason at all for thinking His existence is *logically* necessary or "there is a God" is logically true; and there is prima facie, though perhaps not decisive evidence, for asserting that God's existence is not logically necessary, namely that existential statements do not appear to be logical truths and that more specifically, "there is no God" does not at all appear to be self-contradictory or in any way contradictory. When believes say, as many of them do, that God's nonexistence is wholly unthinkable in any circumstance, they need not be taken to be holding a theory about the logical status of "there is a God," namely that it is self-contradictory to deny that God exists. They can be taken to be asserting that the presence of God is so evident to them that, given their conception of Him as an eternal being, they could not, as a matter of psychological fact, in any way find it thinkable that God should not exist. God's actuality is so vividly present to believers that they could no more, except in a purely logical sense,

---

[12] This is nicely shown by John Hick, "Necessary Being," *Scottish Journal of Theology* 14 (1961): 355–369 and Alvin Plantinga, "Necessary Being," in *Faith and Philosophy*, ed. Alvin Plantinga (Grand Rapids, Michigan: Wm. B. Eerdmans Co., 1964), pp. 97–108.

[13] G. E. M. Anscombe and P. T. Geach, *Three Philosophers: Aristotle, Aquinas and Frege* (Oxford: Oxford University Press, 1961), p. 114.

come to doubt for one moment the reality of God than I could doubt that the earth has existed for many years and that I have been on or near to the surface of that earth during my life. I recognize that I can significantly deny these propositions (after all they are not analytic) but, like Moore, I am quite certain of them and I find it quite unthinkable that they might be false. When certain believers tell us that the non-existence of God (that reality given to them through faith) is quite unthinkable, it is very plausible to take him to be making such an assertion.

God's existence is thought to be necessary; that is, if God exists the existence of God is without beginning or end and without dependence for existence upon any reality other than himself. But this necessity is not a logical necessity but the *aseity* of the scholastics or what Hick calls a factual necessity.[14]

Thus it will not do to try to evade my contention that, given a non-anthropomorphic conception of God, "there is a God," is not an intelligible factual statement by claiming "there is a God" is logically true and asserts a "logical fact." There is no convention in English or logical rule which makes "there is no God" a contradiction. One might, by suitable stipulations and a little ingenuity, set up an artificial "ideal language" in which, given certain stipulative meaning-postulates, "there is no God," when interpreted by that "language," would be a contradiction, but this would only prove that certain people with certain needs and a certain amount of logical ingenuity had constructed such an artificial language. It would show nothing at all about whether "there is no God," which after all is part of the corpus of English, or its German, Spanish, or Swahili equivalents, is used to make a contradictory statement. In short, it would be of absolutely no avail in showing that the statement that there is no God is a contradiction and its denial a logical truth. Thus there are good grounds for thinking that "there is a God" is *not* a logical truth and there are no good grounds for thinking that it is; but, as even Clarke (a defender of the above view) insists, "there is a God" is surely taken to assert something and it is a statement around which ultimately all theistic discourse revolves.[15] It is not a logical statement asserting a "logical fact"; it is rather intended by believers as a factual statement asserting what, logically speaking, is a "contingent fact." But then our initial questions about confirmation and disconfirmation are perfectly relevant and this criticism of my argument fails. Consider the following: (1) there is a God; (2) there is an eternal being; (3) there is an infinite, non-spatio-temporal individual who never began to exist and never shall *cease* to exist and upon whom all other beings depend. When (1) and (2) are asserted by non-anthropomorphic believers and when (3) is asserted, their asserters do not know what, even in principle, would confirm or disconfirm these putatively factual assertions. Since this is so they are

[14] John Hick, p. 365.
[15] Bowman Clarke, p. 376.

bogus, pseudo-factual statements, devoid of the kind of intelligibility that believers rightly demand of them.

Once we leave a simple but false or highly improbable anthropomorphic theism, we find that the key claims of non-anthropomorphic, truly transcendent theistic beliefs are thought by those who accept these beliefs to be beliefs which are expressed in mysterious yet genuinely factual, non-analytic statements; but these key theological statements, unfortunately, are not factual claims for, being unverifiable in principle, they are devoid of factual significance. In short, key doctrines of Judaism, Christianity, and Islam, doctrines without which these religions would be radically transformed and thoroughly undermined, are confused beliefs, parading as factual beliefs but actually functioning as bits of ideology that distort our understanding of the world and give a delusory support to certain peoples' basic commitments by making them appear to be based on facts, written so to say in the stars.[16] If what I have said in this essay is generally correct one ought to be an atheist and reject religious belief, anthropomorphic or non-anthropomorphic, as irrational and unnecessary.

This brings me to my third and final thesis, namely my thesis about atheism. Kierkegaard and Tillich and many like them claim atheism is impossible. Atheism, in their view, is something like a contradiction for, in their very seriousness, in their very concern to destroy idols, atheists exhibit their belief, i.e., exhibit that in a profound sense they are *not* atheists. There is, as I shall show, an inordinate amount of confusion in such a claim. Atheism is not a kind of religion: it is not incoherent or contradictory; it is a reasonable belief that we all ought to adopt.

But before I go into that there are some important terminological distinctions that ought to be made. The first I owe to my colleague Paul Edwards and the second to the British philosopher Alasdair MacIntyre. Edwards points out that there are two ways in which the word "atheism" is used. Sometimes when a man maintains that there is no God he *simply* means that "there is a God" or "God exists" is false. This rather traditional atheism, as Ayer noted long ago, runs into the difficulty that the putative statement "there is a God" is factually meaningless when "God" is used in its straightforward religious ways. Since this is so there is an important respect in which such putative factual statements are unintelligible. But if "there is a God" is so unintelligible the parallel statement "there is no God" is likewise unintelligible. It does not express a false factual statement. Such an atheism is as nonsensical as such a theism! But, Edwards reminds us, there is a second way in which "atheism" is used, and this use of "atheism" is not entangled in these difficulties: ". . . a person is an atheist if he *rejects* belief in God, regardless of whether his rejection is

[16] Attention to my remarks about ideological statements will help make the nature of such claims clearer.

based on the view that belief in God is false." [17] I think of myself as an atheist in this broader sense. To put the matter more precisely, "God exists" seems to me, depending on how "God" is used, either absurdly false, of such a low order of probability that belief in such a being is superstitious or, in its more characteristic uses, it is devoid of factual content and is thus in a significant sense unintelligible and unworthy of belief. To reject the concept of God for any of these reasons is to be, in this second broader sense, an atheist.

Yet even, acknowledging this important distinction, there are atheists and atheists. As MacIntyre points out, atheism of any of the above types tends to be what he calls a speculative atheism; that is to say its interests are theoretical: it is concerned with pointing out the fallacies in arguments for the existence of God, the unintelligibility of God-talk and the like. Its patron saints are Hume, Russell, and Ayer. But there is another kind of practical-activist atheism, an atheism that *presupposes* the truth of some form of speculative atheism, but goes far beyond it. We indeed must, such atheists argue, remove the mask of supernaturalist error, but, as Nietzsche and Feuerbach stressed, we must also transform man. We must develop the vision and the intelligence to live in a world without God; we must come to understand in some concrete detail how to give significance to our lives in such a world.

We need to see more clearly than most speculative atheists have that it is not argument or speculative wonder that stokes religion in the first place; rather it is emotional need that fathers religious belief. "Religion," as MacIntyre puts it, "is misunderstood if it is construed simply as a set of intellectual errors; it is rather the case that in a profoundly misleading form deep insights, hopes, and fears are being expressed." [18] We must cure man of his need for religion, and not just show the intellectual absurdity of it. We must, as Feuerbach and Marx stressed, transform society so that men will no longer need to turn to religious forms to give inspiration to their lives. We must show how men's visions and aspirations can be de-mythologized, can be embodied in purely secular *social forms.* We must, as Feuerbach, the greatest of all these activist atheists, puts it, change "the friends of God into friends of man, believers into thinkers, worshippers into workers, candidates for the other world into students of this world, Christians, who on their own confession are half-animal and half-angel, into new men—whole men." The patron saints of this kind of atheism are Feuerbach, Marx, Nietzsche, David Strauss, and Freud.

I count myself as such an atheist too—though certainly not as a patron saint. I hope in defending and advocating atheism, without personally engaging in any ideology or propagandistic moves, to establish the

[17] Paul Edwards, "Some Notes on Anthropomorphic Theology," in *Religious Experience and Truth,* ed. Sidney Hook (New York: N.Y.U. Press, 1961), p. 242. See also my "On Being an Atheist," *The Personalist* (Winter 1970).

[18] Alasdair MacIntyre, "God and The Theologians," *Encounter* (September 1965), p. 3.

theoretical untenability of theistic beliefs, to show we do not need them
to justify our moral convictions or to give significance to our lives, and to
show that there are other ways of life, other ways of thinking and acting,
that are more desirable, more admirable, more *worthy* of allegiance than
our religious ways of life. In carrying out this last task, a philosopher must
indeed do a little normative ethics and he must dirty his hands with a
few empirical facts, but I see no reason why he should not do these
things, if only he does not confuse normative ethics with meta-ethics.[19]
In this essay I have tried to do something toward establishing the first
two points. To establish the third point, one must go into the nasty *detail*
of normative argument and into an examination, in some concreteness
and with some honesty, of the messy details and harassments of living.

Now I am in a position to examine the rather frequent charge that such
atheism, and sometimes indeed all atheism, is not a denial of religion,
but in effect and in reality its affirmation, an *Ersatz*-religion of its own.

Will Herberg, reasoning much as Kierkegaard, Tillich, Bultmann, and
Bishop Robinson do about these matters, stresses the fact that we should
see the "problem of God" not as a speculative affair but as an existential
concern. Viewed in that way, he argues there are "on the existential
level . . . no atheists." [20] Why not? Because, according to Herberg, "the
structure of a human being is such that man cannot live his life, or
understand himself, without some ultimate concern that he takes as the
that-beyond-which-there-is-nothing of this world. That is indeed his god,
and the articulation of his life in terms of it his religion. . . . In this
sense every man, by virtue of being human, is *homo religiosus;* every
man has his religion and his god. On the existential level, then, the question is not god or no god, religion or no religion; but rather: what *kind*
of god? What *kind* of religion?" [21] Luther remarks that "whatever your
heart clings to and confides in, that is your god." And Robinson and
Tillich tell us that belief in God is a matter of what you take seriously
without any reservation. That which ultimately concerns us, that which
we finally place our trust in, that is our God. But since every man, and
the atheist most fervently, places his trust in something, has some intimate
and ultimate concern, no man is *existentially* an atheist or, if you would
rather talk that way, atheism is a religion or at the very least an *Ersatz*-
religion. "The atheism," Herberg argues, "of a Feuerbach or a young
Marx was existentially not atheism at all, but the deification of Man; just
as the 'atheism' of the later Marx, and so many Marxists, was actually a
quasi-Hegelian deification of the Dialectic of History." [22]

There is a whole evening's worth of confusion in these Kierkegaardian-

[19] For some of the crucial distinctions here and for some of the ways in which we
may do normative ethics see my "Speaking of Morals," *The Centennial Review* 2
(1958): 414–444 and Hans Albert, "Ethik and Metaethik," *Archiv für Philosophie* 2
(1961): 28–63.
[20] Will Herberg, "God and The Theologians," *Encounter* (November 1963), p. 57.
[21] Ibid., p. 56.
[22] Ibid., p. 57.

Tillichian arguments. I shall only have time to expose a few of them, but that will be quite enough.

1. How do we know, or do we know, that all men or even most men have these *ultimate* concerns? It is truistic that human beings care about things, if only booze, the opposite sex, and getting a new sports car. But does such a concern count as an ultimate concern? Well if it does we are well on our way to making "All men have ultimate concern" stipulatively, but arbitrarily, analytic. If we do not play with words in this way, we certainly need a little raw empiricism, a little sociological and anthropological evidence, that all men have such ultimate concerns and thus man is *homo religiosus*. But these religious apologists do not give us such evidence.[23]

2. Let us, however, suppose we have such evidence. Let us suppose that all men everywhere have their ultimate concerns, have something they are deeply devoted to, committed to and finally put their trust in, it still does not follow at all that all such men are religious, that all such men believe in God, have a god, some sense of a *numinous* reality, or a sense of the divine or anything of that sort. We should beware of essentialist definitions of "religion."[24] Theravada Buddhism, a religion of spiritual liberation, has no God or object of worship and devotion.[25] To achieve nirvana (literally the "going out" as of a flame) is to finally achieve liberation (*moksa*) from the endless series of rebirths of a life that is full of suffering. But the goal of this religion is also a spiritual one; nirvana is a very different concept than God, but like the concept of God it is a transcendental concept, e.g., the Buddhist faithful will not allow that naturalistic accounts of it can be fully adequate. In this way, all religions, besides being matters of ultimate concern, have some concept of the sacred or some concept of spiritual reality. But the atheist repudiates nirvana as fully as God; he rejects thinking in terms of sacred, divine, or spiritual realities. If like Nietzsche, Feuerbach, and Freud, he is what I have called an activist atheist, he too has his commitments, has his vision of what a good world would be like, has—if you will—his ultimate concerns. But this does not make him religious, except in the perfectly trivial sense that to be religious about anything is to be deeply involved with it and the like; it does not give him a religion or a god, except in another *metaphorical* sense. To place your trust in something, to be ultimately concerned, to be concerned about the meaning of your existence is at best a *necessary* but most surely not a sufficient condition for being religious or having a religion. To have a religion is to have a distinctive ethical outlook, to accept a certain Weltanschauung, but the converse need not be

[23] I have said something more about this in my "Is God So Powerful That He Doesn't Even Have to Exist," in *Religious Experience and Truth*, pp. 270–282.

[24] Ninian Smart, "Numen, Nirvana and The Definition of Religion," *Church Quarterly Review* (April–June 1959), pp. 216–225.

[25] Ninian Smart, "Buddhism and Religious Belief," *The Humanist* 76, no. 2 (1961): 47–50. See also his *A Dialogue of Religions* (London: 1960).

the case. Ethics is not religion and religion is not simply ethics, or ethics touched with emotion, or associated with parable. A practical activist atheist has a normative view, has a Weltanschauung, but no religion. "A religious way of life" is not a redundancy; "a religious Weltanschauung" is not a pleonasm and "an antireligious or areligious ethic or way of life" is not a contradiction, a logical oddity or a deviation from a linguistic regularity.

Herberg argues that on the existential level there are no atheists for atheism is itself a religious affirmation. He has not shown how this is the case and I have given good reasons for denying that it is the case. But Herberg goes beyond this, for according to him atheism is not only religious, it is an idolatrous religion for it deifies man, the dialectic of history or the state. Herberg again confuses having a certain way of life, having a set of ethical and aspirational ideals, with having a religion. But I think it must be admitted that *some* atheists, not sufficiently emancipated from religious thinking, did stupidly deify man. Comte and Saint-Simon are offenders here, and this most surely is ideological thinking and ought to be resisted most strenuously. But no atheist *must* think this way; no atheist should think this way; and most atheists do not think in this confused way. Commitment yes; ideology and religion no. A commitment to a way-of-life need not be a religious commitment or an ideological commitment.

How this is so can be brought out most economically by contrasting a remark Herberg makes about Christianity with a remark I would make about religion. Herberg remarks that "the fundamental conviction of Christianity is the belief in the insufficiency, nay impotence, of man to straighten out his life or achieve anything worthwhile through his own powers and resources, without reliance on the God beyond." [26] Now I am perfectly aware that there is corruption in the palace of justice; all my life I have felt keenly in myself and in others the deeply perverse Dostoevskian ambivalences of the human animal. Man is, in Pascal's magnificent phrase, but a frail reed; however, I would still reply to Herberg that it is either false or factually meaningless to assert that there is "a God beyond" as the ground of being and meaning, or as the reality transcendent to the cosmos. Such beliefs are ideological and mythological, and man, frail though he be, has no such reality to place his trust in or to rely on. Furthermore, man does have some knowledge of good and evil that not only is but must be independent of any knowledge of a transcendent reality, being-as-such, or a ground of being. Some men have straightened out their lives, given meaning to their own existence and helped to give meaning to the lives of others by using their own puny powers and the help of others similarly situated. To believe that this is so for some men, to *hope* that it may be so for others, and to work to bring about social and psychological conditions under which this will be so for

[26] Will Herberg, p. 57.

as many as possible is not to engage in ideology, to *deify* man, or to make
for oneself an idolatrous religion, an *Ersatz* religion, or for that matter
any religion at all.

RELIGIOUS HUMANISM

Erich Fromm

ERICH FROMM is Director of the Mexican Institute for Psychoanalysis,
affiliated with the National University of Mexico. He has written
extensively on existential humanism, Marx, and psychoanalysis.

. . . .

What is the principle of authoritarian religion? The definition of religion given in the *Oxford Dictionary*, while attempting to define religion
as such, is a rather accurate definition of authoritarian religion. It reads:
"[Religion is] recognition on the part of man of some higher unseen
power as having control of his destiny, and as being entitled to obedience,
reverence, and worship."

Here the emphasis is on the recognition that man is controlled by a
higher power outside of himself. But this alone does not constitute
authoritarian religion. What makes it so is the idea that this power, because of the control it exercises, is *entitled* to "obedience, reverence and
worship." I italicize the word "entitled" because it shows that the reason
for worship, obedience, and reverence lies not in the moral qualities of
the deity, not in love or justice, but in the fact that it has control, that is,
has power over man. Furthermore it shows that the higher power has
a right to force man to worship him and that lack of reverence and
obedience constitutes sin.

The essential element in authoritarian religion and in the authoritarian
religious experience is the surrender to a power transcending man. The
main virtue of this type of religion is obedience, its cardinal sin is disobedience. Just as the deity is conceived as omnipotent or omniscient, man
is conceived as being powerless and insignificant. Only as he can gain
grace or help from the deity by complete surrender can he feel strength.
Submission to a powerful authority is one of the avenues by which man
escapes from his feeling of aloneness and limitation. In the act of surrender he loses his independence and integrity as an individual but he
gains the feeling of being protected by an awe-inspiring power of which,
as it were, he becomes a part.

In Calvin's theology we find a vivid picture of authoritarian, theistic
thinking. "For I do not call it humility," says Calvin, "if you suppose that
we have anything left. . . . We cannot think of ourselves as we ought to
think without utterly despising everything that may be supposed an ex-

cellence in us. This humility is unfeigned submission of a mind over-whelmed with a weighty sense of its own misery and poverty; for such is the uniform description of it in the word of God.". [1]

The experience which Calvin describes here, that of despising every-thing in oneself, of the submission of the mind overwhelmed by its own poverty, is the very essence of all authoritarian religions whether they are couched in secular or in theological language. [2] In authoritarian reli-gion God is a symbol of power and force, He is supreme because He has supreme power, and man in juxtaposition is utterly powerless.

Authoritarian secular religion follows the same principle. Here the Führer or the beloved "Father of His People" or the State or the Race or the Socialist Fatherland becomes the object of worship; the life of the individual becomes insignificant and man's worth consists in the very denial of his worth and strength. Frequently authoritarian religion postu-lates an ideal which is so abstract and so distant that it has hardly any connection with the real life of real people. To such ideals as "life after death" or "the future of mankind" the life and happiness of persons living here and now may be sacrificed; the alleged ends justify every means and become symbols in the names of which religious or secular "elites" con-trol the lives of their fellow men.

Humanistic religion, on the contrary, is centered around man and his strength. Man must develop his power of reason in order to understand himself, his relationship to his fellow men and his position in the universe. He must recognize the truth, both with regard to his limitations and his potentialities. He must develop his powers of love for others as well as for himself and experience the solidarity of all living beings. He must have principles and norms to guide him in this aim. Religious experience in this kind of religion is the experience of oneness with the All, based on one's relatedness to the world as it is grasped with thought and with love. Man's aim in humanistic religion is to achieve the greatest strength, not the greatest powerlessness; virtue is self-realization, not obedience. Faith is certainty of conviction based on one's experience of thought and feeling, not assent to propositions on credit of the proposer. The prevailing mood is that of joy, while the prevailing mood in authoritarian religion is that of sorrow and of guilt.

Inasmuch as humanistic religions are theistic, God is a symbol of *man's own powers* which he tries to realize in his life, and is not a symbol of force and domination, having *power over man*.

Illustrations of humanistic religions are early Buddhism, Taoism, the teachings of Isaiah, Jesus, Socrates, Spinoza, certain trends in the Jewish and Christian religions (particularly mysticism), the religion of Reason

---

[1] Johannes Calvin, *Institutes of the Christian Religion* (Presbyterian Board of Christian Education, 1928), p. 681.

[2] See Erich Fromm, *Escape from Freedom* (Farrar & Rinehart, 1941), pp. 141 ff. This attitude toward authority is described there in detail.

of the French Revolution. It is evident from these that the distinction
between authoritarian and humanistic religion cuts across the distinction
between theistic and nontheistic, and between religions in the narrow
sense of the word and philosophical systems of religious character. What
matters in all such systems is not the thought system as such but the
human attitude underlying their doctrines.

One of the best examples of humanistic religions is early Buddhism.
The Buddha is a great teacher, he is the "awakened one" who recognizes
the truth about human existence. He does not speak in the name of a
supernatural power but in the name of reason. He calls upon every man
to make use of his own reason and to see the truth which he was only the
first to find. Once man takes the first step in seeing the truth, he must
apply his efforts to live in such a way that he develops his powers of
reason and of love for all human creatures. Only to the degree to which
he succeeds in this can he free himself from the bondage of irrational
passions. While man must recognize his limitations according to Buddhistic teaching, he must also become aware of the powers in himself.
The concept of Nirvana as the state of mind the fully awakened one can
achieve is not one of man's helplessness and submission but on the
contrary one of the development of the highest powers man possesses.

The following story of Buddha is very characteristic.

Once a hare sat under a mango tree and slept. Suddenly he heard a
loud noise. He thought the world was coming to an end and started to
run. When the other hares saw him running they asked, "Why do you run
so fast?" He replied, "The world is coming to an end." Upon hearing this
they all joined him in his flight. When the deer saw the hares running
they asked them, "Why do you run so fast?" and the hares answered,
"We run because the world is coming to an end." Upon which the deer
joined them in their flight. Thus one species after another joined the
animals already running until the whole animal kingdom was in a
panicky flight which would have ended in its destruction. When Buddha,
who at that time was living as a wise man, one of his many forms of
existence, saw all the animals running in their panic he asked the last
group that had joined the flight why they were running. "Because the
world is coming to an end," they answered. "This cannot be true," Buddha said. "The world is not coming to an end. Let us find out why they
think so." He then inquired of one species after another, tracing the rumor
back to the deer and then at last to the hares. When the hares told him
that they were running because the world was coming to an end, he asked
which particular hare had told them so. They pointed to the one who had
started the report, and Buddha turned to him and asked, "Where were
you and what did you do when you thought the world was coming to an
end?" The hare answered, "I was sitting under a mango tree and was
asleep." "You probably heard a mango fruit fall," Buddha told him.
"The noise awakened you, you got frightened and thought the world

was coming to an end. Let us go back to the tree where you sat and find out whether this was so." They both went to the tree. They found that indeed a mango had fallen where the hare had sat. Thus Buddha saved the animal kingdom from destruction.

I quote this story not primarily because it is one of the earliest examples of analytic inquiry into the origins of fright and rumors but because it is so expressive of the Buddhistic spirit. It shows loving concern for the creatures of the animal world and at the same time penetrating, rational understanding and confidence in man's powers.

Zen-Buddhism, a later sect within Buddhism, is expressive of an even more radical anti-authoritarian attitude. Zen proposes that no knowledge is of any value unless it grows out of ourselves; no authority, no teacher can really teach us anything except to arouse doubts in us; words and thought systems are dangerous because they easily turn into authorities whom we worship. Life itself must be grasped and experienced as it flows, and in this lies virtue. Characteristic of this unauthoritarian attitude toward supreme beings is the following story:

"When Tanka of the T'ang dynasty stopped at Yerinji in the Capitol, it was severely cold; so taking down one of the Buddha images enshrined there, he made a fire of it and warmed himself. The keeper of the shrine, seeing this, was greatly incensed, and exclaimed: 'How dare you burn my wooden image of the Buddha?'

"Tanka began to search in the ashes as if he were looking for something, and said: 'I am gathering the holy sariras [a kind of mineral deposit found in the human body after cremation and believed to correspond to the saintliness of life] from the burnt ashes.'

" 'How,' said the keeper, 'can you get sariras from a wooden Buddha?'

"Tanka retorted, 'If there are no sariras to be found in it, may I have the remaining two Buddhas for my fire?'

"The shrine-keeper later lost both his eyebrows for remonstrating against this apparent impiety of Tanka, while the Buddha's wrath never fell on the latter." [3]

.   .   .   .

The distinction between authoritarian and humanistic religion not only cuts across various religions, it can exist within the same religion. Our own religious tradition is one of the best illustrations of this point. Since it is of fundamental importance to understand fully the distinction between authoritarian and humanistic religion I shall illustrate it further from a source with which every reader is more or less familiar, the Old Testament.

[3] D. T. Suzuki, *An Introduction to Zen Buddhism* (Rider and Company, 1948), p. 124. Cf. also Professor Suzuki's other works on Zen, and Ch. Humphrey, *Zen Buddhism* (W. Heinemann, Ltd., 1949). An anthology of religious documents expressive of humanistic religion, drawn from all the great sources of the East and West, edited by Victor Gollancz, will be published this year. Here the reader will find a wealth of documentation on humanistic religious thinking.

The beginning of the Old Testament [4] is written in the spirit of authoritarian religion. The picture of God is that of the absolute ruler of a patriarchal clan, who has created man at his pleasure and can destroy him at will. He has forbidden him to eat from the tree of knowledge of good and evil and has threatened him with death if he transgresses this order. But the serpent, "more clever than any animal," tells Eve, "Ye shall not surely die: For God doth know that in the day ye eat thereof, then your eyes shall be opened, and ye shall be as gods, knowing good and evil." [5] God proves the serpent to be right. When Adam and Eve have transgressed he punishes them by proclaiming enmity between man and nature, between man and the soil and animals, and between men and women. But man is not to die. However, "the man has become as one of us, to know good and evil: and now, lest he put forth his hand, and take also of the tree of life, and eat, and live for ever," [6] God expells Adam and Eve from the garden of Eden and puts an angel with a flaming sword at the east "to keep the way of the tree of life."

The text makes very clear what man's sin is: it is rebellion against God's command; it is disobedience and not any inherent sinfulness in the act of eating from the tree of knowledge. On the contrary, further religious development has made the knowledge of good and evil the cardinal virtue to which man may aspire. The text also makes it plain what God's motive is: it is concern with his own superior role, the jealous fear of man's claim to become his equal.

A decisive turning point in the relationship between God and man is to be seen in the story of the Flood. When God saw "that the wickedness of man was great on the earth . . . it repented the Lord that he had made man and the earth, and it grieved him at his heart. And the Lord said, I will destroy man whom I have created from the face of the earth; both man, and beast, and the creeping thing, and the fowls of the air; for it repenteth me that I have made them." [7]

There is no question here but that God has the right to destroy his own creatures; he has created them and they are his property. The text defines their wickedness as "violence," but the decision to destroy not only man but animals and plants as well shows that we are not dealing here with a sentence commensurate with some specific crime but with God's angry regret over his own action which did not turn out well. "But Noah found grace in the eyes of the Lord," and he, together with his family and a representative of each animal species, is saved from the Flood. Thus far the destruction of man and the salvation of Noah are arbitrary acts of God. He could do as he pleased, as can any powerful

---

[4] The historical fact that the beginning of the Bible may not be its oldest part does not need to be considered here since we use the text as an illustration of two principles and not to establish a historical sequence.

[5] Genesis 3:4–5.

[6] Ibid., 3:22.

[7] Ibid., 6:5 ff.

tribal chief. But after the Flood the relationship between God and man changes fundamentally. A covenant is concluded between God and man in which God promises that "neither shall all flesh be cut off any more by the waters of a flood; neither shall there any more be a flood to destroy the earth." [8] God obligates himself never to destroy all life on earth, and man is bound to the first and most fundamental command of the Bible, not to kill: "At the hand of every man's brother will I require the life of man." [9] From this point on the relationship between God and man undergoes a profound change. God is no longer an absolute ruler who can act at his pleasure but is bound by a constitution to which both he and man must adhere; he is bound by a principle which he cannot violate, the principle of respect for life. God can punish man if he violates this principle, but man can also challenge God if he is guilty of its violation.

The new relationship between God and man appears clearly in Abraham's plea for Sodom and Gomorrah. When God considers destroying the cities because of their wickedness, Abraham criticizes God for violating his own principles. "That be far from thee to do after this manner, to slay the righteous with the wicked: and that the righteous should be as the wicked, that be far from thee. Shall not the Judge of all the earth do right?" [10]

The difference between the story of the Fall and this argument is great indeed. There man is forbidden to know good and evil and his position toward God is that of submission—or sinful disobedience. Here man uses his knowledge of good and evil, criticizes God in the name of justice, and God has to yield.

Even this brief analysis of the authoritarian elements in the biblical story shows that at the root of the Judaeo-Christian religion both principles, the authoritarian and the humanistic, are present. In the development of Judaism as well as of Christianity both principles have been preserved and their respective preponderance marks different trends in the two religions.

The following story from the Talmud expresses the unauthoritarian, humanistic side of Judaism as we find it in the first centuries of the Christian era.

A number of other famous rabbinical scholars disagreed with Rabbi Eliezar's views in regard to a point of ritual law. "Rabbi Eliezar said to them: 'If the law is as I think it is then this tree shall let us know.' Whereupon the tree jumped from its place a hundred yards (others say four hundred yards). His colleagues said to him, 'One does not prove anything from a tree.' He said, 'If I am right then this brook shall let us know.' Whereupon the brook run upstream. His colleagues said to him, 'One does not prove anything from a brook.' He continued and said, 'If the law is as I think then the walls of this house will tell.' Whereupon the

8 Ibid., 9:11.
9 Ibid., 9:5.
10 Ibid., 18:25.

walls began to fall. But Rabbi Joshua shouted at the walls and said, 'If scholars argue a point of law, what business have you to fall?' So the walls fell no further out of respect for Rabbi Joshua, but out of respect for Rabbi Eliezar did not straighten up. And that is the way they still are. Rabbis Eliezar took up the argument again and said, 'If the law is as I think, they shall tell us from heaven.' Whereupon a voice from heaven said, 'What have you against Rabbi Eliezar, because the law is as he says.' Whereupon Rabbi Joshua got up and said, 'It is written in the Bible: The law is not in heaven. What does this mean? According to Rabbi Jirmijahu it means since the Torah has been given on Mount Sinai we no longer pay attention to voices from heaven because it is written: You make your decision according to the majority opinion.' It then happened that Rabbi Nathan [one of the participants in the discussion] met the Prophet Elijah [who had taken a stroll on earth] and he asked the Prophet, 'What did God himself say when we had this discussion?' The Prophet answered, 'God smiled and said, My children have won, my children have won.'" [11]

This story is hardly in need of comment. It emphasizes the autonomy of man's reason with which even the supernatural voices from heaven cannot interfere. God smiles, man has done what God wanted him to do, he has become his own master, capable and resolved to make his decisions by himself according to rational, democratic methods.

The same humanistic spirit can be found in many stories from the Chassidic folklore of more than a thousand years later. The Chassidic movement was a rebellion of the poor against those who had the monopoly of learning or of money. Their motto was the verse of the Psalms: "Serve God in joy." They emphasized feeling rather than intellectual accomplishment, joy rather than contrition; to them (as to Spinoza) joy was the equivalent of virtue and sadness the equivalent of sin. The following story is characteristic of the humanistic and anti-authoritarian spirit of this religious sect:

A poor tailor came to a Chassidic rabbi the day after the Day of Atonement and said to him, "Yesterday I had an argument with God. I told him, 'Oh God, you have committed sins and I have committed sins. But you have committed grave sins and I have committed sins of no great importance. What have you done? You have separated mothers from their children and permitted people to starve. What have I done? I have sometimes failed to return a piece of cloth to a customer or have not been strict in the observance of the law. But I will tell you, God. I will forgive you your sins and you forgive me mine. Thus we are even.'" Whereupon the Rabbi answered, "You fool! Why did you let him get away that easily? Yesterday you could have forced him to send the Messiah."

This story demonstrates even more drastically than that of Abraham's

[11] Talmud, Baba Meziah, 59, b. (My translation.)

argument with God the idea that God must live up to his promises just as man must live up to his. If God fails to put an end to the suffering of man as he has promised, man has the right to challenge him, in fact to force him to fulfill his promise. While the two stories quoted here are within the frame of reference of monotheistic religion, the human attitude behind them is profoundly different from that behind Abraham's readiness to sacrifice Isaac or Calvin's glorification of God's dictatorial powers.

That early Christianity is humanistic and not authoritarian is evident from the spirit and text of all Jesus' teachings. Jesus' precept that "the kingdom of God is within you" is the simple and clear expression of non-authoritarian thinking. But only a few hundred years later, after Christianity had ceased to be the religion of the poor and humble peasants, artisans, and slaves (the *Am haarez*) and had become the religion of those ruling the Roman Empire, the authoritarian trend in Christianity became dominant. Even so, the conflict between the authoritarian and humanistic principles in Christianity never ceased. It was the conflict between Augustine and Pelagius, between the Catholic Church and the many "heretic" groups and between various sects within Protestantism. The humanistic, democratic element was never subdued in Christian or in Jewish history, and this element found one of its most potent expressions in the mystic thinking within both religions. The mystics have been deeply imbued with the experience of man's strength, his likeness to God, and with the idea that God needs man as much as man needs God; they have understood the sentence that man is created in the image of God to mean the fundamental identity of God and man. Not fear and submission but love and the assertion of one's own powers are the basis of mystical experience. *God is not a symbol of power over man but of man's own powers.*

Thus far we have dealt with the distinctive features of authoritarian and humanistic religions mainly in descriptive terms. But the psychoanalyst must proceed from the description of attitudes to the analysis of their dynamics, and it is here that he can contribute to our discussion from an area not accessible to other fields of inquiry. The full understanding of an attitude requires an appreciation of those conscious and, in particular, unconscious processes occurring in the individual which provide the necessity for and the conditions of its development.

While in humanistic religion God is the image of man's higher self, a symbol of what man potentially is or ought to become, in authoritarian religion God becomes the sole possessor of what was originally man's: of his reason and his love. The more perfect God becomes, the more imperfect becomes man. He *projects* the best he has onto God and thus impoverishes himself. Now God has all love, all wisdom, all justice—and man is deprived of these qualities, he is empty and poor. He had begun with the feeling of smallness, but he now has become completely powerless and without strength; all his powers have been projected onto God. This mechanism of projection is the very same which can be observed in interpersonal relationships of a masochistic, submissive character, where one person is awed by another and attributes his own powers and aspirations to the other person. It is the same mechanism that makes people endow the leaders of even the most inhuman systems with qualities of superwisdom and kindness.[12]

When man has thus projected his own most valuable powers onto God, what of his relationship to his own powers? They have become separated from him and in this process he has become *alienated* from himself. Everything he has is now God's and nothing is left in him. *His only access to himself is through God.* In worshiping God he tries to get in touch with that part of himself which he has lost through projection. After having given God all he has, he begs God to return to him some of what originally was his own. But having lost his own he is completely at God's mercy. He necessarily feels like a "sinner" since he has deprived himself of everything that is good, and it is only through God's mercy or grace that he can regain that which alone makes him human. And in order to persuade God to give him some of his love, he must prove to him how utterly deprived he is of love; in order to persuade God to guide him by his superior wisdom he must prove to him how deprived he is of wisdom when he is left to himself.

But this alienation from his own powers not only makes man feel slavishly dependent on God, it makes him bad too. He becomes a man without faith in his fellow men or in himself, without the experience of his own love, of his own power of reason. As a result the separation between the "holy" and the "secular" occurs. In his worldly activities man acts without love, in that sector of his life which is reserved to religion he feels himself to be a sinner (which he actually is, since to live without love is to live in sin) and tries to recover some of his lost humanity by being in touch with God. Simultaneously, he tries to win forgiveness by emphasizing his own helplessness and worthlessness. Thus the attempt to obtain forgiveness results in the activation of the very attitude from which his sins stem. He is caught in a painful dilemma. The more he praises God, the emptier he becomes. The emptier he becomes, the more sinful he feels. The more sinful he feels, the more he praises his God—and the less able is he to regain himself.

Analysis of religion must not stop at uncovering those psychological processes within man which underly his religious experience; it must proceed to discover the conditions which make for the development of authoritarian and humanistic character structures, respectively, from which different kinds of religious experience stem. Such a sociopsychological analysis goes far beyond the context of these chapters. However, the principal point can be made briefly. What people think and feel is rooted in their character and their character is molded by the total configuration of their practice of life—more precisely, by the socioeconomic

---

[12] Cf. the discussion about symbolic relationship in *Escape from Freedom*, pp. 158 ff.

and political structure of their society. In societies ruled by a powerful
minority which holds the masses in subjection, the individual will be so
imbued with fear, so incapable of feeling strong or independent, that his
religious experience will be authoritarian. Whether he worships a punish-
ing, awesome God or a similarly conceived leader makes little difference.
On the other hand, where the individual feels free and responsible for
his own fate, or among minorities striving for freedom and independence, humanistic religious experience develops. The history of religion
gives ample evidence of this correlation between social structure and kinds
of religious experience. Early Christianity was a religion of the poor and
downtrodden; the history of religious sects fighting against authoritarian
political pressure shows the same principle again and again. Judaism, in
which a strong anti-authoritarian tradition could grow up because secular
authority never had much of a chance to govern and to build up a legend
of its wisdom, therefore developed the humanistic aspect of religion to a
remarkable degree. Whenever, on the other hand, religion allied itself
with secular power, the religion had by necessity to become authoritarian.
The real fall of man is his alienation from himself, his submission to
power, his turning against himself even though under the guise of his
worship of God.

From the spirit of authoritarian religion stem two fallacies of reasoning
which have been used again and again as arguments for theistic religion.
One argument runs as follows: How can you criticize the emphasis on
dependence on a power transcending man; is not man dependent on forces
outside himself which he cannot understand, much less control?

Indeed, man is dependent; he remains subject to death, age, illness,
and even if he were to control nature and to make it wholly serviceable
to him, he and his earth remain tiny specks in the universe. But it is one
thing to recognize one's dependence and limitations, and it is something
entirely different to indulge in this dependence, to worship the forces on
which one depends. To understand realistically and soberly how limited
our power is is an essential part of wisdom and of maturity; to worship
it is masochistic and self-destructive. The one is humility, the other self-
humiliation.

We can study the difference between the realistic recognition of our
limitations and the indulgence in the experience of submission and powerlessness in the clinical examination of masochistic character traits. We
find people who have a tendency to incur sickness, accidents, humiliating
situations, who belittle and weaken themselves. They believe that they get
into such situations against their will and intention, but a study of their
unconscious motives shows that actually they are driven by one of the
most irrational tendencies to be found in man, namely, by an unconscious desire to be weak and powerless; they tend to shift the center of
their life to powers over which they feel no control, thus escaping from
freedom and from personal responsibility. We find furthermore that this
masochistic tendency is usually accompanied by its very opposite, the

tendency to rule and to dominate others, and that the masochistic and the dominating tendencies form the two sides of the authoritarian character structure.[13] Such masochistic tendencies are not always unconscious. We find them overtly in the sexual masochistic perversion where the fulfillment of the wish to be hurt or humiliated is the condition for sexual excitement and satisfaction. We find it also in the relationship to the leader and the state in all authoritarian secular religions. Here the explicit aim is to give up one's own will and to experience submission under the leader or the state as profoundly rewarding.

Another fallacy of theological thinking is closely related to the one concerning dependence. I mean here the argument that there must be a power or being outside of man because we find that man has an ineradicable longing to relate himself to something beyond himself. Indeed, any sane human being has a need to relate himself to others; a person who has lost that capacity completely is insane. No wonder that man has created figures outside of himself to which he relates himself, which he loves and cherishes because they are not subject to the vacillations and inconsistencies of human objects. That God is a symbol of man's need to love is simple enough to understand. But does it follow from the existence and intensity of this human need that there exists an outer being who corresponds to this need? Obviously that follows as little as our strongest desire to love someone proves that there is a person with whom we are in love. All it proves is our need and perhaps our capacity.

.   .   .   .

The foregoing considerations show that the answer to what constitutes the threat to religion today depends on what specific aspect of religion we are referring to. The underlying theme of the preceding chapters is the conviction that the problem of religion is not the problem of God but the problem of man; religious formulations and religious symbols are attempts to give expression to certain kinds of human experience. What matters is the nature of these experiences. The symbol system is only the cue from which we can infer the underlying human reality. Unfortunately the discussion centered around religion since the days of the Enlightenment has been largely concerned with the affirmation or negation of a belief in God rather than with the affirmation or negation of certain human attitudes. "Do you believe in the existence of God?" has been made the crucial question of religionists and the denial of God has been the position chosen by those fighting the church. It is easy to see that many who profess the belief in God are in their human attitude idol worshipers or men without faith, while some of the most ardent "atheists," devoting their lives to the betterment of mankind, to deeds of brotherliness and love, have exhibited faith and a profoundly religious attitude. Centering the religious discussion on the acceptance or denial of the symbol God blocks the understanding of the religious problem as a

[13] See *Escape from Freedom*, pp. 141 ff.

human problem and prevents the development of that human attitude which can be called religious in a humanistic sense.

· · · · · · · · · · · · · · · · · · · ·

While it is not possible for man to make valid statements about the positive, about God, it is possible to make such statements about the negative, about idols. Is it not time to cease to argue about God and instead to unite in the unmasking of contemporary forms of idolatry? Today it is not Baal and Astarte but the deification of the state and of power in authoritarian countries and the deification of the machine and of success in our own culture which threaten the most precious spiritual possessions of man. Whether we are religionists or not, whether we believe in the necessity for a new religion or in a religion of no religion or in the continuation of the Judaeo-Christian tradition, inasmuch as we are concerned with the essence and not with the shell, with the experience and not with the word, with man and not with the church, we can unite in firm negation of idolatry and find perhaps more of a common faith in this negation than in any affirmative statements about God. Certainly we shall find more of humility and of brotherly love.

SUGGESTED READINGS

A good overview of the radical theologies can be found in Thomas Ogletree, * The Death of God Controversy (Nashville: Abingdon, 1966p) and Ved. Mehta, The New Theologian (New York: Harper & Row, 1966p). Besides the works of the key figures, too numerous to itemize, the student may consult the following anthologies as a way into the material. T. J. J. Altizer (ed.), * Toward a New Christianity (New York: Harcourt, Brace & World, 1967p); Altizer and Hamilton (eds.), * Radical Theology and the Death of God (Indianapolis: Bobbs-Merrill, 1966p). W. R. Miller (ed.), The New Christianity (New York: Dell Publishing Co., 1967p) contains not only material from current death of God theologians but materials from the historical roots of the movement in Nietzsche, Hegel, Freud, Feuerbach, et al. Murchland, The Meaning of the Death of God (New York: Vintage, 1967p); C. W. Christian and G. R. Wittig (eds.), * Radical Theology: Phase Two (Philadelphia: J. B. Lippincott, 1967p); and J. L. Ice and J. J. Carey (eds.), The Death of God Debate (Philadelphia: Westminster, 1967p) all contain essays on the debate that was originally stirred up by Altizer, Van Buren, and Hamilton. See Altizer, The Gospel of Christian Atheism (Philadelphia: Westminster, 1966p); Hamilton, The New Essence of Christianity (New York: Association Press, 1961); and Paul Van Buren, The Secular Meaning of the Gospel (New York: Macmillan, 1963p). A Jewish radical theologian relying heavily on Freud is Richard L. Rubenstein, After Auschwitz (Indianapolis: Bobbs-Merrill, 1967p) and The Religious Imagination: A Study in Psychoanalysis and Jewish Theology (Indianapolis: Bobbs-Merrill, 1971).

On atheism see Richard Robinson, An Atheist's Values (Oxford: Clarendon Press, 1964); S. Freud, Future of An Illusion (London: The Hogarth Press, 1928); Erich Fromm, Psychoanalysis and Religion (New Haven: Yale, 1950p);

MacIntyre and Ricoeur, *The Religious Significance of Atheism* (New York: Columbia University Press, 1969). Charles Bradlaugh's lecture, "A Plea for Atheism," in *Charles Bradlaugh —Champion of Liberty* (London: Watts, 1933) is still a classic. Ludwig Feuerbach's, *The Essence of Christianity* (New York: Harper & Row, 1953p) is still very influential in theological circles as well as atheistic circles. See also a popular atheism (or agnosticism) in Bertrand Russell, *Why I Am Not a Christian* (New York: Simon & Schuster, 1967p). The most complete history of atheism in English is C. Fabro, * *God in Exile: Modern Atheism* (New York: Paulist-Newman, 1968). For sympathetic treatment of atheism from a Christian point of view, see Henri de Lubac, *The Drama of Atheist Humanism* (New York: World Publishers, 1965p); Ignace Lepp, *Atheism in Our Time* (New York: Macmillan, 1964p); W. A. Luijpen, *Phenomenology and Atheism* (Pittsburgh: Duquesne University Press, 1964); and J. M. Gonzalez- Ruiz, *Atheistic Humanism and Biblical God* (Milwaukee: Bruce, 1969). Paul Edwards has two fine essays on atheism: see his article in *Encyclopedia of Philosophy,* op. cit., and "Difficulties in the Idea of God" in E. H. Madden, R. Handy and M. Farber (eds.), *The Idea of God* (Springfield, Ill.: Thomas, 1968). Franklin L. Baumer, * *Religion and the Rise of Scepticism* (New York: Harcourt, Brace & World, 1960p) traces the rise of scepticism over the last four centuries.

The problem of evil is probably the strongest reason for atheism. For a comprehensive review of traditional attempts at solution from a theistic view, see John Hick, *Evil and the God of Love* (New York: Harper & Row, 1966). A biblical point of view is found in John James, *Why Evil? A Biblical Approach* (Baltimore, Md.: Penquin Books, 1960). Other attempts that have had recent impact are A. Farrer, *Love Almighty and Ills Unlimited* (New York: Doubleday, 1961); J. S. Whale, *The Christian Answer to the Problem of Evil* (London: SCM, 1957p); C. S. Lewis, *The Problem of Pain* (New York: Macmillan, 1950p); Langdon Gilkey, *Maker of Heaven and Earth* (New York: Doubleday, 1959p). For a contemporary view out of the analytic tradition see Alvin Plantinga, *God and Other Minds* (esp. Ch. 5, 6 and 7) (Ithaca, N.Y.: Cornell University Press, 1967). A good anthology of recent essays is Nelson Pike (ed.), * *God and Evil* (Englewood Cliffs, N.J.: Prentice-Hall, 1964p). R. A. Tsanoff, *The Nature of Evil* (New York: Macmillan, 1931) is a good overview. Albert Camus, *The Rebel* (New York: Vintage Books, 1956); *The Plague* (New York: Modern Library, 1948); and Sartre, "The Flies" in *No Exit and Three Other Plays,* op. cit., represent the atheistic existential standpoint.

CHAPTER SIX

Process Thought: Toward a New Theism?

Whitehead once said that Buddhism is a metaphysics generating a religion while Christianity is a religion in search of a metaphysics.[1] Down through its history Christianity has been wed to a number of metaphysical grammars, prominent partners being Platonism, Aristoteleanism, Hegelianism and existentialism. In particular the creeds of the Church and much classical theology shows the use of Christian theology of Platonic and Aristotelean catagories. But, so the proponents of a new mate argue, Christianity has outlived these partners, or, at least, needs a new partner for the new time.

Why does Christianity need a new metaphysics? The followers of [2] Whitehead argue that the classical metaphysics is no longer viable. The new physics has changed our conception of the world. But there are also theological reasons. The nature of God as defined in this metaphysics makes it difficult to speak of God acting in the world. The problem of evil is also inadequately treated. This chapter, then, deals with the new metaphysics of Whitehead and how it provides a new and more adequate way to talk about God, his relation to the world, and how evil in the world does not contradict the existence and nature of God. The reader will recall from previous chapters that these issues are central to philosophy of religion.

---

[1] Alfred North Whitehead, *Religion in the Making* (New York: Macmillan, 1926), p. 50.

[2] For a detailed survey of the material written in the Whitehead tradition, see D. Brown, R. E. James, Jr., and G. Reeves (eds.), *Process Philosophy and Christian Thought* (Indianapolis: Bobbs-Merrill Co., Inc., 1971), Chapter One, Section Two.

For Whitehead, philosophy is not reduced to a description of the parts of reality, particularly the workings of our language. Although the "lure of the past" dominates much Anglo-American philosophy, Whitehead sees the philosophical task as an *interpretation* or "vision of the whole." When an analyst describes philosophy as "seeing" he means seeing clearly and precisely. Philosophy *begins* with a puzzle and ends with a solution. For Whitehead "seeing" is more like "vision." Exactness is a fake. Philosophy begins with things being clear, ends up where clearness is impossible. "Philosophy is an attempt to express the infinity of the universe in terms of the limitations of language." Philosophy is therefore, a continuing attempt to interpret experience by framing a coherent, logical, necessary system of general ideas in terms of which every element of experience can be interpreted.

Whitehead's method is imaginative generalization. A metaphysician takes some root metaphor and then sees if he can imaginatively apply this metaphor to everything. For Whitehead *process* is basic. "The organic starting-point is from the analysis of process as the realization of events disposed in an interlocked community. The event is the unit of things real." [3] The universe is made up of events, not things and their qualities. Given this starting point, Whitehead takes off [4] and generalizes so as to include *everything* under this metaphor of process-event.

The *test* of such a system of ideas is its ability to interpret individual facts, although it is not *judged* by individual facts. A metaphysical system must be *logical*, that is, self-consistent; and *coherent*, that is, the system must be an interconnected whole such that no one idea can be abstracted from the rest. Each idea presupposes the others and is significant only in relation to the others.

But a metaphysical system is open-ended. The goal of complete generalization is never achieved because of the weakness of insight and the deficiency of language. A metaphysical system requires an imaginative leap to be entertained. It is not tested by clarity or certainty but a general success at interpreting *all* kinds of experience. It is, therefore, *broadly empirical*, being tested by its adequacy in interpreting experience, and *rational* in that the system of ideas is also tested by logic and coherency.

The most fundamental fact about the world is that it is ever moving on. The universe at this moment is not what it was a moment ago. Each item in the universe is perpetually in process. The universe is not made up of things (substances) that have qualities that move around in space and time. That is the old physics. Contemporary physics teaches us that everything is an energy-event, constantly moving.

This process is universal. In this process something new is constantly

---

[3] *Science and the Modern World* (New York: Macmillan, 1925), p. 212.

[4] In *Process and Reality* Whitehead compares doing metaphysics to a plane ride. A metaphysician takes off with a root metaphor (i.e., universe made up of droplets of process) and sees how many areas can be interpreted by that metaphor (land in other areas such as religion, ethics, and so on).

coming into being only to die as yet another new movement comes into being. What now is, was not before. Novelty characterizes each new movement. But for novelty to occur the old must die away. Process involves on the one hand something new always coming into being and on the other hand, what was, passing out of existence.

But processes do not just pop into existence. If everything were absolutely original, borrowing nothing from the past, for example, then anything might appear anywhere. Order and continuity in the universe require that the present borrow from the past. But the present is also related to the future in that it *conforms* to certain possibilities that are set for it. The present cannot be understood without reference to the past and to the future. The universe is not an aimless drift, but creativity. The present creates out of the matter of the past in terms of the forms of the future. The universe at any moment is an integration of past, present, and future.

As Stephen Ely describes this process,

In the first phase of the growth of an event, influences from the whole universe pour in upon it; or, to put it in another way, the event is born by feeling the many items of the universe that have already come into being. It is born into a phase of confusion and conflict, and it grows by bringing order and sanity into the welter of discordant feelings. The chaos of feelings derived from the world is, by such devices as emphasizing some feelings and subordinating others, contrasting these and combining those, worked up into an integrated and determinate single feeling of the universe. Then the event has fully become, its growth is at an end, and the microscopic process is completed. It has grown into a stubborn fact of the universe, but by becoming a fact in the world, a something that all succeeding events must take account of, it dies to itself. Its job was to become a definite and determinate individual feeling of the world; once this has been accomplished, its work is over and its life is at an end. From then on it "lives" not for and in itself but only as an influence upon succeeding events. Thus in the internal process of the event the many become one, and then this one is added back to the many and so adds its mite to the complex of influences which are focused on the initial phases of all future events. This flux and reflux of the many and the one is a fundamental metaphysical character of the universe. Thus it has always been, and this it will always be. God himself cannot tinker with the basic machinery of existence. . .[5]

Barry Wood [6] has shown that our culture is primarily noun oriented. But our new physics sees "thing" as process and, therefore, better understood through *verbs*. There are whole cultures that view things as happenings, for example, the Hopi Indians. We say, for instance, "the light flashed," thereby creating a thing (the light) that flashed. The Hopi language just says, "flashing." As Whorf has noted, "we are constantly reading into nature fictional acting entities, simply because our verbs

---

[5] Stephen L. Ely, *The Religious Availability of Whitehead's God* (Madison: University of Wisconsin Press, 1942), pp. 16–17.

[6] Barry Wood, *The Magnificent Frolic* (Philadelphia: Westminster Press, 1970), ch. 4 and passim.

must have substantives in front of them." [7] How different our standpoint would be if we viewed the world as a series of events. "For, in a world where every event is a 'happen-*ing*' and every thing is a 'th-*ing*,' we must learn to talk of man as 'manning,' nature as 'naturing'—and, perhaps, of God as 'godding.'" [8] The Whiteheadian metaphysical grammar provides just such a way of looking at the world.

The essay by Delwin Brown, written especially for this volume, introduces the reader to the Whiteheadian vision without the use of Whitehead's technical language. The essay by Ian Barbour compares the process metaphysics of Whitehead with the evolutionary metaphysics of Teilhard de Chardin. L. Bryant Keeling's essay introduces the reader to the neoclassical theism of Charles Hartshorne, probably the most influential advocate of the philosophical movement associated with Whitehead. We have seen that the problem of evil is one of the most serious obstacles to theism. Process thought claims to be able to deal with this problem in a manner that avoids the weaknesses of classical theism. The essays by Charles Hartshorne and Lewis S. Ford defend process thought against critics of its specific solution to the problem of evil.

THE WORLD AND GOD: A PROCESS PERSPECTIVE

Delwin Brown

DELWIN BROWN is an Associate Professor of Philosophy and Religion at Anderson College. He is co-editor of *Process Philosophy and Christian Thought*. The following essay was written especially for this volume.

Basic to the process perspective is the rather uncommon view that the ultimate constituents of reality are processes or becomings, not substances or inert and abiding bits of matter. Beyond this basic agreement, however, the types of process thought vary considerably. This essay provides an interpretation of one process perspective, that of Alfred North Whitehead.[1] Whitehead, who began his professional life as an important mathematician at Cambridge University, enjoyed an extraordinary career as a historian of ideas, philosopher of science, and metaphysician at Harvard University from 1924 until his death in 1947. His system—especially as developed by the American philosopher, Charles

---

[7] Quoted by Barry Wood, ibid., p. 97.
[8] Ibid., p. 99.
[1] The works of Whitehead cited in this essay (all published in New York by Macmillan) are abbreviated as follows: *AI, Adventures of Ideas* (1933); *FR, The Function of Reason* (1929); *MT, Modes of Thought* (1938); *PR, Process and Reality* (1929); *RM, Religion in the Making* (1926); and *SMW, Science and the Modern World* (1925).

Hartshorne—is the most comprehensive and influential statement of the process viewpoint in contemporary philosophy.

The primary purpose of this chapter is to present a Whiteheadian understanding of religion and God. This interpretive description, Part II, is intended as a relatively independent discussion that may be read separately from Part I. Nevertheless, because process theology depends significantly upon process philosophy, a fuller grasp of the Whiteheadian idea of God requires some awareness of the mood and character of Whitehead's philosophical system. Thus, Part I describes in broad outline Whitehead's understanding of the world.

PART I: THE WORLD IN WHITEHEAD'S PHILOSOPHY

A. The Motivation of Whitehead's Thinking

The motivations behind Whitehead's philosophy are numerous. One is the theory of evolution, so his system could be introduced as an attempt to state in philosophical terms an evolutionary view of the universe. Another is the theory of relativity; consequently his work may also be seen as a philosophical statement of the perspectival and relational character of things. But still another motivation—the one from which we shall begin our consideration—is Whitehead's conviction that human experience is a fundamental reality, such that any adequate account of things must not end up explaining experience away. We see colors and hear sounds; we feel compassion, indignation, and obligation; we love and hate; we are moved by music, poetry, and paintings; we touch; we decide. These statements call to mind that which we know best—our own private process of experiencing. Whitehead's contention is that this is a fundamental part of the world. Human experiences are not mere chimeras; feelings are not the mere psychic additions with which we somehow clothe a *more real* world of atoms without qualities moving mechanically in a void without value. Our experiences—moral, aesthetic, religious, sensory—belong as much "to the nature of things" as do the phenomena investigated by the physicist, chemist, biologist, or sociologist. An adequate account of things has no more license to explain away the felt qualities of human experience than it has to dismiss the relativity of space-time or the evolutionary origins of the species. This, at least, is what Whitehead believes.

Of course, Whitehead may be wrong. It might be, for example, that the experienced element of freedom in deciding is dispensable—that no human choice could in the same circumstances have been other than what it was. It might be that the aesthetic emotions elicited by a symphony or the moral wrath provoked by genocide tell us nothing about things as they "really" are—that the lived realities of experience are reducible without remainder to their chemical or physiological concomitants in the brain and other parts of the body. Some reductive account of things might be true, but should we assume that it is? It clearly does not seem to be the case. Our instinctive conviction is that our experiences are as "real" as anything could possibly be. Surely, without compelling evidence to the contrary, a philosophy that diverges from this conviction is simply not being empirical—it is not talking about our world.

Reductivism, to be sure, is often pursued because it does seem required by some compelling evidence. In those instances its pursuit, even if misguided, is an admirable expression of intellectual honesty. Whitehead is convinced, however, that faithfulness to the data of science —for example, the predictability of the physical correlates to human emotion, or the regularity of human behavior patterns—does not require the dismissal of experience. The "flux of energy" and the "red glow of the sunset"—fact and value—may each be viewed on its own terms as an element of the same world. Without rejecting the standpoint of science, the world of experienced emotion may be affirmed as fully and equally real. This is Whitehead's contention. But how this affirmation, so intuitively self-evident, can be maintained must now be shown.

The place to begin is with Whitehead's account of the nature of human experience. Then we will discuss Whitehead's concept of the natural world. This background will enable us to consider how Whitehead proposes to relate physical nature and human experience, that is, to examine Whitehead's philosophical understanding of the world.

B. An Analysis of Experience

Some of our most common assumptions are terribly superficial. These prejudices, occasionally correctable through educated reflection, no doubt affect philosophy also. One such superficiality is manifest, Whitehead thinks, in our habit of equating experience with conscious sensations such as seeing trees and hearing voices. To understand Whitehead's viewpoint let us follow his analysis of human experiencing.

Consider the present moment of your experience. What is there? The most prominent factor in the present is the immediate past moment of experience. The ideas entertained and emotions enjoyed in that experience of, say, a quarter of a second ago have now moved vaguely but massively into the present. So pervasive is the past's ingredience in the present, indeed, that we commonly think of the present as continuing its preceding moments. The continuity cannot be denied. We are what we were. Even so, that is only part of the story; there also is a degree of discontinuity. New elements insinuate themselves, and elements of the past moment disappear into irrelevance as new purposes reorganize the contents of the present. We are what we were, but also we are more and less than what we were. There is continuity and discontinuity. Present and past experiences seem to be a kind of unity of diverse moments. The past is in, yet somehow other than, the present.

But the present moment of experience, as the element of discontinuity implies, is not simply what is inherited from the past. There is also sense perception—the conscious apprehension of the external world. Yet to move directly to sense perception, says Whitehead, is to ignore the important factor of our bodiedness. We feel with our fingers and see with our eyes. When called to our attention, this dependence of our perceptual experience upon bodily functionings is obvious. Yet the body is more than a mere medium enabling perception of the outside world. Some elements of our experience are more or less directly dependent upon the body itself, the proper or improper functioning of bodily organs. Like the past moment(s) of experience, the just-past activities of the body contribute massively to the experienced present. So fully indeed, and yet with such vagueness, that we are unable to distinguish clearly events of the body from those of the mind. Consider, for example, our perception of a hard surface. The initial phase is the sensation registered by the nerve endings in our finger tips; the final phase might be the idea of hardness in what we call mental reflection. But at what point does physical sensation become mental apprehension? To be sure, one might arbitrarily select such a dividing point, and for certain purposes that division might be useful. But experience disavows clear delineations. Body and mind seem different, yet their boundary eludes us. They are discontinuous, yet continuous. The relationship of mental experience and bodily events is not unlike that of present and past experiences—there is some sort of unity among discrete elements.

The same can be said, so far as the experiential evidence is concerned, with respect to the relationship of our present experience to the world. Roughly speaking—but perhaps correctly nevertheless—the world is in the mind and the mind in the world. The latter relationship is obvious. The phenomenon of experience must be included in any full account of the world; the mind is a part of the world. But is the world not a part of the mind, too? Because it is impossible to separate with microscopic finality our bodies and their immediately outlying world, and because our bodies are in some important way ingredient in the present experience, the same thing can be denied of the extra-bodily world only gratuitously. In fact, we know immediately that somehow the world "out there" is not purely out there; to know the world is to have it given over to us, to have it become ingredient in our experience. Once again sharp divisions, so abundantly useful for certain purposes, do not stand firm under scrutiny.

In view of the foregoing analysis, what are we to conclude about experience?

Human experience is a stream of moments or occasions occurring in rapid succession. Each moment is essentially related to its past. It is so heavily indebted to its immediate predecessors, in fact, that clear divisions between it and its mental, bodily, and natural background are quite impossible. The present experience does not appear as something in itself which in addition is merely related to things outside itself; it *is*

the coming together into one of manifold givens. The factor of relatedness with the past, then, is integral to the constitution of the present
reality. Even so, however, present experience is not simply the sum of
convergent influences. The paths of givenness (the-tablet-for-me, the-
bodily-feelings-for-me, the-voices-in-the-dim-background-for-me, the-pur-
poses-of-the-past-moment-for-me) are actively received. In the emergent
synthesis they are simplified and modified, and they are emphasized or
de-emphasized under the duress of the present's purpose. Indeed, even
the purpose acclaimed supreme in the immediate past, e.g., my aim at
the completion of this line of thought, must now stand before the emergent purpose of the present in some uncertainty, however minute,
awaiting its own disposition. As paradoxical as it sounds, the present experience is the self-directed creator of itself; it is the artist of its own
becoming.

C. Experience and Nature: A Comparison

When we compare experience, so conceived, to nature it is at first
hard to see what the two can have in common. What has a fleeting
momentary synthesis of feeling to do with abiding rocks and atoms?
What can essentially relational events share with static, self-contained
bits of matter? How can dynamic experience and lifeless nature be conceived as part of the same world?

The solution, Whitehead believes, lies in a full awareness of the
nature of the physical world according to modern physics. He writes:

The modern point of view is expressed in terms of energy, activity, and the
vibratory differentiations of space-time. Any local agitation shakes the whole
universe. The distant effects are minute, but they are there. The [pre-modern]
concept of matter presupposed simple location. Each bit of matter was self-
contained, localized in a region with a passive, static network of spatial relations,
entwined in a uniform relational system from infinity to infinity and from
eternity to eternity. But in the modern concept the group of agitations which
we term matter is fused into its environment. There is no possibility of a
detached, self-contained local existence. The environment enters into the
nature of each thing. Some elements in the nature of a complete set of agitations
may remain stable as those agitations are propelled through a changing environment. But such a stability is only the case in a general, average way. This
average fact is the reason why we find the same chair, the same rock and the
same planet, enduring for days, or for centuries, or for millions of years. In this
average fact the time-factor takes the aspect of endurance, and change is a
detail. The fundamental fact, according to the physics of the present day, is that
the environment with its peculiarities seeps into the group-agitation which we
term matter, and the group-agitations extend their character to the environment.
(*MT*, 188f.)

Because the outmoded categories of Newtonian physics are so firmly
embedded in our thinking and forms of speech, we are prone to overlook the very striking similarities between "mind" and "matter"—be-

tween, that is, the moments of activity constituting experience and the quanta of energy constituting the physical world. The members of each emerge under the influence of the past, and they project their own characters into succeeding becomings. Both the mental and the physical are essentially relational. Yet, too, each type of entity is something for itself, that particular synthesis and no other. The realms of mind and matter are both composed of small atomic unities.

The assumption of an absolute distinction between mind and matter is no longer possible. And because of this, those strategies which, in the interest of a cosmic unity, reduce one to the other are no longer necessary. Ultimately, the world is not composed of substantial things; it is a single, though fantastically complex, web of happenings. Each such event is a unity that flows from its past and into its future. The variations of complexity presented in these events is utterly extraordinary—there are the occasions constituting "empty" space, and those constituting the richness of human experience. Still the variations are not absolute. Dynamic mentality and inert matter represent not two entirely different modes of being, but two extremes in the one continuum that is reality.

To say that things are one, however, is not to describe how that oneness is to be conceived. What we now require is a philosophical understanding of the world that incorporates both the theories of the physical scientist and the data of human experience.

D. Experience and Nature: A Philosophical Understanding

According to Whitehead, "the key notion from which . . . [philosophical] construction should start is that energetic activity considered in physics is the emotional intensity entertained in life" (*MT*, 231f.). This point is crucial, and it is easily misunderstood. Whitehead is *not* saying that physical things are composed of little minds, or are conscious, or have emotions. He is suggesting that reality even at its so-called lowest levels exhibits modes of functioning remotely analogous to those patterns of activity characteristic of human experience. This is true because human experiences or feelings, unlike other entities (such as the stones and billiard balls long taken as the philosophical models of a "thing"), are essentially relational. A feeling is of something other than itself; it somehow includes its object within itself; it remains nevertheless other than its object. Subject, object, and the relationship are in some sense inseparably present in one reality. It is clearly not a question of there being consciousness at non-living levels of reality, for even in human experience consciousness is flickering and often absent. Even on the human level we postulate unconscious feelings, though by definition none of us has ever witnessed such a feeling. Whitehead's point is simply that human feelings, divorced from the accompaniment of consciousness, furnish us with the most adequate model for understanding those events that constitute the energetic activities of the physical world.

1. ACTUAL ENTITIES AND SOCIETIES OF ACTUAL ENTITIES

Whitehead calls the ultimate units or events, of which all things are constituted, "actual entities" or "actual occasion." They are microcosmic pulses existing momentarily, summing up anew patterns of synthesis inherited from the past, then giving themselves as data for succeeding momentary becomings. Overwhelmingly, passage from actual occasion to occasion is characterized by simple repetition. Repetition means the reenactment of possibilities (or, as Whitehead often calls them, "eternal objects"). In successive moments of my experience, for example, the possibility of "anger" or "sympathy" is the predominating realization in syntheses that actualize manifold other possibilities as well. Similarly there is the repetition of, say, "grayness" in the actual entities constituting the atoms of a stone. At all levels, repetition predominates. Occasionally however, even if very rarely, repetition is joined by significant novelty. Mutations occur in nature; novel emotions or new ideas emerge in experience. The cosmic process is enriched or impoverished.

The abiding, macrocosmic entities of ordinary experience, e.g., men, flowers, and buildings, are groupings or societies of actual entities. In such a society each "generation"—that is, the actual entities existing at a given instant—exhibits characteristics or common elements of form derived from previous generations. Societies of actual entities are structured in radically different ways. Some are "inorganic," which means that their members exhibit neither diversity of characteristics nor functional hierarchies of importance. Some are "living," which means that at least some of their members are significantly characterized by novel adjustment to their environment. In lower organisms, e.g., the flower turning toward the sunlight, the adjustment is devoid of conceptual awareness. In higher organisms, e.g., the student turning his attention back to the textbook, the adjustment emerges out of a conceptual awareness of contrasting possibilities, such as reading and staring out the window.

Some living societies, most of whose members are virtually equal in their influence on the whole, do however sustain within themselves a society of peculiarly dominating occasions. This dominant strand, no two members of which are temporally overlapping, is a society of "presiding occasions." A tomato and a human body, for example, are both more or less egalitarian in organization, but the latter also includes a linear society which maintains significant control over the subordinate democracy. This society of presiding occasions in the human body is what we may refer to as the psyche.

2. MENTALITY AND THE HUMAN PSYCHE

The psyche is fundamentally mental; that is, it is distinguished by the degree to which it generates and entertains novel contrasts in re-

sponse to environmental givens. It inherits dominant patterns of order;
it conceives novel alternatives; it contrasts the alternatives to the inherited options; it chooses. Sometimes significant novelty is chosen, but
even repetition at the level of higher mentality is never simply repetition, for conceptual novelty is now irrevocably present as the nagging
awareness of other paths of becoming. Whitehead writes:

> Mental experience is the organ of novelty, the urge beyond. It seeks to vivify
> the massive physical fact, which is repetitive, with novelties which beckon.
> Thus mental experience contains in itself a factor of anarchy. . . .
> But sheer anarchy means the nothingness of experience. We enjoy the con-
> trasts of our own variety in virtue of the order which removes the incompatibility
> of mere diversity. Thus mental experience must itself be canalized into order.
> In its lowest form mental experience is canalized into slavish conformity. . . .
> This lowest form . . . pervades all nature. It is rather a capacity for mentality,
> than mentality itself. But it *is* mentality. In this lowly form it evades no dif-
> ficulties: it strikes out no new ways: it produces no disturbance of the repetitive
> character of physical fact. It can stretch out no arm to save nature from its
> ultimate decay. . . .
> But when mentality is working at a higher level, it brings novelty into the
> appetitions of mental experience. In this function, there is the sheer element
> of anarchy. But mentality now becomes self-regulative. It canalizes its own
> operations by its own judgments. It introduces a higher appetition which
> discriminates among its own anarchic productions. Reason appears. . . . Reason
> civilizes the brute force of anarchic appetition. . . . Reason is the special
> embodiment in us of the disciplined counter-agency which saves the world.
> (*FR*, 33f.)

Actual entities and their social organizations at every level exhibit certain factors: there is the past with its resources and limitations, the self-
creativity of the present over and above inherited preferences, and
the element of novel possibility. At the simplest levels novelty is minuscule—the bare unactualized possibility of there being possibility. But
complexity increases with the increase of novel appetition, i.e., with mentality. Mentality—again, not to be simply equated with consciousness—is
thus the agent of richness, diversity, and complexity. And, at its broadest
reaches, mentality begets civilization.

3. NOVELTY AND THE ADVENTURE OF CIVILIZATION

Civilized life is not devoid of a strong tie to the past or to the sustenance of surrounding stability. But its special quality is the degree to
which self-creativity cherishes the integration of newness. "Apart from
some transcendent aim," says Whitehead, "the civilized life either wal-
lows in pleasure or relapses slowly into a barren repetition with waning
intensities of feeling" (*AI*, 108). It should be absolutely clear that civilization requires the full satisfaction of basic necessities—"Prometheus did
not bring to mankind freedom of the press. He procured fire, which . . .
cooks and gives warmth" (*AI*, 84). Whitehead's sense of transcendence

implies no diminution of natural needs and functionings. But the satisfied body requires for its enrichment the adventurous soul. Adventure is the quest of imagination:

The world dreams of things to come, and then in due season arouses itself to their realization. . . .

Sometimes adventure is acting within limits. . . . Such adventures are the ripples of change within one type of civilization, by which an epoch of [a] given type preserves its freshness. But, given the vigor of adventure, sooner or later the leap of imagination reaches beyond the safe limits of the epoch, and beyond the safe limits of learned rules of taste. It then produces the dislocations and confusions marking the advent of new ideals for civilized effort.

A race preserves its vigor so long as it harbors a real contrast between what has been and what may be; and so long as it is nerved by the vigor to adventure beyond the safeties of the past. Without adventure civilization is in full decay. (*AI*, 359f.)

Thus adventure, embryonically present even in the most rudimentary forms of reality, emerges with power only in the life of the human mind. Even here, though, its assertiveness is sporadic. And here, too, its accomplishments are subject to temporal decay. No levels of fine achievement are immune to subsequent loss. But neither are there limits set in advance to what, eventually, may be achieved.

4. REQUISITES OF ADVENTURE: FREEDOM

What are the requisites of adventure? One condition, as Whitehead's concept of mentality makes clear, is freedom—freedom from total bondage to the dictates of the past. "It is for this reason that the notion of freedom haunts the higher civilizations" (*AI*, 362). Thus, integral to Whitehead's philosophy is a doctrine of freedom in some ways far more radical than that of any existentialist. Whitehead—convinced that freedom is an essential element of human experience, and that experience is our model of reality—postulates some measure of freedom, however primitive, in every actual entity at every level of the universe. But Whitehead's concept of freedom is also more qualified than that of most existentialists. Freedom, though in some sense universal, is always operative within a context of effective influences. The past is influentially present. The past is presently felt heavy with preference for modes of present becoming. But the role of the past, at the basic level of actual entities, is persuasive and not coercive. In the final analysis, however forceful the imprint of the past upon each becoming actual entity, there still lurks within the present an element of self-creativity.

One naturally asks what sense can be given to the claim that freedom in some form is present throughout nature, that the past influences but does not determine the present. The answer is no sense at all, *if* we approach the matter from the standpoint of a Newtonian conception of causal relationships. So long as the interaction of billiard balls or the movement of machine parts is retained as our basic model of causal relationships, these relationships must be viewed either as strictly determined or as strictly undetermined. Whitehead frankly seeks a middle course between these two options. He believes that the universe exhibits too much order for the latter and too little for the former to be true. He further believes that neither conforms to our actual experience. In experience, the past pervades the present luring it toward repetition. And the present must receive, must take account of, the past. But what ensues is scarcely analogous to the crisp movements of a balance scale responding automatically to the heaviest weight—nor would we be attracted to a mechanistic model were its authoritative character not already assumed. Experientially, causal relatedness appears as the efficacy of persuasion. Even repetition is acquiescence to persuasion. Hence, assuming the reality of experienced freedom, and assuming, even as determinists have contended, the unity of nature, the conclusion seems apparent: neither "determinism" nor "indeterminism" is absolute; each is an extreme in the single continuum of persuasive causality. The capacity for freedom, which is itself a form of freedom, is pervasive.

5. REQUISITES OF ADVENTURE: GOD

Whitehead thus roots civilization in nature. The minuscule freedom of non-human nature begets the fuller freedom of man, and human freedom gives rise to that form of adventure which is the distinguishing mark of civilization. Adventure is the adventure of the free. But why are the free adventurous? And what is the significance of the adventurous quest? That is, how are we to understand the urge to adventure? The answer, for Whitehead, lies in religion and God.

PART II. GOD IN WHITEHEAD'S PHILOSOPHY

The world is a web of momentary events and process is its fundamental character. The cosmic process throbs antiphonally—now as the manifold past merging into the several unities of feeling, then as each such unity contributing to a subsequent multiplicity, and again as the many merging into diverse onenesses for other manys. Related in extraordinarily diverse ways, the momentary instantiations of the process extend everlastingly.

A. God and the Cosmic Order

One may contend that to seek explanations for the existence of the cosmic process is to misunderstand the meaning of "explanation," to commit a "category-mistake." But surely we are not remiss to try to explain the character of that process. That quest is not obviously illegitimate, the problem is its difficulty, for no single characterization of the world seems adequate. There is order but also disorder. There is gain but also loss. Structures arise from simpler forms of life, their emergence halting and uncertain. Often, born out of season, they fail to endure. Sometimes they subsist. Occasionally they blossom forth, fortunately housed in a sustaining environment. But only occasionally. The cosmic process is not like the finely tuned coordinations of the human eye, to which it is frequently compared. For every integrated and relatively self-sustaining system produced, the evolutionary struggle has generated scores of failures. The world is rather like a mysteriously half-cultivated garden found in an apparently uninhabited forest—it is too poorly tended to have a gardener, but too well tended not to. To be adequate, an account of the cosmic process must consider both the dull repetition and blind gain, and the occasional creative leaps toward higher forms of order.

Whitehead contends that there is too little order and progress in the world for traditional theism to be very plausible, and too much for atheism. The cosmic process suggests a God, but it does not, as we shall see, give evidence of a cosmic monarch presiding omnipotently over the course of temporal affairs. Traditional theism is without support. However, in Whitehead's view, atheism is no more adequate to the evidence. The garden reflects some planning, some care. Amidst adventitious meanderings, a universe did mysteriously groan into being. Man's eloquent odes to cosmic order and value are not wholly groundless. It is not manifestly foolish to see in things some measure of intentionality. Indeed, much as the largely habitual and chaotic dimensions of human experience are granted an element of ordered progress by our own intentionality, the circuitous wanderings of cosmic evolution seem to mask a faint but persistent urge toward order. The evidence is by no means decisive, nor could it be. But this interpretation of evolution is a plausible one, and it accords well with the supposition discussed in Part I that human experience is as fully a part of the world as are molecules and electromagnetic waves. It is strained to suppose that purposiveness at the human level altogether lacks remote antecedents at the more primitive levels from which it arises, and the price of such a bifurcation, namely, the expulsion of human experience from the world of nature, is too great to pay so needlessly.

That there is some ordering element in the cosmic process seems highly reasonable. The issue is where it is to be located. The urge toward order cannot, for Whitehead, be placed in some transcendent realm of abstract, self-contained principles. Like Aristotle, Whitehead rejects the Platonic notion of wholly non-actual, disembodied realities. Principles do nothing, explain nothing; they merely describe a pattern of action, a way something is being done. In process philosophy causal efficacy is tied to actuality; only actual entities act. But it does not seem sufficient to locate the persistent cosmic urge toward order in the individual "decisions" of the self-creative actual occasions themselves. It is precisely the tendency toward order and progress evident in these manifold decisions that needs explaining. Nor can the coordination of purpose be explained entirely in terms of the efficacy of the past. The past is often a conglomerate of divergent, sometimes incompossible, urgings; and even when it does manifest itself as a unity, the present not infrequently deviates from its coaxing in pursuit of other aims. Thus, Whitehead reasons, there must be some one actuality which, because its intimacy with the rest is uniquely complete, pervades the temporal process with an urging toward order and the increase of value.

Whitehead's doctrine, more precisely put, is as follows: Every actual entity has as its data the full diversity of the past. Its task is to create itself as some one of the many possible syntheses of this given multiplicity. Among these manifold feelings of the past there is a "prehension" of God. The object of this feeling is God's own evaluation of those possibilities relevant to that occasion's becoming. By virtue of the interrelatedness of all things, God's preferences too are always ingredient, however dimly, in the data for every present becoming. That divine preference constitutes the ideal possibility realizable in that actual occasion. The physical organization of chaos, the human realization of value, and the adventure of civilized experience—all are the fruit of God's ceaseless presence as the persuasive lure toward nobler, richer forms of achievement.

B. The Nature of God

We now may see some basic ways in which the God of process (or neoclassical) theology differs from that of classical theism. The first has to do with God's power. Traditionally God has been thought capable of determining the course of the temporal process in its detail. Even if God has chosen to limit himself, we are told, he can alter that choice at will because essentially God is all-powerful.

Process thinkers raise two objections to the doctrine of divine omnipotence. One is a conceptual problem. What can "all-powerful" mean? The very idea of power presupposes some resistant force over which power is effective. But such a counter-force, itself embodying some degree of power, is denied by the claim that one being possesses, or even could possess, all power. Hence, the concept of an all-powerful God is self-contradictory. The second objection to God's omnipotence is based on the reality of evil. If an omnipotent deity controlled pre-human evolution, why was there so much unproductive experimentation, so many disastrous divergences, so much failure and loss? And now, why so much *unnecessary* suffering? Could any morally credible divine plan necessitate every moment of every instance of human agony? Consider what is by no means the most gripping example: the last agonizing minute before, finally, death relieves the torturous assault of cancer. Surely some one such minute of suffering has been pointless. And if God could have eliminated such a moment, he should have done so. Of course we can give up the effort to understand, and perhaps we ought to do so. But short of that retreat (in which, though, truth and error stand equal, both without justification), we must, it seems, eschew a doctrine of divine omnipotence. Even if such a view were coherent, both unnecessary suffering and the waywardness of the evolutionary advance stand as evidence against it.

God, in process theism, is supremely powerful by virtue of his pervasive presence as a lure toward higher forms of order. But while God's aims are universally active, their realization is not guaranteed. The autonomy of temporal entities is real. God's purposes in the world have no power except that of persuasion, except as their intrinsic worth elicits a creaturely adherence to the divine bidding. Whitehead thus seeks to explicate in philosophical theory the spirit of that "brief Galilean vision of humility" that "dwells upon the tender elements in the world, which slowly and quietly operate by love" (PR, 520).

Classical and process theism also differ with respect to God's knowledge. The traditional view maintains that God knows what has happened and what will happen in the world. Process thinkers reject the doctrine of God's foreknowledge because it entails the denial of human freedom and the real contingency of the future. If God knows what will occur in the future, and if God cannot be wrong, then the future cannot be different than God now knows it. But if the future must come to pass as it is now known by God, the future is predetermined. Consequently for any view like Whitehead's that affirms freedom and contingency, it follows that God cannot foreknow the future.

God's omniscience, in process theism, is his perfect knowledge of the past as actual, and of the future as a complex of possibilities. Given his perfect awareness of what has occurred, God is capable of anticipating the relative likelihood of possible future developments. Some of these, especially the more proximate ones, will be more precisely calculable than others. But even for God what is not yet actual cannot be known as actual, only as possible. And that which is merely possible is to some extent open and, in the same measure, uncertain. Hence for God as well as man, the future holds both opportunity and risk.

The most fundamental difference between traditional and process theism has to do with their understandings of God's perfection. The divine perfection, in traditional theology, is understood in terms of God's completeness, the absence of any lack in God. One consequence of this is that God, lacking nothing, is incapable of being contributed to or affected, i.e., God is impassible. The classical idea of perfection also entails God's immutability or changelessness. A perfect being could not change, for because he is already utterly complete, any change would be to something less than perfection.

Process theologians stress the difficulty of reconciling this view with
the Hebrew-Christian affirmation that God knows and loves the changing
world. How can God's knowledge not change if the world he knows
changes, and how can God love the world without being affected by it?
The doctrine that God is immutable and impassible is firmly at odds with
the Biblical perspective. From the process perspective, too, it is unacceptable: as we showed earlier, to be actual is to be relational and
dynamic; this can be no less true in the case of God.

God, in process thought, is dipolar: in one respect he is changing and
passible and in another respect he is unchanging and impassible. The
fundamental character of God's experience—the fact that he always fully
knows and loves the world—is unchanging and unaffected. But precisely
because this is the nature of God's abstract character, the content of
God's experience—his concrete relatedness to the changing world—is itself changing and supremely sensitive to temporary affairs. Thus, God's
perfection entails not his completeness, but instead the unsurpassable
fullness of his love. It is a love that fully knows the world, tirelessly seeks
its good, and, as we shall see, endlessly preserves its achievements in
God's abiding life.

Whitehead's doctrine of God is philosophically derived. It is a conclusion to be elucidated strictly in terms of the nature of the natural process.
If convincing at all, it is because this view is a reasonable speculative
account of the observed world. But with respect to God, Whitehead also
offers another kind of consideration, having to do more specifically with
the nature of religion. We now turn to it.

C. God and Religion

"Religion," Whitehead said, "is what the individual does with his own
solitariness" (*RM*, 16). This statement, though often quoted, remains
relatively obscure apart from the following passage: "The great religious
conceptions which haunt the imaginations of civilized mankind are scenes
of solitariness: Prometheus chained to his rock, Mahomet brooding in
the desert, the meditations of the Buddha, the solitary Man on the Cross.
It belongs to the depth of the religious spirit to have felt forsaken, even
by God" (*RM*, 19f.). In its profoundest dimensions religion is rooted in the
experience of cosmic loneliness. Antecedent to the sense of solitude, historically speaking, there are no doubt rituals and emotions that also may
be called religious. But these persist barely distinguishable from other
human interests. They give rise to beliefs, then to the rational assessment
of beliefs, then to the liberating realization of individuality wrought by
rationality. Reason frees one from uncritical immersion in the life and
meaning of the tribe or race. Self-hood comes as its gift. The gift, however, is also a curse. Traditional wells of meaning run dry and the parched
thirst of futility appears. "In its solitariness the spirit asks, What, in the
way of value, is the attainment of life?" (*RM*, 60). Life's significance is

opened to question at the deepest levels of human feeling. Individuality
is haunted by the sense of being forsaken.

Even so, religion is not solitariness; it is what one does with his
solitariness. The emphasis, however, is not to be put on the volitional
connotations of "doing," for, as Whitehead says in a slightly different
context, the "doing" (or better, the "seeing") "comes as a gift" (AI, 368).
Religion is the intuition, mysteriously given amid the temporal clash of
value and loss of achievement, that "inherent in the nature of things. . . .
is a character of permanent rightness" (RM, 61). It is the mingling of
solitariness with the conviction that "fine action is treasured in the nature
of things" (AI, 353).

The peculiar character of religious truth is that it explicitly deals with values.
It brings into our consciousness that permanent side of the universe which we
can care for. *It thereby provides a meaning . . . for our own existence, a
meaning which flows from the nature of things.* (RM, 124; italics added)

Religion is the confidence that our lives have an abiding significance not
vitiated by the vicissitudes of time or the caprice of fate. The manifold
religions and their rational superstructures give an account of this confidence in varying ways, with more or less internal consistency and adequacy to experience. But religion underlies its expressions. It is a sense, a
feeling of the ultimate decency of things. From this point of view, then,
the finest strivings of humanity have their conformity to, their rootage
in "the nature of things." Hence religion moves from the communalism
of the tribe, to the solitariness of the individual, to individuality participant in the cosmic community.

How Whitehead's "poetry" of cosmic belongingness is to be construed
must be discussed. But first it must be said that the religious confidence
does not vanquish the awareness of tragedy and finitude ingredient in
solitude. For one thing, religion's rational justification hinges perilously
upon the validity of metaphysical analysis, in which undertaking intellectual certainty is a dangerous chimera. What is more, for Whitehead at
least, the tragedy of tragedy cannot be expelled. No Camus was ever more
broodingly attuned to the genuine lostness of "what might have been, and
was not" (AI, 369). To be sure, the religious vision attempts to discern a
meaning in tragedy—to see it "as a living agent persuading the world to
aim at fineness beyond the faded level of surrounding fact." But "the
understanding of tragedy . . . [is] at the same time its preservation" (AI,
368). This, the undiluted reality of tragedy, as well as the religious intuition
that strives to take tragedy into itself, must be explained.

Whitehead's account of the religious vision is grounded, philosophically,
in his principle of relativity: "it belongs to the nature of a 'being' that it is
a potential for every 'becoming'" (PR, 33). And the viability of this
principle rests upon the compellingness of Whitehead's analysis of an
actual entity, discussed in Part I. Given the essentially social character of
actuality, it follows that we must attribute to every actual entity, includ-

ing God, an aspect that is consequent upon its relationship to the past temporal world. Just as God contributes something to the becoming of each actual occasion, so as each occasion contributes something to God. The world enriches the life of God.

In process thought, therefore, life's meaning is tied to the relativity of things. To be meaningful is to make a contribution to some subject of experience. The meanings we find in life reside in our contributions to the future of the human race, to the more immediate community, to those we love, and indeed even to our future selves. Though it does not diminish the immediate importance of these meanings, the fact remains that they are transient—movements fail, memories dim, and men die. Thus if our lives are to have an abiding meaning it can only be their contribution to the abiding life of God. And just as one may reasonably (though, to be sure, not of logical necessity) feel that the finite meanings of his life for, say, his children or his causes give to his life a finite worthwhileness, so also he may reasonably (though, again, not of logical necessity) feel that the contribution of his life to the divine life gives his efforts an abiding worth they would not otherwise possess.

The two dimensions of meaning, transient and abiding, are not at odds. "The purpose of God," for process philosophy, "is the attainment of value in the temporal world" (*RM*, 100). Therefore one can only contribute desirably to the life of God by contributing to the achievement of temporal good. Conversely, to support the increase of value at any level of life is to contribute to, to have meaning for, God. *This* world, indeed the *whole* of this world, has an abiding significance.

Nevertheless, tragedy remains. "What might have been, and was not"— that too is contributed to the life of God. Temporal tragedy enters into God's experience as an ineradicable fact. As we pain those who know us incompletely, so we would pain all the more one whose awareness of things is complete. God's sensitivity to the world is unreserved; his love is unbounded. And he who loves most, risks most and suffers most. Loss in the temporal process, therefore, means genuine loss in the life of God. Suffering in the world means suffering in the life of God. God takes the world into himself—its triumphs and joys, its failures and griefs. "God is the great companion—the fellow-sufferer who understands" (*PR*, 532).

What evidence is there that the religious vision is reliable, that our lives are in fact ultimately meaningful? Philosophically, the religious claim rests on the adequacy of some supportive metaphysic, for example, Whitehead's social conception of reality. At this level the issue is whether the philosophical categories offered are consistent, coherent, and adequate to our experience and to the world as understood by science. But there is, in assessing religion, another kind of consideration, namely the special experience of mystic insight. The suggestion is not that such experiences prove any doctrine to be true. Indeed, Whitehead himself is particularly sensitive to the fact that interpretations of these experiences are always relative to the tradition of the visionary—Christians experience Christ,

Hindus experience Vishnu, and Buddhists experience a Beatific Emptiness. Still, religious experiences are not wisely dismissed from philosophic
consideration. Common to them all is a "direct apprehension of a character exemplified in the actual universe" (*RM*, 86), a "rightness in things,
partially conformed to and partially disregarded" (*RM*, 66). The mere
fact that such intuitions occur in so widespread a fashion is important.
At the least, it continually throws into question the systematic denials
of ultimacy based on the flatness of human experience in historical epochs
such as our own. But more than that, to the extent that the convictions
of special religious intuition and the conclusions of secular philosophical
analysis (such as Whitehead's) conform—to that extent, the credibility
of each is strengthened.

D. God and Civilization

There is yet a third factor to be considered in assessing the religious
vision. It is a pragmatic consideration, approached from the standpoint
of civilization. The problem of a viable civilization is that of balancing
individuality and community. The former represents the creative force
of a culture; the latter represents the conserving element. Each is necessary. Without the often chaotic impulses of individual creativity, on the
one hand, the social process becomes pallid and repetitious—law, order,
and boredom. Thus, as Whitehead says, "on the whole, the great ages
have been unstable ages" (*SMW*, 299). Without some social cohesion, on
the other hand, the richness introduced by creativity is abortive, deprived
of the context of diversity that both enhances and sustains it. A fruitful
social cohesion, though, cannot be coerced; it must be elicited by a mutual
sense of worth among its members. There must be some conserving community deemed worthy of creativity's gifts.

In periods when genuine cultural cohesion widely prevails, the need
of worth has its immediate satisfaction, for the reward of fine action is
close at hand. But few generations could know better than our own how
devastatingly the worth of a society can be questioned. And when communal desire and individual vision are sharply at odds, the polarity productive of civilized vigor is broken. Then the quiet urge toward creativity
is muffled by a sense of futility, unless the rejected community is quickly
replaced by another, or unless the creative adventure is sustained by a
sense of peace.

Whitehead defines "Peace" as "a quality of mind steady in its reliance
that fine action is treasured in the nature of things" (*AI*, 353).

The Peace that is here meant is not the negative conception of anaesthesia.
It is a positive feeling which crowns the 'life and motion' of the soul. It is hard
to define and difficult to speak of. It is not a hope for the future, nor is it an
interest in present details. It is a broadening of feeling due to the emergence
of some deep metaphysical insight, unverbalized and yet momentous in its
coordination of values. Its first effect is the removal of the stress of acquisitive

feeling arising from the soul's preoccupation with itself. Thus Peace carries with
it a surpassing of personality. . . . It is a sense that fineness of achievement
is as it were a key unlocking treasures that the narrow nature of things would
keep remote. There is thus involved a grasp of infinitude, an appeal beyond
boundaries. Its emotional effect is the subsidence of turbulence which inhibits.
More accurately, it preserves the springs of energy. . . . (*AI*, 367)

Peace preserves the springs of creative energy because it is the conviction
that, *somehow,* fine action has a meaning not dependent only upon its
contribution to some finite and fallible community. But how? For Whitehead, the answer is found in the doctrine of God.

God, we have seen, lures the temporal process toward the creative
realization of higher levels of order. But also, God treasures achieved
value in his abiding experience. Therefore, whatever its temporal fate,
"fine action" makes its ultimate contribution to, and has its ultimate
significance in, the unsurpassably worthy life of God. The God who
inspires the creative advance sustains its consequences everlastingly. In
this way, religion at its most profound dimension is the fountain from
which springs civilization.

TEILHARD'S PROCESS METAPHYSICS

Ian G. Barbour

IAN G. BARBOUR is Chairman of the Department of Religion and
Professor of Physics at Carleton College. He has written extensively
on the relationship of science and religion.

The writings of Teilhard de Chardin [1] can be read in a variety of ways:
as evolutionary science, as poetry and mysticism, as natural theology, and
as Christian theology. There is, however, one aspect of his thought to
which little attention has been given, namely, his undeveloped *process
metaphics*, which, I have suggested, plays a crucial role in his synthesis
of scientific and religious ideas.[2] In this paper I will explore some of Teil-

[1] The works of Teilhard most frequently cited below (all published in New York
by Harper & Row) are abbreviated as follows: *AM, The Appearance of Man* (1965);
DM, The Divine Milieu (1960); *FM, The Future of Man* (1964); *MPN, Man's Place
in Nature* (1966); *PM, The Phenomenon of Man* (1959); and *VP, The Vision of the
Past* (1966). The Whitehead works cited (all published in New York by the
Macmillan Co.) include: *AI, Adventures of Ideas* (1933); *MT, Modes of Thought*
(1938); *PR, Process and Reality* (1929); *RM, Religion in the Making* (1926); and
SMW, Science and the Modern World (1925).
[2] Ian G. Barbour, "Five Ways of Reading Teilhard," *Soundings,* Vol. I, No. 2
(Spring, 1968), reprinted in *The Teilhard Review,* Vol. III, No. 1 (Summer, 1968).
In Section V of "Five Ways" I discuss the treatment of Teilhard's metaphysics by
several of his recent interpreters.

hard's metaphysical categories which reflect both evolutionary and bibli-cal assumptions. Successive sections will be devoted to. (1) reality as temporal process, (2) the "within," (3) freedom and determinism, (4) continuing creation, (5) God and time, (6) the problem of evil, and (7) the future of the world.

Teilhard's thought can be illuminated by comparing it with that of Alfred North Whitehead, the most systematic exponent of a philosophy of process. The striking similarities may help to show the character of Teilhard's ideas. The significant differences may make more evident the points at which his contribution is distinctive, or in some cases may suggest ambiguities or limitations in his approach. I will not deal directly with his Christology, which is a major point of divergence from White-head; but by showing the influence of Teilhard's temporalistic metaphysics on his interpretation of a number of biblical themes, I hope to point the way to a subsequent study of his *process theology*. By concentrating on his conceptual thought, I will of course be neglecting many aspects of his complex personality, including the profound spirituality and mysticism which were his most impressive characteristics.

Theilhard's style is very different from Whitehead's. He was not a philosopher; he used vivid analogies and poetic images where Whitehead used carefully defined philosophical abstractions. Yet their underlying insights were often very similar. I will not dwell on the historical reasons for these parallels. Neither man was familiar with the work of the other, but both acknowledge great indebtedness to Henri Bergson.[3] Both were deeply impressed by the status of time in modern science—primarily in evolutionary biology in Teilhard's case and in relativity and quantum physics in Whitehead's. Our task, however, will be to examine the content rather than the genesis of their ideas. Let us start from their reflections on the general structure of the world.

I. REALITY AS TEMPORAL PROCESS

Teilhard and Whitehead both adopt a radically temporalistic outlook in place of the static viewpoint which has dominated most of Western thought. For Teilhard, "the universe is no longer a State but a Process."[4] "Taken at this degree of generalisation (in other words where all experi-mental reality in the universe forms part of a *process*, that is to say, is *born*) evolution has long ago ceased to be a hypothesis and become a *general condition of knowledge* (an additional *dimension*) which hence-

---

[3] See M. Barthelemy-Maudale, *Bergson et Teilhard de Chardin* (Paris: Éditions du Seuil, 1963). Cuénot says that in 1945 Teilhard "songe á lire Whitehead, *La science et le monde moderne*"—which may mean that he actually read it; see Claude Cuénot, *Pierre Teilhard de Chardin* (Paris: Libraire Plon, 1958), p. 292.

[4] *FM*, p. 261.

forth all hypotheses must satisfy." [5] Teilhard asserts, in a variety of contexts, that "this new perception of time" alters all our ways of looking at
things. We live in "a world that is *being born* instead of a world that
is." [6] Ours is an embryonic and incomplete universe; change and development are its pervasive features.

Teilhard suggests that we have usually thought of *time* as a kind of
neutral container in which self-sufficient objects could be rearranged
without being affected, "a sort of vast vessel in which things were
suspended side by side." [7] But now one must acknowledge that "duration permeates the essence of every being." Reality does not consist of
inert objects moving through successive instants, but of processes having
temporal extension. "Every particle of reality, instead of constituting
an approximate point in itself, extends from the previous fragment to
the next in an invisible thread running back to infinity." [8] For Whitehead also the world is made up of events and processes. He rejects both
the scholastic view of unchanging substances with changing attributes
and the Newtonian picture of unchanging particles which are rearranged
but never altered in themselves. Whitehead and Teilhard both employ
categories of becoming and activity rather than of being and substance.[9]

Teilhard refers frequently to the organic interdependence of all
entities. The world is not a collection of self-contained objects related
only externally to each other, but a network of mutual influences spread
through time and space. Every entity is constituted by its relationships;
"every element of the cosmos is woven from all others." "However narrowly the 'heart' of an atom is circumscribed, its realm is coextensive
at least potentially with that of every other atom." [10] The "web of life"
is a fabric of interactions, "a single process without interruption." A close
parallel is Whitehead's rejection of "Simple Location," the mechanistic
assumption that independent particles can be completely described "apart
from any essential reference of the relations of that bit of matter to other
regions of space and to other durations of time." [11] Whitehead proposes
"a social view of reality" as a community of interacting temporal events.

Despite this emphasis on interdependence, neither author ends with a
monism in which the parts are less real than the total process. Every
entity is a center of spontaneity and self-creation contributing distinctively to the future. But in Whitehead this *pluralism*, which counter-
balances the idea of unity, is carried much further. He starts from a
plurality of beings whose individuality and integrity are always preserved.
Whitehead wants us to look at the world from the point of view of each

[5] *AM*, p. 211, n. 1; cf. *VP*, p. 246.
[6] *FM*, p. 88.
[7] *VP*, p. 128; cf. *FM*, p. 59.
[8] *FM*, p. 84; cf. *VP*, p. 129.
[9] *SMW*, pp. 71–77, 157 ff., 188–89; *PR*, pp. 122–23, 317–22.
[10] *PM*, p. 41; cf. *FM*, p. 85.
[11] *SMW*, p. 84.

entity itself—considered as a moment of experience which inherits its data from previous events, yet is radically on its own during the moment it responds: Each occasion or "concrescence" is a unique synthesis of the influences on it, a new unity formed from diversity. Only as it perishes does it influence other events.[12] Whitehead thus envisages not a continuous process but an interconnected series of discrete events. Continuity is accounted for by the succession of individual units of becoming, each of which is completed and then superseded by other units.[13] There is no agency except that of a multiplicity of actual occasions, including God. Whitehead has none of Teilhard's "temporal threads running back to infinity," but only a network of threads connecting each event with its immediate predecessors. This greater pluralism in Whitehead's scheme has repercussions which we will note in his treatment of mind and matter, freedom and determinism, and God's relation to the world.

In Teilhard, the balance between pluralism and monism is tipped in the opposite direction. "Everything forms a single whole," an integral cosmic process.[14] We will find that in some passages the whole of cosmic history seems to have a unified structure not unlike that of a single Whiteheadian concrescence; Teilhard predicts the "convergence," "centration," and "involution" of the universe. Where Whitehead is concerned to give a generalized account of the growth of all particular entities, Teilhard tries to delineate the patterns of universal history. While these two tasks overlap considerably, they tend to encourage differing emphases. At a later point, we will see that Teilhard's belief in the unity of creation was strengthened by his own mystical sense of experienced oneness and by the biblical hope of a single eschatological goal of history.

Both authors portray *continuity* as well as *discontinuity* between the levels of reality, but Teilhard puts somewhat greater stress on continuity. There are no sharp lines between the non-living and the living, or between life and mind. Each level has its roots in earlier levels and represents the flowering of what was potentially present all along, though these roots are "lost in darkness as we trace them back." The higher was already present in the lower in rudimentary form: "*In the world, nothing could ever burst forth as final across the different thresholds successively traversed by evolution (however critical they be) which had not already existed in an obscure and primordial way. . . .* Everything, in some extremely attenuated version of itself, has existed from the very first." [15] Yet within this continuity there were thresholds and critical points. These "crises" were not gaps or absolute discontinuities, but each marked a major breakthrough. There was real novelty at each new level (life, thought, society), even though each was anticipated in previous levels. Teilhard gives the analogy of a gradually heated liquid which reaches a critical tempera-

12 *PR*, pp. 95, 188.
13 *PR*, p. 53.
14 *DM*, p. 30.
15 *PM*, pp. 71, 78.

ture, a boiling point at which a change of state suddenly occurs.[16] He uses the words "metamorphosis" and "transformation" to describe these changes in which new properties emerged.[17]

Whitehead shares Teilhard's assumptions concerning the historical continuity of the past, though his attention is directed to the ontological similarities among differing types of entities today. For him also the higher is present in the lower in rudimentary form. Since he takes metaphysics to be the search for interpretive categories of the widest generality, these categories must be applicable to all entities. Yet the modes in which they are exemplified may vary widely; "there are gradations of importance and diversities of function." Whitehead makes greater allowance than Teilhard for the diversity of events which occur at different levels of reality.[18] Let us look in particular at their views of mental life.

II. THE "WITHIN"

In Teilhard's philosophy every entity has a "within." Even among atoms there was a tendency to build up molecules and then cells of more highly centered complexity; he attributes this to a "radial energy" which produced and maintained very improbable systems in violation of the law of entropy. Next there was an elementary responsiveness which was a forerunner of mental life. He does not, of course, ascribe self-awareness or reflection to simple organisms; their "psychic life" was infinitesimal, a rudimentary beginning of perception, anticipation, and spontaneity "in extremely attenuated versions." [19]

We have seen that Teilhard mentions "critical points" at which novel phenomena occurred for the first time; there were "metamorphoses" of the "within" to new forms, which were "quite different." But his terminology tends to blur any such distinctions. With the exception of reflective thought (which is imputed to man alone), Teilhard's various terms are used interchangeably all the way down the scale from man to cell: the "within," interiority, psychic life, mentality, consciousness, etc. He sometimes says that in simple organisms these are all *potentially* present (though he provides no specific analysis of the concept of potentiality). More often he says they are *actually* present in infinitesimal degree. At higher levels, consciousness is said to be proportional to the development of the nervous system and brain; at lower levels, it is said to be proportional to complexity, even in the total absence of a nervous system.[20]

16 *PM*, pp. 78, 168; *VP*, p. 180.
17 *PM*, pp. 79, 88.
18 *PR*, pp. 127–67.
19 *VP*, p. 235; *PM*, pp. 54 ff.
20 *PM*, *pp*. 53–66, 71, 88, 149–52; *VP*, pp. 227–28; *MPN*, pp. 32–33.

Whitehead's "subjective pole" resembles Teilhard's "within." In general, every entity takes account of previous events, responds to them, and makes a creative selection from alternative potentialities. But Whitehead's basic categories characterizing all events have very diverse exemplifications. A stone has no organization beyond the physical cohesion of its parts and hence it has no "subjective pole" at all; it is a "corpuscular society" which is not the locus of any unified events. A cell has only an incipient psychism, which is so vanishingly small that for all practical purposes it may be considered absent; its response to changing stimuli testifies at most to an exceedingly attenuated form of aim or purpose. Only with animals is there a single "dominant occasion" of awareness. Whitehead holds that there is *no* consciousness, even in a rudimentary form, in lower animate beings, much less in inanimate ones.[21]

Clearly, both Teilhard and Whitehead do use human experience, with various qualifications, as a model for the interpretation of other entities. Why do they make this generalization from man? Their reasons appear to be similar:

1. *The unity of man with nature.* Man is part of nature; he is a product of the evolutionary process. "The roots of our being," says Teilhard, "are in the first cell." Human experience is a fact within nature. We cannot be content with a physical description "which leaves out thought, the most remarkable phenomenon which nature has produced." "The apparent restriction of the phenomenon of consciousness to the higher forms of life has long served science as an excuse for eliminating it from its models of the universe. A queer exception, an aberrant function, an epiphenomenon—thought was classed under one or other of these heads in order to get rid of it." [22] Whitehead likewise defends man's unity with nature and shows the inadequacy of accounts which omit the most distinctive features of human experience. A world of particles-in-motion would be a world to which man's purposes and feelings would be totally alien.[23] We must not ignore the part of the universe we know most directly—our own experience.

2. *The continuity of the world.* We have seen that in spite of the occurrence of thresholds Teilhard traces a continuous evolutionary development. There was an unbroken spectrum of complexity from cell to man; one can set no absolute limits at which the basic features of human experience may have been present. Nature is an integral process: "Since the stuff of the universe has an inner aspect at one point of itself, there is necessarily *a double aspect to its structure,* that is to say in every region of space and time. . . . *In a coherent perspective of the world, life inevitably assumes a 'pre-life' for as far back before it as the eye can see."* [24] Teilhard gives another analogy: Just as we assume (in relativity theory)

21 *PR*, pp. 164–67; *MT*, p. 38; *AI*, p. 164.
22 *PM*, p. 55; cf. *VP*, p. 162.
23 *SMW*, pp. 78 ff.
24 *PM*, pp. 56–57.

that a change-in-mass too small to detect occurs in objects moving at low velocity, since a detectable change-in-mass is found at high velocities, so also can we assume a "within" in beings of low complexity, since its effects are noticeable in those of high complexity.[25] The force of the analogy depends on the assumption that the "within" is, despite its "metamorphoses" into differing forms, a single continuous function of complexity. Whitehead likewise defends the continuity of historical development, but we have noted that he gives greater prominence to the emergence of genuinely new phenomena at higher levels of organization.

3. *The coherence of interpretive categories.* The search for a coherent metaphysics presupposes the unity of the world, but it directs attention to the consistency and generality of one's conceptual system. Whitehead holds that metaphysical categories should be applicable to all events, including our awareness as experiencing subjects; human experience is taken to exhibit the generic features of all experience. "An occasion of experience which includes a human mentality is an extreme instance, at on end of the scale, of those happenings which constitute nature." [26] In order to give a unified account of the world, he seems in effect to employ concepts most appropriate to a "middle range" of organisms; these concepts can in very attenuated form be applied to lower entities, and yet they are capable of further development when applied to human experience. A similar concern for intellectual coherence in our understanding of the world seems to have been one of Teilhard's motives.

4. *The inadequacy of mind-matter dualism.* Both authors want to overcome the dualism which has been prominent in Western thought since Descartes. They seek a unitary ontology, not by reducing mind to matter (materialism) or matter to mind (idealism), but by making organic process primary. "Mind" and "matter" are not two distinct substances, but two aspects of a single complex process. Whitehead finds them inseparably interwoven in human experience—for instance, in the bodily reference of feeling and perception. Teilhard reacts not only against the mind-matter dualism, but against the dichotomy of matter and spirit which Christian thinkers have supported. Here he adopts a biblical view of the unity of man as a whole being and rejects the assumption that matter and spirit are separate substances or antagonistic principles.

The two authors differ considerably, however, in their representations of the relationship between the "within" and the "without." In Whitehead's system, subjectivity and objectivity occur in *distinct phases* of the concrescence of an event. Every momentary subject first inherits objective data from its past. It is then on its own in subjective immediacy, appropriating this data from its unique perspective, selecting among alternative possibilities, and producing a novel synthesis. The resulting outcome is then available as objective data to be appropriated by subsequent mo-

25 *PM,* pp. 54, 301.
26 *AI,* p. 237.

ments of experience. Efficient causality characterizes the transition between such events, while final causality dominates the internal growth
within the concrescence as it actualizes its own synthesis. Teilhard pictures no such successive phases; for him every entity is *simultaneously*
subjective and objective.[27] He stresses the continuity of experience,
whereas Whitehead stresses its fragmentary character.

This difference has a significant methodological consequence. Whitehead claims that the scientist, relying on sense perception, can deal
directly only with the outcome of a past event; the isolated moment of
present subjectivity is inaccessible to him: "Science can find no individual
enjoyment in nature; science can find no aim in nature; science can find
no creativity in nature; it finds mere rules of succession. These negations
are true of natural science; they are inherent in its methodology." [28]
Teilhard agrees that the "within" of another being is not itself directly
observable; but he seems to think that its effects are among the "phenomena" which a more open-minded science will in the future be able to
analyze. But he has perhaps given insufficient consideration to the
epistemological problem of how an inherently private mental life expresses
itself in the public world.

III. Freedom and Determinism

For Teilhard, then, all beings are temporal, interdependent, and characterized by a "within." But is their activity free or determined? In many
contexts, Teilhard seems to reject determination by either natural laws
or divine omnipotence. In discussing evolution he repeatedly mentions
"random mutations," "blind chance," and "billionfold trial and error."
Particular combinations of atoms or configurations of species were "accidental," "fortuitous," and "unrepeatable." "Even if there were only one
solution to the main physical and physiological problem of life on earth,
that general solution would necessarily leave undecided a host of accidental and particular questions, and it does not seem thinkable that they
would have been decided *twice in the same way*. . . . The genesis of life
on earth belongs to the category of absolutely *unique* events that, once
happened, are never repeated." [29] Whereas the scholastics interpreted
the actualization of potentiality as the unfolding of what was there all
along, Teilhard speaks of *alternative potentialities* not all of which are
actualized. He gives the example of a molecule which could exist in either
of two forms (mirror images of each other); it is today found in all living
organisms in only one of these forms—which presumably represents the

[27] Cf. Richard Overman, *Evolution and the Christian Doctrine of Creation* (Philadelphia: Westminster Press, 1967), p. 227.
[28] *MT*, p. 221.
[29] *PM*, p. 100; cf. *PM*, pp. 74, 307.

way in which the atoms happened to collide in the primeval molecule from which all the samples today are descended. The present world "exhausts *only a part of what might have been.*" [30]

With the advent of simple organisms there was novelty and spontaneity, according to Teilhard. With reflective consciousness came moral choice and responsibility. Man's destiny is now in his own hands; he can "grasp the tiller of evolution" and steer his own course. Teilhard makes frequent reference to the "choices," "options," and "crossroads" which we face. His political philosophy indorses individual freedom and diversity despite the need for collectivization and global unity.[31] He grants that in the future, man's free decisions may thwart the progress of the universe toward union; final success "is not necessary, inevitable or certain." Some men may fail to co-operate, for man has the power to refuse to love.[32]

On the other hand, many of Teilhard's statements sound completely deterministic. Various stages of past evolution were "inevitable," "inexorable," or "necessary." The future convergence of the cosmos is "inescapable." There is an "over-riding super-determinism which irresistibly impels Mankind to converge upon itself." [33] He even suggests that it would be futile for anyone to try to oppose global socialization, since it is inevitable. The total process is one of "sure ascent" and "irreversible movement." How can one reconcile Teilhard's apparently contradictory declarations of freedom and determinism? There seem to be three ways in which he attempts a reconciliation:

1. *The law of large numbers.* Events such as the tossing of a coin can be individually random yet statistically lawful; the individual case is unpredictable but the group can be accurately predicted. Teilhard applies this principle to chance in evolution and extends it to human freedom. He holds that each person considered separately may fail, but "by a sort of 'infallibility of large numbers,' Mankind, the present crest of the evolutionary wave, cannot fail." [34] "It is statistically necessary that in any large number of letters there will regularly be mistakes: stamps forgotten, addresses incompleted, etc. Yet each sender is free not to make mistakes." [35] Teilhard makes the rather dubious assumption that chance and freedom are subject to the same kind of statistical consideration. There are, he says, "two uncertainties related to the double play—the chance at the bottom and freedom at the top. Let me add, however, that in the case of very large numbers (such, for instance, as the human population) the process tends to 'infallibilise' itself, inasmuch as the likelihood of success grows on the lower side (chance) while that of rejection and

---

[30] *PM*, p. 95; cf. *FM*, p. 220.
[31] *FM*, pp. 194, 241.
[32] *PM*, pp. 288, 306; *FM*, p. 232.
[33] *FM*, p. 128; cf. *FM*, p. 71.
[34] *FM*, p. 237.
[35] See Christopher Mooney, *Teilhard and the Mystery of Christ* (New York: Harper & Row, 1966), p. 127.

error diminishes on the other side (freedom) with the multiplication of the elements engaged." [36]

2. *The Universe as a unified power.* Teilhard sometimes speaks of the cosmos as a single agency which will prevail in its purposes regardless of the vagaries of individuals. In the past, evolution has won over all obstacles and found a way out of all impasses; it would be absurd for it to abort now after it has gotten this far. The subject of the following propositions is "the world": "To bring us into existence it has from the beginning juggled miraculously with too many improbabilities for there to be any risk whatever in committing ourselves further and following it right to the end. If it undertook the task, it is because it can finish it, following the same methods and with the same infallibility with which it began." [37] Teilhard's confidence undoubtedly rests ultimately in the power of God, but he often writes as if the cosmic process is itself a trustworthy and purposeful agency which will determine the outcome:

No doubt it is true that up to a point we are free *as individuals* to resist the trends and demands of Life. But does this mean (it is a very different matter) that we can escape collectively from the fundamental set of the tide? . . . The earth is more likely to stop turning than is Mankind, as a whole, likely to stop organising and unifying itself. For if this interior movement were to stop, it is the Universe itself, embodied in Man, that would fail to curve inwards and achieve totalisation. And nothing, as it seems, can prevent the Universe from succeeding—nothing, not even our human liberties, whose essential tendency to union may fail in detail but cannot (without "cosmic" contradiction) err "statistically." [38]

3. *God's control of the world.* Teilhard's conviction of the inevitable convergence of the world rests finally on his Christian belief in the omnipotence of God. "Only Omega can guarantee the outcome." To the Christian, "the eventual biological success of Man on Earth is not merely a probability but a certainty, since Christ (and in Him virtually the World) is already risen." [39] In later sections we will examine Teilhard's views of evil, progress, and eschatology. At the moment, we may note that in his doctrine of providence he faces the difficulty with which so many theologians of the past wrestled: How can one consistently believe in both human freedom and divine determination? On this problem he throws little new light.

Whitehead, by contrast, is specific in rejecting all forms of determinism. He holds that the existence of genuinely alternative potentialities is incompatible with predestination. God radically qualifies but does not determine the action of each actual entity. "It derives from God its basic conceptual aim, relevant to its actual world, yet with indeterminations

[36] *PM*, p. 307.
[37] *PM*, p. 232; cf. *PM*, p. 276.
[38] *FM*, p. 152.
[39] *FM*, p. 237.

awaiting its own decisions." [40] God provides a cosmic order within which there is self-determination by each being. Whitehead attacks the idea of a predetermined and fixed divine plan; God has unchanging general purposes, but his goals for particular events are modified as individual entities take their own actions in response to his initiative. Whitehead thus departs further than Teilhard from the traditional doctrine of divine omnipotence.

Teilhard has been accused of adopting pantheism, which in the past has often taken deterministic forms. But the accusation is unjust. Teilhard is critical of the Eastern "mysticism of identification," in which the individual seeks absorption in the All, hoping to merge "like a drop in the ocean." He adheres to the Western "mysticism of union," in which individuality and personality are not lost.[41] Convergence will be achieved "not by identification (God becoming all) but by the differentiating and communicating action of love (God all *in everyone*)." [42] Ultimate reality is neither an undifferentiated unity nor an impersonal structure, but a supreme person. Nevertheless the reader may easily forget, amid Teilhard's frequent references to "the All" and "the whole," that God is to be distinguished from the cosmos. In Whitehead's writing, on the other hand, it is always clear that God is one among a plurality of entities. Each occasion retains its individuality and self-determination, even in relation to God.[43]

IV. CONTINUING CREATION

For Teilhard, as for Whitehead, the understanding of the world as temporal process outlined in the preceding sections has important implications for the representation of God's relation to the world. God is not the external fabricator of an essentially static system but a creative influence immanent in an evolutionary development. Teilhard urges us to think of creation not "as an instantaneous act, but in the manner of a process or synthesizing action." [44] "Creation has never ceased. Its act is a great continuous movement spread out over the totality of time. It is still going on." [45]

Teilhard proposes that creation consists in *the unification of the mul-*

[40] *PR*, p. 343.
[41] *DM*, p. 94.
[42] *PM*, p. 308; cf. *PM*, p. 262, and *FM*, p. 207. See Henri de Lubac, *The Religion of Teilhard de Chardin* (New York: Desclee, 1967), pp. 143–60.
[43] See William Christian, *An Interpretation of Whitehead's Metaphysics* (New Haven, Conn.: Yale University Press, 1959), pp. 403–9.
[44] "Christologie et évolution" (1933), scheduled for publication in *Oeuvres*, Vol. XI; quoted in Robert L. Faricy, "Teilhard de Chardin on Creation and the Christian Life," *Theology Today*, Jan. 1967, p. 510.
[45] "Le milieu mystique," in *Écrits du temps de la guerre (1916–19)* (Paris: Éditions Bernard Grasset, 1965), p. 149.

tiple. Whereas Bergson conceived of an original unity which differentiates and diverges into multiplicity, Teilhard assumes a primeval multiplicity which converges toward a final unity. In several of his early writings, he speaks of creation as "a struggle against the many," but he maintains that in its disunity "the many" represents only a potentiality for being rather than an independent reality over against God.[46] In an essay written in 1948, he imagines four "moments" in which the world originated. Initially there was only a self-sufficient First Being. Second, according to revelation, there was a movement of internal diversity and union in the divine life understood as "trinitization" rather than static unity. I quote in full his speculation concerning the third and fourth "moments," since it is controversial and not yet published:

By the very fact that he unifies himself interiorly, the First Being *ipso facto* causes another type of opposition to arise, not within himself but at his antipodes (and here we have our third moment). At the pole of being there is self-subsistent Unity, and all around at the periphery, as a necessary consequence, there is multiplicity: *pure* multiplicity, be it understood, a "creatable void" which is simply nothing—yet which, because of its passive potency for arrangement (i.e. for union), constitutes a possibility, an appeal for being. Now everything takes place as if God had not been able to resist this appeal, for at such depths our intelligence can no longer distinguish at all between supreme necessity and supreme freedom.

In classical philosophy or theology, creation or participation (which constitutes our fourth moment) always tends to be presented as an almost arbitrary gesture on the part of the First Cause, executed by a causality analogous to "efficient" and according to a mechanism that is completely indeterminate: truly an "act of God" in the pejorative sense. In a metaphysics of union, on the contrary—although the self-sufficiency and self-determination of the Absolute Being remain inviolate (since pure, antipodal multiplicity, is, I insist, nothing but pure passivity and potentiality)—in such a metaphysics, I say, the creative act takes on a very well defined significance and structure. . . . To create is to unite.[47]

This idea of "creative union" is not in itself incompatible with the idea of "creation out of nothing." Teilhard says that God is "self-sufficing" and initially "stood alone." He denies the need for a "pre-existing substratum" on which God operated and holds that matter is not eternal. As North points out,[48] the multiple is little more than potential-for-being;

[46] "L'union créatrice," Les noms de la mattière," "La lutte contre la multitude," in *Écrits du temps de la guerre;* also "Mon univers," in *Oeuvres,* (Paris: Éditions du Seuil), Vol. IX.

[47] "Comment je vois" (1948), scheduled for publication in *Oeuvres,* Vol. X; quoted in Mooney, op. cit., pp. 172–73. Alternative renditions in Robert Faricy, op. cit., pp. 510–77, and Piet Smulders, *The Design of Teilhard de Chardin* (Westminster, Md.: Newman Press, 1967), pp. 79–81. A letter from Teilhard to my father accompanying a copy of this essay and commenting on it is given in George B. Barbour, *In the Field with Teilhard de Chardin* (New York: Herder & Herder, 1965), pp. 125–26.

[48] Robert North, *Teilhard and the Creation of the Soul* (Milwaukee, Wis.: Bruce Publishing Co., 1967), pp. 88–91.

union is equated with being and disunion with non-being. DeLubac argues that Teilhard's "creative union" takes place moment by moment *within* the process and that one can still consider the *whole* process as created *ex nihilo*.[49] But Teilhard does treat the ongoing process (the fourth moment) rather than an instantaneous beginning as the really creative stage of God's work. In effect he seems to assume that the cosmic process has a convergent and unifying character; therefore he extrapolates to a primeval state of "pure multiplicity," whose relation to the prior unity of God remains problematical.[50]

Whitehead shares Teilhard's themes of continuing creation and unification, but he explicitly rejects "creation out of nothing." He holds that time is infinite. There was no first day, no initial act of origination, but only a continuing bringing-into-being in which past, present, and future are structurally similar. God has a priority in ontological status but no temporal priority over the world. God "is not *before* all creation but *with* all creation."[51] However, no ready-made materials were given to God from some other source, and nothing can exist apart from him; he is the ground of order as well as novelty in the world. As Cobb suggests, Whitehead attributes to God a fundamental role in the birth of each new event, though there is no event which he alone determines absolutely.[52]

I would submit that even though Whitehead rejects and Teilhard qualifies the idea of "creation out of nothing," both men share the *motives* which led the church fathers to the formulation of the traditional doctrine. The formula is not of course itself scriptural; Genesis does not open with "nothing" but with the primeval chaos of a watery deep prior to God's acts of creation. *Ex nihilo* was first propounded in the intertestamental period and was later elaborated by such theologians as Irenaeus and Augustine, in order to exclude the Hellenistic idea that matter on which God imposed form existed independently of him and constituted the source of evil in the world.[53] But Teilhard and Whitehead are as insistent as the church fathers that matter is in itself basically good rather than evil.[54] An additional motive in the *ex nihilo* doctrine was the assertion of the total sovereignty and freedom of God. Teilhard and Whitehead do limit God's omnipotence, but neither of them adopts an

[49] De Lubac, op. cit., pp. 195–200. See also Smulders, op. cit., pp. 77–85.

[50] North, op. cit., p. 116, claims that, without intending to, Teilhard adopts an implicit emanationism in which the world is made from the substance of God. North argues that if there is a temporal symmetry between Alpha and Omega, and if Omega involves "absorption in divinity," then creation must have arisen "by a sort of sifting out of divinity." However, he never shows that Teilhard's thought entails such an assumption of symmetry. See also Robert North, "Teilhard and the Problem of Creation," *Theological Studies*, XXIV (1963), 577–601.

[51] *PR*, p. 531.

[52] John B. Cobb, *A Christian Natural Theology* (Philadelphia: Westminster Press, 1965), pp. 211–12.

[53] Langdon Gilkey, *Maker of Heaven and Earth* (Garden City, N.Y.: Doubleday & Co., 1959), chap. iii; Bernhard W. Anderson, *Creation Versus Chaos* (New York: Association Press, 1967).

[54] For example, *DM*, pp. 81–84.

ultimate dualism or imagines a Platonic demiurge struggling to introduce order into recalcitrant matter; this is no cosmic carpenter who must use the materials on hand. Even Whitehead agrees that nothing has ever existed in independence of God.

In regard to creation as a continuing process, it is not altogether clear how Teilhard thinks of divine activity in relation to the order of nature. He avoids claims of God's intervention at specific points; he advocates "a creation of evolutionary type (*God making things make themselves*)." [55] Such passages would be consistent with the assumption that evolution is in principle scientifically explicable in terms of natural forces. In such a framework God's functions would be (1) to design and effect a set of natural laws which would of themselves gradually produce the fore-ordained cosmic progression and (2) to preserve and sustain this natural system in operation and concur in its results. If this is Teilhard's view, it would be essentially the scholastic notion that God as *primary cause* works through the operation of law-abiding *secondary causes*.

However, Teilhard's terminology frequently suggests that God's role is more active than this. He says that God "animates" and "vivifies" the world, "controls" and "leads" it to fulfillment. There are passages in which God is invoked to explain phenomena held to be scientifically inexplicable: "In Omega we have in the first place the principle we needed to explain both the persistent march of things toward greater consciousness, and the paradoxical solidity of what is most fragile." [56] God's action is not simply that of an Aristotelian "final cause" which is built into the functioning of all beings as they follow their inherent natures. Teilhard seems to believe that the "within" is a more effective vehicle of divine influence than the "without," but he does not clarify the modes of causality involved.

Whitehead, on the other hand, does assign to his equivalent of the "within" the crucial role in God's action on the world. He gives a detailed analysis of causation which includes the influence of past causes, present initiative, and divine purpose in the coming-to-be of each event. [57] Briefly stated, every new event is in part the product of the *efficient causation* of previous events, which in large measure—though never completely—determine it. There is always an element of *self-causation* or self-creation as an entity appropriates and responds to its past in its own way. In the creative selection from among alternatives in terms of goals and aims, there is *final causation*. By structuring these potentialities, God is the ground of both order and novelty, but the final decision is always made by the entity itself; at the human level this means that man is free to reject the ideals which God holds up to him. Whitehead thus works out in much greater detail than Teilhard a set of categories which allow for

[55] *VP*, p. 154.
[56] *PM*, p. 271.
[57] See, for example, Ivor Leclerc, *Whitehead's Metaphysics* (New York: Macmillan Co., 1958), pp. 170–74.

lawfulness, spontaneity, and divine influence in the "continuous creation" of the world.

V. God and Time

Teilhard, like Whitehead, holds that there is reciprocal interaction between God and the world. Both men criticize traditional thought for making creation too arbitrary and the world too "useless" and "ontologically superfluous" to God.[58] In place of what he calls the "paternalism" of the classical view, Teilhard substitutes "a functional completing of the One and the Multiple." [59] He maintains that the idea of the complete self-sufficiency of God makes him seem indifferent and leads to a deprecation of the value of the world and human endeavor in it. "Truly it is not the notion of the contingency of the created but the sense of the mutual completion of God and the world that makes Christianity live. . . . God, the eternal being in himself, is everywhere, we might say, in process of formation for us." [60]

Does Teilhard imply that God experiences change? There are a number of texts which speak of "the fulfillment of God," who "consummates himself only in uniting." "God is entirely self-sufficient, and nevertheless creation brings to him something vitally necessary." [61] In the world viewed as the object of "creation," classical metaphysics accustoms us to see a sort of extrinsic production, issuing from the supreme *efficiency* of God through an overflow of benevolence. *Invincibly*—and *precisely* in order to be able to act and to love fully at one and the same time—I am now led to see therein (in conformity with the spirit of St. Paul) a mysterious product of completion and fulfillment for the Absolute Being Himself.[62]

Teilhard has received considerable criticism for this idea. Thus, Tresmontant comments:

[58] For example, "Contingence de l'univers et goût rumain de survivre" (1954), scheduled for publication in *Oeuvres*, Vol. XI. Whitehead uses almost identical terms, e.g., *AI*, pp. 213 ff.

[59] "L'étoffe de l'univers," in *Oeuvres*, VII, 405.

[60] "Contingence de l'univers . . ."; "Trois contes comme Benson," in *Écrits du temps de la guerre.*

[61] "Comment je vois," quoted in Smulders, op. cit., p. 276; "Christianisme et évolution" (1945), scheduled for publication in *Oeuvres*, Vol. XI.

[62] "Le coeur de la matière" (1950), scheduled for publication in *Oeuvres*, Vol. X; quoted in Claude Tresmontant, *Pierre Teilhard de Chardin: His Thought* (Baltimore: Helicon Press, 1959), p. 93. On p. 30 of the mimeographed version given by Teilhard to George Barbour, the phrase "a mysterious product of *completion* and *fulfilment* for the Absolute Being Himself" is replaced by "a mysterious product of *satisfaction* for the Absolute Being Himself" (italics added). Smulders, op. cit., p. 276, n. 17, mentions this difference between the two versions of the essay and considers the latter "less shocking."

In order to avoid the Charybdis of a universe created in a purely contingent and arbitrary way, Teilhard falls into the Scylla of a well-known mythology. According to it, God fulfills Himself in creating the world. God engages in a struggle with the Many (the ancient chaos) in order to find Himself again, richer and pacified, at the terminus of this world. This is an old gnostic idea which is found in Boehme, Hegel and Schelling.[63]

Mooney suggests that Teilhard's statements are less objectionable if one notes that God's "need of the world" and "dependence on man" are the results of his own sovereign decision and free self-limitation rather than of a necessity imposed on him. He also points out that some of the statements about the world as "completing" God can be interpreted as referring to man's co-operation in building up the Body of Christ in the world. I would submit, however, that Teilhard's ideas do entail a revision of the traditional understanding of God's relation to temporality.

Whitehead goes further than Teilhard in modifying the classical assertion that God is timeless and immutable. God's purposes and character are eternal, but his knowledge of events changes as those events take place in their own spontaneity; he cannot know the future if his creatures have genuine freedom. God contributes to the world and is in turn affected by it (Whitehead calls this the "consequent nature" of God). Yet in his "primordial nature" he is independent of events, unchanging in character and aim; his timeless envisagement of pure possibilities is unaffected by the world. Of all actual entities, he alone is everlasting, without perishing, without beginning or end. He is omniscient in that he knows all that is to be known, all ideal potentialities, and a past which is preserved without loss.[64]

Whitehead's idea of God's "primordial nature," like Teilhard's Alpha, refers to God's eternal purposes for the world; the "consequent nature," like Teilhard's Omega, includes the world's contribution to God. For Teilhard, however, Omega is primarily in the future, though it exerts an attraction on the present. For Whitehead, the two aspects represent two continuing roles of God which are abstractions from his unity:

But God, as well as being primordial, is also consequent. He is the beginning and the end. He is not the beginning in the sense of being in the past of all members. He is the presupposed actuality of conceptual operation, in unison of becoming with every other creative act. Thus by reason of the relativity of all things, there is a reaction of the world on God. . . . God's conceptual nature is unchanged, by reason of its final completeness. But the derivative nature is consequent upon the creative advance of the world.[65]

Whitehead holds that there is successiveness and becoming within God, since he prehends worldly events which come into being successively. But God is a non-temporal single occasion who does not perish and lose

[63] Tresmontant, op. cit., p. 94. For Mooney's comments, see n. 35 above.
[64] See Christian, op. cit., pp. 364–403.
[65] *PR*, pp. 523–24.

immediacy as every temporal entity does. Thus, creatures in the world are *temporal,* and God's "primordial nature" is *eternal* (unaffected by time), but his "consequent nature" is neither temporal nor eternal but *everlasting,* in Whitehead's terminology. One wonders whether Teilhard might not have found such a formulation acceptable.

VI. THE PROBLEM OF EVIL

Let us consider next Teilhard's assertion that evil is an inevitable by-product of an evolutionary process. There can be "no order in process of formation that does not, at all its stages, involve disorder." [66] The pain of growth and the presence of failure and death are structural concomitants of evolutive development; in any advance, much must be left behind. Ours is "a particular type of cosmos in which evil appears necessarily and as abundantly as you like in the course of evolution—not by accident (which would not matter) but through the very structure of the system." "Pure unorganized multiplicity is not bad in itself; but because it is multiple, i.e. essentially subject in its arrangement to the play of chance, it is absolutely impossible for it to progress towards unity without producing evil in its wake through statistical necessity." [67]

Teilhard is particularly concerned to show that suffering is an integral part of any evolutionary system. "The world is an immense groping, an immense attack; it can only progress at the cost of many failures and much pain." [68] Suffering and death are not in themselves products of human sin or means to its expiation:

Following the classical view, suffering is above all a punishment, an expiation; it is efficacious as a sacrifice; it originates from sin and makes reparation for sin. Suffering is good as a means of self-mastery, self-conquest, self-liberation. In contrast, following the ideas and tendencies of a truly cosmic outlook, suffering is above all the consequence and price of a labor of development. It is efficacious as effort. Physical and moral evil originate from a process of becoming; everything which evolves experiences suffering and moral failure. . . . The Cross is the symbol of the pain and toil of evolution, rather than the symbol of expiation.[69]

In answer to the charge that his interpretation limits God's power, Teilhard replies that a world in evolution and a world without disorder are simply contradictory concepts:

We often represent God to ourselves as being able to draw a world out of nothingness without pain, defects, risks, without "breakage." This is con-

[66] "Le Christ évoluteur" (1942), in *Cahiers* (Paris: Éditions du Seuil, 1965); scheduled for republication in *Oeuvres,* Vol. XI; cf. *DM,* p. 58, n. 1.
[67] "Comment je vois," quoted in Mooney, op. cit., p. 108.
[68] "La signification et la valeur de la suffrance," in *Oeuvres,* VI, 63.
[69] "La vie cosmique," in *Écrits du temps de la guerre.*

ceptual fantasy which makes the problem of evil unsolvable. No, it is necessary instead to say that God, despite His power, *cannot* obtain a creature united to Him without necessarily entering into struggle with some evil; because evil appears *inevitably* with the first atom. . . . Nobody has ever been astonished because God could not make a square circle or set aside an evil act. Why restrict the domain of impossible contradiction to this single case? [70]

Teilhard holds that evil is intrinsic to an evolutionary cosmos as it would not be in an instantaneously produced one; like Whitehead, he claims that this insight exonerates God from responsibility for evil. He points out also that the failure and death of individuals contribute to the advance of the total process. God can make use of patterns which entail evil; he "transfigures them by integrating them into a better plan." [71] Sin is one more form of a universal and inevitable imperfection. Original sin is a result of structural conditions, not of an accidental act on the part of Adam and Eve. I cannot at this point discuss the theological adequacy of this view of sin; it is considered here only as a form of the wider phenomenon of evil—concerning which, his position is summed up in the following sentence: "Evil, in all its forms—injustice, inequality, suffering, death itself—ceases theoretically to be outrageous from the moment when, *Evolution becoming a Genesis,* the immense travail of the world displays itself as the inevitable reverse side—or better, the condition—or better still, the price—of an immense triumph." [72]

For Whitehead, too, evil is an inescapable concomitant of temporal process. "The nature of evil is that the characters of things are mutually obstructive." [73] But he sees evil as arising not simply from the incompatibility of alternative potentialities or the unavoidable conflict among a multiplicity of beings; it also stems from the choice of less valuable alternatives by individual beings. Whitehead's stress on the freedom of each creature in choosing evil seems more compatible with the traditional idea of sin than Teilhard's ideas of statistical necessity. But has Whitehead exonerated God from responsibility for evil at the cost of leaving him powerless to do anything about it? Whitehead's God cannot insure that what is chosen will be the ideal or even the best of the options open, but he can hold out the higher option as a possibility, and he can achieve some positive value from every event. He shows how evil can be turned to good account by integration into a wider pattern of harmony which is everlastingly preserved in his memory. He "loses nothing that can be saved." [74]

Here again Whitehead limits God's power more drastically than Teilhard. Both men object to the idea of arbitrary divine acts. But

[70] "Note sur les modes de l'action divine dans l'univers" (1920), quoted in Tresmontant, op. cit., p. 96.
[71] *DM*, p. 27.
[72] *FM*, p. 90.
[73] *PR*, p. 517; cf. *AI*, pp. 333 ff.
[74] *PR*, p. 525.

Whitehead reacts more vehemently to the image of the "absolute monarch" which he sees in much Christian thinking.[75] His assumption of a pluralism of actual occasions leads him to a greater emphasis on the world's freedom. "The divine element in the world is to be conceived as a persuasive and not a coercive agency."[76] God lures every being toward co-operation in the production of value; he is a transforming influence in the world without determining it omnipotently. But he is ultimately in control through the power of a love which respects the integrity and freedom of his creatures; like human love, it influences by the response it evokes. Even more than in Teilhard's writing, the future actualization of the divine ideal is understood to be dependent on the world's activity.

VII. THE FUTURE OF THE WORLD

Consider, finally, Teilhard's expectations of the future. Evolution continues; its next stage will be the convergence of mankind into an interthinking network, the "noosphere." The new level of planetary consciousness will require global unification and the interpenetration of cultures.[77] Teilhard is confident that such a "social organism" will not submerge individuality and diversity in totalitarian uniformity. He seems to base this vision of the future on three kinds of assumptions:

1. *Extrapolation from the convergent past.* He projects into the future the previous trend toward greater complexity, consciousness, and personalization. This trend will now continue at the level of culture, which is the extension of biology; man's past is today transmitted by education more than by genes. Man has not followed the pattern of most creatures, namely, divergence into separate species. Moreover, convergence is now aided by the "planetary compression" imposed by the globe's limited surface and by improved intercommunication. Teilhard also introduces a more pragmatic argument: Faith in a convergent future and in human solidarity is a condition of mankind's continued survival. Teilhard's apologetic interest in addressing the unbeliever leads him to seek grounds for hope independent of revelation, even though it would appear that his own optimism had primarily Christian roots.

2. *The unity of the world process.* Teilhard's belief in interdependence and unity is expressed in his portrayal of a convergent cosmos. Whitehead, by contrast, visualizes *each* event as converging from multiplicity toward a new unity, which serves in turn as part of the multiple data inherited by its successors. Teilhard sees the *whole* cosmic process as one slowly culminating event with a single goal. Here, as elsewhere, the

---

[75] *PR,* pp. 146, 519; *RM,* pp. 55, 74–75; *SMW,* p. 266.
[76] *AI,* p. 213.
[77] *FM,* pp. 119, 167, 228 et passim.

monistic elements in his thought predominate over pluralistic ones, whereas in Whitehead the relative balance is reversed. (If space permitted, we could explore how their differing assumptions concerning pluralism are reflected in their political philosophies—e.g., their views of the relation between the individual and the collective.)

3. *The unity of all things in Christ.* Teilhard's idea of the "cosmic Christ" combines his conviction of the organic interdependence of the world and his biblical belief in the centrality of Christ. Redemption is not the rescue of individuals from the world but the fulfillment of the world's potentialities; the corporate salvation of the cosmos is integral with the activity of continuing creation. The world converges to a spiritual union with God in Christ, whose relation to the world is organic and not merely juridical and extrinsic. The incarnation reveals God's participation in matter and his universal involvement in cosmic history. The mystical side of Teilhard is expressed in his extension of the imagery of the Mass; the sacramental transformation of matter which occurs in the Eucharist is the paradigm of the universal "Christification" of matter. In a prayer written in Asia on an occasion when he had neither bread nor wine, he offers the whole creation as "the all-embracing Host." [78]

Teilhard's vision of the culmination of cosmic history in the Parousia shows once more the influence of his process thought on his reinterpretation of biblical doctrines. One change, of course, is the time scale; no imminent end is expected, and Teilhard speculates that we may have "millions of years" ahead of us. Again, he is more concerned about the salvation of the cosmos as an integral enterprise than about the salvation of individuals considered separately. In Teilhard's eschatology, moreover, the Kingdom will be a transformation of our present world, not the substitution of a new world. It will not come by an arbitrary intervention of God but by the consummation of a universe already prepared for it. The actualization of the potentialities of creation is a necessary condition for the final advent of the Kingdom, even though the *eschaton* is a gift from God and not simply the world's own achievement. Man and nature collaborate with God in bringing the cosmos to completion:

We continue from force of habit to think of the Parousia, whereby the Kingdom of God is to be consummated on Earth, as an event of a purely catastrophic nature—that is to say, liable to come about at any moment in history, irrespective of any definite state of Mankind. But why should we not assume in accordance with the latest scientific view of Mankind in a state of anthropogenesis, that the parousiac spark can, of physical and organic necessity, only be kindled between Heaven and a Mankind which has biologically reached a certain critical evolutionary point of collective maturity? [79]

Whitehead agrees that there will be a long future which will involve quite new types of orders. To this novel future both man and God will

[78] See *Hymn of the Universe* (New York: Harper & Row, 1965); *DM*, pp. 102 ff.; *PM*, p. 297.

[79] *FM*, p. 267; cf. *FM*, p. 22, *DM*, pp. 133–38, "Comment je vois," etc.

contribute. "Man's true destiny as cocreator in the universe is his dignity and his grandeur." For Whitehead also, God is primarily fulfiller of the world and only derivatively its judge. But Whitehead differs greatly from Teilhard in expecting no integrated cosmic convergence and no final consummation of history. He departs from classical Christianity in his assumption that time is infinite. Moreover he disavows any detailed fixed divine plan. God has an unchanging general purpose, the maximum actualization of value and harmony; but he does not determine the world's free activity, and much that happens is contrary to his will. Within an over-all teleology, God envisages a plurality of goals which he continually revises in the light of the world's response to his initiative. Whitehead speculates that there may be various "cosmic epochs," some having types of orders unlike those with which we are familiar.[80] His vision of God does not guarantee any final victory of good in the world. But it does assure us that God is concerned for the world, that the future is not the product of human effort alone, and that God will not be finally defeated. Moreover, it does provide the confidence that whatever is of value will be preserved everlastingly in the divine memory. The only permanence lies in the world's contribution to God's consequent nature—which treasures without loss all that has been achieved, even while it remains open to further enrichment.[81]

In summary, Teilhard's process metaphysics, though not systematically developed, shows striking similarities with Whitehead's, especially in his views of temporality, interdependence, continuity, and the "within." There are close parallels in their presentations of continuing creation, interaction between God and the world, and the idea that the world's maturation is a condition for the fulfillment of God's purposes. However, Whitehead's ontology is fundamentally pluralistic, whereas Teilhard has stronger monistic tendencies which are particularly evident in his deterministic statements and in his expectation of cosmic convergence. Teilhard's beliefs in a beginning and end to history are closer to traditional representations of creation and eschatology, and his qualification of divine omnipotence is less extreme than Whitehead's. On some issues, however, Teilhard's monistic leanings seem to take him further from the biblical tradition—in his treatment of freedom, evil, and sin, for example, or in his apparent exaggeration of the unity and continuity of the world, or in his terminology concerning "the whole" and "the All," which often sound pantheistic despite his intentions. I hope to explore in another paper Teilhard's process theology in which is reflected the influence of his process metaphysics on his interpretation of such biblical themes as the integral nature of man, the significance of secular life, the unity of creation and redemption, and above all the idea of "the cosmic Christ."

[80] Cf. *PR*, pp. 139, 148, 171, 442; *MT*, pp. 78, 212. See last paragraph of *RM*.
[81] Cf. Cobb, op. cit., pp. 218–23.

THE PANENTHEISM OF CHARLES HARTSHORNE

L. Bryant Keeling

L. BRYANT KEELING is Associate Professor of Philosophy at Western
Illinois University. This essay is published here for the first time.

We must try to discover what might be meant by "God," and to see which
meaning is most adequate. To do this will require the application of strict
logical principles in order that we may be sure we have not accidentally
excluded the correct alternative. This is especially important in dealing
with the doctrine of God because everyone comes to the issue with so
many prejudices that they are apt to settle on one form without even
considering what the other possibilities are. Hartshorne [1] begins by pick-
ing out what seems to be a central idea that has almost universal consent.
He writes:

To discuss God is, by almost universal usage, to discuss some manner of
"supreme" or "highest" or "best" individual (or super-individual) being. As a
minimal definition, God is an entity somehow *superior* to all others (*MVG*, 6).

Now perfection might be taken in one of two different ways. It might
mean superior to absolutely all entities actual or potential. This is called
absolute perfection and designated by the symbol A. It might also mean
(although this possibility has generally been overlooked) superior to all
actual entities and superior to all possible entities except itself in some
future state. This second formulation would make the distinction between
potentiality and actuality real for even a perfect being. This is called
relative perfection and is designated by the symbol R. Imperfection that
is, lack of superiority is designated by the symbol I. Now if we recognize
that perfection is applied to beings in different respects, we can apply the
"all, some, none" trichotomy to our two meanings of perfection and come
up with seven different logically possible combinations. These will formally exhaust the possible alternatives, so that if the idea of a perfect
being is meaningful at all the truth must lie with one of them. These can
be conveniently listed in the following way (*MVG*, 8): (X stands for the
negation of A, and thus the disjunction of R and I.)

---

[1] The works by Hartshorne cited in this essay are abbreviated as follows: *BH*,
Beyond Humanism (Chicago: Willett, Clark and Co., 1937); *DR*, *The Divine Rela-
tivity* (New Haven, Conn.: Yale University Press, 1964); *LP*, *The Logic of Perfection*
(LaSalle, Ill.: The Open Court Publishing Co., 1962); *MVG*, *Man's Vision of God*
(Hamden, Conn.: Archon Books, 1964); *PSG*, *Philosophers Speak of God* (Chicago:
The University of Chicago Press, 1953, with William L. Reese); *PPS*, *The Philosophy
and Psychology of Sensation* (Chicago: The University of Chicago Press, 1934); and
RSP, *Reality as Social Process* (Glencoe, Ill.: The Free Press, 1953).

Group	Symbol	Case	Symbol	Interpretation
I	(A)	1	A	Absolute perfection in *all* respects.
II	(AX)	2	AR	Absolute perfection in *some* respects, relative perfection in all others.
		3	ARI	Absolute perfection, relative perfection, and imperfection. . . , each in *some* respects.
		4	AI	Absolute perfection in *some* respects, imperfection in all others.
III	(X)	5	R	Absolute perfection in *no* respects, relative perfection in all.
		6	RI	Absolute perfection in *no* respects, relative in some, imperfection in others.
		7	I	Absolute perfection in *no* respects, imperfection in all.

It seems fairly obvious that the alternatives in Group III are inadequate as applied to God because a being who has absolute perfection in no respects has no guarantee that it will continue to be superior in any. It also seems fairly clear that numbers 3 and 4 of group II are inadequate as applied to God, for if God has the greatest conceivable perfection he cannot have any imperfections unless it can be shown that the conception of a being with no imperfections is meaningless. A being with no imperfections would be greater than a being with some imperfections. Hence we are left to choose between numbers 1 and 2, God as A or AR, as the two most plausible possibilities.

Of course A represents classical theism. This view is based on a denial that God can in any sense change. The argument is that if God could change this would imply either deterioration or improvement. God certainly cannot be conceived as deteriorating and if he improves this means that he presently lacks some perfection. The most perfect being must have all perfections; hence God must be conceived as being changeless.

This view presupposes that it is meaningful to speak of a being possessing all possible perfections and values. Hartshorne argues that some values are "incompossible," that is, that there are positive values that are not capable of all being actualized. The actualization of one possibility always means that some other possibility has not been actualized. This is the meaning of choice. And, "if the possibilities we reject are not left unactualized, any more than those we accept, then our choices are cosmically null" (*RSP*, 99). The idea of a being possessing all conceivable positive values is meaningless because the idea of a totality of conceivable values is meaningless.

Everyone is aware of some of the serious difficulties with the A position (we will consider some more of these when we look at the relation of God to the world), but the question may arise whether or not the introduction of the R factor in God does not imply a God who is less than the greatest that can be conceived. In a short section in *Man's Vision of God* Hartshorne describes this view in this way:

God, for both old and much new theology, is the being whose uniqueness consists in his unrivaled excellence, or whose amount of value defines a necessarily one-membered class (and so in a sense not a class). In some respects he is absolutely unexcelled, even by himself in another conceivable state; in all other respects he is (to state the view reached in this book) the only individual whose states or predicates are not to be excelled unless he excels them with other states or predicates of his own (MVG, 47; cf. DR, 20).

Does the AR view envisage God as a less perfect being than the A view? On the contrary, Hartshorne argues, the A view is truncated and is therefore not a description of the greatest conceivable being. This can perhaps be most simply shown by appealing to Morris Cohen's "law of polarity." Hartshorne states it like this: "According to this law, ultimate contraries are correlatives, mutually interdependent, so that nothing real can be described by the wholly one-sided assertion of simplicity, being, actuality, and the like, each in a 'pure' form, devoid and independent of complexity, becoming, potentiality, and related contraries" (PSG, 2). Classical theism has arbitrarily selected one set of poles (simplicity, being, actuality, etc.) as being superior to the other set (complexity, becoming, potentiality, etc.) and has thus said that only the former can be applied to God. They have thus excluded from God the perfections implied by the latter set of polar terms. If the classical theist argues that these are not perfections, Hartshorne replies that there is considerable evidence that we treat them as such, and it therefore must be demonstrated that they are not. For example, a great man is not one who is wholly impassive and unaffected by other people. Rather, he is a person who is sensitive to his fellows, who sympathizes with them in their sorrows and rejoices with them in their joys. At the human level there are perfections associated with both the active and passive roles. What warrant have we for saying that the values of activity are greater than the values of passivity? As Hartshorne says:

Sympathetic dependence is a sign of excellence and waxes with every ascent in the scale of being. . . . The eminent form of sympathetic dependence can only apply to deity, for this form cannot be less than an omniscient sympathy, which depends upon and is exactly colored by every nuance of joy or sorrow anywhere in the world (DR, 48).

The classical theist might argue that to make God dependent upon the world is to place God at the mercy of the world, and this certainly is not a perfection. To this charge, Hartshorne replies that it is certainly a perfection to be independent in some respects, and that in these respects God is independent. Thus God might have the power absolutely to guarantee his existence through all change and yet be dependent upon the world for the particular character that this existence has (MVG, 108, 164). He might have absolute power to know whatever is the case, to know the actual as actual and the possible as possible, and yet still be dependent upon the world for the particular content of his knowledge (DR, 135); he might be omnipotent, and yet still in some ways be influenced and limited by these agents because "omnipotence or 'perfect power' is by no means the same as pure impassivity, and does not imply it" (*MVG*, 105). Thus it seems to be the case that God as AR is greater than God as A in the sense in which the abstract is less than the concrete (*DR*, 83; *RSP*, 203). The limitation of God as A as compared with God as AR might be put like this: if God does not include the world then there is a greater than God, viz., the whole that is the world and God taken together; if God does include the world then God must be described as AR not just A.

The contradictions in the view of God as A have religious significance also. Hartshorne points out that the religious attributes (omniscience, love, etc.) contradict the view of God as A (*MVG* 95–96, 121) so that not only is this view self-contradictory, but it is unable to provide adequate expression for the most fundamental religious insights into the nature of God. Paradoxes abound when we try to speak of a God who knows and loves the world and yet is in no sense changing (*DR*, 8). Of course, supporters of classical theism will reply that they are aware that their view is paradoxical, but that such paradoxes are the natural and necessary result of trying to speak of the divine in human terms. There are, however, a number of difficulties with this position that Hartshorne is quick to point out. First of all, he can ask the question, "And if paradoxes are not accepted as signs that we are thinking badly, what sign would we recognize" (*DR*, 4)? If we are willing to admit patent contradictions into a system of thought, what standards do we have to determine when our descriptions are even approaching adequacy? If categories like "process" and "potentiality" are not to be applied to God because they indicate finitude, how can we know that categories like "permanence" and "actuality" can be any more aptly applied? After all, they also are human categories. If the supporter of classical theism replies that we cannot attribute any positive characteristics to God because he is so far beyond all that we can know that we can use only negative attributes (immutable, immaterial, etc.), then Hartshorne can raise the question as to whether these unqualified negative attributes are compatible with any positive meaning whatsoever for the term "God" (*MVG*, 122). Why not negate all categories to arrive at nothingness instead of to arrive at God? Not only is it the case, Hartshorne argues, that the traditional religious insights into the nature of God contradict the view of God as A, but they imply the view of God as AR. For example if God is absolutely impassive, completely unaffected by what happens in the world, then it is not possible for man to serve God. As Hartshorne puts it:

For if God can be indebted to no one, can receive value from no one, then to speak of serving him is to indulge in equivocations. Really it must, on that assumption, be only the creature who is to be served or benefited (*DR*, 58).

If God is wholly impassive then the worst sinner serves him as much as the greatest saint. It simply makes no sense, on the view of God as A, to speak of God caring for man, of God loving man, of God desiring good for man, or of God acting in any way on behalf of man, for all of these would imply at least some degree of change. On the other hand, if we think of God as AR, we can speak quite literally of God loving man, and of man serving God. Man can genuinely serve God on this view because by actualizing the greatest values in his own life he contributes value to God, values that God eternally preserves and enjoys. God can genuinely love man on this view because perfect love means adequacy to the object loved (*MVG*, 165), and God is the one being who is absolutely adequate to all objects. God would, on the AR view, exemplify categorical supremacy. That is, he would be the supreme instance of every positive category of relation. Man knows only imperfectly but because God's relativity is unrestricted his knowledge is perfect (*DR*, 10–11). Human love is imperfect, but the divine being can be completely concerned with the welfare of one of his creatures. Hartshorne puts it like this:

We do not "love" literally, but with qualifications, and metaphorically. Love, defined as social awareness, taken literally, is God. . . It is by self-flattery that we imagine we exemplify the category, say, of "knowledge" *simpliciter*. We guess, we have probable opinions, we unclearly feel, but know . . . ? It is God who knows. Why then the negative theology? Our own natures it is which (partially) negate the categories, not God's (*DR*, 36).

This view, Hartshorne believes, does far greater justice to all genuinely religious insights than does the view of God as A which is primarily imported into Christian theology from Greek philosophy. If the supporter of classical theism objects that it is a genuine religious insight that God is unchanging, Hartshorne replies that his view (God as AR) recognizes that a God who changes through all time may yet have an immutable aspect, and that it is to this aspect that such insights refer. Thus God, though continually in process, may still be characterized by love, faithfulness, and other ethical attributes in an absolutely unchanging way (*MVG*, 110–11; *RSP*, 120 ff.). This is possible because we can speak of God as having two natures, an abstract and a concrete nature (what Whitehead calls the primordial and consequent natures of God). The abstract nature of God is the unchanging, self-identical, and absolute aspect of God. It is to this aspect of God that all absolute perfections are attributed, such as absolute goodness, and absolute power to know perfectly whatever there is to be known. But God also has a concrete aspect. As concrete, God grows, increases in value, enjoys new experiences, and knows new objects as they come into being. Thus the view of God as AR preserves all the values of classical theism that were based on genuine religious insight, while enriching the idea of God by including much that classical theism was not able to include.

I have in the foregoing discussion presented many basic features of Hartshorne's understanding of the relation of God to the world. There are, however, yet a few features of this problem that deserve more explicit consideration. As we have already seen, Hartshorne believes that it is necessary to conceive of the relation of God to the world "by analogy with relations given in human experience" (*MVG*, 174). But there is one particular relation that is of special importance, and that is the relation of a human to his own body. A human being, we have pointed out, is a monarchial society, with the mind as the dominant individual. The human mind does not, for Hartshorne, directly encounter the "external world," but most immediately experiences the cells in its own body. It experiences their experiences of other objects. As Hartshorne puts it:

The immediate object of effective human volition is a change in the human body . . . . We thus arrive at the far-reaching conclusion: the power-relation in man which alone can be used as the basis for the theological analogy is the mind-body relation, or rather a part of this relation (*MVG*, 179).

That part of the body to which the mind is immediately related is, of course, the brain. It is the cells in the brain that respond immediately to our volition and transmit our decisions to the rest of our body (which for some purposes might be considered as that portion of our environment with which we have the most intimate relations). So Hartshorne argues that God is related to the world in much the same way that we are related to our own brain cells (*MVG*, 185). A man has an "essence," that which makes him who he is in spite of various external changes; so God has an "essence," a set of permanent features enduring through all the changes that the universe undergoes (*MVG*, 230). The essence of man must be the essence of a body, and the man has many particular features as a result of having the body he has. The same is true for God:

Thus God may depend, even for his essence, upon there being creatures, but he may have power to guarantee absolutely that there should be such; while beyond his essential characters he may necessarily have accidental ones, just *which* ones being contingent and depending upon which creatures exist—and since the creatures are partly self-determining this means, depending partly upon what the creatures may choose to do (*MVG*, 108).

This analogy, if taken seriously, will prove very helpful in understanding Hartshorne's view of God, and his relation to the world.

But if God is related to the world as mind is related to body, and if mind cannot exist totally disembodied (it makes no sense to say that it does or might) then we are led to the conclusion that God cannot exist apart from the world. This means that, strictly speaking, there cannot have been a creation out of nothing. The notion of God as Creator must be interpreted to mean that God is essentially creative. He is always creating, but he creates out of that which exists prior to that particular act of creation. Hartshorne observes that all human uses of the word "create" involve making something out of some antecedent substance, so that a creation out of nothing is a self-contradiction. The difference between divine and human creation is that it is never the case that God must create out of material that is completely foreign to himself. The material he uses in creation has already been influenced by himself in a previous state. If we cannot make sense out of an infinite regress of actual beings (although Hartshorne believes that this may be possible) we will simply have to affirm what we know: that God is creative in any given instance by serving as the ground and goal of the creative processes in a situation that has been similarly influenced by his presence in the past.

But God is not just Creator; he is also Preserver. New values are added through creation, but nothing is lost. Hartshorne puts it like this:

> The upshot is that reality as a whole of real events, together with whatever there may be besides events, is a growing whole. It surpasses all other beings; for all parts of it grow in being and value. It acquires new members but loses none. It increases but does not decrease; it is mutable but incorruptible (*RSP*, 119, cf. *PSG*, 20).

God is the cosmic memory that forgets nothing. Human minds have imperfect memory. They remember only a fraction of what they have experienced. The analogy of God to the world as human mind to human body leads to the notion of God as conscious preserver of all value as man is the partial and imperfect preserver of the values he experiences.

One more issue must be considered briefly before we can leave the question of the relation of God to the world, and that is the problem of evil. Evil, for Hartshorne, is the choice of some one of the creatures to realize a value in a given situation that was less than the maximum value that could have been realized in that situation. There is no actuality that does not have some measure of goodness. Evil is simply the realization of a lesser good. Of course such evil may still be quite radical because the difference between what is and what might have been can be vast. In terms of panentheism, two things can be said about the relation of God to evil. First, evil is the result of the free decision of the creatures and not of God. God does not completely determine every event (as he does in some versions of classical theism) and therefore it does not follow that he is in any way responsible for evil. "What God can do, and because he is good does do, is to set the best or optimal limits to freedom . . . where the definition of 'optimal limits' is that they are such that, were more freedom allowed, the risks would increase more than the opportunities, and were less freedom allowed the opportunities would decrease more than the risks" (*RSP*, 41). Secondly, God can suffer with the world. For panentheism (as opposed to classical theism at least by implication), evil is real for God. God is genuinely sorry when evil occurs for as a consequence he is deprived of value that he might have had. But because God does receive into himself whatever value is realized, and because all events have some value (zero degree value equals zero degree actuality), even the worst tragedies are not wholly unmitigated. For Hartshorne, Christ is the supreme example of this sympathetic character in God (*RSP*, 24).

In conclusion, I wish to treat briefly the question of the existence of God. I shall not discuss the proofs for God's existence in detail because this will be handled in a separate essay. I wish only to indicate the place that the proofs have in Hartshorne's system as a whole.

It is important to recognize that, for Hartshorne, belief in God is always a matter of degree, and that such belief is possessed always by all men to some extent (*BH*, 37; *MVG*, 79; *DR*, 70). This is because "The import of the word 'God' is no mere special meaning in our language, but is the soul of significance in general, for it refers to the Life in and for which all things live" (*LP*, 297). This means that wherever man seeks to find meaning he will find it only insofar as he finds God. Suppose man is trying to understand the world. "The point is that God is nature, envisaged as rationally and concretely as man can envisage her; and therefore to fail to see God is always in some way to fail to achieve adequate understanding of nature. . . ." (*BH*, 163). Suppose a man merely wants to work out some kind of salvation for himself (salvation considered simply as the integration of his personality), then he will find that even to achieve this he will need to think theistically (*BH*, 12). The reason for this is:

Faith in man is absurd without faith in nature as an enduring, and for man tolerably convenient, system of activities. It is also absurd without an implicit trust, which need not be verbalized, that the future, however remote, will leave intact something of the value of one hour of achievement. This is a part at least of what is meant by Providence (*BH*, 71).

Because this is so, the proofs for God's existence are not an effort to coerce a person intellectually into believing something rather strange and difficult; rather "they (the proofs) are merely ways of making clear that we already and once and for all believe in God, though not always with clearness and consistency" (*MVG*, 274). Hartshorne believes that most of the classical arguments (ontological, cosmological, teleological, etc.) can be useful if revised and cast into a form compatible with panentheism. These arguments will rest upon insights into the meanings of the fundamental categories of reality (*MVG*, 19), and their function will be to lay bare these meanings and thus clear up confused thinking with relation to the question of the existence of God. . . . We begin with something concrete. We seek to explain our experience of it, and logic and the meaning of language will lead us to affirm the existence of a supreme social being, the God of panentheism.

THE MODERN WORLD AND
A MODERN VIEW OF GOD

Charles Hartshorne

CHARLES HARTSHORNE received his degree from Harvard University, where he was Whitehead's assistant. He has taught at Harvard, Chicago, and Emory Universities and is now Ashbel Professor of Philosophy at the University of Texas. He is the author of many books and articles that develop neo-classical theism.

Why is the idea of religion without God so widespread today? One reason, without doubt, is the boost which technology has given man's self-esteem. Instead of turning to a superhuman power to influence nature in his favor he can turn to the engineer. Man apparently needs no outside help, he can help himself. Then there is the power of the human mind shown in pure science. Instead of thinking with awe how mysterious life is, we can think how, step by step, the hidden causes of all that happens to us are being unravelled. Not only can man do almost all things, but it more and more seems that he can know almost all things. He is himself potentially something like what God was believed to be actually. So man begins to worship his own kind. This self-deification of man is a chief rival in our time of what I regard as true religion. For I agree with the old Greeks, who agreed with the Hebrews at this point, that one of man's greatest enemies is his own vanity, *hubris*.

There are, however, several excuses for modern man's falling deeply into *hubris*. Not only are his technology and pure science wonderful achievements, truly deserving to be glorified; but also these new powers encourage habits of thinking which in some respects make it more difficult to see grounds for belief in the superhuman. Science is our great theoretical accomplishment; yet it seems to uncover no evidence of anything divine. We have learned, or think we have learned, that what science cannot discover is very likely not there, at any rate cannot be known to be there. If fairies and demons and witches were real, science would have had to invoke them to explain events. But it has found no occasion to do so. Hence we cease to take such ideas seriously. The idea of God seems to many to belong in the same class. And we feel a certain obligation to be on the side of science, against fairy tales and nightmares.

Now I wish to argue that while all these reactions to the modern scene are natural enough, some of them do not withstand careful criticism, and represent indeed aspects of a sort of fairy tale of science, not a tested scientific hypothesis.

So far as influencing nature is concerned, man has certainly immensely increased his resources. But the chief results of this change are: (1) The total number of people on earth has multiplied many times over, and has even become one of our gravest anxieties, a threat which only fatuous optimists belittle. (2) Newborn babies have several times as good a chance of reaching maturity as they used to have. (3) Those who reach maturity can expect to live a decade or two longer than formerly. (4) A minority of people on earth have luxuries undreamt of in older days even for kings. (5) When things go wrong, there is usually something we can do besides pray—we can look for an expert, medical or other, and we have better reason to trust our modern experts than the primitive had to trust his elders and medicine men. However, do these differences amount to anything, relative to the problem of God? I say that, relative to that problem, they are negligible. Each man is still born and dies, he is still throughout his life subject to accidental death or grievous injury, and he is still but a negligibly small part of a stupendous whole, which for all he knows infinitely precedes and will infinitely outlast him. Though armed with atomic power man is yet almost nothing in physical power compared even to the sun. And there are billions of billions of suns! On this earth now man is powerful, but what is he in the vastness of reality? So close to nothing we can scarcely say how small, or how weak.

In what I have just said, I have employed facts of astronomy. I think, indeed, that the *proper* result of science is to increase man's humility, to make his inveterate conceit seem even more absurd, if possible, than the Greeks and ancient Hebrews could know it to be. Think of millions of galaxies, each probably with millions of planets. Suppose we do reach a few of these planets in space ships. The ones we do not reach will be practically the same in number as all those which exist. Thus the races of rational beings which, according to all reasonable probability, people the great spaces, will be virtually unknown to us forever. The Greeks could explore but a small portion of this earth; they estimated the total universe as a billion miles in diameter. We talk in billions of light-years. True, we expect to explore our solar system, and eventually perhaps a bit beyond, but our solar system dwarfs the area of the earth which the Greeks could reach no more than our present estimate of the universe dwarfs that of the Greeks. Understating the case, no larger part of the universe, relatively speaking, seems to astronomers today open to human exploration than ancient astronomers supposed was open to it. Our relative insignificance, therefore, according to our best knowledge, has not diminished. Only human vanity has enabled us to imagine otherwise—to talk, for example, of conquering space.

I am not, please note, belittling science. It is one of man's noblest, most glorious accomplishments. But one of the chief origins of science—Einstein has said it—is a deep humility. Man is the only terrestrial animal, though surely not the only animal, who can see himself as but an item in the scheme of things, not the center about which all must or can be made to turn.

There is another consideration. Ancient man might dream of his kind existing forever on earth. He did not know that the sun's fires are but temporary, and must eventually burn out. We do know. We also know that the sun might become unbearably hot, and destroy us in that way. We know that man has but a temporary dwelling on this earth. Of course some men may colonize other planets and even solar systems. But still, every such venture will be risky, many will fail, success can never be guaranteed, and certainly there is no guarantee that the successful colonists will be such as we would be able to consider in significant degree our own descendents, or even that our influence will have been helpful to them. Add to all this the fact, which we know far better than ancient man, that human folly or wickedness could bring human life to an end at almost any time—in the near or distant future.

Man is not God and is infinitely far from being so. Rather he is a tiny, and for all practical purposes ultimately temporary, as well as an unreliable and often very cruel, creature. Now there are two possibilities and only two: this tiny, temporary episode of nature called man either exists merely for its own sake, or also for the sake of something greater than man. If man in his own eyes exists merely for himself, then so far as his valuations go, the rest of the universe exists for him. We must either serve, or be served by, the larger cosmos. We cannot but use the cosmos, so far as accessible to us, just as the cells in our bodies cannot but profit by our organic existence enclosing them. But the cells in our bodies also serve us, as we at least know, whether or not they have any feeling of doing so. One way to put the religious question is simply: "Do we in turn stand in an analogous relation to anything greater than ourselves in space time, and can we have any awareness of this relation?"

This question has no proper analogy to that of fairies. Fairies at most were incidental conveniences, or nuisances. But the question, "Is the part for the whole, or the whole merely for the part?" is not an incidental question. It is *the* question, if we set aside our natural self-centeredness and look at life objectively, as the astronomer does. Is man to live and die merely for man, and are the species of rational animals on other planets to live and die merely for themselves? Or do they, and all creatures, live and die for the whole encompassing them, as our cells do for us?

Science as I view it could not possibly favor the self-centered answer to this question. Science is not anthropomorphic. It does not assume any peculiar importance of man. The famous "rejection of final causes" was really, in one aspect, a rejection of man-favoring causes. Nothing cosmic turns, for science, upon human values in particular. Does it follow that nothing turns upon values of any kind? I believe this is a non sequitur. The ends of nature could only be incomparably vaster than merely human ends, and therefore man in his amazing vanity cannot easily conceive these ends. But they can be conceived, as we shall see.

But still, you may say, it remains true that science finds no evidence of anything divine, and where there is no scientific evidence, have we not learned to admit that there is no evidence at all? Here it is pertinent to inquire what it means to speak of scientific evidence. The highest, or at least, a very high, authority on the scientific method, in my opinion, is Karl Popper. His view is that an hypothesis is scientific if it can be observationally falsified. Not, please note, if it can be verified. For it is doubtful if, *strictly* speaking, any scientific generalization has been verified, that is, shown to be exactly true as it stands. So-called crucial experiments are not those which have a chance of proving some theory, since no experiment can wholly establish a positive theory; but rather, those which have a chance of disproving a theory. One instance clearly not in accordance with a supposed law refutes the law, but many instances in conformity with the law still do not prove it. Accepting this test of falsifiability, we may remark that the idea of God either could, or could not, be falsified by some conceivable observation. If it could not, then theism is a view which science is in no position to test; and the fact that science has not "verified" theism is irrelevant. For, as Popper persuasively argues, to confirm a view by scientific evidence is only to conceive ways of falsifying it, and then to find that the falsifying observation fails to result from the suitable experimental or observational conditions. Who, then, has told us what an observation incompatible with theism would be like? Is it the observation that there are evils? In that case, science is not needed to evaluate theism, for this fact has always been known. And theists have always denied that the existence of evils contradicted their belief. If they are right in this, then how could science find evidence against the divine existence? Is any fact, other than evil, incompatible with that existence? Is it the reign of law in nature? But theists say that the laws of nature express the divine power and consistency.

What are we to conclude from the apparent fact that theism, as theists understand it, is not scientifically testable at all? We might conclude that theism has no consistent meaning, and hence could not be true. Or, we might conclude that it has some meaning, but of a sort whose true is untestable by human means. Finally, we might conclude that it has meaning, and that science is not the only human means of testing truth. This last is my position. I hold that the relevant test of ideas of God is their ability to integrate, not facts of science, but the principles which all science and all life presuppose, principles without which we could not understand how there could be facts at all, or why it is worth knowing what the facts are. Not facts, but the idea of fact, not values but the idea of value, not truths but the idea of truth, is what theism tries to elucidate. The study which investigates such questions is philosophy. To suppose that natural science can substitute for philosophy in this task is logical confusion; it is pseudoscience, not science.

Are theists right, however, in holding that the facts of evil and of the orderliness of nature are consistent with theism? I hold that they are right. However, I do not think that the classical, or best known, theologians and theistic philosophers have given us a very clear and consistent account of this matter. And I cannot blame anyone who concludes that they have failed to make their case. I shall now try to show how the case can be made. First, some ways in which it cannot be made.

It is useless to maintain that all evil is divinely designed and is but good in disguise. For on that principle all human choice is absurd. Do as you please, the result is exactly what divine wisdom saw to be needed for the perfection of the world plan. True, it may be a part of the plan that you should be punished for what you do, but still your deed is quite as it should be. For if it were not, it would not have been included in the providential design, and would not have happened. On this view, serving God means doing whatever you happen to do. You cannot go wrong. In addition to this absurdity, is the difficulty of distinguishing between such a God and the sadist who finds evil to his liking. God deliberately designs the evils, for they are necessary to the world's being pleasing to him.

It is also useless to explain evil as the result of human freedom alone. For all animate nature involves conflict and presumably suffering. Surely human choice throws no light upon this fact.

The root of the trouble is in failing to note the starting point of the problem of evil. This starting point is the notion that God creates. What is it to create? It is to determine the otherwise indeterminate. Out of the vagueness of chaos of the merely possible, comes the definiteness of the actual. There might be all sorts of worlds: yet *this* world came into being. Similarly, the poet might write all sorts of poems, but actually he writes this poem, or this set of poems. Now suppose the divine poet includes in his poem a description of a lesser non-divine or human poet creating non-divine poetry. The divine poet can choose the description of this other and lesser poet and his poetry just as he pleases, can he not? No, this will not do, for the divine poet creates not just poems, but poets who create poems; and, since to create is to decide how the vagueness of possibility is to pass into definite actuality, if the created poets really exist as poets, as creators, then they, and not the divine poet, must decide in some degree what the non-divine poems are to be. I wonder if you see already how, according to this analysis, the problem of evil results from an equivocation of terms. According to the view which gives rise to the problem, God is to decide precisely what lesser agents decide; but then there can be no lesser agents, and all decisions are divine decisions. The supreme artist would thus create, not lesser artists, but mere descriptions of artists, mere dreams of lesser creators. The one agent is, on that view, the only agent, but he imagines others. We are these divine imaginings of lesser agents. But in that case, we could from our own experience have no concept of creation, of agency, of decision, with which to ascribe the supreme form of these powers to deity. The whole business is a play with ambiguities, and I believe it is nothing more.

Once admit that the supreme artist must create lesser artists, with genuine, though inferior capacities for deciding what no one else has wholly decided for them, and you will see that the perfection of divine power cannot consist in a monopoly of creative freedom. However well and powerfully God may decide, he must leave something for the creatures to decide. Hence it cannot be right to attribute the details of the world to divine decree, and it need not be wrong to attribute the evils of these details to decisions other than divine. Nor is it merely human creatures who must in some measure have creative power. For what could the supreme creative agent produce but lesser forms of creativity? There is no absolute difference between human originality and that of an humble animal tracing the design of its own individual life, in fine details unique and never to be repeated. The jump from infinite creativity to the creature, even the humble creature, can hardly be from the infinite to zero; it must rather be from the infinite to the finite, from supreme creative freedom to lesser creative freedom, not no freedom. Any creature is thus somewhere between the total absence of discretionary power, and its eminent or divine form. In this way creaturely freedom explains, not only evils which man produces, but those which animals and atoms produce. The entire world, on a consistently theistic view, is pervaded by an element of self-determination in each and every individual whatsoever. Myriads of agents other than God have had a hand in any result, and it is therefore illegitimate to ask, why God made that result as it is. He did not "make" it, if that means, decide it. For the creatures are all, in part, self-decided.

Does it follow that we must renounce the perfection of the divine power? Not if words are used carefully. The perfection of divine power does not consist in the ability to make merely unilateral decisions, for this is meaningless. Every agent and every creator produces results beyond itself only by influencing the self-determination of other agents, or other creators. Decision is always *shared*, so far as effects upon others are concerned. The perfect form of this shared decision means, not ideal ability to decide detailed results, but ideal ability to decide general outlines. These outlines are the laws of nature. Who but God could have decided these? They set the limits within which the lesser agents can effectively work out the details of their existence. Without such limits the universal creativity would mean universal chaos and frustration. With these limits, elements of chaos and frustration remain, but subordinate to general order and harmony.

The orderliness of nature is essential to creaturely freedom. It can then without inconsistency be considered providential. That some evils result is not the fault of the order, for any order must stop short of destroying freedom, and freedom means risk.

To put the matter another way: the atheistic argument from evil holds that God must be weak or wicked because he does not use his freedom to maximize harmony and reduce discord to zero. This means nothing if not this, that the chances of harmony and those of discord could and should be made to vary *inversely*. But we can, rather clearly, understand that this is logically impossible. Harmony and discord, as values, have the very same source, freedom. Harmony in freedom is good, conflict in freedom is evil, and the greater the freedom the greater the chances both of good and of evil. God is held deficient for not doing what logically could not be done. To avoid the evil of suffering and discord, he should have a world of pure puppets, incapable of getting off their designated tracks; to avoid the evil of deadly monotony and insipidity, to make existence interesting by causing free agents, able to make their own decisions, to flourish he should not have a world of puppets at all, but self-determining creatures, with some faint spark at least of creativity analogous to his own supreme creativity.

I see nothing in the classic "problem of evil" but this confusion or equivocation between creatures both puppets and free, or both lesser forms and not even lesser forms of the power of decision eminently ascribed to their creator.

The ideal power and wisdom of God does not, then, imply a perfection of detailed results, for no power could guarantee the detailed actions of others, but rather an optimal excess of opportunity over risk, as arising from the laws of nature.

I cannot give anything like all my reasons for accepting this conception. But I wish to return to our previous question: "Is the part for the sake of the whole, or the whole merely for the sake of the part?" To me it seems wonderfully irrational to suppose that the enduring universe exists merely for its transient parts. But if the parts exist for the whole, then the whole must contain the values of the parts. Since it is unintelligible that values can exist except for some being able to value or enjoy them, the cosmos should be thought of as able to value all that falls within it. The supreme creator is then the whole, evolving and appreciating its own parts, somewhat as the human body evolves new molecules, and in many cases new cells, from time to time. But the supreme Whole must have full appreciation, such as we cannot have, for the details of the parts. The idea of the cosmos as conscious, and evolving its own details, subject to their proper freedom is, I believe, compatible with all the results of science. True, there are many puzzles which may arise in this connection. But it is striking how few among the sceptics see that this is the question to which theists, if they understand themselves, give an affirmative answer. Most theists are unclear about this also, and many will say that I am quite on the wrong track. But I believe I have read these people with more care than they have read me, or anyone who thinks as I do.

I said above that science excludes not all final causes, but man-favoring or anthropocentric final causes. I shall now try to explain this. We must first understand, once and for all, that no teleology can exclude unfortunate accidents and frustrations, for goals have to be reached through multiple acts of freedom, none of which can be entirely controlled, even by God. The point is not that he cannot control them, but that they cannot be controlled. It is not his influence which has limits, but their capacity to receive influence. Absolute control of a free being, and there can be no others, is self-contradictory. Hence exceptional monstrosities and incidental sufferings are to be attributed to the chance results of freedom, not to the teleology of nature. Only the general plan, the structure of laws, the normal pattern of nature can be wholly purposive.

If you ask, must not the laws and the antecedent conditions entirely determine the detailed phenomena, the answer is, not if law is conceived as physicists now incline to conceive it, as essentially statistical, a matter of averages in large groups of similar cases. The new outlook in physics thus fits our doctrine of pervasive freedom, as the Newtonian outlook did not.

Granting then that details are not necessarily purposive, what are the goals which nature is realizing? Here older discussions, both theistic and anti-theistic, suffered from arbitrary assumptions. For instance, it was thought strange that all living creatures are subject to death, that species die out, that creatures live by destroying other creatures. I find all of these things less strange than the more or less unconscious beliefs which made them appear strange. Is it desirable for an individual to live forever? If the individual has no long run memory and foresight, it cannot matter to it that it will not live forever. And if the individual does have long range memory and foresight, then in the long run continuation within the limits of its individuality will prove increasingly monotonous, lacking in interest and zest. All young animals show more evidence of being thrilled by life, the novelty of things, than old animals. Human beings are not exceptions, in principle. They only think they are. One has but to observe life to see this. So I conclude, endless continuation of the individual is either of no value to the individual, or it is undesirable, even unendurable. That species do not last forever is even more obviously not an evil. Species other than man cannot know that they are temporary, and man can understand how his temporary existence can contribute to what is not temporary, the all-encompassing Whole.

You may suppose that even the Whole, according to the same principle of diminishing novelty, must finally grow old and tired. But the whole is the supreme reality, with no external conditions limiting it; whatever novelty it may need, it should have full power to evolve. Only ideal power, divine power, can either sustain, or make desirable, endless continuation. So I think we can, quite consistently, conceive God as immortal, without giving up the argument that mortality for creatures is no evil for them. Something in reality must be permanent, and God, I submit, is precisely that something.

But should creatures live, while they do live, by destroying others? Is this not vicious or cruel? This too I deny. We have granted that creatures should not live forever. How then are they to die? The only causes must be other creatures, either within, as parts, or without as members of the external environment. And what harm does it do a deer that it dies through the attack of a lion, rather than of old age? Old age is a dull mode of existence; if death generally came that way, then instead of the species being composed mostly of creatures enjoying the prime of life, it would

be more largely composed of half-bored elders. The sum of intense enjoyment would be less, not more.

What, we now ask, are the over-all goals of nature? We have argued
that the parts live not merely for their own sakes but for that of the whole.
What does the whole get from the parts? Well, what do we get from our
parts, our bodily cells and molecules? We get the sensory and emotional
content of our experience. When our cells thrive we feel physical pleasure,
when they are injured we often feel physical pain. Thus their health
contributes to our joy, and their ill health to our sorrow. We seem to
participate in their weal and woe in whatever sense they are subject to
weal and woe. And cells are living—I believe sentient—individuals. The
"love of God" has often been spoken of; but men may overlook the full
meaning of their own words. To love is, at least, to participate in the life
of another. It may be more than that, but we should not use the word for
less. We love, then, our own cells, though without distinct consciousness,
so far as the single cells are concerned. We have a vague sense of good
and evil enjoyed by the parts of the body. Imagine this vague sense
flooded with the light of full consciousness and you have an analogy for
the love of God.

It is a well-known law that the value of experience as coming to us from
the body depends upon the variety and intensity of activities which can
be harmonized. We know that lack of variety and contrast kills interest;
we also know that variety and contrast may in some cases confuse and
disturb. Harmonious variety is essential to value. What is nature if not a
wondrously varied pattern of forms. Is it an harmonious pattern? Not in
the sense of excluding all conflict, discord, or suffering; but this we have
seen to be inherent in the pervasiveness of freedom, without which there
could be no world at all. But essentially nature is harmonious, things fit
together in an ecological web which naturalists admire the more they
study it. The laws of nature articulate the harmony of nature. Some of the
greatest scientists have tried to tell us how their more or less mystical
reverence for and enjoyment of the cosmic harmony inspires their work.
But we have often been too dull to believe them. I take them at their
word.

Nature is a harmony in variety, ultimately for the enjoyment of the
whole, but proximately for the enjoyment of each and every part, in
proportion to its awareness of this harmony. Variety is in space as well as
in time. That individuals and species die and others take their place is
variety in time. Those who lament the passing of species want to limit the
variety to be enjoyed by the whole. Truly they know not what they would
have.

But can God love us if he allows us to cease, while he lives on? The
answer lies in a simple ambiguity in the world "cease." That our lives are
finite in time as well as in space does not mean that at death we become
nothing, or a mere corpse. For our past experiences are not cancelled out.

The past is indestructible, ever-living. Persons who truly love those who have died feel this vividly, though they usually, thanks to the strange blinders worn by philosophers and theologians who have taught them no better, misconceive the nature of the feeling. The past reality of the person is not dead and cannot die. It "lives forevermore," in Whitehead's phrase. Where? How? In the Whole, whose appreciation is infinitely tenacious of every item it once has appropriated. God forgets us never, and this is our immortality. We are imperishable items in his consciousness.

Our vanity is perhaps not satisfied by this? I can only speak for myself. I wish no further immortality, either for myself or for those I love. It is this earthly life which should be dear to us, for which we should be grateful. And this life is deathless. For what we and those we have influenced, have done and felt cannot ever not have been done and felt. But the ultimate summing up and treasuring of this imperishable reality is not in our memory of consciousness; it is in God's.

There will be those who say that the view I have been presenting is pantheistic, implying that this is enough to condemn it. However, the term "pantheism" has been used to cover doctrines as far apart from each other as from views commonly called theistic, and the habit of trying to put an end to reasonable discussion by the use of this label is on a par intellectually with terming every economic policy with which we disagree "communistic." The communism which properly deserves rejection on principle is something much more definite than those who misuse the term have in mind; so with the pantheism which deserves rejection on principle. Or, in other words, if my view is pantheistic, then perhaps so much the better for (one form of) pantheism, not necessarily so much the worse for my view.

The foregoing conception of God, or something like it, can be found, apart from my own writings, in Fechner's *Zend Avesta,* written a century ago, in Berdyaev's *Destiny of Man,* in the last chapter of Whitehead's *Process and Reality.* Many other writers have pointed in its direction. It is the great neglected alternative to classical theism, the stone rejected of the builders, whose ultimate destiny has by no means been decided by this rejection.

But how, you may ask, can we know any such view to be true? The answer to this question is a long story. But it can be summarized in brief as follows: That philosophy is true which contains in itself the explanatory power of its rivals, plus additional power of its own. The theory of pervasive freedom explains evil at least as well as any other view could do, for freedom is always risk. But the theory explains good better than any other view, provided we admit a supreme or divine level of freedom, by whose influence all lesser freedom can be benignly guided and coordinated, for freedom thus coordinated is primarily opportunity, and only secondarily risk. Thus freedom, if taken as both divine and non-divine is self-explanatory, accounting alike for its failures and its successes. It is the only self-explanatory principle. Order is due to the over-ruling supremacy of divine freedom, disorder to the multiplicity of lesser freedoms.

It is an interesting, but complicated, matter to reconsider the historic proofs for the existence of God in the light of this modern doctrine. I find that they can all be restated so as to have a certain cogency, in spite of the attacks of Hume, Kant, and others.

These attacks rest upon assumptions incompatible with the theory of pervasive freedom, and of divine freedom as that of the all-inclusive reality. The entire problem of God must be viewed afresh, if we are not to be victimized by mistakes of our ancestors. I deeply believe that the idea of a God who determines all things is an absurdity; and I also deeply believe that religion without God is a poor second best, an irrational self-deification of man in his dangerous pride. Our life is on earth, not elsewhere; but the eventual importance of earthly life consists in its contribution to the cosmic Life, which alone is truly immortal, and alone deserves to be worshipped.

DIVINE PERSUASION AND THE TRIUMPH OF GOOD

Lewis S. Ford

LEWIS S. FORD is Associate Professor of Philosophy and Religion at Pennsylvania State University. He is a leading exponent of process philosophy.

In Archibald MacLeish's *J. B.*, Nickles hums a little tune for Mr. Zuss:

> I heard upon his dry dung heap
> That man cry out who cannot sleep:
> "If God is God He is not good,
> If God is good He is not God;
> Take the even, take the odd,
> I would not sleep here if I could . . ."

These words epitomize the unyielding difficulty confronting classical theism, for it cannot seem to reconcile God's goodness with his power in the face of the stubborn reality of unexplained evil. The process theism of Alfred North Whitehead * and Charles Hartshorne was clearly designed to circumvent these persistent difficulties. The time has now come, perhaps, to probe the adequacy of this solution. While it may handle the problem of evil, does not process theism's critique of classical omnipotence

---

* The works of Whitehead cited in this essay (all published in New York by Macmillan) are abbreviated as follows: *AI*, *Adventures of Ideas* (1933); *MT*, *Modes of Thought* (1938); *PR*, *Process and Reality* (1929); and *RM*, *Religion in the Making* (1926).

open up a Pandora's box of its own? If God lacks the power to actualize his own ends in the world, how can we be certain that the good will ultimately be achieved? In a recent article, Edward H. Madden and Peter H. Hare contend that process theism lies shipwrecked in the very same shoals it sought to avoid.[1] If God's power is curtailed in order to absolve him of responsibility for evil, they suggest, then the guarantee for the ultimate triumph of good has been undermined. The process theist may say that

natural events do not thwart [God] but are the occasions for his exercise of creative power, but he still must admit that on his view of the matter God is still limited in the sense that he neither creates nor wholly controls actual occasions. Moreover, if God does not wholly control actual occasions, it is difficult to see how there is any real assurance of the ultimate triumph of good. The two elements of traditional theism reinforce each other. The unlimited power of God insures the triumph of good, and the latter requires the notion of God's unlimited power. The mutual reinforcement, however, is wholly lacking in Whitehead's system. The absence points up a fundamental difficulty with his quasi-theism.[2]

Madden and Hare implicitly construe divine power to be coercive, limited by the exercise of other coercive powers in the world. We contend that divine power is neither coercive nor limited, though we agree that God does not wholly control finite actualities. This means we must recognize their contention that process theism does preclude any *necessary* guarantee that good will triumph on the stage of worldly endeavour. Yet should there be such a guarantee? Far from being required by theism, we shall argue that such a philosophical guarantee would undermine genuine religious commitment, and that the ultimate redemption from evil moves on a very different plane. With respect to any such guarantee we find, as Kant did on another occasion, that it becomes "necessary to deny knowledge, in order to make room for faith." [3]

I

Now clearly, if power is exerted only to the extent that control is maintained, then Whitehead's God is limited. But power may be defined

---

[1] E. H. Madden and P. H. Hare, "Evil and Unlimited Power," *The Review of Metaphysics*, XX, 2 (December 1966), 278–289. This article has been revised and reprinted in Hare and Madden, *Evil and the Concept of God* (Springfield: Chas. C Thomas, 1968). Throughout the revision the original phrase "triumph of good" has been softened to "growth of value." In the present essay we shall quote from the original article, adding in parentheses a reference to the corresponding passage from the book.

[2] Ibid., 281f. (117).

[3] Immanuel Kant, *Critique of Pure Reason*, B xxx. Norman Kemp Smith, trans. (London: Macmillan, 1929), 29.

more broadly as the capacity to influence the outcome of any process of actualization, thereby permitting both persuasive and coercive power. Coercive power directly influences the outcome, since the process must conform to its control. Persuasive power operates more indirectly, for it is effective in determining the outcome only to the extent that the process appropriates and reaffirms for itself the aims envisioned in the persuasion. Thus the measure of control introduced differs; coercive power and control are commensurate, while persuasive power introduces the additional variable of acceptance by the process in actualization. That God's control is in fact limited by the existence of evil would signify a limited coercive power, but it is compatible with unlimited persuasive power.

Whitehead's thesis is that God possesses no coercive power at all. Whether limited or unlimited, such power is incompatible with divine perfection. In the official formulation of Christian doctrine, Whitehead complains, "the deeper idolatry, of the fashioning of God in the image of the Egyptian, Persian, and Roman imperial rulers, was retained. The Church gave unto God the attributes which belonged exclusively to Caesar" (PR, 520). The concept of divine coercive power, both in its pure and modified forms, has led to grave difficulties.

Consider the extreme instance in which God is conceived as exerting unlimited coercive power, thereby controlling and determining all things. God is the master potter, moulding the clay of the world by the force of his creative activity, except that God has no need of any clay with which to work; he makes his own. On this exception the analogy breaks down, for the potter's vase asserts its own reality apart from the human potter precisely because it had already existed separately as clay. Could a world moulded completely by God's coercive power assert any independent existence of its own? To do so the world must possess some power. Pure coercive power transforms *creatio ex nihilo* into *creatio ex deo,* with the world possessing no more independent actuality than an idea in the divine mind would have. Even if it were to exist apart from the divine mind, it could not enrich God's experience, for he fully experiences in imagination any world he could completely determine.

Most views of divine power are less extreme, but they all share the same basic defects insofar as they ascribe coercive power to God. To the extent that God exercises such power, creaturely freedom is restricted, the reality of the world is diminished, and the divine experience is impoverished. Creaturely freedom is all important, for without it God is deprived of the one thing the world can provide which God alone cannot have: a genuine social existence. Abandoning the angelic marionettes who merely echo his thought as further extensions of his own being, God has elected to enter into dialogue with sinful, yet free, men.

Divine persuasive power maximizes creaturely freedom, respecting the integrity of each creature in the very act of guiding that creature's development toward greater freedom. The image of God as the craftsman, the cosmic watchmaker, must be abandoned. God is the husbandman in

the vineyard of the world, fostering and nurturing its continuous evolutionary growth throughout all ages; he is the companion and friend who
inspires us to achieve the very best that is within us. God creates by
persuading the world to create itself. Nor is this persuasion limited by
any defect, for as Plato pointed out long ago, the real good is genuinely
persuasive, in contrast to the counterfeit of the apparent good we confront on all sides.

This vision appears to many as too bold, for its seems to ascribe mind
and consciousness to all beings. In ordinary discourse only those who
are consciously sensitive to the directives and promptings of others can be
persuaded, although we are beginning to recognize the subliminal influence of the "hidden persuaders." Whitehead is urging us to broaden our
understanding of persuasion, for otherwise we lack the means for penetrating the nature of creation. Without the alternative of divine persuasion,
we confront two unwelcome extremes: divine determinism or pure chance.
In neither instance can God create. If determined by God, the world lacks
all ontological independence. It makes no difference even if God only
acts through the secondary causes of the natural order. To exist apart from
God, either the world as a whole or its individual parts must possess a
self-activity of its own. This self-activity is denied to the world as a whole
if God is its primary (coercive) cause, and it is denied to the individual
parts if they are determined by the secondary causes of the natural order
acting in God's stead. Chance, on the other hand, ignores God's role in the
evolutionary advance entirely and renders this advance itself unintelligible. We need not anthropocentrically imagine the evolutionary process
to culminate in man, for it is quite conceivable that in time it might bypass man and the entire class of mammals to favor some very different
species capable of a greater complexity than man can achieve; if not here
on earth, then in some other planetary system. Nevertheless it seems
impossible to deny that there has been an evolutionary advance in the
sense of increasing complexity of order over the past several billion years.
This increasing complexity cannot be satisfactorily accounted for simply
in terms of the chance juxtaposition of component elements, and calls for
a transcendent directing power constantly introducing richer possibilities
of order for the world to actualize. God proposes, and the world disposes.
This response is the necessary self-activity of the creature by which it
maintains its own existence. The creature may or may not embody the
divine urge toward greater complexity, but insofar as that ideal is actualized, an evolutionary advance has been achieved. Any divine power
which so influences the world without violating its integrity is properly
called persuasive, while the necessary self-activity of the creature insures
the spontaneity of response. This spontaneity may be minimal for protons
and electrons, but in the course of the evolutionary advance, sustained
until now, it has manifested itself in ever richer forms as the vitality of
living cells, the conscious activity of the higher animals, and the self-
conscious freedom of man. Spontaneity has matured as freedom. On this

level it becomes possible for the increasing complexity of order to be directed toward the achievement of civilization, and for the means of divine persuasion to become ethical aspiration (see *RM*, 119). The devout will affirm that in the ideals we envision we are being persuaded by God, but this self-conscious awareness is not necessary for its effectiveness. Not only we ourselves, but the entire created order, whether consciously or unconsciously, is open to this divine persuasion, each in its own way.

II

The model of divine coercive power persisted so long primarily because God's activity is usually conceived in terms of efficient causality. The effect must conform to its cause; this is the basis for all causal law. Yet Aristotle's insight that God influences the world by final causation is more insightful, though it must be reformulated so that God can *act* to provide each actuality with its own final cause, and not just inspire the world as a whole through the perfection of his *being*. Whitehead suggests that God experiences the past actual world confronting each individual occasion in process of actualization, and selects for it that ideal possibility which would achieve the maximum good compatible with its situation. The occasion's past actual world consists in the totality of efficient causal influences impinging upon it which it must take into account and integrate into its final actualization. The efficient causal influences provide the means whereby actualization occurs, but the way in which they may be integrated can vary, depending upon the complexity of the situation. God's directive provides an initial aim for this process of integration, but unlike the efficient causal influences, that aim can be so drastically modified that its original purpose could be completely excluded from physical realization in the final outcome.[4] Insofar as the occasion actualizes its initial aim, the divine persuasion has been effective. God furnishes the initial direction, but the occasion is responsible for its actualization, whether for good or for evil.

In presenting this theory of divine activity, Whitehead unfortunately concentrated his attention upon the primordial nature of God as the locus of possible values to be presented to individual occasions, at the expense of the consequent nature's role in determining which possibility would be most appropriate for the particular contingent situation. As John B.

[4] The subjective aim cannot be rejected in the sense that the aim could be excluded (i.e., negatively prehended) in its entirety at some phase in concrescence, thereby leaving the occasion bereft of any direction whatsoever. There must be continuity of aim throughout concrescence, for the process of unification is powerless to proceed in the absence of some direction. Nonetheless it is possible for the subjective aim to be so continuously modified in concrescence that the final outcome could express the contrary of the initial aim. Though genetically related to the initial aim, such a final outcome has excluded that initial purpose from realization.

Cobb, Jr. has convincingly demonstrated,[5] Whitehead's "principle of concretion" only gradually takes on flesh and blood as he subjects his conception of God to the categoreal obligations of his own metaphysical vision during the years 1924–1929. Any statements taken from *Science and the Modern World* or *Religion in the Making* about the nature of God are systematically worthless unless proleptically interpreted in terms of Whitehead's mature position. Taken in isolation they only serve to muddy the waters.[6] Even in *Process and Reality* the transformation of God into an actual entity is not wholly complete, and to that extent there is some truth in the assertion that "what little influence Whitehead's God has on the actual world . . . he has as a principle, not as a being or person, and insofar as God is a personal being, he is without any effect on the actual world." [7] On the other hand, it is possible to modify Whitehead's presentation in the direction of greater consistency with his own categoreal scheme, indicating the very active role the consequent nature plays in providing the initial aim. William A. Christian recognizes the interweaving of the primordial and consequent natures when he writes:

As prehended by a certain actual occasion. God is *that* unity of feelings which result from the integration of his primordial nature with his prehensions of the past actual world of *that* actual occasion.[8]

Cobb also develops this point:

Whitehead speaks of God as having, like all actual entities, an aim at intensity of feeling. . . . This aim is primordial and unchanging, and it determines the primordial ordering of eternal objects. But if this eternal ordering is to have specified efficacy for each new occasion, then the general aim by which it is determined must be specified for each occasion. That is, God must entertain for each new occasion the aim for its ideal satisfaction.[9]

Cobb recognizes that his account goes "a little beyond the confines of description of Whitehead's account in *Process and Reality* in the direction of systematization," [10] but he is prepared to defend his interpretation in detail.[11] What is important for our purposes is the fact that the involve-

[5] John B. Cobb, Jr., *A Christian Natural Theology* (Philadelphia: Westminster, 1965), 135–185.

[6] *Contra* Madden and Hare, 282f. (118).

[7] Ibid., 285f. (121).

[8] William A. Christian, *An Interpretation of Whitehead's Metaphysics* (New Haven: Yale University Press, 1959), 396; italics his. See also pp. 268, 275.

[9] Cobb, 156. He continues: "Such an aim is the feeling of a proposition of which the novel occasion is the logical subject and the appropriate eternal object is the predicate. The subject form of the propositional feeling is appetition, that is, the desire for its realization." We agree, except for the identification of the logical subject, which we take to be the multiplicity of actual occasions constituting the past actual world of the novel occasion, as reduced to the status of bare logical subjects for God's propositional feeling.

[10] Ibid., 157.

[11] Ibid., 157–168, 176–185. (The latter section is reprinted in this volume, pp. 215–221.)

ment of God's consequent nature in divine persuasion renders that activity intensely personal. For God thus serves as a dynamic source of value, personally responding anew to the concrete situation confronting each creature in turn, and providing it individually with its own particular initial aim. Through this ever ongoing activity God becomes the ultimate source for all value, though not one which is static and impersonal like Plato's Form of the Good.

III

If there is no fixed, final end towards which God and the world are moving, what governs God in his choice of the good? Socrates once asked Euthyphro (10 A), "whether the pious or holy is beloved by the gods because it is holy, or holy because it is beloved of the gods?" In response to the corresponding ethical question, Duns Scotus declared that what God wills is good because God wills it, rather than that he wills it because it is good. If in affirming God as the dynamic source of value we agree with Scotus, what prevents our God from being utterly capricious in what he chooses to be good?

In order to grapple with this question we must first appreciate White-head's analysis of the good. Because he subordinates goodness to beauty, he runs a serious risk of being misunderstood. He has been accused of a general aestheticism which fails to take seriously the tragic conflict between good and evil, though his own motives are quite different. He does not seek to trivialize the good, but to enhance it by placing it in relation to an all-embracing value which would not be restricted to the limited context of human conduct. Beauty, the name of this all-embracing value, cannot be interpreted simply in terms of aesthetic categories. It is evoked by nature occurrences and by works of art, to be sure, but also by conduct, action, virtue, ideas, and even by truth (AI, 342f.).

Goodness is essentially subordinate to beauty for two reasons. As White-head uses these terms, goodness is primarily instrumental while beauty is intrinsically valuable, actualized in experience for its own sake. It is a quality of experience itself, while that which occasions our experience of beauty (such as the good) is more properly called "beautiful" (AI, 328). Moreover, goodness is rooted in Reality, the totality of particular finite actualizations achieved in the world, while beauty pertains also to Appearance, our interpretative experience of Reality:

For Goodness is a qualification belonging to the constitution of reality, which in any of its individual actualizations is better or worse. Good and evil lie in depths and distances below and beyond appearance. They solely concern interrelations within the real world. The real world is good when it is beautiful (AI, 345).

We are apt to dismiss appearance as unimportant in contrast to reality, regarding it as largely illusory. Appearance need be neither unimportant nor illusory. It is presupposed by truth, which as "the conformation of Appearance to Reality" (AI, 309) could not exist without it. It is the basis for the intelligibility of our experience, and as we shall see in the final section, appearance plays a crucial role in the establishment of the kingdom of heaven. In any event, whether appearance is significant or trivial, that value which includes it along with reality is clearly the more inclusive.

The good, therefore, is to be understood in terms of its contribution to beauty. Beauty, in turn, is described as "the internal conformation of the various items of experience with each other, for the production of maximum effectiveness" (AI, 341). This effectiveness is achieved by the conjoint operation of harmony and intensity. Harmony is the mutual adaptation of several items for joint inclusion within experience, while intensity refers to the wealth and variety of factors jointly experienced, particularly in terms of the degree of contrast manifest. In effect, then, actuality is good insofar as it occasions an intrinsic experience of harmonious intensity.

By the same token, evil is the experience of discord, attesting to the presence of destruction. "The experience of destruction is in itself evil" and in fact constitutes its meaning (AI, 333). This definition is fully serviceable, once we realize that what is destroyed is not what is but what might have been. We tend to think of existence only in terms of continued persistence of being, but whatever has once achieved actual existence remains indestructible as determinate fact, regardless of the precariousness of its future continuation. In like manner, we ordinarily restrict destruction to the loss of anticipated continuing existence. Such continuing existence, however, if destroyed, never was but only might have been. As such it is merely a special case of what might have been, along with lost opportunities, thwarted experiences, disappointed anticipations. Whenever what is is less than what might have been there is destruction, no matter how slight.

Whitehead is emphatic in insisting upon the finitude of actuality, which in its exclusiveness affords the opportunity for evil.

There is no totality which is the harmony of all perfections. Whatever is realized in any one occasion of experience necessarily excludes the unbounded welter of contrary possibilities. There are always 'others', which might have been and are not. This finiteness is not the result of evil, or of imperfection. It results from the fact that there are possibilities of harmony which either produce evil in joint realization, or are incapable of such conjunction. . . . History can only be understood by seeing it as the theatre of diverse groups of idealists respectively urging ideals incompatible for conjoint realization. You cannot form any historical judgment of right or wrong by considering each group separately. The evil lies in the attempted conjunction (AI, 356f.; see AI, 375, MT, 75).

This conflict of values in attempted actualization is experienced as discord, and engenders destruction. "There is evil when things are at cross purposes" (*RM*, 97). "The nature of evil is that the characters of things are mutually obstructive" (*PR*, 517).

While evil is the disruption of harmony, it need not detract from intensity. In fact, the intensity of evil may be preferred to the triviality of some dead-level achievement of harmony, for the intense clash may be capable of resolution at a much higher level of complexity. The unrelieved "good life" may be rather dull, yielding no more zest of value than the perfectly harmonious repetition of dominant fifth chords in C major. "Evil is the half-way house between perfection and triviality. It is the violence of strength against strength" (*AI*, 355).

In his consequent nature God experiences both the good and the evil actualized in the world. His own aim, like that of the creature, is at beauty. "God's purpose in the creative advance is the evocation of intensities" (*PR*, 161), but these intensities must be balanced to overcome the mutual obstructiveness of things. God therefore seeks in his experience of the world the maximum attainment of intensity compatible with harmony that is possible under the circumstances of the actual situation. In order to insure this richness of experience for his consequent nature, God therefore provides to each occasion that initial aim which, if actualized, would contribute maximally to this harmonious intensity. This is the aim God wills as good for that creature in his role as the dynamic source of value. It is not capricious for it seeks the well-being both of the creature and of God. Were God to select any other aim for that occasion he would be frustrating his own aim at beauty.

Because of the intrinsic unity of the divine experience, all the finite actualities of the world must be felt together in their measure of harmony and discord. Insofar as they are individually intense and vivid, these occasions contribute to the maximum intensity of experience for God. Insofar as the several occasions are mutually supportive of one another, they also contribute, but should they clash, or be individually trivial, they detract from this final unity of all actuality within God. Divine love and justice may serve as primary symbols for God's aim at the harmonious intensity of beauty. Love expresses God's concern and appreciation for the particular intensity achieved by each individual, who finds ultimate significance in this divine feeling of appreciation for its particular contribution. Justice, on the other hand, expresses God's concern for the social situation of the togetherness of all occasions, since his experience of the world necessarily includes all the harmonies and clashes between individual achievements. Human justice tends to be cold and impartial, because our own partiality is so imperfect and limited to permit fair adjudication. Our sympathy and participation in the needs and claims of one party usually precludes any adequate participation in the rival needs and claims of others, particularly if the rival claimant is "society as a whole." Divine justice, on the other hand, is not abstract, following inexorably from the character of the primordial nature, but is concrete, the natural and spontaneous activity of the consequent nature integrating God's individual appreciations of the several occasions. Far from being impartial, God is completely partial, fully participating in the needs and claims of every creature. But because he is partial to all at once, he can judge the claims of each with respect to all others, valuing each to the extent to which this is consonant with all rival claims. Justice is ultimately the divine appreciation for the world, that is, the divine love simply seen in its social dimension.

This analysis of divine activity as the source of human value enables us to make sense out of the competing claims of rival ethical theories by assigning each a subordinate role within a wider explanation. Hedonistic and emotivistic theories emphasize the necessity to locate intrinsic value solely in subjective experience, though they tend to ignore the divine experience in this connection. Utilitarian theories stress the need for individual achievements of value to support and enhance one another. Their rule of "the greatest happiness for the greatest number" is strictly applicable, but it is spontaneously and non-calculatively calibrated to balance the claims to individual experience both qualitatively and quantitatively in the divine experience. Theories of duty, including Plato's vision of the Forms, see both the ideal character of the initial aim for each individual as well as the transcendent character of its source.

Religion seeks to enhance the role of ethical aspiration embodied in initial aims by concentrating upon their source in God. God is supremely worthy of worship because he is the ultimate source of value, as well as being that actuality in which all other actualities achieve their ultimate significance. The metaphysical description of God serves to purify the religious tradition of accidental accretions, while the religious experience of God gives concrete embodiment to these philosophical abstractions.

IV

Is there then any ultimate triumph of good? The Christian and the Jew alike wait with confident expectation for that day when the wolf shall lie down with the lamb. Classical theism, construing omnipotence in terms of coercive power, provides a philosophical guarantee that that day will in fact come to pass, or argues that it is already taking place (Leibniz' best of all possible worlds). This guarantee, however, transforms a confident expectation into a determinate fact, whether that fact be regarded as present or future. From the standpoint of faith, this appears to be nothing more than an emphatic underscoring of an intense trust in God. From the standpoint of logic, however, the fact of the triumph of good vitiates all need to strive for it. As in the case of the Marxist vision of a classless society, if its coming is inevitable, why must we work for it?

In process theism the future is an open risk. God is continuously directing the creation toward the good, but his persuasive power is effective only insofar as the creatures themselves affirm that good. Creaturely evil is an ever-present contingency, unless Origen is correct that we cannot resist the grace of God forever. On the other hand, the absence of any final guarantee now makes it genuinely possible for the expectation of the good to become a matter of faith. By faith I do not mean its rationalistic counterfeit: a belief based upon insufficient evidence. Rather I mean what Kierkegaard meant by truth for the existing individual: "an objective uncertainty held fast in an appropriation-process of the most passionate inwardness." [12] Faith is belief in spite of doubt, sustained by trust, loyalty, and devotion. The future is now doubtful, risky, uncertain. Yet the theist is sustained by his confident expectation that if we as creatures all have faith in God, that is, if all rely upon his guidance (given in the initial aim of each occasion), trusting him sufficiently to actualize the good which he proposes as novel possibility, then the good *will* triumph. The continued persistence of evil, both in man and in the natural order, testifies to the very fragmentary realization of creaturely faith in God. Nonetheless we may hope that the grace of God may be received and permeate all beings, and in that hope do our part in the great task. Such hope prohibits other worldly withdrawal, but calls upon us to redouble our efforts to achieve the good in this world with all its ambiguities for good and evil.

Faith in this sense is reciprocal. Just as the world must trust God to provide the aim for its efforts, so God must trust the world for the achievement of that aim. As Madden and Hare point out, "he is apparently so weak that he cannot guarantee his own welfare." [13] This is true to the

[12] Soren Kierkegaard, *Concluding Unscientific Postscript*, David F. Swenson, trans., (Princeton: Princeton University Press, 1944), 182.

[13] Madden and Hare, op. cit., 288 (125). In *Evil and the Concept of God*, 121f., Madden and Hare insert three paragraphs summarizing and criticizing the argument thus far of this paper (except for the discussion of evil in section II). Their summary is succinct and accurate, and they introduce the interesting analogy that Whitehead's God is like "an especially effective leader of an organization . . . who is powerful enough to guarantee the success of the organization *if* most of the members pitch in and help." They propose two objections to the existence of such a conditional guarantee of the triumph of good. "First, if cases can be found in which there has been widespread human cooperation and yet there has been no success, these cases would count as evidence against the existence of such a conditional guarantee. Such cases seem easy to find." Yet none are mentioned. I suspect all such instances would turn out to be problematic, for the theist and the naturalist would evaluate "widespread human cooperation" and "success" rather differently. Only widespread human cooperation *with God* can count as the proper fulfillment of the condition attached to the guarantee. Here the Christian might point to the rise of the early church, and the Muslim to the initial spread of Islam, both of which were eminently successful. Ancient Israel always understood her success in terms of her obedience to God, and her failures in terms of a widespread lack of cooperation with him. Secondly, they argue that the amount of evil in the world suggests that God is not a very persuasive leader. "It is a little too convenient simply to attribute all the growth to God's persuasive power and all the evil to the world's refusal to be persuaded." Now convenience, by itself, is not objectionable; in this instance, it may indicate that we have hit upon a proper solution. The measure of persuasion, moreover, is not how many are actually persuaded at any given time, but the in-

Biblical image of God's vulnerability toward man's waywardness. We read that "God repented that he had made man, and it grieved him to his heart." [14] Israel remembers God's suffering and anguish over his chosen people,[15] a suffering most poignantly revealed to the Church in the crucifixion of Jesus of Nazareth. The world is a risky affair for God as well as for us. God has taken that risk upon himself in creating us with freedom through persuasion. He has faith in us, and it is up to us to respond in faith to him.

V

Thus far we have spoken concerning the actualization of the good in the world. Here the good will not triumph unless we achieve that victory. Nevertheless there is an ultimate consummation, not in the world but in the divine experience, that accomplishes our redemption from evil.

Whitehead provides an extremely detailed analysis of experience as a process of integration whereby an initial multiplicity of direct feelings of other actualities fuse together with the help of supplemental feelings to achieve a unified outcome. This distinction between initial, physical, conformal feelings and supplemental, conceptual feelings can be significantly applied to the divine experience. In this initial phase God experiences each actuality just as it is for itself, with all its joy and/or suffering. As Christian documents indicate, God's initial conformal feelings are perfect, re-enacting the same feeling with all of the intimacy and poignancy that the creature felt, without any loss or distortion.[16] Here God is completely vulnerable, completely open to all the evil and the tragedy that the world has seen. "God is the great companion—the fellow-sufferer who understands" (PR, 532). Moreover, the early phases in his integration of these several conformal feelings introduce dimensions of suffering the world has not known. God experiences fully the discord between incompatible achievements of value, since he honors and appreciates the value of each wholeheartedly, refusing to moderate the cause of any party in the interests of easy compromise. He also faces the disappointment of the disparity between the initial ideal he proposed for any

---

trinsic value of the goal envisaged. The only really satisfactory motive for action must be the achievement of the good, which alone is purely persuasive. All other "persuasion" is mixed with apparent, counterfeit goods and with indirect coercion. Divine persuasion may be a "still, small voice" amid the deafening shouts and clamourings of the world, but it is most effective in the long run—it brought this mighty universe into being out of practically nothing.

[14] Genesis 6:6.

[15] Hosea 11:8, Jeremiah 31:20, Isaiah 63:15. See also Kazoh Kitamori, *Theology of the Pain of God* (Richmond: John Knox Press, 1965), and Abraham J. Heschel, *The Prophets* (New York: Harper & Row, 1962), chaps. 12–15.

[16] Christian, 351–353.

occasion and its subsequent faulty actualization. God is a most sensitive individual, with the highest ideals, constantly thwarted at every turn, yet who resolutely refuses to give up his grip on either ideality or actuality. At the same time, however, he is also a most imaginative being, whose unlimited conceptual resources enable him to transmute this suffering into joy and peace.

In his analysis of beauty and evil, Whitehead discusses four ways of dealing with the suffering of disharmony (*AI*, 334f.). The first three are inhibitory, directly or indirectly, excluding and rejecting some elements for the sake of the final harmony. Since God is hospitable to all, refusing none, none of these approaches is finally satisfactory. Yet there is hope in the final approach.

This fourth way is by spontaneity of the occasion so directing its mental functionings as to introduce a third system of prehensions, relevant to both the inharmonious systems. This novel system is such as radically to alter the distribution of intensities throughout the two given systems, and to change the importance of both in the final intensive experience of the occasion. This way is in fact the introduction of Appearance, and its use to preserve the massive qualitative variety of Reality from simplification by negative prehensions [i.e. by inhibitory exclusions] (*AI*, 335).

Here we can best understand Whitehead's point by analogy with works of the imagination, since this fourth way calls upon the resources of conceptual possibility to heal the wounds inflicted by actuality. Art and poetry transform the dull, ugly, irritating commonplaces of life into vibrant, meaningful realities by inserting them within fresh and unexpected contexts. Dramatic insight at the hands of Sophocles can suffuse the tragic deeds and suffering of Oedipus the King with dignity and honor by skillfully weaving these actions into an artful whole. Imaginative reason in the form of a speculative philosophy such as Whitehead's can surmount the interminable conflicts between man and nature, mind and body, freedom and determinism, religion and science, by assigning each its rightful place within a larger systematic framework. The larger pattern, introduced conceptually, can bring harmony to discord by interrelating potentially disruptive elements in constructive ways. Since God's conceptual feelings as derived from his primordial nature are inexhaustible, he has all the necessary resources to supplement his initial conformal feelings perfectly, thereby achieving a maximum harmonious intensity from any situation.

As the last sentence of our quotation indicates, the shift from initial conformal feelings to supplemental conceptual feelings marks a shift from reality to appearance. The objective content of conformal feelings constitutes reality as experienced, for it embodies our direct confrontation with other actualities (*AI*, 269). The difference between this objective content and the content arising out of the integration of conformal feeling with supplemental conceptual feelings (the "mental pole") is felt as "appearance."

In other words, "appearance" is the effect of the activity of the mental pole, whereby the qualities and coordinations of the given physical world undergo transformation. It results from the fusion of the ideal with the actual—The light that never was, on sea or land (*AI*, 270).

Appearance plays little or no role in simpler actualities, for they tend simply to conform to the realities of the immediate situation. Appearance becomes of the utmost importance with the emergence of sensory perception, for this complex mental functioning provides the means whereby the bewildering bombardment of causal influences can be reduced to a vivid awareness for perceptive discernment. We tend to despise appearance for its occasional lapses from reality, but this is short-sighted thinking. Appearance, Whitehead argues, is the locus for perception, novelty, intelligibility, and even consciousness. We constantly strive to encounter reality directly, but such an effort simply takes us back to a preconscious physical interaction with our surroundings. What is needed is not reality but truthful appearance, that is, conscious perceptive experience which is directly derived from and rooted in reality. Appearance becomes illusory only to the extent that the final integration achieves completion by the inhibitory exclusion of some elements of reality.

Clearly, divinely experienced Appearance is thoroughly truthful, incorporating all Reality within its comprehension, yet infusing it with an intensity and harmony that Reality failed to achieve for itself. Goodness, as pertaining solely to the achievement of Reality, is left behind in this final experience of Beauty, though its contribution forms its necessary basis. In this way Truth, as the conformation of Appearance to the Reality in which it is rooted, enhances Beauty (see *AI*, 342f.). In Beauty the goodness of the world is saved and preserved whole, while its evil is redeemed and purged of all its wickedness.

Hopefully this technical analysis will illuminate Whitehead's lyrical words towards the end of *Process and Reality:*

> The wisdom of the divine subjective aim prehends every actuality for what it can be in such a perfected system—its sufferings, its sorrows, its failures, its triumphs, its immediacies of joy—woven by rightness of feeling into the harmony of the universal feeling. . . . The revolts of destructive evil, purely self-regarding, are dismissed into their triviality of merely individual facts; and yet the good they did achieve in individual joy, in individual sorrow, in the introduction of needed contrast, is yet saved by its relation to the completed whole. The image—and it is but an image—the image under which this operative growth of God's nature is best conceived, is that of a tender care that nothing be lost.
>
> The consequent nature of God is his judgment on the world. He saves the world as it passes into the immediacy of his own life. It is the judgment of a tenderness which loses nothing that can be saved. It is also the judgment of a wisdom which uses what in the temporal world is mere wreckage (*PR*, 525).

(The last two sentences recall to mind the ancient vision of a law-giver, the leader of a second exodus, who humbly fulfills the task of the suffering servant:

> A bruised reed he will not break,
> and a dimly burning wick he will not quench,
> he will faithfully bring forth justice.) [17]

George F. Thomas, while most sensitive to the metaphorical power of these words of Whitehead, offers a searching critique which must be answered:

> The nature of the process by which God "saves" the world is not entirely clear. "He saves the world," says Whitehead, "as it passes into the immediacy of his own life." This means that in some way the values realized by actual entities are saved by being included in the experience of God as a "completed whole." But does it mean that the world is transformed and the evil in it overcome, or only that it is included in the harmony of God's experience? The method by which it is "saved" is said to be rationality rather than force. . . . But the "over-powering rationality of his conceptual harmonization" (PR, 526) seems to be effective not in transforming the *world* and overcoming its evil but in harmonizing its discords in the experience of *God*.[18]

Yet is it God's task to transform the world? Clearly the ancient Hebrew looked to Yahweh to bring about the prosperity of his nation. Thomas reaffirms that hope, but is it a realistic and justifiable expectation?

Samuel H. Beer argues that this expectation was transformed by the proclamation of Jesus:

> The gospel of the kingdom is that there is another order beyond our earthly existence. Things of the world as we find it are mortal and so without consequence and meaning, except as they may be preserved in that saving order. Here the covenant with man is not that he and his children shall thrive and prosper in history. It is rather that they shall sooner or later die in history but that they shall yet live in an order which transcends history. The meek, the merciful, the pure in heart, shall inherit it, not on earth, but in heaven.[19]

We are to seek "a kingdom not of this world" (PR, 520), a kingdom which both Beer and Whitehead find exemplified in the consequent nature of God (PR, 531).

Were God to transform the world, he would usurp our creaturely function in the moral economy. Yet suppose he were to usher in a perfected world tomorrow, the fulfillment of all our wishful dreaming. That would certainly redeem the world from all the evil which it would otherwise fall heir to tomorrow, but would it purge the world of today's evil? Remembering Ivan Karamazov's words, would such a perfect world even

[17] Isaiah 42:3.
[18] George F. Thomas, *Religious Philosophies of the West* (New York: Charles Scribner's Sons, 1965), 368.
[19] Samuel H. Beer, *The City of Reason* (Cambridge: Harvard University Press, 1949), 131. Beer is Professor of Government at Harvard and very distinguished in that field, yet quite versatile. In this remarkable book he sought "to state a philosophy of liberalism based on A. N. Whitehead's metaphysics of creative advance (p. vii). See particularly chap. 12, "A Saving Order," which considers most of the themes of this final section.

compensate for the innocent suffering of one baby in today's world? For
what has already happened is past and cannot be altered; no future
transformation can affect it. Nevertheless it can be transformed in the
divine experience of the world, and this is where its redemption is to be
sought. Finite actualization is necessarily transient. Far from saving and
perfecting the past, the present blocks out the immediacy of the past by
its own presence. If "the nature of evil is that the character of things are
mutually obstructive" (PR, 517), then the constant displacement and loss
of the past through the activity of the present is most evil, however unavoidable, and no present or future achievement of the world can remedy
that situation. "The ultimate evil in the temporal world . . . lies in the
fact that the past fades, that time is a 'perpetual perishing'" (PR, 517).
This perishing can only be overcome within a divine experience which
savors every occasion, no matter how distantly past with respect to ourselves, as happening now in an everlasting immediacy which never fades.

Each actuality in the temporal world has its reception into God's nature.
The corresponding element in God's nature is not temporal actuality, but is
the transmutation of that temporal actuality into a living, ever-present fact
(PR, 531).[20]

Finally, however, it may be objected that this ultimate consummation
of all things is fine for God, but has no value for us. Thomas argues that
Whitehead's God is not "the *Redeemer* of the world who transforms His
creatures by the power of His grace and brings new life to them." [21] In
response Whitehead speaks of "four creative phases in which the universe
accomplishes its actuality" (PR, 532),[22] which culminates in the impact
of God's consequent experience upon the world.

For the perfected actuality passes back into the temporal world, and
qualifies this world so that each temporal actuality includes it as an immediate
fact of relevant experience. For the kingdom of heaven is with us today (PR,
532).

This follows from his general 'principle of relativity,' whereby any actuality whatever causally influences all subsequent actualities, however
negligibly (PR, 33). As it stands, this brief description of our intuition
of the kingdom of God in the last two paragraphs of *Process and Reality*
is exceedingly cryptic, and must be explicated by means of the final
chapter of *Adventures of Ideas* on "Peace." In this chapter, however, there
is a tentativeness, a suggestive inarticulateness struggling with a far wider
vision than we can possibly do justice to. Whitehead tells us he chose

[20] For a detailed development of this point, see my article, "Boethius and Whitehead on Time and Eternity," *International Philosophical Quarterly*, VIII, 1 (March
1968), 38–67.
[21] George F. Thomas, 389.
[22] The first three phases are (a) God's originating activity in providing initial
aims, (b) finite actualizations in the world, and (c) God's complete experience of
the world in his consequent nature.

"the term 'Peace' for that Harmony of Harmonies which calms destructive turbulence and completes civilization (*AI*, 367). The experience of Peace is largely beyond the control of purpose. It comes as a gift" (*AI*, 368). I take it to be the way in which we participate in the divine life through an intuitive foretaste of God's experience. "It is primarily a trust in the efficacy of Beauty" (*AI*, 367), presumably that Beauty realized in God's perfected experience of all actuality. It is here that the good finally triumphs in all her glory—or, more precisely, as engulfed by all the divine glory as well.

SUGGESTED READINGS

An extensive bibliography can be found in D. Brown, R. E. James, Jr., and G. Reeves (eds.), * *Process Philosophy and Christian Thought* (Indianapolis: Bobbs-Merrill, 1971p). Whitehead's *Process and Reality* (New York: Macmillan, 1969p) is basic to understanding his metaphysics, but the student should begin with easier material, for example, *Adventure of Ideas* (New York: Macmillan, 1967p); *Science and the Modern World* (New York: Macmillan, 1967p); *Modes of Thought* (New York: Macmillan, 1968); *Concept of Nature* (London: Cambridge University Press, 1964p). Because of the difficulty of Whitehead's thought the student is urged to use the following as commentaries: W. A. Christian, *An Interpretation of Whitehead's Metaphysics* (New Haven: Yale University Press, 1967p); Ivor Leclerc, *Whitehead's Metaphysics: An Introductory Exposition* (New York: Macmillan, 1958); Victor Lowe, *Understanding Whitehead* (Baltimore: Johns Hopkins Press, 1962); and especially Donald W. Sherburne, *A Key to Whitehead's Process and Reality* (Bloomington: Indiana University Press, 1966p). Two new studies deserve mention. John W. Lango, * *Whitehead's Ontology* (Albany: State University of New York Press, 1972) and Lyman T. Lundeen, *Risk and Rhetoric in Religion* (Philadelphia: Fortress Press, 1972). The latter volume deals with Whitehead's theory of language, especially relating to religious language. The journal *Process Studies* contains articles and book reviews dealing with those philosophies in the process tradition.

Charles Hartshorne's development of neoclassical theism is articulated in *The Logic of Perfection and Other Essays in Neoclassical Metaphysics* (LaSalle, Ill.: Open Court, 1962p); *The Divine Relativity: A Social Conception of God* (New Haven: Yale University Press, 1964p); *A Natural Theology for Our Time* (LaSalle, Ill.: Open Court, 1967p); *Reality as Social Process: Studies in Metaphysics and Religion* (Boston: Beacon Press, 1953); *Man's Vision of God and the Logic of Theism* (Hamden, Conn.: Anchor Books, 1964); and *Creative Synthesis and Philosophic Method* (LaSalle, Ill.: Open Court, 1970). Good introductions to Hartshorne include the following: E. H. Peters, * *The Creative Advance* (St. Louis: Bethany Press, 1966p) and his * *Hartshorne and Neoclassical Metaphysics* (Lincoln: University of Nebraska Press, 1970); and R. E. James, Jr., * *The Concrete God* (Indianapolis: Bobbs-Merrill, 1967). Brown, op. cit., contains a good bibliography on Hartshorne.

Three anthologies that contain more detailed essays on process thought are W. L. Reese and E. Freeman (eds.), *Process and Divinity: Philosophical*

Essays Presented to Charles Hartshorne (LaSalle, Ill.: Open Court, 1964);
Delwin Brown, op. cit.; and P. A. Schilpp (ed.), ° *The Philosophy of Alfred
North Whitehead* (New York: Tudor, 1941).

John B. Cobb, Jr., Schubert M. Ogden, and D. D. Williams have written
extensively using Whitehead and Hartshorne within the Christian standpoint.
See especially John Cobb, Jr., *A Christian Natural Theology* (Philadelphia:
Westminster, 1965); *God and World* (Philadelphia: Westminster, 1969p);
The Structure of Christian Existence (Philadelphia: Westminster, 1967). S. M.
Ogden's *The Reality of God* (New York: Harper & Row, 1966) is a very
important book in this tradition. D. D. Williams, *The Spirit and Forms of Love*
(New York: Harper & Row, 1968) is an excellent study. William A. Beardslee,
A House for Hope (Philadelphia: Westminster, 1972) relates process thought
to biblical thought. Henry Nelson Wieman writes out of the process tradition
with a more naturalistic stress. Other writers that may be consulted are
N. Pittenger, B. Meland, and B. Loomer. While Teilhard de Chardin is not a
Whiteheadian, there are striking similarities. His books are currently widely
read. Barry Wood's *Magnificent Frolic* (Philadelphia: Westminster, 1970p) is
a delightful book for the beginning student. *Hope and the Future of Man*,
edited by E. Cousins (Philadelphia: Fortress Press, 1972p), contains a number
of essays combining theology of hope, process philosophy, and the thought of
Teilhard de Chardin.

CHAPTER SEVEN

Rumor of Angels: [1] New Forms of Transcendence

Something is happening to the whole structure of what we mean by human consciousness. We are living *on the verge* or *threshold* of a new [2] consciousness. As Matthew Arnold poeticized,

> Wandering between two worlds, one dead,
> The other powerless to be born,
> With nowhere yet to rest my head. . .[3]

In this last chapter the reader confronts a number of standpoints that speak out of *and* contribute to that emerging consciousness.[4]

While this "new consciousness" is a complex phenomenon, the following items are included in most of the discussions. The new consciousness emphasizes:

1. Immediate and sensual experience, the "sensate." "If you can't feel it through the skin it is unreal." *Authority* no longer resides in tradition or is mediated through an intellectual conceptual frame.

---

[1] Peter L. Berger, *A Rumor of Angels:* Modern Society and the Rediscovery of the Supernatural (Garden City: Doubleday & Co., Inc., 1969). An excellent discussion of some of the themes of this chapter.

[2] A case could be made that "new consciousness" is a persuasive definition. By calling this consciousness "new" the proponents of this standpoint are not only stipulating the time factor, but are making an *evaluation*. Who would want an *old* consciousness? The components of the new consciousness have been around before!

[3] Quoted by Martin Marty, *Varieties of Unbelief* (New York: Holt, Rinehart and Winston, 1964), p. 38.

[4] See bibliography for works on this theme.

The *individual's immediate experience* is the ultimate court of appeal.[5]

2. Recognition of mystery, for example, the interest in the occult, the affirmation of "something more" than the strictly empirical. The rational mind is at the end of its tether. The emerging culture is caught up in a Dionysian frenzy. As one guru of this phenomenon says: "The power which makes all things new is magic. What our time needs is mystery: what our time needs is magic." [6] Harvey Cox has also made this point by stressing the importance of play. When man plays he is open to mystery; when man does not play he requires everything be worked through what is feasible (rational).[7]

3. High value of novelty and creativity. Again we notice the stress on the new, the emerging and the individual's contribution to this process. The aesthetic of experience is central, not morality understood in the tradition sense. "Who wants to be good! I want to be 'beautiful!' " By "beautiful" the new consciousness is not stressing physical beauty, but a beautiful life-style, i.e., loose, graceful, spontaneous, loving, open, etc. Moral values are caught up in this higher state of being.

4. Quest for new and expanding levels of consciousness (transcendence). Human beings have no fixed nature. "Man is a rope stretched from the ape to the Overman." (Nietzsche) There are levels of consciousness beyond the rational which will determine the future of human consciousness.

5. Openness to views other than one's own, for example, Oriental thought, polymorphic diversity is not perversity.[8]

6. Strong feelings of solidarity with the earth, for example, concern with ecology and nature mysticism.

7. Strong feelings of community with all of humanity. "Human first; Christian second!" [9]

8. Concern for authentic communication. Communication between humans is larger than verbal exchange. Indeed, authentic communication goes beyond linguistic activity. Feelings and actions

[5] Two books that survey the material, relate this phenomenon to religion, and criticize its ultimate value as a lasting life-style, are John Passmore, "The New Mysticism: Paradise Now," from his book *The Perfectibility of Man* (New York: Charles Scribners' Sons, 1970) and Richard King, *The Party of Eros* (Chapel Hill: University of North Carolina Press, 1972). Part of the latter was reprinted in *Psychology Today* (August 1972).

[6] Norman O. Brown, "Apocalypse: The Place of Mystery in the Life of the Mind," *Harper's Magazine* (May 1961). See essays by Harvey Cox and Sam Keen in Chapter One and Chapter Seven, respectively.

[7] Harvey Cox, *Feast of Fools* (Cambridge: Harvard University Press, 1969); "Feasibility and Fantasy: Sources of Social Transcendence," *Transcendence,* edited by H. W. Richardson and D. R. Cutler (Boston: Beacon Press, 1969). These two books deal with many of the themes of this chapter.

[8] The reader will remember the essay by Robert Lifton in Chapter One in this regard.

[9] M. Novak's essay in *Time to Build,* op. cit.

are more important than words. Grooving or being in rhythm with another is central.

9. Concern with the "not-yet" of humans, i.e., the future.

Because of the diversity of these items I have, rather than briefly touching on all of them, centered in this chapter on items 4, 6, 9 (transcendence, the earth, and the future). The other items mentioned on the list come into the essays chosen for this chapter, although they are not central.

TRANSCENDENCE

Whether achieved through chemical or natural means, many today believe that there are levels of consciousness beyond the simply rational. These experiences of "something more" have made many today open to religion and metaphysics. The amazing fact about the contemporary scene in philosophy and theology is that while some go on announcing the death of metaphysics and God-talk, both have made an amazing recovery, particularly among the young. As William James remarked,

. . . our normal waking consciousness, rational consciousness as we call it, is but one special type of consciousness, whilst all about it, parted from it by the filmiest of screens, there lie potential forms of consciousness entirely different. We may go through life without suspecting their existence; but apply the requisite stimulus, and at a touch they are there in all their completeness, definite types of mentality which probably somewhere have their field of application and adaptation. No account of the universe in its totality can be final which leaves these other forms of consciousness quite disregarded. How to regard them is the question—for they are so discontinuous with ordinary consciousness. Yet they may determine attitudes though they cannot furnish formulas, and open a region though they fail to give a map. At any rate, they forbid a premature closing of our accounts with reality. Looking back on my own experiences, they all converge toward a kind of insight to which I cannot help ascribing some metaphysical significance.[10]

THE EARTH

The concern with ecology is not simply a concern for physical survival. A whole new [11] understanding of *nature* is required. The Judeo-Christian

[10] William James, *The Varieties of Religious Experience* (New York: Modern Library, 1902), pp. 378–379. For a contemporary treatment of levels of consciousness see "The Natural Mind" by Andrew Weil in *Psychology Today* (October 1972). The latter is excerpted from *The Natural Mind: A New Way of Looking at Drugs and the Higher Consciousness* (Boston: Houghton Mifflin Co., 1972). See also Theodore Roszak, *Where the Wasteland Ends* (New York: Doubleday, 1973).

[11] By "new" I mean in terms of emphasis. The alert reader will have noted that many of these so-called new ideas are old ideas in new dress. For example, Taoism is particularly important to the new consciousness in its stress on the sacredness of nature. Yet Taoism is one of the oldest of all philosophies.

concern with history has resulted in the rape of the earth. *History* [12] is where humans find God. Nature is seen only as the backdrop for the human drama. Nature is man's tool. M. Novak's essay in this section exemplifies a reaction to this excess. Nature also has its sacred dimensions. God is also to be found immanent in the process of nature. This belief has been called pagan. Maybe what we need is to become pagan again.

CONCERN WITH THE FUTURE

Before Toffler came out with his best selling *Future Shock*, philosophers and theologians were already preoccupied with the "future" as a key dimension of experience from which to understand God and Man. Ernst Bloch with his eschatological [13] philosophy has become the current rage in German theology.[14] Theologians are arguing that God is not the "Ground of Being" (Tillich), the God up there, or the God who acted back then. God is the "power of the future." God's mode of being is in the future. The creation is not a past mythological event, but belongs to the future, a coming eschatological event. While this is difficult to grasp, God as future exists prior to the past and the present.

The first standpoint in this anthology represents the view that the *past* illuminates the present. Because God *has* spoken to us in times gone by and *has* given us his promises, we can see this present event as an incident of a promise kept.[15] This anthology ends with the thesis that we must look from the *future* (end) to the now if we are to understand the nature of our existence. The "now generation" has given way to the "on the verge generation." What man is "not-yet" is crucial to discovering what he is. And therefore man's *hopes* are crucial to understanding who he is. Because God is the power of the future, man can live in hope. In this way the theology of hope speaks to the concern of many today that man is *homo viator* (man on the way); that our present cannot be justified by what was, but only by what is to be.

The following essays explore these three themes: earth, transcendence, and the future. Michael Novak's essay raises the issue of nature *and* history. Do Christians need a greater openness to nature? Why? Sam Keen's essay argues that theology is too rational (Apollonian). The non-rational elements have been downgraded with a consequent death of vitality. If theology is to recover, the Dionysian element must be nurtured. How does the Dionysian revolt effect theology? Abraham Maslow and

[12] See Chapter Two for a discussion of the centrality of history in the Judeo-Christian tradition. An excellent discussion of the tension between Western and Eastern thought on nature can be found in John Cobb, Jr., *Is It Too Late?* (Beverly Hills: Bruce, 1972). Process thought provides a way to mediate between these two traditions. See Chapter Six.

[13] Concern with the last (or future) days.

[14] Ernst Bloch is to Moltmann, Pannenberg, Braaten, et al. as Martin Heidegger is to Bultmann, Tillich, et al.

[15] See essays in Chapter Two by Herberg and Brown.

Huston Smith investigate forms of transcendence. Are there levels of consciousness? Is religious experience a manifestation of higher levels of consciousness? The essays by Harvey Cox, and Carl Braaten explore the philosophy of Ernst Bloch. If man is the animal who hopes, how does religion manifest this future orientation? What does it mean to say that God is "the power of the Future?" What does it mean to call Jesus the "anticipation of the Future?"

THE BEAUTY OF EARTH

Michael Novak

MICHAEL NOVAK is Associate Professor of Philosophy and Religious Studies at the experimental Old Westbury campus of The State University of New York. He is the author of many novels, books, and articles. His latest books include *Ascent of the Mountain, Flight of the Dove* (1971), *Experience of Nothingness* (1970), and *Theology for a Radical Politics* (1969).

We seek a revolution in consciousness—a religious task. Yet for many college students in America, talk about Christian faith has been hopelessly compromised by unpleasant experiences with organized religion. A "religionless Christianity" often seems to them just as irrelevant as a "religious" Christianity. On the other hand, many of the brightest students have had experiences which they find it difficult to speak of in the categories of pragmatism and science. With each year that passes they are becoming more open to religious discourse. Nevertheless, for various reasons they reject the language of American Christianity and Judaism. In this context I would like to argue that certain human experiences are ordinarily prerequisite for an understanding of Christianity and, further, that one malaise in contemporary Christian theology is due to inattention to certain kinds of human experience. Consequently, I wish to argue for a greater openness to the lessons of nature, a greater responsiveness to actual human experience, apart from any reference to Christianity. Christians do not need more Christianity, but less; Christians need a greater openness to nature.

1. The Importance of Nature

Let me begin by citing four exceedingly important movements. (1) Probably the most significant development in the contemporary religious world is the growing attraction which Eastern and other world religions are beginning to exert upon the consciousness of Christian nations. (2) The hippie culture of California is becoming a prototype of non-pragmatic experience for an increasing number of young people. (3) The often destructive use of psychedelic drugs does provide new experience, which cries out for expression in religious language. (4) The growing emphasis placed upon myth and symbol by contemporary sociology, psychology, and anthropology seems to signify the end of the Protestant, rationalistic, pragmatic, and scholastic era. These four movements are all interrelated. No doubt they depend upon the affluence and electronic technology of the present period. They mark, I believe, the beginning of a new age in the history of religion. They may be characterized by the reëmergence of the category of "nature" in human consciousness. A study of the work of a man who received the Nobel prize for illuminating the conscience of our time may make this point plain.

No writer is so widely read and so profoundly cherished by American young people as Albert Camus. Yet one aspect of Camus' writing which critics have consistently overlooked, an aspect indispensable for understanding the contemporary consciousness, is his turning away from the Christian man of northern Europe to his "Mediterranean man," the man of the noonday sun.[1] Many writers interpret the modern period as a conflict between secularity and Christianity, between the German secular discovery of "historical consciousness" with its ideology of "the future" and more static Christian political and philosophical concepts. Camus reads modern history in a different light: "The profound conflict of this century is perhaps not so much between the German ideologies of history and Christian political concepts, which in a certain way are accomplices, as between German dreams and Mediterranean traditions . . .—in other words, between history and nature."[2] Camus links together Germanic devotion to the future and Christianity. He regrets the loss of Hellenism and its respect for nature, its view of man as an organic fruit of nature, a child of earth. "When nature ceases to be an object of contemplation and admiration, it can then be nothing more than material for an action that aims at transforming it."[3] Camus understood very well the lesson John Updike has drawn from the most future-oriented of all countries, the United States: "We in America have from the beginning been cleaving and baring the earth, attacking, reforming the enormity of nature we were given, which we took to be hostile. We have explored, on behalf of all mankind, this paradox: the more matter is outwardly mastered, the more it overwhelms us in our hearts."[4] In brief, Camus' diagnosis of our illness is precisely the opposite of those who ask Christianity to take on an

[1] See " 'Greece in Rags' and the Young Barbarians," in Parker's *Albert Camus: The Artist in the Arena*, pp. 25–45.

[2] *The Rebel*, p. 299.

[3] Ibid.

[4] *Pigeon Feathers and Other Stories* (New York, 1962), p. 248.

even more one-sided orientation toward the future. For Camus, we have drunk too much history and have repressed nature.

Let us dwell on Camus' analysis a little longer—it is a point he made in his *Notebooks,* in the *Myth of Sisyphus,* and also in the *Rebel.* Camus used the phrase "German ideology" to refer to "the violence of eternal adolescence," "romanticism," a "nostalgia rendered more acute by knowledge and by books." "Despite its pretensions," he says, "it begins in the absolute and attempts to mold reality." It uses the future as a lever against the present. By contrast, "rebellion" is grounded in "Mediterranean traditions," in "virile strength," in "courage reinforced and enlightened by the experience of life," and "it relies primarily on the most concrete realities." [5] In this contest between history and nature, German ideology, he writes,

has come into an inheritance. It consummates twenty centuries of abortive struggle against nature, first in the name of a historic god and then of a deified history. Christianity, no doubt, was only able to conquer its catholicity by assimilating as much as it could of Greek thought. But when the Church dissipated its Mediterranean heritage, it placed the emphasis on history to the detriment of nature, caused the Gothic to triumph over the romance, and, destroying a limit in itself, has made increasing claims to temporal power and historical dynamism. When nature ceases to be an object of contemplation and admiration, it can then be nothing more than material for an action that aims at transforming it. These tendencies—and not the concepts of mediation, which would have comprised the real strength of Christianity—are triumphing in modern times, to the detriment of Christianity itself, by an inevitable turn of events. That God should, in fact, be expelled from this historical universe and German ideology be born where action is no longer a process of perfection but pure conquest, is an expression of tyranny.[6]

The source of the death of God, for Camus, does not lie in the use of the Hellenic category of "being," nor in any of those other places where theologians whose nourishment comes from northern European sources divine it. God dies because man has been uprooted from nature, historicized, and rendered a tyrant over and an alien in his own environment. Yet there is, Camus senses,

an irrepressible demand of human nature, of which the Mediterranean, where intelligence is intimately related to the blinding light of the sun, guards the secret. . . . In the common condition of misery, the eternal demand is heard again; nature once more takes up the fight against history. Naturally, it is not a question of despising anything, or of exalting one civilization at the expense of another, but of simply saying that it is a thought which the world today cannot do without for very much longer.[7]

Camus, of course, is not interested in rehabilitating the notion of God, only in making human life more possible for man. He finds it humiliating that for twenty centuries the West has had a Christian image of man.

[5] *The Rebel,* pp. 289–299.
[6] Ibid., pp. 299–300.
[7] Ibid.

"Who can say what we should be if those twenty centuries had clung to
the ancient ideal with its beautiful fate?" [8] Camus has hold here of
something extremely important—the vitality and the power of man's biological life. How shall we ever regain our sanity as a culture unless we
become reconciled to our body? Man is not, in the phrase of Alan Watts,
an ego trapped in a bag of skin, alien to his environment. Man is a part
of nature, brought forth from the universe like fruit from a tree. The
universe is a *thou* to him, inseparable from his own self, part of him, and
he is in dialogue with it. As an apple tree *apples,* so the universe *peoples*—
if again we may use a phrase of Alan Watts'.

Thus Camus saw with joy and urgency the need for a return to nature.
He saw the need for a return to nudity and simple delight in the beauty
of the flesh.

For the first time in two thousand years the body has appeared naked on
beaches. For twenty centuries men have striven to give decency to Greek
insolence and naïveté, to diminish the flesh and complicate dress. Today,
despite that history, young men running on Mediterranean beaches repeat
the gestures of the athletes of Delos. And living thus among bodies and
through one's body, one becomes aware that it has . . . a psychology of its
own. The body's evolution, like that of the mind, has its history, its vicissitudes,
its progress, and, . . . its deficiency. . . . How can one fail to participate,
then, in that dialogue of stone and flesh in tune with the sun of seasons? [9]

One senses in California today, as in Algeria so loved by Camus, the
burgeoning renewed trust in the human body. One finds young people,
as it were, trying to put Humpty-Dumpty together again, beginning with
the things closest to them, the things that their hands can touch, learning
the meaning of community, dignity, sadness, joy.

I have the mad hope that, without knowing it perhaps, these barbarians
lounging on beaches are actually modeling the image of a culture in which the
greatness of man will at last find its true likeness. This race, wholly cast into
its present, lives without myths, without solace. It has put all its possessions on
this earth and therefore remains without defense against death. All the gifts
of physical beauty have been lavished on it. . . . And yet, yes, one can find
measure as well as excess in the violent and keen face of this race. . . . Between this sky and these faces turned toward it, nothing on which to hang a
mythology, a literature, an ethic, or a religion, but stones, flesh, stars, and
those truths the hand can touch. [10]

There is something of penetrating beauty in this natural return to paganism, this wholehearted sense of nature in its measure and its limitations.

At a time when doctrinaire attitudes would separate us from the world, it is
well for young men in a young land to proclaim their attachement to those few

---

[8] *Notebooks 1942–1951* (New York, 1966), p. 8.
[9] *The Myth of Sisyphus* (New York, 1955), p. 106.
[10] Ibid., p. 111.

essential and perishable possessions that give meaning to our lives: the sun,
the sea and women in the sunlight. They are the riches of the living culture,
everything else being the dead civilization that we repudiate. If it is true that true
culture is inseparable from a certain barbarianism, nothing that is barbaric can
be alien to us.[11]

Moreover, Camus sees in this modest sense of nature the solid base of
a revolutionary ethic. He well realized that within a few miles of the
beaches of Algeria on which his maroon athletes lounged, there were
villages where people, scabbed with various diseases, starved to death.
Camus wished to find a way of wedding political consciousness to respect
for nature. He found this way in his concept of rebellion. The Greek myth
of Nemesis guided his thought here, as the myth of Sisyphus had earlier.
"The revolutionary mind, if it wants to remain alive, must therefore return
again to the sources of rebellion and draw its inspiration from the only
system of thought which is faithful to its origin: thought that recognizes
limits. . . . Rebellion, at the same time that it suggests a nature common
to all men, brings to light the measures and the limit which are the very
principle of this nature." [12]
He wrote further:

Analysis of rebellion leads at least to the suspicion that, contrary to the
postulates of contemporary thought, a human nature does exist, as the Greeks
believed. Why rebel if there is nothing permanent in oneself worth preserving? . . . The slave asserts himself when he comes to the conclusion that a
command has infringed on something in him which . . . is common ground
where all men—even the man who insults and oppresses him—have a natural
community. . . . From this point of view human solidarity is metaphysical.[13]

For Camus, in short, the rebel rejects and disputes history in the name
of nature. Camus does not deny that man is responsible for history. He
only wishes to make plain that man is part of nature. Man may possibly
be "evolution become conscious of itself," but Camus wishes us to be
certain that we do not become conscious in an alienated, rootless, un-
natural way. Nature lives in us, and we in it. Nature is historical, and
history natural. To wave a banner either in the name of history against
nature or of nature against history is to misunderstand our own identity.

For some time the entire effort of our philosophers has aimed solely at
replacing the notion of human nature with that of situation, and replacing
ancient harmony with the disorderly advance of chance or reason's pitiless
progress. . . . Nature is still there, however. She contrasts her calm skies and
her reason with the madness of men. Until the atom too catches fire and history
ends in the triumph of reason and the agony of the species. But the Greeks
never said that the limit could not be overstepped. They said it existed and

[11] "Presentation de la revue 'Rivages'," *Rivages*, No. 1 (1939), 1, as quoted by
Parker in *Albert Camus*, pp. 40–41.
[12] *The Rebel*, p. 294.
[13] Ibid., pp. 16–17.

whoever dared to exceed it was mercilessly struck down. Nothing in present history can contradict them.[14]

2. IN DEFENSE OF RELIGION

What is the bearing of the new paganism of Camus upon the problem of God? It suggests that the problem of God is not to be solved by seeking a "religionless Christianity," but by a move in quite the opposite direction. We might say that Christianity has been weakened because it has had too high a component of "Christianity," and because its component of "religion" has been exhausted. Christianity may be a good seed; but it cannot thrive in thin, sandy, or rocky soil. It is religion which makes the human heart fertile. We need more religion and less Christianity.

"The Greek myths," I have recently heard a student say, "speak much more powerfully to me than Christian myths." Another student wrote in his term paper: "Christian stories never impressed my imagination so vividly as stories of the American Indian gods: tales of thunder and the Presence in the mighty rivers. It was in *those* stories that I first understood the meaning of 'God,' which I later lost in Christian education." Herman Hesse's *Siddhartha* startles many students into awareness, and the wisdom of the East begins to speak directly to their hearts.[15] Why is this? I believe that Camus' theory is correct. German ideology—its emphasis on man's future projects—rests upon too cerebral, too egoistical and too tyrannical a view of man. The organic, biological, and imaginative life of Americans and other future-oriented people has been starved. "God" has not died because the Hellenic concept of being was used to speak of him. "God" has died because the word "being" has lost its roots in human biology, human experience, and human imagination. The great, profound *Om* which Siddhartha labored long to find deep in the pit of his stomach says much more adequately what "being" used to say. We do not need to dehellenize the word "God." We need to turn to nature and myth as the Greeks did, in order to give human depth to our faith.

There is, of course, an ambiguity in the word "religion." When Bonhoeffer attacked "religion," he attacked a widespread kind of inwardness, separateness, artificialty—a piety which led religious people out of the center of life.[16] But why did religion do that? Because religion had lost its roots in nature—lost its roots in sea, wind, the nudity of beautiful human beings, sunlight on beautiful women, courage, political consciousness. It may clarify matters to recall that just as Bonhoeffer was working out his vision of a religionless Christianity, Camus was working out his

---

[14] *The Myth of Sisyphus*, pp. 136–137.
[15] See, for example, Alan Watts, *The Way of Zen* (New York, 1957).
[16] *Letters and Papers from Prison* (New York, 1953), pp. 162–166.

vision of secular sanctity. The basic momentum in both arguments is to turn men toward the center of life—toward the kiss of lovers, the coolness of the evening air, the demand today for quiet courage in rebellion against the manipulators of the future.

It is because Americans dread the public use of four-letter words, insist on cleanliness and neatness, think human genitals are dirty, fear controversy, will not admit drinking and gambling into public life, refuse to imagine that their leaders could ever lie or use power tyrannically or kill innocent people—it is because Americans try in the name of "religion" to cover up reality that "religion" has atrophied and God has died. Christianity without raw nature, Christianity without reality, is the *Logos* who never became flesh. Genuine religion, honest religion, is the flesh which the Word assumes, the soil in which the seed is sown.

Thus the tack taken by those who follow uncritically in the path of Bonhoeffer is, I believe, a mistaken and sterile one. If there is no God, the figure of Jesus is without interest. So long as we do not turn to nature, there can be no God. But how, we are certain to be asked, does turning to nature lead us to God?

3. THE GOD WITHIN

A series of insights or orientations is needed if an American is to discover God in his own experience. For example, an American student will commonly imagine that "turning to nature" means turning to objects "out there" in the environment. The ordinary American student has been taught to think of himself as a center of consciousness imprisoned subjectively in a sheeting of thin flesh and confronted with an environment full of objects out there to be observed objectively and mastered. In brief, the American has been taught to view the universe as made up of two kinds of stuff, conscious and unconscious, of which the first is an alien, an intruder, an outsider. It comes as a surprise to many to recognize that this "myth of the objective observer" is in fact a myth, and that they are free to look at themselves in a quite different way, living as organically in their environment as an apple lives on a tree. Nature courses through them and shares its consciousness with them. They are free to feel "at one" with nature. They may speak to nature as to themselves. They may imagine that the imaginative form for presenting their relationship to the ocean, to trees, to buildings, to chairs, to desks is not the form "it" but the form "thou." Consciousness, intelligibility, presence—we fumble for the telling word—pervades all things. "*Tat tvam asi:* That art Thou." Thus does the famous Hindu expression articulate the identity of the soul and God, an identity whose presence extends to every moment and to every place.

It is important, I would argue, for Westerners to begin to recover

ancient experiences of man's relation to the world and of men's relations
to one another. It is not true that metaphysics is at an end; it is only at a
beginning. The functional patterns of scientific thinking have their place;
they serve the purposes of prediction and control, so that man is able to
extend the power of his aims and purposes over his environment. But the
logic of science is the logic of tyranny: as Francis Bacon saw, scientific
knowledge is power. The scientific model for action is the manipulation
of objects. Scientific thinking applied to metaphysical questions destroys
metaphysics.

However, the expansion of scientific information and its extension
through technology is bringing about a major correction in the assumptions of recent generations. Questions about nature and about man's
nature are regaining their primacy in the most technologically advanced
nations. As men begin to take responsibility for building the urban
centers of the future, they are forced to ask the questions: "What sort of
cities do we desire? What forms best realize human potential? Who do
we think we are?" Anthropological and sociological societies have discovered in recent years that while their methods may in some sense be
value free, their employment on real human beings has empirical, social
effects and hence involve investigators in serious value commitments.
Among engineers who dream not only of the constructs which will be
operational in a few years, but of those not yet realized even in design,
the fundamental questions is: "*Should* we do X? By what values should
we decide which *X*'s to do?"

In brief, what Aristotle called architectonic questions or politics and
ethics are beginning to dominate human consciousness. And the mysteries
of the human self, the multiplicity of future possibilities, and an almost
universal identity crisis are reasserting their primacy. The fundamental
question for the children of an affluent society, trained to technical skills,
is: *Who are we? What do we wish to do with ourselves, and with our
power?*

A second series of insights emerges when students try to answer the
question, *Who am I?* If they keep a diary, or attempt to write out who they
think they are and what they think their values are, they speedily discover
that what they commit to paper one day seems woefully inadequate the
next. The self is elusive. Its values and sense of identity refuse to be
condensed in words. In answering the Socratic question, they begin to
understand the point of the Socratic method. Knowledge is not power;
it is knowledge of ignorance. Moreover, the self is inextricably and
organically linked to its environment to its societies. The question "Who
am I?" launches a dialectic that leads to discoveries about one's economic,
social, political, mythical, and biological history. The Hindu insight, "*Tat
tvam asi:* That art Thou," is verified in greater richness than one had at
first anticipated.

Thirdly, it is commonly impossible for young Americans to deal with
the Socratic question or with the question of God unless they have first

shared the experience of communion with at least one other person. This experience, for young Americans, is more rare than one might expect. There has perhaps never been a generation for whom the sense of loneliness is so acute. Their parents, after a fashion, love them, but the family is no longer, nor can it be, the nest it used to be. Moreover, young people have been taught that other people are their competitors, objects whose friendship and influence they must try to win. Achievement is rewarded. Popularity and acceptability are established as criteria for human relations. The Beatles comment accurately: "She's leaving home/After living alone for so many years." It is not unusual for college students, suddenly aware of one another, to fall into one another's arms, to hug one another tightly, and to cry both from fear and from joy. Many young people from "good middle-class homes" have never known the sense of community with another human being. They are "uptight" about touching one another.

Moreover, Christian society in America has publicly treated the human genitals as organs of embarrassment and shame, the *pudenda*. Consequently, the genital organs are surrounded by taboos; "breasts," "nipples," and "penis" are suppressed words, and the actions of lovemaking are thought to be "obscene." Nevertheless, the mutual revelation of two people to each other gives rise to the most poignant sense of the sacred in our society. In sexual openness one "transcends" the stultifying mores of society; in intimacy and tenderness one "transcends" the acquisitive, impersonal human interchange of our society. For many persons it is only, or chiefly, in sexual love that one encounters the category of an end in itself, the category of the sacred. Everything else in our society appears to be a means; the commercialization of sexuality—and the common ecclesiastical view of sex—threaten to degrade even sexual love into a means. Yet for many of the young no human experience is more full of awe, joy, and holiness than sexual intercourse. It is from this experience, for many, that religious language becomes meaningful again. The honesty, community, and absolute respect for the other which good lovers are led to share takes them beyond the categories of the pragmatic, the rationalistic, and the isolated self.

Why is it, then, that Christian society tolerates violence and murders by the dozen in movies and on evening television, but outlaws manifestations of sexual love? Is it moral to strike a man in the face in a barroom brawl, but not to caress a woman's breasts? Is it clean to plunge a knife into a man again and again, but dirty for a man to enter into a woman with gentleness? Christian society has come to prefer repression of vital and sacred instincts, and has conceived of God as the transcendent, all-seeing Eye who detects every violation of sexual taboos. The God of American Christianity has been the idol of inhibition, repression, and shame. The death of this God should have been predictable.

Conventional American society, in short, has been hostile to every basic human experience from which language about God commonly springs. If conventional American society is "religious," then by all means we need a "religionless Christianity." Yet I have been trying to suggest that American society is not genuinely religious; it is self-contained, repressive, uncritical, and idolatrous. The question which remains to be answered is why the experiences of nature, the self, community, and sexual love lead many young Americans to a religious language. Why do these experiences constantly break through the ordinary patterns of life and establish the sacred in the midst of man's strength?

Perhaps the best way to understand the emergence of religious categories is to grasp the character of technological, pragmatic life in advanced countries like the United States. From the perspective of studies in Marx and Freud, Herbert Marcuse in *One Dimensional Man* has come to describe such life as effectively totalitarian; people think that they are free, but they are only free within the limits established by the pragmatic concensus. Technical society awakens false needs and false consciousness; it is virtually impossible not to be inwardly determined by such needs and such consciousness, much more so than at earlier stages of man's development. M. Garaudy, the famed Marxist interpreter of Christianity, continually assaults Christianity for its "inwardness" and "subjectivity." [17] Christian critics, unfortunately, appear to concede too much to Garaudy on this point. For it is the strength of Christianity and the weakness of Marxism that the criteria of humanistic life are centered in the human person and the critical community, not in the impersonal processes of technical, pragmatic life. On the other hand, the inwardness of existentialism and of Christianity is by no means contained within the private sphere. Sartre and Camus possess an acute social and political consciousness; there is an existentialist politics.[18]

The heart of existentialist politics, in fact, lies in its rejection of the presuppositions of the present technical consensus, which it judges to be inhuman and irrational. It is not a mistake in government, nor the fault of any one administration, that the United States and Russia spend so many billions of dollars for destructive armaments. The irrationality of the Cold War springs from the dominance of pragmatic and technical considerations over a radical humanistic critique of the system under which the secular city is being built. Consequently, it appears to be a mistake for Harvey Cox and Johannes B. Metz to surrender the strength of subjectivity and inwardness because of Marxist objections.[19] A certain kind of private inwardness is pale and sickly, to be sure, an interior life oblivious to the power of institutions and economic structures and irresponsible in social and political affairs. A great many sins of this sort have been committed by Christians.

---

[17] See, for example, "Christian-Marxist Dialogue," *Journal of Ecumenical Studies,* IV (1967), 207–222.

[18] See Michel-Antoine Burnier, *Choice of Action* (New York, 1968).

[19] See *The Secular City* (New York, 1967); *Journal of Ecumenical Studies,* IV (1967), 223–234.

The cure for sickly inwardness, however, is not pragmatism, nor a zest for technique, nor devotion to the future of man. The cure for sickly inwardness is a conversion to social and political responsibility. But *why* should a man be concerned about other men? Why should he become involved? The history of our time seems to indicate that political life is murderous and that society is impervious to intelligence and courage. The great leap of faith is faith in man. One must, despite appearances, trust in the power of critical intelligence, courage, and compassion. One must, despite odds, go on struggling for a more brotherly city. Solace between individuals is not enough; community structures must be changed. A reconstruction of the economic, social, and political order is called for if men are to develop into men.

Thus openness to nature, to the Socratic question, to the experience of community, and to sexual love become *models* for what it is to be a man, and *sources* of faith in man. It is only when persons become awakened from their sleep and recognize that the assumptions of a technical, pragmatic society have blinded them to their inner possibilities that hope for a political revolution can be generated. The awareness of the mystery of the self and the mystery of community becomes the criterion by which social, economic, and political realities are judged: do they stultify or do they stimulate this awareness?

But to become aware of the mystery of the self and of the mystery of communion with others is to gain a sense of "participation" and of "unity," a sense of being part of something in which one does not lose one's own identity but does lose one's alienation and isolation. In being honest, one has the sense of being honest *against oneself* and yet somehow in the name of oneself—not as if under the glare of an all-seeing Eye, but as if by "participating" in a light greater than one's own emotions, interests, or rationalizations. In loving another as other, one has the sense of responding outside the categories of subject and object, or interest, or need, or stimulus and response. In moments of courage one has the sense of surrendering the interests of the self, not exactly for an abstraction or even a value, but for a self more important than the interested self. From such experiences of honesty, community, and courage, religious language is bound to spring. Human life is not self-contained. Who has belief in man has already made the giant leap of faith, compared to which the leap to religious language is only a step. The sense of man as an end in himself suggests that the radical structure of the universe in which we live is not hostile nor even impersonal; those who treat men as ends in themselves seem to live most fittingly. Why is this so? One cannot help wondering. One may reject the repressive, transcendent "God" of false religiousness; but the wonder which is the every-fecund source of true religion springs up like clear water in the heart. No one sees God. All that we encounter is the sense of human experience leading beyond pragmatic and technical categories, out of the area of means and ends. Here arises the sense of the sacred and the darkness of which the mystics wrote.

4. JESUS IS NOT ENOUGH

What are some of the fruits of turning to nature? Thomas J. J. Altizer
has been telling us eloquently that the God of history is dead. Who is the
God of history? He is the transcendent One, Providence, the Repressor,
the Father. Altizer takes seriously the crisp affirmation: "God was in
Jesus." The transcendent God "emptied himself," negated himself, becoming so immanent in history that the only legitimate way of speaking
of him is through affirmations about Jesus. I believe that Altizer is making
several most important points. But I think it is necessary to go beyond his
position in two ways.

In the first place, Jesus is not, of himself, especially attractive. A man
among other men, he suffers too many liabilities—too many innocents
died on account of him, too many horrors have been for centuries committed in his name (upon Jews and Arabs, for example, but also upon
the sexual and psychological life of countless Christians, too). Moreover,
his own character and deeds are ambivalent; not all men are attracted to
him, not all admire him in every respect.

In the second place, a common Protestant understanding of the transcendence of faith is—it seems to me—faulty. On this understanding, a
man cannot come either to experience or to knowledge of God except
through the historical, in-breaking grace of Jesus. Any knowledge of God
at which man arrives through his own experience and understanding apart
from Jesus is idolatrous. Yet we are told in the prologue of St. John's
Gospel that in the beginning was the Word, and that all things were made
through him. The vision behind this prologue seems to suggest that every
person, thing, and event in history has been made in the image of the
Word. We should expect, then, that every culture, every person, every
moment of history reveals the creative presence of the Word. Thus the
grace of the Word does not only break into history through the historical
Jesus; *all* things have been made in him, through him, and with him. All
things are graced—"Everything we look upon is blest" (Yeats). Thus, I
think we must say that even the historical Jesus can be used idolatrously;
that is to say, in a manner that overlooks the omnipresence and the
efficacy of Jesus insofar as he is the Word by whom, through whom, and
with whom were made all the things that were made. Nature itself is a
word mirroring and echoing the Word. Like the castle of Albee's *Tiny
Alice* it is a castle within a castle within a castle: its reverberating air
shaped by a Word.

Thus Teilhard de Chardin is able to step with swift strides from evolutionary nature and the Omega Point to Jesus as the Word. Is not the Alpha
also the Omega, and does not abyss cry out to abyss in glory? Teilhard de
Chardin, like Dostoevsky and Berdyaev, drew his nourishment from Greek
Christianity, which saw a dynamic universe flowing forth from the

Pantokrator, the *Logos,* the *Risen Lord.* What has come to be despised in
scholasticism as "Hellenization" is, in fact, "Latinization." It is Latin
categories rather than Greek, based on commerce and jurisprudence rather
than upon potent, dynamic nature, that have led to the death of the
transcendent God.

In nature itself, the nature known to physical science and the nature
known to ordinary human experience, there are, if Christianity be true,
elements leading the reflective man to honesty rather than to dishonesty,
to creativity rather than to destruction, to courage to be rather than to
anomie, to community rather than to atomic isolation. The universe in
which we live often seems impersonal, indifferent, hostile, and even cruel.
Yet our experience within it often fills us with reconciliation, with a sense
of unity and peace, with a profound stirring of ecstasy and the desire to
create. The transcendent is immanent in the world as yeast in dough, as
powers of growth in a mustard seed, as shaping word in air. It is through
nature as it is that God is to be found. Such a conviction is profoundly
Oriental, profoundly Greek, and profoundly Christian. Who says the
Buddha's *Om* says *Word.*[20]

What Christianity adds to Greek and to Oriental religions is a responsibility not only to reflect the world, but also to change it. Creation is
unfinished; each man, in the image of the creative Word, must utter a
creative word. But man was separated from his environment and history
was separated from nature by the first cycle of modern science, by the
printing press, and by Germanic eschatology. Modern science has entered
a new cycle, the printing press has been replaced by electronic media,
and now it is time to turn from Germanic eschatology [21] to Mediterranean
nature. Camus refused to surrender the present moment to the future.
Visions of the future must share time with the world of total present
experience, experience of the senses, the imagination, the emotions, and

[20] Nancy Wilson Ross, *Three Ways of Asian Wisdom* (New York, 1966), p. 24.
Western men cannot simply accept Eastern religious themes, of course. Western
experiences and Western questions must be accounted for. In order to experience the
world as one, for example, it is not necessary to understand concrete realities as mere
maya. What I mean to argue for is the interpenetration and mutual criticism of
Eastern and Western concepts. A *coincidentia oppositorum* is necessary, if we are
to experience an international wisdom in our time.

[21] When completing this paper, I had not yet read Jürgen Moltmann's *Theology of
Hope* (New York, 1967). There are powerful passages and useful distinctions in the
book. The treatment of nature and present experience is inadequate—the restlessness
and self-driving, self-expanding impulse are characteristically German and (I would
say) dangerous. The treatment of Camus is only of the early Camus and far too facile.
Moreover, although the argument of the book is carried out in theological words, its
moving spring is quite clearly the cultural pressure arising from a new stage of
science, technology, and international politics—a fresh perception of man's experience
of his own present. Its key values like "more justly, more humanely, more peacefully,
and in mutual recognition . . . of human dignity and freedom" (pp. 337–338)
seem to have their ground in human experience not limited to Christians. In America,
Babbitt was a "booster," there are Optimist Clubs, and hope is often a mask by which
present horrors are evaded and the compulsion to master history, space, and matter
is legitimized. Theology played on one string is not an orchestra.

the intelligence and will. Man is coming to life again; taste and see that the taste of life is sweet! When man regains his roots in nature, the God immanent in nature courses through his consciousness again. The dead God rises. The arrowhead breaks through into a new, creative, period.

MANIFESTO FOR A DIONYSIAN THEOLOGY

Sam Keen

SAM KEEN is currently a free-lance writer and lecturer. His books included *Apology for Wonder* (1969) and *To a Dancing God* (1970).

> *I would believe only in a god who could dance.*
> Nietzsche.

Philosophers holding tenure, theologians committed to the preservation of orthodoxy, intellectuals captivated by ideas, and citizens dedicated to establishing a perimeter of defense against insecurity are reluctant to yield to the rhythm-induced ecstasy of the dance. It is understandable, therefore, that the strange music coming from the wilderness far removed from the academy and the marketplace has not been noted with acclaim in professional journals or the popular press. But the music will go on, for Dionysus is again issuing an invitation to the dance, to ecstasy, enthusiasm, and a touch of divine madness.

Middle-class wisdom looks to Apollo, demands sanity, and accurately maintains that it is dangerous to heed the intoxicating call of Dionysus. Culture depends upon discipline and order; civilization requires civility; even creativity involves sublimation and repression—all of which Dionysus tempts us to forget. In fact, both Dionysian and Apollonian elements are found in any culture, past or present; both chaos and order, ecstasy and discipline are woven into the fabric of all life. Most cultures provide for periodic return through game, festival, and orgy to the chaos that underlies the veneer of civilization (Saturnalia, Mardi Gras) while maintaining the legal order and the social discipline necessary for daily life.

Yet chaos must be domesticated for human community to be possible; the city must build its walls of stone to defend itself against the barbarians without and its structures of law to protect itself from the chaotic passions of its own citizens; the ego must erect defenses against the insistent arational demands of the id. But if order must prevail over chaos, chaos must also have its rights or else vitality is killed by restraint, spontaneity falls prey to the necessity to do everything "decently and in order" (one of the higher laws of Presbyterians), and laughter fades before the spirit of seriousness. When Dionysus is not given his due, Apollo becomes a tyrant, a god to be killed.

Western culture has become increasingly Apollonian and the time has come when the rights of Dionysus must be reasserted. This tyranny of Apollo is especially evident in Western theology and religious institutions, which have for the most part identified with the status quo and been fearful of the chaos of psychological and political revolution. The religious establishment has put its weight behind maintaining the present boundaries, the present forms of personality and social organization. It has counseled that the impulses of the id must either find satisfaction within the existing structures of marriage and society or be repressed, and likewise that political revolution (from the left at any rate) must conform to the rules of capitalism and parliamentary procedure.

If we could once pretend that an Apollonian theology was adequate we no longer can. Both the social revolutions in the underdeveloped countries and the encounter with depth psychology have given irrefutable evidence that the repression of the "lower" classes and the "lower" passions leads only to social and personal sickness. The only way toward health is in learning to live creatively with the chaos within. An integral society, like an integral personality, is the product of a democratic organization within which opposites may coexist in mutual creative interaction. Pluralism is the condition of authentic life, and hence the quest for wholeness, for social and individual healing (salvation), must involve our learning again to praise Dionysus. For when Dionysus is denied the honor due him, the healing power of reformation, ecstasy, wonder, and grace is lost.

From the fringes of contemporary thought is coming a renewed vision of Dionysian way of life. While it would be too much to claim that there is a self-conscious school of Dionysian thinkers, Thomas Altizer, Norman O. Brown, Nikos Kazantzakis, Herbert Marcuse, and Alan Watts are all centrally concerned with themes which can fairly be called Dionysian, as in a lesser degree are Heidegger, Marcel, Tillich, and Whitehead. This essay will trace in broad outline the worldview and life style of the Dionysian way with special reference to theology. We will first contrast the Apollonian and the Dionysian ways and, after suggesting a corrective in the Dionysian understanding of the self, will advocate the necessity of recovering the Dionysian element in theology. Our concern is to discover what it might be like if we had the courage and/or folly to accept the invitation to dance our way through life.

THE APOLLONIAN WAY

Apollo is the god who most fully incarnates the ideals we associate with classical Greek thought. He is the god of the ego, of light, youth, purity, reasonableness, order, discipline, and balance. Perhaps the most characteristic maxim of the Apollonian way is the one that Socrates adopted from the oracle at Delphi as the basis of a philosophy of life—"Know thyself!" Know thyself to be a man, to be limited in time and space; above all do not commit the folly of *hubris,* do not in pride presume to exceed the limits of mortality and aspire to the conditions of the gods.

Wisdom, in the Apollonian tradition, consists of learning the rules and boundaries and in distinguishing with clarity between that which belongs to mortality and that which is immortal, between the knowable and the unknowable, the possible and the impossible, man and God, I and thou, mine and yours. The happy man, having learned the proper limits of humanity, follows the way of moderation and seeks to govern the rebellious forces of the senses and the wayward imagination by the imposition of discipline. The psyche of man is a commonwealth which the wise man will subject to the rule of reason. One might well see in Plato's figure of the Demiurge one model for the Apollonian view of man.

Like the architect of the universe, man also must be a craftsman, a fabricator (*homo faber*) who grasps the ideal of reason and by force of will imposes it upon the recalcitrant and chaotic givenness of life. Man shares with the gods the responsibility for creating a cosmos in which reason and order prevail. The rule of law is the path of wisdom. Man must distinguish between the good and the evil, the permissible and the impermissible; and then, as a citizen in a commonwealth under law, must take the responsibility for tailoring his inner and outer life to conform to what is required, to the laws governing nature, society, the psyche, and the relationship between God and man. Whatever impulses, desires, or actions run counter to the order necessary to a harmonious commonwealth must be repressed.

The Apollonian way has come to dominate Western culture. Science and technology rest upon distinguishing, clarifying, and gaining controlling knowledge over the environment. The world of science is the realm of law and regularity where personal desires and impulses are disciplined and brought into conformity to the objective and verifiable modes of thought of the scientific community. Western political and psychological organization also tends to stress private property, individual responsibility, and the unique identity of the individual. We have come to see man as an atom living in a society of atoms cut off both from the natural order below and the "super-natural" order above.

The Apollonian organization of modern life is visible as one flies across the United States or any Western country. Where man is, order is obvious. The geometric patterns which we impose on our fields and cities reveal our passion for neat boundaries, for the discipline of ownership, for distinguishing between my possessions and yours. Our laws which stress individual responsibility and guilt show that we organize psychic space in the same way we structure physical space. Guilt before the law implies that one is in *full possession* of the personal faculties which make for responsibility.

The dominance of the Apollonian way has been especially evident in theology. Western theology has always been strongly theistic in its doctrine of God. God is *a* being, transcendent and separate from his creation; he must not be confused with the world or with any part of the world. Both Kierkegaard and Barth are typically Apollonian in their insistence that we must recognize "an absolute qualitative distinction between time and eternity," between man and God. God must keep his boundaries sacrosanct, and the theologian as the explicator of his revelation must be jealous to destroy any theology which suggests that anything finite can mingle with God. Pantheism and mysticism are theologically suspect, as both Niebuhr and Brunner have argued, because they teach an unseemly confusion of God and the natural order, either as God becomes wholly incarnate in the world in pantheism, or as man finds a point of identity with God in his own soul in mysticism.

The Apollonian God is a jealous God. Those who would trespass on his omnipotent and transcendent glory must be reminded that "good fences make good neighbors." God alone can overcome the distance between himself and everything finite, and because he is a God of love he has chosen to leave his isolation and reveal himself to man in special places and times. In certain "mighty acts," such as the exodus of the Israelites from Egypt and the life, death, and resurrection of Jesus, God has chosen to be Emmanuel (God with us), to overcome the distance that otherwise separates the creatures from the Creator. The traditional theistic understanding of God's revelation in special acts, events, and persons has created a dichotomy between the sacred and the profane and has led to the segregation of the experience of the holy from the realm of the everyday.

One other aspect of a dominantly Apollonian theology must be noted. Nietzsche, Sartre, Altizer, and others have charged that an Apollonian concept of a creator God is necessarily repressive of human dignity and freedom. The God of theism is a creator who fabricates the world out of nothing through the instrument of his reason (*logos*). Like a good craftsman, God gives the world order, structure, rationality, and law. Man as a creature can find authentic life only by discovering God's plan for his life, only by actualizing the essence which he was potentially given in creation, only by obedience to the "will" of God.

Thus the creator God becomes the omniscient judge who rewards and punishes those who obey and those who rebel against the standards which he has programmed into his created order. As the one who oversees the whole course of history, God is the critical audience before whom the drama of life is played. (Billy Graham: "Remember when you read those sexy magazines—God is watching you.") Such a God may be merciful and forgiving, the eye which watches may be kindly, but he is responsible for the "oughts," he is the definer of what human life should be. Man is authentic in obedience, not in self-creation. Increasingly modern man has felt that he must rebel against such a God and assert his right to be for himself, to create his own oughts, to define for himself the nature of good and evil. This rebellion has been carried on with the help of Dionysus, to whom we now turn.

The Dionysian Way

Dionysus was a strange and wild god, an import both to the Greek countryside and the Greek spirit. He seems to have originated in Thrace, where he was a god of fertility and the energy of nature. On Greek soil he became associated with wine as well as with the metamorphosis which is symbolized in the cycle of the seasons. The worship of Dionysus was literally enthusiastic; it involved ecstasy, license, revelry, and direct participation by eating in the life of the dying and reborn god. In the ecstasy induced by wine and dancing the worshipers lost their own personalities and were merged with Dionysus. Thus the boundaries separating man, nature, and the divine were erased.

The essence of the Dionysian way is that it dares the extreme and hence leads to a form of consciousness which is alien to the law-abiding and mean-regarding character of the Apollonian mind. The Dionysian way exalts ecstasy over order, the id over the ego, being possessed over a possessive orientation, the creative chaos of freedom over the security of inherited patterns of social and psychological organization, and divine madness over repressed sanity. As Nietzsche pointed out in his study of the Apollonian and Dionysian types, it is Prometheus who is the model of the Dionysian way. Prometheus transgressed the boundaries of *hubris* in stealing the fire from the gods and was, therefore, condemned to punishment. The hard lesson he teaches is: "Man's highest good must be bought with a crime and paid for by the flood of grief and suffering which the offended divinities visit upon the human race in its noble ambition." [1]

Both the Genesis myth and Freud's mythology teach the same lesson: man becomes man only by breaking the laws which would refuse him the personal knowledge of good and evil, only by "killing the father," the source of authority and power, who would keep him forever in a state of childhood and dependence. Only in abolishing the "law," in denying any authority that dictates what he must become, does man become free.

Wisdom in the Dionysian tradition consists of continuing openness to the diverse and sometimes contradictory streams that flow through the depths of man. Man is not a property whose boundaries must be guarded against the intrusion of chaos by the watchful eye of the ego and its symbolically masked agents, but it is a nexus (Whitehead), a field of awareness where all dimensions of reality converge. The boundaries are created by the possessive instinct, by the cultural ideologies which sacri-

---

[1] Friedrich Nietzsche, *The Birth of Tragedy* (New York: Doubleday, 1956), p. 64.

fire vividness to security and ecstasy to order. In yielding to possession by the god, one is inhabited by a holy power that informs all life, and the boundaries are broken down between I and thou, man and nature, man and God, ego and id.

The self exists by its mystical participation in the power of being, which is in all things. Once the boundaries of the ego are broken down, the self is understood not so much as a substance that has its own resident source of power but as one focus of a universal power, taking, for the moment, the form of an individual man. Nietzsche has spoken of the Dionysian way as one in which the principle of individuation is lost:

Not only does the bond between man and man come to be forged once more by the magic of the Dionysiac rite, but nature itself, long alienated or sub-jugated, rises again to celebrate the reconciliation with her prodigal son, man. The earth offers its gifts voluntarily, and the savage beasts of the mountain and desert approach in peace. . . . Now the slave emerges as a freeman; all the rigid, hostile walls which either necessity or despotism has erected between men are shattered. Now that the gospel of universal harmony is sounded, each individual becomes not only reconciled to his fellow but actually at one with him—as though the veil of Maya had been torn apart and there remained only shreds floating before the vision of mystical Oneness. Man now expresses himself through song and dance as the member of a higher community; he has forgotten how to walk, how to speak, and is on the brink of taking wings as he dances.
Each of his gestures betokens enchantment; through him sounds a super-natural power, the same power which makes the animals speak and the earth render up milk and honey. He feels himself to be godlike and strides with the same elation and ecstasy as the gods he has seen in his dreams. No longer the *artist*, he has himself become *a work of art;* the productive power of the whole universe is now manifest in his transport, to the glorious satisfaction of the primordial One. . . .[2]

This loss of individuality, which is at the heart of the Dionysian way, has been expressed by modern thinkers in diverse terminology. Heidegger makes a complete analysis of the human condition without using the word "man." Man becomes *dasein*, "being there," an instance of Being, not a hermetic substance with an autonomous power of being. Norman O. Brown understands authentic life as requiring the death of the ego and a passivity by which *we are lived,* inhabited.

The *id* is instinct; that Dionysian "cauldron of seething excitement," a sea of energy out of which the ego emerges like an island. The term *"id"*—"it"— taken from Nietzsche (via Groddeck), is based on the intuition that the conduct through life of what we call our ego is essentially passive; it is not so much we who live as that we are lived, by unknown forces. The reality is instinct, and instinct is impersonal energy, an "it" who lives in us. I live, yet not I, but it lives in me; as in creation, *fiat.* Let it be; no "I" but an it. The "I-Thou" relationship is still a relation to Satan; the old Adversary; the Accuser; to whom we are responsible; or old Nobodaddy in the garden, calling Adam, where art thou? Let there be no one to answer to.[3]

[2] Ibid., p. 24.
[3] Norman O. Brown, *Love's Body* (New York: Random House, 1966), p. 88.

Alan Watts, drawing on the insights of Zen and Eastern mysticism, makes substantially the same point as Brown. The authentic life, which Buddhism has spoken of as *nirvana*, involves losing the illusion of the ego as a separate agent.

Nirvana is a radical transformation of how it feels to be alive: it feels as if everything were myself, or as if everything—including "my" thoughts and actions—were happening of itself. There are still efforts, choices, and decisions, but not in the sense that "I *make* them"; they arise of themselves in relation to circumstances.[4]

If the more characteristic models for the Apollonian way are the activities of fabrication (God making the world in conformity with his *Logos*, man making himself in the image of some ideal) and legislation (God and man projecting laws which hold chaos in check and allow community), the model for the Dionysian way is the dance. Life is flux, movement, a dynamic power which assumes form for a moment and then changes. There is no end-point, no complete product. In the strict sense of the word there can be no integrity (a state of being complete, whole, unbroken) of individual life. Everything is a fraction, incomplete without its counterpart.

In the dance of life, male and female, work and play, creativity and fallowness, day and night, life and death belong together in a *rhythmic* unity. Identity is in movement, in the economy of fractions which create a community in diversity. Authentic thought is, as Nietzsche said, thought which dances. Kazantzakis' figure of Zorba the Greek might well be taken as a concrete illustration of the Dionysian way and of the centrality of dance as an organizing metaphor for life. Zorba dances when the joy or the tragedy of life overflows the capacity of his words.

Two other metaphors are also frequently used to characterize the Dionysian way: fire and war. Fire, like a dance, is always moving and consuming what it touches; life is not being but becoming, not substance but process, as Heraclitus said at the beginning of Western philosophy and as Hegel and Whitehead have reminded us more recently. Fire and dance are also war, because in the flux of experience the opposites belong together. Life is dialectic, hence thesis and antithesis are bound together in conflict. True warfare, like dance, like sex, like contest (*agon*), requires friendly enemies, requires the love of the enemy. Human communication at its best is, as Jaspers has said, "loving combat." We wrestle together in dialogue (which is polite warfare) in order that the whole truth may emerge from the incomplete and fractured individual perspectives.

The Dionysian way is one of iconoclasm or of what might be called "muraloclasm" (breaking down the walls). In destroying the traditional boundaries and limits that inform our accepted notions of personality and society, the Dionysian way flirts with madness. As psychoanalysis has

[4] Alan Watts, *Psychotherapy East and West* (New York: Mentor Books, 1966), p. 60.

demonstrated, there is at the depths of every person a wilderness, a chaos never domesticated by the "Identity" we assume or the "personality" we put on "to meet the faces that we meet." The Dionysian wisdom is that we must immerse ourselves in this wilderness, which we usually repress and know only in dreams, daydreams (both brief psychotic episodes), and in the cultivated symbols of art and religion. The source of the power for vivid life lies locked in the unconscious. To be vital we must risk madness, as Zorba the Greek points out in his criticism of the life style of his Apollonian "Boss."

"No, you're not free," he said. "The string you're tied to is perhaps longer than other people's. That's all. You're on a longer piece of string, boss; you come and go, and think you're free, but you never cut the string in two. It's difficult, boss, very difficult. You need a touch of folly to do that; folly, d'you see? You have to risk everything! But you've got such a strong head, it'll always get the better of you. A man's head is like a grocer; it keeps accounts: I've paid so much and earned so much and that means a profit of this much or a loss of that much! The head's a careful little shopkeeper; it never risks all it has, always keeps something in reserve. It never breaks the string. Ah no! It hangs on tight to it, the bastard! If the string slips out of its grasp, the head, poor devil, is lost, finished! But if a man doesn't break the string, tell me what flavor is left in life? The flavor of camomile, weak camomile tea. Nothing like rum—that makes you see life inside out!" [5]

Norman Brown gives the same speech as Zorba, changing only the rhetoric:

Dionysus, the mad god, breaks down the boundaries; releases the prisoners; abolishes repression; and abolishes the *principium individuationis*, substituting for it the unity of man and the unity of man with nature. In this age of schizophrenia, with atom, the individual self, the boundaries disintegrating, there is, for those who would save our souls, the ego-psychologists, "The Problem of Identity." But the breakdown is to be made into a breakthrough; as Conrad said, in the destructive element immerse. The soul that we call our own is not a real one. The solution to the problem of identity is, get lost. Or as it says in the New Testament: "He that findeth his own psyche shall lose it, and he that loseth his psyche for my sake shall find it." [6]

We are here at the heart of the Dionysian view of man. And a problematic heart it is! If the boundaries established by the ego are to be broken down in order that direct participation in the divine power which pervades all may be experienced, what of the self who remains the focus of experience? The Dionysian way has never been able to offer an adequate doctrine of the person. Norman Brown and Alan Watts both make frequent use of the Buddhist idea of no-self. Once the self strips off those items of its identity which are accumulated from the repressive demands of parents and culture, from the defense mechanisms which insist upon

[5] Nikos Kazantzakis, *Zorba the Greek* (New York: Simon & Schuster, 1965), p. 300.
[6] Brown, op. cit., p. 116.

uniqueness and separateness, there is no ego left, no unique identity which distinguishes one man from another.

Our illusions of uniqueness and separateness arise out of our internalization of masks (personalities) and models. Our ego is a theater, and it is the masks we wear and the roles we feel compelled to play that separate us. Once the masks drop and the performance before the audience of the introjected parental figures—and others from whom approval is necessary—ceases, there is no more ego, no more internal theater, no defense mechanisms. There remains only a perceiving mind that now realizes its oneness with all things.

By way of criticism we must insist that while it is evident from the therapeutic success of the psychoanalytic method that psychic health demands openness to the unconscious, to the repressed awareness of the totality of experience, it is equally evident that some principle of identity or selfhood is necessary for authentic and vivid life. When Norman Brown advocates schizophrenia as the divine madness appropriate to the Dionysian way of life, he ignores a crucial distinction between garden variety insanity and that divine madness which is the essence of creativity and joy. There is a vast difference between a schizophrenic who has no ego strong enough to screen the chaotic intrusions from the unconscious, and hence is submerged in a state of chaos in which there is neither clarity nor joy, and the person who has learned to be open to the depths of emotion and feeling and to the whole range of symbolism which lies beneath the surface of daily preoccupations. The schizophrenic has no person; he is lacking in the unity and the sense of limits which are necessary to even minimal functioning in a social context. The healed schizophrenic, if we may use that term for the Dionysian type of personality organization, is aware of the glory and horror of being human. He knows that the difference between himself and the murderer is only that he dreams what the murderer does, as well as what the saint does. He is aware of the diverse possibilities which exist within himself, of the underworld of hatred and the overworld of dreams and ideals, of the hope and the despair, of the child that remains within. Yet the healed schizophrenic is also in touch with some principle of unity within himself. Call this principle of unity the self, the person, or whatever, but unity there must be if we are to distinguish between that insanity in which there is no transcendence but only tragedy and that divine madness in which the individual knows himself to be a part of that unifying power which binds together the kaleidoscope of reality.

My suggestion is that we call the Dionysian form of consciousness in which there is tolerance of the plurality within the self *inclusive self-consciousness,* as distinguished from the Apollonian *exclusive ego-consciousness* in which the ego is felt as a sensitive enclosure whose boundaries must be protected from all that is alien or strange. Inclusive self-consciousness is, in Marcel's terms, available (*disponiblé*); it keeps open house for strange visitors from far and near without being threatened by the new, the unexpected, or the disorienting. The authentic Dionysian consciousness prefers astonishment to possession; wonder is its rule of life, its charter of organization.

The principle of organization that gives unity to the inclusive self-consciousness of the Dionysian person is the rhythmic oscillation between the formation of models or self-images and iconoclasm. The authentic self continually sets boundaries and limits by its introjection of ideals and images of what it is and what it would like to be and then it destroys these boundaries as experience overflows them. Psychological and spiritual health does not consist in having no self but in keeping the process of self-formation flowing, of continually enlarging the images by which we understand ourselves and our world. In this way the Dionysian self is always in process of becoming more open, more wondering, more permissive of that strangeness and novelty which renews the sense of limitless possibilities and increases the capacity to hope. Dionysian man is *homo viator* (Marcel), a pilgrim, a gypsy, a dancer. His security lies in learning to be at home on the road. By contrast Apollonian man is a homesteader who stakes out a territory with defined limits and possibilities and finds his security in the defense of this territory. He lives by what Robert Ardrey called "the territorial imperative."

DIONYSIAN THEOLOGY

Just as the Apollonian way had an appropriate theological expression in traditional Western theism, the Dionysian way also has its characteristic understanding of God, revelation, and the style of the religious life.

The symbol of dance best captures the unique emphasis of a Dionysian theology's idea of God. Nietzsche's statement may serve as a starting point.

I would believe only in a god who could dance. And when I saw my devil I found him serious, thorough, profound, and solemn: it was the spirit of gravity—through him all things fall.
Not by wrath does one kill but by laughter. Come, let us kill the spirit of gravity!
I have learned to walk: ever since I let myself run.
I have learned to fly: ever since, I do not want to be pushed before moving along.
Now I am light, now I fly, now I see myself beneath myself, now a god dances through me.[7]

In order to understand the significance of the symbol of a dancing God we must go back briefly to the Apollonian theological tradition. Western theology, until modern times, has never been free of the Aristotelian con-

---

[7] Friedrich Nietzsche, *Thus Spake Zarathustra*, in Walter Kaufmann, *The Portable Nietzsche* (New York: Viking Press, 1954), p. 153.

cept of God as the Unmoved Mover. God has been a giver, never a receiver, a frigid God to whom no value accrued from the world. Even where Christian theology has spoken of God's death upon the cross, it has never allowed suffering, change, or time to be taken into the life of God himself. When the Apollonian tradition has allowed movement within God it was not because he was understood as being intimately related to the chaotic and tragic flux of time, but because he was trinitarian and thus, being a plenum of perfection and reality, had internal relations between the "persons" of the Godhead.

God's self-sufficient perfection has precluded his passionate involvement in the movement and suffering that is human history. Many theological dodges have been thought up to allow God both the static perfection of his eternal being and the semblance of a relation to time, but always the Apollonian tradition has come out on the side of the perfection, aseity, and impassability of God. As the Methodist discipline reminds us: God is without "body, parts, or passions." That which is perfect cannot change, that which suffers cannot be God; hence God is ultimately beyond change and suffering; he is an unmoved mover; he does not dance; he is substance not process.

Modern theology has increasingly rejected the notion of an unmoved mover, of a God in whom there is "no shadow of change," and has come to speak of a dancing God, a God whose perfection is in process, whose life is involved in the relativities of relationship. A static God is dead. Under the impact of scientific categories which show that all "substance" is process, that mass is energy, that being is relationship, theology has rejected the Apollonian God of defined boundaries and self-sufficient life; the God whose sole activity was knowing himself, whose mode of creation was through the instrumentality of *logos*, whose "ideas" formed the essence of all things. The thinkers associated with this change are many. Other than those we have mentioned as seeking to create a Dionysian theology, process theologians such as Whitehead and Hartshorne have made the most substantial contribution.

A God who is changed and relativized by a real relationship with the moving face of human history is no longer the theistic God of Apollonian theology. A Dionysian theology tends in the direction of pantheism or panentheism. God is not a being but Being itself, or the ground of being. Whether God transcends the world is a moot question (this being the issue between pantheism and panentheism), but the immanence of God is stressed. God is not a strange being enthroned beyond time and space in unchangeable glory who occasionally condescends to invade our planet by means of a mighty act or an incarnation. God is the creative power at the heart of all things. As the Oryxhynchus Papyrus reports Jesus as saying: "Wherever there are two, they are not without God; and where there is one alone I say I am with him. Lift up the stone and there shalt thou find me; cleave the wood, and I am there."

One of the reasons a Dionysian theology finds it necessary to reject the traditional Apollonian concept of a monarchical God isolated in eternity and revealed primarily in an inaccessible past (and these ideas logically involve each other, for it is only a distant God who must occasionally make himself known in an otherwise secular world by way of mighty acts) is that such a theology is inevitably both *repressive* and *regressive.* Before the face of the God who is the Absolute Monarch of the Universe man always stands under scrutiny and judgment. Nietzsche, Sartre, Brown, and Altizer have all stressed the repressive nature of the traditional concept of God. Before the omniscient eye we are reduced to objects who may only obey or rebel; we become artifacts of a Cosmic Artisan devoid of any real freedom to give meaning to our own lives. Life becomes a performance before an all-seeing spectator. As Norman Brown notes, such a transcendent judge is really the projection of the image of the father, the superego ideal made absolute. As long as such an idea of God is held:

the distinction between public and private disappears; we are on stage at all times. Christianity will not be rid of the performance principle, will not become a pure principle of invisible grace, until it gets rid of the specter of the Father, Old Nobodaddy, the watching institution.[8]

The God who is really for man must genuinely be *with* him, he must leave the boundaries of his own isolation (always a sign of defensive weakness) and incarnate himself in the movement of human history. Altizer, using language that is still Christocentric, finds the unique meaning of Christian theology in its radical incarnational principle. He can go so far as to insist that the old God is dead and therefore the transcendent ground of repression and guilt is broken. Christianity is the good news that the distant and transcendent God who showed himself only in the sacred preserve of some past time is dead.

The Christian Word appears in neither a primordial nor an eternal form; for it is an incarnate Word, a Word that is real only to the extent that it becomes one with human flesh. If we are to preserve the uniqueness of the Christian Word, we cannot understand the Incarnation as a final and once-and-for-all event of the past. On the contrary, the Incarnation must be conceived as an active and forward-moving proceess, a process that even now is making all things new. . . .[9]

A Dionysian theology says that a man must lose his life if he is to gain it, that the defensiveness of the ego must give way to inclusive self-consciousness that acknowledges the communion of the self with the whole world, that the rigid boundaries of our "unique" personalities are the product of a possessive and repressive orientation to life. Such a theology cannot worship a God who is understood on the model of that isolated

[8] Brown, op. cit., p. 106.
[9] Thomas Altizer, *The Gospel of Christian Atheism* (Philadelphia: Westminster Press, 1966), p. 40.

life which in man arises out of weakness and fear. God is God in giving himself, in losing his boundaries, in entering into the dance of history.

If God loses himself in the dance of history the radical question of the appropriateness of retaining "God" language arises. If the boundaries separating God, nature, and man are abolished does it make any sense to continue speaking of God? The Dionysian "God" is not a transcendent object or person to be known by the inbreaking of revelation at certain unique points, but rather the power of "the creative good" (Wieman) or the "power of being" in all things (Tillich). The justification for continuing to speak about God is pragmatic and epistemological. Man must have symbols which grasp and articulate his intuition of what he experiences as ultimate. The symbols are always objectifying but the reality they point to overflows all conceptual boundaries. "God" language functions to focus celebration and adoration on those sacred dimensions of reality which are known in the ecstatic experiences of love, creativity, hope, joy, and thanksgiving.

What is ultimately the case about the whole of reality is beyond human powers of perception. At best man can only yield to those experiences in which he senses the presence of a power which urges human life toward a richer harmony. If he names this power "God" it is because he confesses that the power by which life is sustained and invited toward wholeness is no human creation and abides and remains steadfast even in a world where death does have dominion over every individual. To speak of God is to safeguard man against the pathetic arrogance which presumes to possess this power rather than be possessed by it.

In a Dionysian theology, revelation, which is merely man's awareness of the presence of the holy, is not limited either to special events in some past history of salvation or to any special realm of the sacred. Reality as a whole is sacramental. Any tree, person, or event may become transparent to the holy power that informs every living thing. Revelation is always new; it is a process not a product. The world is the vocabulary of God. In opening ourselves to life as a gift to be enjoyed and utilized with responsibility, we may find that which makes us whole, which undergrids our lives with the certainty of dignity and value at any point in our experience.

A Dionysian view or revelation moves in what Tillich called a radically "theonomous" direction. The ordinary is seen as holy. There are no special times and places, no privileged sections of history. Revelation is homogenized into the quotidian; it is found in the ordinary rather than the *extra*ordinary. Van Gogh's paintings reveal clearly the Dionysian vision of the reality of the everyday permeated with the presence of the holy. In a letter he stated:

I can very well do without God, both in my life and my painting, but I cannot, ill as I am, do without something which is greater than I, which is my life—the power to create. . . . And in a picture I want to say something comforting as music is comforting. I want to paint men and women with that something

of the eternal which the halo used to symbolize, and which we seek to give by
the actual radiance and vibration of our colorings.[10]

In the same spirit Norman Brown writes:

Dionysus calls us outdoors. . . . Out of the temple made with hands; out of
the ark of the book; out of the cave of the law; out of the belly of the letter.
The first tabernacle in Jerusalem; the second tabernacle the universal Church;
the third tabernacle the open sky.[11]

The Dionysian way understands theological language as arising out
of those experiences which are dense with meaning and value. In love,
trust, wonder, hope, and other such experiences having what Marcel
called "ontological weight," we find life a holy gift and identify its source
as "God." Theological language is a way of giving form to those wondering moments when we find ourselves possessed by a power which makes
life whole and holy. The language is merely a handle we use to understand and to maintain ourselves in a condition of openness to this power.
As such it must always be a means, an instrument which is abandoned
when it ceases to function creatively. A living theology demands a constant process of iconoclasm and renaming of the holy. There are no holy
words, not even the word God.

A valid theology constantly orders and extrapolates the implications of
the experience of that power of being which gives meaning and value to
life. The traditional symbols of theology are not a correct system of language to be memorized but a museum of models or linguistic maps of the
way in which the religious intuition has been articulated in the past.
Loyalty to the tradition does not mean that we accept the adequacy of
past models and maps; only that we learn from them the principles of
theological mapmaking. Theological language is a way of handling experiences, of clarifying and orienting ourselves. It is a creation of man
and hence it is a human responsibility to make the language function in a
way which maximizes the creative potentials of the human community.

To admit that theological language is a projection, a creation of man,
is neither to deny that it makes cognitive claims concerning God nor is it
to reduce theology to an illusion. It is merely to admit that the sources of
all that is, the holy power which we apprehend as the foundation of
human dignity and meaning, can only be conceived in human terms, in
stories, myths, symbols. The God from whom human life is a gift can
never be adequately named, hence we are responsible at a minimum to be
flexible in our adherence to symbols for the ultimate, lest our allegiance
turn into idolatry and we give our loyalty to symbols which have become
repressive.

Theologically as well as psychologically man must remain a pilgrim, a
wayfarer; epistemologically and linguistically he is *homo viator*. Recognizing the relativity of all his modes of perceiving and articulating, the

---

[10] Quoted in Herbert Read, *The Meaning of Art* (London: Faber & Faber), p. 206.
[11] Brown, op. cit., p. 229.

religious man must strike his theological tents and move on when the
waters of life dry up where there has traditionally been an oasis. Man
must give names to the ultimate if he is to possess and understand his
experience, but he must be willing to undergo the painful process of
iconoclasm and reformation.

Perhaps the real sin against the holy spirit is the refusal to move to new
linguistic and institutional forms that keep things verdant when the old
names and organizations have become parched and devoid of life. A
living theology is a dance, the rhythmic oscillation between the experiences of the nameless power that gives life and invites us to wholeness
and the domestication of that power through language and institutions.
The same principle which governs the organization of inclusive self-
consciousness governs an authentic Dionysian theology—there must be
continual reformation of the images and models by which we understand
and give shape to our lives.

Apollonian theology, with its assumption that the decisive revelation of
God took place in the past, has always been oriented around the *hearing*
of the word in which the memory and witness of God's mighty acts is
preserved. Tradition, which is the codified memory of the sacred time of
the distant God's inbreaking in history, is the instrument of revelation;
the ear is the organ of religious perception. By contrast, a Dionysian
theology assumes that the decisive revelation of God's presence in history
takes place in the present. God is perceived as the source of the gift of
life and the power which invites us toward wholeness in every present
moment of experience.

Tradition is illustration; the memory of God's acts that is preserved in
the literature and discourse of the theological community (the church or
synagogue) is important to the present-day believer only to the extent
that it helps him interpret *his own personal and social history* as revelatory, as undergirded by that which assures dignity and meaning to human
existence. This means that Dionysian theology is oriented toward the *eye*,
the senses, and the body. It seeks the fullest possible participation in the
present moment; it urges that we taste and see and feel the world, that
we penetrate to the abiding dimensions of meaning and value that are
within the immediate moment of experience.

In assuming that the present moment is the time of revelation we
become involved in a theology of affection and emotion. Our basic feelings of wonder or possession, trust or mistrust, expectation or boredom,
hope or despair, nostalgia or satiety, love or fear, potency or impotency
are far more fundamental to the way we actually position ourselves in
and experience our world than the linguistic systems and ideas that we
articulate. A God whose revelation *was* in the flesh but for the contemporary believer primarily *is* in the Word will be absent from the substance
of human life and present only in its rationalizations and ideologies. To
the degree that our primarily religious perception is a matter of memory,
God is dead. If we are unable to identify any power which we may call

God in our present feelings and experience then we had best let God language be "antiqued" and preserved for its decorative value.

The God of past mighty acts cannot fill our need for a sanctifying power which makes us whole in the present moment. To isolate God either in transcendence or in past history is to destroy him. Since that is what most western theology has done it is little wonder that the secret has been let out—"God is Dead." Either we learn how to use our theological language to identify the action of God in the dynamics of present experience or we capitulate. The dominant emphasis of contemporary theology on the revelation of the transcendent God in special mighty acts in history is built upon an empty slogan. There is no such thing as history divorced from nature or experience. All theology has arisen from man's effort to interpret the world given to him in experience. "God" and "act of God" are interpretations of experience.

The real question separating Apollonian and Dionysian theologies is "In whose experience is the holy normatively revealed for our time? In our forefathers or our own?" A Dionysian theology proclaims that we must return to basic experiences and attitudes, such as trust, love, wonder, joy, sorrow, hope, and despair, in order that we may learn again how to speak with integrity about what is holy and sacred. It may well be that in recovering a wondering openness to our total experience we may discover that ours is a holy place, that the events of our own personal histories tell a story of promise and fulfillment and give testimony to the presence of a power within human history which makes for wholeness and freedom.

To accept the Dionysian invitation to the dance is not without danger. Revolution is a radical solution. It only remains to consider whether in this time of psychological and political crisis anything less than a radical solution is adequate. Should we by foolishness or courage discover that we may celebrate the holiness of life in any time and place, we might be induced to question that other form of madness which has brought us to the edge of moral and political nihilism—the unquestioned Apollonian assumption that impulse must be repressed and revolution be dealt with by violence, even at the cost of napalmed innocence. If out of timidity or the desire for security we refuse the ecstasy of allowing our ideas, our bodies and our institutions to dance, perhaps there remains only that form of insanity which expends its substance in defending some absolute qualitative distinction between U.S. defense of freedom and communist aggression or in insisting on some 17th parallel dividing time from eternity.

Summary

Without denying that an adequate philosophy or theology will partake of both Apollonian and Dionysian elements, we have maintained that our time is predominantly in need of recovering the Dionysian element. The respective emphases of these two ways may be summarized:

The Apollonian Way	*The Dionysian Way*
Man-the-maker, fabricator, molder and manipulator of environment.	Man-the-dancer responding to the givenness of life in its multiplicity.
Domination of the ego, emphasis upon erecting boundaries, giving form, intellectual and material possession. The will and the intellect are central.	Domination of the id. Emphasis upon destroying boundaries, exploration of diversity, chaos, vitality. Feeling and sensation are central.
Value is created by action. Authentic life is aggressive, "masculine," active.	Value is discovered, it is given as we encounter the world in wonder. Authentic life involves passivity, accepting, responding.

As translated into theological idiom the two ways yield an emphasis upon:

Theism or deism. God is *a* being encountered as a Thou, revealing himself in unique acts in history.	Pantheism or Panentheism. God is being itself, the encompassing, the power of being in all, known in the density of experiences in which value is discovered.
A theology of the Word, work, action, speaking, willing, thinking, consciousness, order.	A theology of the spirit, leisure, play, listening, waiting, feeling, chaos, the unconscious.

RELIGION AND PEAK-EXPERIENCES

Abraham Maslow

ABRAHAM H. MASLOW was Professor of Psychology at Brandeis University until his death in 1970. He was the author of many articles and books, see especially *Religions, Values and Peak-Experiences* (1964).

THE "CORE-RELIGIOUS," OR "TRANSCENDENT," EXPERIENCE

The very beginning, the intrinsic core, the essence, the universal nucleus of every known high religion (unless Confucianism is also called a religion) has been the private, lonely, personal illumination, revelation, or ecstasy of some acutely sensitive prophet or seer. The high religions call themselves revealed religions and each of them tends to rest its validity, its function, and its right to exist on the codification and the communication of this original mystic experience or revelation from the lonely prophet to the mass of human beings in general.

But it has recently begun to appear that these "revelations" or mystical illuminations can be subsumed under the head of the "peak-experiences" or "ecstasies" or "transcendent" experiences which are now being eagerly investigated by many psychologists. That is to say, it is very likely, indeed almost certain, that these older reports, phrased in terms of supernatural revelation, were, in fact, perfectly natural, human peak-experiences of the kind that can easily be examined today, which, however, were phrased in terms of whatever conceptual, cultural, and linguistic framework the particular seer had available in his time (Laski).

In a word, we can study today what happened in the past and was then explainable in supernatural terms only. By so doing, we are enabled to examine religion in all its facets and in all its meanings in a way that makes it a part of science rather than something outside and exclusive of it.

Also this kind of study leads us to another very plausible hypothesis: to the extent that all mystical or peak-experiences are the same in their essence and always have been the same, all religions are the same in their essence and always have been the same. They should, therefore, come to agree in principle on teaching that which is common to all of them, i.e., whatever it is that peak-experiences teach in common (whatever is *different* about these illuminations can fairly be taken to be localisms both in time and space, and are, therefore, peripheral, expendable, not essential). This something common, this something which is left over after we peel away all the localisms, all the accidents of particular languages or particular philosophies, all the ethnocentric phrasings, all those elements which are *not* common, we may call the "core-religious experience" or the "transcendent experience."

To understand this better, we must differentiate the prophets in general from the organizers or legalists in general as (abstracted) types. . . . (I admit that the use of pure, extreme types which do not really exist can come close to the edge of caricature; nevertheless, I think it will help all of us in thinking through the problem we are here concerned with.) The characteristic prophet is a lonely man who has discovered his truth about the world, the cosmos, ethics, God, and his own identity from within, from his own personal experiences, from what he would consider to be a revelation. Usually, perhaps always, the prophets of the high religions have had these experiences when they were alone.

Characteristically the abstraction-type of the legalist-ecclesiastic is the conserving organization man, an officer and arm of the organization, who is loyal to the structure of the organization which has been built up on the basis of the prophet's original revelation in order to make the revelation available to the masses. From everything we know about organizations, we may very well expect that people will become loyal to it, as well as to the original prophet and to his vision; or at least they will become loyal to the organization's version of the prophet's vision. I may go so far as to say that characteristically (and I mean not only the religious organizations but also parallel organizations like the Communist Party or like revolutionary groups) these organizations can be seen as a kind of punch card or IBM version of an original revelation or mystical experience or peak-experience to make it suitable for group use and for administrative convenience.

It will be helpful here to talk about a pilot investigation, still in its beginnings, of the people I have called non-peakers. In my first investigations, in collaboration with Gene Nameche, I used this word because I thought some people had peak-experiences and others did not. But as I gathered information, and as I became more skillful in asking questions, I found that a higher and higher percentage of my subjects began to report peak-experiences. I finally fell into the habit of expecting everyone to have peak-experiences and of being rather surprised if I ran across somebody who could report none at all. Because of this experience, I finally began to use the word "non-peaker" to describe, not the person who is unable to have peak-experiences, but rather the person who is afraid of them, who suppresses them, who denies them, who turns away from them, or who "forgets" them. My preliminary investigations of the reasons for these negative reactions to peak-experiences have led me to some (unconfirmed) impressions about why certain kinds of people renounce their peak-experiences.

Any person whose character structure (or Weltanschauung, or way of life) forces him to try to be extremely or completely rational or "materialistic" or mechanistic tends to become a non-peaker. That is, such a view of life tends to make the person regard his peak- and transcendent experiences as a kind of insanity, a complete loss of control, a sense of being overwhelmed by irrational emotions, etc. The person who is afraid of going insane and who is, therefore, desperately hanging on to stability, control, reality, etc., seems to be frightened by peak-experiences and tends to fight them off. For the compulsive-obsessive person, who organizes his life around the denying and the controlling of emotion, the fear of being overwhelmed by an emotion (which is interpreted as a loss of control) is enough for him to mobilize all his stamping-out and defensive activities against the peak-experience. I have one instance of a very convinced Marxian who denied—that is, who turned away from—a legitimate peak-experience, finally classifying it as some kind of peculiar but unimportant thing that had happened but that had best be forgotten because this experience conflicted with her whole materialistic mechanistic philosophy of life. I have found a few non-peakers who were ultra-scientific, that is, who espoused the nineteenth-century conception of science as an unemotional or anti-emotional activity which was ruled entirely by logic and rationality and who thought anything which was not logical and rational had no respectable place in life. (I suspect also that extremely "practical," i.e., exclusively means-oriented, people will turn out to be non-peakers, since such experiences earn no money, bake no bread, and chop no wood. So also for extremely other-directed people, who scarcely know what is going on inside themselves. Perhaps also people who are reduced to the concrete à la Goldstein, etc. etc.) Finally, I should add that, in some cases, I could not come to any explanation for non-peaking.

If you will permit me to use this developing but not yet validated vocabulary, I may then say simply that the relationship between the prophet and the ecclesiastic, between the lonely mystic and the (perfectly extreme) religious-organization man may often be a relationship between peaker and non-peaker. Much theology, much verbal religion through history and throughout the world, can be considered to be the more or less vain efforts to put into communicable words and formulae, and into symbolic rituals and ceremonies, the original mystical experience of the original prophets. In a word, organized religion can be thought of as an effort to communicate peak-experiences to non-peakers, to teach them, to apply them, etc. Often, to make it more difficult, this job falls into the hands of non-peakers. On the whole we now would expect that this would be a vain effort, at least so far as much of mankind is concerned. The peak-experiences and their experiential reality ordinarily are not transmittable to non-peakers, at least not by words alone, and certainly not by non-peakers. What happens to many people, especially the ignorant, the uneducated, the naïve, is that they simply concretize all of the symbols, all of the words, all of the statues, all of the ceremonies, and by a process of functional autonomy make *them*, rather than the original revelation, into the sacred things and sacred activities. That is to say, this is simply a form of the idolatry (or fetishism) which has been the curse of every large religion. In idolatry the essential original meaning gets so lost in concretizations that these finally become hostile to the original mystical experiences, to mystics, and to prophets in general, that is, to the very people that we might call from our present point of view the truly religious people. Most religions have wound up denying and being antagonistic to the very ground upon which they were originally based.

If you look closely at the internal history of most of the world religions, you will find that each one very soon tends to divide into a left-wing and a right-wing, that is, into the peakers, the mystics, the transcenders, or the privately religious people, on the one hand, and, on the other, into those who concretize the religious symbols and metaphors, who worship little pieces of wood rather than what the objects stand for, those who take verbal formulas, literally, forgetting the original meaning of these words, and, perhaps most important, those who take the organization, the church, as primary and as more important than the prophet and his original revelations. These men, like many organization men who tend to rise to the top in any complex bureaucracy, tend to be non-peakers rather than peakers. Dostoevski's famous Grand Inquisitor passage, in his *Brothers Karamazov,* says this in a classical way.

This cleavage between the mystics and the legalists, if I may call them that, remains at best a kind of mutual tolerance, but it has happened in some churches that the rulers of the organization actually made a heresy out of the mystic experiences and persecuted the mystics themselves. This may be an old story in the history of religion, but I must point out that it is also an old story in other fields. For instance, we can certainly say today that professional philosophers tend to divide themselves into the same kind of characterologically based left-wing and right-wing. Most official, orthodox philosophers today are the equivalent of legalists who reject the problems and the data of transcendence as "meaningless." That is, they are positivists, atomists, analysts, concerned with means rather than with ends. They sharpen tools rather than discover truths. These people contrast sharply with another group of contemporary philosophers, the existentialists and the phenomenologists. These are the people who tend to fall back on experiencing as the primary datum from which everything starts.

. . . .

To summarize, it looks quite probable that the peak-experience may be the model of the religious revelation or the religious illumination or conversion which has played so great a role in the history of religions. But, because peak-experiences are in the natural world and because we can research with them and investigate them, and because our knowledge of such experiences is growing and may be confidently expected to grow in the future, we may now fairly hope to understand more about the big revelations, conversions, and illuminations upon which the high religions were founded.

(Not only this, but I may add a new possibility for scientific investigation of transcendence. In the last few years it has become quite clear that certain drugs called "psychedelic," especially LSD and psilocybin, give us some possibility of control in this realm of peak-experiences. It looks as if these drugs often produce peak-experiences in the right people under the right circumstances, so that perhaps we needn't wait for them to occur by good fortune. Perhaps we can actually produce a private personal peak-experience under observation and whenever we wish under religious or non-religious circumstances. We may then be able to study in its moment of birth the experience of illumination or revelation. Even more important, it may be that these drugs, and perhaps also hypnosis, could be used to produce a peak-experience, with core-religious revelation, in non-peakers, thus bridging the chasm between these two separated halves of mankind.)

To approach this whole discussion from another angle, in effect what I have been saying is that the evidence from the peak-experiences permits us to talk about the essential, the intrinsic, the basic, the most fundamental religious or transcendent experience as a totally private and personal one which can hardly be shared (except with other "peakers"). As a consequence, all the paraphernalia of organized religion—buildings and the like—are to the "peaker" secondary, peripheral, and of doubtful value in relation to the intrinsic and essential religious or transcendent experience. Perhaps they may even be very harmful in various ways. From the point of view of the peak-experiencer, each person has his own private religion, which he develops out of his own private revelations in which are revealed to him his own private myths and symbols, rituals and ceremonials, which may be of the profoundest meaning to him personally and yet completely idiosyncratic, i.e., of no meaning to anyone else. But to say it even more simply, each "peaker" discovers, develops, and retains his own religion.

In addition, what seems to be emerging from this new source of data is that this essential core-religious experience may be embedded either in a theistic, supernatural context or in a non-theistic context. This private religious experience is shared by all the great world religions including the atheistic ones like Buddhism, Taoism, Humanism, or Confucianism. As a matter of fact, I can go so far as to say that this instrisic core-experience is a meeting ground not only, let us say, for Christians and Jews and Mohammedans but also for priests and atheists, for communists and anti-communists, for conservatives and liberals, for artists and scientists, for men and for women, and for different constitutional types, that is to say, for athletes and for poets, for thinkers and for doers. I say this because our findings indicate that all or almost all people have or can have peak-experiences. Both men and women have peak-experiences, and all kinds of constitutional types have peak-experiences, but, although the content of the peak-experiences is approximately as I have described for all human beings, the situation or the trigger which sets off peak-experience, for instance in males and females, can be quite different. These experiences can come from different sources, but their content may be considered to be very similar. To sum it up, from this point of view, the two religions of mankind tend to be the peakers and the non-peakers, that is to say, those who have private, personal, transcendent, core-religious experiences easily and often and who accept them and make use of them, and, on the other hand, those who have never had them or who repress or suppress them and who, therefore, cannot make use of them for their personal therapy, personal growth, or personal fulfillment.

RELIGIOUS ASPECTS OF PEAK-EXPERIENCES

Practically everything that happens in the peak-experiences, naturalistic though they are, could be listed under the headings of religious happenings, or indeed have been in the past considered to be only religious experiences.

1. For instance, it is quite characteristic in peak-experiences that the whole universe is perceived as an integrated and unified whole. This is not as simple a happening as one might imagine from the bare words themselves. To have a clear perception (rather than a purely abstract and verbal philosophical acceptance) that the universe is all of a piece and that one has his place in it—one is a part of it, one belongs in it—can be so profound and shaking an experience that it can change the person's character and his Weltanschauung forever after. In my own experience I have two subjects who, because of such an experience, were totally, immediately, and permanently cured of (in one case) chronic anxiety neurosis and (in the other case) of strong obsessional thoughts of suicide.

This, of course, is a basic meaning of religious faith for many people. People who might otherwise lose their "faith" will hang onto it because it gives a meaningfulness to the universe, a unity, a single philosophical explanation which makes it all hang together. Many orthodoxly religious people would be so frightened by giving up the notion that the universe has integration, unity, and, therefore, meaningfulness (which is given to it by the fact that it was all created by God or ruled by Gor or *is* God) that the only alternative for them would be to see the universe as a totally unintegrated chaos.

2. In the cognition that comes in peak-experiences, characteristically the percept is exclusively and fully attended to. That is, there is tremendous concentration of a kind which does not normally occur. There is the truest and most total kind of visual perceiving or listening or feeling. Part of what this involves is a peculiar change which can best be described as non-evaluating, non-comparing, or non-judging cognition. That is to say, figure and ground are less sharply differentiated. Important and unimportant are also less sharply differentiated, i.e., there is a tendency for things to become equally important rather than to be ranged in a hierarchy from very important to quite unimportant. For instance, the mother examining in loving ecstasy her new-born infant may be enthralled by every single part of him, one part as much as another one, one little toenail as much as another little toenail, and be struck into a kind of religious awe in this way. This same kind of total, non-comparing acceptance of everything, as if everything were equally important, holds also for the perception of people. Thus it comes about that in peak-experience cognition a person is most easily seen per se, in himself, by himself, uniquely and idiosyncratically as if he were the sole member of his class. Of course, this is a very common aspect not only of religious experience but of most theologies as well, i.e., the person is unique, the person is sacred, one person in principle is worth as much as any other person, everyone is a child of God, etc.

3. The cognition of being (B-cognition) that occurs in peak-experiences tends to perceive external objects, the world, and individual people as

more detached from human concerns. Normally we perceive everything as relevant to human concerns and more particularly to our own private selfish concerns. In the peak-experiences, we become more detached, more objective, and are more able to perceive the world as if it were independent not only of the perceiver but even of human beings in general. The perceiver can more readily look upon nature as if it were there in itself and for itself, not simply as if it were a human playground put there for human purposes. He can more easily refrain from projecting human purposes upon it. In a word, he can see it in its own Being (as an end in itself) rather than as something to be used or something to be afraid of or something to wish for or to be reacted to in some other personal, human, self-centered way. That is to say, B-cognition, because it makes human irrelevance more possible, enables us thereby to see more truly the nature of the object in itself. This is a little like talking about god-like perception, superhuman perception. The peak-experience seems to lift us to greater than normal heights so that we can see and perceive in a higher than usual way. We become larger, greater, stronger, bigger, taller people and tend to perceive accordingly.

4. To say this in a different way, perception in the peak-experiences can be relatively ego-transcending, self-forgetful, egoless, unselfish. It can come closer to being unmotivated, impersonal, desireless, detached, not needing or wishing. Which is to say, that it becomes more object-centered than ego-centered. The perceptual experience can be more organized around the object itself as a centering point rather than being based upon the selfish ego. This means in turn that objects and people are more readily perceived as having independent reality of their own.

5. The peak-experience is felt as a self-validating, self-justifying moment which carries its own intrinsic value with it. It is felt to be a highly valuable—even uniquely valuable—experience, so great an experience sometimes that even to attempt to justify it takes away from its dignity and worth. As a matter of fact, so many people find this so great and high an experience that it justifies not only itself but even living itself. Peak-experiences can make life worthwhile by their occasional occurrence. They give meaning to life itself. They prove it to be worthwhile. To say this in a negative way, I would guess that peak-experiences help to prevent suicide.

6. Recognizing these experiences as end-experiences rather than as means-experiences makes another point. For one thing, it proves to the experiencer that there are ends in the world, that there are things or objects or experiences to yearn for which are worthwhile in themselves. This in itself is a refutation of the proposition that life and living is meaningless. In other words, peak-experiences are one part of the operational definition of the statement that "life is worthwhile" or "life is meaningful."

7. In the peak-experience there is a very characteristic disorientation in time and space, or even the lack of consciousness of time and space. Phrased positively, this is like experiencing universality and eternity.

Certainly we have here, in a very operational sense, a real and scientific meaning of "under the aspect of eternity." This kind of timelessness and spacelessness contrasts very sharply with normal experience. The person in the peak-experiences may feel a day passing as if it were minutes or also a minute so intensely lived that it might feel like a day or a year or an eternity even. He may also lose his consciousness of being located in a particular place.

8. The world seen in the peak-experiences is seen only as beautiful, good, desirable, worthwhile, etc. and is never experienced as evil or undesirable. The world is accepted. People will say that then they understand it. Most important of all for comparison with religious thinking is that somehow they become reconciled to evil. Evil itself is accepted and understood and seen in its proper place in the whole, as belonging there, as unavoidable, as necessary, and, therefore, as proper. Of course, the way in which I (and Laski also) gathered peak-experiences was by asking for reports of ecstasies and raptures, of the most blissful and perfect moments of life. Then, of course, life *would* look beautiful. And then all the foregoing might seem like discovering something that had been put in a priori. But observe that what I am talking about is the perception of evil, of pain, of disease, of death. In the peak-experiences, not only is the world seen as acceptable and beautiful, but, and this is what I am stressing, the bad things about life are accepted more totally than they are at other times. It is as if the peak-experience reconciled people to the presence of evil in the world.

9. Of course, this is another way of becoming "god-like." The gods who can contemplate and encompass the whole of being and who, therefore, understand it must see it as good, just, inevitable, and must see "evil" as a product of limited or selfish vision and understanding. If we could be god-like in this sense, then we, too, out of universal understanding would never blame or condemn or be disappointed or shocked. Our only possible emotions would be pity, charity, kindliness, perhaps sadness or amusement. But this is precisely the way in which self-actualizing people do at times react to the world, and in which all of us react in our peak-experiences.

10. Perhaps my most important finding was the discovery of what I am calling B-values or the intrinsic values of Being. When I asked the question, "How does the world look different in peak-experiences?", the hundreds of answers that I got could be boiled down to a quintessential list of characteristics which, though they overlap very much with one another can still be considered as separate for the sake of research. What is important for us in this context is that this list of the described characteristics of the world as it is perceived in our most perspicuous moments is about the same as what people through the ages have called eternal verities, or the spiritual values, or the highest values, or the religious values. What this says is that facts and values are not totally different from each other; under certain circumstances, they fuse. Most religions have either explicitly or by implication affirmed some relationship

or even an overlapping or fusion between facts and values. For instance, people not only existed but they were also sacred. The world was not only merely existent but it was also sacred.

11. B-cognition in the peak-experience is much more passive and receptive, much more humble, than normal perception is. It is much more ready to listen and much more able to hear.

12. In the peak-experience, such emotions as wonder, awe, reverence, humility, surrender, and even worship before the greatness of the experience are often reported. This may go so far as to involve thoughts of death in a peculiar way. Peak-experiences can be so wonderful that they can parallel the experience of dying, that is of an eager and happy dying. It is a kind of reconciliation and acceptance of death. Scientists have never considered as a scientific problem the question of the "good death"; but here in these experiences we discover a parallel to what has been considered to be the religious attitude toward death, i.e., humility or dignity before it, willingness to accept it, possibly even a happiness with it.

13. In peak-experiences, the dichotomies, polarities, and conflicts of life tend to be transcended or resolved. That is to say, there tends to be a moving toward the perception of unity and integration in the world. The person himself tends to move toward fusion, integration, and unity and away from splitting, conflicts, and oppositions.

14. In the peak-experiences, there tends to be a loss, even though transient, of fear, anxiety, inhibition, of defense and control, of perplexity, confusion, conflict, of delay and restraint. The profound fear of disintegration, of insanity, of death, all tend to disappear for the moment. Perhaps this amounts to saying that fear disappears.

15. Peak-experiences sometimes have immediate effects or aftereffects upon the person. Sometimes their aftereffects are so profound and so great as to remind us of the profound religious conversions which forever after changed the person. Lesser effects could be called therapeutic. These can range from very great to minimal or even to no effects at all. This is an easy concept for religious people to accept, accustomed as they are to thinking in terms of conversions, of great illuminations, of great moments of insight, etc.

16. I have likened the peak-experience in a metaphor to a visit to a personally defined heaven from which the person then returns to earth. This is like giving a naturalistic meaning to the concept of heaven. Of course, it is quite different from the conception of heaven as a place somewhere into which one physically steps after life on this earth is over. The conception of heaven that emerges from the peak-experiences is one which exists all the time all around us, always available to step into for a little while at least.

17. In peak-experiences, there is a tendency to move more closely to a perfect identity, or uniqueness, or to the idiosyncrasy of the person or to his real self, to have become more a real person.

18. The person feels himself more than at other times to be responsible,

active, the creative center of his own activities and of his own perceptions, more self-determined, more a free agent, with more "free will" than at other times.

19. But it has also been discovered that precisely those persons who have the clearest and strongest identity are exactly the ones who are most able to transcend the ego or the self and to become selfless, who are at least relatively selfless and relatively egoless.

20. The peak-experiencer becomes more loving and more accepting, and so he becomes more spontaneous and honest and innocent.

21. He becomes less an object, less a thing, less a thing of the world living under the laws of the physical world, and he becomes more a psyche, more a person, more subject to the psychological laws, especially the laws of what people have called the "higher life."

22. Because he becomes more unmotivated, that is to say, closer to non-striving, non-needing, non-wishing, he asks less for himself in such moments. He is less selfish. (We must remember that the gods have been considered generally to have no needs or wants, no deficiencies, no lacks, and to be gratified in all things. In this sense, the unmotivated human being becomes more god-like.)

23. People during and after peak-experiences characteristically feel lucky, fortunate, graced. A common reaction is "I don't deserve this." A common consequence is a feeling of gratitude, in religious persons, to their God, in others, to fate or to nature or to just good fortune. It is interesting in the present context that this can go over into worship, giving thanks, adoring, giving praise, oblation, and other reactions which fit very easily into orthodox religious frameworks. In that context we are accustomed to this sort of thing—that is, to the feeling of gratitude or all-embracing love for everybody and for everything, leading to an impulse to do something good for the world, an eagerness to repay, even a sense of obligation and dedication.

24. The dichotomy or polarity between humility and pride tends to be resolved in the peak-experiences and also in self-actualizing persons. Such people resolve the dichotomy between pride and humility by fusing them into a single complex superordinate unity, that is by being proud (in a certain sense) and also humble (in a certain sense). Pride (fused with humility) is not hubris nor is it paranoia; humility (fused with pride) is not masochism.

25. What has been called the "unitive consciousness" is often given in peak-experiences, i.e., a sense of the sacred glimpsed *in* and *through* the particular instance of the momentary, the secular, the worldly.

THE REACH AND THE GRASP:
TRANSCENDENCE TODAY

Huston Smith

HUSTON SMITH is Professor of Philosophy at Massachusetts Institute
of Technology. His works include *Religions of Man* (1958) and
Condemned to Meaning (1965).

Man lives forever on the verge, on the threshold of "something more"
than he can currently apprehend.

This "more" presents itself most conspicuously in space. The center of
the universe is where I happen to stand at any moment. From this center
space spreads. I can move into it in any direction I please: forward or
backward, right or left, even, with more difficulty, up or down. I lift my
eyes and space stretches toward a horizon. If I try to approach this
horizon, it recedes indefinitely, backstopped by light years.

In time, too, I sense myself enveloped by more than is evident. Moment
by moment I slide from a past that is vanishing into a future that has yet
to appear. Most of yesterday is gone already; tomorrow has not yet
arrived. And beyond these proximate "befores" and "afters" stretch pasts
and futures that may be infinite.

If we were content with the obvious we might stop here and regard
man as a boundary creature only in these physical respects. Actually,
however, our existence is endlessly liminal and adumbrative. Philip
Wheelwright suggests that an entire "metaphysics of the threshold" might
be needed to do justice to the ineluctable fact that as human beings "we
are never quite *there*, we are always and deviously on the verge of being
there." [1] The Marxist philosopher Ernst Bloch proposes a comparable
"ontology of the not-yet-being" built on categories of possibility, the new,
and futurity. [2] Though Asia is generally considered to be oriented to the
past or present, she too looks toward More: "To feel . . . that all is at
peace, to set ourselves down in a state of so-called satori, means there is as
yet no real understanding of Buddhism. If we are really receptive to
Buddhism there is always the feeling of not enough, not enough; limitless
endeavour and striving continued age after age, that must be the spirit of
Mahayana." [3] Nietzsche's Zarathustra was right; "man is a bridge and not
an end."

I propose to use "Transcendence" to name the *there* with respect to

---

[1] *The Burning Fountain* (Bloomington: Indiana University Press, 1968), p. 272.
[2] See *Philosophische Grundfragen. Zur Ontologie des Noch-Nicht-Seins* (Frankfurt:
Suhrkamp Verlag, 1961).
[3] Trevor Leggett, ed., *The Tiger's Cave* (London: Rider and Co., 1964), p. 64.

value which we sense as encircling our present existence; the Value More that exceeds our current possession; the presentiment that salvation, while not identical with our present stance, is nevertheless at hand.

Whether this Value More exists independent of and prior to our awareness of it, like space, or *per contra* is, prior to detection, only a possibility, like things that can but need not emerge in time—this question I shall finesse. Ontological realists, like Plato, espouse the former option; emergent evolutionists, like Bergson, the latter. The dispute isn't pointless, for if something already exists the prospect of laying hold of it seems greater than if we must take our chances on its coming into being in the first place. But if we read "possibility" here as "real possibility," equal in probability to the probability of our connecting with values that in some way do already exist, we can bypass the ontological dispute in favor of issues concerning Transcendence that are more metaphysically neutral.

Though the ontological status of the Value More can be left undetermined, other aspects of the category need to be pinned down. Each new moment adds *something* to our value store. If Transcendence designated only such an incremental "more" everyone would acknowledge its claims and the concept would cease to be interesting. Transcendence is not "more of the same." We do not encounter it in the form of another good dinner added to the list of all the dinners we have previously enjoyed. Even if the dinner is the best ever—or the experience, whatever its character, better than any to have previously come our way—Transcendence has not appeared. Experiences of Transcendence are probably of a very high order—"peak experiences" in Maslow's designation—but to *define* them by their position in a hierarchy of values lays one open to all the unresolvable difficulties of "hedonic calculus."

Transcendence should be defined neither quantitatively as "more of the same" nor qualitatively as "better than anything previously experienced" but in terms of the *kind* of value it designates. The effect of its appearance is to counter predicaments that are ingrained in the human situation; predicaments which, being not fully remediable, are constitutional.

What are these predicaments? Existentialists have described them adequately but have produced no résumé as compact as Gautama's "Three Signs of Being." As I wish to explore the transcendence of life's predicaments, not their description, I shall work with the Buddhist formulation. The predicaments which man must come to terms with in one way or another are:

a. *Dukkha*, suffering.
b. *Anicca*, transitoriness.
c. *Anatta*, no soul. Read "no personal significance." Individually we are nothing.

How does Transcendence counter these predicaments? To begin with, it counters them categorically rather than piecemeal. Dentistry remedies certain evils without affecting others. By contrast, transcendence, when it touches *dis*value, alters the entire field. It is a gestalt phenomenon, changing nothing within the field unless in some way it changes the field as a whole. Secondly, it counters *dis*values paradoxically. Instead of eliminating them, it transmutes them. If a man hits his thumb with a hammer, the fact that he lives *sub species transcendentia* doesn't keep his thumb from hurting. Transcendence doesn't work on suffering like anaesthesia does, by simply blotting it out. The pain remains; it is the quality (significance, import) of pain that has been affected. Thirdly, transcendence effects its results noetically, through insight. Noetically here differs from emotively, through emotion. Emotion is involved, but it is consequent upon insight, like the joy brought on by the discovery that "she loves me." Thus, transcendence is a state of actual or potential being, the discernment of which counters categorically, paradoxically, and noetically the *dis*values of suffering, transience, and insignificance or futility (as implied by Ecclesiastes' "Vanity of vanities! All is vanity").

IMMANENCE

Before proceeding with Transcendence it is worth noting that there is one condition in which all talk of Transcendence is superfluous. This condition is Immanence, capitalized to indicate that it embodies all the values of Transcendence minus the sense that those values await realization. Elsewhere in this volume (p. 89) Robert Bellah quotes Wallace Stevens'

> . . . times of inherent excellence,
>
> As when the cock crows on the left and all
> Is well, incalculable balances,
> At which a kind of Swiss perfection comes. . . .[4]

Such moments of inherent excellence transcend the need for transcendence itself, for when one is totally fulfilled one asks for nothing more, neither that one live forever, nor that the past be eternally preserved, nor that one's life count; all such concerns, being extrinsic, disappear. Meister Eckhart wrote that while he was in the source of the Godhead no one asked him where he was going or what he was doing. "There was no one there to ask me." It was only after he emerged that "the world of creatures began to shout: 'God.'" That is the point. Only when Immanence dissolves does the world begin to shout "God" and the issue of Transcendence descends upon us.

Let us consider what Immanence does to transitoriness, leaving its parallel operations on vanity and suffering to be dubbed in by the reader. Immanence transfigures time into eternity. Peter Munz argues that all religion is essentially such "a search for the *salus* that consists in knowing

---

[4] Wallace Stevens, *Collected Poems* (New York: Alfred A. Knopf, 1955), p. 786.

how transience can be transcended." [5] "Man's greatest disease is the consciousness of transience. Nothing is so likely to produce despair as the awareness of the contingency and vanity of life. A powerful cure . . . is . . . a perception of eternity. . . . The theologian who helps us to this perception is the great physician." [6]

"Eternity" here doesn't denote everlastingness—continuance in time forever—but rather total presence in the present: Eckhart's "Now moment," Buddha's "single instant awakening." Wittgenstein's "He lives eternally, who lives in the present." It names those moments in time in which the present emerges as a single point in the stream that flows from the past into the future. Eternity is an instant in which past and future disappear.

Since our empirical ego is the sum total of the desires, urges, and plans that we pursue and satisfy in time, the transfiguration of time into eternity —the moment in which time gives way to the present—is concomitant with the transcendence of the empirical ego. Or perhaps it is better to put it the other way around; transcendence of the empirical ego transfigures time. Remorse drags us back into the past; worry projects us into the future. To be released from both is to be free to live in the present, like lilies of the field, taking no thought of the morrow. To live in eternity is to live from moment to moment; to live not in the realm of means but in the realm of ends in which every act is an end in itself and has no purpose beyond itself.

If eternity requires transcending the empirical ego, it also requires release from the idea of physical time which stands as a screen between ourselves and the present, blocking communion and forcing us to care and plan for a future in which we nevertheless know all our achievements will be transient. Only when physical time dissolves in the emptiness of *sunyata*—the void as the Buddhists would say—can we "find that sublime flavour, that direct experience, at each step in our path . . . step after step." [7]

When Buddhists speak of throwing away their rafts after their rivers have been crossed and the *Lankavatara Sutra* tells us that there is really nothing to be acquired, nothing to be delivered from; no Way, no Goal, no Round, no Nirvana, nothing at all needing to be done or undone; it is from this state of Immanence, realized or envisioned, that they speak. It is, as we have said, from *outside* this condition that Transcendence appears, in something like the way that oxygen jumps to notice when we lack it. It may be that the further a life or culture stands from intrinsic fulfillment, defined as desiring nothing to be different from the way it is,[8] the more

[5] *Problems of Religious Knowledge* (London: SCM Press, 1959), p. 22.
[6] Ibid., p. 129.
[7] Leggett, op. cit., p. 69.
[8] Cf. Hakuin's Song of Zazen:
> At this moment what do you lack?
> As Nirvana presents itself before you,
> The place where you stand is the Land of Purity,
> And your person, the body of the Buddha.

prominently Transcendence will figure in its outlook, provided vitality doesn't decline. A related point would be: the further the remove from Immanence, the more dramatic the experience of Immanence if achieved. "The deeper the clinging to life, the more clearly is release known. The stronger the passions show themselves to be, the deeper the experience of the Buddha salvation." [9] If so, this would explain, for example, why apocalypticism appeared and reappeared in Judaism's most difficult periods. What we can say more confidently is that the *guise* in which Transcendence appears varies with the mode of life's deficiency. Those who suffer from bondage and confinement see it as promising liberation and expansion. Those who suffer from darkness look to it for light. To those who groan under the weight of death and transitoriness it intimates eternity. To those who are restless it betokens peace.

This-Worldly Transcendence

The fact of Immanence proves that men do not always seek Transcendence. When they do they can either seek it within the world's confines— meaning the confines of reality as usually envisioned—or test to see if these confines are final. Transcendence within our normal worldview I shall call this-worldly Transcendence; outside it, ontological Transcendence.

1. *Love.* The clearest instance of this-worldly Transcendence is occasioned by love. Kierkegaard better than anyone else has explained the dynamics of this solution to the human problem. The self, being dichotomous (composed of two halves, finite and infinite, temporal and eternal) is incapable of uniting itself by itself. Only when something outside the self takes possession of it, causing it to become fully absorbed with this outside something, can the self's two parts be aligned. In living with the princess day by day, the swain fulfills the temporal half of his being; at the same time, she fulfills his need for eternity, for something that doesn't change and isn't in flux, by "gestalting" all the time in his life. This gestalt is experienced as constant and is in this sense eternal: the time before he encountered the princess was prelude, her entry into his life was decisive climax and everything subsequent has been consummation.

The dynamics are similar with respect to finitude and infinity. The princess fulfills the swain's finite yearning; he can touch her and delight in her beauty which is concrete and particular. But she fills equally his infinite need. She provides him with something (herself) to which he can give himself infinitely (totally, completely).

There is no questioning the effectiveness of this solution to man's dilemma. The problem is to keep it working, that is, to keep the swain's passion for the princess infinite. Berdyaev thinks most marriages are

[9] Leggett, op. cit., p. 90.

unhappy. One need not go with him that far to concede that few experience the clear-cut before-and-after effect respecting fulfillment that Kierkegaard wants. Romantic love can effect Transcendence, but once love settles into fondness and companionship it does no disrespect to what these add to human happiness to admit that at the level at which they usually function, they fail to keep people from wanting additional solutions to the human situation.

2. *Hope* can be one of the supplementing solutions. Hope redeems the present and makes it significant and enduring by tying it to a meaningful future. As with love, no one doubts that hope can counter *dis*values; one perceptive psychologist thinks that most human happiness actually derives from hopeful expectations concerning the future. St. Paul thought enough of hope's redeeming power to rank it with faith and love, and Georges Bernanos valued it enough in *Diary of a Country Priest* to consider sin against it the deadliest sin of all.

The question is not whether hope can redeem but whether it can be sustained. To youth, whose life consists more of promise than of actualization, hope exists naturally. Later, it is more difficult. Personal hope comes up against the question, with time running out and life possibilities narrowing in number, what reason is there to expect that the fulfillment (Transcendence) that hasn't reached me yet will come in the future? And collective hope that historical advances will improve the human condition across the board runs into the fact that each age seems to find itself with new problems as great as those recently solved.

These difficulties besetting hope in both its personal and collective expressions raise the question whether hope can in the long run be sustained within life seen through ordinary, mundane, objective eyes. This question is at the forefront of the current debate by philosophers and theologians, Marxists and Christians, on hope and the future, Ernst Bloch (*Das Prinzip Hoffnung*) representing one side and Jurgen Moltmann (*Theology of Hope*) the other.

The answer is probably, "Some can, others cannot." For those who cannot, hope requires "another world" and faith in its existence. Indeed, the deeper one explores hope the more it begins to *resemble* faith in some form. St. Paul lists the two (and love) separately, but this may be a theological variant of outmoded "faculty psychology." Psychologists used to treat mind, will, and emotion as distinct human faculties; today they are impressed by the overlap. It may be that the separation of faith, hope, and love is provisional only, and that to sustain the division is to produce "faculty theology." The closer one approaches life's vital center, the more human faculties converge.

3. *Commitment to a cause* represents a third avenue to this-worldly Transcendence. "Ah, if only one could die suddenly as he is serving a Purpose," Kazantzakis cries. In *The Devil and Daniel Webster*, Stephen Vincent Benét makes the same point less directly. Having been cheated out of Jabez Stone's soul by Webster's oratory and legal agility, the

Devil offers to tell Webster's fortune, taking this opportunity to bury Webster's hopes.

The forecast is that Webster has a great ambition to be President but he will not succeed; lesser men will be chosen and he passed over. He wants to establish a dynasty, but both his sons will die in war. He is proud of his oratory, but his last great speech will turn many of his fellows against him; they will say he has turned his coat and sold his country, and their voices will be loud against him until he dies. Webster hears the Devil out and then puts one question to him: The Union, will it endure? When the Devil has to concede that it will, Webster retorts,

Why, then, you long-barreled, slab-sided, lantern-jawed, fortune-telling note shaver . . . be off with you to your own place before I put my mark on you! For, by the thirteen original colonies, I'd go to the Pit itself to save the Union!

ONTOLOGICAL TRANSCENDENCE

Immanence, being self-contained, is the best mode of life, but it is difficult to sustain. This worldly Transcendence is occasioned by something within the ordinary world: a loved one, a specific hope, or a cause that commends itself as deserving. Such Transcendence works for everyone at times, and perhaps enough, for some to preclude their asking for any other mode. But there are others who do not find in Immanence or this-worldly Transcendence the fulfillment they seek.

Such persons exist and I think it as probable that their "this-worldly" discontent is divine (engendered by exceptional sensitivity) as that it is neurotic (the result of failure of nerve or warped childhoods). I extend my typology, therefore, to include ontological Transcendence, defined as Transcendence deriving from the possibility that reality houses reservoirs of value qualitatively different from what we normally perceive or assume. To pursue the possibility of ontological Transcendence is, of course, to fly in the face of recent "secular theology," but this pursuit requires no apology. The secular theologians' request that we stop speaking of God as "out there" may be useful, for geography never applies literally to spiritual affairs. But their proposal that we drop all talk of a "behind the scenes" reality seems curious. Secular theologians tend to be science enthusiasts, yet "behind the scenes" sounds like precisely what the scientists have been uncovering as they penetrate deeper and deeper into nature's undersurface. In human experience, probability waves and anti-matter aren't exactly at stage center.

Anthropologists generally agree that in situations of life crisis and emotional stress primitive man experienced rescue through myths that showed him a way of escape where empirically none had existed.[10] The need for

[10] B. Malinowski, *Myth in Primitive Psychology* (London: Norton, 1926), pp. 23ff.

such transempirical ways has not disappeared. Mankind continues to be cramped enough by the limits of worldly existence to warrant asking if there is conceivably a more commodious existence. We need not approach the question apologetically as if ontological Transcendence were a crutch for the maimed. Physicians are becoming interested in the concept of positive health, a state of well-being as much above what we consider normal health as disease falls below it. Transcendence has comparable creative possibilities. The sustained secret excitement implicit in the speech of Socrates and his friends throughout the Platonic dialogues is one example of ontological Transcendence working, in that case taking the form of the Idea of the Good, to heighten the vitality of men who before they caught sight of it were, at the very least, perfectly normal.

Immortality is one possibility which, if actual, would instance ontological Transcendence. Another possibility is that reality is personal, that, in William James' formulation, we can "legitimately say *thou* to the universe." Classical theism affirms that we are loved by personal reality. A third possibility would occur in relation to an impersonal perfection, so self-contained that it doesn't know men as individuals and hence is not directly concerned with their well-being. The power of such an impersonal perfection—Nirguna Brahman, Sunyata, Plato's Idea of the Good, the Godhead—to effect transcendence has often been challenged, but without warrant. If such a perfection exists, it could afford a vision so stupendous that to glimpse it would be to find one's attention totally riveted, slicked to its object, with no remainder left for oneself and such residual questions as whether one is known or loved.

I have nothing against any of these possibilities. They have been explored thoroughly for centuries, however. It is perhaps more promising to ask if there are other reasonable ways reality's "more" might be envisioned. I wish, of course, that I could induce other modes of Transcendence to disclose themselves directly; since revelations can't be engineered I must fall back upon reason's service: to provide propaedeutics. Negatively, reason can remove obstacles to accepting ontological Transcendence; positively, it can fashion conceptual forms through which such Transcendence can be convincingly imagined.

Via Negativa. Dionysius the Areopagite, Avicenna, Maimonides, and the mystics in general represent an important theo-philosophical tradition which claimed that the difference in kind between finite and infinite precludes man from knowing anything about God's nature save what it is not. Current epistemology holds resources for a comparable *via negativa*, but with a different slant. Whereas the burden of traditional negative theology was that the Transcendent is, in its nature, unknown, the contemporary version must be that there is an unknown, aspects of which may be Transcendent. This neo-"negative theology" doesn't prove Transcendence; however, it does make room for it.

From the radiant energy of the total electromagnetic spectrum, human eyes register only a slender band. Similarly, we hear only a fraction of sound waves. Radio, X-, and gamma rays don't register with our senses at all; in this respect they are like magnetic fields. Given different sense receptors, we would perceive an unimaginably different world. From a wide range of possible directions, life, it appears, has traversed one among innumerable possibilities; it is the world we experience.

So much for our senses, their relativity, and the correspondingly relative world they offer for perception. But the world of our *conception*, which we can know even if we cannot directly perceive it, has turned out to be equally relative. The physical world, which prior to the rise of modern science seemed to be the only world, now turns out to be macro, or middle-sized. It is enveloped by the megaworld of astronomy and contains the microworld of quantum physics.

Each of these three physical worlds—the mega, the macro, and the micro, set one within another like Chinese boxes—has a distinct logical structure and mechanics in part independent of hierarchies above or below. The megaworld is expanding, its space is curved, and its geometry is non-Euclidian. In the microworld, matter is mostly empty and can be massless (the photon and neutrino). It can function somewhat like a particle, wave, or force (the latter instanced by mesons which act like glue to hold protons and neutrons together in nuclei). It can have life spans under a ten-billionth of a second or, where more stable, it can execute disappearing acts, appearing only at certain points as it moves along a line. It can be created (from energy) or destroyed (when, for example, positive and negative electrons collide and disappear in photons of light), and it has its mirror image in antimatter.

There is no reason to presume that these three "worlds" are exhaustive. Scientists are presently looking for new worlds beyond mega and micro: a transstellar, gallactic space whose distinctive mechanics may explain the quasars brightness 10,000 times that of a billion suns; and a subquantum level where we expect to find the quarks. There are difficulties, of course. The deeper we burrow into the interstices of matter the stronger we find the bonds that unite its elements; indeed, their strength increases exponentially rather than arithmetically, which has led Philip Morrison to calculate that to break matter apart at its quantum level would, by present methods, require an accelerator larger than the earth itself. Presumably new methods will be found, in which case we will be exposed to matter acting in five distinctive ways in each of five distinguishable dimensions.

David Bohm thinks the total number of dimensions is infinite.

Recognition that the way matter behaves on the human scale is only a special instance of nature's total repertory does bear some relation to negative theology's goal of ventilating our views of reality, but in the end neither this nor the preceding point about the partiality of sensory knowledge touches the *value* question. Not even J. B. S. Haldane's hunch that "the universe is not only queerer than we imagine; it is queerer than we *can* imagine" or James Coleman's verdict that relativity theory isn't difficult to understand, only difficult to believe,[11] implies that what strains imagination or belief pertains to value. Instead of tailing science to reach value we must backtrack and show that in the interest of control science ultimately turns its back on values and meanings in favor of what can be known objectively.[12] In the long run the most important task for neo-"negative theology" is to demonstrate in detail that: 1) epistemologies are hyphenated to the purposes for which they are designed; 2) contemporary epistemology is vectored by science whose primary purpose is to control nature; and 3) since this purpose is partial, epistemologies tailored to it are correlatively partial and incapable in principle of doing justice to reality's full (specifically value) dimensions.

The aim of neo-"negative theology" is not to prove Transcendence, but rather to make room for Transcendence if it shows a disposition to enter through extrarational channels. This may be the greatest service reason can render faith in our age, namely, to loosen the clods of prevailing modes of thought which welcome so little the seeds of faith. "Only that life is worth living," Nietzsche has Zarathustra say, "which develops the strength and the integrity to withstand the unavoidable sufferings and misfortunes of existence without flying into an imaginary world." Granted. What, however, is imaginary, and what real but elusive? "One world at a time," we hear, and fair enough, but not half a world. Reason operates in contemporary life under such heavy unconscious conditioning from science that it might be good for us if at certain times, for certain purposes, we had a Western equivalent of the Zen *koan* to decommission reason, to simply knock it out, allay it, so it wouldn't get in our way.

Conceptual forms. Though this negative service may be the greatest contribution reason can make to ontological Transcendence at this time, reason can also do something positive. It can formulate conceptions consonant with (though not implied by) the most sophisticated contemporary information, in which Transcendence can with dignity take lodging if Transcendence presents itself. I call these formulations "conceptual forms" and think of them as complementing the symbols Robert Bellah finds "unavoidable but provisional" in man's confrontation with reality: poetic symbols like those Bellah extracts from Wallace Stevens, religious symbols, including God, Lord, Nothingness, and Nirvana.

I shall try three formulations which involve, respectively, a spatial image, a temporal image, and an image from neurophysiology.

A spatial image. Are the three usual dimensions of space exhaustive? Edwin Abbott's *Flatland* raised this question intriguingly, and Karl Heim has built a full-scale theology on the premise that they are not. Mathema-

---

[11] *Relativity for the Lawman* (New York: William-Frederick, 1954), p. 48.

[12] Cf. Munz, *Problems of Religious Knowledge,* op. cit., pp. 128–129: "The scientist approaches the world with a well-defined aim. He wishes to understand the world so that he can manipulate it. This aim guides his investigations. He has framed the concept of truth in such a way that he can apply it to that kind of knowledge which enables him to manipulate events."

ticians refer to abstract "configurational space" and "Hilbert space" (where "quarks" rotate in special unitary transformation in six dimensions); their work moves from three to four to "n" dimensions without hesitation. Physicists speak of electrons that disappear, then reappear elsewhere. Could this involve dropping out of our space and subsequent reentry? Hoyle's "continuous creation of matter-energy in space" has had to be greatly modified, but the conception must still be reckoned with; could matter-energy enter from another dimension?

What is the value-import of additional dimensions? If a dot extended through time produces a line, a line extended through time in a different dimension produces a plane, and a plane extended through time in still another dimension creates a solid, by extrapolation a solid extending through time in a fourth dimension would produce a four-dimensional body. As our sight is three-dimensional, we couldn't see such a four-dimensional body any more than two-dimensional sight could see an elongating block; to two-dimensional sight its advancing surface would appear as no more than a moving plane. *Mutatis mutandis:* if there *are* additional dimensions, our three-dimensional sight doesn't preclude us from having four-dimensional bodies created by the summation of all the past moments we have lived.

Conceptually, such a body might be described as the sum of all its intersections in three-dimensional space as it passes through time. We couldn't hope to visualize it, but William Witherspoon has suggested that imagining the dimension might be likened crudely to reconstruing a moving picture film of a bud opening into a full-blown flower. If we cut apart each frame of such a film, stacked the whole film together frame by frame, and then looked at the unfolding flower simultaneously through all the frames, that might be the most we could do to appease our yen for imagining the fourth dimension.

The concept of a four-dimensional figure would, of course, apply to a physical object, animate or inanimate. But if we have gone this far, there is no need to stop. Living things might differ from the nonliving by their involvement in a fifth dimension. Death, then, would be the cessation of movement in the fifth dimension while the corpse continued its movement in the fourth. Spirit, as distinct from life alone, could be the product of a sixth dimension. A four-dimensional body would expand to a fifth dimension by being alive and to a sixth if it were evolving spiritually. Ample dimensions remain, of course, for God.

It may be no accident that William Pollard, a theologian-physicist—as theologian, sensitive to value questions; as physicist, schooled in the extent to which reality differs from common sense—finds this spatial image meaningful. For the rest of us, time may lubricate our imaginings better than space.

A temporal image. Whatever one may think of the specifics of *The Phenomenon of Man*, the reception accorded that book indicates that Teilhard de Chardin tapped an immense potential in the contemporary mind for expanding its value perspective through the imagery of time.

Evolution was first a historical concept. It was applied next to biology and then to cosmology. We live not only in an expanding universe but in a universe that is evolving. This notion affects value most directly through the evolution of consciousness. At every stage evolution has brought to view a world which qualitatively as well as quantitatively would have been completely inconceivable from the vantage point of the preceding rung on the evolutionary ladder. What reason is there to suppose that we have reached the apex?

If the emergence of memory counters transience to some extent, might a further development not counter it more? If human consciousness enables us to step back from consciousness one step in *self*-consciousness, might not further developments enable us to step back a second step into ecological-consciousness and a third into cosmic-consciousness, thereby progressively countering insignificance? Perhaps we can no more imagine what such expanded states of consciousness would feel like than a dog can imagine what it would feel like to be self-conscious or to think abstractly. On the other hand, those moments when we sense within us "a self that touches all edges" (Wallace Stevens again) could be foretastes of a future which today man can sustain no longer than protoamphibians could endure unhydrated oxygen.

A neurophysiological image. The human brain contains over 10 billion cells. Any single cell can be connected with up to 25,000 other cells. The possible paths through the cortical computer exceed the number of atoms in the universe. Something like a billion impulses flood up to it each second. A huge constriction process seems to work to reduce this prodigious information-processing device to manageable proportions. This is as it should be, for if we had to attend to a billion optional things, we might not attend sufficiently to the few things that require our attention if we are to survive: cars that bear down on us, pantries that need restocking, and the like.

If we had to nominate a group that faces in the rawest form life's three *dis*values as enumerated at the start of this essay, terminal cancer patients would be a logical choice. Their suffering tends to be acute and unrelieved. Their time is fast running out, and with it their personal significance. When their neural circuitry is rerouted by LSD, however, surprising things happen in about fifty per cent of the cases. The following descriptions are quoted from Sidney Cohen's "LSD and the Anguish of Dying":

The pain is changed. I know that when I pressed here yesterday, I had an unendurable pain. I couldn't even stand the weight of a blanket. Now I press hard—it hurts, it hurts all right—but it doesn't register as terrifying.

I could die now, quietly, uncomplaining—like those early Christians in the arena who must have watched the lions eating their entrails.

I see that the hard deaths too, must be borne—like the difficult births, it is a part of you.

When I die I won't be remembered long—there aren't many friends and hardly any relatives left. Nothing much accomplished—no children—nothing. But that's all right, too.[13]

Has the chemical recircuiting anaesthetized these patients or opened the doors of perception to enable them to see more of reality, or reality more objectively, than they and we normally do?

Conclusion

There seem to be two routes to human fulfillment, psychological and ontological. The former accepts more or less standard views of reality and seeks psychological resolution within those limits; when successful the result is either Immanence or this-worldly Transcendence, the difference being that in the latter fulfillment derives from something specifiable, a loved one, hope, a cause, or whatever. Ontological Transcendence, for its part, accepts the permanence of psychological tensions that cannot be resolved within reality as normally conceived, and so presses the possibility that reality includes surprising corridors of worth that elude ordinary eyes. Things are as they seem; things are not as they seem: that is the great divide.

This essay takes no position as to which side is right. The two types of fulfillment are equal both in worth and in difficulty. It is precisely as difficult to maintain genuine faith in ontological Transcendence as to achieve Immanence or this-worldly Transcendence. With respect to ontological Transcendence, my claim is not that it is superior or easier but that it *is* legitimate. There is no more reason to assume that reality conforms to the "man in the street's" suppositions of its worth than that it conforms to his notions of its physical complexity. A further claim is that the creation of conceptual forms through which man's imagination can grapple with ontological Transcendence is a useful enterprise. More important than the individual's right to believe, which concerned James, is his capacity to believe. Conceptual forms cannot deliver this capacity, but like background advertising, they can work the soil. The distinctions that have structured the paper—between Immanence and Transcendence, between this-worldly and ontological Transcendence, between psychological and ontological fulfillment—are probably themselves provisional. But this is not the last analysis; it is an analysis of where our thinking stands today.

[13] *Harper's Magazine*, September 1965.

ERNST BLOCH AND "THE PULL OF THE FUTURE"

Harvey Cox

HARVEY COX is a Professor of Church and Society at the Harvard
Divinity School. His books include *The Secular City* (1965) and
Feast of Fools.

. . . .

After years of hearing about him indirectly, American readers will now
be able to taste some of the fruits of Ernst's Bloch's long and productive
career for themselves. These essays, drawn from Bloch's more recent
writing, will hopefully whet so many appetites that the translation of his
major works will occur before too long. Ranging over an incredibly wide
variety of subjects, from musicology to epistemology, from social and
literary criticism to political theory, Bloch's books will eventually delight
and stimulate many different people. Why, then, it might reasonably be
asked, should this first book-length collection of his ideas be introduced by
a theologian, and a so-called "young theologian" at that? Whatever else
Ernst Bloch may be he is not a "young theologian." He misses that condition on two counts. First, he is an octogenarian, an alert and hard working
one but nevertheless a man born in 1885 (of Jewish extraction in Ludwigs-
hafen am Rhein). Also, Bloch is not a theologian—even though some of
his critics have occasionally hurled that epithet at him. Bloch is a philosopher—and an atheist at that, at least in his own terms.

Still there are reasons why a theologian should introduce Bloch to
English speaking readers. Bloch's delayed "discovery" has been largely the
work of theologians. This became especially clear in 1965 when Bloch
reached his eightieth birthday and a group of friends and admirers published a *Festschrift* in his honor (*Ernst Bloch zu Ehren,* Suhrkamp
Verlag). To the astonishment of many readers, who knew Bloch as an old
Marxist, nearly half the contributors to the volume turned out to be
theologians, among them some of the youngest religious thinkers of
Europe. Why this interest in Bloch among younger theologians?

Bloch himself might enjoy trying to answer that question. One of
the continuing interests of his life has been the riddle of why certain
insights emerge at one point in history and not at another, why some
men appear "before their time" and others seem to live in an age which
has already disappeared. As a theologian it seems to me that while Bloch's
work is certainly not of exclusive interest to theologians, there are compelling reasons why he is particularly relevant for us today.

The first reason Bloch fascinates us is that we feel very strongly, and
quite correctly I think, that the world today stands *"zwischen die Zeiten,"*
between two ages. We disagree on how those two ages should be defined.

Some see us emerging from Christendom into a "post-Christian era." Others see us moving from the religious to the secular epoch in theology. Still others insist that God is dead, that all forms of theism are passé and that we are already in the period of post-theistic Christianity. Yet, despite the disagreements, most agree that we are now leaving one identifiable period behind but have not yet arrived at the next. We are experiencing what Bloch calls a period of "Zeitwende."

Such periods, claims Bloch, are particularly fruitful to study because during them, if often only very briefly, we catch a glimpse of man as he really is. In such periods we live in radical anticipation, hope and expectation. This is valuable, says Bloch, because existence in hope should not be a periodic episode in man's life; it should be the basic posture of his existence at all times. Man *is*, Bloch contends, that creature who hopes, who phantasizes, who dreams about the future and strives to attain it. These features are not merely accidental to his nature but are utterly constitutive of it. To be human is to be on the way to something else. To be man is to be *unterwegs*. Man's nature eludes definitive description because by the time it is described it has already begun the transmutation into something else. Thus Bloch helps us to seize the day, to enjoy and profit from the discomfort of transition, to see in the dislocations of our own period an epiphany of what is real in history at large. Consequently theologians, for whom the changes of today are especially momentous, see Bloch as especially significant.

But what does Bloch help us to see? How would his thought be capsuled if it had to be described in a few words? Bloch himself, Adolph Lowe reports, was once faced with this challenge. A few years back at a late afternoon tea in the home of a friend, someone challenged the old man to sum up his philosophy in one sentence. "All great philosophers have been able to reduce their thought to one sentence," the friend said. "What would your sentence be?" Bloch puffed on his pipe for a moment and then said. "That's a hard trap to get out of. If I answer, then I'm making myself out to be a great philosopher. But if I'm silent then it will appear as though I have a great deal in mind but not much I can say. But I'll play the brash one instead of the silent one and give you this sentence: S is not yet P."

"S is not yet P"? Is this a mere evasion? No, in a sense Bloch had succeeded, despite himself, in passing the test of being a great philosopher. His life work has been built on the contention that the dynamic reality always eludes even the most supple agility of language, that it outraces words even while they are being spoken. Thus to say "S=S" is already to falsify the situation since in the time it takes to utter even a short phrase, the inexorable movement of reality toward a still undefined future has relativized the statement.

Does this mean that for Bloch the venerable law of identity in classical logic is passé? Yes it does. For Bloch's ontology, to claim that S must be S and nothing else is to fall into a static view of reality, a condition which can only result in hindering and slowing down the onward march of history, though it can never halt it. In short Bloch is suggesting a logic of change, a new logic appropriate to a time when we have discovered at last that change itself is the only permanent thing we have.

There is another clue in Bloch's one-sentence summary. It is the words "not yet." Just as other philosophers have written at length on the vast worlds that open to our imagination if we examine such tiny words as "love" or "is" or "time," Bloch peers into the creative sources of human existence by examining the words "not yet." Man is not for Bloch principally a product of his past either individually or as a race. Man is not to be described as "thinker" or "symbol maker" or "tool maker" or even as "worker." Man is the "hope-er," he-who-hopes. His essential existence tiptoes along the narrow ridge between the disappearing "now" and the ever newly appearing "not-yet." And his basic stance, when he is true to himself, is that of creative expectation, a hope that engenders action in the present to shape the future.

What is the nature of the "not-yet"? The future that makes man free? Bloch's answers are never fully satisfying. With a trace of teutonic titanism he proclaims himself the discoverer of this new continent. But like Columbus, he admits that the full exploration of the new world must be left to others. He is content to plant his flag in its sand, let his gaze follow its vast horizons and speculate on what may lie behind its towering mountain ranges. Like that great investigator of the unconscious, Sigmund Freud, with whom Bloch likes to compare himself, he can demonstrate how the charting of the new land mass might proceed. But he does not pretend that the rough charts he has made are definitive.

The comparison between Bloch and Freud is an interesting one. Both are secularized Jews. Both thought of themselves as atheists but could not shake off their interests in religious problems. Both offended middle class sensibilities, Freud by meddling with sex and Bloch by becoming a Communist. But both retained in their private lives a conventional bourgeois style. Freud loved to play cards with old cronies in his anti-macassar Vienna home. Bloch thrives on the *Gemütlichkeit* of Tübingen. Freud studied what Bloch has called the *Nichtmehr-Bewusst*, that which has come to consciousness but has now passed into unconsciousness. Bloch has discovered the *"Noch-nicht Bewusst,"* that which scampers teasingly on the threshold of consciousness, sensed only in anticipation, not yet fully realized. While Freud was interested in night dreams, Bloch is fascinated by daydreams. Fantasy, for Bloch, is not a mere frippery, not a waste of time, but a crucial key to how human beings think. Perhaps the most significant difference between the two is that while Freud did develop a method for examining the no-more-conscious, psychoanalysis, Bloch has not produced its equivalent for the not-yet-conscious. Or perhaps in Bloch's own spirit we should say he has *not yet* produced it.

In theology, the study of the "not-yet," although we do not usually employ Bloch's phrase, is called "eschatology." Although it has usually been the poor step-sister in the household of theology, eschatology, the study of the Christian hope, is today once again claiming a central place. Theologians such as Jürgen Moltmann and Johannes Metz are working today with the assumption that Albert Schweitzer was right when he saw Christianity as essentially eschatological. They see the need not just to recover eschatology but to rethink the whole theological tradition from the perspective of hope. As Moltmann says, eschatology is not just one doctrine among others; it is the *key* in which everything is set, the glow that suffuses everything else. Therefore eschatology cannot be merely part of Christian doctrine; it must be the determining characteristic of all Christian existence and of the whole church.

But how does Christianity recover its lost eschatological stance? Its daring hope for the future which has now been taken over and distorted by revolutionary movements? The trouble is that Christian hope has been either so postponed or so underplayed in the history of Christian thought, that theologians today have an enormous job on their hands. How can we restate that hope, expressed in the New Testament in symbols of the resurrection of the dead and the triumphant return of Christ on the clouds, in images that modern man can understand? For centuries Christianity has persistently minimized any notion that the future would overturn the religious or political institutions of the day. Consequently the church has often become an objectively conservative force in the society. Yet the early Christians hoped for something that *would* transform this world, and today secularized forms of this hope are altering the face of the earth. How does Christianity regain a posture of radical hope, a hope for *this* world? How can the church regain the *stance* that was unswervingly oriented toward the future, but transmute the content of their hope so that it becomes available to contemporary man? With this task set before us it is natural that we should be impressed by a man whose life has been spent examining the "*futurum*," the idea of the new, the "*Impuls der Erwartung*" and the "principle of hope."

The interest in Bloch among theologians is not merely an unrequited love. Like any really significant philosopher, Bloch recognizes that he must deal with religion, so the interest moves both ways. Still Bloch remains, for his Christian suitors, a little hard-to-get and perhaps ultimately even unavailable. But this resistance, in the intellectual as in the romantic, often seems to excite interest rather than to dampen it. How does Bloch deal with religion?

As a Marxist, he knows as Marx did that "all criticism begins with the criticism of religion." Unlike most Marxists, however, Bloch approaches religion neither with distaste nor with condescension, but with genuine sympathy and untiring fascination. He has displayed an interest in religion since his earliest years, and that interest continues to the present day. For Bloch, all religion finds its source in the "dichotomy of man between his present appearance and his non-present essence" (*Prinzip Hoffnung*, page 1520)—a statement that calls to mind Marx's own assertion that religious misery is not only the expression of real misery in a distorted and mystified way, but is also a protest against real misery. Marx, however, emphasized the narcotizing effect of religion (the "opiate of the people"), whereas Bloch is more interested in why and how religion functions as an expressive form of protest.

What about Christianity? Unlike some 20th century theologians who insist on a qualitative distinction between "faith in Christ" and religious belief, or between "religion" and "the Gospel," Bloch sees a continuity between religion and Christianity. More in the style of a 19th century theologian, or of recent theologians influenced by contemporary phenomenology of religion, Bloch speaks of Christianity as the purest and most consistent expression of this irreduceable content of all religion. In its universal messianism and its inclusive eschatology Christianity becomes the religious expression par excellence of the hope-laden dissatisfaction which spurs man on toward the future. Bloch also believes, however, that there is a crucial difference between Christianity and many other religions in the way it copes with the present. While some religions stress the mythical and thus tend to become static and to serve as an apology for the status quo, Christianity's messianism gives it a critical perspective on the present and loads it with explosive potential.

Both friends and foes of Christianity may rightly suspect at this point that Bloch's estimate of its significance seems unduly generous. They should realize at once that Bloch is not talking about Christianity as currently preached and practiced. He has in mind what might be called the "essential meaning" of Christianity, a meaning which for Bloch burned brightly in the early church but emigrated into non-Christian movements when the church surrendered to the wiles of Constantine, sacrificed its eschatological hope and allowed itself to become the sacral ideology of the Empire. He believes that Christianity's great gift was to introduce the "principle of hope" into the world, that is, a way of seeing things from the perspective of the future, what they could become. He says that this essential Christian impulse, although it was throttled by the church, has popped out again here and there in such renegades as Thomas Münzer and Joachim of Fiore, but that its major vehicle in recent years has been movements of revolutionary social change. Christianity kindled a revolution which, instead of devouring its children, disavowed them.

In Bloch's view, not only man but the cosmos itself is an existence moving toward a still unfulfilled essence. Indeed he insists on this point so avidly that one cannot help being reminded of St. Paul's famous assertion in the eighth chapter of Romans that not only man but the creation itself groans and travails waiting for its redemption. But here Bloch adamantly stops short of any agreement with St. Paul. It is not God who is the source of this discontent or the ground of this hope. Drawing on the same "left-wing Aristotelianism" that nourished Marx, Bloch contends that this restlessness of matter, its longing for form, is an inner characteristic of matter itself. Here he seems closer to the vision of Teilhard de Chardin than he does to those theologians who posit a God who beckons to the cosmos from a radically other future. Yet even here his position is not entirely unequivocal.

Bloch is a troubled atheist. He rejects the Christian propensity to hypostasize the future into an existent God. But he is also bothered by the nihilist alternative which sees man's hope merely as wishful projection into the void. Bloch wants to guard the unconditional openness of this future by arguing that it transcends all images and schemes that seek to give it content, but he refuses to assign it any viable facticity. He attempts to escape from this dilemma by talking about a "vacuum," an unfilled area which exerts a certain magnetic pull on man and on the cosmos. This moving point ahead of human history was once the cinema screen on which religious projections were flashed. Now we must no longer be deceived by the pictures. Still, for Bloch the moving point is no mere oasis, no cruel deception luring man on into destruction and frustration. But at the same time it has no substantial or existent reality. It is the constantly receding threshold over which existence passes in its endless quest for essence, a quest which, for Bloch, is never satisfied as long as man remains man.

Here the point of fruitful encounter between Marx and contemporary theology zooms into focus. Bloch balks at saying this open window to the future "exists." He is understandably afraid that to concede this would drag back into the picture all the static ontologies and superstitious notions of God that Christianity has for centuries erected, thus contributing to the constriction and stupefaction of man. But what Bloch does not realize clearly enough is that many Christian theologians today are equally reticent to claim God "exists" in the sense that makes Bloch so uncomfortable. Tillich, for example, vigorously refuses to allow the verb "exists" to follow the noun "God." For Tillich the phrase "God does not exist" was central to his thought since an existent being could not be the ground of all being and all existence. There is no real difference, therefore, between Tillich and Bloch on the question of the "existence" of God—they both deny it. The point of their essential disagreement is over the question of where the reality Tillich calls "God" and Bloch does not, touches man. For Tillich it was "in the depths," as the source of our being. For Bloch, on the other hand, it is at the "forward edge," where man moves from the present into the future.

The truth is, however, that Tillich's influence in modern theology is now waning. The dialogue with Bloch is now in the hands of a younger group of theologians with somewhat differing emphases and interests. . . .

. . . .

From Bloch we might learn that a horizon is always formed by something, not by nothing. The hidden God, whose very hiddenness is disclosed in Jesus of Nazareth, provides history with its "frame," with what

Marshall McLuhan might call its "anti-environment." Bloch helps us to see that this *saeculum,* this world-age, is bounded by the future toward which it hastens every day, a future it never attains but which continually prevents it from accepting itself as finished and final. With Bloch's help, we can be unremittingly concerned with the secular without sacrificing the transcendent. God is not above, or beneath us, or even just "within" us. He is ahead. Christian existence is defined by hope and the church is the community of God's tomorrow, eternally discontent with today.

This tiny volume of essays may begin a new chapter in the career of English language theology. It will certainly bring to many people the voice of a man whom cold war politics and ephemeral intellectual fads have kept from us for far too long. I have often speculated on how different theology would be today if Ernst Bloch, rather than Martin Heidegger, had been our conversation partner for the past twenty years. Would we be as miserably lacking as we are in a theologically grounded social ethic? Would we be as disastrously out of touch with the revolution that is transforming the third world and burning the centers of our American cities? Would we have needed the catharsis of the death-of-God theology? Would we have allowed the ecclesiastical furniture shuffling of recent years to pose as a real renewal of the church? Might we have produced a theology that was truly radical in its impact on the world and not just in its rhetoric?

These questions cannot of course be answered today. Nor can we expect Bloch to do for us the work we must do for ourselves. Bloch is not just a Christian *manqué.* He does not help us much when we seek to spell out the *content* of hope for today's man. For Christians, that must come from a vision of what is possible for a world in which the God of Exodus and Easter is still alive.

THE CANCELLATION OF HOPE BY MYTH

Carl Braaten

CARL BRAATEN is Professor of Systematic Theology at the Lutheran
School of Theology in Chicago. His works include *The Future of God*
(1969), *The Futurist Option* (1970, with Robert Jenson), and *Christ
and Counter-Christ* (1972).

Hope is not man's only possible response to the future. The unknowns of the future may quench hope, wither courage, and very likely evoke a response of anxiety and fear. When hope is driven out, despair takes over. Despair comes from *de sperare*—to be without hope. Anxiety in face of the future triggers off the attempt to find security for life in the past, to return to a paradise above time or at the beginning of history. It is anxiety that causes man to shed tears for the good old days, that makes him surrender his perceptions of the present and hopes for the future to his glorious memories of the past. Nowhere is this anxiety more conspicuously at work than in religion and politics. The utopias of hope are then slipped into the past and the mythical mood of "once upon a time" penetrates the religious rituals and political dreams. In Christianity this takes the fatal form of appealing to the faithful to remember some golden age, which actually did not exist in the first five centuries, as Anglicanism imagines, or in the High Middle Ages, as Roman Catholicism believes, or in the period of Luther and seventeenth-century orthodoxy, as Protestantism pretends, at least on anniversary occasions. Christianity is absolutely tied to memory, of course, but the genuine appeal to memory is a call of hope to remember the future which has been promised in the past and which the church is to prefigure through her faith and love in the present.

The deadliest enemies of hope are not, as one might think, doubt, despair, and death. Hope can cope with these; that is its mission. The deadliest enemy always appears with the friendliest face. In this case the friendly face is religion, not religion per se but religion as mysticism and archaism. The function of hope is to keep faith active in history and to keep history moving forward until the future itself overcomes the negativities of existence. Mysticism is an unhistorical way of thinking. What is truly real for it is not what comes in and through history but what lies behind or beyond the flux of time in the abysmal ground of being. Now "ground" is a spatial symbol. Salvation comes by leaving the plane of history, by sinking in this moment into the depths of the motionless ground of being, into the eternal womb which summons all her children into formlessness.

In archaism we have the cancellation of a historical hope by the myth of return to eternal origins. The biblical attitude of anticipating a new future far superior to any sunken island or lost paradise in the past is incompatible with the myth of eternal recurrence. Yet, Christian theology is far from having drawn the consequences of this incompatibility. In this myth we see the expression of a flight from history, and an inability to be sustained by hope toward a future which has not yet divulged all its mystery. Mircea Eliade has written the classical account of this myth of eternal return. This myth is the triumph of anxiety in the sphere of religion. Only what is perennial is real; only what is repeatable is meaningful. Religion is imitation and repetition of what possesses original, that is, archetypal, validity. Everything that counts in religion must have been done from the beginning *ab origine*. Religion needs to find its precedents among the ancestors; ultimately everything must go back to a sacred "once upon a time"—*in illo tempore*. Salvation comes by suspending the duration of history, just as in mysticism, and by participation in a timeless event in a mythical epoch. Eliade observes that the whole intent of this myth is to abolish history, to cancel time, to live in an eternal present, by making the future nothing more than a recurrence of the past.

Corresponding to this mythical archaism is a futurism which also abolishes the significance of hope in historical experience. Not every attention to the future can be reconciled with the Christian eschatology of history. A futurism which tries to overcome anxiety by taking a leap out of the present should not be confused with the futurism of Christian hope which presses for change all along the line. Some Christian theologians, Origen, for example, adopted the Platonic axiom that "the end is always like the beginning." This axiom is a rationalization of the mythical idea of eternal recurrence. Its symbol is the circle; it transposes into time the image of the cycle based on observing the seasonal rhythm of nature. If time is interpreted in analogy with nature, it is made to turn back to the beginning.

Another expression of this *Urzeit/Endzeit* axiom is the interesting fact that many of the great utopianists have located their ideal world in the past. Utopia is the creation of hope; it portrays "home, sweet home," and "happy days." All the negativities of existence are negated. What then is the difference between utopian hope and eschatological hope? Both of them seem to use the principle of negating the negative and maximizing the positive in human experience. The contents are, therefore, often quite comparable. The difference is history. Utopias that are projected backward into some mythical past disregard the temporal dynamics of hope at work in biblical eschatology.

There has been a tendency in the Christian tradition, never completely victorious, of interpreting the entire history of salvation on the model of the myth of eternal return. Then the future is a correlate of the past, the end a restoration of the beginning, redemption a regaining of a lost paradise. The myth of the fall of Adam has misshaped the structure of Christian theology, not primarily because it was for so long taken as real history, but for two other reasons: first, because it was taken as an explanation of the origin of evil in the human race, and second, it was viewed as a "fall" from an originally perfect condition. Kierkegaard said all that needs to be said on the matter of explaining sin in the fantastic terms of a biological inheritance from the first ancestor of the human race. Even more damaging, however, is the idea of Adam's fall from the perfect state of paradise. This places all later historical movement within the structures of the primeval past. Everything that is new is a recovery of the past; the history of grace is a restoration of a preestablished condition. Mankind is struggling in history to catch up to where it once stood in the figure of Adam. Eden is a paradise of archetypes; everything that happens later, so far as it is true, good, and beautiful, is an imitation and repetition of the original state of mankind. In the patristic tradition the Platonic essences were given an earthy embodiment in the way things were before the fall. The category of the old became virulent in Christian thinking, crowding out the place of preeminence that belongs to the now in an eschatological faith. The new began to be couched in words prefixed by a *re*. The history of Israel, of Christ, of the church, of the world, is going forward only to re-discover, re-collect, re-turn, re-store, re-vive, re-new, re-pristinate, and re-establish what existed once upon a time— *in illo tempore*. For the concept of hope, this means to cast it in the mold of memory. Memory in the Christian tradition was taken out of the biblical framework in which the initiatives of promise lead history into the open field of new reality. Instead it was placed in a Platonic cave where the shadows cause us to recollect an ideal world to which the events of history can contribute nothing really new.

In the tradition of Christian Platonism it was not at all essential to maintain the historicity of the myth of the fall. It was not modern historical science which first discovered the mythical character of the story of paradise, of Adam and Eve. Clement and Origen of Alexandria, for example, acknowledged without any hesitation that the early chapters of Genesis were not an account of historical facts. The myth could be dehistoricized, then ontologized in such a way as to retain the primacy of the original point of departure. It matters very little to real history whether it is made to proceed from a heavenly paradise above us or from an earthly paradise behind us. In either case, the essence of man is something ready-made, perfectly given in its original form and substance. Philosophically the primacy of origin is expressed in the slogan: Essence precedes existence. There is, I think, a sense in which the classical order must be maintained over the existentialist innovation: "Existence precedes essence." For the existentialist's point is not merely to reverse the Platonic order but to deny any transcendent point of reference in the self-determination of man. Existentialism is as inimical to an eschatological as to a protological orientation of man. On the other hand, from a historico-eschatological viewpoint, essentialism and its existentialist antithesis are both examples of antihistorical thinking. There is no room in either view for existence in hope toward a future determination of man's essence. History cannot really mean anything at all, if with existentialism the future of man's essence is collapsed into the present of his momentary existence, or if as in essentialism the future of existence is but a return to an already fixed essence. The choice between these twin philosophical options has been set forth in categories basically unrevised by the eschatological vision of reality as history whose truth is revealed from its future and whose meaning is not locked in the structures of what already is or always has been. The essence of a thing is neither in its past nor in its present but in its future. Man is an experiment in the laboratory of a history whose goal, according to the Christian hope, is new life in a new world.

Suggested Readings

The volumes listed in the bibliography at the end of Chapter One also relate to the topics of this chapter. Two works that brilliantly detail what Novak calls the collapse of the American myth are R. W. B. Lewis, *The American Adam* (Chicago: University of Chicago Press, 1955p) and Leo Marx, *The Machine in the Garden* (New York: Oxford University Press, 1964p). Michael Novak's *Theology for a Radical Politics* (New York: Herder and Herder, 1969p); *Ascent of the Mountain, Flight of the Dove* (New York: Harper & Row, 1971p); *The Experience of Nothingness* (New York: Harper & Row, 1970p), plus his many articles, serve as a good introduction to the continuing quest for the sacred in the secular. To see the shift in emphasis from the 1960s to the 1970s one should first read H. Cox, *Secular City* (New York: Macmillan, 1965p) and then *The Feast of Fools* (New York: Harper & Row, 1969p). Follow the footnotes in these two books for more books and articles on these themes. For more material by Sam Keen see his *To a Dancing God* (New York: Harper & Row, 1970p) and *Apology for Wonder* (New York: Harper & Row, 1969). He tells me that he has a book coming out on storytelling.

The recovery of transcendence has been an unexpected phenomenon in this decade. See Peter L. Berger, *A Rumor of Angels: Modern Society and the Rediscovery of the Supernatural* (New York: Doubleday, 1969p); H. W. Richardson and Donald R. Cutler (eds.), *Transcendence* (Boston: Beacon Press, 1969p), and Theodore Roszak, *Where the Wasteland Ends* (New York: Doubleday & Co., Inc., 1973). A good selection of materials from current proponents of higher consciousness is John White (ed.), *The Highest State of Consciousness* (Garden City: Doubleday, 1972p). The latter volume introduces the student to the works of Norman O. Brown, Aldous Huxley, R. D. Laing, Allan Watts, Houston and Masters, Abraham Maslow, P. D. Ouspensky, and others, all of who may be consulted for material on the issue of transcendence. The books of Carlos Casteneda are currently widely read on campus. They, along with some of the above, raise the issue of drugs and religious experience.

Two other anthologies that deal with the "inward movement" and quest for transcendence are Charles T. Tart (ed.), * *Altered States of Consciousness* (Garden City: Doubleday & Co., 1972p) and B. Aaronson and H. Osmond (eds.), * *Psychedelics* (Garden City: Doubleday & Co., 1970p).

Carl E. Braaten's *The Future of God* (New York: Harper & Row, 1969) is a good introduction to the Theology of Hope. Jürgen Moltmann's, *Theology of Hope* (New York: Harper & Row, 1967) and the works of Wolfhart Pannenberg may be consulted for primary materials. *New Theology No. 5* is a good introduction to diverse elements in this new school. For an atheistic perspective see the works of Ernst Bloch, particularly *Man on His Own, A Philosophy of the Future*, and *The Principle of Hope*, all published by Herder and Herder. Three paperbacks that contain dialogues within the school are C. Braaten and R. Jenson, *The Futurist Option* (New York: Newman Press, 1970p); E. H. Cousins, *Hope and the Future of Man* (Philadelphia: Fortress Press, 1972p); and W. H. Capps (ed.), *The Future of Hope* (Philadelphia: Fortress Press, 1970p).